Reflections on the Fall of Modern Civilisation

Francis Vairley

New Generation Publishing

Contents

Preface

This has been a difficult book to write – a long and relatively isolated but not altogether unfulfilling exercise. Started five years ago, chapters have been written and rewritten, parts moved and the order changed. It now, hopefully, follows a reasonably logical sequence. The main difficulty was that what in the outside world are many different discourses and disciplines, don't normally sit together in one book. Indeed, almost all readers familiar with parts of the discussion will surely find themselves in very unfamiliar territory elsewhere in the text. This, however, had to be, insofar as our world, in its complexity, has become incredibly fragmented in its compartmentalization of information and discourses so that an overview that enables vital connections to be made is lost. This book is, in a sense, an attempt to retain basic information from many discourses whilst achieving some kind of integrated whole. One of the results of this attempt is that there is much material that might seem repetitive. This is not an oversight but is done in order to ensure that central messages are reinforced and set in different contexts as the argument unfolds.

This is only up to a point an 'academic' book in that full research on all the topics would have required either a whole team to write the book or else many more years of my work. This means that whilst many books have been studied (thank you, Amazon, also for second hand books going well back into the 20th century), there is often a danger of missing important niceties of ongoing discourses. Of course today (briefly) we have the wonders of internet search engines, without which this would have been an entirely different book.

There is still in academia a certain conservative, though diminishing, scepticism about using material from the internet in academic publications. And it is true that much 'information' floating on the web is relatively specious or misleading. But it is now usually possible to 'triangulate' between sources and get a feel for which source is nearer the truth. We should never forget that even rock-hard sources produce data in forms that satisfy better their political masters. The fact is that almost all but the simplest data require complex inputs and even judgments that can make results significantly different in their impact. A good example is the way in which in 2012 the UN Food and Agriculture Organisation revised their calculating method regarding the incidence of undernourishment in the world today, making it now seem that things are not as bad as many people — including themselves — had been saying. But in many areas, such as how much land is under organic production and above all how much food is being produced through Urban and Peri-Urban Agriculture, different sources give extreme differences in statistics depending on the approach that has been used to measuring these phenomena in the context of what the authors are interested in or would like to use to legitimise what they want to say.

It will be found below that in spite of their extensive use, few web sites are actually referenced as these are constantly changing and so unlikely to exist when if and when researchers try to find them. Books are, however, fully referenced – for in the more distant future, when electronic data bases are no longer accessible and thence disappear as a consequence of the demise of electricity systems, books should still exist to be referred to!

The upshot is that maybe there may be deemed to be many small mistakes and misinterpretations of data and information in this text — and maybe I will be informed of these in time. Maybe the book should have gone through a more rigorous peer review process that would have meant a number of readers from different disciplines scrutinising the parts relating to their knowledge. In fact the review process must be admitted to have been minimal, in part because my own circle of academic colleagues are hardly into much of what I have written about and in part that no formal publisher was prepared to publish the book. If they had, then they would have seen to it, as with many of my previous academic publications, that the book was adequately reviewed. However, it should be evident that neither the main nor even few of the lesser arguments in the book stand or fall by detailed data. The perspective, prospective and calls to action require relatively little by way of 'solid facts' to support and justify.

The book is actually being 'self-published' by one of the many self-publishing presses that have popped up in recent years. I thus have to thank New Generation Publishers for taking on the task, albeit the ball is in my court to prepare the material in publishable form most of the time. A dozen traditional publishers were contacted but it seems maybe that there is seen to be little prospect of selling the book. However, we have to realize that formal publishers always have their outlook and niche. This book is not seen as mainstream academic ('it doesn't fit any of our lists' being a usual response). In addition, when these publishers did agree to look at some of the text, they might have worried about the rigour of the research over so many topics and with so many potentially contentious statements lacking solid references. The book also includes advocacy that is generally frowned upon by the academic press unless it is supportive of something in the region of the status quo or other well-worn discourses.

More 'radical' publishers, were also approached, where it seems this book is neither orthodox 'leftist' nor 'new age' and so drops through the cracks. There are, as of recently, a few publishers looking seriously at the consequences of the emerging depletion of energy ('peak oil'); however, the book isn't about this at all, but rather on the far broader issue of the evolution of civilisation and where ours might be heading, written in a rather academic way. In this context, 'the end of oil' becomes but the key precipitating factor of the end of our civilisation.

Regarding the fate of the book, as this is the first attempt to market it, it is surely a difficult and long read so we will have to see whether the traditional publishers were correct in their surmise that it will raise little interest in a world that has no time for long-winded argumentation and little stomach for to focus on the momentous troubles ahead. What occurs to me is that a book of this kind, taking a somewhat Olympian view of life and the world, might have been expected in the 19th century to be widely debated. It is a small personal joke that the title merges parts of Gibbon's *Decline and Fall of the Roman Empire* with Burke's *Reflections on the Revolution in France,* where in the latter case I am radically vindicating, rather than denigrating, the need for fundamental political and social change. Today, such broad writing about the 'the predicament and future of civilisation' is not in favour and even before anything gets read, today the concept of civilisation tends to be avoided as too sweeping.

This comes with the fact that there is an extremely widespread fear of what lies ahead of us with the problems of global warming at the head of the worries and then also what is seen as a deepening economic crisis and beyond this the implications of 'peak oil'. Quite simply, very few people indeed want to think at any great depth about the roots of the problems we are facing and where they are heading. It is amazing how these problems are increasingly screened out by the mainstream media in the United States, abetted by a small industry of books and articles and statements by 'people in the know' that the problems are not so bad and anyway not heading for the apocalypse that so many fear. Elsewhere in the world, beyond the Occident, excitement with what is happening today entirely obliterates any thought about what the future might hold.

Of course the general proposition of the book, that we are about to experience 'the fall of modern civilisation' might be entirely wrong. Maybe there *is* a high-tech future ahead that will miraculously appear over the horizon in the next few years and facilitate continued

9

economic growth ever onwards and upwards, rendering the ostensible pessimism of the book misjudged. More likely is that the problems we face as a consequence of global warming, that are not just the warnings of an inspired individual but, rather, a consensus of thousands of scientists contributing to the work of the Intergovernmental Panel on Climate Change, will be played out in full over the coming decades. We see levels of greenhouse gases rising inexorably and it is clear that the political process is no longer prepared to do anything meaningful to slow this down. And so the book, with its presumption that we might reorganise life over the coming decades in something approaching a reasonable way, may be nothing but romantic nonsense as humanity purposefully destroys the biosphere and in the process commits suicide.

We are in this book certainly considering extreme problems requiring extreme measures and an attempt is being made here to encourage those already thinking and acting in ways aimed at ameliorating these problems - particularly the Transition Movement - to understand in more depth the full scope of the predicament we find ourselves in. It is hoped also to reach a far wider audience of people so far too fearful of – or not caring about - the future to think more coherently about how we might constructively address the problems we face and what steps will need to be taken to address these in a realistic and effective way.

Finally, I am sad that the book lacks any fulsome acknowledgements. I am grateful for the love of Julie and the support of friends and colleagues for generally making my life a reasonably happy one, but the writing of the book has been from this point of view almost completely 'time out'. As noted above, I have had very little direct intellectual critique so much as informal conversations that generally came round easily to an acknowledgement of the probable correctness of the overall thrust of the book but provided little regarding content. So I thank all those who know of and have been sympathetic concerning the writing of the book and the far greater numbers who unknowingly fed me with the information and experiences that facilitated its writing.

Introduction

In the early heroic years of modernity, as science came into focus as a path to acquiring absolute knowledge, new steps were taken to understand in depth the structure of the universe. Starting with the solar system, it all seemed quite simple, once the right attitude had been acquired and the system of knowledge acquisition set out, it would just be a matter of time before everything was known, with an ultimate theory of everything expressed as a set of mathematical relations. The earth, with all its teeming life, was just a ball, circulating around the sun which imparted its energy to give motion and life to all that took place thereupon.

As the quest for knowledge advanced in one field after another, scientific laws threw light into all corners of nature and facilitated its manipulation where hitherto it had been a sea of riddles and an exacting master upon whom work had to be exerted to produce the basis for human life. Science yielded knowledge that enabled the construction of machines to lighten the burden of work and open vistas of an easier life in which human potential could be realised as never before.

However, as time advanced, the more knowledge that was acquired, the more complex everything became both in terms of being able to master nature in the understanding and in terms of the manipulation that progressed with the harnessing of nature in the framework of knowledge. The search for knowledge, impelled by the beguiling things that could be done with her and the lifestyle that this could yield, blinded society to the foundations that allowed all this to happen and the dangers that might lie in ignoring these as progress took its course.

Science always had difficulties capturing the meaning of energy in the framework of knowledge. Boltzmann's laws of thermodynamics possessed a kind of contingency to them that refused to be brought into the fold of true science. Energy, after all, is what moves everything and is therefore not of a kind of the rest of nature as matter and as 'things'. And yet all of life is a function of energy. Perhaps we should say that energy *is* life, existing only when things come alive as heat, light and movement. And as life itself, it has a will — *is* the will of all that happens in the universe. Perhaps the universe is but a battle – no, just a game – endlessly entrapping and manipulating energy in its attempt, as described in the Second Law of Thermodynamics, to disperse into the void and there find peace. Entropy.

In contrast to our nearest neighbours in the universe — our moon, the planets of Venus and Mars, and for all we know about the more distant planets of our solar system with their many moons — the earth has hosted an extraordinary phenomenon of the capture of tiny amounts of the energy that flees in an endless stream in every direction from the sun, manipulating this in complex ways before releasing it to its destined place in the emptiness of space. Somehow, once brought into motion, this complexity of the biosphere, which created and maintains the existence of the oceans and of the wafer-thin layer of the earth's atmosphere, continued to evolve. Crises arose with sudden destabilisations of the atmosphere that left a depleted remainder of the biosphere but in each case there was a recovery with a different configuration of species but the same complexity of capturing and passing on the energy of the sun in the cycles and metabolism of multitudes of biological species in their ecosystemic contexts.

And then a new dimension entered the game, where dying biological organisms took with them part of the energy accumulating in the swamps in which they had lived and with geological evolution became entrapped deeper and deeper under the earth's crust. This meant nothing to the ongoing evolution of species and ecosystems on the surface, in the oceans and in the atmosphere as it accumulated and went to sleep, pending the end of the world, whenever this might come about.

That is until the advent of the invention in the course of the ongoing evolutionary process of the phenomenon of consciousness, produced by the physiological configuration of the species homo sapiens sapiens. Consciousness could in principle be configured in a myriad of ways; necessarily, however, spending its energies on the organisation of human social life in nature: figuring out ways to make a living and then living life on the principles and practices which fragments of social existence invented. Sometimes these lifestyles and the cultures that defined them would have been capable of continuing indefinitely, integrated into the parts of the biosphere which they inhabited. But in the way in which the biosphere never ceases to evolve, so also cultures came and went, both in response to changing natural and climatic conditions and as a consequence of conflict and destruction wrought by the interaction of cultural entities themselves.

In the first instance, the sleeping lodes of energy hidden in the depths of the earth were discovered as one of a myriad manifestations of the inquisitiveness of human cultures and for millennia small amounts found near the surface, whilst finding minor uses, made no significant impact on the way in which the cultures making the discovery worked, even insofar as these were harnessed as one of the multitude of nature's resources that gave structure to the lives of these societies.

This situation continued until the advent of modern civilisation, when these hidden stores of energy made themselves evident as a source of power harnessed to the evolution of society. Taking a step back, we might see the motivation of energy working through human consciousness to break down the walls of the prison under the earth in which nature had so cunningly incarcerated it. Energy will out, and be released into the emptiness of space and here the opportunity and the machinery had arrived to facilitate its ambitions. Consciousness, in its configuration as modern civilisation, lacked entirely the knowledge - or the wisdom - needed to understand the way in which the rapid release of this entrapped energy would affect the systems of nature and with this the very viability of the civilisation itself that had made the discovery and thus freewheeled into a deep obsession with 'Progress' and 'Development' as a process of complexification of human social systems and of consciousness itself, fuelled by the release of the energy entrapped beneath the earth's surface.

When knowledge did at last come to focus on the dangers of what was happening, it was, apparently, too late in that the trajectory of Development and the degree to which the whole of, by now, global society was beguiled and intoxicated by the fabulous – the bizarre – products of modernity produced with the aid of fossil energy, that attempts to bring some wisdom to bear and to change the trajectory of the Development process – the path dependence - in a way that would stem the release of the subterranean energy store seemed increasingly to be in vain. And so, today, it is not only the end of a particular human civilisation that faces us but also the sixth major crash of the earth's ecological systems[1]. It can only be conjectured where this might end. How much of the entrapped energy will be released — maybe just a tenth, and at maximum a quarter — depends on how far the trajectory of modern civilisation is able to survive both as a rapidly complexifying system of organisation, collapsing under its own weight and exhaustion in the ingenuity of technology to continue exploiting fossil energy, or destroyed as a dimension of the destruction of the systems of nature, the very foundation of our existence, through changes in the earth's atmosphere brought about through the burning of fossil fuels.

As each day passes, another nail is driven into the coffin of modern civilisation by the way in which it has come to function. The massive extraction and burning of fossil fuels constantly adds gases to the atmosphere, changing its constitution, raising the earth's temperature, precipitating in stages changes to ecosystems and to the geology of the surface of the earth. Processes started by the metabolism of modern civilisation are freewheeling into a situation where within a century the robust ecosystems from which we make a living may be reduced to a precarious rump that will support only a small residue of humanity that, if it fails to adapt, may be eliminated well before the start of the next biospheric revival — if it should revive at all. It may, indeed, revert instead to the conditions found on the moon and the neighbouring planets where the fecundity, the serendipity, the beauty of the game of nature is laid to rest from this corner of the universe.

Or - and this is the assumption that informs this entire book - modern civilisation will fall, ceasing in the process the extraction of fossil energy and so reducing the severity of the collapse of the biosphere. Whilst not even the immediate future can be foretold, we may make assumptions as a basis for attempting to make the stages of the descent less catastrophic for those who will have to suffer it and to start to lay the foundations of a viable future for humanity, initially amongst the ruins of modernity and the depredations wrought upon nature, but then in the more distant future creating human cultures that have learned the lessons of the fallacies of Civilisation.

Civilisation

In a real sense this will be the end of civilisation as such. The immediate reason is that the very word 'civilisation' is derived from the Latin word *civitas* denoting city. In spite of the fact that until the brief flowering of modern civilisation - and for the majority of the world population right up to the turn of the 21st century - urban life involved a minority and for most of the time, if we refer to the population that was not engaged in producing food from the land and the seas, a truly tiny minority of people alive at any one time,[2] the assumption was that urban life, as the centre of power and the higher expressions of civilisation, was what really mattered and that the rural was of little account in terms of political and cultural life. And this was in spite of the objective, abject dependence of cities on food, water and energy from rural hinterlands and further afield, facilitated by the labour of those who peopled the countryside and sailed the seas.

There is little chance that the mega-urbanisation that has been a feature of the availability of fossil fuel will survive the decline and end of fossil energy exploitation. Any viable future for the remains of humanity oriented to its survival and the revival of viable cultural entities, will recognise the importance of the rural as our essential relations with immediate nature and physical resources, to human existence. Thus cities, if they continue to exist at all, will in future be of modest dimensions and of necessity have but a measured space in the total consciousness of the re-emergent societies. But much else that has been a constant of civilisation since cities by this name, came into being, will also be put behind future generations if viable forms of human culture are to re-emerge following the fall of modern civilisation. Primarily this will be a corollary to the supersession of the separation of societies into hierarchies and class divisions and the struggle for superior status and power that eventually led to what became the ludicrous complexity and self-indulgence of modern civilisation itself.

So what was this thing 'civilisation'? In common parlance it denotes a certain complexity and sophistication in the organisation of life, embodying physical comforts and the development of intellectual life and the arts. In the past this has been contrasted with 'primitive' life and barbarism — in the 19th century seen as stepping stones in the 'triumphal march of history' — denoting simpler ways of life assumed to be inferior to civilised life. In recent years, a creeping question as to whether civilisation really is a route to the better life has led to a more circumspect use of the term as representing some kind of ideal or even better state of being. Whilst the messianic presumption that European civilisation was the culmination of the triumphal march and hence that in spite of the evidently different paths which this had taken in different parts of the world, all would be resolved in the eventual unity of a global civilisation led by the Occident. In fact, this presumption is today as strong as in the past, now un-analysed but clearly embedded in the obsessive striving for 'economic growth' and 'Development' and as such poses immense problems which are the subject of this book.

We might conjecture that civilisation was simply a matter of finding appropriate formulae for the cooperation of human communities inhabiting particular ecosystems or series of contiguous ecosystems, to establish sets of social relations and productive processes that would support their existence and self-understanding through time, through the seasons and the decades. This was, however, already accomplished early in the evolutionary emergence of humans, with the formation of small bands adapted to particular ecosystems and with their own particular understanding of these and lifestyles that interacted in a sustainable way with these. Through most of the 150,000-200,000 years of the presence in the world of Homo Sapiens Sapiens – human beings physically identical with ourselves - with no significant further evolutionary change in physical and mental machinery beyond this point in time[3], this was achieved without the existence of cities, in conditions referred to as 'prehistoric', given the lack of any written history, but evidenced by the archaeological record as having satisfied their needs, living lightly in their immediate environment[4] and gaining sustenance through hunting and gathering.

Whilst, without written records, there can only be very restricted evidence of how language, social self-understanding and organisation emerged and evolved, the ingenuity of present-day archaeological research[5] has revealed a great variety of cultures that arose under these circumstances as Homo Sapiens Sapiens groups moved out of Africa, starting some sixty thousand years ago[6], and spread across Eurasia, eventually crossing the land bridge between Asia and America in the receding millennia of the last ice age, around sixteen thousand years ago. Cultures came and went that produced impressive cave painting in what is present-day Spain and France, but also in Australia, South Africa and Patagonia. Cultures also came and went that produced monumental structures as widely distributed as Stonehenge — built earlier than the Egyptian pyramids — and other megalithic structures scattered across Europe, monumental mounds in the south-central United States and the structures of Great Zimbabwe in southern Africa: all these cultures came and went, without the building of significant concentrations of settlement or the development of agriculture.

Proliferation and refinement of tool-making, means of human adornment, the production of sculptures and long-distance trade are all in evidence in prehistoric times with substantial variation from area to area indicating in some cases exchange of capacities and in others local invention and reinvention of technologies and probably also of forms of social organisation and interaction. What is evident is that there was not a smooth, generalised evolution in any particular direction but rather cultures that had adopted particular lifestyles, adapting and responding to environmental and climate change - particularly to the emergence and then retreat of the last great ice age and the greening and then re-desertification of the Sahara desert - nevertheless were sustained in many places over many thousands of years.

Civilisation is generally seen as having emerged some eight thousand years ago, defined as the emergence of fixed settlements of more substantial structures — an 'Urban Revolution,' albeit for several thousands of years involving what today we consider no more than villages and towns. It also involved the institution of organised agriculture - termed the 'Neolithic Revolution' - the invention of basic technologies of the sedentary life, pottery and fabric production, writing and of greatest importance, the organisation of societies hierarchically into definite classes[7]. All of these attributes except writing could be found in certain pre-civil societies but the conjuncture of all of these together set civilisation apart from what went before. Whilst, portrayed often enough as the triumph of human ingenuity and capacities over ignorance and submission to the will of nature, civilisation at the same time expressed itself as the exploitation of the majority of people by elites, sometimes relatively benignly but often enough brutally — and the incessant waging of wars[8]. Whilst the powers of humans had been discovered and expressed as changed relations with nature, now this became systematic, as agriculture, and was then transmitted to power relations between humans, within and between societies.

Archaeologists have asked rhetorically, under the title of the 'sapiens paradox,' why, if our species had already inhabited the biosphere for so many thousands of years, it took so long for civilisation to emerge. One view is that gradual population increase encouraged intensification of food production, resulting in organised agriculture[9] and as an extension of this, the organisation of irrigation systems that emerged in Mesopotamia, Egypt and China. These precipitated the difference between those organising the irrigation systems over against those who farmed the fields[10] and these rapidly emerged as social hierarchies from which the division of labour proliferated. Notwithstanding the fact of intensively communally-organised irrigation systems to be found in many parts of the world today, this might nevertheless, seen from a functionalist perspective, have been an important route to the emergence of civilisation.

There can be no doubt that when the main characteristics of civilisation came together that these cohered in kinds of synergy and, indeed, functional interconnections that maintained them through time. But above all, the emergence of hierarchy and the division of labour introduced means for elites to purloin resources — surplus production — that could be directed to feed artisans who manufactured goods for the use of elites, to employ labour forces to build monuments and generally employ ideological means to secure allegiance of the under-classes. It also provided resources to finance armies used to conquer other nations and civilisations and generally to establish nation states and empires that were the hallmark of civilisation.

In recent years, the assumption that civilisation is a superior state of being to that of pre-civilised peoples has been increasingly challenged, confirmed in a major conference in 1966 that brought together a large number of researchers on pre-civil societies[11], where copious evidence from analysis of the surviving hunting and gathering societies indicated that 'prehistoric' ways of life could be perfectly congenial and certainly well-adapted to their environments and hence inherently sustainable. It seems, furthermore, that across much of the era of civilisation, even where there was proximity between civilised peoples and pre-civil groups, the latter failed to adopt the ways of civilisation being, it appears, content with their way of life. Their elimination comes from the crowding out by agriculture, facilitated by the evident technological and organisational means that comes with the civilising process[12].

In the past, arguments raged over whether all civilisations stem from the copying of a root civilisation. However, whilst across Eurasia there was certainly some communication, each civilisation emerged as a coherent expression of local culture that might spread through conquest but which had its own life and eventually death. The emergence of civilisation in Mesoamerica with no contact to Eurasia is definitive evidence for civilisation as an autonomous locally-emergent phenomenon and not one that spread from any one centre.

Clearly civilisation brought with it a total change in the human understanding of the world the inhabitants lived in and of their place in nature; what we might call a revolution in socio-psychological state of which religious conversion is an essential dimension. It has been one of the central concerns of philosophy since the 19th century as to the way in which human consciousness perceives the world is shaped by the context of social relations and relations with nature in the sense of the means of satisfying our existential conditions, in Marxist terms the 'Mode of Production' but involving also attitudes towards nature, to other species and to landscapes. The emergence of civilisation could only have taken place where minds were receptive to changes actually taking place. As the components of civilisation came together and lifestyles and productive systems changed, so also attitudes would have solidified into new systematic ways of understanding and reacting to the social and natural world. This is most evident in the changes in the structure of religions and the way in which these provide a framework of meaning to societies and orient the ways in which they cohere and function.

The religions of civilisation came in many forms which we can loosely classify between early and late. The initial break from animistic understanding of the human condition that seems to have prevailed in various forms through pre-history and in a few cases well into modernity, came in the form of many variants on Polytheism that could be found in all early civilisations throughout Eurasia, including ancient Egypt and also Mesoamerica; subsequent displacement left Hinduism as the only major survival of these religions[13]. These are characterised by a focus on epic stories and myths involving heroes of the past, or of parallel worlds of gods and fantastical creatures,

18

confirming political and social rules in the governance and everyday lives of the people and their orientations and understanding of the structure and purpose of life. Already there is a distancing from nature in the mind that clearly synergises with the establishment of agriculture as the means of gaining food, including the domestication of animals, which indicates the capacity of humans to control nature, hence reducing the mystery and danger that once defined relations between human communities and their environment.

The later religions emerged in the West starting with Zoroastrianism and via Judaism and thence Christianity and Islam and in the East, Buddhism, Confucianism and Taoism. These started some two thousand seven hundred years ago up to one thousand four hundred years ago (Islam) with many subsequent branches out of these. These were all initiated by single Prophets or teachers who laid foundations on which social rituals, moral codes and eventually detailed rules of political and social life were built or adapted and fused from those inherited from the past. A dimension of fatalism in the sense that life must be accepted as it is characterised the earlier religions of civilisation. However, in the cases of Buddhism and incipiently in Judaism and Christianity, there was a notion of an ideal life beyond civilisation, around a notion of Enlightenment, which should be striven for.

It is useful already here to note as an aside that the focus of these religions, with their distant gods and moral abstractions, were concerned almost entirely with the human condition, paying little attention to the biospheric context which had produced humanity and which would need a degree of empathy and understanding if it was to continue to nurture the species. At best the concern was one of good stewardship, eventually, in the Occidental case, giving way, in the context of the emergence of science, to a forthright notion of conquest as expressed by the early ideologue of science, Francis Bacon[14]. And it should be clear that the hierarchical nature of civilisation as a means of organising human life was confirmed and became more deeply embedded, in Confucianism clearly stated, but perhaps more perniciously in the Abrahamic religions with the notion of an almighty (male) God and Lord under whom all of life is given meaning and structure, suggesting, and in the case of Islam and its laws forthrightly setting out, the rules of hierarchically governed life.

The Eastern religions generally offered themselves to adherents in ways that allowed them to pick and choose the aspects they would adhere to - with Confucianism, as more a socio-political philosophy than a religion - eventually defining the ground rules according to which mode of governance worked in the Far East until the tidal wave of Occidental modernity swept these aside. In this context, Buddhism offered a way to enlightenment that was essentially individual and thus had nothing to say about how politics and society should function. Notwithstanding the monastic life that it brought into being, it could therefore never have had more than a marginal impact on the way in which societies were run at a practical level and certainly never posed a threat to established socio-political power hierarchies.

Not in the name of enlightenment but nevertheless concerned with bringing rational rules to bear on the organisation of socio-political life, Confucianism evolved in China and the Far East into a comprehensive moral system that provided foundations for life in that part of the world for over two thousand years. In the West, the extraordinary flowering over some three hundred years of Greek philosophy, laid a foundation that fed, some two thousand years later, into the various discourses generated by the European Enlightenment.

The European Enlightenment, emerging from the reinterpretation of Christianity and the rediscovery of Ancient Greek philosophy was an altogether different notion of enlightenment to that of Buddhism, banishing the spiritual and opening rational discourses on both the way in which the socio-political system should be organised as well as laying the foundations of science that set Occidental civilisation on the path that gave us our modern technological, fossil-fuelled world. We might say that, given the ambitions of much of the early discourse of the Enlightenment, and the many utopian proposals and experiments of the 19th century, that by the early years of the 20th century this had definitively failed in its loftier ambitions, as expressed by the sociologist Max Weber and the Frankfurt School of Philosophy. Any meaningful debate concerning what the Enlightenment might involve by way of resolving the 'human condition' had virtually disappeared from intellectual life by the end of the century.

What is particularly problematic is how social hierarchy came to be accepted by the majority of civilised peoples who suffered its negative consequences. There were clear steps from the egalitarian bands and confederations of primitive life to the state of civilisation[15] and whilst rebellions and revolutions have occurred regularly throughout history, coercion and violence, promotion of ideologies of power and subservience and today seduction into compliance on the part of organised elites, have perennially reformulated and maintained unequal social relations. Nevertheless, as already noted, for most of the era of Civilisation, primitive egalitarianism, and much simpler forms of social and political organisation persisted over much of the earth and in spite of the elimination of these communities under the impact of modern civilisation over the last few hundred years, some persisted even to the end of the 20th century.

In fact there have been very large variations on what civilisation has meant amongst different peoples and these have, besides the survival of significant numbers of primitive communities, included lacunae, particularly of peasant communities in many parts of the world that have been to all intents and purposes egalitarian whilst possessing many of the de facto benefits associated with civilisation. These are particularly important, and are later discussed, as illustrating that social hierarchy is not a necessary attribute of cultures that can possess a high level of education, artistic expression and production of finely crafted objects. It is important to stress this over and against a certain American literature that would insist that the only long-term viable cultures are ones living from hunting and gathering[16]. A central issue of this book is how social hierarchies might be eliminated and egalitarian communities established in the context of the fall of modern civilisation, and with it the destabilisation of present-day elites, as the central means to ensuring that the excesses and extravagances of modern civilisation do not re-emerge.

Throughout this book we will be focusing on the last few hundred years of the phenomenon of civilisation, as the emergence and realisation of modern civilisation. In this context we would already stress the instability and the self-illusions of civilisation as a phenomenon. The fact of the fall of civilisations is well-enough known, with notable examples from every continent — of Rome, of the Khmer, of the Maya and many more. Joseph Tainter, in studying the collapse of nineteen different 'complex societies', concluded that civilisation as such eventually inevitably reverts to small-scale organisation that we might associate more with pre-civil (or maybe post-civil?) forms of organisation[17]. Jared Diamond warns against the assumption that civilisation may be assumed to be attainable as an ultimate stable state without constant adaptation to the changes to which it is — largely of its own making — subjected to through time[18]. The precariousness and the unsustainability of modern civilisation becomes a further important focus of this book.

Modern interest in understanding the phenomenon of civilisation, starting in the debates of the European Enlightenment some two hundred and fifty years ago, has been intimately connected to the ideology of 'progress' and the notion that it is evolving along a passage that will ultimately resolve the 'riddle of human existence' and end in a world in which human life is one of ease and enlightened understanding. Rapid changes over the 19th and 20th centuries lent justification to this notion, in spite of all the wars and ideological conflict that accompanied these changes, that civilisation was going somewhere meaningful. In the popular mind there were ideas of a resolution to 'the human condition' whereby technology would provide the basis of the 'good life' and with the eventual conquest of the universe.

Enough has now been researched about civilisations of the past that led to the abandonment of notions of a single evolutionary past or, indeed, that later civilisations, and particularly Occidental civilisation, are superior to earlier civilisations. Later civilisations, where there was communication, learned some things from earlier ones, but did not accept all to which they had been exposed and insofar as they maintained and evolved their own priorities, only ever partially accepted what was available to be learned that might have been to their advantage. We might say that each had its own highlights and problems and that in general we really cannot speak of progress in any linear way. Civilisations came, evolved and went, and might have continued to do so for millennia, until Occidental civilisation, for reasons internal to its own particular Development parameters, came to harness fossilised energy sources to its own evolution.

It is truly bizarre to contemplate the absence of any self-understanding of this civilisation as to how its development — and eventual overrunning of all other Civilisations — was a function of the extraction and burning of this finite energy resource from below the earth and that once the accessible portion of this resource came to an end, the greater part of the insanely complex means of organising this civilisation and with it its whole self-image, might come rapidly to an end.

Discussion throughout this book attempts to face up to this blindness and then seek ways to go beyond into a future that does not need constant increases in energy or indeed the amounts of energy consumed today. At this point it is simply necessary to emphasise that it was not inevitable in some teleological sense of evolution, but was, like all other aspects of evolution, a just-so story of 'one thing leading to another' and thus with no necessary structure or conclusion. It could well have been diverted by events emanating from nature, such as major volcanic activity that is thought to have created one or more mass extinctions in the geological past, or elsewhere in the universe such as an asteroid striking the earth[19] but, more importantly, by reconfiguration of ideology and socio-political organisation. The importance of this insight is that it is necessary to address what will become a deep disorientation that we can expect upon the fall of our vaunted civilisation and open up the possibility to see that alternatives are always possible if the social imagination and initiative are there.

So our task is to make clear where we stand today in terms generally of the organisation of human life, but more specifically regarding modern civilisation. It is increasingly feared that our civilisation is not a triumphal march into a glorious future but, on its current trajectory, is a road, in relatively short shrift to, at best, a state of chaos of the kind that many civilisations of the past have experienced, only this time on an unimaginable scale that could well end up eliminating humanity altogether.

It was pointed out earlier in this discussion that civilisation has been a particular way of organising human life in terms of producing what we need to live comfortable lives with something of a pretence of creating the best of all possible worlds, marred only by the struggles for power that often interrupted life. The European notion of Enlightenment did contain the hope and even ambition to produce a civilisation that would truly realise the capacities of humankind to live in peace and harmony as well as, if not in wisdom, at least in comfort and the elimination of ignorance. In the last paragraphs we wish to point to how easily, whilst producing beautiful artefacts and events, the illusions of civilisation could precipitate obsessions that have constantly marred the lives of some and eventually of whole civilisations that have brought about their downfall. This is presented as a warning so that this propensity to illusion and obsession might be guarded against in any future attempts at reconstructing cultures.

Civilisation is thus defined simply as the concentration and striving for power and wealth — the right of some to take decisions over other people's lives and the prerogative to decide how physical resources and the produce of others should be generated and used. On the one hand, civilisation has generally been portrayed in heroic and noble terms with respect to the beautiful, wonderful, amazing states and things that have been produced (we think of today's tourism, in part fed by the built residue of past civilisations, the museums containing evidence of their artisanal and artistic achievements and the libraries of books of fiction, technical explanation and philosophy as expressions of the intelligence and imagination of civilisations). It is, on the other hand, at the same time easy enough to see how badly civilisations have treated the great majority of humanity most of the time in terms of exploitation, hardship, stress and often mass brutality in the context of wars.

And how easy it seems to have been to pervert the creative and playful expressions of humanity as art and crafts, turning these around in the context of civilisation to become extensions and confirmation of the concentration of power. The catalogue of absurdities and obsessions, sanctioned by the modes of social, economic - and military - organisation and woven into religions, totems and taboos, is endless. The weary path trodden by humanity trapped in its own particular civilisations, attempting to make sense out of life and of elites maintaining their power, privilege and prerogative, can indeed be characterised as a monumental tragedy.

The drive for power and status repeatedly generated obsessions and taboos, confirming the power of the powerful, from ordinary men within family hierarchies to leaders of nations or of powerful institutions and corporations. They spanned from such peripheral cultural expressions as the Chinese practice of binding women's feet or the practice of female genital mutilation, to broader phenomena of religiously-inspired murders such as Mesoamerican bloodletting rituals and the sacrifice and burial, in India, of wives and servants with their dead masters, to encouragement of the mass-suicide of Japanese Kamikaze pilots to the catastrophic expressions of power epitomised by Genghis Khan's organisation of the mass destruction of cities right across Eurasia, and by the Holocaust. But above all, the culture of organised war, so often deemed to be heroic activity, has been a truly bizarre — and yet constant — dimension of civilisation.

Although present as a constant dimension of civilisations since its emergence, the formalisation of the concept and actuality of private property, where resources and commodities become an essential extension of the individual persona indicating the class status to which individuals belong, including the capacity to own as expressed in incomes, has become the hallmark of modern civilisation[20]. The freedom to wield power with and in the confines of one's own property and the use of property as an instrument to intervene in social intercourse and to express who one is, are deeply embedded foundations of the very understanding by modern people of the world we inhabit – and it is this that has to be understood in its origins and workings, and which must be exorcised in rebuilding any kind of viable world post fall of civilisation, so that it will not be repeated; this therefore becomes another important focus of inquiry as this book proceeds.

With the emergence of property as the foundation of social status, hitherto prevailing social relations of power, sanctified by religion (the Divine Right of Kings) and the bonds of blood relations expressed in the configurations of power and obligation within the family which beguiled ethnographers in their studies of different societies, became secondary to the 'capitalist mode of production' that saw property owners employing workers to produce more property in the form of commodities, the sale of which, in the context of an ever more consolidated 'commercial ideology', became the main basis for power, as wealth, in modern civilisation. Karl Marx's sometime use of the term 'Commodity Fetishism' says much that is crucial to understanding the ruling obsession of modern civilisation: the proliferation of things and situations, referred in today's common parlance as 'stuff', augmenting status by their accumulation.

To understand this as the central obsession of the modern world is crucial to understanding in turn the suicidal trajectory of modern civilisation both in terms of its unsustainability and beyond this the destruction of the physical basis of the future existence of any form of human existence and organisation. We can see how inegalitarian power, today predominantly in the form of wealth, relations are maintained by the *flow* of commodities that gives the vast majority of humanity today a sense that their own powers are in process of augmentation. What is obsessive about it is the inability to sense in any meaningful way clearly, even where it is understood intellectually, the consequences for ourselves individually and as society of this obsession.

The foundation of this is totally screened out from the process: the explosive energising of the whole trajectory of modern civilisation through the exploitation and bringing into the life process of fossilised energy resources. These resources were known even at the outset of civilisation in that they appeared on the earth's surface in Mesopotamia and whilst bitumen was widely used for construction and waterproofing, oil was deemed to be of no use — though it may have been the basis for incendiary weapons in subsequent eras. It was only from the mid-17th century that this has been harnessed significantly to the augmentation of power and wealth. Already in the 16th century, enough coal was reaching London from Northumbria and used in industry to the point where a regulation was passed to limit its use due to air pollution. This was the start of the trajectory of modern civilisation both to fuel, initially in Britain and then spreading across the Occident, a massive augmentation of productive capacity through industrialisation and to power the transport systems and war machine of colonialism to extend the range and depth of exploitation.

There is enough evidence to point to something happening in the 18th century that triggered the integration of fossil energy exploitation into the very creation of the civilising process. The term 'modern' arrived in the late 17th century as a term to contrast thinkers and actors,

25

termed 'ancients' who looked upon the past and present as providing a model of stability and sufficiency upon which to organise life, with a new attitude that saw the future as opening new vistas and chances to somehow improve on the past. Eventually 'modern' came to mean the bursting of the bounds of social convention, as 'creative destruction', relativising public morality to release the adventure of progress and Development. As discussed in detail in Chapter Three, this coincided also with the emergence of property, as totem, as never before - and what later is referred to as the Commercial Ideology - as the state of mind and being that spread to become the ruling framework of modern civilisation.

It is truly bizarre how little attention has been paid over the past two centuries to the deepening dependence of the whole revolutionary upending of social and political relations and the physical world in the process that came to be called Development, on the ever increasing flow of fossil energy resources. The modern imagination saw only the wonders of technological development and the harnessing of the scientific imagination to accelerate progress as industrialisation, and with it, urbanisation. But without coal, the industrial revolution could not have happened and the processes of urbanisation that have so closely followed in the train of industrial growth would have ceased, as in past civilisations, when the resources of the urban hinterlands, together with modest flows of imported food and materials, reached the limits set by the power of animals, biomass and the winds.

The path into an eventually technology-dominated world facilitated by the various dimensions of liberal philosophy and the realities of free trade and the freedom of the realisation of entrepreneurial ambition to feed the processes of wealth accumulation, left little room to question where the process might lead. Indeed, it was a deep article of unquestioned faith that continued even through the eventual division of modern civilisation, for a period, into two visions: 'capitalist' and 'communist'. The future would be industrial, urban and, above all wealthier, erasing almost entirely[21] any concern for the possible unsustainability of this march into the unknown. As this civilisation deepened and through the 20th century spread, so also the faith in the path it was following became ever more deeply confirmed as a 'path dependence'. And as the impossibility of continuing for very much longer along this trajectory becomes empirically ever clearer, rather than questioning the wisdom of attempting to continue, a deep denial of this impossibility is becoming ever more insistent.

The conviction that our civilisation is something inevitable that cannot be questioned is almost absolute today, right across our globalised world. For almost all the world's population the possibility of alternative worlds never occurs, given the urgency of the present and their embeddedness in a rapidly changing everyday life. Even the few who do take time to consider possible alternatives, these are either denied as a possibility or are defined as a plethora of small incremental changes far short of the capacity to adjust to the kinds of rapid changes that actually lie ahead of us. In fact, European intellectual and political history is littered with proposals for quite other ways of organising society and attempts — in the extreme, revolutions — that, in the end, came to very little indeed in deflecting what can be seen in retrospect an almost predictable trajectory seen from within the machinery, both intellectual and political, that has brought us through the last few centuries.

But this does not mean that alternatives cannot exist, nor that these cannot be conceived, rationalised, debated and implemented. As we have been discussing, different civilisations come in many shapes and sizes and different arrangements of human societies have been created and thriven over long periods. In the text which follows, these are discussed in terms of how we got to be where we are today, what alternatives were pushed aside and what alternatives actually existed in other civilisations that have been eclipsed in recent times by the hegemony of the modern civilisation.

The book is also intended to provide some elements of thought processes and thence activities that might be helpful in the difficult passage down from the absurdities of modern civilisation to something more viable. Viable in this context also means putting civilisation as such behind those who survive the downward passage, to create forms of society that, like Civilisation, may come in many shapes, and sizes (the end of any notion of empire and even nation is fundamental), that will, in the sense of so many utopian proposals of the past, resolve the human condition as a return to a viable relationship with the rest of nature and ways of life that are congenial for all, realising the potential inherent in being human as a social being.

Purpose and Structure

The third section of this Introduction provides a synopsis of the complete book, chapter by chapter. Given the wide range of topics dealt with in the book, many readers will surely wish to focus attention just on particular chapters. However, it is important to see the book as a complete argument from A to Z and at least readers should take the time to read straight through this synopsis to see how the discussion builds up from problematic to ways and means to ameliorate the downward passage from modernity and by the end of the passage create societies that are truly sustainable into the distant future, in which life may be enjoyable and fulfilling, not just for elites but for all of the human population and for the natural world in which they will be able to thrive.

Chapter One: The Consequences of Unustainable Development

This Chapter opens with a discussion of the cacophony of contemporary life with, under the surface, widespread yet inchoate, a foreboding of looming crises, confirmed in fragmentary events: financial and economic crisis with fluctuating but incipiently rising prices of energy and food, water shortages, flooding on ever larger scales and sudden and incipient pollution events affecting ecology and human health. These come and go in the public consciousness as presented by the media but are not apprehended in any coherent way with respect to where the whole is leading. Since the early 1970s, the 'Green Movement', given initial impetus by a number of studies, above all *The Limits to Growth,* developed attempts to bring the unsustainability of the modern world into perspective and into the political process as a basis for confronting the challenges it posed. The history of the movement and its ultimate failure is described.

There is then a systematic analysis of the key dimensions of the unsustainability of the present trajectory of the human world and what each of these and their interaction might mean for the future. These are: failure of the global economic system through its own internal dynamic; the limits to energy and water production and use, together with looming inability to meet global food needs; the increasing difficulty of accessing mineral resources without increased access to energy; questions concerning the impacts of continuing human population growth in this context; the impacts of pollution, particularly global warming and the negative impacts of this, and the impacts of 'Development' on biodiversity.

The last section of the chapter sketches three overall scenarios and some of the major negative interactions of the various crises in causing, within the coming decades, the falling apart of the modern world and how the global and national socio-political systems might respond as the 'downward passage' accelerates. A Coda summarises the problematic and focuses on the question of how our civilisation got to this point, noting that the frame of mind in which this is happening will have to change fundamentally in the future. The assumption is that the

28

impacts of climate change will be modest enough to leave sufficient opportunity to formulate entirely new ways of understanding what life is about and how to organise society in this context.

Chapter Two: How we got to be here – a Critique of Modernity

The main terms to be used in the discussion are defined: Civilisation, Culture, Society, Ideology and Community. This is followed by a discussion of the notion of the evolution of civilisation. The European belief in progress and its origins in the Christian apocalyptic is contrasted with the ideologies that underlay and provided structure for other complex civilisations, focusing on India and China. The way in which 'class struggle' has fuelled progress and how this became concretised in a particular format as capitalism is set out. The details of how the ideological framework that defines the modern world came about in the context of the European Enlightenment is described, contrasting the two contenders for ideological hegemony of 'Possessive Individualism' and 'the Perfectibility of Man'.

The second half of the chapter documents the development of the modern world in real terms over the past two hundred years. The discovery of fossil energy provided the foundation for modern Development, opening the door to industrialisation. Whilst this unfolded as the development of capitalism, notions of alternative ways of organising the social process were battled out across the 19th century with utopian proposals and experiments, culminating in the challenge of Marxist Communism and thence the establishment of the Soviet Union. Possessing ostensibly fundamentally different views on the aims of social and political life, in practice both capitalism and communism pursued the same Developmental goals across the 20th century. The chapter describes how coercion and cooptation brought all other cultures into the same frame of mind and Development path, culminating, with the failure of what became known as 'actually existing socialism', in the 'consumer society'.

Chapter Three: Socio-Political Life and Institutions

The collapse of modern civilisation won't happen from one day to the next. However, in the coming decades we can expect the structures of our globalised world, including both the technical capacities to continue running our industrial systems and the political machinery that hold our societies in place, to fall apart. Whilst this will mean reformulating radically the ways we produce our living, it will also leave a void in the expectations, the ideological underpinnings and thence the ways in which the socio-political world functions.

The chapter confronts this situation as a discussion of systems of governance that we might expect to be viable under the changing circumstances. To do this requires a thorough examination of the systems of government that have held cultures together in the past, the events and debates that brought them into being and at a more theoretical level what alternatives have been considered and implemented over the past centuries. The discussion surveys the evolution of government from primitive societies through Hellenic Greece (Plato's discourses) and sideways to other complex cultures, on to the debates of the 18th and 19th centuries that led us to the forms of government that prevailed throughout the 20th century.

A major thesis is that whilst elite governance – with, today, commerce dominating the political process - has been maintained throughout the evolution of civilisation, and with its wellsprings in Christian teaching, the idea of an ultimate solution to the human condition being the elimination of hierarchical society, expressed in the modern era as the idea of Utopia, supplying us with the most promising route to forms of governance that can provide a solid foundation for the reconstruction of viable and sustainable societies post-fall of modernity. The reasoning for this and what would be involved is presented, but the chapter ends in a discussion of the ways in which this may well not be achieved in practice.

Chapter Four: Ecology – Resources – Production

The discussion now focuses on the ecological side of concern for the future of humanity and immediately encounters the tragic divide throughout Occidental history between concern for humanity and concern for nature. This has its origins in Ancient Greece, with the distinction becoming evident between the concerns of natural scientists contrasted with intellectuals concerned with the human condition and political life. Reaffirmed in the revival of Greek thought in the Renaissance and into the European Enlightenment, this divide became a hallmark of modern thought up until today. Nature has simply been ignored as sentient life and even adequate concern for its maintenance as the basis of long-term human survival has been continually discounted.

This chapter is episodic insofar as it returns to the human impacts on nature discussed in the first chapter and documents the systematic step by step subjugation and eventual plunder of ecosystems and tearing up of the surface of the earth to gain access to whatever was deemed necessary to promote Development. Inadequate thought was given to how the natural environment in more benign places and times guided into being cultures that coexisted and empathised with the surroundings which they inhabited. Occidental culture, by contrast, was determined to conquer nature while at the same time deriding cultures that empathised with her and that merged into their natural surroundings. The end product has been the grotesque efflorescence of the Consumer Society with lamentably inadequate space for deeper reflection on the impact which this is having upon nature.

Science and technology then are seen as being the heart of the cultural problematic which promoted and facilitated this aggressive attitude to nature, made conscious by Francis Bacon. However, since the advent of the Green Movement that identified the folly of Occidental civilisation in respect of its attitude to nature, a stream of attempts to find a new understanding of the human predicament in nature unfolded which, however, became solipsistic in the sense of tiny numbers involved in the discourse on environmental philosophy and ethics with no resonance in wider society. The chapter ends by analysing the use of the earth's resources for Development, the inevitable end game that this involves, already identified by Jevons in the mid-19th century and by other forlorn voices over the ensuing decades, and thence evolution in the exploitation of resources used in the context of modern industry and the Consumer Society.

Chapter Five: Life after Modernity – some General Considerations

This chapter starts with a history of 'de-localisation'. Long-distance trade goes well back into pre-history. However, the vast majority of daily consumption — viz food, building materials and basic manufactures — was very locally produced almost everywhere, well into the 20th century. Modern de-localisation is closely associated with the rise in the use of fossil energy, fuelling ever more efficient transport systems and with them the concentration of manufacturing in particular places around the world. It is only over the past half century, however, that the almost complete dispersal of trade in materials and goods has been effectuated, with — what in future may become the most serious problem once re-localisation commences — the radical loss of practical knowledge and skills at the local level.

Two sections of the chapter then analyse questions that will be key to the re-localisation of economies as the consequence of the decline of energy resources and related dimensions of the unsustainability of modernity, namely the 'Mode of Production' (MoP) that will emerge, and the question of how social movements have, in recent years, already pointed in the direction of 'alternative' ways of organising social, economic and political life. Past MoPs are analysed and contrasted with the cooperativism that emerged in the 19th century and of which there is by now much experience, demonstrating this as a possible main route to the reconstruction of local economies. Recent social movements, including 'Intentional Communities' and 'Bioregionalism', present possible models of social and political reconstruction Meanwhile, the recent emergence of the 'Transition Movement', with already well over a thousand groups around the world, is anticipating re-localisation and taking initial steps towards this.

The last section of the chapter looks at practical means of realising the social and political process of re-localisation, analysing the reasons and then the stages through which re-localisation is likely to take place. It then suggests ways in which, as materials cease to arrive in cities, populations might form local communities that initially ensure efficient production and distribution of goods and resources to their members but then organise to leave cities and suburbs to find places with land near at hand where they can return to farming, whilst developing their capacity to process local resources and manufacture locally to satisfy their needs — as did most communities only one or two generations ago.

Chapter Six: A More Detailed Look at Life after Modernity

The chapter starts by noting that before the coming of modernity, the means to life was created almost entirely from the land adjacent to the villages and towns where people lived. Modernity severed this connection and although wealth can still be counted in terms of ownership of land and the income accruing to it, this has diminished progressively to just a minor part of what the rich today consider to be their wealth, with suburban lots comprising the 'wealth' of ordinary citizens. In the future, land proximate to settlements will again loom large as the basis of most life-sustaining resources and so how this is 'owned' and managed will be crucial to the revival of communities. Notwithstanding the real possibility of reversion to some version of neo-feudalism, it is argued that the holding of all land in the form of what is currently referred to as Common Pool Resources Management Regimes (CPRMR), as defined by Elinor Ostrom, will become the only happy social resolution of this problematic that will enable Communities to plan the reconstruction of sustainable settlements.

The chapter continues by presenting how, in this context, local economic (re)development (LED) might proceed as a participatory planning process. This looks at the future economies of communities in terms of primary, secondary and tertiary sectors, noting that in the first instance, recovery of materials from the detritus of modern civilisation may provide a bridge to future times when a return to the harvesting of local natural resources — particularly the re-growth of woods and forests — can be effectuated. Major attention will need to be focused on reviving skills and modest tools that are relevant to reconstructing local economies that will produce most of what is locally needed to sustain life.

The chapter goes on to focus on what future settlements might be like, replacing the unviable cities and suburbs of today, noting the way in which communities in the past planned their settlements and built these, as the vernacular, out of local resources. New forms of vernacular building may be expected to emerge, perhaps learning from the past, to replace modern ways of building that have come to require so much by way of energy-intensive components and materials imported from afar and then massive energy resources to function as settlements. The chapter ends by summarising the future problems of communities obtaining basic resources, given the diminishing flows of energy, water and food into cities and suburbs. This focuses on how reasonable lifestyles can be rebuilt using a fraction of today's per capita energy resources and implementing new ways of obtaining resources at the local level.

Chapter Seven: Changed World, Changed Understanding, Changed Life

The last chapter starts by picking up the thread set out in the Introduction and analysing both what we mean by Civilisation and how this came into being as a mode of human existence and organisation. Setting out the key parameters of civilisation, the first sections of the chapter focus on the stages in the evolution of forms of inegalitarianism in society and how these have been maintained through time as rank and then stratified societies. The origins and uses of the concepts of Alienation and eventually self-commodification are used to understand the problematic of fragmentation of self-understanding as civilisation has evolved. The issue becomes the way in which inegalitarian relations hinder more rational ways of organising societies which can answer both deeper human needs and empathise with the need to maintain the natural environment.

Here a philosophical discussion develops, asking if inegalitarian forms of social existence are in any way prefigured in what it is to be human. The biological facts and the emergence of human consciousness and how this structures our capacity to understand nature and cooperate socially are investigated. This provides a view both of how open human consciousness, as social understanding, is to different possibilities of self-consciousness and how this has evolved through history. How to escape from the alienated condition of hierarchical societies becomes the focus of the following sections, looking at this not only as a problematic of social self-understanding but also an understanding of social self-consciousness and the human presence in nature. This makes reference to recent discourse both on social philosophy and the recently emerged environmental philosophy concluding the need to return to something analogous to the self-consciousness of societies before the advent of civilisation, of the annulment of the distinction between subject and object in what Freya Mathews refers to as the 'Ecological Self'.

The final sections of the chapter revisit the notion of 'community' and how this will necessarily re-emerge with the demise of global culture, but it will need to be understood and practised in a new light, not simply as a reversion to a close-knit class society and what could become some form of neo-feudalism, but as truly egalitarian, cooperative entities where maintenance of the other and of nature become second nature. The history of utopian ideas regarding the organisation of such societies, and an outline of what this involves, becomes the focus of the last section of the book with a notion that in the long run, revival of human organisation following the fall of modernity could become, at the same time, the positive 'resolution of the human condition' that sometimes was understood as the ultimate goal of the European Enlightenment.

Chapter 1: The Consequences of Unsustainable Development

As I write, I am overwhelmed by the sheer cacophony of the world we are living in. All on the surface is motion, colour, noise. There seems no time or place to reflect on what is unfolding. At the same time we are assailed by 'information', most of which we welcome; we absorb it, we are carried away by the sheer excitement, the frisson. But perhaps because of the rapidity with which the information passes over us, because of the increasing din, the increasing complexity — perhaps also for layers and layers of deeper reasons which we will be discussing —all is increasingly fragmented and the possibilities of connecting things up and making more coherent sense out of what is happening escape us. Multifarious voices speak out that are clear in their warnings that serious problems — maybe catastrophe on an unimaginable scale — lies immediately ahead and there are flashes of light where we seem to be moving towards coherence in understanding what is happening. But interest passes on and these moments are lost in the general noise.

The word 'crisis' abounds but is quickly lost in the context of things seeming, nevertheless, to work in marvellous ways, where the trains and planes turn up and leave like clockwork; somehow, almost all the time, fast moving traffic avoids accidents, the internet delivers instant information and television endless entertainment, with instant communications through twitter and blogs, with vast crowds preening themselves with mutual admiration via facebook; the supermarkets and department stores deliver an incredible array of goods and cities give themselves over regularly to festivals where citizens can lose themselves in gay abandon.

Yet for thirty years, the notion of the 'unsustainability' of this trajectory, of this way of organising the world and its increasingly globalised lifestyles has been asserted with increasing insistence and, under the surface, this is accepted as true by an ever wider population. The means to obviating what it means not to be sustained, that all this will come to an end in the foreseeable future, is put off, fails to come into perspective as anything but fragments and incoherent actions. A vast literature and a vast media outpouring has emerged, documenting and analysing what is unsustainable about our world trajectory and, in fragments, suggesting what should be done to bring it onto a sustainable track.

However, these and even the immediate crises we see unfolding around us are drowned out by the increasing noise. Ever more concrete evidence is provided: on the impossibility of maintaining escalating real estate prices and unmaintainable banking practices, the emergence of global warming and increasing natural disasters, depleting biodiversity, increasing water stress and the incipient decline in food and of energy resources. The connections between the different facets, however, fail to be made and there is no perspective on the relative importance of each dimension as they rise to the surface and then are soon eclipsed by another dimension and generally disappear below the surface of frenetic life. Few agreements can be reached on taking effective action to reduce the dangers revealed by the crises. There is a distinct sense of active denial, of not wanting to hear or to know, underlain by a fear of what this might bring and an unreflected acceptance of the growing risks. This is resulting in practice in a systematic ignoring of issues that renders it well-neigh impossible to focus coherent attention on what lies ahead.

Meanwhile, the crises are precipitating proliferating personal tragedies – increasing by millions in sudden events that hit the headlines and then disappear again from view. Hundreds of thousands of employees are being relieved of their work overnight and joining what was already ever longer-term unemployment amongst school-leavers, precipitating creeping poverty even amidst the florid affluence of the northern countries; sudden natural disasters are instantly killing thousands and rendering hundreds of thousands homeless. This can, in part, be put down to populations increasingly locating in hazard-prone areas, joining those suffering from creeping water-scarcity and, fleeing to the cities. Indeed, in the global South, we can witness a gentle descent over past years into urban un- and underemployment, ever larger populations scratching a living and constructing their own slums without access to sanitation and yet in the main seeing the world from their perspective as improving whilst the statistics indicate undernourishment topping the billion mark in 2009 and accelerating in the context of deepening crises. Meanwhile, whilst there are less organised armed conflicts today than in past decades, random crime and lawlessness makes life for all in many southern cities increasingly precarious. But on a day-to-day basis, there is no perspective on problems that are systematic in their unfolding and where, even in the medium term, matters are leading.

The Failure of the Green Movement

Across the past few decades, however, there have been initiatives and individuals who have attempted to work through the complexity to present for discussion ways of understanding the roots of the malaise and what might be done to obviate it, with small initiatives demonstrating possible escape routes. Although there had been well-articulated concerns as far back as the mid-1950s, publication of *The Limits to Growth* at the beginning of the 1970s[22] can still be seen as the clearest analysis of what lay, and still lies, before us if 'development' in the form being pursued is allowed to continue along its current trajectory. Some way into the 21st century, the authors contended, growth as generally understood — of the economy, of population, of capital —will come to an end, followed by a rapid collapse. The authors of the study attempted to indicate broadly what would have to be done to avoid collapse. At the time, this raised widespread debate in the media and in political circles with some further academic research, and even government research, following on. Within two years, however, this had died down to little more than academic memory. A quarter of a century later, very few of the younger generation have even heard of the study.

Nevertheless, *The Limits to Growth,* amongst related publications at that time, was key to bringing to life the multifaceted Environmental Movement, joining and being joined by other radical movements to produce a continuous stream of information and solutions that appeared — particularly towards the end of the 1980s — to be precipitating a broad change in attitude. Each wave, each new manifestation, however, ended in failure to make any real impact and each was quickly relegated to the memory of those who maintained a particular interest but forgotten by the general public and ignored by the mainstream political process, to be reinvented as if there had been no precedents, and then to suffer a similar fate as the growth machine and Consumer Society rolled onwards and upwards[23].

In the broad political consciousness of the Northern countries, the concerns of *The Limits to Growth* were quickly shunted into a siding under the title of 'environmental concern' and even more narrowly to concern with 'pollution of the environment' which was certainly a serious distortion of what had been intended. The introduction of the notion of 'Sustainable Development' in the early 1980s then carried the flag of the idea of a coherent view of the emerging 'limits'. But this, too, splintered into many different concerns and lost its way in the details. Although *The Limits to Growth* also had borders to what might be considered sustainability issues, nevertheless, the authors identified not only environmental impacts but also ecological and physical resource limits and the global financial system as embodying eventually incipient tendencies to contribute to the eventual collapse.

Already in 1970, under the rising pressure of the first manifestation of the Green Movement in the United States, the administration created the Environmental Protection Agency. This was not a Ministry, and remained steadfastly within the limits of its remit to improve environmental management, overwhelmingly meaning limiting environmental pollution. This was certainly well short of any critique of the wider society that was producing increasing amounts of pollution and an escalating call on non-renewable resources. Over the following decade, most countries emulated in one way or another this initiative, establishing Ministries and agencies responsible for environmental management. Everywhere, however, these remained weak agencies, the main task of which was to do little more than claim that governments were responding to the call by the Environmental Movement to address deteriorating environmental conditions. They possessed no remit to look more broadly at the economic and social impacts of deteriorating environmental conditions and not at all at the crucial issue of the long-term availability of resources to support the ongoing Development process.

Environmentalists — who re-named themselves 'Greens' — were often accused of doing no more than disseminating warnings of apocalypse to come if nothing was done. The truth is that relatively few focused serious interest on coherent alternatives to the social and political arrangements and the layers of ideology, conviction, everyday assumptions and practices that would need to be altered if the 'growth paradigm' were to be effectively halted and superseded. Nevertheless, over the forty years between the launching of the movement and the point we have arrived at, many thousands of books and an even larger outpouring of pamphlets and more ephemeral expressions were cast upon society, with conferences, sporadic serious media interventions and many school systems introducing elements of education that would alert the public to the 'environmental' problems being generated by modern life, the need for improved environmental management and countless proposals for how this might be achieved.

The structure of the Green Movement was complex, with a great proliferation of 'environmental non-governmental organisations, or 'civil society groups, academic programmes and less coherent or organised expressions. The nearest the movement came to attempting both strategic thinking and effective action, however, was through the Green political parties that started in the early 1970s (in Britain and New Zealand) and proliferated to most European countries from the early 1980s (Green politics made no headway in the incredibly elaborate, formalised and highly-financed electoral rituals of the United

38

States). The most effective was the German Green Party that emerged from a coalition of some older left-wing fragments and the new upswing in commitment to addressing the 'environmental problematic'. Achieving five per cent of the votes in Germany meant that the Greens entered the parliament , calling themselves 'the party that is not a party', thus indicating that they aimed eventually to make fundamental political changes. During the halcyon years of party, they produced a series of serious policy papers out of research carried out with the funding they received from the Government as a formal political party, aimed at taking the country down a Development path that would obviate the mounting environmental problems.

At the time in Germany, the Green Debate raged between the 'Fundis' and the 'Realos', the former believing that change had to move swiftly beyond conventional politics and into changing the ideology and thence the whole structure of modern society. The most well-articulated Green theory emerged from this milieu, with the name of Rudolph Bahro[24], a renegade East German who, released from prison and migrating to the West, for a short period becoming the chief theoretician of the movement in Germany. The Realos grew from strength to strength in the Parliament and by the 1990s were well-enough respected by the electorate to be a significant political force that agreed to form a governing coalition with the Social Democratic Party and in this sense briefly was part of the Government of Germany. However, in the process of becoming established, the debate between the Fundis and Realos snapped and the Green politicians increasingly compromised their position, conforming to the general format of conventional politics, holding out with a few policies, such as opposition to nuclear power and promotion of organic farming, that they felt they might be able to succeed with in this milieu.

The Green Movement nevertheless produced other manifestations that attempted to point in the direction of how the world should be changed to head off the collapse predicted by *Limits* and attempting to design in part or whole basic changes that would need to be undertaken. Perhaps the most coherent manifestation in the United States was the short-lived 'Bioregional Movement' of the mid-1980s[25]. In addition there was the occasional project undertaken by the more effective non-government organisations, notably the International Forum on Globalisation (IFG), that was a gathering of a number of radical intellectuals from many countries, which included numbers with 'green credentials' and also many from the global South. The group presented a coherent manifesto to change the direction which the global political and economic system was taking[26]. These, however, made no palpable headway in the media and as a movement — or dimensions of a movement — remained in the shadows of the increasingly bellicose Consumer Society.

At the level of international development discourse, environmental concern and the concept of Sustainable Development were picked up in a number of initiatives. The first of these was an international conference on environment, held in Stockholm in 1972, that first disseminated the concerns of the Environmental Movement in the North to the interlocutors in the South, and initiated what became a shadow of the Environmental Movement, with its 'Non-Government Organisations' pursuing local environmental issues. This led to the establishment of the United Nations Environment Programme (UNEP), an agency that came to be located in Nairobi, but one that has remained throughout its life marginal in the context of the International Development system. It was the International Union for Conservation of Nature and Natural Resources (IUCN), a collaboration between international agencies and environmental organisations, that created, with the support of UNEP, the first international manifesto concerning the environmental problems of ongoing Development, in the process coining the term 'Sustainable Development'[27].

Out of apparent concern for the increasingly obvious environmental depredations and looming resource exhaustion resulting from 'economic growth' at the international level, the World Commission for Environment and Development was established, leading, following a period of study and negotiation, to the publication of *Our Common Future*[28], known as the Brundtland Report after the Chair of the Commission. From there the International Conference on Environment and Development (UNCED) was organised, taking place in Rio de Janeiro in 1992.

Arguably this was the high point of international awareness of the problematic nature of the ongoing Development path, issuing and seeking the commitment of all the world's Governments to implement a four hundred page manifesto entitled Agenda 21[29]. Over the ensuing years many national Governments produced their own national Agenda 21 and, in yet more cases, national Conservation Strategies, Action Plans and lists of documents with promises and proposals, none of which were framed in anything like a coherent analysis of what should have been a turn in Development that would have confronted the issues effectively. In the event, very little of the contents of even these weak documents made any significant impact on governmental policy that might have steered the development process into more benign pathways.

Arguably the most effective outcome of Agenda 21 was the enthusiasm with which Chapter 28, concerning local government responsibilities, was taken up by local governments and civil society groups, particularly in some European countries. Eventually some six thousand Local Agenda 21 processes were initiated at the local level, proposing changes intended to head off the depredations of the Development path through local actions. In the end, these amounted to little insofar as they remained marginal to local authority actions as 'additions to' ongoing activities rather than modifying these in any meaningful way. By the early years of the new century, the movement had been routinised into the framework of conventional local administrative action without any more strategic concern with the deepening problems for the development path.

In general, mainstream 'green', and related 'radical' action, moving out of a consciousness of the problematic nature of the present, created different, overlapping foci and milieux. Important among these was concern for healthy living, extending to support for benign farming, expressed in purchase of 'green products' which, however, raised only fragmented questions as to what the true impacts of the production and marketing of even these products was and in any case attracting the commitment of only a small proportion of consumers. Whilst initially ignored by governments beyond their regular public health remit, in time, in some countries, some weak government support, for instance for organic farming, was forthcoming. Concern for wasteful use of resources produced local and eventually complex nation-wide systems for 'recycling' waste — which, however, did pitifully little to stem the continued growth in the use of resources and the production of domestic waste and remained relatively energy-intensive.

Concern to substitute the use of fossil hydrocarbons with energy from renewable sources also generated long debates, eventually producing landscapes scattered with giant wind turbines, particularly in California, Denmark and Germany and later in Texas, Spain and China as well as the proliferation of a range of other renewable energy technologies, making, however, even in countries that became known for their apparent commitment to 'renewables,' only marginal impacts on the growing thirst for energy. In very few countries did these, including older hydroelectric and all other renewable energy investments, ever supply more than ten per cent of available energy.

All these and many more initiatives which blossomed, were assumed to be pointing in the direction of Sustainable Development, but outside the confines of the Green Movement almost no efforts were made to analyse in any coherent way how much more effort would be

41

needed to achieve results that would avoid the collapse foreseen in *The Limits to Growth*, and with no steps being taken to connect the few attempts at coherent analysis with activities on the ground. Thirty years on, the authors of *Limits* published an evaluation that indicated how close the world was to the 'uncontrolled' scenario they had originally produced[30], indicating that the envisaged collapse was by now quite close at hand.

It is now clear, as we stand close to the pinnacle of *The Limits to Growth* curve, poised to make the descent, that all the attempts, from global studies through high-level national sustainability committees and action programmes and through political manifestos and academic work on environmental ethics, politics, economics and engineering and thence the overlapping manifestations of the Green Movement, made no meaningful impact on the 'growth trajectory'. Beguiled, seduced and co-opted into participating in the ever-widening offer of consumer goods and activities, in the blossoming political world of neo-liberal democracy, very few people indeed (the exception being a few scattered 'permaculture communes') could claim to live lives that were not overwhelmingly defined in terms of the mainstream consumerist mass.

The global North had succeeded in what was, after all, the central vision of the 20th century: widespread individual affluence within a socio-political framework that promoted and facilitated this. Steps to make this sustainable were an added luxury that inspired little more than passing concern and minimal gestures. In the global South, with small 'middle classes' and elites having achieved affluent societies, much of the rest were decanting rapidly out of traditional rural societies into urban slums, living between harrowing poverty and the delusion that one day they, too, might arrive. Concerns with the unsustainability of these developments had little appeal, being indeed, entirely unknown to all but a few educated minorities.

What is 'Unsustainable' about our present World?

Whilst the burgeoning academic literature found many ways of conceptualising Sustainable Development, constantly bringing new dimensions, in fact the core of the matter is very simple. We live on a finite planet but have pursued over the past two centuries a course of Development that demands constantly increasing amounts of resources. Someday, there must either be an abandonment of this 'growth paradigm' or the resource base will become exhausted, or destroyed through 'pollution' - breaking the growth trajectory and resulting in what these days is referred to as 'negative growth'.

This term already hints at the notion that Sustainable Development is an oxymoron. We will discuss this in considerably more depth in the following chapters because we are clearly looking at a concept that many – maybe most - people have been keen to agree with but in reality very few have been prepared to countenance in practice. It is in this way that obfuscation entered the arena, with widespread incantations of an agreement that our socio-economic trajectory is unsustainable but deflecting the bald facts by making things too complex to be graspable or otherwise simply ignoring them.

A favourite diagram, oft reproduced, asserts that Sustainable Development combines social and economic dimensions as well as 'the environment'. The diagram sees each of these in a circle with the intersection containing the words 'sustainable development' Indeed, whilst the term Environmentally Sustainable Development already obscured the centrality of the abuse of resources, prima facie it was surely necessary also to question whether the prevailing social and economic system, or paradigm, was worthy of sustaining. Other components of the radical movements of the present were very insistent that profound changes would be required in the social and economic systems on grounds of social justice and fair distribution so that wishing to sustain these systems would be highly questionable on moral grounds; furthermore, economic growth was precisely the problem that Sustainable Development was supposed to eliminate[31]. This famous diagram epitomised the way in which, by the end of the 20th century, the discourse on Sustainable Development, whilst having broadened out had, in practice, become a truly perverse, obfuscatory discourse.

The problem here was, again, quite simple: that few wanted to even think about the roots of the problems they were facing, being quite happy with how life was evolving around them and the cultural and ideological framework that made sense out of their lives. Hence the descent into obscure abstraction and discussions that entirely lost sight, not only of the fundamental problematic of the cultural context in which their lives were playing themselves out but even any meaningful perspective on what were major and what minor problems with respect to sustainability.

The literature on Sustainable Development nevertheless identified a long list of concerns raised by the Environmental and subsequently Green Movement as needing to be addressed. Here we take a short list of these to indicate in part why, in relation to each of these, the Development path was not yet in a state of collapse and how, once the downward passage accelerates, each of these will be likely to come into play. The point here is the interconnectedness of various dimensions that were already identified in the *Limits* study. The dimensions discussed here are:

- the financial and economic system
- energy
- water
- food
- mineral resources
- population
- environmental pollution
- global warming
- biodiversity

The Economic and Financial Systems

There is a very widespread belief, deeply embedded in modern ideology, that the health of the economic system is somehow a kind of autonomous entity outside physical reality and thus of the health of ecological systems and resource availabilities. It follows that poor economic management and sharp financial practices are the prime cause of economic problems without any need to refer to wider influences. As the global economic system falls apart over the coming decades, it is to be hoped that it will become more evident that our economic system sits squarely upon the availability and effective exploitation of physical resources and the environments with which these interact.

In the past there has been nothing to indicate that financial and economic collapses that have taken place in modern history have been in any way linked to resource shortages or environmental problems of any kind. Certainly, in the more distant past, there have been many cases where resource and environmental problems have been one and even the major cause of the collapse of whole civilisations.[32] Nevertheless, in modern times, oscillations in financial and economic conditions have been almost entirely due to the ideologies and related mechanisms through which national and international financial institutions and economies, and the political manipulations that have underlain these.

The potential instability of international financial systems has been known since the great financial crashes in the early 18th century, for

44

instance the South Sea Bubble and crash of France's Banque Royale. However, although measures were subsequently taken to guard against recurrences of these, the processes of industrial development and growth in size and complexity of modern economies, gave opportunities that, during the 19th century, resulted in relatively frequent 'booms and busts' that within countries and increasingly overflowing boundaries led to periods of widespread economic malaise.

The most profound case of autonomous economic collapse was, of course, in the United States in the 1930s, following the 1929 'Wall Street Crash'[33] that spread its effects right across the industrialised world, and into all countries where the national economy had become significantly interdependent with the industrialised economies. This created the Great Depression. We can say with some certainty that the severity and duration of this economic state had clear ideological roots in the notion of economic liberalism and the inability of political leaders to understand, and above all accept, the mechanisms easily available for the state to intervene in ways that would have 'restored business confidence' and revived the economy.

The Soviet Union, the economy of which grew strongly throughout the Great Depression, showed clearly what state economic planning and management could achieve to obviate the causes of the Depression. Furthermore, some European Governments, particularly fascist Germany,[34] were prepared to take steps already in the 1930s to intervene in order to control and direct the financial and industrial systems and the owners of capital in charge of these, and to create employment and with it incomes for the broad masses. Certainly the effort of fighting the Second World War, demanding the production of a vast flow of war materials, had the effect of eliminating the causes of the Depression. After the war, it was the theoretical framework for economic management developed by the economist John Maynard Keynes, and the way in which this framework was, at least in part and in different ways in different countries, implemented following the war that moderated economic oscillations in the immediate post-war decades.

The 'Neo-Liberal Counterrevolution' of 1979-80, that returned in certain respects to the ideological framework of the 19th century economy, might have been expected, sooner or later, to repeat the problems of the Great Depression insofar as regulatory controls were rolled back, exposing the system to the possibilities of runaway speculation that had been the cause of the Great Depression. Indeed, many economists and many books written on the subject, and in recent times even the World Bank, had warned about this possibility, even inevitability, given some of the more arcane means used to extend the mechanisms of economic speculation through the 1990s, that there would at some stage be a major collapse of the international financial, and with it the economic system.

Whilst there were some partial banking crises during the 1990s, it was clearly the 2008 financial collapse that brought much of the unrealistic financial speculation back to a more realistic level of activity. Widespread comment on its aftermath was that whilst some of the banks involved in the speculation and collapse disappeared and the US and some European banking systems as such only survived through government support, still far from sufficient attention was being paid to reintroducing strong regulatory measures to head off a new wave of speculation[35]. In the light of this, a further round of 'boom and bust' could be expected sooner or later to erupt.

In the end, financial and economic management and the Development process that this has contributed to facilitating over the past two centuries, could become a sustainability issue if the political conjuncture evolved into a situation where a particular faction were to decide to implement measures explicitly designed to undo development or to restrict its benefits to a small group or class. However, in the present world this appears to be an extremely unlikely scenario even though in practice control over financial resources, economies and their ostensible benefits have in recent years accrued predominantly to a very small group of super-rich and powerful citizens. In the end, the economy is not exogenous to the political system but a function of it, including the oscillations which it manifests.

Nevertheless, the substance of economies that, we might say, are the raison d'être and finally the measure of the economic success of modernity, are the products and services that they deliver and these are themselves reliant on the increasing flow of material resources, rather than the decisions of bankers or industrialists. Could it be that underlying the health of the modern economy, out of sight of the everyday discussion and the whole superstructure of financial and economic management, the flow of resources plays some kind of a role in determining the health of the economic system?

Famously, Barnett and Morse in a book entitled *Scarcity and Growth* published in the early 1960s[36] made the case for the dismissal of natural resource flows as determinants of economic health. They argued from past evidence not only that natural resource prices would fall continuously into the future but that 'diminishing returns' (rising prices) that might be expected as resources become more scarce would always lead to substitutes being found and exploited (improvements in accessing previously inaccessible resources or finding other resources to fulfil the same purpose). Diminishing returns became in this view a non-issue.

On the whole, resource prices did, in fact, decline consistently from the 1950s into the new millennium (with a brief spike in the early 1970s coinciding with the OPEC-engineered oil price rise)[37]. However, from the early years of the new century, these began an upward trend. This was particularly the case with energy, and especially petroleum, such that there was by now widespread agreement that these price rises were a contributing (as yet not seen as the main) factor in the financial crash of 2008 and the subsequent downward passage of the international economy. The issue then becomes not that the financial and economic systems themselves are sustainability issues but whether the flow of resources that become the commodities delivered by the economy will continue to flow, as the real focus of economic sustainability.

Energy

In retrospect, it must be deemed a strange anomaly that throughout the era of environmentalism, few environmentalists have focused on the possibility that the key to non-sustainability might lie in the eventual inability to supply the increasing amounts of energy demanded by the global economic system, which would never free itself from abject dependence on fossilised hydrocarbons and would therefore eventually collapse as access to what remains of these became increasingly difficult. The simple fact is that the whole development process from the mid-17th century until today - in short, industrialisation and urbanisation - has been built upon the exploitation of fossilised hydrocarbons and appears increasingly to stand or fall on the continued growth in the supply of these.

Traditional sources of energy, notably biofuels and water power, continued to be exploited and in the latter case, developed strongly with the introduction of electricity. However, these were left behind by the continued increase in the exploitation of fossil hydrocarbons upon which development and everything to do with modern life became increasingly dependent. With the invention of the means to exploit nuclear power it seemed briefly as if this would, one day, take over as the source that would satisfy all the energy needs of modern civilisation. However, from the mid-1970s, this dream was eclipsed as the high cost of nuclear electricity and realisation of the disasters that could, and eventually did, result from accidents, resulted in an almost complete cessation of investment in these technologies. Today, over three quarters of global energy use is satisfied by fossil hydrocarbons and in the case of transport, over ninety per cent.

How did we come to this pass? A short history of the supply of energy to fuel modern civilisation is useful. Until the middle of the 18th Century – just two hundred and fifty years ago – all civilisations were fuelled overwhelmingly from biofuels, wood and agricultural residues, with, starting already in ancient times, curious inventions that yielded tiny amounts of energy from the flows of wind and water, most importantly, of course, to power ships. Significant exploitation and use of fossil fuels, in the first instance in the form of coal, started in the late 18th century and accelerated in Britain across the 19th century, thence spreading, particularly to Germany and the United States, as the power behind industrialisation.

The exploitation of oil started in the second half of the 19th century, growing simultaneously in what is today Azerbaijan, and in Pennsylvania, to become a significant industry by the turn of the 20th century, though it was not until the middle of the 20th century that oil came to eclipse coal and in the ensuing decades that natural gas grids spread throughout Europe and North America. Following the oil crisis of the 1970s, the use of coal began again to climb, as an increasingly significant fuel for electricity production. The fact that it is possible to produce oil and gas from coal is well enough known through the experience from the mid 19th century where 'town gas' was produced and distributed throughout the towns and cities of Europe and North America and that during the Second World War, Germany, possessing no oil resources but substantial reserves of coal, initiated production of oil from coal to power its war machine.

The notion that fossil hydrocarbon as the main source of energy to fuel the world economy might one day run into problems of access (there will always remain large quantities in the ground which are, however, no longer accessible) was first explored in a book by the then renowned economist William Stanley Jevons, entitled *The Coal Question*, published as long ago as 1865. Whilst his predictions of exhaustion were clearly premature and little thought was given in the ensuing decades as to exactly when these resources might fall short, the general thesis, whist being ignored, was nevertheless unassailable: assuming fossil hydrocarbons continue to fuel our society, sometime in the future, what remains of these resources will be become inaccessible — and sooner rather than later, in the context of exponential growth in demand, as could be seen throughout the 20th century. There always seemed to be alternative energy sources waiting in the wings that might be assumed to substitute for fossil hydrocarbons when exhaustion began to reveal itself in earnest.

Plucked recently from obscurity, it was M King Hubbert who, in a paper published in 1956, explored the issue of the longevity and probable profile of easily accessible petroleum exploitation[38]. This was important as petroleum had, by then, become the backbone of modern energy supplies. His calculations led to predictions, based on the history of discoveries of oil in the US, of a rise and decline in production, that would more or less follow a regular bell-shaped curve; this implied that decline in production (the cusp being known as 'peak oil') would come already when only half the accessible resources had been exploited. His prediction of such a growth and depletion profile for the United States, based on an assessment of extensive knowledge of the geology of the country, proved to be close to correct and he went on to construct from the available evidence a similar curve for global oil production.

Whilst his prediction was somewhat disrupted by the temporary drop in oil consumption consequent upon the OPEC-instigated price rises of 1973 and 1979, this merely pushed the predicted global oil production peak from the end of the 1990s to around 2010. In the event, by 2010 most of the oil producing countries had already peaked, with production on the descent and global production increasingly reliant upon the major Middle East oil producing countries.

Meanwhile a new perspective on the descent in oil production had arisen where it had become clear that the efficiency of production was constantly in decline. This is expressed in terms of the declining energy return on energy invested (EROEI). Being concentrated sources, fossil hydrocarbons, at least in their fluid and gaseous state, require in the first instance little investment to yield substantial amounts of useful energy. The original oil discoveries had an EROEI of a hundred to one - one hundred units of energy available for other uses per energy unit invested. Gradually this has declined so that today the best oil wells produce at a rate of twenty to one.

The wells in the United States are down to around fifteen to one. Furthermore, almost everywhere the amount emerging from the ground is in decline. Once the ratio approaches one to one then clearly exploitation no longer makes sense, even if there are still considerable resources in the ground and in fact, even with 'enhanced recovery', being the best practice in terms of oil extraction, something less than half the oil in any well can be recovered at an 'energy profit'. The result of this is that in the coming years the downward slope of *accessible and usable* fossil energy could, in practice, be substantially steeper than the upward slope, as increasing amounts of energy are used simply to access what is left of the resource rather than being put to other uses.

In principle, similar curves to those produced for oil exploitation could be expected, also for other fossil hydrocarbons, notably gas and coal, albeit the profile of exploitation has been more erratic in past years, making it difficult to make anything like an accurate assessment from the evidence of when the peak might occur. Changes in production methods, for instance the sudden increase in the tapping of 'shale gas' in the United States, discussed further below, are likely to make more difficult any simple forecasting by modelling or other systematic forms of estimation. The problem of diminishing EROEI, i.e. the increasing amounts of energy needed to exploit new sources and the remainder of the old, eventually becomes relevant in all cases.

Until the emergence of the debate concerning the advent of peak oil, statistics on the potential future availability of fossil hydrocarbons given out by established bodies were provided in terms of total future availability in number of years, assuming current consumption rates. However, if the exponential growth in demand plus Hubbert's theory that decline in availability would start to set in when only half the accessible resource has been exploited are taken into account, then the picture changes radically. Although Hubbert was a respected oil geologist, his theory of growth and decline of oil availability was dismissed by his colleagues. Clearly what should have started to happen, had his research been taken seriously, would have been comprehensive explorations of where energy might come from once decline in fossil hydrocarbon availability set in.

The 1970s did see much research in this area, in the context of the then relatively high oil prices precipitated by the control of global oil supply by the OPEC countries, leading to sharp increases in oil prices in 1973 and then again in 1979. The issue became how to use less energy to achieve the same ends through efficiency measures and a start was made on the development of tools to be able to analyse energy use more coherently so as to be able to plan future use. Also a start was made to more in-depth research and development of renewable energy production technologies. This did not, however, last very long, reducing greatly in interest and financial support as the OPEC control of oil prices fell apart and the real price of oil dropped to pre-1973 levels.

It is truly bizarre just how silent the 1990s were when it came to analysing where global energy demand was heading and, at this rate of acceleration and the increasing reliance on fossil hydrocarbons, and particularly oil, how rapidly 'Hubbert's peak' was approaching. Energy supply was simply not an issue and one may look far and wide for any literature from the 1990s that had any significant concern about potential future energy shortages. Fear amongst European governments that Middle Eastern regimes might turn off the oil tap was an important factor in energy policy from the 1950s to the mid 1980s. This was a major impetus behind the development of nuclear power in Europe, and particularly in France, in the 1960s. The fear was made more concrete through OPEC's success in raising the international traded price of oil. This high price, plus efforts to destroy the power of OPEC, led to the development and exploitation of petroleum resources in many countries, most notably from the North Sea and Alaska's North Slope that, in succeeding in undermining OPEC, triggered the decline in oil prices in the 1980s. It also had the effect of substantially reducing structured thought on the future of energy supplies generally. Production from most of these minor sources of oil and gas is now in decline as a consequence of diminishing accessibility of what is left.

The possibility of displacing the use of fossil fuels with energy from renewable sources had, of course, been a major issue pursued by the Green Movement since its emergence in the 1970s. All manner of means had been deployed by the movement to bring the issue to the surface, via numbers of academic analyses, and with small industries developing and offering various technologies. However, these remained almost entirely ignored. By the early years of the new century, little had been done to deploy renewable energy sources that were, by now, yielding less than fifteen per cent of global energy supplies — eleven per cent from biofuels, three per cent from water power and less than one per cent via wind, solar and sundry other marginal sources. Meanwhile energy from nuclear power stations was going into decline as a consequence of decommissioning and lack of new investments throughout the 1980s and 1990s, satisfying no more than seven per cent of global energy demand.

In recent years, regular pieces in the media have implied that a crash programme in investment in renewable sources could substitute for the loss of energy from fossil hydrocarbons, allaying worries amongst that part of the public that didn't want to hear of problems ahead. These, however, lent a fallacious sense of optimism for two reasons. Firstly, apart from hydroelectric dams where the lion's share of the available sites have already been exploited, energy from renewable sources — the sun, wind and waves — is extremely dispersed so that investments in harvesting it have to be over vast surfaces to achieve anything more than modest results relative to the massive throughput of energy fuelling the modern world and again, with the exception of hydropower, the EROEI is very modest, requiring massive investments for relatively small energy outputs.

We can see this in the already impressive landscapes of huge wind turbines in Germany and to a lesser extent in other countries, and also in a few cities the proliferation of solar arrays which, however, produce only a very modest proportion of the energy consumed and do nothing to substitute for the massive use of oil to fuel transport systems. Related to this is the fact that any crash programme to invest in renewable sources, at the rate of decline in fossil hydrocarbons which may be expected over the coming decades, would firstly need to be sure that the technology choice is sound and well-developed and then be available in truly vast quantities that would take decades to ramp up but which are as yet hardly on the horizon.

In practice, there is little urgency to develop sources of renewable energy. A brief boom in investments in the United States, fuelled by subsidies relating to the 'recovery' from the 2008 economic crisis (tiny by comparison with capital continuing to be poured into facilitating the flow of fossil fuels), collapsed again in 2012. Chinese investment had now become the greatest growth area in renewable sources, including now the largest producers of solar and wind technologies; these installations, however, pale into insignificance (supplying less than five per cent of national energy consumption) when contrasted with continuing massive growth in the consumption of oil for transport and coal to generate electricity.

The actual mix of energy sources varies substantially between countries. While, for instance, a handful of countries possess significant nuclear capacity, a few others that happen to possess substantial sites for hydroelectric dams gain a significant proportion of their electricity from this source and then a few governments took the decision to subsidise wind power so that this has become a modest source of electricity. Biofuels remain the main energy source in the poorest countries but, although even at the peak of global development, they supply as much energy as was the case two hundred years earlier when this was virtually the only source of energy for the whole of humanity. As noted, these now satisfy just eleven per cent of global energy demand.

In spite of the warnings of the International Energy Agency (IEA), the global agency responsible for monitoring energy supply and use, the precarious situation with regard to the future source of energy for Development - and for supporting current lifestyles - remains entirely absent from mainstream political debate. Instead, there has continued to be loud announcements on new energy finds, new discoveries and investments in renewable sources and in nuclear power, suggesting that there is nothing to worry about, when in practice none of these could make more than a very modest impact on the expected accelerating decline in energy, following the general curve of diminishing fossil hydrocarbons.

Warnings that peak oil would soon be upon us came first not from the oil companies or government energy agencies but, rather, from individual oil geologists and investors. Starting at the end of the 1990s, public debate arose — notably initiated by ex-Shell executive Colin Campbell who went on to found the Association for the Study of Peak Oil and Gas (ASPO) in 2002 — followed by a number, initially of American academics, from a proliferation of disciplines. These insights, however, remained marginalised, in an extraordinary level of denial, in spite of clear evidence provided by oil companies of the problematic[39]. Only in 2008, in the midst of the then rapid rise in the price of oil, did the International Energy Agency, that had hitherto avoided the issue by only presenting expected demand and avoiding the issue of potential supply, reveal imminent problems in the supply of both oil and gas. The November 2008 release of their flagship World Energy Outlook[40] report opened with the statement that:

Current Global Trends in Energy Supply and Consumption are patently unsustainable – environmentally, economically, socially.

It went on to announce that if the current oil demand trends were to be satisfied, it would be necessary to bring on line the equivalent of six times current Saudi Arabian supply by 2030 — just 21 years ahead. Whilst the IEA noted that part of this need would be satisfied from known reserves, these were far from what they expected by way of demand. In the event, however, the 2008 economic recession brought demand for energy down rapidly, ahead of even the most dire predictions, and the resulting glut of oil brought the oil price tumbling down to be followed, however, by a relatively rapid climb back up to levels that continued to have debilitating effects on the global economy.

However, a further change in perspective on the depletion of oil and gas has arisen as increased evidence of the peak in easily accessible oil and gas approaches. This has brought into the equation resources referred to as 'unconventional' oil and gas. It is important for the interpretation of matters throughout this book to understand what this means and what the implications are or could be. A little known fact is that besides the easily accessible resources of liquid oil, gas and the

53

concentrated energy in coal, there remain vast quantities of hydrocarbon locked in various rock formations that are generally classified as 'tar sands' and 'oil shales'. These have been known for many centuries and oil shale, mined and burned in the same way as coal, has featured as a low-grade fuel (with calorific value less than half that of coal), at least since the 17th century. We might imagine that as remaining coal resources become increasingly difficult to access later in this century, the vast resources of oil from these sources will, in principle, come into their own to fuel the final stages of modernity.

The mining of tar sands started in Canada in the 1970s and by the early years of the 21st century had grown into a significant industry in the sense that a substantial area of land had been subjected to open cast mining and was, by 2008, producing petroleum at a rate contributing three per cent to global oil consumption. Loud environmentalist objections were being systematically overridden as the industry continued to expand. Economic analysis, which sees the matter entirely in terms of comparative costs, asserts that as the price of conventional oil and gas increases, so this industry will rapidly expand, both in Canada and in other countries (such as Venezuela) where significant deposits are to be found.

Global estimates of recoverable amounts of oil and gas produced from oil shale are considered to be more than the remaining recoverable reserves of oil extracted by conventional means. However, the production of oil and gas from this source presents considerable problems such that what is or is not truly recoverable remains a very open question. Historically, various petrochemical substances, including fuels, have been produced in very small quantities from oil shale in many countries and whilst this almost entirely ceased with the growth of the modern petrochemical industry, interest increased again during the 1970s oil crisis and again in recent years. A large number of technologies have been developed to extract the oil from oil shale, which have yet to produce methods that will yield up the oil to mass extraction at a reasonable cost in economic and energy terms. Currently 0.025 per cent of global petroleum production is derived from oil shale mainly in China and Brazil but only in Estonia does shale oil satisfies a significant amount of the national energy demand.

The most dramatic development with respect to oil shale has been the recent growth in the extraction of gas in the United States through hydraulic fracturing – a technology that has been used already for many decades in 'enhanced recovery' of oil from declining oil wells - that has entered the popular media as 'fracking'. Over the past fifteen years huge investments in many thousands of wells have come to yield significant amounts of gas that have reversed what was a rapid decline in gas production in the United States. As with exploitation of tar sands, the environmental impacts of fracking are considerable — polluting groundwater with the chemicals used in the fracturing process and releasing considerable quantities of methane contributing to global warming — which does not mean that the industry cannot or will not continue to expand. But what is also evident is the short-term life of the wells that yield more than half their production within one year and yield little gas beyond a few years[41].

Furthermore, this method is good for extracting only those resources close to the surface and hence may access only a small fraction of the potential yield. It can be seen that this is certainly no long-term answer to the decline in available fossil energy. However, technological means of accessing more of the resource may well emerge in the coming decades. And finally, the EROEI of exploiting the 'unconventional sources' is extremely low, in comparison with 'conventional' oil and gas exploitation, meaning, as discussed above, ever increasing amounts of fossil energy needing to be extracted for a given yield in usable energy.

The upshot is as follows: Whilst substantial effort and imagination is going into devising technologies that maximise output whilst minimising the need for environmentally problematic inputs and pollution caused by extraction and processing of unconventional oil and gas, the simple matter of the modest amounts of energy per ton of material in the ground mean that even if the massive investments implied become available, the industry will grow only slowly and in all probability never be able to extract more than a small fraction of oil and gas as a consequence of technical inaccessibility and emergent decreasing EROEI.

The IEA indicated this in their assessments of where energy might come from between now and 2030 and it is clear that as the downward passage of conventional oil and gas accelerates over the coming decades, attempts to replace this from unconventional sources will look increasingly forlorn, whilst laying waste to vast landscapes and greatly exacerbating the production of greenhouse gases in the attempt. Of course one would wish that this path is not followed and that, rather, the changes outlined in the later parts of this book terminate the attempts, leaving in the ground in perpetuity what in the end will be more than eighty per cent of what were the global hydrocarbon deposits prior to the advent of the extraction industries.

We turn now to take a final look specifically at the production of electricity. Whilst a few countries have been favoured with substantial hydropower sites and less than a handful of countries have developed nuclear power to become a significant source of their electricity, in most countries electricity generation has always been based predominantly on fossil hydrocarbons, with coal as the main source supplemented by oil and then natural gas. The decline in gas may come within a relatively short space of time although this has been allayed at least in the United States by the development of shale gas. However, coal should be available for many decades ahead and where this is the mainstay of electricity generation (currently fifty per cent in the United States and ninety per cent in China), coal-fired generation plants could continue to function possibly until significantly beyond the middle of the century. This would have the effect of progressively exacerbating the greenhouse effect and, as noted, this could continue into the more distant future, as long as the economies in which the power stations are located can continue to support them with the burning of oil shale.

Insofar as there is open discussion on the coming decline in energy, this mainly focuses on the threats to the cost of transport and other dimensions of everyday lifestyles. The impacts will, however, be no simple matter of a new frugality in energy-using habits. Barnett and Morse noted that access to adequate (and cheap) energy resources is a prerequisite for the diminishing cost of accessing all other resources — that is to say that energy is the key to access all other resources and then of the processing of these and the manufacturing from these of all products needed to sustain human life. Cheap and abundant energy, and specifically hydrocarbon resources, is thus clearly a prerequisite for continuing to run the globalised economy. Hence, prima facie, falling energy availability must be seen as the primary dimension of the sustainability of our current world. Rapid decline in the availability of energy is clearly catastrophic from the point of view of any hopes of continuing the century-long aspiration to grow economically and beyond that to live affluent, modern lives.

Water

Water was not one of the early concerns of the Environmental Movement but attention grew over the years, more as an international development issue than one associated with the Green Movement. After 1990, the concept of 'water stress' became common currency, denoting the amount of available water per head of population that, with population growth, was inexorably falling, precipitating water crises in country after country. The issue was, in practice, extremely complex and multi-dimensional with battle lines drawn between burgeoning international water companies asserting that water is a commodity versus environmentalist (or non-government water organisations and coalitions) campaigning for a global policy of water as a basic human right, directing governments to ensure that populations were supplied with the water they needed. The fact of the matter was that good management and adequate investment could, and in northern countries had hitherto, allayed water crises that would otherwise have manifested themselves in the form of water stress.

Water was big business and big national government programmes were where the battle lines were often drawn between different claimants to the same water source — for urban and industrial water supply, irrigation and hydroelectric power. All of these proponents could claim superficially to be investing in Sustainable Development: urban water supply undertakings alleviating urban water shortages, irrigation authorities extending the productive capacity of agriculture, and power authorities asserting hydropower as the primary renewable energy source. However, all of these — and particularly the dam-builders — came within the critique of the Green Movement as precipitating serious problems, through displacement of populations and damage to, or complete elimination of, valued ecosystems to make way for reservoirs and other infrastructure such as inter-basin water transfers.

The struggle to halt the development of major water infrastructure, focusing on analysis of immediate impacts and actions, reflected little on the longer-term unsustainability of much that was happening. High dams would eventually silt up, some major reservoirs silting in less than a half century due to deforestation and erosion of mountainsides upstream. Irrigation systems were, in some very extensive cases (most dramatically, the Ogallala aquifer underlying several middle-American states), mining fossil water (water collected underground in past eras and replenished only slowly or not at all) and so would in just a matter of decades cease to flow. Meanwhile, many irrigation systems were losing their effectiveness through salinisation and waterlogging of the irrigated areas so that, again, these could only be productive for a matter of decades. In cases where irrigation water is produced by pumping ground water, this too will run into increasing problems as energy resources become scarce. Clearly this spells immense problems for maintaining food production.

Finally, the massive transfers of water to supply cities in water-poor areas required substantial inputs of energy to pump the water, which in a situation of diminishing energy supply would cease to serve the needs of urban settlements for which they were built, so that the cities will only survive as long as the energy supply systems continue to function. The cities that have recently grown around the Arabian Gulf and in a few other areas 'solved' their water supply problems by building desalination plants that extract sweet water from seawater. Although in a few places this is accomplished on a small scale using solar power, all the larger cities rely on the use of fossil fuel and are thus clearly unsustainable within the coming decades. However, even large cities in areas where there are considerable sweet water resources have come to rely on massive pumping, ergo significant amounts of energy, to operate and are in this sense unsustainable.

Urban water systems have suffered an additional problem of pollution of water sources by wastewater. In addition, the almost universal application of agrochemicals on farmland has consistently had a similar effect of polluting ground and surface water, sometimes over wide areas and affecting urban water supplies downstream. Severe water pollution problems arose in the growth of cities in Europe in the course of the 19th century, resulting in epidemics of water-borne disease that triggered the invention and construction of urban sewerage systems. By the turn of the 21st century, however, although cities in the global North were largely equipped with such sanitation systems, at the global level, still 90% of urban wastewater was entering the environment untreated.

Furthermore, even where elaborate sewerage systems existed, these worked to remove and dispose of human waste that should have been returned to the soil as nutrients, where in practice artificial agrochemicals were being applied to all but the very small percentage of soils that were under organic agriculture. Both of these practices will reveal themselves as unsustainable under conditions of the loss of energy to run urban water supply and sewerage systems and with the loss of agrochemicals as the 'fuel' of modern agricultural systems. In the opening years of the 21st century, explicitly addressing the unsustainability of these practices, a new movement under the titles of 'sustainable sanitation' or 'ecosan' came into existence to demonstrate alternative sanitation systems[42]. However, this does no more than illustrate the path which will have to be trodden to undo the dysfunctional sanitation systems of modern cities.

It is thus evident that over the coming decades, whilst in principle water for human use is a renewable resource and may be accessed indefinitely, in practice modernity has manipulated the flow of water resources in multiple ways that are clearly unsustainable *per se* and as energy resources decline this will have a major impact on the productivity of much of the world's agriculture and the viability of life in most of the world's cities.

Food

The concern that food production can at any time fall short of needs is as old as there has been any coherent thought about Development. That is to say that most places in the world have at some stage throughout civilisation, and usually periodically, suffered famine. In the short term this has generally resulted from fluctuations in weather conditions exacerbated by population growth in a situation of inadequate investment – mental and financial. In the past the productivity of soils has, in many places, deteriorated radically over time as a consequence of unsustainable farming practices, the most renowned case being the collapse over a period of two centuries of the Maya civilisation in Central America, which failed to understand what was happening in terms of the exhaustion of soil fertility through monoculture, and in the light of this to change their farming practices.

Amongst the early publications of what became the Environmental Movement, one of the major themes was possible future shortfalls in food supply, linked to a concern that the world population was growing too fast or eventually beyond the capacity of the global food production system to be able to cope[43]. Sometimes furious academic arguments went back and forth and the United Nations Food and Agriculture Organisation (FAO) and World Food Programme took up the challenge of promoting policies and programmes to obviate food shortages in the long term and address short-term food supply crises.

Global programmes, including the 'Green Revolution' where international research institutions succeeded in developing and disseminating higher yield grain species, seemed to address these problems in the public mind and in practice to greatly increase the production of food, so that over the following decades, occasional shortages in particular countries due to failed harvests or other internal maladjustments in the food production system did not result in famines. The concern about possible shortfalls in food supply and, in the extreme, famines, remains, however, not far below the surface of politics in most southern countries where hunger is a reality for significant and growing populations, resulting in periodic food riots. Food security was indeed for three decades following the Second World War the primary concern behind the European Common Agricultural Policy. However, increasingly the ideology asserting that 'the market' would resolve any problems came to the fore, shifting the focus of food policy (in all probability temporarily) away from concern with possible food shortages.

Thus, from the 1970s, the Environmental Movement shifted its concern with food supply, coming to refocus on the increased use of agrochemicals in farming, worldwide, exacerbated by the demands of new, highly productive grain strains. The promotion by the movement of organic farming in various forms as a central focus, and in time with permaculture as the eventual 'solution' to food production in terms of truly sustainable production, became one of the hallmarks of the movement. The concern here was both the eventual unsustainability in the supply of agrochemicals and also the health impacts of agrochemical residues in food.

Whilst the farming community and their support in government, with agrochemical industry influence in the background, was hostile to the organic farming lobby well into the 1990s, eventually, with public pressure emanating from what became one of the successes of the Green Movement, most European government agencies responsible for agriculture policies and programmes came to accept, and in a small way support, organic farming. The fact that nevertheless, the global food production system continued to be heavily dependent on petrochemicals for the high yield of food production per hectare of land, and that therefore decline in availability of petrochemicals would lead to decline in food production, did not re-emerge as a key concern of the movement.

The decline in availability of fossil hydrocarbons will signal also the decline in productivity of soils (though it may contribute to the revival of rich soils damaged by agrochemicals). As discussed later in the book, it is not, however, merely the productivity of the soils but the immense inputs of fossil energy into the whole modern food chain, including mechanised farming methods and food transport, processing and distribution that will come to an end in the coming decades. It will therefore, be necessery to organise farming at a relatively local level. In this way, the levels of global food production we see today will decline substantially, with obvious consequences for the maintenance of today's global population. Meanwhile, food production in many places around the world is already being negatively affected by climate change and much study is going into estimating what this might mean into the future for the general decline in food production — which will be in addition to that resulting from the decline in energy resources.

Besides farming, a significant source of food, and particularly protein, was in the past yielded from the harvesting of fish from the seas, with many coastal communities heavily dependent on this for their sustenance. The increase in fish harvesting, both from the competition between local and international fishing fleets and thence the increasing sophistication of fishing technologies, led progressively to the over-fishing of fishing grounds around the world. This meant that more fish were being harvested than the rate of reproduction with a profile of a downward slope that came to a point of sudden radical decline over a few years. By the turn of the 21st century it was estimated by the UN Food and Agriculture Organisation (FAO) that half the world's fisheries were fully exploited and incipiently over-exploited, and a further third were some way into the curve of collapse with little being done to stem the decline.

On the other hand, there was a rapid increase in fish farming, focusing on relatively few species and, in many cases, with poor practices that led to collapse also of fish farms over just a few years, consequent on increase in disease and polluted ponds. This was not, however, a necessary phenomenon but simply a matter of poor management practices. Within two or three decades, with the future decline in energy resources, ocean fishing is likely to decline greatly. However, experience into the 21st century indicated that even when fishing of particular grounds ceased entirely, these did not 'bounce back' rapidly in terms of the return of fish stocks. This is probably because the entire ecological balance of these grounds has collapsed, so that it may take many decades and even centuries, long after the capacity of humans to exploit the oceans except on the small scale such as happened prior to fossil hydrocarbons, for these to recover their ecological richness. Global Warming could, however, lead to a far longer-term decline in fish stocks as a dimension of a general planetary ecological collapse.

Mineral Resources

Concern that mineral resources would someday be exhausted in the context of increased mining activity arose strongly in the 1950s in the United States; this was primarily seen in the simplistic thinking of the era in terms of the Soviet Union 'winning' the Cold War and establishing a global empire by possessing access, for longer, of key resources. We might say that it is prima facie rather obvious that minerals cannot continue indefinitely to be dug out of the ground and so this is clearly a problem for sustainability of a society that insists on continually expanding production of resources. However, whilst the detailed studies carried out at the time tended to see exhaustion of many resources happening within decades, we might ask why these studies did not trigger a deeper questioning of the Development process and its faith in continued growth. Whilst the well-known, but controversial economist Kenneth Boulding was to quip:

Anyone who believes exponential growth can go on forever in a finite world is either a madman or an economist.

As already noted, economists Barnett and Morse confirmed the prejudice of the mainstream economics profession as a whole, and in the process set the public mind at rest, concluding that as exhaustion of one resource is approached, the price will rise, triggering a search for and investment in substitutes. However, the fact that the search for and exploitation of mineral resources will always demand plentiful and cheap energy into the indefinite future will surely show in the future the fallacy of this thesis. How and why this should have been accepted as dogma becomes part of a broader discussion in Chapter Four.

Population

The growth in human population was a further sustainability issue that surfaced strongly at the outset of the Environmental Movement but which faded into the background of the movement's concerns during the course of the 1970s[44]. From the 1950s through to the early 1990s, there were, however, strong, open debates about the wisdom of allowing the human population to continue to grow at the rapid rate that has been witnessed at least since the middle years of the 19th century. This was seen as a central problem in the debates surrounding the production of *The Limits to Growth* and a few governments — notably the Chinese but also the Indonesian and Indian Governments — took population control seriously and implemented more or less successful policies to bring down the rate of population growth with, not far in the back of the mind of policy-makers, the potential problem of producing enough food to feed growing populations.

Following a pivotal summit held in Cairo in 1994 on the subject of population, this debate was brought almost to a complete halt with a residue pursued by the almost invisible UN Population Fund (UNFPA). It became evident that a wide array of political opinion, ranging from governments that equated more population with more political power, through to religious groups — particularly Catholics and Muslims — and radical women's 'body politics', who presented reasons rooted in their own dogmas, effectively silenced those arguing the dangers of continued population growth.

We can, nevertheless, be certain that increased populations, thanks to greatly increased survival rates facilitated by modern medicine and hygiene, have been central to the depletion of ecosystems and hence reduction in biodiversity, greatly exacerbated by changing practices in terms of farming, general modern production processes, and, above all consumption lifestyles. It is vanishingly improbable that, in the face of declining energy resources and hence both decline of irrigation systems and in the availability of agrochemicals and in addition the depredations of climate change, the world will be able to continue to support even the present world population, which is approaching seven billion, even presupposing considerably more frugal lifestyles.

The United Nations was, until the end of the first decade of the 21st century, confidently expecting the world population to continue upwards from the then six billion to some nine or ten billion by the middle of the century. Certainly, attempts to sustain the spread of modern lifestyles with such an increasing population should have been brought into question, at least allowing for debate and the possibility of other scenarios. It is clear that nobody would wish to think or talk about the notion of forced population decline: everyone might conjecture 'would this mean my own premature death?' Nevertheless, in the context of the unsustainability of energy and water resources and the consequent decline in food production it is extremely difficult to envisage even the maintenance of the present world population, let alone the continued increase projected by the United Nations.

In parentheses, it should be added that with the collapse of the Soviet Union in 1990, the collapse of its economy led to local solutions to food production of the kinds we will be discussing later in this text. It also led to decline in the population that was not simply through hunger, but through disorientation, particularly of the male population, as a consequence of the loss of employment and more generally the fundamental change in the goals of the society. It was estimated by the United Nations that some three million 'premature deaths' resulted in this context[45]. The diminution of population over the coming decades will in all probability not merely result from hunger or famine but have other complex causes in the inability of large numbers to be able to make the physical or mental transition to the very different kinds of society that will inevitably result from the fall of modernity and which are the main focus of the second half of this book.

Environmental Pollution

One of the main foci of the early Environmental Movement, together with resource and population concerns, was that modern life and economic growth were increasingly polluting the environment. What this meant was that ecological systems were increasingly impaired and human health affected by the waste products of modern industry, lifestyles and the testing and use of new military technologies. In practice, this was not a new concern but had been the subject of attention of waves of earlier social movements. Urbanisation and industrialisation in the 19th and early 20th centuries in Europe and North America led to severe contamination of water and air of cities and in the proximity of heavy industries[46]. Although ignored for many decades, the poor health condition of growing urban populations and the deterioration of ecological and agricultural production systems in the vicinity of cities eventually encouraged the growth of social movements insisting that serious steps be taken to reduce or even eliminate pollution.

The first major step taken from the middle of the 19th century was the invention and thence construction of urban sewer systems that spread throughout Europe and North America over the ensuing century. However, these dealt only partially with the problems, often simply taking the contaminated water to the edge of the city where it was deposited in rivers or the sea, where rural populations would have to contend with the smells and health dangers. By the beginning of the 21st century still only ten per cent of human waste was being treated before discharge into the environment. Generally, it took major accidents or clear signs of impacts on human health, such as the 'smogs' of London through the late 19th to the mid-20th centuries that in most winters resulted in increased mortality rates, for steps to be taken to reduce the problems. And in all cases, it took vocal social movements to raise the issues enough to precipitate political action.

The late 20th century Environmental and thence Green Movements took the concern about pollution from being something local and relevant to particular cities and industrial plants, to a concern for the way in which pollution in the late 20th century had become a global problem. This is to say that pollutants were now spreading throughout the earth's atmosphere and seas and that legacies of past industrial activity were not just local but were now having widespread effects. The World Bank made a useful distinction between what it termed the 'brown agenda', where particularly southern cities were growing without the benefits of the kinds of environmental controls that had been implemented in northern cities, and the 'green agenda' which described the concerns of the Environmental Movement regarding global pollution.

The existence of the Environmental Movement, doing the necessary research and raising issues in the political arena, did have its effects and considerable legislation and control systems were put in place that were, to an extent, effective in eliminating some problems and reducing others. However, these could never be completely effective in the context of constantly proliferating development, and release into the environment, of new chemicals with inadequate testing of what effects these might have[47]. In addition, there was always a danger of accidental releases which, on occasion, did create havoc — famously, but by no means isolated, being the case of a ruptured chemical tank in Bhopal in India in December 1984 that released gas resulting in some 4,000 immediate deaths, 4,000 severely and permanently disabled and eventually 25,000 premature deaths as a consequence of the accident[48].

One example amongst many illustrating the problematic of more widespread but insidious dangers was the case of the release over a long period of oestrogen-related chemicals used in a variety of household applications (for instance in cleaning fluids which find their way into sewage and thence via treatment plants that do not remove them, into water bodies) which caused changes in fertility of animals in the environment with potential threats to certain species directly and thus indirectly to the ecosystems of which they are an integral part[49].

More dramatically, the use and thence release into the environment of chlorofluorocarbons and related chemicals (again in a variety of applications, including aerosol propellants and refrigerants) was discovered in the 1960s to be destroying the stratospheric ozone layer which, it became evident, if continued, would have increasingly negative consequences on human health and the integrity of ecosystems . International agreement to phase out the use of these chemicals was reached in the late 1990s with the Vienna Convention and Montreal Protocol largely eliminating the problem.

Arguably, before the rise to prominence of the issue of climate change as a result of greenhouse gas emissions, the most serious pollution problem raised by the Environmental Movement was radioactivity. Atmospheric radioactivity was rising globally across the late 1950s as a consequence of the atmospheric testing of nuclear bombs, on the part mainly of the US and Soviet Governments. This was contained and thence reduced once the nuclear test ban treaty came into effect following vociferous public campaigns[50]. However, the potential for radioactive pollution through the development of nuclear power and the inability to find satisfactory procedures for the disposal of spent nuclear fuel from power stations lay at the heart of Green Movement campaigns, resulting by the late 1970s in the secession of construction of nuclear power stations in the United States and although national programmes continued elsewhere, particularly in France, the Soviet Union and latterly some Asian countries. Generally, the political enthusiasm for the development of nuclear power declined and construction of nuclear power plants remains modest with, since the turn of the century, older stations closing down and hence an absolute decline in electricity production from nuclear stations.

The possibilities and consequences of an accident at nuclear plants was clearly demonstrated by the explosion of a nuclear power station at Chernobyl in the Ukraine in 1986 that led over the years to over seven million people dying or diagnosed as suffering debilities as a consequence of the accident. This confirmed the negative stance that many governments had towards further development of nuclear power. Then again, in 2010, in a situation where some governments were once again advocating new nuclear power programmes as a response to growing fears of future threats to energy security, an accident at the Fukushima nuclear power station in Japan caused massive radioactive releases that laid waste to extensive areas of countryside with the complete evacuation of the population in the area. This reconfirmed the caution of Governments to re-enter the arena of nuclear power.

Reference must also be made to the way in which already in the final decades of the 20th century, many sites were discovered, particularly in Britain, Germany and the United States, where factories and chemical disposal sites in the past had left legacies of polluted soils, that, when re-used, people living and working over or in the vicinity of these contracted serious health problems and birth defects appeared in their children. Considerable work was done to map these and to clear them of the pollutants. And finally, the exploitation of unconventional fossil fuels promises not only to accelerate the production of greenhouse gases (carbon dioxide and leaked methane) but current modes of production have serious - potentially devastating - effects in terms of water pollution. Some of this can be treated, depending on ever weaker government environmental regulatory agencies' ability to enforce, but in the case of fracking, a large number of chemicals are injected into subterranean shale formations which in time can spread throughout extensive aquifers. Already in limited areas, these chemicals are showing up in drinking water, in the vicinity of gas wells, and clearly insofar as shale gas and oil exploitation grows in attempts to meet declining conventional gas and oil supply, these effects will also spread.

In the future we can expect the staged demise of the modern chemical industry that should reduce the need for effective controls on environmental emissions of the kind in place today. However, some kind of effective systems to monitor, control and clear polluted sites will continue to be needed to ensure that pollution from defunct chemical plants and other industries, and above all the remains of nuclear power stations, are contained. Populations living in the vicinity of these, with receding knowledge of the dangers hidden in these sites, will need some kind of reminder and control systems that will defend them against future debilitating effects, sudden or creeping. However, when adding up the untold millions of people killed and maimed through pollution accidents and the insidious spread of the polluting side-effects of modern development, we might say that in the past these rarely escalated into long-term sustainability problems and then only very local (Bhopal and Chernobyl being the most serious). In the future, however, there will be many places in the world, particularly in what will have been industrialised countries, where future populations will be in need of obviating debilitating health problems with, in all probability, little or no capacity to analyse the sources.

Global Warming

Increasingly evident changes in climatic conditions around the world, precipitated by ongoing 'greenhouse gas' emissions from human activity, especially carbon dioxide (CO_2) from the burning of fossil hydrocarbons, seemed to reach the top of the political agenda by the end of the first decade of the 21st century. Understood as a problematic that holds catastrophic dangers for humanity and the biosphere in the future, nevertheless, it became increasingly apparent that no national political system was prepared to take serious effective action to stem the releases. The 'greenhouse effect', through which these gas emissions cause the evident increase in the earth's temperature, was discovered in the early 20th century and was initially seen as a good thing in so far as northern temperatures might become milder, signifying a more pleasant climate.

Significant research into atmospheric change started in the late 1950s and the first serious studies of the potential impact of global warming were undertaken in the early 1970s. By the mid-80s, enough was known of the fact of rising levels of greenhouse gases, especially CO_2, which has been measured since 1958, at Mauna Loa in Hawaii.

From the first explorations of possible future climate change, made possible by the introduction of powerful computer-simulation models, the dangers were clarified and it became evident that considerably more attention should be paid to the phenomenon and means found to halt the rise of greenhouse gases.

The impact on the earth's climate of rising levels of greenhouse gases showed themselves to be complex, with accumulating research investigating a wide range of relevant interrelated issues. This growing body of research was brought together with the formation in 1988 of the Intergovernmental Panel on Climate Change (IPCC) that, initially cautiously and thence into the new millennium with greater confidence, indicated the dangers of rising greenhouse gases and resultant climate change[51].

By the end of the first decade of the 21st century, the warnings were firm in stating the limits to which levels of greenhouse gasses in the atmosphere might reach before catastrophic events would be precipitated. These include rise in sea levels gradually inundating major cities and vast areas of agriculturally productive land, and major changes in weather patterns, severely damaging or destroying whole ecosystems and greatly reducing food production with further repercussions on human health and the capacity of the earth to support the present population or, indeed, a significantly reduced population.

Major international events were organised to devise plans and mechanisms to contain the growth in greenhouse gases and thence to bring them back down to levels experienced in history prior to the anthropogenic emissions beginning in the 18th century. The 'Kyoto Protocol', being an international agreement on at least stabilising greenhouse gas emissions, was adopted in 1997 and brought into force in 2005. Most national governments signed up to this — though not yet the United States or China that by 2010 were together producing the greatest amounts of greenhouse gas. This took matters as far as governments were prepared to accept the problem and create policies and programmes at the national level, initially to stabilise emissions. These promises were, however, far short of what the IPCC had indicated would be the minimum steps necessary to head off catastrophe. In the event, even the feeble targets adopted in the Kyoto framework were achieved by few of the countries that had signed up to the convention.

In December 2009 the 15th Conference of the Parties to the United Nations Framework Convention on Climate Change took place in Copenhagen with extensive media coverage and a hope in the air that at last effective targets would be set on limiting and reducing the emission of greenhouse gases. The conference ended with the adoption of a short 'Accord' in which it was stated simply that emissions should be kept below levels that would limit temperature increase of the earth by two degrees centigrade. How this might be achieved, however, was left to further work by the Parties — meaning the government representatives who had signed up to the convention. A group of NGOs, headed by the Worldwide Fund for Nature (WWF), attended the conference, bringing with them a much longer document, spelling out what would have to be done to maintain this limit and how this might be achieved. The measures that would have to be taken were summarised as follows[52]:

- *industrialised countries' fossil fuel and industrial greenhouse gas emissions would have to drop from present levels rapidly and almost be fully phased out by 2050;*
- *deforestation emissions would need to be reduced globally by at least 75% or more by 2020;*
- *developing country fossil fuel and industrial greenhouse gas emissions would need to peak before 2020 and then decline, which emphasizes the need to provide high levels of binding support by industrialized countries.*

Part of the problem of governments setting more radical limits was the fact that mechanisms were hard to find in a liberal-democratic world, which might be effective in controlling sources of emission, and especially emissions by ordinary householders who, together, are major emitters. Means were being experimented with and discussed to capture the carbon dioxide that results from burning fossil hydrocarbons (known as Carbon Capture and Sequestration, or CCS), but even a crash programme to implement such systems would never be able to deal with billions of small point sources of households and automobiles and hence would never make much of an impact. By 2012 these attempts had been largely abandoned as requiring commitment and capital to implement that was way beyond what any government was prepared to pledge. By now the international media had largely lost interest in the annual Conference of the Parties.

The clear fact was and remains that the only realistic route to cutting greenhouse gas emissions significantly is to rapidly reduce the burning of fossil hydrocarbons, especially coal, starting now[53]. Three quarters of the 'forcing effect' that is the cause of global warming comes from carbon dioxide emissions due to burning fossil hydrocarbons. Almost nobody, neither governments nor enterprises nor individual citizens, want to hear this because it would clearly have a massive impact on reducing economic activity, making the 2008 economic recession look like a small perturbation and with no hope for any return to the life we currently 'enjoy'. There has thus been an accelerating discourse of denial that global warming is a problem and even that it exists [54]. However, 'peak oil' and thence availability of energy resources *per se* can be expected in any case to be declining over the coming years.

Insofar as this stems the growth in greenhouse gas production, so much the better because at the present rate of growth in the earth's temperature, the likelihood of reaching a point where this is self-accelerating is increasing. Beyond a certain point (indeed, this may now have been reached), the rising global temperature will trigger the release of vast quantities of methane hydrates currently frozen in the northern tundra, which is liable to melt. Even greater quantities are to be found in places on the ocean floor that may also be released as a consequence of changing ocean temperatures. Although relatively short lived in the atmosphere, methane is nevertheless a powerful greenhouse gas and the release in great quantities of the methane hydrates will, without doubt, trigger a continuing increase in the earth's temperature in a self-generating process that is almost certain to lead to catastrophic general die-back of ecosystems later in this century and into the next.

Such an ecological collapse due to global warming has occurred several times in the history of the earth, with the last such occurrence being 250 million years ago, almost extinguishing the biosphere altogether[55]. Should this happen again then it is unlikely that there will be any future at all for humanity. So we have to hope, and in the rest of this text we assume, that the decline in energy resources described above happens faster rather than slower and that the conditions described above do happen, rather than that modernity continues until a collapse that extinguishes all hope of establishing the kind of new world where hope and happiness prevail.

Biodiversity

The reduction of biodiversity due to human activity can be considered, for the longer term, amongst the most devastating dimensions of the unsustainability of present-day developments. Extinction is forever, although in practice, over millennia rich ecosystems have regenerated themselves following mass extinctions. The geological record indicates five major (and many lesser) mass extinctions that took place more or less suddenly and which are by no means all well-explained. The era of human presence is already revealing itself to be another period of mass extinction[56]. This started immediately when humans came to occupy new territory, in the form of the elimination of larger species through over-hunting and possibly from obsessive killing for its own sake. Some areas of the world have at various stages in past history been severely depleted of biota and hence of their original biodiversity, affecting the sustainability of the societies perpetrating these actions and in some cases leading to the collapse of these societies — meaning severe reduction also of human populations[57].

Deforestation, primarily displaced by agriculture, has progressed in sudden surges for at least the last ten thousand years, with the result of ecological depletion, the scale of which has become increasingly evident through recent archaeological research. Once gone, such as happened in Mediterranean cultures between 500 BCE and 500 CE, these by no means always revived after the decline or destruction of the cultures that had destroyed them. As Occidental culture spread around the globe from the end of the 15th century, the transfer of species from one place to another almost always had the effect of disrupting and hence depleting local biodiversity[58]. In a few cases this was severe, such as the introduction by European sailors of goats to many islands around the world, to live and reproduce as a source of meat for the crews of later visiting vessels, the animals then proceeding to eat their way through the local biodiversity.

The rate of extinctions accelerated from the mid-eighteenth century, with the take-off of industrialisation and sudden surge in human populations. With the rapid decline in forest cover, in some cases of selected trees, in others clear felling of forest products, leaving rough grassland and eroding soils, to clearance for farming, global forest cover had diminished by the 21st century to a rump of its former coverage. What we are witnessing today is a generalised global loss of biodiversity, continuing to accelerate, albeit progressing at different rates in different places, and remembering that many areas have already suffered whilst partially recovering from past depletions[59].

More devastating is that global warming is set to have further effects of degrading ecosystems even, as outlined above, where there is minimal human presence, or independent of what humans are doing directly in and to the affected ecosystems. Clearly this is a sustainability issue for the long-term and in some areas even for the short-term where human activity, which is often intended to increase production by introducing modern agricultural systems and methods, has resulted in degradation of the resilience of local ecosystems. Whilst this might not be immediately evident, such ecosystem weakening, which could accelerate into local or regional ecological collapse, may not immediately affect agricultural productivity, but is likely to do so when people are forced by dwindling energy resources to revert to organic farming methods.

The Denial of Environmental and Resource Issues

As the fall of the modern world sets in, we can say in a very general way that humanity has made a tragic mistake in pursuing unsustainable Development. However, what is analysed above is the fact that a whole series of different kinds of mistakes have been made. At its best, the ambition of the Green Movement was to attempt to look right across these mistakes and forge an ideology that would facilitate a coherent overview of the problematic, that in turn would open the door to a coherent approach to addressing all the mistakes in one, that would mean providing a simple enough concept that could be understood and disseminated right across the planet and through this to forge a fundamentally different way of organising life. However, in practice, almost all those involved in the Green Movement found the complexity too daunting and hence focused on one or a few of the problems with a hope to forge tools to deal at least with these. A small corps of environmental theoreticians, on the other hand, ruminated on the philosophical issues but in the process lost sight of the concrete, and particularly social, dimensions of the problematic.

In some cases there were genuine mistakes in the sense of what seemed to be sensible and sometimes even conscientious decisions taken either in complete ignorance of the consequences, or of an expectation of outcomes that was misguided. However, in all too many cases, decisions were taken out of ideological positions that excluded the possibility of seeing negative consequences even when these could clearly be expected with little need for rational logic or imagination. And there was a very short path between this kind of ignorance and outright denial and thence belligerence against those who would simply point out the errors in judgement. In many cases this was simply a matter of those profiting by this apparent ignorance using whatever means, ideological or in the end, force, to secure their actions.

Finally, there was thoughtless or even purposeful destruction in order to assert power, to gain wealth or, in the case of war, to vanquish enemies. The real problem in recent decades, however, was that so many of these mistakes, cumulatively, would increasingly have negative consequences not just for people other than those who took the decisions but also for the decision-takers themselves. Ultimately this would involve the collapse of the whole culture out of what Jared Diamond refers to as an inability or unwillingness to face up to the accumulating problems and make the necessary adaptation to the realities of the situation[60].

It became apparent that there was, somewhere, a fundamental fault in the ideology and functioning of the culture that allowed so many mistakes to blossom unchecked. An important contribution to understanding the way in which this happened in the case of modern society was Ulrich Beck's analysis of what he termed 'risk society'[61]. He contended that even in Europe up to the era of the 18th century Enlightenment, life for the vast majority of populations everywhere was contained in structures that limited the possibility of decisions that would be contrary to the interests of the society as a whole, and its institutions of the Church and of everyday life and then inside extended families.

From the early 19th century, in Northern Europe these structures progressively failed, with the scope for individuals to pursue their own putative interests increasing and whilst new institutions arose that might constrain the increasingly destructive direction things were taking, these were more fragmented in the controls they exerted over individual action. In the early 20th century, governments took on the main role of structuring the life of the individual, who had been increasingly distancing her or himself from any constraints of family and Church and in the final phase, the most important institutions became the corporate structures that gave employment and income and hence could demand allegiance with, on their side, only limited goals of profit-making and their encouragement of people to consume, constrained increasingly weakly by government regulation and the vigilance of *ad hoc* environmental community and civil society organisations.

In this context, the propensity across the complete society to take risks and ignore or play down negative consequences of their actions progressively increased. That is to say, that in the past experience had indicated the limits to acting outside the constraints of social and religious morality and in terms of actions that might have negative consequences inside the society and with respect to the environment, such as the famines that had been a regular feature of European societies in the past - and many similar examples can be found in other places and societies around the world. Much of what we observe with regard to the dimensions of unsustainability today can be understood in the light of an increasing propensity for risk-taking that was usually perpetrated by organisations and individuals who reasoned that they would not be affected by negative consequences even if it was evident that others could be or were being affected. Of course, much of this risk-taking has a long history, as noted in particular cases and some, such as the Catholic dogma against abortion, go back in history to periods when having many children was, if not a necessity, not much of a threat to the sustainability of society.

What was new was the means available, in terms of technologies and the energy to fuel their use, to expand the whole framework of civilisation and pursue deeply ingrained dogmas and prejudices whilst at the same time increasingly relaxing the constraints that might have encouraged criticism of what was happening. Hence the loss of the capacity or inclination to construct institutions that would have addressed all the problems and that could have led to societies that would have been sustainable in the sense of there being continuity into the indefinite future. The purpose of the immediate following chapters of this book is to look more precisely and critically at how the current situation came to pass and then what avenues are available to make the transition that should have taken place two centuries ago. Over the early decades of modernity, abundant utopian proposals arose to reconstruct society, indicating what this might comprise of. This is, indeed, a process which we need to repeat to define and construct a future that works — assuming there is any room left, post-fall, for cultural reconstruction.

For the remainder of this chapter, however, we need first to take a hard look at how ignorance and dogma has escalated in recent years to outright denial, through 'considered silence' and perverse, belligerent argumentation aimed at closing minds to the clear problems faced by modern society[62]. It is particularly this perverse resistance to rethinking our social and political systems that makes it ever more difficult to work out and agree means to ameliorate the consequences of the fall of modern civilisation. Although nothing like exact predictions can be made of the steps through which the fall will take place, we nevertheless deem it to be useful to examine some of the dimensions in order to bring into focus the kinds of difficulties we — already in the immediate future, but particularly over the coming decades, the younger generation today — will have to face and negotiate.

****

If we look at the list of problems that have not been adequately responded to in recent years, we can distinguish three main avenues of what the think tank FEASTA referred to as 'ritualized maintenance of collective denial'[63]. The first concerns deep-seated traditional values that modern life has failed to unseat. Whilst this includes aspects of environmental exploitation that were benign under conditions prior to the modern age but are now systematically depleting environments, centrally this concerns population growth. Whilst in the heartlands of modernity, population growth did decline to the point of stasis (births equalling deaths and in a few cases beginning to decline); however, as we will see, this was still at high levels relative to the local resource base necessary to support this. But in a few southern countries, in a situation of cultural predilection towards large families, the overlay of modern institutions was too weak to formulate and therefore to execute policies to halt population growth.

The second avenue arose out of the growing power of corporate enterprise, being in the first place only interested in profit albeit under some pressure from institutions based on goals more oriented towards the social good. Most of the sustainability problems outlined above have come about and reached the extremity they have through corporate entities successfully pursuing what they consider to be their interests over the interests of civil society and with the connivance or silence of governments that ostensibly are there to protect the general interests of society[64]. We discuss in the following chapter how the rise to domineering power of corporate production entities has been permitted and facilitated by the deeply embedded ideology of modern Occidental culture.

And we cannot let it be assumed that we are necessarily talking only of capitalist enterprise. Enterprises in the Soviet Union (we can speak also of nationalised enterprises, particularly utilities, in Western European countries) were in an even better position to be able to pursue aims that might not have been financial profits but profits in the sense of the power they were able to wield over the financial resources of governments, being themselves a part of government.

But the third, and in the end ultimately fatal avenue is to be found is in the minds of modern populations themselves. As already implied by Ulrich Beck, and discussed in considerably more detail in the chapter to follow, the degeneration of social institutions, the rise of single-minded individual pursuit of wealth and status had, with the spread of the Consumer Society, an increasingly debilitating effect on the capacity — or maybe we should say the willingness — of populations to level critical thought and to form or support institutions that might have the will and strength to address the problems effectively. This we will address further in the final chapter, where we come to discuss institutions in the future that will have the capacity to motivate

75

responsible thought and action by members of society in their own best long term interest.

Turning now to how this endemic lack of responsibility worked in recent practice, we focus first on the issue of global warming. Since the establishment of the IPCC and the regular international conferences on the subject, the public has been subjected to information in the mainstream media about global warming, its causes and consequences, and it is in this light that denial must be discussed. The point here is that it becomes difficult to look in any way clearly at the evidence and not see that to combat global warming effectively will result decisively in the end of the modern lifestyle. This is never made clear by the IPCC itself, nor by any of the governments attending the meetings, that in any case were nowhere near proposing anything like effective measures to reduce greenhouse gas emissions to levels that would arrest the upward passage of the global temperature. It is only civil society organisations that have been prepared to address the problematic clearly and effectively, but which, however, possess no authority to take action.

Given the clarity with which the problematic of global warming was spelled out across the media (the most widely viewed presentation being the film *An Inconvenient Truth* made by ex-Vice President of the United States Al Gore) it took much for the general public to dismiss it from their minds. Whilst the whole previous generation had contributed towards the creation of 'democratic' government, ostensibly beholden to responding to public demand regarding policy, now was the time to hold it to account and now was the time that the public turned away from responsibility, implying that it was the government that should act, whilst it was clear that any government that *did* take relevant action would immediately be voted out of office. Thus, as we have seen, nowhere were governments prepared to take any effective action.

As if this were not enough, a number of organisations, funded by corporations, conceived it as being in their interest to deny the problem, together with wealthy individuals who took this up as a cause, — right wing think tanks, financed media and ostensibly more than a hundred 'scientific' books aimed at undermining the veracity of the 'science' of the IPCC in its insistence that global warming was in the process of actually happening.[65]

Alerting the public with a view to encouraging some kind of rational response to the coming diminution of energy supplies was faced with even more barriers than the issue of global warming, more in terms of silence than of structured denial. There is copious evidence from informal literature and transcripts of the meetings of politicians and their advisors that already by the final years of the last century the Presidents of the United States were fully appraised of the impending decline in oil and other resources within the foreseeable future. There were no structured statements on what kind of problem this might represent and thence what policies might be pursued in order to respond meaningfully to the problematic. It is unlikely that any politicians in the leadership of Northern countries would not have been exposed to this information.

United States Presidents, going back over several decades, had from time to time made brief statements on the need to reduce reliance on oil from the Middle Eastern countries and George W. Bush managed to accuse the American people of being 'addicted to oil'. But no directives were given to government agencies that might have taken some kind of action to respond to or amplify this rhetoric, which certainly made no reference to any kind of future crisis in global supply. The only structured statement on the issue came from the National Energy Technology Laboratory of the Department of Energy where three well-respected researchers, having identified peak oil as a potential problem for the United States, wrote a report, indicating some steps that the US Government would need to take in order to address energy shortages that would surely appear within the coming decade[66]. The key statement in the report ran as follows:

... the problem of the peaking of world conventional oil production is unlike any yet faced by Modern industrial society. The challenges and uncertainties need to be much better understood. Technologies exist to mitigate the problem. Timely, aggressive risk management will be essential.

Scepticism amongst their peers concerning the probability of an imminent peak in oil production motivated the researchers to write a further report noting the widespread confirmation of this amongst experts, oil company spokespeople and politicians in producing countries responsible for oil matters [67]. In an interview in 2009, the main author of the report, Robert Hirsch, stated that when oil production goes into decline, it will be 'the defining issue for humanity'. He spoke of the difficulty of getting clearance to publish their report. He went on to note in the interview that the research group was under a good deal of pressure not to be 'bearers of bad news' and as the profile of the work rose, this pressure, both from higher up the Department hierarchy and from both political parties, led to the research being halted. There was no response to the report from the administration.

The British Government, from the late 1990s, produced more than one policy document , that in general called for prudence in the use of energy that did not specifically identify why this might be a problem and then advocated nuclear power as a potential solution to any future energy supply problems. There is evidence that the American President and British Prime Minister specifically discussed the issue of peak oil as early as 2003, with no public statement resulting from this [68]. The subsequent British Prime Minister was stimulated to commission a policy document on energy security that was published in August 2009, which asserted that the market would be capable of addressing any problem of rising oil prices as these would stimulate investments necessary to relieve any pressures. Orthodox economic dogma restated.

Meanwhile, in the early years of the century, an 'All Party Parliamentary Group on Peak Oil' (APPGOPO) was formed as part of the machinery of policy generation by the British Parliament, to enquire into the potential problems suggested by the rising issue of peak oil. Following commissioning of various consultants' reports, the Chair of the Group, in the introduction to one of these, wrote:

...I have raised the issue with the Government many times. Regrettably, the Government is still unable to grasp how serious the threat of peak oil is, and so the UK remains inadequately prepared to cope with this looming crisis.

In late 2010, the German Government was briefly confronted more directly with the problematic of peak oil, when a research institution of the Bundeswehr (the German army) produced a report entitled *Peak Oil: Security Policy Implications of Resource Shortages*[69] which spelled out in detail the problems which the German polity is likely to face in future years with the decline in petroleum resources. The Green Party faction in the German parliament used this as a basis for launching an inquiry addressed to the government, and did this by posing twenty-five questions exploring what the government intended to do by way of response to the difficulties which the decline in oil will pose for the country[70]. The written response came back, dated the 26th November[71]. Noting that the Bundeswehr report was a draft as yet not adopted by the Government, reference was made to the 2010 IEA forecasts asserting that, whilst the situation needed to be kept under review, at the present time there was no need to take any structured steps to allay possible problems arising from future reduction in the availability of oil.

Following the release of the 2009 International Energy Agency annual *World Energy Outlook (WEO)* on the prospects for energy, a 'senior IEA official' had informed the *Guardian* newspaper (9th November 2009) that, under pressure from the US Government, the decline in existing petroleum reserves had been underplayed in the WEO and the prospects of finding more had been overplayed 'in order to stop panic buying' and because '…the Americans fear the end of oil supremacy because it would threaten their power over access to oil resources'.

Whilst these are isolated incidents, they are illustrative of the way in which governments avoided wherever possible raising the topic of the coming peak and decline in oil production, and when it was raised, spending efforts on minimising the impact of the statements that were made.   The public did, however, have access to information freely available on the internet and increasing numbers of publications, albeit sites and literature promoting information on peak oil and its consequences, were matched by those of organisations dedicated to throwing doubt on the issue and reducing any feeling of the need to structure thinking and action to ameliorate the impacts and plan for the different world that will inevitably result as the decline in energy supply and availability of fossil hydrocarbons sets in.

What might we expect as the decline in energy sets in?

The mindset of denial makes it extremely difficult for even the more thoughtful members of society to imagine just how far our civilisation has to fall and the difficulties we will meet as the fall unfolds[72]. It is evident that the fall will not happen in one apocalyptic event as many seem to wish for, so that they do not have to take responsibility for what will happen, but will unfold in steps that will be different, and painful in different ways and with very different human impacts, in different places[73]. Before looking at a number of dimensions of what we might expect to happen along the way, it is useful first to consider three general possible paths as follows[74]:

1. The downward passage could proceed in a fashion analogous to the fall of Rome, which has generated a huge literature over the centuries with much new work being carried out through sophisticated archaeology in recent years, demonstrating just how thorough the collapse was in the west[75]. It is recognised

that many factors contributed to the fall of the Western Roman Empire, some of which are relevant to the present situation and others which are not. The point here is simply that as the combination of impacts hit the empire over a period of centuries, so the capacity and competence to administer it led to the falling apart of the management of even the simplest of political and social relations, from urban systems to the manufacture of the accoutrements of everyday life; even the basics of farm productivity fell apart[76]. Given the complexity and precariousness of modern civilisation, such a process could proceed much faster than was the case with ancient Rome.

This could be accompanied by a reversion to (by this time entirely dysfunctional) religion and, in terms of social relations, a reversion to rigid hierarchy and even some form of neo-feudalism. This characteristic of the collapse of many complex societies in the past was the main theme of the research of Joseph Tainter[77], who concluded that there is a usual downward path ending in simple village life and subsistence farming, with little or nothing left by way of urban life. The city of Rome, which by the first century AD had grown to over a million people, collapsed by the middle of the sixth century to a few tens of thousands and continued the downward passage, so that by the twelfth century it was little more than a village. In places modern civilisation could fall even further, to nomadic life or even hunting and gathering. It seems from the present perspective that such a collapse would be the dominant passage taken in most parts of the world — but not necessarily so.

2. Another possibility is that at least some places, even countries and certainly towns and sub-regions will learn rapidly to take what Howard and Elizabeth Odum refer to as a 'prosperous way down'[78]. The only national government to have in some way recognised the need to retreat from oil and base life on other energy sources is Sweden[79], albeit this appears to have been but a passing initiative. As yet this by no means recognises the complexity of the decline of oil for the global economy and how this will reflect also on the economy of Sweden, but the possibility is that a few nations may, within the coming decade, recognise the depth of the changes that will be necessary and will attempt to coordinate a national 'way down'.

The situation is more promising at the level of localities where the 'Transition Movement', starting in Ireland[80] and the

UK, and rapidly spreading across Europe, North America and a few places beyond, is being inventive of actions that have to be taken at a relatively local level to forestall collapse and, rather, rebuild local life on a different footing[81]. In the United States, the 'post-carbon cities' are attempting to play a similar role[82]. In France, in addition to the spread of 'francophone' Transition Towns, the Colibris movement, starting from concerns with agriculture (organic and bringing it back to the local level) is expanding into other transition issues. At first these initiatives, whilst being enthusiastic, were small-scale and fragmented, as a consequence of a lack of ability amongst proponents to conceive of the profundity and complexity of adaptation that will be called for. However, dense networking through the social media is spreading messages and experiences. As the downward passage accelerates, planned transition will only work where this covers a reasonable size of region with adequate resources and the accompanying planning and administrative capability to organise predominantly self-reliant communities and polities that integrate initiatives into more comprehensive re-localisation initiatives, as discussed in Chapter Six.

3. A final possibility is that some way into the collapse a broad movement emerges analogous to the rise of the socialist movement in the 19th century, with an entirely new view in terms of cultural goals, definitively rejecting liberalism and forging a coherent vision, informing new ways of organising social and political life based on a fundamentally altered existential self-understanding. Whilst this might be analogous to religious revelation for which we might coin the term 'secular revelation', it would not be a revival of existing religions but rather displace these definitively by a process of thinking and action that accepts the new conditions of life and forges ways of organising, caring and sharing within and between communities and with the particular part of nature in which the communities rebuild themselves. What this might comprise is implied by some of the emerging US literature and is the central subject of the final chapter of this book.

If, simplistically, we assume the downward passage of modern civilisation to follow the systematic diminution of fossil hydrocarbon availability, we would expect this to start gradually with the levelling off of oil production starting now, where symptoms are more or less already clear, given that oil production levelled off already in 2005 and seemed to start a halting downward passage in 2009, and with a peak for fossil hydrocarbons as a whole around 2020. The downward passage would then accelerate to a point by 2040 that depletion would be around three per cent annually and by the end of the century production would be around the level of the 1920s with, as then, coal being the major source of energy. Factors altering this trajectory include on the one hand increased efforts to exploit unconventional sources of energy, slowing the descent in the early years, and on the other hand the impact of diminishing EROEI absorbing ever greater amounts of energy in accessing what is left and hence accelerating the downward passage of energy actually available to do work.

However, such a smooth downward passage is very unlikely and two alternatives have been conjectured that stem from experience of the collapse of ecological systems and which in practice reflect the interconnection of parts of modern systems where, beyond certain points, there are systematic collapses. These may be partial, involving oscillations in economic activity with, after each crash, attempts to stabilise and reconstruct, resulting in a new upward passage that then encounters the new ceiling of energy availability, precipitating a further crash down to a lower level of activity and so on all the way down, stretching across this century and into the next.

The third possibility is that that there be a gradual downward passage with minor oscillations, illustrated by the 2008 events, up to a point in two or three decades where suddenly there is a major disjuncture resulting in free-fall to a considerably lower level of energy use and related economic activity. In the language of chaos theory this is referred to a 'catastrophic bifurcation', being a sudden departure from one coherent state to another entirely different state[83]. This would represent the definitive termination of globalisation, with the trade in oil and other fossil hydrocarbons disrupted and with individual nations and even localities becoming largely self-reliant, as was the case for all countries but Britain up to the 20th century. This dislocation might be expected around the middle of this century but could happen considerably earlier for reasons that are elaborated in the following paragraphs.

The major impact of energy depletion will be the diminishing availability of oil and following from this of gas, with some amelioration consequent on the exploitation of unconventional sources, leading to escalating competition and hence rise in price. Price spikes, as in 2008, may occur at regular or irregular intervals, each time reducing demand that will not be able to return to previous levels even when prices again recede at a lower level of activity. There is actually considerable wastage across the full spectrum of energy usage at present, such that major disruptions may be avoided through energy conservation measures and carrying out activities with greater efficiency, as was started but then failed with the energy crises of 1973 and 1979 and the subsequent collapse of oil prices.

Continuing the reduction in movement experienced in 2008-9, people may be expected to drive and fly less and some industries will work to reduce energy per unit of production, going initially through short cycles as experienced between 2006 and 2012. The most serious emergent impact will, however, be on the rising cost of feedstock for industrial production, resulting in rising prices of a wide range of products that are made directly from fossil hydrocarbons or their derivatives[84]. At the same time almost all products not actually made from fossil hydrocarbon derivatives, including notably steel, aluminium and cement, make very heavy demands on fossil hydrocarbon with their price therefore closely linked to the price of these.

The underlying downward spiral would thus be economic. The general impact of diminishing availability of oil would be an increasingly coherent negative Keynesian cycle where increasing prices leads to decreasing demand, reducing economies of scale, further increasing production costs and so further decreasing demand. Increase in unemployment, that started with the first jolt in the United States in 2008 and has since ricocheted, particularly through southern European countries, would, in this scenario, proceed in further jolts up, down and up but with a general downward trend in availability of jobs. In the decade ahead, a wide range and number of companies, including, dramatically, multinational companies which are household names, already today on the edge of bankruptcy, who would cease operations as a consequence of inter-linkages where production companies are no longer purchasing services and the diminishing of consumer purchasing power results in lack of demand for almost everything, so that sunk costs and extended chains collapse under their own weight. Governments with diminishing tax revenues as a consequence of decreasing economic activity would be increasingly incapable of intervening to support either business or the unemployed or to support any kinds of social services. The downward spiral into personal destitution would, in this scenario, be expected to spread from the already precarious poor to ever wider circles of population.

Production of goods would return in stages to the local level to make up for the increasing failure, not just of dispensable but increasingly of essential goods to arrive from the global economy. In the first instance this would mean local food production. Already there is a rapid increase almost everywhere in what is known as Urban and Peri-Urban Agriculture (UPA), proceeding out of different kinds of initiative resulting from economic crisis or, in the richer countries, both a general enthusiasm and an anticipation of escalating food insecurity in the coming years; this is the one area where already the current ongoing decline in economic activity is bringing this into focus for increasing numbers of people[85].

Already in the 1980s the weak economic development of African cities precipitated the growth of UPA that has grown gradually in subsequent years. The fall of the Soviet Union and the failure of the Soviet economy precipitated a rapid growth of local own-production — famously also in Cuba — that has continued[86]. Starting in Japan and spreading to Northern Europe and North America, social movements have been increasingly organising 'farmers' markets' and 'Community-Supported Agriculture' (CSA) that now covers several thousand initiatives. In China, UPA has also been supported by the Government since the 1960 and continues to evolve. Large numbers of these initiatives are no more than small beginnings and even where they are substantial, such as in China and the ex-Soviet sphere, whilst producing much of the vegetable intake and some of the fruit, dairy products and meat, these remain a long way from satisfying carbohydrate requirements and over the coming decades, this would be expected to show itself to be the central issue in spreading undernourishment and famine.

Some new local production of goods may be initiated by existing companies or new enterprises formed out of a realisation of the direction things are taking, recognising gaps in the supply of materials and goods and responding through internal reorganisation and revised production methods. However, as the contraction of the global and national economies proceeds, the difficulty of obtaining components and thence raw materials from beyond the locality would increase, requiring rapid changes in products and production methods likely, as long as production is carried on by profit-dependent capitalist methods, to result in rapid and regular business failures, that might start deeper processes of questioning with regard to how local populations might organise access to the materials and goods they need for their survival.

Under any circumstances, the escalation of violent reactions to the emergent situation certainly cannot be ruled out. Mild political manifestations objecting to economic developments in Europe and North America from around 2005 and increasing in the following years were not, however, truly massive demonstrations, in spite of the brief spread from New York to many other US cities of the Occupy Wall Street (OWS) manifestations. Nor were they aggressive, resulting in few deaths and injuries, and almost no concrete forms of more permanent organisation around the demands being made. 'Food riots' escalated in poorer countries, which also had no effects in terms of new organisations of more substantial movements lasting beyond the manifestations. It is entirely unclear whether in the future these types of manifestation will continue, as these clearly will produce little to satisfy demands where governments are faced with diminishing resources as was clearly the case in Greece in the years from 2007 to 2012[87].

However, violence could escalate where groups within countries attempt in a more concerted way to exert their perceived interests and demands, and then confront governments in more organised ways with weapons. Some governments may well attempt to use organised violence to maintain their legitimacy through internal repression or through external wars over resources[88]. It is, however, difficult to see how such manifestations will be sustainable in situations where energy resources are declining, making conventional modern forms of police and military violence difficult to sustain over any extended period. Outbreaks of organised violence might then be expected to be relatively short-lived — which is not to say these would not be started, nor that these would not result in possibly massive loss of life as death from war is added to death from the exacerbated economic disjuncture of the downward passage. War has always, in net terms, been dysfunctional. But this fact has rarely, if ever, been a reason to desist.

Another scenario is that a 'Great Depression' may descends upon the world as a response to the fading away of the cornucopia of Stuff[89] that has been the hallmark of the global society that has spread around the world over the last few decades[90]. Perhaps most salient with respect to the frame of mind that will prevail will be the fading away of virtual worlds, of instant electronic communication, of twitter, facebook and e-mail. Handphones and eventually television and the entertainment industry will decline and flicker out, leaving populations with the task of rebuilding face-to-face communication as the limit of their daily universe. There may be periodic tastes of this failure where electronic systems go silent for days and even weeks, as has been the experience even in recent years in some southern countries, but as the collapse deepens, these manifestations of Modernity can be expected to disappear permanently.

This brings us to the point at which sudden collapse may occur. Two clear dimensions can be discerned. One is the collapse of electricity systems and, as a consequence, much of the infrastructure of modern life, from urban water supply and rural irrigation systems to transport and general long-distance supply systems and maintenance, including sanitation systems. The collapse might be early in some places and later in others but as it proceeds, it will feed upon itself as failing energy supplies sever communications and control systems, inventories necessary for organising supplies of goods and materials, security systems and the capacity to maintain what remains functional of large-scale infrastructure. Whilst it has been suggested that these systems have in recent years been incipiently 'splintering'[91], and hence that many facilities will continue to be able to function through ad hoc decentralised provision of infrastructure, the core, even of apparently decentralised systems, remains highly centralised and focused, from the supplies of oil from the Middle East to the giant power stations and grids that are central to the functioning of the modern world, and in particular of cities and urban regions.

The second dimension concerns the collapse of modern governments. The failure of financial resources, which modern governments collect and distribute to maintain the coherence of the whole, will reach a point where government structures will have to be modified substantially to be able to function at all, with considerably fewer activities focused on revised interpretations of the purpose of Government. However, before this takes place, it is likely that in most countries — maybe as an international domino effect analogous to the way in which the brief 'Arab Spring' spread throughout the region as an attack on the particular formula of governance at the national level — will undergo radical reformulations, possibly in cycles or as a process of slow-motion collapse.

As a form of government, modern representative democracy is unlikely to survive as national governments either adopt authoritarian structures, holding countries together through simplified, military or quasi-military regimes or, and this is more likely in the face of their inability to address the needs of the people and hence escalating loss of legitimacy central governments will become incoherent not only in terms of modern functions, but also as centres of leadership and governance. This can be expected to signal the total collapse into structures of organisation or self-organisation of sub-regions and localities, with the possibility of different formulae in different sub-regions ranging from 'war lords' to local participatory-democratic government at a very local level. There may even be in some areas the total dissolution of governance structures with the dispersal and disappearance of populations into 'bands' or isolated individuals and households struggling to survive off severely diminished resource flows by foraging for food and without fixed communities.

Although this might be witnessed as a sudden collapse over a number of months, it is more likely to proceed everywhere in stages that might be over a few years or a whole decade. When oil ceases to reach countries, possibly because a few nations (and the United States Government is the most likely candidate to close off oil shipments to other countries as it attempts to continue to maintain a semblance of its own coherence) may requisition dwindling supplies whilst others will necessarily fall back on their own resources, in some cases including fossil hydrocarbons, in others returning overwhelmingly to the use of biofuels — which in any case is the experience even today of the poorest regions and countries.

Here we must refer to the widespread, in the 'most developed countries' almost absolute, incompetence that will be encountered to make the necessary transition to local productive economies. In most cases it will be easier for the populations of the 'poorer' nations to make the transition to whatever lies in wait for us as the transition deepens. The reason for this is simply that poor populations throughout the South have either not adapted themselves in any very meaningful way to modernity (this 'resistance' is almost the meaning of 'poverty' today) or, within local informal economies, they have continued to maintain a mentality to produce things by hand and, to some degree, the manual skills accompanying this.

Skills in the North today are overwhelmingly those learned to work in service areas; where more practical skills are involved, these are aimed at using machines and power-tools and installing and maintaining ready-made objects and components. The design of the essential things of life, for example - fabric and clothing, buildings and furniture, kitchenware and the hand tools to make these - exists nowhere as these things are made by machine and the skills of those involved in the production processes are fragmented to a point where nobody has complete knowledge of anything of practical value. The skills to design by computer, programme machines or package and sell the results will be useless and the 'skills' of such service workers as accountants, real-estate brokers and business managers will be rendered in stages increasingly irrelevant.

Hence a rapid and probably overwhelmingly spontaneous re-skilling process will be necessary. Crucial to this will be the will to make such a transition; to acknowledge that present-day education and training are almost entirely useless and that other skills must be learned and practiced, and other attitudes accepted within the local society of the worth and status of manual work. In short, education and training programmes will have to be reformulated from their very foundations and then the means to organise these to render populations effective to serve the needs of the emergent local polities and communities, will be crucial to the success of localities being capable of making the transition.

At the same time, 'information' will be decimated as electronic data bases and information systems become inaccessible through the failure of electricity supplies necessary to maintain global information systems and the internet. It seems entirely unlikely that much will be done to maintain libraries of books, though universities everywhere will again become the focus of information and, whilst 'old books', have in many libraries been displaced by more recent publications, these all too often contain 'information' that will be of little or no use for a practical, workable future. Nevertheless, we might hope that some reoriented research will be effectively carried out. This should recover practical information from the past to rebuild useful knowledge and skills so that, in spite of the emergency conditions, some useful information will spread to help rebuild useful skills.

Historically, the migrations of populations have never ceased, in spite of there being times and places where it seemed that some kind of permanent settlement pattern had been achieved. Today's perspective asserts that urbanisation that has been ongoing for the past century will continue and somehow find a plateau once the vast majority of populations around the world are living in cities. However, the viability of cities as the main location of populations is now reaching its peak and the decline in energy will certainly bring urban living deeply into question leading, as the century progresses, to the decline of cities as populations return to tilling the land and producing most of their own goods at a relatively local level using local resources.

Already in the early years of this century a small group of researchers in the United States had concluded that suburbia in the form in which today the majority of people in the United States live has no future. It is overwhelmingly dependent on cars to bring people to work and undertake all forms of social and economic activity and the demise of the automobile lifestyle, as a consequence of the decline in availability and escalating price of petroleum, will be the demise also of the viability of suburban living[92]. Suburbia as a lifestyle and use of land can be expected to disappear as well in Europe, where it is by now also widespread, and in its lesser manifestation in Asia and Latin America.

On the other hand, high-rise city centres and residential living will also become unviable as electricity supplies fail, and internal lighting and ventilation as well as lifts cease to function, initially sporadically, where auxiliary power units have been installed, and thence entirely as a consequence of the lack of fuel for these. One thinks particularly of cities in the United States being so afflicted, but today, high-rise development has spread also to Latin American and Asian cities. Chinese cities have been utterly transformed in just the past twenty years to 'high-rise jungles', and the cities that have arisen in the oil-lands of Arabia will in the most extreme way end their lives as ghost cities of monumental towers, as witness to the hubris (or perhaps foolishness) of modernity, as the oil ceases to flow and the oil-fuelled desalination of water that is the life blood of these cities comes to an end.

It can be speculated on how populations will disperse out of cities, continue in small numbers to dismantle and remove the resources, cluster in areas where there is sufficient vacant land to farm and move to outlying areas where they can join existing smaller communities or found new ones[93]. In principle, movements could be planned by existing planning agencies but there seems at this stage to be a vanishingly small likelihood that this will happen anywhere in the context of a chaotic collapse of modern civilisation and the deep prejudice almost everywhere that the city is where things happen and where one should be. Furthermore, there will be long-distance migrations, possibly of substantial populations, out of areas such as the south-west of the United States, which supports cities only through massive transfers of water that will cease to flow, into areas that will support small-scale agriculture. Such migrations are already under way in a small way out of Siberia and the Russian Far East into the west of the country and substantial migrations can be expected throughout much of the Americas. By contrast, in the overpopulated areas of Europe and Asia, there will be little room for mass-migrations beyond urban-rural population adjustments.

The unhappiest dimension of the collapse concerns the way in which over much of the globe, existing population levels will not be supportable from the resource base as water supply systems fail and as petrochemical agricultural inputs diminish in availability. UPA as a spontaneous reaction to problems of growing food insecurity and undernourishment will not support large urban populations anywhere in terms of their carbohydrate demand. Today most countries are completely or largely self-sufficient in terms of calorie provision — just 18% of wheat, 12.5% of corn and 6.5% of rice is internationally traded — but what trade there is now will be diminishing almost from today and fade away rapidly in the coming decades with, at the same time, local production declining for lack of input.

The most dramatic reversal will be in the United States, which produces by far the largest agricultural surpluses globally, supplying about half the world's traded grain. Even today, vast areas in the United States are farmed unsustainably in the medium term in terms of the diminished local ecology, even without yet contending with the diminution of supplies of water – such as over the fossil waters of the massive Ogallala aquifer, along the San Joaquin Valley and so on - and of agrochemical inputs.

The level to which the global population will decline and over what length of time cannot in any way be predicted. However, it may be expected that the current global population will be decimated with very few if any countries spared their share of the decline.

But it is not only food for which communities will have to find new sources. The global economy sources all materials and goods from particular places, ships these to yet other places across the globe for processing and then distributes them to yet many other places around the world. As this system falls apart and materials and goods cease to flow, new sources or resources nearer home will have to be sought. An interim solution will be the increasing growth and importance of the second-hand and recycling industries that are evolving everywhere around the world. Already in many Southern cities recycled materials and goods satisfy substantial markets so that their lives are prolonged and adaptations are made to new uses.

This can be expected to spread to a point where in the North the vast amounts of Stuff that is already subject to 'built-in obsolescence' will be joined by abandoned buildings and cars and household goods, now no more than mountains of detritus, that might be considered storehouses of material. These could facilitate the transition to later years in the century when practically all materials, from building materials to timber for furniture, fibres for making cloth and basic minerals, will have to be sourced relatively locally, as was the case until less than two centuries ago. Small amounts of trade in vital materials such as metals, medicines, condiments and luxuries have been the subject of long-distance trade since pre-history and can be expected to continue as long as human communities exist. But these will once again revert, in terms of weight, to the margins of material life.

A final consideration is what, in the conditions described above, will be the impact of the legacies of pollution left behind by modern civilisation. Mention was made earlier and will be repeated here that today we have agencies with their programmes to clean up old sites polluted by past industrial activity and then measures are taken to secure ongoing activity — particularly of the chemical industry and of nuclear facilities to minimise the possibility of leakage of lethal pollutants. In a future where governments break down due to the lack of resources, this will undoubtedly include resources to guard over leakage of pollutants and to clean up the consequences. With radically decentralised polities, it can only be hoped that those communities in the vicinity of potential sites of future leakage, particularly chemical plants and above all the skeletons of nuclear power stations of the past, will continue to maintain an awareness of the dangers residing in these and if necessary take measures to prevent future leakage and the consequences for health and life that this could have.

Global warming will certainly continue, however rapidly the burning of fossil hydrocarbon declines. It can only be hoped in this respect that the collapse in the burning of fossil hydrocarbons comes earlier rather than later, for all the pain that economic collapse will cause; there can be little doubt that as the concentration of carbon dioxide in the atmosphere increases, so the danger of a runaway rise in global temperature will also increase. In any case, it can be expected that extreme weather conditions, for instance severe droughts, storms and flooding, already escalating in prevalence, will increase over the coming years, further prejudicing the capacity of communities affected, to recover from the collapse.

Sea level rise has been widely discussed as having potentially catastrophic impacts on coastal cities with, however, IPCC estimates indicating a very gentle increase, by little more than one metre by the end of the century. This may turn out to be conservative and in any case, in conjunction with extreme weather conditions, numbers of cities may be subjected to the kinds of catastrophic events experienced by the city of New Orleans in August 2005 and Bangkok in January 2012. However, this may be the least of the problems faced by cities in the coming decades as populations decant in search of agricultural land and the formation of new forms of community. Nevertheless, climate change from the rising global temperature already in train will certainly accelerate the reduction in biodiversity over the coming decades and, in conjunction with severe weather conditions, will hamper new developments in agriculture and in areas where transhumance predominates now or in the future, also reducing the productivity of grassland. Runaway temperature rise could, over the next one or two centuries, eventually reduce the biomass of the biosphere to a point where human populations, returned to their original place in the global ecological balance, might number but a few million.

Coda

This chapter started with a description of the surface of our world as being carried away by excitement and diversion from facing up to an imminent future of the fall of modern civilisation. As the chapter unfolded, the evidence of the unsustainability of the 'Development Path' of what has become a global society was analysed. As each dimension is scrutinised, the accumulation of problems faced by our global society seems overwhelming and in the end the way in which the dangers are ignored, dismissed and then denied comes to seem bizarre — almost a race to perform a purposeful mass-suicide.

The proximate reason for this would appear to be simply that almost nobody wants to face up to the bad news. The present is fun, engaging, enthralling and the idea that it is coming to an end is uncomfortable and for some who do spend longer investigating and thinking about it, frightening and depressing where, as individuals in an individualistic and at the same time insanely complex world, there is little or nothing they feel they can do about it. This, however, points in the direction of the problem being one that arises out of deeper causes concerning the social and cultural outlook of the present times, of modernity as a cultural phenomenon. Much has been written about this by the academic branch of the Green Movement, or just academics with a bent for attempting to understand how the world got to be like this in terms of multiple sustainability problems, but above all the cultural self-understanding that has systematically failed to face up to the problems and thence take meaningful action to forge a different direction.

For many decades now, the Green Movement has made countless proposals on what could be done in practical ways to obviate the problems by simply changing our lifestyles. Later in this book, there will be a summary of some of these because, as is evident from the above analysis of the probable trajectory of collapse, there will be a great need for effective practical ways to reorganise life in a situation where the environment and availability of resources has radically changed . It is, however, often stated by those who take the time and effort to understand the problems described above, that our society is in need of a good deal more than practical solutions. Before these can progress very far, there will need to be profound changes in cultural outlook to make sense out of the world that will be emerging and to be able to organise life in ways that will have meaning for the emergent communities. And in order to do this, it will be very helpful to analyse how the present-day state of mind and cultural outlook came to possess the global population to submit themselves to what, in the end, has become a truly bizarre, even ludicrous condition.

The following three chapters therefore investigate the origins of the culture that has produced modern society. The underlying supposition is that cultural attitudes are constructed through time, and can be maintained over long periods and then change, sometimes quite suddenly, to yield the foundations of what populations and communities deem to be important in life and providing them with direction with regard to how they act as social entities, components and as individuals. We will see in this light how modern society was constructed, including alternative directions that arose and failed, but which, it is contended, give leads as to how a radical change in cultural outlook that will surely be needed for the reconstruction of viable societies for those who survive the coming collapse may be achieved.

Chapter 2: How we got to be here: A Critique of Modernity

The intention of this chapter is to inquire into the reasons why our civilisation has come to the point of imminently destroying the basis of its existence, with all the pain that this will involve at the personal level, by ignoring and eventually denying the increasingly clear evidence of what is threatening to happen and in this knowledge what might be done to ameliorate the situation. Whilst our society has prided itself from the 18th century on being 'enlightened', meaning consciously rational in our dealings with one another and our environment, here is evidence of an extreme irrationality in terms of action. The ultimate purpose of the chapter is then to reveal 'what went wrong' as a prelude to proposing ways to reconstruct what will be left of the world following the fall of our civilisation.

The use of Key Terms

Writing about 'what happened in history' is of course always a question of choices amongst a myriad of 'facts' and, in spite of many historians attempting to hide the fact, in the end what is chosen and how it is presented always has a purpose: perhaps to criticise the past so as to clear the way for a different future, to justify and perhaps glorify present social and political arrangements to prevent unwanted change, and so on[94]. As already made clear, the choice of 'facts' and the interpretation given to these here is undertaken with the hope that it will help illuminate the problems which the trajectory of our civilisation has created that will need to be resolved in the coming decades as modern civilisation falls apart and if humanity is to survive at all. There are terms used here already that need to be better defined and understood before we proceed much further. Here we provide a basic definition and then in Chapter Seven we will be taking a much closer look to be able to find a terminology and set of concepts that will be of use to a very different understanding of the world and of human existence that will necessarily emerge following the end of modern civilisation.

   We do not need to define the concept 'civilisation' as used here as this was already accomplished in the Introduction. But it is necessary to sketch what we mean in terms of human existence by the terms 'culture' and 'society'[95]. To do this requires a preliminary assertion — difficult to swallow for persons brought up in the present age of liberalism and individualism — that very little that we think or do is not pre-defined by the cultural and social context in which we are born, live and die and this proposition becomes a vital focus of the final chapter of this book. People may seem individually different and, insofar as we have a language in common, we can discuss existential matters with people from any part of the world and think we are thinking the same things. But in practice, and this is the central problematic we face in the coming decades when radical change in direction will be called for, even in our 'globalised' world, cultures are universes of thought and action that have a certain internal coherence that has a different complexion one from the other and that motivates people to act in different ways when faced with the same circumstances. Communication of some sort is always possible, and may involve anything from proactive desire to emulate the thoughts and actions of people of other cultures through mild detached interest or the necessity to adapt, to situations of conflict and assertion or defence of one's own culture.

This chapter is concerned throughout to relativise culture, and above all to help readers brought up in Occidental culture to see our culture more objectively and particularly to see where the faults that have brought us to where we are today originate and are located in our thinking processes, latterly dragging the rest of the world with us. Fundamentally, we should be able to see how other cultures, complex and less complex, also have characteristics that are clearly superior to ours — even being able to see that 'primitive' societies might be more capable of satisfying basic human needs far more successfully than 'complex cultures' as well as being sustainable with respect to their impacts on the environment in which they subsist.

We then come to the point of clarifying the difference between civilisation, culture and society and the role of ideology. Civilisation, as noted in the Introduction, whilst apparently simply a word to describe how we all work together to produce our world, has, in fact, a strong normative dimension that implies that some people are better ('more civilised') than others and that implies also what 'better' means. The term 'culture' can also have normative overtones ('to be cultured') but has been used in anthropology enough to be rid of any assertions of superiority and inferiority[96]. The word is used here simply to denote different, more or less coherent worlds of thought and action in which we all live out our lives and above all the structures they create around them in terms of institutions and thence artefacts and lifestyles.

The term 'society' is sometimes used interchangeably with 'culture' — partly because some anthropologists like to restrict the term culture to just the ways in which people think rather than including how they actually organise their lives around institutions and through the creation and use of artefacts and hence through their actions. Of course the term 'society' also goes beyond what people think and say, denoting how people in a particular culture relate to one another regarding positions of individuals within social structures, motivating what they do with themselves and the limits of what they may or may be expected to do with their lives as defined by social relations and institutions. The term 'society' tends to end with human interaction and, unlike the term 'culture', is disinterested in the relationship with the physical environment and how this is utilised and moulded to yield the physical necessities and create the ambience of particular lifestyles.

We then come to the term 'ideology', invented following the French Revolution by a group that wanted to forge a new way of thinking. The notoriety and contentiousness of the term came from Karl Marx's accusation that the idea was intended to promote the interests of the bourgeois class as a weapon against working class emancipation[97]. Even within the Marxist camp, however, Lenin decided that the term 'ideology' might be applied to any coherent way of thinking and that 'class struggle' was also a 'clash of ideologies'. The use of the term here – discussed at greater length in Chapter Seven – is that adopted by Lenin and which recently has become the common usage of the term[98]. Ideology in this text thus denotes the configuration and orientation of ideas that inform the ways in which particular societies and cultures work in practice. This means also that religions, philosophies, encompassing indeed science, are ideologies or certain, usually key, components of ideologies. It can also be seen in terms of a way of thinking that one group within a society might wish others also to think, as was the case with the original ideologues.

Ideologies are not just passive configurations of ideas; they are the ideas that give meaning to life and through which people are motivated to act and to understand joy and sadness, humour and tragedy, influencing what is deemed to be important or not important, fact or fiction and in general articulate understanding. One thing insisted on here is that there is no such thing, as Marx would have liked to think, as a post-ideological culture. Cultures — and human beings as such — cannot survive without relatively coherent, overlapping and interwoven cultural *and* ideological contexts, and it is indeed the collapse or degeneration in recent centuries and particularly the last few decades, through infestation of non-Occidental ideologies with modern (ergo Occidental) ideology that has been one of the most tragic outcomes of the expansion of European culture to all other parts of the world, and these are discussed at length as this book proceeds.

The concept of ideology here thus covers religion, in its system of belief, the related social customs, and also philosophy. Ideologies are inherited and all members of particular cultures learn these as the basis of their education, formal and informal. Whilst ideologies generally survive over more or less long periods, they also evolve, sometimes quite radically over a short time, which is an essential dimension of revolutions[99]. However, they are best understood as being layered structures with surfaces easily changed but with deeper layers that have lost any notion of their original rationale but nevertheless persist in terms of orienting whole societies to particular ideas. It is this that we will be looking at in most detail as this chapter unfolds: the way that our 'liberal' society came about in terms of orienting thinking and how this evolved into what is termed here the 'Commercial Ideology' that in its ultimate form, today, is generally referred to as 'consumerism'. Then, in the following chapter we discuss the issue of ideology as it relates to political ideas and their organisational manifestations.

Even though in recent years we have seen the dissolution of many cultures, with the disappearance of many hundreds of discrete languages[100] (these being an essential indicator of ideological and cultural difference) nevertheless, we can still identify many almost incommensurably different worlds all on the same planet. Most people have no interest in this because they live happily (or unhappily) within their own cultural universes, although globalisation and in particular the global media, but also increasing numbers of 'foreign' communities living outside their native communities where the differences can be encountered directly - have come to expose almost everyone to cultural difference which might be reacted to in terms of adaptation or hostile rejection as prejudice (e.g. the popularity in Britain of Indian food or the banning of the wearing of the burqa in France).

But it is useful for our purposes here to examine ways of understanding the variety of cultures and particularly the notions of simplicity and complexity in cultural development and expression. Even today, there exist simple cultures in the sense of occupying limited territory and being predominantly self-contained in their interaction with the local environment, from which they construct and maintain their lives, and administer these in logistical terms and in terms of satisfying their abstract ideological needs including moral questions of right and wrong and existential questions about the origins and meaning of life. More geographically extensive and complex cultures appear in the historical record starting some ten thousand years ago and have arisen and declined or been destroyed right across Eurasia and North Africa and also in Central and South America.

Stages in Cultural Evolution and an Ultimate Resolution to the Human Condition?

It is clearly possible to see the development of civilisations as some kind of progress using different dimensions, in the sense of 'one thing leading to another'. Thus there may be stages in technological development or the efflorescence of the accoutrement of lifestyles or stages in administrative capacity to hold larger territories within the same 'empire'. Or civilisations may be classified according to social differentiation — the division into classes or castes defining who does what in the production of life, from the family through to the economy and the state in an overall system of the development of unequal power relations.

We can start by noting three broad stages in the development of religion that are reasonably consistent in their typology, not only across Eurasia but also quite independently — at least the first two stages — in the Americas prior to the arrival the Europeans. We start with Animism, which, whilst being displaced by later manifestations of religion, nevertheless resurfaced in various forms throughout civilisation as Pantheism. This imputes spiritual meaning and ways of understanding beyond the empirical, diffused throughout natural events and artefacts, people and relationships, where human consciousness and the rest of nature are fused into an organic unity with a configuration that sees human understanding and the actualities of the environment in which particular groups lived to be a single, articulated entity. We then see the emergence in the early stages of civilisation of Polytheism, where meaning and direction is given to the world and human relations through the mythical acts of discrete gods and mythical heroes personified as animal, humans or hybrids, associated with particular places and artefacts where, in other words, the separation between human social consciousness and nature in general has taken place, whilst particular places continue to possess sacred qualities.

Finally we see the emergence of the meaning of life emanating from sacred texts and the preaching of prophets that present an altogether more abstract notion of God or of Nothingness: the nominal, the mystical and the transcendental experience as the context within which we are supposed to understand our existence, by now almost entirely severed of referents within the physical, natural context. That meaning might be derived directly from human reason starts with the decanting of moral precepts, previously sacred rules of conduct, into the worldly administration of family and politics, starting some two thousand five hundred years ago with the teachings of Confucius and in certain respects, Siddhartha Gautama (the Buddha).

This was also to be found clearly in the speculative debates, preserved in written form, of the ancient Greek philosophers. The notion that religious belief — the mystical source of socio-economic and political organisation — might be displaced by reason in the organisation of life was then a fundamental (and we can now see fundamentally chimerical) hope of the 18th century European Enlightenment. At the same time, nature, already divested of spirituality, and already long before starting its career as quarry and larder, becomes the instrumental matter to supply the needs of humanity with all too few questions asked[101].

It is instructive, however, to contrast the two attempts made in the history of two of the major religions to define an ultimate solution to the human condition under the title of 'Enlightenment'. On one side we have the Buddhist notion of Enlightenment as a quietist *condition* attainable in real time by consistent personal thought, sensibility and action. On the other side we have the European notion of Enlightenment as an active *process* involving social, economic and political progress, deficient in large measure of anything very concrete by way of a coherent moral framework in the sense of guidance on what the good society or the morally virtuous individual or community might entail. We must pause for a moment to drive this point home and to look at the origins of this orientation.

Although academic debates on the stages of cultural development (the stages of history) have flourished and languished at different times across the 20th century for reasons we will discuss further in the following chapter, it is clearly the 19th century where one has to look for the Great Debate on this issue[102]. First sketches start in the late 18th century with the Frenchman, Turgot, and the Scot, Adam Smith (the two were acquainted) seeing progress as a question of Development of more productively effective economic activity, summed up as the capacity to accumulate wealth, passing from hunting and gathering through herding, farming and on ultimately to urban commerce. The Marquis de Condorcet, mentored by Turgot, then envisaged a humanist progression — essentially following the Progress of European history from its predecessors — to an eventual enlightened society, under the title of the 'Perfectibility of Man', that would comprise a liberal economy, free and equal public education, constitutionalism, and equal rights for women and people of all races[103].

British intellectual self-understanding in the 19th century was saturated with evolutionism,[104] which always confirmed the present situation of British hegemony[105] as the ultimate stage of history, crowned by Darwin who gave a particular slant on natural evolution that indicated that all is a question of (power) struggle and, as a kind of inevitability so not morally questionable, that the 'fittest' win: 'might is right', regardless of what it might want to achieve by way of a lifestyle or fairness and the pain that might be imposed on those who suffer the will of the mighty. Notwithstanding utopian ideas and movements described further below, there was precious little in this version of mainstream consciousness by way of wisdom or moral introspection or any notion of what might comprise in any sense a good society. This evolutionism was, however, quickly forgotten in the light of Karl Marx's notion that the next stage of evolution would see the overthrow of 'bourgeois' culture that so self-confidently expressed its superiority.

Karl Marx's notion of cultural evolution as progressing through 'Modes of Production' has been both influential and is at least in part a useful way to look at how societies are constituted[106]. This fuses ideas about the social and political organisation of society and the exploitation of natural resources to produce the physical livelihood of particular cultures. Whilst this grew out of a clearly very effective analysis of the transition from feudalism to capitalism in Europe, attempts to lump what had gone before and what continued to happen elsewhere as being all of a kind of feudalism (i.e. a past 'Mode of Production' which will be superseded by capitalism and eventually communism) was a crass presumption, in the face of the sheer fecundity of cultural evolution, to fit the purpose of the exercise: this was to promote a 'World Revolution' that would create a single, enlightened society led by the messianic progress of European society. Cultural difference was to disappear, indicating a gross violation of the meaning of life for the peoples beyond the borders of Europe and a breathtaking naiveté with respect to the very possibility of moving whole cultures with ease, through one mighty revolution, from one self-understanding to something entirely other. It is of considerable interest to note in parentheses just how far this messianic programme, taken up in their own interpretation by cultures as diverse as Cuba, Tanzania and China, was able to change these cultures and what, now that this is in the past, were its limits.

Marx's 'materialism' inclined him — and even more so, his followers — to assert that it is primarily a matter of the way in which cultures generate their livelihood in the form of the social means of organising production processes that determines the nature of the society, and that the broader framework of ideas and institutions that informs the everyday functioning of societies, right up to the religions they espouse, are but epiphenomena or 'superstructure'. Whilst the Mode of Production clearly provides important dimensions of the self-consciousness of societies and the way in which they express themselves in terms of culture and ideology, anthropology provides us with enough evidence that ideas and social structures possess their own evolutionary dynamics that in turn can constrain and inform the Mode of Production so that we cannot speak of a foundation and a superstructure but, rather, of the interconnection of all these dimensions making up and providing coherence to the whole. The coherence of these can, however, break apart and be reformulated through the decay or destruction of any of the parts, leading to 'evolution' that might be 'progressive' but which has also, in many cases, resulted in 'collapse' into less economically productive and in general simpler societies[107].

The Peculiarity of a Progress-Oriented Culture

The view underlying this chapter is that the construction of cultures and the understanding that societies have of the world they inhabit and how to act in it are overwhelmingly consequent upon what went before. One thing leads to another. In general, Stephen Jay Gould's notion of 'punctuated equilibria' is useful to understand how civilisation evolved, where complex cultures have emerged in a particular configuration, often through relatively rapid transformations and then functioned, notwithstanding periodic crises and recoveries, as more or less stable configurations over longer periods. We can see such an equilibrium of four thousand years in the case of Ancient Egypt and well over two thousand years in the cases of Hindu India and Confucian China.

Of course many an empire has survived for much shorter periods before collapsing or, classically in the case of Aztec and Inca cultures, being destroyed through external attack. The amazing march of Alexander and his armies to Asia and back; struggles between Germanic tribes in destroying the Western Roman Empire. The waves of Mongol and Turkic invasions and supersessions embodied little by way of coherent aspiration to achieve a more permanent lifestyle and organisational configuration[108], albeit facilitating trade and communication between China and Europe that led both to the European colonial expansion — initiated by the search for a direct trade route to China — and the scientific revolution, where a long list of technical and technological inventions and improvements in life found their way from China to Europe[109]. The Eastern Roman Empire nevertheless survived a further thousand years, developing the first extensive Christian culture[110]. Eventually the Islamic settlement also developed definite cultural characteristics that changed little in their basic orientation, lifestyle and organisational principles, lasting well over a thousand years, strong features of which survive even today in spite of the overwhelming power of present-day Occidental - so-called global - culture, with the powerful means available to change cultural outlooks and the messianic inclination to destroy other cultures and to refashion them after ours.

What has emerged as modern Occidental civilisation is a unique case, in being informed by a time-oriented philosophy/ideology that we think of as 'progressive' where there has been an expectation of continuous change that has become a self-fulfilling prophesy[111]. We just have to think of the meaning and feeling of anything today that is deemed to be 'progressive' as somehow at the forefront of 'inevitable' change and somehow better than what went before; and the notion of 'stagnation' applied to the sophisticated and enduring cultures, for example Indian, Chinese, or Islamic, that did not consider change to be a valuable cultural attribute but, rather, were happy when they achieved what they considered to be a sophisticated level of culture. In practice, an orientation to progress could only be expected to last for a limited time-span before eventually running into limits that would destroy the apparent forward march and with it the underlying orientation and belief.

The end of the road of this phenomenon – that might have happened in the 19th Century - was, however, forestalled by the discovery and exploitation of fossilised energy sources. This led to an astonishing explosion of developments that also someday has to come to an end, which is what we see now immediately ahead. As we shall see in the analysis that follows, it is an extraordinary phenomenon that the fact of the latter years of our civilisation, accelerating into a bizarre complexity, being a function of the exploitation of fossil energy has been simply overlooked, ignored, invisible, not only to the ordinary people but to the whole intellectual consciousness of the civilisation. The way in which this fact has come in recent years, not only to be ignored but actively screened out was analysed in the foregoing chapter. Here we look more broadly at the development of this Civilisation as a whole where we see more clearly the role that this one-time concentrated injection of physical energy has played.

The Christian Roots of the Idea of Progress

The idea of progress can be seen to be rooted in the Judaic and thence Christian eschatology. Although it has been disputed that what today

102

are considered the sinews of progress (economic growth, scientific discovery technological advance, and human development) has much to do with Christianity and is, rather, a child of the Renaissance and more so the Enlightenment[112], nevertheless, Judaism and Christianity set themselves well apart from all other 'great religions' in suggesting a linear idea of the condition of humanity on earth, that emanates from key biblical texts and the exegesis of these in the context of Christian belief and practice. Whilst one thousand five hundred years ago Saint Augustine put any notion of salvation firmly into the 'other life' – the City of God - and thus, together with the fact of the fall of Rome, closed the door upon any assertion that progress might be attainable in the here and now, this Christian foundation, as understood by many of the great writers and philosophers of the 17th to the 19th centuries from Newton[113] to August Comte, as researched over the past decades[114], is difficult to avoid.

The issue for Christians and their modern heirs is the notion of the Second Coming of Christ and the Judgement, associated with the notion of the millennium and apocalypse. One interpretation, known as pre-millennialism, sees His arrival at the nadir of a deterioration of the moral condition of the world, and, following the Judgement, a thousand years where the saved will live a beatific life. The second, known as post-millennialism, sees life improving over a thousand year period after which will come the Judgement. In fact, not only does belief in the idea of the millennium live on in Christian minds and communities, but efforts went consciously amongst academics in the late 17th century to secularise Millenarianism as the notion of progress and we saw strongly across the 19th and 20th centuries the clear distinction between the liberal ameliorative notion of improvement as pre-millennialism and the revolutionary path as an interpretation of post-millennialism.

We cannot separate the ideological orientation from the social and political structuration of cultures. Thus the Occidental ideology of progress is intertwined with the actuality of progress, or rather the expectation of constant change and the complexification of Society and polity. Max Weber, whose comparison of the different complex cultures of Eurasia is further discussed below, although not overtly aware of Progressivism as a uniquely Occidental phenomenon, was insistent on the way that religious ideology is intertwined with the structure and functioning of society, seeing how the social process in all the societies he examined was informed by and hence operated within the ideological structures given or adopted. Whilst in the case of Indian Hindu culture (as a society organised around castes that have a fixed place in the organisation of society and polity, this also being the origin

103

of so much by way of religious and mystical thought and spiritual sensibility) there never developed any intellectual approach to designing social and political process: what is, has to be, as determined by fate, and cannot be changed. By contrast, Confucianism, arising some five hundred years before Christ, came about through the teachings of Confucius and his followers as a conscious effort to define an end state in terms of how society and polity should be organised, being largely a rationalisation and reformulation of traditional moral and organisational principles and structures[115].

We must stress here that Confucius' concern was to counter the growing insecurity of a society developing rapidly with commerce, war and the intrigue amongst elites, destabilising traditional Chinese society. The conditions under which he developed his ideas had definite parallels to the developments we have seen in Europe over the past four centuries. Confucius, and the sages who followed his lead, worked out and then taught arrangements for social and political process that would bring what they saw as the negative effects of Development to a halt in a format that would provide an abrogation of violence and an acceptable way to organise the life of the entire society from the family to the State as embodied in the 'Mandate of Heaven'.

It took four centuries for this formula to become generally accepted and then adopted by the Han Dynasty as state and social ideology that gave structure and orientation to Chinese society for almost two thousand years and, with interruptions, did provide stable ('sustainable') arrangements for most of the centuries between. Such a concern — we might refer to it as wisdom — regarding the dangers of progress motivated Confucius, but never had any purchase in the context of Christian Millenarianism and so we find ourselves confronted with a mountain of problems that has resulted from this lack of wisdom, still unable to see the cultural underpinnings that blind us to the urgent need to dismantle the belief in progress and purposefully seek a genuinely sustainable socio-political and economic system that will provide a congenial way of life for all and which maintains the ecological foundations that sustain the system.

Class Struggle fuels Progress

The rhetorical opening of the Communist Manifesto states that: *The history of all hitherto existing society is the history of class struggle*[116]. This is certainly questionable when it comes to societies where class positions are deeply enculturated and hence accepted. But we can see that in Europe the collapse of feudalism initiated what became an ongoing social struggle in conditions of social instability fuelled by the hopes embedded in the notion of progress. It is now generally recognised that the Great Plagues of the middle to late 14th century loosened the grip of what throughout Europe was a form of caste society, embodied in the village hierarchy, with Monarchy, the baronage and the Church maintaining strategic control.

Villages and towns emptied out as populations died of the plague, leaving everywhere a shortage of labour that gave opportunity for the 'lower orders' (generally more than one rank) opportunity to escape their bondage, often to the towns where, as became the slogan, 'the air is free', and obtain enhanced status. Trade was increasing and the rising urban commercial classes were demanding rights to pursue their interests and able, with their growing wealth, to buy their way to power step by step, pushing aside aristocracy and Church, much of the time incrementally and then in sudden rebellious outbreaks, many of which were explicitly connected to biblical exegesis, and then in the great secular revolutions that attempted to change the political and social conjuncture in one fell swoop[117].

Each of the revolutions brought into the open different groups, combining different interests with different ideas of how the political settlement should be reorganised. The mid-seventeenth century English Revolution was a classic case where on the one hand the Monarchy and aristocracy were pushed aside by the 'gentry' with at least three concrete, increasingly radical, visions amongst the common people, pursued respectively by the Levellers, the Diggers and the Ranters, with their own agendas and approaches to implementation[118]. None of these survived the repression following the end of the Cromwellian Republic and re-installation of the Monarchy — except, perhaps, the Quakers, whose mode of thinking survived to become a significant voice in the more passive, educational, 'alternative' and peace movements of the 20th century.

The French Revolution, following on from the multifaceted discourses of the Enlightenment, had models enough to reorganise the political and social settlement, taking its own course through the different tendencies and the struggles to realise these. Whilst even today there exists a deep hypocrisy embedded in French society regarding the vanquishing of an elite, the genuine achievement here was the establishment of a technocracy that even today is unique amongst Occidental nations[119]. Finally, the Russian Revolution, whilst growing out of increasingly radical political movements and manifestations throughout the second half of the 19th century[120] was dominated by one clear ideological alternative — albeit in the first instance seriously lacking any defined programme. In all cases, the outcome of these revolutions was inconclusive, leaving the process of struggle and competition between classes and interests — and indeed nations — continuing and fuelling insecurity and a mentality that expected 'progress' to continue, perhaps until a World Revolution would resolve everything...

Throughout this process of change, lay a range of mythologies. At one end were those who saw the abolition of absolute Monarchy and disempowering of the aristocracy as sufficiently radical, thence promotion of the interests of the next class down the hierarchy — the gentry or bourgeoisie. At the other end was the notion of an ultimately egalitarian society where no class or group would possess priority or prerogative over any other. Unlike in India, China or the Islamic world, in Europe the social and political organisational rules were not deeply enough embedded to hold the political settlement in place. The idea of progress fuelled hope that someday there would arrive an ideal settlement, come the Millennium. Whilst ruling elites asserted regularly that the ultimate arrangements had now been attained, there was inadequate cultural cement to maintain this position for long.

Thus, from the dissolution of feudalism, the most radical proposal for an ultimate settlement was the notion of a classless, egalitarian society that clearly has its roots in the teaching of Christ (and for obvious reasons had, until the growth of Occidental influence in the past hundred years, no purchase at all in Asian cultures). Whilst today this is associated in most minds with the Marxist notion of Communism, the idea was in practice expressed many times over the past centuries of Occidental history with many different ways to arrive there and what could be expected as the result[121]. We might say that the non-achievement of egalitarian social arrangements in the Occident is a crucial component of the trajectory that is taking us to the collapse ahead. 'Social struggle' fuels 'progress' as those below attempt to achieve 'Social Justice' and an abstract notion of 'Freedom'; and the privileged classes constantly invent new ways to block the achievement of justice for the masses, blinding all parties to the wider impacts of the struggle.

Capitalism as the Concretisation of the Ideology of Progress

Marx's notion of capitalism as the 'current Mode of Production' can be viewed more broadly as a particular combination of ideology and productive relations that evolved in a contingent way out of many historic threads of Western European cultural history, in the context of a particular set of geographic and environmental conditions, and here we will try to unravel these, all the time contrasting what happened here to the evolutionary paths taken by cultures elsewhere in Eurasia. In this chapter we will look at the social side of the process of cultural configuration. In Chapter Four we will look more closely at the role that nature and the environment played in generating the specific characteristics of western European culture together with the particular interpretation of human-nature relations that emerged under these conditions.

Max Weber, whose intercultural studies have already been referred to above, was attempting to understand how it was that Western Europe had invented capitalism by contrasting this with other complex cultures that did not develop this particular mode of interaction between society and nature which, is an important insight for our purposes[122]. This was the first time since the Enlightenment that other complex cultures had been taken into serious consideration in European social inquiry without bellicose prejudices that accompanied the deepening colonialism of the 19th century, indicating systems of organisation other than that which had evolved in Europe as being equally legitimate qua cultural systems. Whilst this is prima facie an absolutely essential piece of research to provide some kind of objectivity on European culture, it was only the critique of capitalism that Weber published under the title of *The Protestant Ethic and the Spirit of Capitalism*[123] which was widely read and cited.

The rest of Weber's research explaining why capitalism did not develop under Islam, Hinduism and Confucianism (Weber saw religion – but as adjunct to this, legal and institutional and social structures and ideologies - as the foundation of cultural outlooks and motivations) is rarely read. Subsequent, predominantly Marxist-inspired, cross-cultural research at this macro scale, whilst, as in the case of Perry Anderson correcting[124] the bland Marxist presumption that all complex non-capitalist societies displayed the some form of 'pre-capitalist' structure, nevertheless implicitly accepts the universalist notion of an eventual single, Occidentally-led culture and hence has lacked the capacity to use other cultures as a platform from which to understand Occidental culture critically.

What Weber failed to see was the power that the notion of progress has on the European consciousness and the way that this motivates the complete cultural process. For, as outlined above, European culture takes for granted that culture as such is something on the move in an upward direction and capitalism, concerned as it is with the continuous accumulation of wealth expressed in 'commodities', can easily be interpreted not just as a piece of economic and social machinery but one that specifically fulfils the requirements of the belief in progress and through this gains its own immense ideological power, translating this belief into concrete reality.

Weber's analysis showed that the other cultures he examined did not display this belief, thus potentially opening the door to the possibility of questioning the wisdom of such a belief as a possible additional dimension to the critique of capitalism. He himself, whilst expressing a clear personal dislike of capitalism did not, however, question the wisdom of the belief in progress and even today, as we see the rapidly accumulating problems of the pursuit of progress (generally focussed obsessively on the pursuit of growth in Gross Domestic Product), our culture displays a fatally inadequate capacity to be able to look critically at what is happening as a consequence of this belief[125].

This is in no way intended to regret that Europeans are neither Hindu nor Buddhist, neither Confucian nor Muslim, nor to imply that conditions were not sometimes unhappy in these contexts — for many reasons, not necessarily to do with the social and ideological systems themselves. What it is saying is that other visions of the way in which our socio-political life may be organised, qua complex cultures, are not only feasible but exist and have been viable over significant periods of history. And it implies that surely the aim of religion, philosophy or whatever it takes to design and provide the ideological framework of cultural structures, should be to seek and attain 'the good life for all', in the context of a sustainable relationship with its environment, of which there are many examples from which to choose or which we could eventually experiment with and hone from there. By contrast, Occidental progressivism, ultimately in its guise as capitalism, is a formula that constantly regenerates dissatisfaction, pushing cultural self-expression into the unknown and that, prima facie, will inevitably end in tears.

The Triumph of the Commercial Ideology

The rest of this chapter, in examining what did actually happen and how this led to the current situation focuses on the struggle between the 'idealist' version of progress and that part of the elite that has sometimes come to the surface in the pursuit of this, also the 'commercial classes,' and eventually the obsessive pursuit of wealth (or the accumulation of commodities and personal status) that has at other times come to dominance. It is the struggle between these and, on the part of both, against the notion of an egalitarian society, and with the ultimate triumph of commerce and what is here referred to as the 'Commercial Ideology'(the essence of which is 'buy cheap, sell dear' and the promotion of consumption) that has brought us to where we are now. We need to look in detail at how this unfolded.

Before starting down this path, it is useful again to contrast the role that commercial interests, and the Commercial Ideology, has played in India and China as opposed to the Occident. Whilst having a specific, recognised place in Hindu and Confucian Society, commerce was always kept in check through a combination of ideology and the configuration of social interests which this supported. India's 'Mode of Production' was and in significant measure remains one that allocated functions by caste, with commerce relegated to a relatively minor space (involving Hindus but also Jains and other religious and ethnic groups outside the Hindu system) that had no chance of expanding. It was only under, and subsequent to, British rule that a modern commercial class rose to significance and later even dominance in the formal political sphere.

The Chinese Mode of Production, over some two thousand years, might be said to have possessed two components within the overall Confucian socio-political structure and hierarchy. One was the system of tribute whereby taxes were used to carry out public works and the other was social space allocated for small businesses that, being outside the dominant status hierarchy that was organised through the public exam system, relegated commerce to a low status[126]. Indeed, whilst in the course of the Sung Dynasty (10th to 13th Centuries AD), commerce expanded and traders were now travelling to India, Arabia and the African coast, which could have led to the growth of a distinct class of wealthy merchants who might have used their wealth to increase their social and political status. The government retained tight control by requiring that merchants sell much of their merchandise only to them, by levying substantial taxes and then maintaining monopoly of key industries. Today, of course, in the spirit of Deng Xiao Ping's memorable aphorism that: *it doesn't matter what colour the cat as long as it catches the mouse*, the Commercial Ideology has been let loose in China, with the Chinese showing themselves, now the course is set, to be masters of modern commerce[127].

Returning now to Max Weber's inquiries, we discover how commerce came to be accepted into the Christian universe in the course of the Reformation. It has been asserted that Weber exaggerated the crucial role played by the reformer Jean Calvin, in the middle years of the 16th century, in marrying capitalism to religion. Be that as it may, we should not forget that Calvin expounded his doctrine in Geneva where the citizenry, as in much of Northern Europe, were keen to rid the Church of the corrupt state into which Catholicism had descended, but that at the same time Geneva had been, as a key European crossroads since at least Roman times, an important centre of commerce. In the past, Christian doctrine had not held commerce in high regard, had not condoned wealth or generally the matter of making money. As already noted, following the demise of feudalism, the urban commercial classes had been gaining in political power and the question was how they could at the same time be seen to be morally upright — or even better, to usurp the Divine Right of Kings.

Calvin's bitter pill was the introduction of supervision of moral behaviour, but this was amply compensated for by embracing the notion that personal wealth, produced through righteous work, was not only acceptable but was a sign of the elect in the eyes of God. In its original Calvinist form, this smiling upon wealth was to be accompanied by what Weber termed 'worldly asceticism', popularised as the notion of the Protestant work ethic, which condoned accumulation but not the exuberant self-expression of this. The profits should rather be reinvested in further productive activity. This is the essence of the meaning of the term capitalism and although it might have started inchoately much earlier in the history of civilisation, from here on it becomes a conscious piece of *social* machinery.

Marx, who had other ideas concerning the genesis of capitalism — that this simply condensed out *deus ex machina* from the structurally determined drive of the emergent bourgeoisie and the emergence of the free market in labour — was enthusiastic, even concerning the socially destructive dimension of capitalism because he saw this as building the foundations of an ultimate beatific society beyond World Revolution. Weber, on the other hand, hated the accumulation of dead things and the bureaucratic structures that had come about to administer the whole of what he considered to be a joyless process. Of course, neither of them lived to see the ultimate casting off of worldly asceticism, now embedded in the machinery creating the Technostructure as an autonomous, extra-societal process, facilitating and providing structure for the final fatal explosion of accumulation at the personal level and the ransacking of the earth, that is the modern (not yet 'post-Modern') Consumer Society.

The Emergence of 'Possessive Individualism'

However, the seeds of this can already be seen in debates at the end of the 17th century, re-evaluating the question of consumption. By then, trade, along with the plunder of what became Latin America, had yielded an increasing flow of consumer products that enriched in the financial sense but also, where the products of Asia were concerned, graced the lives of the European aristocracy and a few others who managed to move in the circles of court and government. The golden age of Holland across the 17th century had shown what could be achieved also by a flowering bourgeoisie and elsewhere pressure came to break up royal monopolies, and onerous taxation to allow the rising bourgeoisie also to live in style. In London, puritan values of parsimony and frugality still exerted a major influence on the society, whereas the rich, nevertheless, lived in luxury. Trading interests argued that encouraging growth in consumption would benefit everyone in terms of providing work, and hence improved income for the poor, via a general upward spiral of wealth. Desire should be encouraged to stimulate trade which, in turn, should be free of government restriction[128].

The most effective advocate of this tendency was Bernard de Mandeville, a Dutchman settled in London, who expounded his views in a series of pamphlets and a book entitled *The Fable of the Bees*[129]. His thesis was that whilst human beings are driven by their passions, in practice the way in which these are expressed is determined through competitive consumption, restrained, however, by moral precepts and government restrictions. If the ultimate goal of progress in the social sphere is the accumulation of wealth, as was believed to be the essential truth by the milieu amongst whom he circulated, then moral principles and government restrictions should not be allowed to constrain the will to consume or, indeed, actual consumption because people will always strive to conform to social norms, as this is the framework within which they obtain their status and by this means satisfy their desires.

Status objects and expressions are socially given and hence striving for status is at the same time to strive towards what is deemed *by society* to be of superior status. This was very much a psychologistic argument about how society works — or should work — that we might see in retrospect to be something close to advocacy of a social 'philosophy of sleaze' and beyond this, addiction to money and all that it can buy. This is not in itself identical with liberalism (freedom of the individual to seek satisfaction of her or his individual desires by whatever means) but can be seen as a natural corollary in the sense of creating machinery through which individual liberty can be pursued in a dynamic way. Freedom is achieved through the accumulation of status of which wealth is the most important dimension or component.

It is necessary to elaborate on this principle and practice in greater detail, given the central role this plays in the way in which modern society works (with, as discussed later, the radical exception of the communist states over the period when they existed). Put simply, it is life where individuals and corporations (institutions) strive to maximise their income, profits and other benefits whilst minimising their costs. This means in the business world negotiating deals and contracts but it also applies to career climbing bureaucratic hierarchies and the 'collective bargaining' of trade unions (and eventual strikes as part of this machinery). On the underside it is a matter of minimising wages, including offshoring production to non-unionised poor labour countries and negotiating resources flows at lowest cost.

Most of this is legalised and negotiated, clearly with a dimension of political power, which can be deemed to be political even on the smallest scale of discussions about pay rises but escalates to the subsidisation so widely practiced in the United States (that ostensible bastion of the liberal economy) of particular produce and products through the pressure of particular interest groups. Looking at the ethical side, it radically sidelines the principle of fairness and clearly equality beyond that: on the contrary, it is precisely about increasing social difference. And also, consideration of environmental consequences becomes at best weak even where there is evidence that these might in the longer run have negative impacts even on those winning in the struggle. Adam Smith, as philosopher and professor of ethics and the chief prophet of this principle, clearly had little concern for the social differentials that this might create, and whilst acknowledging that entrepreneurs, when they get the chance, will collude to raise prices, nevertheless asserted that in the end the world will become a better place through this competitive process by creating wealth and lowering costs — for those who can afford to buy what the system produces.

We should dwell for a moment on this in the light of the way in which it created a kind of social psychology where status has both an external aspect — being better than one's neighbour — and an internal, narcissistic dimension where wealth and commodities attaching to one's self, confirm one's self-identity, in place of older notions relating to one's relation to God and one's moral worth as a social being. Moral worth is now embodied in what Marx referred to in passing as 'commodity fetishism'. Whilst developing in stages in the ensuing centuries, by the end of the 20th century this pursuit of inner and outer status had become the dominant characteristic of the whole of Occidental society, seducing the rest of the world into accepting this as the driving principle of life through the sophisticated machinery of the modern media.

It is imperative to stress at this point, given the ease with which Occidentals today casually refer to this 'natural' corollary to 'greed' as a human attribute, that this orientation to life is very specifically the outcome of the evolution of the European belief system. Accumulation of wealth is *not* the ultimate goal of other cultures and nor was it even in, say, the European Middle Ages where we just need to reflect on the enormous resources lavished on building cathedrals and as far as the organisation of society was concerned, how wealth creation as status was subordinated to the complexities of power relations in societies with distinct classes. The importance of realising this now is to gain some perspective on the extremity to which the Mandevillian outlook came to dominate social relations and intercourse during the 20th century, culminating in the extraordinary machinery of Stuff production, its vicarious use and disposal, the frantic pursuit of which crowds out any meaningful sense of the suicidal consequences of this orientation for us today.

Whilst Mandeville's thesis generated moral outrage at the time on the part of the guardians of public virtue, it is this basic analysis that became the foundation of the commercial ideology, as succinctly expressed in the most famous passage in Adam Smith's *Wealth of Nations*[130] which is generally acknowledged to be the founding text of what became political economy and thence the 'economic way' of understanding and indeed organising the world, that speaks so loudly to us today:

...every individual necessarily labours to render the annual revenue of the society as great as he (sic) can. He generally, indeed, neither intends to promote the public interest, nor knows how much he is promoting it... he intends only his own security; and by directing that industry in such a manner as its produce may be of the greatest value, he intends... only his own gain, and he is in this, as in many other cases, led by an invisible hand to promote an end which was no part of his intention... By pursuing his own interest he frequently promotes that of the society more effectually than when he really intends to promote it.

As he advocated matters, Smith made much of what he called:

...a certain propensity in human nature which has in view no such extensive utility; the propensity to truck, barter, and exchange one thing for another.

This ostensible natural tendency was seen in a positive light as something that should be given free reign, regardless of the role it played in generating social inequality. As we stand at the edge of unbelievable catastrophe for the society which this idea produced, we can see just how sickeningly perverse it is in encouraging the abrogation of responsibility for future generations and even our own welfare, as the 'invisible hand' leads us perhaps to the peremptory destruction of the biosphere and the end of any possibility of future civilisation. Put simply, the striving for individual status in the form of commodity wealth has become the ultimate goal of our culture, relegating to the shadows all else, including even the destruction of the very world that supports this culture, as irrelevant.

All of the foregoing fed into what, by the 19th century, became the 'philosophy' informing - at least Anglo-Saxon - social and political process and we might jump ahead and see how today this has swept all before it, driving onward and upward the machinery of globalisation. In terms of more substantial philosophy, we start with Thomas Hobbes's *Leviathan*[131]. Hobbes's proposition is widely enough known to hardly need stating:

The life of man in a state of nature [i.e. prior to becoming a member of society] *is at war with all others.*

In other words, human nature is basically individualistic and competitive. Hobbes's solution was the necessity of the existence of power above the society that would constrain individuals and steer conflict into non-destructive channels.

John Locke, writing some forty years later at the end of the 17th century, and party to the debates that produced Mandeville's *Fable*, asserted that in fact it was not necessary for there to be a power over society but rather that individuals willingly give up powers to governments to protect their interests[132]. Locke's focus was, however, on how Hobbes's individual operationalises himself, focusing on the concept of property. This did not only refer to private property in the sense of land and commodities but to the essential individual: that we create ourselves as property — or as a commodity — and, as we would say today, market ourselves in the marketplace of society, yielding what Macpherson, in characterising the result in political terms, referred to as 'Possessive Individualism'[133]. It is difficult to avoid the notion that this is abetting universal prostitution!

This clearly links into the Calvinist concept of the work ethic, which Weber saw as the centre of the Calvinistic universe. Hence today, if asked who we are we answer: 'teacher' or 'surgeon' or 'actor' as a 'calling' — but this can also be day-labourer or dustman or worse, unemployed in the context of an imposed social necessity to earn a living, however meagre, by selling our labour — and it is in this way, through the importance of spending time 'working'[134], that we commodify ourselves. This defines us, as human beings, so differently from pre-capitalist and other societies where identity and worth are achieved by one's context in the structure of society and relationship with God and, in primitive society, also the relationship with the surrounding nature as living world and not as dead property. And thus ultimate proof of worth in this society is the income and wealth that come our way as a consequence of the status of what we are and how well we have marketed ourselves as commodities.

It is important at this stage to be clear about what these theoreticians overlooked. In the first instance, it has been argued untold times that Hobbes's notion of human nature is a travesty of reality and whilst the counter-argument has been that this was only intended as a foil upon which to build his edifice, the fact is that it becomes the heart of the matter, and, indeed, is the basic tenet upon which the discipline of classical economics is based[135], and which is held very widely today as the 'truth' about 'human nature': that individuals are basically competitive and this is what matters about life and what moves the whole social process. It is extremely unlikely that this thought could have ever occurred in any other society as (not possessing any idea of progress and hence that there was any 'original state') people are born into, live and die within an actual society of which they are first and foremost a component part or function, however it might be organised in practice.

Nevertheless, had the whole of British society at the end of the 17th century taken the blossoming theories of individualism and liberalism seriously, then very rapidly the whole society would, indeed, have fallen apart in a Hobbesian war of all against all. What in practice held it in thrall was the fact of enculturation: that individuals grew up in and stayed within their social position because this was the universe in which they were confident to live and where they found the necessary social support, but also sanctions, in any attempt to break loose. At a quite fundamental level, humanity cooperates through learned and enculturated habit, even in situations that prima facie are undignified such as India's 'scheduled castes' or in 17th century Europe the life of the servant or the landless farm labourer. In fact the English and French Revolutions had encouraged the 'lower orders' to imagine and even take action to change the social order, not as a war of all against all but to institute social arrangements that would take the rich and powerful off their backs.

Then for most of the latter half of the 17th century, dissidents in English society were subjected to a police state determined to crush the radical ideas and sentiments that had arisen in the Revolution, so that by the end of the century, the underclass — the vast majority of the society — had become obedient and thus irrelevant to the implications of emergent liberalism, subsisting at a very modest level of consumption and, when not living in dire poverty, could learn to be happy enough in this condition however unfair it might be, because it was perceived as being inevitable or beyond the powers of the individual or collectivity to change. The commodification of those occupying the 'lower orders', rather than voluntary, was forced upon them in the making of a 'working class' that sold its labour to the burgeoning capitalist system. This situation was confirmed in Britain following the French Revolution, when radical ideas and movements resurfaced, unleashing again a police state, followed by another wave of liberal philosophising against the cowed working class — the creation of which was so masterfully analysed by EP Thompson in his *Making of the English Working Class*[136].

What in practice liberalism has done at times when it has become the dominant political ideology, such as in 19th century Britain or as the ideology unleashed upon the world since the 1980s under the title of 'globalisation', is that it has produced increasingly inegalitarian, increasingly stratified, societies which are, indeed, an essential foundation for the struggle for wealth and status. Quite simply, marked differences in wealth and their expression as the lifestyles of the rich and powerful are essential as incentives in a system that promotes competitive individualism. At the same time, the ethos and practice of personal competition shuts down the critical faculties that might indicate that things are going wrong, as the notion of seeking status, even amongst those with modest means, magnifies self-concern at the expense of social consciousness and responsibility.

This attaches to political machinery that is well illustrated by taking a brief look at the process of industrialisation and urbanisation from the middle of the 19th century. As the cities, first in Britain and thence

116

particularly in Germany and the United States, grew, not only in size but in the industrial activities taking place in the cities, so with deteriorating sanitation and problems of mobility and thence the demand for increasing energy supply. The cities, therefore, became seriously dysfunctional with the urbanising poor living in increasingly squalid conditions. Pragmatically, steps began to be taken to address these problems, generally through municipal reform, the raising of public funds and the invention of relevant infrastructure technologies.

However, there was a constant attack on the part of private enterprise that in the extreme the Economist magazine (already peddling its Mandevillian/Smithian ideology) argued perversely that nothing should be done to ameliorate conditions if this meant raising taxes and if private profits could not be made out of it: let the people die of dysentery and cholera — the problem being, of course, that cholera did not respect class boundaries! In Britain[137], the actions that were taken to implement urban infrastructure systems became known eventually as 'municipal socialism,' denoting the synergies between the social movement and activities that improved the living and working conditions of the cities, not only for the rich.

But this is running ahead of the story. What is important to repeat here, however, is that the notion of Possessive Individualism is a peculiarly British (these days we say Anglo-Saxon) ideology that could not have occurred in societies beyond the fringes of northern Europe because the individual assumes already that they exist in a social context — at a minimum, the extended family. But the tragedy, as we shall see below, is the way in which the rest of the world has been coerced and seduced into accepting this ideology through the instrument of constantly increasing flows of commodities — meaning even for the poor, *relative* increase in wealth.

Fossil Energy Resources - Foundation of actual Progress in the Modern World

At this point we need to look at three intertwined aspects of the progress of Occidental culture that facilitated its expansion and so, as it were, make progress a self-fulfilling prophecy, rather than that it would have reached some kind of limits or collapse as was the usual passage of over-ambitious empires. These are: the exploitation of the resources of other cultures and territories, the development of technology and the discovery and exploitation of fossil energy resources.

The first of these is generally the conventional focus of how Occidental culture grew[138]. Some — though relatively little — attention has been focused on the role played by technological development[139]. Virtually no attention has, however, been paid to the crucial role played by the growth in exploitation of energy resources[140] which, as we are discovering here, has not only been the most important but also the fatal ingredient that allowed the process to expand far into territory from which, one day, it would have to retreat. In so far as there was concern in recent decades that this was an unsustainable path, the answer was seen increasingly as lying in the promise that technological development would substitute for the failure of non-renewable energy sources if and when the day were to come.

Looking first at the expansion of European culture, superficially we see a process of empire-building recognisable throughout Civilisation, at least as far back as Ancient Mesopotamia and Egypt. It is true to say that each previous empire, be this Egypt or Rome, China or Mongolia, Maya or Inca, had particular traits and developed different dimensions that cannot be directly compared with others. However, we can certainly say that these were all enabled and then limited by the efficiency with which they were organised and administered and the technological means and access to physical resources available to the empire. Some empires cared little for longevity and, having the organisational means and technological capacity to invade, lived in the short term on plunder. This was particularly the case in the process of the fall of Rome and the 'Dark Ages' of Western Europe up to the final Mongol invasions in the 13th century.

We can see clearly from the 16th century how commerce had become a primary and hence particularly pronounced feature of the European empire(s) relative to previous empires and those flourishing in the same period, and the way that this promoted increased production efficiency and hence technological development. The competition between European powers was also a feature that gave impetus to the expansion. We can contrast this with similar rivalries between empires in other parts of the world where, however, the commercial dimension was less dominant. For instance in Southeast Asia between the Khmers and Mons, pushed back by the Vietnamese and Thais, the latter eventually jousting with the Burmese. These were hardly, however, further 'advanced' in terms of organisation and technological capability than the Ancient Egyptians or the Incas. And, indeed, nor were the European nations prior to the growth of commercialism, the learning of technologies developed in China[141] and thence the exploitation of fossil energy sources.

The technology of large sailing vessels and gunpowder (both of which were developed earlier in China, albeit applied more efficiently in the Occident) clearly played an important role in European expansion. But these had reached their limit by the middle of the 18th century, with territory under their sway little more extensive, save for the Americas, and certainly no more affluent than other Eurasian empires, and contrasting with the phenomenon of India that throve with relatively restricted 'technology of Empire' on petty states sitting relatively lightly upon a dense matrix of local self-sustaining cultures. It was only with access to and exploitation of fossil energy sources that the process could move to a new stage of expansion. China, by contrast, once consolidated as the centre of East Asia (Zhong Guo) from the Han Dynasty, whilst sometimes expanding and at other times retracting its boundaries, exacting tribute from border states and sometimes splintering into multiple states and then becoming reunited, largely remained in place for millennia without the insatiable growth ambitions that were ever present over the past millennium in the European realm[142].

Surveying the substantial literature on the industrial revolution, which clearly provided the cumulative development of technology in Europe[143] there is very little reference to the way in which this was facilitated − we might say driven - by the increased harnessing of energy resources. Thus there was an absence of any sense of the abject dependence of the industrialisation process and the quest for modernity, that became Schumpeter's 'creative destruction' as the upward journey to we know not where. Somehow, the excitement and the sweeping of all hitherto existing cultures before it and the human drama which unfolded in this context, relegated into the deep background any focus on the energy resources that were driving the process forward.

The horrendous conquest, destruction and plunder of the pre-Columbian American cultures by the European powers was facilitated by a certain cultural incommensurability that destroyed almost instantly the inner coherence of the great Meso- and South American civilisations. This was greatly intensified by the lack of immunity of the peoples of that continent to the diseases brought by the Europeans that is thought today to have reduced the population by as much as 95 per cent within one and a half centuries of the arrival of the Europeans and enabled the latter to assert that this was an empty continent awaiting their coming to develop and exploit its resources[144]. This was not, however, yet the result of the increased power of Europe through physical resources.

However, from the mid-18th Century the whole story is driven by increasing harnessing and availability of fossil energy resources with almost no trace in the Occidental intellectual record of the centrality of this dimension and specifically on how the evolution of technology from the path-breaking 'invention' of the steam engine — initially to improve efficiency in coal mining — through the increased density and efficiency of all forms of mechanised movement and production and thence communication to the electronic revolution, could not have happened without this deepening dependence. The writing of history, having advanced in the 20th century from the notion of the development trajectory being driven by 'Great Men' to more socially and process-aware explanations, particularly under the influence of Marxism, still remained at the level of social forces, capitalism and at the edges, the role of technological prowess.

Fernand Braudel (focusing particularly on the Mediterranean region[145]) was, perhaps, the most prescient of the great historians to focus also on the geographical and environmental dimensions of the 'why' of European expansion, drawing on Enlightenment explorations of the way in which environment influenced cultural outlooks and attitudes (further discussed in Chapter Four below). British historiography might have noted the widespread availability of coal as facilitating the industrial revolution, and might have gone further to marvel at the sheer range of useful mineral resources below the soil of that country that were available for the (re)invention of steel[146] and other industrial metals and materials that all contributed. And the absence of this wealth of resources below the soils of France might be a contributory reason for the weakness of France's participation in the early stages of industrialisation. But this is not really the point. It is indeed hard, in the almost absolute absence of any focus on the issue of fossil fuel-dependence, to find a suitable language to draw out and provide an adequate picture of its central role to the development of European, then Occidental, and finally, global, culture.

Utopia: Alternatives to Abstract Progress

Could European culture have evolved in a different way? It was noted earlier that the Enlightenment produced essentially two different orientations: one, based on the British notion of Possessive Individualism and its connection with commercialism and the other envisaging, as imagined by the Marquise de Condorcet, writing in the final years and summarising the dominant French facet of Enlightenment thought, a progression towards 'the Perfectibility of

Man' that opened the door to notions of an ideal future by design. It should be stressed that Christian Millenarianism had encouraged from the Middle Ages a vast number of imaginings, inspirations and movements[147] that we might generally label utopian, of which Thomas More's (1516) version from which the term derives, was by no means the first, albeit it was the first modern attempt, stated as a 'rational' approach to socio-political organisation more or less free of the mystical and millenarian Christian versions that went before.

These included both imagined futures in literary form, theoretical and practical proposals for political and institutional change and experiments in living an ideal community life. In the course of the 19th century many of these sketched alternatives of greater or lesser coherence to the emergent dominance of bourgeois liberalism, including notably Godwin's and Proudhon's Anarchist visions, Saint Simonian technocracy, Owenite mechanisms of Cooperativism and socialism, Fourierist 'Phalanstères' and Kropotkin's decentralised Communitarianism. Marx, although rejecting utopianism on account of what he considered to be too puny a vision against the grandeur of the Enlightenment vision of Progress, nevertheless developed his own prophecy, together with his partner Frederick Engels, in full knowledge of these proposals and experiments.

Rather than see Marxism as a unique alternative to capitalism and the ideology of Possessive Individualism, it is helpful to see the 'alternative movements' as a whole as presenting what might have been a coherent alternative path, which may have something to say to us of great relevance for the reconstruction of viable societies following the fall of modernity. None of these alternatives criticised progressivism as such, generally seeing themselves as the *ne plus ultra* of progress. However, what they had in common was a vision of an end state to the development of the times that would de facto bring progress to a halt as being unnecessary.

In the case of Marx, this would come in the form of a post-revolutionary society that, by eliminating social struggle in egalitarian social arrangements, would allow for the society to determine how it should organise itself to satisfy the human needs of everyone through the *withering away of the State* and a social and economic process that would assure *from each according to his (sic) ability and to each according to his need.* This was classic post-millennialism in contrast to the pre-millennialism of the standard version of Progress as an open-ended process. And in general this is the paradigmatic framework in which all 'alternative' proposals for social and political organisation in the context of Occidental culture should be understood.

The 'mainstream' Utopians were more explicitly concerned with how they thought the ideal society should be organised, increasingly synonymous with the political ideology of anarchism. All were inclined – already key dimensions appearing in More's Utopia but increasingly explicitly – towards a classless, egalitarian society where women also had an equal status (not so obvious in the 19th century). Arrangements for education and the organisation of productive activity are to be found in their writings, generally focusing strongly on universal education and local productive activity and in most cases stressing the importance of art and the aesthetic. Most were predominantly social and political, economic and cultural visions, there being nowhere any particular concern for the 'conservation of nature'. There was still a presumption, shattered only in very recent times, that nature is there for our use, implying that a utopian society would have more rational consideration that would *de facto* maintain the health of the environment and ensure the sustainable use of resources. These alternatives are analysed further in the final two chapters.

Emergence of the Politics of Cooptation and Diversion

In the course of the 19th century, the alternative utopian paths, though sometimes applauded by mainstream intellectuals and even statesmen, were brushed aside by the rapacious and competitive process of industrial development and colonial expansion under an insistent assertion of bourgeois class prerogative. And then when the emergent 'working class' started to organise in terms of syndicalism and around the mechanisms of political organisation implicit in the vision of Marx, concerted reactions within the ruling elites arose to outflank, appease, and/or divert the movements. Cooptation was achieved by introducing (what became known as Bismarckian) welfare systems, whilst the trade union movement was steered into narrow channels of 'wages and conditions' instead of 'worker's control' (universal Cooperativism). Ultimately nationalism was invoked, diverting the movements into the horror of the First World War and thence challenged by the petty bourgeoisie in the context of fascist movements.

We can see the Commercial Ideology as having to a degree been eclipsed for almost a hundred years (1880 to 1980). However, the hopes for the triumph of Utopia were dashed, both in the failure of post-First World War attempts at revolution and, above all, in the authoritarianism that emerged in the Soviet Union, eliminating anarchist manifestations (Makhno's Ukraine, the Kronstadt uprising, the Tolstoy Commune, Kropotkin's return) as aggressively as bourgeois manifestations. With its alternative elite and with a vision no further than attempting to exceed capitalist progress, participation of the working class in realising Utopia ('all power to the Soviets') was lost in the struggle to equal in terms of production and consumption the achievements, particularly of the culture of the United States.

We see here the perverse way in which the aspiration of the Enlightenment to organise human life on a rational basis was systematically subverted. The Soviet case is the classic version of how elites have constantly asserted their prerogative to rule and in the process to take the best of the fruits of Development, in terms of status, for themselves. But more problematic is the way in which Anglo Saxon Possessive Individualism was promoted by elites in the United States as an 'anti-communist' ideology to convince the masses, who prima facie would have been the beneficiaries of Utopia, that they would be better off pursuing their own individual interests under the flag of 'Freedom'.

Of course it was relatively easy to build this orientation on the foundations of the notion that brought so many to America: that here, they could improve their status. The perverseness of the emotional rejection by much of the American mass of the benefits of social provision to satisfy basic needs, and indeed the love and care of their fellow humanity, can be seen to work only as a consequence of the insistent ideological propaganda driving on the notion that the meaning of life is to increase personal status through the accumulation of commodity wealth. This succeeded as a consequence of the escalating throughput of tangible commodities as 'possessions,' as both goods and more ephemeral symbols of status ('that's real cool, man!').

This is the true meaning and motor of the current stage of modern society — and the primary reason why the increased obviousness of the depredations on nature of this supply system have been systematically undervalued and the inevitability that someday the game would have to end, have been ignored. It is often said that Development is necessary before people can afford to worry too much about 'the environment'. The reality is, however, that the day will never come for this culture where Development needs have been fully satiated as long as consumption remains a race without end to gain status. In this way, Mandeville's ribald provocation has become a quasi-religious pursuit in the sense of throwing reason to the four winds and placing faith in a system that would yield status in the eyes of our fellow men (and, according to Calvin in the eyes of God) in the here and now.

The Coercion and Cooptation of Other Cultures

Turning now to the issue of other cultures in the maelstrom of European expansionism: it is only in very recent years that anything like a notion of an equality of cultures has achieved wider acknowledgement in the Occidental mind. There continues, nevertheless, the implicit tendency in the media, the public mind and unfortunately in the elites of other cultures themselves who have 'turned traitor' to consider themselves to be 'subordinate Occidentals' — to continue to see all other cultures as inferior to what today is called 'global culture' but which is, in reality, the ultimate extension of the logic and actuality of Occidental culture.

Traditional cultures, now shoehorned into the uniform category of 'nation-states', are relegated to a place in the global hierarchy of GDP as set out in the annual World Development Report produced by the World Bank. Occidental hegemony (that of Europe and progressively peoples of other continents, initially of European descent) can be described as nothing but messianic in its insistence that our version of how life should be lived is Right and Good. Faint voices, particularly those of anthropologists deemed to be expressions of romantic sentiment towards the dying past, could be heard to lament the passing of other cultures, but with few warnings that this could involve losses that might be regretted in the future[148].

Colonialism came together with the dissemination of religion — forcefully in Latin America, resulting in, at least superficially, the conversion of the remaining indigenous population as part of the total subordination of their cultures. But the rationale of European colonialism was predominantly commercial and carried out by turns as rapacious exploitation, sometimes in terms of more or less fair trade (at the negative extreme, forcing 'trade' in opium on the Chinese people to rectify trade imbalance) and occasionally to the benefit of local people — notably in the construction of irrigation systems in some Asian countries.

Besides what since the 17th century have been relatively minor attempts at direct religious conversion, that made little impact in Africa and even less in Asia, the conviction that European culture was superior, and indoctrinating local elites in European thought-patterns and lifestyles, was far more effective as a tool of ideological conversion and subordination. The French were particularly keen to demonstrate and disseminate the superiority of their culture in their colonial territories (and this continues in the 'Francophone' ex-colonies even today) and whilst the British were generally more instrumental in focusing on economic exploitation, in India, the crown of British colonialism, following the Rebellion of 1857 more effort was put into 'cultural conversion' amongst the elite classes[149] that continued seamlessly with the rise to world dominance of the culture of the United States.

It is impressive to see how, when from the late 19th century indigenous rebellions against European colonialism arose, few of these showed much interest in anything like a forthright reassertion of indigenous culture. The leaders in most cases had been educated in Europe and anti-colonialism was often inspired by European socialist movements and hence had Marxist tendencies, if not being directly Marxist. In so far as both 'capitalist' and 'communist' systems pursued the same developmental ends, there seemed no way out, no way to assert hitherto existing cultural norms and standards.

One might have expected China, as the most robust and into the 19th century the most self-confident and independent of 'other cultures' to have maintained a resistance to European culture. In the event, the first major rebellion against Occidental incursion to China, the T'ai P'ing, whilst extremely alien to modern culture, nevertheless adopted a form of Christianity. Mahatma Gandhi (who was no simple Indian traditionalist but well aware, particularly through years spent in South Africa, of Occidental ideological and political developments and was particularly influenced by the philosophy of Tolstoy) might have been tolerated but never stood a chance of turning the Indian elite away from 'Modernisation' and 'Development'.

However, the tragedy we have seen over the past few decades is the rapidity with which the 'Mandevillian disease', pushed through high-powered commercial indoctrination disseminated particularly through the modern media, has infected even the poorest groups in the global South to wish to participate in the ethos of the Consumer Society, in pursuit of material goods and appearances of increased status, however impoverished the lives of those living in 'urban slums' might seem, prima facie, to be[150].

The Specifics of Progress in the 20th Century

But this is again running well ahead of the story where it is necessary to scrutinise more closely the events of the 20th century and how these unfurled to yield the tragic — or perhaps more truthfully, ludicrous — situation we find ourselves in today. We have seen accumulating in the foregoing pages, the forces that defined the trajectory taken by modern civilisation across the 20th Century. Overarching, we see two kinds of

125

phenomena. On the one hand, the tensions that had built up during the 19th century with respect to the two visions of the Enlightenment hardened into two competing political systems, ostensibly pursuing different routes towards whatever Progress was supposed to yield: the post-millennial liberal path and the pre-millennial revolutionary path.

The second dimension is that of the development of technology. As has been discussed above, technological change was facilitated, even driven, by the availability and application of increasing quantities of energy. And this in turn interacted in the first instance with the processes of production, introducing mass production and thence changing the nature of social interaction, first in terms of the workplace and then through the impacts of technology on consumption patterns and lifestyles, precipitating what almost amounts to the dissolution of anything we might refer to in a coherent way as society[151]. It is only very recently, and by no means widely acknowledged, that the dialectical movement between social change and technological development has come into focus, chiefly through the insights of Bruno Latour[152].

Looking at the first of these phenomena, it is not necessary to do more than sketch the stages of its development and then highlight aspects of particular interest to our overall objective. We can see a general metamorphosis of Occidental societies as a consequence of an accelerating shift from farming and associated traditional rural culture to a new urban culture associated with industrialisation. Ideological structure was provided for the emerging working classes by proliferating ideas around socialism, communism, anarchism and syndicalism.

Out of this conjuncture there condensed new forms of organisation: powerful private industrial corporations and conglomerates, political parties organised to promote the interests of hitherto excluded lower classes and trade unions through which the working classes could exert their supposed interests. One of the ironies of this was the way in which 'liberal' political parties and elites considering themselves to live by liberal principles shifted from advocacy of free enterprise and free trade to advocacy of government support for welfare. 'Liberal' came simply to mean 'progressive' and progress was changing direction!

The hard-line repression of the nascent British working classes in the first half of the 19th century gave way to appeasement in the later years of the century. As other European societies industrialised, this became an important approach adopted by elites attempting to run ahead of the growing resolve of the lower classes to achieve 'social justice' by, in the extreme, resolving to eliminate class difference to create an anarchist world without leaders or class prerogative. Such a future would be consciously planned and organised to produce and distribute the fruits of Development to all. Thus working class opposition to liberal ideology grew between 1880 and the end of the First World War.

This resulted in truly radical changes in the complexion of politics and broader social outlooks and structure and with it lifestyles characterised above all by an accelerating process of urbanisation. Nevertheless, whilst the first half of the 20th century is seen as an era of fundamentally opposed ideological systems, in practice there was a distinct convergence towards modes of national organisation that had far more in common, relative to the pre-1880 and post-1980 situation, than they had differences and a common trajectory in 'civil life' involving the loosening of social ties and rigidities in structured social hierarchy.

On the other hand, an increasingly comprehensive, technocratic process of Government regulation, coordination and planning of economic and social life emerged, responding to various stimuli. Welfare measures, public housing, in general increasingly sophisticated infrastructure and thence tripartitism (implemented through the founding of the International Labour Organisation) were introduced to appease and co-opt the working classes and deflect the increasingly evident trajectory towards revolution. But this was also to the great benefit of corporate enterprises, gaining negotiating frameworks and also widening markets for their products as a result of the success of trade unions to negotiate higher wages that meant higher incomes with which to buy the fruits of burgeoning industries.

Whether in the communist or capitalist world, hierarchical production 'organisms' emerged, articulated in terms of the increasingly complex internal division of labour and the application of technology to increase output efficiency — 'Taylorist scientific management' and 'Fordist mass production' were embraced equally by capitalist corporations and by Lenin. The First World War pushed the warring governments to coordinate industries to develop technologies, produce war materials and transport these more efficiently. Even in the United States, where commercialism continued to play the leading role right up to the Wall Street Crash of 1929 and the Great Depression that followed this, as early as the turn of the century, the 'First Conservation Movement'[153] introduced regulation in the use of resources and expanded government budgets to build a coherent national infrastructure.

127

The Soviet Union was clearly the most extreme in almost eliminating 'private' initiative and with it the commercial mentality, planning the complete process of social and economic development. German National Socialism, generally thought of as the opposite of Soviet Communism, was in practice the pioneer amongst 'non-communist' Occidental cultures of high levels of social welfare and strict regulation of economic activity as well as high spending levels on infrastructure and technological development, eventually oriented towards the fighting of the Second World War.

The collapse of the US economy in 1929 was the final step in universalising relegation of commercialism and the fuelling of consumption to the interstices of the tightening bindings of the technocratic state, forthrightly planning in the communist sphere and with Keynesian macroeconomics displacing the ideology of commercialism in the capitalist sphere. It is important to see how this eclipsed the creed of classic economics, based as it is squarely on the Hobbesian dogma and the orientation, expressed in the quotation of Adam Smith cited earlier, that if individuals look to their personal interest, that the social interest will look after itself.

For this period, the conviction spread right across Occidental society that the social and economic process had to be consciously steered. Even at the extreme end, in the United States, New Deal policies, the subsequent organisation of the Second World War and thence a combination of encouragement and planning such as the organisation of national water resources and the construction of the 'interstate highway system' and facilitating the financing of suburbia through Veteran's Administration administered mortgages, amount to a predominance of state organisation in spite of the deep-seated individualism of that culture and the McCarthy witch hunts of communists.

The Global Spread of Modernisation and Development

It is important at this point to pause and contemplate a little the outlook and orientation of this period of Occidental history. European cultural expansionism came to a halt in the form it had taken through the 18th and 19th centuries, frozen at a particular level and with colonial administrations coordinating whatever activities — political, administrative and economic — that were already in position. International trade as a percentage of the world GDP declined. This was also the period in which independence movements were born in the South and, following the Second World War, succeeded in throwing off direct domination. However, the 'independent' states that emerged across Asia and Africa were ruled by elites — socialist or 'liberal' — thoroughly educated into Occidental culture and lifestyles, who governed their states within a global system in accordance with Occidental rules regarding the sovereignty of nation states and the structures of government.

'Development', 'Modernisation' and 'Economic Growth' had become the universal, unquestioned creed. The idea that leaders would come to the fore who would turn their back on 'Modernity' and defend or reconstruct traditional culture and society was unthinkable — and at the extreme, where the Chinese annexed Tibet, the issue was to help a deeply traditional society to modernise. Indeed, the Han Chinese have at various stages in over two thousand years of history made efforts to 'develop' the considerable numbers of minority nationalities within the territory they have claimed and over the past decades this attitude has become almost universal in the 'developing' countries[154]. Thus most of the 'independent' regimes turned actively against their own traditions and traditionalists, imposing their interpretation of Occidental culture upon their own people. Over most of the 'underdeveloped' and thence 'developing' world, this was also, in effect, the mission of the international development agencies.

However, other cultures were far from dead. Although a few had been virtually entirely eliminated, particularly in the Americas and Australia, and most had been more or less severely subverted, even after the Second World War the majority of the populations of the South still lived rural ways of life little changed from the days before the arrival of the Europeans and even amongst the elites, with much of inherited cultural and particularly social and religiously inherited attitudes continuing de facto to guide their everyday lives.

We might refer to this as the era of Developmentalism. Throughout the first half of the 20th century, industrialisation changed fundamentally the constitution of the pioneering Occidental cultures (or we should perhaps speak of sub-cultures) with the decanting of rural populations into urban areas and lifestyles. We are generally unaware of how a substantial proportion of the populations of even Germany and France were still living traditional rural lives until after the Second World War and this was even more the case in Eastern Europe with as much of 60% of the workforce still working in agriculture, albeit the collectivisation of farming once communist regimes were installed actively destroyed and severely disoriented the rural population leading, instead of the hoped-for increase in productivity, to serious failure of the agricultural production systems (not for the first or the last time).

In short, the presumption, orientation and action of national governments and with the establishment of the United Nations, World Bank and proliferating Development institutions and organisations , was that the world would one day follow in the footsteps of the Occident, industrialising and urbanising. One could imagine a situation where, had this notion been taken seriously, that major resources would have flowed from North to South to facilitate such development. In fact, as a percentage of global GNP, more capital flowed into South America from Europe and the United States in the 19th century to make more profits than in the third quarter of the 20th century in the context of a committed international Developmentalist ideology. However, the attention of the northern countries continued almost wholly to be on their own development, focusing particularly on provision of infrastructure upon which private investment could more readily expand business. Meanwhile, many national governments in the South did take seriously the Developmentalist ideology and invested in base industries in emulation of the Soviet model and/or with assistance of the World Bank or other development mechanisms. Very few were, however, able to make any significant progress in this respect.

Superficially a notion prevailed that Development is a 'good thing' and that it was therefore the right thing to do to promote it. There was certainly a good deal of idealism around both national policies and actions and particularly in the early years of the new international institutions, oriented towards some notion that whole populations would benefit from Development by achieving Occidental lifestyles. However, the ideology was also driven – we might say predominantly - in the capitalist North by a fear amongst elites that post Second World War, strong measures had to be taken to ward off revolution ('going communist') and that this could be best achieved by facilitating the provision of 'the good life' for all[155].

Provision of better housing became something of a totem, with the facilitation in the United States of the vast extension of 'suburbia' and in both eastern and western Europe the provision of housing directly from the State. This was accompanied by the notion of 'full employment', where workers could expect systematically rising wages. On the communist side, this was also seen as a competition, but one to prove the system was superior (actually 'at least as good as') and on that side to maintain credibility that the elite could deliver and hence remain in power.

Two Illusions of Development

Speaking of the 'classic' Developmentalist years up to the end of the 1970s, we must note two things of great importance that simply were overlooked as a consequence of the thrust and conviction and competitive urgency embodied in Developmentalism over this period. One is that not having an ultimate goal in view, the fact that 'things cannot not go on like this forever' in terms of the availability of resources — above all, energy — was simply not taken into consideration. Technocratic planning was generally fragmented into sectors and looking into the future for planning purposes basically meant extrapolation of the Development path already being trodden, without any consideration of how sensible or reasonable or sustainable this might be.

In the foregoing chapter it was noted that in the 1950s in the United States, concern did arise that the flow of raw materials might fail[156]. This, however, arose out of the competition with the Soviet Union and that sources of materials might become inaccessible, rather than this being a concern for outright exhaustion and, as pointed out in the previous chapter, by the mid-1960s, the notion that resources might become exhausted had been dismissed by theoretical economists. The idea that someday energy might decline in availability was not on the agenda. It is important in this context to see the fate of the *Limits to Growth* initiative[157], coming towards the end of this period, that attempted forcefully to question fundamentally the wisdom of the global Development path, raising a wide discussion that soon died down as a public and political debate, lost through its incommensurability with the Developmentalist ideology and the depth to which this had colonised the Occidental and increasingly the global imagination.

The second illusion refers to the assumption that Development was becoming a universal state of being, whereas even into the 1980s a substantial majority of the populations of the 'developing countries' were still living traditional, sustainable lives. There was a widely held, unreflected expectation that this population would eventually 'become developed' and that the only thing that kept them on the land was their poverty, when they would have preferred to 'develop' as in the North. The politics of the rural South, however, was in great measure one concerned with land redistribution, reflecting the tenacity of peasant society and community as the local existential consciousness. Whilst in China, following communist principles and Soviet precedent, farmers had been reorganised into collectives and cooperatives, swept up in revolutionary hope of great material improvements to their lives[158], throughout most of the global South the aspiration of peasants remained one of wanting no more than sufficient land to farm, to get landlords off their backs and to produce a small surplus that would enable them to buy a modicum of luxuries.

Whilst there were in practice many different situations — such as in South Africa, with farmers and their wives spending periods in mines or as urban household servants respectively, the return to the land to continue farming was widespread. In Latin America and much of Asia, both the peasant way of life and the aspiration to continue it, with marginal improvement and, particularly, sufficient land was the dominant aspiration, and not to 'become developed'. Developmentalism was the ideology only of urban elites, their entourages and the relatively small working classes that had made the transition to those limited urban industries that did develop.

The Neoliberal Counter-Revolution

1979-1980 saw the overthrow of Developmentalism and in a very real sense the final triumph of the Lockeian and Mandevillian interpretation of how the world should be organised and how life should be lived. This is generally seen as the Reagan-Thatcher Counter-Revolution where liberalism — as neoliberalism to distinguish it from the equivocal version of what in the United States had become the recent re-interpretation of liberalism — came back into its own with a vengeance[159]. The power behind this movement was the entry in force of commerce, now in the form of transnational and other powerful corporate interests, into the political arena to dictate the political agenda in accordance with their ideology. The ground was prepared across the 1970s, when lobbying groups and 'think tanks' proliferated in Washington to convince the politicians of the way they should reorient policies to make space for 'private interests' to realise profits by competing to serve 'markets' and ostensibly to bring new life into the Development process[160].

In practice, in the ensuing years, the indicators of economic growth slowed rather than accelerated and what development there was accrued overwhelmingly to the better off, the upper end of which became ludicrously wealthy whilst the ordinary citizen had relatively little to indicate, objectively, that the new arrangements were to their benefit. What mattered, however, was that the constant proliferation of commodities and means of consumption, even for those at the bottom end of the social spectrum, encouraged the impression that status was increasing even for them as a consequence of the systematic reduction in the cost of consumer goods and services.

Whilst intellectually there was objection to what was happening, both on the part of those focusing on social inequality and human rights and the emergent Green Movement, this did not translate into anything approaching a mass 'alternative' political movement and with the collapse of the communist system, Margaret Thatcher could declaim that 'there is no alternative'. Governments that even in the Developmentalist decades had seen provision of infrastructure to facilitate the activities of private economic interests, now shifted more concertedly into this mode, abandoning their role of 'forestalling the revolution' and hence of social provision and with the demise of the Soviet Union removing the threat of an 'actually existing' alternative model.

'Global Culture' and Traditional Residues

A truly massive transformation now took place at the level of non-Occidental cultures. One cannot underestimate the crucial role that the development and dissemination of the means of communication played in what transpired over the last quarter century. This refers both to the easing of movement and the penetration of telecommunications and, above all, television, as a forceful instrument for indoctrination, into the furthest corners of the world. The minds and lives of populations everywhere became bound ever tighter into a unified culture of consumption, of colonisation of desires and the means, if not to satisfy, nevertheless to strive to possess and to experience what the evolving machinery of modernity (now palpable progress) had to offer. Two closely related questions are of interest here.

The first concerns whether television inherently 'corrupts morals' or is a force for education into a more articulated understanding of the world, opening opportunities to realise personal talents. Whilst there is no clear conclusion, it is certain that it could be used as a means to education, particularly in its role as provider of in-depth information on what is happening in the world or, indeed, on providing effective understanding, for instance, of technology or nature. However, in practice television has become predominantly the instrument of those in ownership and control of the media around the world to deliver 'entertainment' that in reality spreads a common set of cultural precepts — not so much as a didactic but simply in what appears to be fed through programming and how this is absorbed by the viewers[161]. The medium became the message; whether moral or not, the international media seemed to succeed where Developmentalism had failed, to instil active adoption of the ideological structures of Occidental culture amongst even the most remote peoples.

The second, closely related question is: are we in consequence seeing the emergence of a single global culture? Are other cultures really being destroyed in the process of globalisation? The answer to this question is clearly complex in that there are certainly active resistances, most clearly in the insistence of elements in Islamic society to maintain what they see as key parameters of their culture. But more passively, rather than resistance, one has witnessed 'conversion' and adaptation almost everywhere outside the Occident only to a certain level, with pre-existing cultural attitudes and practices continuing at the level of the day-to-day amongst the 'ordinary people'.

The net result is, however, evident in 'people voting with their feet'. That is to say that decisions are taken at the level of the traditional village and farm to participate actively in the emergent 'global society' by adopting elements of urban lifestyles — visiting cities, perhaps, only to sell produce to gain an income to pay for the satisfactions of new wants or setting up a stall along an inter-city highway to benefit from sales to passing traffic, or moving to the city[162]. This would not be worth a mention in this text were it not for the fact that this is a mass-movement on a global scale to be found right across what is left of traditional societies. This is generally expressed in terms of rates of urbanisation which indicate the results of this 'flight from the land'.

Economists like to say that it is economic push and pull factors that are inducing this change. This entirely misses the point that 'rural poverty' is perfectly acceptable if the outlook is one where rural life and lifestyles are the mental and social universe of the rural population and lives of modest consumption are accepted as the norm. However, once this is undermined by aspirations to consume more of modern goods — even while remaining in the village — and rural populations become dissatisfied with what they have and are drawn emotionally to urban consumption patterns, then the inclination to migrate to the city, or even in search of work abroad, motivates people to move. In fact the new life may not be better economically, and where most rural-urban migrants end up in the precarious informal economy and with expenditure on housing, food and other things that came free or at little monetary expense in the village. However, they may still prefer the urban life because they have undergone a significant cultural transformation in their heads, in their social relations and in their lifestyle.

Governments — and the ruling elites that de facto orient what governments do and don't do — seem to indicate an awareness that where in the past the social peace in unfair societies was maintained through force and embedded culture and ideology, today the social peace is, it is imagined, maintained through seduction in what has become a treadmill that must be continued at all cost. Nationalism can be and still is used to great effect to secure allegiance, as in Margaret Thatcher's defence of the Falkland Islands and George Bush's Iraq war (and possible encouragement of '9/11') in each case securing long-term adherence of 'the electorate' to these particular politicians. And in many southern countries, nationalism is nurtured by ruling elites as an important contribution to securing allegiance. However, the main thrust of governments today is to use 'economic growth' to secure the social peace.

And in this context, the corporate take-over of global and national politics has been accompanied by and has accelerated the 'competition for markets': to sell your products to accumulate corporate and, within corporations, personal profit, ergo wealth. This is seen at its most ludicrous in the gyrations of the trade negotiations carried out in the context of the World Trade Organisation. Everything aims at selling more, regardless of any notion of need, whether aimed at over-consuming northern populations or undernourished and impoverished southern populations, at cornering markets. Here we see Occidental 'taxpayers' donating billions of dollars/Euros annually to farmers in 'subsidies' to utilize vast inputs of non-renewable agrochemicals and fuel in over-production of food and other agricultural produce (in Europe, farmers are even paid not to produce as a means of lowering surpluses), at the same time forcing free trade on southern polities that do not have the means to subsidise their own producers, in the process undermining the economies of millions of southern peasants, thrusting them into deeper poverty and encouraging them to cease farming and move into the deep dependence of urban informal economies.

So Where do we Stand Today?

Whilst contemplating the impossibility of continuing this paradigm of organising life and the world for much longer, it becomes clear at the same time that the present global political system is deeply disinclined to take effective steps to turn the Development process around to the extent needed to establish a 'sustainable path'. We can look back to the Developmentalist years and remember the notion of the 'planned economy' and the degree to which even in the United States, technocracy and the directing of financial resources was effective in carrying out massive developmental programmes. However, in reality even then, the actions taken were informed at root by the notion of appeasement and beyond that the pursuit of the 'allegiance of the electorate' and hence the inclination to heed reasonable arguments as to why the Development process should be redirected to head off the collapse envisaged in *The Limits to Growth,* showed itself to be extremely weak.

In the context of neoliberal ideology and the restructuring which this has effectuated since the beginning of the 1980s, the inclination is now entirely missing. We are all Mandevillians now, intent on pursuing our individual status in the global social market in the larger framework of Lockeian government, there to protect the sanctity of property, both physical and personal. Already in the 1970s, the nascent environmental movement pointed out the impossibility of the whole world achieving the US 'standard of living'. This has often focused on China, with a quarter of the world's population: the calculation was very simple as to the resources that would be necessary to satisfy such a demand and the answer was clear. Resource-exhaustion and environmental stress would stop the process long before it reached its goal. And yet, in the interim the US appetite for resources having grown vastly, the Chinese regime has been convinced through constant external pressure to assist its population to aspire to the US lifestyle. Surely this is the final, by now insane, phase of the messianic mission of the European Enlightenment, insisting that all other cultures should be like ours and pursue progress to a shining future — or to the bitter end.

On the surface of it, government today has become little more than part of the global entertainment machine. Its real achievement, however, has been the cooperation with corporate power to knit together the extraordinary Technostructure that has, step by step, substituted for what might otherwise have been socio-political structures with some sense of what to do as the process advanced into the impossible. The Technostructure[163] has, however, no intelligence nor, more importantly, any moral judgement that might bring sense into the system and turn it around, from the point of view of a reasonable future, into a benign path. And when the fuel runs out, the machine will simply fall apart, abandoning the passengers to their fate. Or worse, global warming advance to the point of no return and within a century perhaps, a miserable remnant of humanity will subsist in the last vestiges of what was the incredible beauty of nature that evolution created over billions of years...

Chapter 3: Socio-Political Life and Institutions

Whilst Chapter One showed clearly the way in which abuse and overuse of resources and damage to the earth's environment are driving our civilisation to collapse, Chapter Two showed how the fault lies not simply in matters physical but primarily in the ways in which our civilisation is organising the world and our lives and how this came about. Indeed, we can be sure that the fall of our civilisation will not just be a matter of living on less resources in the context of a damaged environment but that the legitimacy and workability of our present social and political systems will also run into a deep crisis demanding fundamental changes.

The main purpose of this chapter is to think through proactively what kinds of social and political organisation may be appropriate to overcome the problems we face, not just in terms of short-term measures but in terms of cutting through the problematic history of modern social and institutional development to penetrate through to systems that might be expected to work 'sustainably' into the future, under the conditions we are likely to find or be able to build, post-fall.

Such a project can be taken at various levels. Conventionally, in the context of modern academic approaches to the subject, the social and political are taken separately, with a further separation of other societies and the past into anthropology. Given the interpenetration today of the economic with the political (what is referred to earlier as the Commercial Ideology) the separation of economics from focus on the social and political is clearly inadequate. Finally, there is the issue of the mythologies, the social psychology and moral presumptions, and beyond this the existential understanding of what life is or should be all about that in practice underpin the particular way in which social and political systems are understood, legitimated and operationalised. These live, intellectually, a more furtive life on the edges of academic debate but must essentially be understood and faced up to in making any more than superficial proposals for change.

In this book the work is divided into three parts. This chapter will take a more technical look at the social and political systems from the responsibilities of the individual, the family, networks and communities through to governance in terms of levels and structures of government and their interplay with organisations of civil society. This means analysing how in the first instance human organisational systems evolved and thence how we came to the 'modern' organisation of society. Proposals and attempts at implementation of alternative systems or institutions in the broadest sense are analysed and 'tested' against a set of basic principles and against the resistances and problems which any proposed reconfiguration of these will have to face. The idea is not to make a definitive proposal but rather an orientation appropriate to the design and implementation of systems that we might expect to be appropriate to future conditions.

It should be emphasised that this is not intended as yet another Occidental attempt to impose systems upon non-Occidental cultures. We might in general hope - and can probably expect - the grip of Occidental dictatorship upon other cultures to loosen as modernity falls apart and local communities across the Occidental world become self-absorbed in attempting to find their own way, initially to survival and thence to build appropriate local social and political arrangements. This being the case, other cultures will again be free to find their own solutions as long as they, in turn, are not imposed on others. We can hardly expect any simple return to pre-modern conjunctures given the deep impact of Occidental culture and in general modernity into the furthest corners of the world. Everywhere there will have to be a reconsideration of what to do with this legacy in the new circumstances and how to build a new culture that will surely incorporate parts of this legacy but also reach back to re-evaluate what was lost and what has survived of traditional culture and what its worth might be in rebuilding an indigenous culture appropriate to conditions that emerge 'post-globalisation'. There will surely be many difficult passages.

In the following chapter we will look at how future societies may come to terms with the much modified environment in which they will find themselves and particularly how to organise life with radically diminished supplies of energy than we have in recent years become used to. The notion of sustainability will have to be thoroughly re-evaluated and taken into practical detail to ensure that whatever societies survive, there is no repeat of what Occidental society has wrought upon the earth and its ecosystems in recent centuries — what may well become known as the horror of modernity. The truth is that the notion of a moral system with respect to the interaction between society and nature has been entirely missing, with the Enlightenment attitude being one predominantly of exploitation (according to Francis Bacon's propaganda contrasting the moral questionability of political conquest set against the approval of the assertion of 'power and domination over nature'). This will have to change and the following chapter takes this as its thematic, reflecting not just on theory but more importantly on praxis.

It was noted above that in discussing socio-political systems, it is also necessary at least to be aware of the mythological, social-psychological and moral beliefs and orientations that underpin and are, indeed, the true life of these. The final chapter essentially re-evaluates philosophical and moral concepts in the light of the orientation provided in the two foregoing chapters. This looks critically at the concepts which guide the every-day understanding of those living the modern life and contrasts these with concepts and tools compatible with the orientation provided in the foregoing chapters aimed at erasing the notion of progress and substituting this with notions that can serve as foundations of 'Utopia': societies that provide an enjoyable existence in a sustainable relationship with their particular local environments.

Some Considerations concerning the Evolution of Socio-Political Systems

We might think that other, simpler, societies have nothing to teach us because their thinking and practices are too distant and, of course, because of the dogmatic presumption that Occidental culture is the culmination of social evolution and hence the best possible society. Anthropology over the past century has, in the main, comprised an endless documenting of disappearing 'simple' or primitive societies for little more than the accumulation of knowledge for its own sake.

As described in the foregoing chapter, during the 19th century there had been much conjecture concerning the 'stages of social evolution' that had led to this apparently superior state of culture. In Britain, being considered at least by its own elite as the pinnacle of progress, a wide range of social theory that included consideration of systems of law and government asserted that the path so far trodden had led to the best of all possible worlds and that things had to be this way, justifying this with the Darwinian theory of natural evolution of which social evolution was but an extension[164].

However, the advent of Marxism posited squarely the notion that 19th century 'bourgeois capitalism' was not necessarily the end of the process of cultural evolution and that society could organise itself on a different basis. This led to an initial conjecture of Marx himself followed by a re-evaluation of notable holistic attempts to find structure in social evolution – by the anthropologists Morgan and Tyler – to sketch an evolutionary process of socio-political development, that was able to demonstrate that other ways of organising society are possible because we can see that this has actually happened in the past and we can still see remnants in the present[165].

At the time, this was used by Marx and Engels to justify not only the possibility of other arrangements but that the arrangements they themselves outlined under the title of communism — above all the abolition of classes and the establishment of an egalitarian society without rank, privilege or prerogative and without economic stratification — were certainly feasible, if extant hitherto only in primitive form[166]. Although they themselves rejected the idea of presenting anything by way of a design of future society, there were many other 'radical' thinkers, also convinced that an alternative was possible, and who sketched essential dimensions – in some cases such as the Owenite communities, Fourier's 'Phalanstéres' and other 'utopian communities' in some detail – of how such alternatives might be implemented in practice.

Of course, these debates might have taken a closer look at more complex and sophisticated societies to 'prove' that other systems are possible and even to help to formulate relevant, sophisticated and complex alternatives to bourgeois capitalism. Of course the reason why this did not happen was that these were seen as being further back along the trajectory of social evolution and, as so forcefully asserted by the then British social evolutionism, by definition, inferior to modern Europe. So how come primitive societies could nevertheless be seen by Marx as the 'vanguard'? The clue to this rests in the almost aesthetic notion of the socialist, communist and utopian movements of the 19th century as harbingers of 'the end of civilisation' and its return to the beginning. This clearly gained its power from Christian Millenarianism and the early egalitarian Christian communities informed by the spirit of the Sermon on the Mount. No reference was made to this in the debates, but it is difficult to understand the messianism in the new movements — and particularly Marxism — without taking this interpretation of history into consideration. The justification rested on the conviction that the organisation of society had to be rethought and rebuilt from its very foundations.

There seems little doubt that the advent of Marx's writing, projected into the world through the emergence of Marxist political movements and the fact of the Soviet Union as a concrete manifestation of his thought, had a deep impact on academic work throughout the Occident. Any discussion of issues that might justify Marxism were censured and counter-arguments developed. This was particularly the case for sociology and anthropology[167]. The motivation of those opposing Marxism — and more generally the radical theorists and movements of the times — was to preserve, over and against the idea of the possibility of a society of equals, the assertion, justified by Darwin as being universal in Nature and going back to the Hobbesian dogma of the 'original state of nature', that humans are inherently egotistical, competitive and possessive and hence, by extension, that social hierarchy can never be extinguished.

For much of the 20th century in the capitalist world, social evolutionist debate and doctrine was, as a consequence of the threatening presence of the Marxist interpretation, successfully suppressed[168]. From the early 1960s, however, 'neo-Marxist' anthropology again picked up the theme of social evolution, now able to call upon a large volume of empirical material that had been accumulating over the earlier part of the century[169]. A rough sequence in the formation of more complex societies could now be discerned with greater clarity than had been the case with the 19th century anthropologists. This led to a conclusion that there have been various evolutionary paths in different parts of the world. One of the more important themes in the debate was the fact that it is quite clear, confirming in detail the findings of 19th century anthropology, that 'pre-civil' societies — the remnants of which were still to be found surviving into the 20th century — did not possess anything that can be deemed to be hierarchical differentiation within their social groups, or 'bands'.

It would thus seem that for the vast majority of the time that humans identical to ourselves have graced the earth, no such thing as social hierarchy, states or even governments existed. It became evident that it was the advent of Civilisation some eight thousand years ago that, in creating class difference and the incipient competition for status ('class struggle'), set the machine of Development in motion and with it the machinery of government that holds the social structure in place. The upshot of the debate was simply that whilst social hierarchy may be a ubiquitous manifestation in various forms of civilisation, it is in no way a 'natural' phenomenon[170]. Hence, the possibility of a non-hierarchical society without government in the conventional sense may be introduced into discourse on 'possible futures', the Hobbesian dogma concerning 'the state of nature' being relegated to a contingent and specious construct[171].

Subtexts of this literature included investigation, notably as presented by Marshall Sahlins in *Stone Age Economics*[172], into how the economy of 'early' societies did not necessarily - as Adam Smith would have it — involve an incipient tendency of humans to 'truck and barter' but that, certainly at the scale of small, early societies, a 'gift economy' where all within, and even between, communities shared in the proceeds of social production, 'according to need'[173]. Furthermore, primitive societies – at least those still in existence – far from existing on the edge of starvation, tended to live an easy life, spending on average only a few hours a day obtaining and making the necessities of life and otherwise living lives of leisure.

A further line of investigation concerned whether humans and human societies were 'naturally aggressive'[174]. The conclusion here was that there are widely differing levels and forms of expression of aggression between different societies and that enculturation in childhood is crucial to determining how this is expressed and how it is contained and channelled. Finally, there also blossomed a feminist anthropology, looking at whether 'male dominance' is universal in all societies or whether this, also, is enculturated[175]. This concluded that whilst male dominance is extremely widespread throughout the history of civilisation, the way and the degree to which it manifests itself is crucially a question of education and culturally embedded attitudes and practices and that it is not a state of humanity in some way imprinted, so to speak, in our genes.

What is, nevertheless, notable is that this literature remained isolated in academia, spreading to just a small circle of the intellectual and concerned public, and extending to small radical social initiatives. The wider media — and indeed the education systems — did not respond to these insights and it can be fairly said that the unconsidered ideology of the by-now global 'middle class' remains social-darwinian, that is to say subconsciously convinced that hierarchy and aggression are inevitable expressions of 'human nature'. This expresses itself particularly in the notion that 'competition is good' appearing in many milieux that include the precept of 'competitivity' in business and between cities and then in extremis the outpouring of popular films, computer games, etc. What amounts to a barrage of propaganda breeds an unthinking scepticism concerning any notion of organising society on the basis of mutualism, of sharing and without significant manifestations of power and aggression.

Background to the Analysis of Modern Systems of Government

Over the past four centuries, what was a wide proliferation of forms of social and political organisation and governance has been steadily brought into line with a single version of how the world should be organised, emanating from the messianic Occidental project. This can be characterised as generally falling in line with the Charter of the

142

United Nations, but today is deeply distorted by the impacts of what is referred to in the previous chapter as the Commercial Ideology, implemented through the assertion of power on the part of corporate empires and the structures they have helped to create and to facilitate this penetration[176].

The mechanisms used to bring the non-Occidental world into line with the one 'True' set of organising principles have been multifarious and we can but give examples.   At one extreme the British confrontation with 'the other' in North America and Australia was in a general sense to ignore, to sweep aside and at the extreme exterminate all cultures that might have stood in the way of their quest for exploitation, importing to the Americas and the Caribbean populations of slaves from Africa to carry out their work of 'developing' the resources. Although remnants of 'pre-civil' cultures survive even until today — and became, as noted, the source of prolific anthropological data — the most meagre consideration has been given to the possible significance of these cultures or their potential relevance to a viable future.

The Iberian invasion of what has become Latin America resulted in the destruction of all pre-existing political organisation, bar in a few remote regions.   Initially the 'conquistadores' simply plundered and abused local populations to facilitate this process[177].   The early formalisation of this exploitative approach was a system known as 'encomienda' that allocated rights in particular territories to favoured individuals to extract tribute and convert the native population to Christianity.   The creation of cities for administrative purposes followed and as time proceeded, the granting of land rights as 'latifundias', 'haciendas' 'estancias', 'fazendas', and so on, which could be used to extract resources in the form of mines, plantations or extracting payment as landlords from peasants. Notwithstanding large areas of territory beyond the extent of colonisation to which slaves and peasants escaped for a while before the frontiers of civilisation caught up with them, resulting in massacre or ejection or exploitation as labour or as tenants, little remained of 'other' means of social and political organisation and a deep reorientation was introduced through the conversion of the remaining population to Christianity. The resulting countries, comprising ex-Portuguese Brazil and the fragments of ex-Spanish colonisation that resulted from the early 19th century 'liberation' movements, are essentially run by the descendants of European colonists and are thus Occidental in the sense of ideological, social and political outlook, rules and practices.

Attempts by the Europeans to repeat in sub-Saharan Africa the performance played out in the Americas came late, with small incursions (nevertheless having major disturbing effects on interior cultures) starting already in the 16th century but the major onslaught coming only in the second half of the 19th century. Once again, there was no thought for the notion that indigenous forms of social and political organisation might have merit and hence Occidental rules and procedures were, and continue to be, everywhere imposed, albeit until very recently much of the African population continued to live in the framework of traditional values, lifestyles and even local political decision-making.

Only in Asia was a real challenge to the superiority of the European outlook and rules of governance perceived and whilst in the 19th century the attitude was overwhelmingly one that only the European had any real worth, nevertheless these cultures (Islamic, Hindu and Confucian, which were the focus of Weber's analysis discussed in the foregoing chapter) demanded to be taken seriously as alternative ways of organising civilisation and the cultural process.

Today we see the remnants of Islamic culture split between an adaptation of modern Islamic, or ex-Islamic, states to modernity, and insurrectionary activity ostensibly aimed at reviving Islamic culture, in particular via the imposition of Sharia law, social structuration (in particular the differentiated roles of men and women) and religious practice. By contrast, as this text was being written, a new wave of 'revolutions' was sweeping the Islamic world, with the international media overwhelmingly seeing this as progress towards modern culture and hence as something to be applauded. Whether, with any deeper reflection and in the light of what was starting to emerge by way of results, this might in any way be seen as an 'improvement' towards modern governance is highly questionable, if not clearly fallacious.

Looking back into the 19th century, attempts on the part of the British colonial administrators of India to 'make them like us' were successful only in indoctrinating a small elite into modern political praxis that gives us today 'the world's largest democracy', with more problematic manifestations in other South Asian countries. Whilst the impacts of modernity have been penetrating down into the society at an accelerating rate over the past few decades, much of South Asian life remains traditional for the majority of the population in terms of social relations and organisation, resting upon ancient religio-social foundations.

Finally, China, and other Far Eastern countries from Japan to Vietnam, where internal decisions and practice over the past century have been aimed at adapting to the aggressive onslaught of the Europeans (and then the United States) have attempted different routes (viz contrasting Japan and China), and are today in a situation almost entirely of possessing modern Government, with a residue of Confucian and religiously-supported attitudes and practices at the family level (albeit almost entirely erased in China during the communist era), extending in a few institutions to the community level. Sophisticated traditional modes of social and political organisation have been relegated to 'the dustbin of history'.

We should not let it go by without emphasising the continuous aggression that the Occident has exerted to erase other cultures, less obviously at the social level, although this has also been a constant theme, but above all at the political level and with economic exploitation never far from the rationale for change. Ostensibly this has been the spreading of what might be considered an internal problem of the Occident, 'capitalism versus communism', where the United States Government — sometimes drawing other Occidental and even non-Occidental governments to participate — has systematically encouraged and in most cases directly compelled all other polities to conform to their vision of what is Right and Good[178].

It is not a question that other forms of social and political organisation 'don't work' but that one formula, emanating from European Enlightenment sensibilities and theories, has been insistently forced on all other cultures, in recent years through a whole set of procedures, ultimately (and often) involving violence in a process of what William Blum appositely referred to as 'killing hope'[179], in so many situations where other peoples would have liked to run their own society on lines determined by themselves. We may consider the forms of governance that were precipitated in different cultural context to be in some way morally reprehensible but the fundamental question is: why should we believe it is our business to decide on behalf of others how they should resolve their problems? In the end, as we approach the fall of modernity, this messianic crusade in pursuit of Progress and Development, whether via US or Soviet aggression, appears, to say the least, deeply reprehensible.

A Brief History of Modern Government

So it becomes necessary to examine critically the system (or systems) that form the body of governance theory and practice as they have emerged in Occidental history and as they appear before us today. The first and foremost issue concerns the concept of 'sovereignty'. Whilst

145

the term emerges from the end of the Middle Ages, we can see states that exhibited the characteristics of sovereign states in Europe (indeed in other parts of the world historically) by the 16th century. But the modern notion of sovereignty, that now encompasses the whole globe in terms of almost 200 sovereign states, precipitated out of the settlement of the Thirty Years War in Central Europe — specifically, the various treaties that constituted the Peace of Westphalia.

Besides adjustments made between the relative power of the various warring states, the treaties succeeded in resolving two problems. Firstly, the hitherto accepted practice of the Catholic Church intervening in the decisions and activities of governments and communities across Europe without their consent, was to be eliminated. The second problem concerned governance of the Holy Roman Empire that stretched across much of Central Europe. This started at the outset of the Middle Ages as something of a unified empire, but was divided into sub-territories of varying different sizes ruled by dukes, princes and kings who had gradually asserted their partial independence and thus where the distribution of prerogative between the Emperor and these rulers was unclear, leading to increasing conflict.

The Peace of Westphalia ended thirty years of continuous war across Western Europe. From then on, the rule of territories (and sovereignty is at root a geographical concept) has been solely the right and responsibility of governments decided upon solely by the peoples of that territory or rather by their rulers, however these might have come by their power. Of course there have since then been countless wars where one state has invaded or otherwise intervened in another sovereign State and even come to dominate their affairs. However, it is a very deep-seated principle of modern governance that people within particular states should be free to — and responsible for — determining how they should run their political lives.

How territories are run thus becomes an internal matter; the nation within the territory may be an absolute Monarchy (a tyranny) or other form of dictatorship or a theocracy or an oligarchy or a constitutional, representative or participatory democracy or a communist government and the legitimate government may devolve selected sovereign powers to regions or localities within their territory. But this is entirely the affair of the people (the rulers) of that nation and it is basically illegitimate for other nations to interfere or intervene unless another nation is undertaking actions that violate their sovereignty. Needless to say, whilst this principle has, since the Peace of Westphalia, been the basis of political 'morality' in the Occident since that date, this was clearly disregarded in Europe's colonial ventures and countless more recent US interventions. Nevertheless, it is this principle that became the basis upon which European colonialism came to an end in the middle years of the 20th century with many, particularly African, states divided up arbitrarily at the whim of the ex-colonists with no respect for indigenous cultural boundaries, but nevertheless constituted as sovereign states.

Already, before the Peace of Westphalia, the mythologies and struggles that characterised European politics concerned where the centre of gravity of decision-making should lie. At the local level, changes took place with the dissolution of feudalism, where in some places the peasantry were truly their own masters but predominantly there remained hierarchies in unequal distribution of property, of work and of benefits both in the countryside and the towns. Governance, either as a stated prerogative or de facto, has in all modern states to some extent, and in many countries to an extreme degree, been concentrated in the hands of small minorities.

The major issue regarding governance in the Occident from the end of the Middle Ages was a more or less universal struggle to divest monarchs of their absolute powers and this is what the great revolutions, attempted to achieve. The deep resonance of the notions of Justice, Liberty and Freedom in the Occidental universe emanates and derives their meaning from this struggle. The answer was to institute laws, rooted in constitutions, and then create 'parliaments,' as structures where group decisions could be taken that would define the political life and direction of a nation. Most countries today have written constitutions that set out the rules and allocate rights and responsibilities to the people at large but also make space, usually by omission, for privileged groups who, in practice, are able to wield considerable power on their own behalf or, in practice, on behalf of their own constituency or class.

The principles of 'constitutionalism' go back at least as far as the formation of the state of Venice in the 7th century, which possessed the rudiments already of the modern idea of republican democracy in so far as the head of state — the Doge — was elected from amongst the elite (in reality a tiny proportion of the whole population). Of course the principles and practice of democracy go back to Ancient Greece — and indeed into the mists of unwritten pre-history — the Greek case being discussed further below. But the history of constitutionalism and written constitutions takes us via the English 'Magna Carta', being a rudimentary written constitution where the barons of the 11th century broke the absolutism of the King, who thenceforth was also subject to law, to the English 'Bill of Rights' of 1688 and thence to the American

Constitution and Bill of Rights. Today the latter is still a model in terms of format and focus both of large numbers of national constitutions around the world (Britain, ironically, being one of the few countries today without a written constitution!) and of the United Nations Charter and Universal Declaration of Human Rights.

At this point we must remind ourselves of the importance of John Locke's notion of property to the development of modern government. It was noted how decades where liberalism has predominated are also decades where poverty has increased. It was Adam Smith, rather than the more radical thinkers of the Enlightenment, who noted candidly (and we should bear in mind the centrality of the concept of 'property' in the post-Lockean world) that:

> *Civil Government, so far as it is instituted for the security of property, is in reality instituted for the defence of the rich against the poor, or of those who have some property against those who have none at all.*

It should thus be borne in mind how the structures and practices of Government over the past two centuries have in significant measure been designed to implement this principle.

The orientation of the Occidental struggle for the 'right' political system within nations takes us back to the English Revolution where the King was executed and a Republic (although in practice a dictatorship) was established, that lasted for eleven years. The eventual 'resolution' (in the 'Glorious Revolution' of 1688) that has become one of the model forms of modern government, was the establishment of a constitutional monarchy with the monarch now possessing only ceremonial powers with 'real power' allocated to two assemblies. One is an assembly voted by 'the people' through 'universal suffrage' whilst the other, in the British case, represents the aristocracy (today an amalgam of inherited rights and 'prominent men and women' appointed by parliament). This format, the majority of countries possessing only one assembly, is the basic structure of government for the majority of the world's nations today, with, in the majority of cases, the monarch substituted by an elected President and, where there are two assemblies, the 'lower house' being elected. In the case of Federal States, the second assembly can represent the interests of local governments at the level of provinces.

This brings us to describing the difference between 'unitary government', that has so far been the focus of this analysis, and forms of government where decision-making powers are devolved. 'Federal government' is generally operationalised through national constitutions that allocate powers and responsibilities to different levels of government, including 'provinces' and 'municipalities' and so can be said to devolve power to a degree and symmetrically reduce the scope of powers of the national government. Notable federations include the United States, Russia, Germany, Brazil and Nigeria.

The extreme case of federation (or confederation) is rare and best described via the case of Switzerland[180]. Generally dismissed as a 'small (insignificant) country' that is 'the exception that proves the rule', in practice this proves, through its existence for over seven hundred years, both the feasibility of an almost total devolution of political power amongst the people — seemingly the ultimate goal of the extreme radicals of all the 'Great Revolutions' — and at the same time gives the lie to the Hobbesian dogma by demonstrating that politics in the modern world *can* be successfully organised on the basis of consensus rather than competition, compromise and the centralisation of power.

The Swiss Confederation is made up of sovereign 'cantons' (provinces), some of which are towns and others rural areas. Discounting the two largest cantons of Zürich and Bern, the average population of the Cantons today is 222,000. Each canton has its own constitution ranging from 'centralised' Republics such as Geneva to confederations of local governments where the locus of power is further devolved to municipalities such as Graubünden (average municipal population 1,000). Where all cantons have some form of representative government, these are everywhere restricted in their powers. In their original form, the cantonal governments are elected by the democratic assembly of the complete male population of voting age gathered together in one place (Landsgemeinde). The number of cantons where this takes place has, however, been diminishing as a consequence of their unworkability as populations have grown and also with the doubling of the electorate following the inclusion of women.

However, a further mechanism that devolves power to the people is the referendum. Whilst these are not entirely unknown in many countries, they are generally used extremely sparingly. In Switzerland, however, the electorate participates in referenda over a great range of issues upon which they vote several times a year. Referenda might be proposed by political parties or by citizens on the basis of numbers of signatures of voters collected — a greater number of signatures is necessary as to whether a local, a cantonal or a national referendum is being called for. What this means in practice is simply that representative government at whatever level cannot expect to be able to take substantive decisions on anything considered by the people to be important without the agreement of the people and the people themselves can bring issues to referendum which, if the proposition is accepted, becomes the duty of government to implement.

The Swiss system never attempted to obviate the principle and fact of private property. We might say that in the 'Friedian' analysis of political systems in the direction of egalitarianism it minimises *rank* whilst paying less attention to economic *stratification*[181]. Furthermore, Switzerland has in recent years had a rather poor reputation for various reasons — the slowness with which women achieved the vote, a reputation for extreme parochialism (clearly connected to the intensity of participatory political traditions and processes), the secretive banking practices, particularly in their encouragement of illegal 'money laundering' and yet other evils. None of these detract, however, from the fact of long traditions of what today are seen as political best practice of subsidiarity, participation and empowerment. Furthermore, this has been associated in the past with a relative – and in some cantons extreme – egalitarianism. In principle, the original three rural cantons and subsequent joining rural cantons have been what amounts to peasant democracies whereas the towns have been run by oligarchies where some families have traditionally been in a position to exert more power than others through cultural practice rather than formal institutions. The critique of Switzerland seems like a case referred to in the gospel of St Matthew where Jesus asks:

Why do you look at the speck of sawdust in your brother's eye and pay no attention to the plank in your own eye? (Matthew 7:3).

Recently economic differences have been growing in Switzerland as elsewhere, in part by the 'importation' of a working class and the grasping, on the part of oligarchic Capitalists, of opportunities opened up by globalisation to create some of the world's largest manufacturing and banking corporations. So it seems that whilst we might think of radically devolved political power to be 'a good thing', this has not been sufficient, or consistent enough in itself to prevent the society from contributing through the activities of these corporations – disproportionately for the size of the country - forcefully to the excesses of the global resource and environmental problematic which we are facing.

However, it is evident that this system of government is fundamentally incompatible with waging war against other states. Perhaps ironically, Switzerland started life with a proven reputation of their male citizens being the best fighters in Europe, whereby their insurance against the poverty of farming the mountains was compensated by hiring themselves out as mercenaries to supplement their income. However, it was this fighting ability that enabled the young independent cantons to defend their independence from the Hapsburgs for four hundred years, where the latter repeatedly attempted to invade but were repeatedly defeated.

These mercenaries, whilst themselves at home 'free citizens', often defending monarchs and oligarchs of other countries, even fought one another in the pay of other country's armies until they saw the horror of this in the course of the 16th century European struggles and agreed they would never again fight on opposite sides. Napoleon, who invaded Switzerland, attempted to create a centralised Swiss state which, however, fell apart following his defeat. Historians have been puzzled as to why Switzerland, clearly capable of organising effective fighting forces, never went the way of all other European countries to build an empire (with one minor exception of Bern in the 17th century invading the Savoie). Clearly there is a direct connection between their decentralist and confederalist sensibilities and culture, their consensus politics and the lack of a propensity for expansionism.

It should be emphasised that the educated Swiss are well aware that their system of government is fundamentally different than that of other modern states and that consensus is something that is of great value and needs to be continually nurtured. In history there have been Swiss individuals who would have drawn the country into the power politics of Europe. However, deep traditions, giving a sense of the problematic nature of the centralisation of power, has in the past resulted in the establishment of political machinery that makes expansionism extremely difficult. This has not obviated small crises arising in this respect. The danger of these in modern times has been severe, with the projection by the international media of the normalcy of liberal democracy, the rise to power behind the scenes of powerful private enterprises and the irresponsibility amongst growing numbers of citizens to whom the consumer mentality encourages lack of participation in political life.

A further difficulty is the way in which parochial xenophobia can, and has, both at the cantonal and national level, resulted in tensions which have in the past created exclusionary policies - at the extreme, with the treatment of the Roma during the Second World War. Whilst this has never resulted in mass violence, the issue of social inclusion becomes particularly salient in such decentralised politics and requires further discussion as a generic issue in the final chapter.

In New England in the United States, 'Town Meetings' that have a different form of organisation from one state and even one town to another, comprise the original forum of political decision-making, where in principle the whole eligible voting population gather together. These have survived into the present day in a few towns and a few states to the west have adopted this institution. Whilst 'home rule' is built into the American political culture as a relative independence of local government within the federal framework, in practice state and particularly national governments retain all major powers. Furthermore, the emergent gigantism of American cities, precluding face-to-face decision-making and added to this the power of commerce, have meant that the scope of decisions that can be taken at a Town Meeting in those towns where this is still practised have dwindled to little more than symbolic gestures of democracy, further underscored by the fact that the majority of local government funding is handed down from above, most of it with strings attached.

As one describes the apparent spreading consensus on how nations should be and apparently are governed, awareness grows that what are essentially political decisions are increasingly being taken outside and far removed from this machinery. It becomes necessary to discuss in more detail below exactly how and on behalf of whom decisions are taken by these government apparatuses. But it is necessary to be aware of the way in which the complexity of government has continually grown over the past century to the point where bureaucracies - Ministries, Departments and other Government and quasi-Government institutions - essentially pre-empt decisions through the logic of what they are mandated to do and, as a consequence of one thing leading to another, has led to the growth of what is referred to in previous chapters as the Technostructure, where the logic of the machinery overwhelmingly dictates how resources should be allocated.

Secondly, further removing decisions from governments, exacerbated by what particularly in recent years has become the enormous political influence of business interests, the Commercial Ideology — the principle of sleaze — has essentially imposed its logic and its machinery upon the political decision-making process, justified as liberalism (or neoliberalism), leading to a decision-making process largely independent of anything approaching the real political interests of 'the people' whom governments are ostensibly there to serve.

This has constituted a major assault on the principle of sovereignty, through the decanting of political decisions into the realms of a growing global economic system and the corporate control of this, reinforced by the activities of the international financial Institutions. This proceeds through the machinery of 'Structural Adjustment' and the 'supervisory' functions of the International Monetary Fund, followed up by the powers of the World Trade Organisation, which is mandated to apply sanctions to nations that violate its rules (thus allowing intervention in the governance of countries where the United Nations organisations lack legal powers to do so in deference to the principle of sovereignty).

In practice, outside the confines of Occidental cultural evolution, through colonialism and thence incorporation into the 'global system' and its ideology of sleaze, and in many cases via direct military and political intervention of the United States Government[182], all other cultures have been distorted and infected in ways that have undermined, damaged and even destroyed existing social values and organisational mechanisms without actually substituting any very structured versions of the assumed 'best system' of Liberal democracy. Whilst there is an assumption that eventually all will be like us, political and media pressure (most obviously through the influence of television and the cinema) is constantly applied to bring this about.

The results, however, have produced 'corruptions' of the assumed 'correct' principles and across much of the global South, a collapse into megacities of slums with small but growing 'middle classes' who emulate their peers in the Occident, as tutored by the media, in terms of lifestyle and eventually political systems that support this — viz, most recently, the 'Arab Spring'. This is underpinned by extremely meagre understanding of the principles upon which Occidental socio-political structures have been built and hence with catastrophic misunderstandings and dysfunctional reactions. This has landed huge populations in a kind of ideological void, reflected in lifestyles that attempt to emulate the Occident but with very little by way of access to the Stuff that is the essential reward of this system and with the disposal end, as garbage, spread about neighbourhoods as a kind of negative proof of arrival.

There has, of course, been a major alternative to the liberal democratic form of government that for much of the 20th century ran in parallel to the so-called 'Communist Government'. Whilst the commitment to the ideals and ideas of Karl Marx obtained a vast following approaching a religious character, the actual copious writings of Marx and his associate Frederick Engels had all too little to say about how political decisions might be reached following the revolution. Whilst Lenin claimed to be the true interpreter of Marx, casting extreme invective at those ('revisionists') who would make other interpretations and look for practical ways to manage communism, he decided, as set out on the eve of the Russian

153

Revolution in *The State and Revolution*[183], that the 'Dictatorship of the Proletariat' (a concept coined in the early years of Marxist communism) should be undertaken by a centralised state apparatus overseen by a 'Communist Party'.

In practice, the Party Leader — and, indeed, 'the cult of the leader' tantamount to personal dictatorship — maintained major powers throughout what became the 'actually existing socialist countries' over who should be members of the Party. How they voted for the Central Committee and in turn for the Politburo, and how in general decisions were reached, remained in the main closed to outside scrutiny and with no hint at any level of participation of people outside the Party in any significant decision with regard to the use and distribution of resources. Indeed, the state proactively dissuaded the public with extreme sanctions from questioning any decisions taken by the Government.

It is important to emphasise that Marx's vision and programme was fundamentally aimed against Lockean governance, with its extreme emphasis on safeguarding property. Marx's early philosophy circulates around the notion of 'Alienation' derived from Hegel but in fact closely attaching to the English language usage of the term in property law applying to land and buildings. Communism – and many other radical doctrines - asserted, as a broad consensus arrived at as the 19th century wore on, that property should be held in common: the era of the commercial ruling classes and their obsession with property and 'commodities' would be over. But how should we define 'in common' and how should this be administered?

The high level of Marx's rhetoric gave no clues apart from the notion of 'collective' ownership. Thus, upon inheriting the reins of power, it became necessary for the Soviet Communist Party to invent it and whilst one might be impressed at how the state planning machinery and the implementation of development through various Ministries came rapidly into being, the omission of 'Worker's Soviets' or any meaningful democracy in planning or in the workplace, meant that a technocratic process with power vested essentially in a new kind of ruling class was implemented.

The practice of centralised decision-making resulted in a situation where the 'abolition of property' had no meaning for the ordinary people who, on the contrary, perceived that they had been robbed of any real sense of ownership or control over the land, the built environment and the means of production with which they lived and worked. Transformation of the pre-revolutionary peasant communes (*obshchina*) into cooperative farms (*kolkhoz*) initially had aspects of self-management but had to fulfil plan quotas and from the 1930s the

154

increasingly brutal 'collectivisation' almost totally eliminated any sense of ownership, with the system eventually being a forthright system of coercion, of wage and forced labour, and thus difficult to distinguish from slavery, albeit with 'owners' being replaced by 'carders'.

Thus, as has been increasingly the case in capitalist and social democratic countries, ministries and government departments took, step by step, what amounted to political decisions regarding the allocation of resources out of the logic of their remit, albeit set out in the framework of national plans, the content of much of which was in practice the result of competing demands of the ministries (and also the military) rather than any meaningful analysis of what 'the people' might want or need and certainly excluding absolutely any consultation of the workers, or 'the common people', in this matter.

Of course, although the Commercial Ideology and the principle of sleaze had no place in communist praxis, it might well be contended that the end of the communist system of government came about through pressure of the people themselves, influenced by the ideology of sleaze emanating from the liberal West and wishing to participate in the resulting Consumer Society, lacking any conviction that the communist bureaucracy was capable of delivering the ineffable joys of modern commodity consumption, which eventually even communist governments came to accept as the goal of communism. Of course, this was aided by elements of the elite who could see that by going over to a capitalist system, and specifically in the way that this was undertaken in practice, they could greatly enhance their own personal wealth and lifestyle.

To all intents and purposes, although certain aspects of communist rule remain in practice in parts of Asia (particularly the important role of the Communist Party) and particularly in terms of opening the doors to the Commercial Ideology and the machinery through which it operates, these countries have capitulated to the general context within which political power is exercised today and there are few who believe that dictatorship (of the proletariat or any other kind) is an attractive or effective form of government (albeit in actuality, and lacking any substantial intellectual critique, it is still common amongst Arab and sub-Saharan African countries).

Alternative Proposals for the Organisation of Society and Politics

Modern government emerged initially out of particular ideological proclivities and the way in which it suited the changing form of elites of Occidental countries and the compromises that emerged from social struggle. As we have seen, there are significant differences in the actual way in which it functions in terms of interpretation and execution of 'democracy'. Over the past two centuries since the general model came to be widely accepted as 'the best system', further modifications have taken place incrementally, largely as a function of the growing size of populations, the process of urbanisation and industrialisation and, particularly over the past three decades, the growing dominance of corporate intervention in what are, de facto, political decisions. As sketched in the first chapter, what we can expect over the coming decades is a falling apart of the global integuments of this system and hence a fragmentation of governance and of governments. In the first instance, one might expect a reversion to a more consistent state sovereignty, but in all likelihood, in time, states will no longer remain coherent in many if not most cases, so that localities or communities will have to learn to a far greater extent than they have been used to, how to govern themselves.

Fundamental changes in the nature of social and economic organisation and thence in governance took place throughout Europe following the collapse of feudalism as a consequence of the Great Plague of the 14th century, ushering in what we refer to as the capitalist era[184]. Probably more analogous to what we see ahead is the collapse of the Western Roman Empire and the devolution in this context to relatively autonomous village and small town life[185]. Certainly, as analysed in the forgoing chapter, these turning points changed fundamentally the organisation and orientation of Occidental society and we can expect such a radical break, on a much grander scale, to be taking place over the coming decades. What we are therefore looking for is potential models and mechanisms for constituting political life on a basis appropriate for the situation which the world will find itself in later this century.

Whilst the following paragraphs look primarily at potential machinery, the assumption is that it is well-nigh useless to make abstract or radical proposals without reference to the process of transformation. This means starting from current understanding and experience of political and social organisation and building out from there using models that are in some way already in the back of the cultural consciousness as proposals made in the past and battles that were lost in the process of arriving where we are today — in other words, reviving past debates and deciding to go along routes previously blocked or abandoned.

As discussed at the outset of this chapter, government in pre-literate societies evolved and the first complex societies developed forms of government seemingly spontaneously and — there being no record of this — without 'rational' debate about what alternatives might be the most appropriate. Above all, there was initially no meaningful dividing line between systems of belief and governance such as hierarchy and headship (the Mandate of Heaven, the Divine Right of Kings, etc.). The organisation of local institutions (e.g. to administer the distribution of water in complex irrigation systems) and the structures and roles of the family and their members were taken as given and sanctioned eternally through sacred laws and the mists of revered tradition.

This mystical or 'ideological over-determination' of political systems is never entirely absent and today we might say this is a strong dimension of what government today ostensibly is, with its rituals of voting and parliamentary debates blinding us to the real ways in which public decisions are arrived at, but at the same time assigning definite powers to particular individuals occupying particular offices. We see for the first time in history in what is known of the writing of Confucius, an avowed absence of mystical ingredients. This came in the form of a very practical notion of how, functionally, and for effectively rational, moral and socio-psychological reasons why society and political organisation should be based on the principles he set forth.

In Occidental thought and praxis we look to Ancient Greece for the emergence of rational debate on what political machinery might be optimal. Plato's *Republic* gives us a discussion of what he saw as four alternatives for the organisation of political systems and a fifth which was his own proposition[186]. What is interesting in view of the evolution of Government after the European Dark Ages is that Plato already dismissed the notion of the Divine Right of rulers and, indeed, any significant mystical or spiritual dimension to the organisation of social and political life. Whilst his five systems are not in any detail relevant to what started to evolve in Europe some fifteen hundred years after his death, a few remarks on his ideas are relevant, particularly because his work (and that of other Greek thinkers) was an important foundation of the debates on politics — and also the utopian propositions and movements that emerged following the collapse of feudalism.

Plato envisaged an evolutionary path starting from the Spartan system of government, where a military elite ruled over a slave mass, through the emergence of oligarchy where slaves were, to an extent, emancipated and thence to democracy and finally, because of the failings of this system, the collapse into tyranny (as indeed happened a little further along European history in the case of Ancient Rome). Whilst we might see this as somewhat fanciful qua an evolutionary sequence, what is particularly interesting is what he saw as the failings

157

of democracy. On the one hand, Plato's Athens was a small enough Community for something like a genuine democracy to exist — that is the whole eligible (in the Athenian case male, non-slave) population gathered together as possessing the sovereign right of political decision-making through simple majority vote, where all could participate in discussion and the formulation of law.

On the other hand, Plato saw that, through suasion, rhetoricians and de facto leaders could all too easily convince 'ordinary people' to take decisions that were against their own real interests, and that the 'tyranny of the majority' could discriminate against the interests of minorities and in the end that the people gained the impression and acted as if the freedom of the democratic state gave them licence to act as they pleased, regardless of the broader, considered social interest. Plato's solution was that a class of philosopher-warriors (the Ancient Greek states were constantly at war with one another, hence 'warriors') should be selected, living an ascetic life apart from the population at large and educated to rule on behalf of the people. Notwithstanding Plato's miserable failure to initiate such a scheme in Sicily, we should perhaps question his elitism and assumption that 'ordinary people' (perhaps when women are included?) cannot be enculturated into an adequate sense of responsibility for their own long-term welfare and wellbeing.

'Rational' analysis of possible improvements in governance in Europe started as Feudalism retreated, first in Utopian writing more imagined than practical. Nevertheless, Thomas More's *Utopia*[187] as the first major volley in what subsequently became a copious Utopian literature taking its generic title from More's book, already highlights key issues that became – and still are – serious contributions to possible reconstructions of social and political life post-fall. Major themes in *Utopia* that are considered in greater detail with respect to potential future practicality are an insistence on a relatively frugal and egalitarian life with no significant hierarchy – albeit *Utopia* did have its King and also slaves (slavery in Utopia, however, was for a fixed period, as punishment instead of prison). Property in Utopia, but for a few modest belongings, was held and management in common. This notion clearly flew in the face of the subsequent insistence of the Enlightenment on the importance of private property.

The theories of Hobbes and Locke were discussed briefly in the foregoing chapter and their writings (particularly Locke's *Two Treatises of Government*[188]) can be seen as major foundations for the subsequent practical debates of the late 18th century that largely gave us the Government systems we have today. The great emphasis on the importance given by Locke to private property, together with the presumption that there is an inevitable distinction between the uneducated and unpropertied mass and the elites, meant that the interests and opinions of the former were absent from the ensuing debates.

In the context of the rich outpouring of the French Enlightenment (that in general was elitist in its proclivities) it was particularly Montesquieu and Rousseau who strengthened the foundations of what became the basic notion of republican governance that emerged subsequently as the model we see around the world today. Whilst Montesquieu clarified the division of powers between legislature and judiciary, Rousseau, in his *The Social Contract*[189], revisited the Lockeian notion of the role of government in relation to civil society as a relationship between the individual and the collective, influencing the reconstitution of government following the French Revolution.

As a proud citizen of Geneva, however (albeit there was a mutual falling out later in his life) Rousseau expressed an admiration for the democratic traditions and relatively simple life of Switzerland. His early essay in answer to the question *Has the restoration of the sciences and arts tended to purify morals?* denigrated the over-sophistication of the society of his age and his subsequent *Discourse on the Origin and Foundations of Inequality among Men* is a profound critique of hierarchical society[190]. His incorrigible utopian sensibilities — the search for a *monde idéal* — poured out in copious subsequent writings which opened the door to the more radical notions of governance, and particularly his anti-elitism that emerged during and following the French Revolution.

It is, however, the debates, particularly as documented in early issues of a set of papers under the title of *The Federalist*[191], around how the emergent United States should be governed that are of vital importance to us today to understand the origins of the divergence between the kind of government that started the modern world down the road that has led to modern national and global government structures, and the possibility of true democratic government as the more radical response to the Enlightenment discourse on governance. Here, the issue of scale is key. There is an essential distinction made in *The Federalist* papers between a democracy where decisions are taken face to face and which therefore restricts political entities to a size that allows for this to actually happen (both Aristotle and Plato wrote on this issue) and Republicanism where the people are represented in the political decision-making process by elected representatives. Very few people are unaware today of the essential novelty at the time of representative republicanism as set out in these papers, as a means of governing large populations and territories and that today is misnamed democracy (or oxymoronically representative democracy).

The authors of *The Federalist* were arguing for a political entity that would be a union of the states — and therefore necessarily a Republic as opposed to a confederation of Democracies — against those who had other opinions. These included voices arguing for sovereignty to be vested in groups of states, yet other strong voices arguing for each state to be independently sovereign and yet others (who were dismissed summarily) who argued for a truly democratic country comprised of very small units (which might then have confederated but on their own terms). As we know, the federalists, clearly relishing the potential power that an eventual mighty United States would give to this new elite, won the day. However, as noted above, New England states maintained the Town Meeting as a genuine democratic forum in the space left for local governance in the Constitution as ratified. It is interesting to note that one of the authors of *The Federalist* papers, Alexander Hamilton, when, many years later, he became President of the United States, was the father of American industrialisation, diverging from the strongly argued views of former President Thomas Jefferson who had envisaged the United States as remaining a rural idyll — albeit worked by slaves[192].

It was in the cauldron of the French Revolution and the subsequent proliferation of radical political discourse and movements that the notions of egalitarian societies, with worker's self-management of the economy and abolition of property with communal ownership and management, and in general the concept of mutualism, came back into their own. The concepts of socialism, communism and anarchism (and yet other 'tendencies') all originated in the early decades of the 19th century.

To a certain extent, these terms were used interchangeably with advocates sometimes collaborating and sometimes in conflict as their proposals and movements evolved. Eventually socialism came to be understood as a stage on the road to communism. And it was in this context that the word 'communism', not originally associated with Marxism, came nevertheless to be the term attaching itself to Marx's ideas. The term 'anarchism' came to denote the ultimate 'end state' to which all these ideas ostensibly strove (in Marx's terminology, the eventual 'withering away of the state') and anarchists are thus those who advocate direct, unmediated implementation of anarchist polity and society as direct democracy.

Already in the foregoing chapter, reference was made to the way in which, despite the strongly expressed notion within Marx's writing that the revolution would abolish property and social class and hence be de facto egalitarian, this remained at the level of philosophy and rhetoric. When it came to discussion with the anarchists regarding how this might be brought about, however, Marx asserted the need in the first instance for 'dictatorship of the proletariat' (again not a term invented by him but one endorsed by him). Whilst the only reference to how this might function was Marx's endorsement of the democratically elected Paris Commune, no further practical proposals as to how this would be organised or how, in time, dictatorship and the state might wither away.

The first international organisation bringing all these tendencies together in the mid-1860s, under the title of the International Working Men's Association (subsequently known as the First International), collapsed in the 1870s in the dispute in which the anarchists (Bakunin) accused the communists of authoritarianism that, it was argued, could only lead to the formation of and perpetuation of new elites. With hindsight we can see how 'communism' or 'actually existing socialism' became in practice 'authoritarian modernisation,' where the elite justified its existence by asserting that only they could bring Russia into the realm of modernity, as it was emerging in Western Europe and latterly in the United States.

The fate of Marxism in practice is well-enough known and was outlined in the foregoing chapter. Concerning the anarchists, who were a strong dimension of the radical discussions and movements of the 19th century[193], it should be noted that there was a rich debate and attempts to organise anarchist initiatives, with divergent views that were more or less resolved in the practical proposals of Piotr Kropotkin, set out in a series of writings around the turn of the 20th century[194]. Kropotkin started his anarchist career in the context of an anarchist movement that, like Marxism, insisted that the change in the constitution of society could only come about through revolution.

But unlike Marxism, practical mechanisms were put forward to create an egalitarian, property-less society in which the State no longer had a role. Inevitably this means decentralising decision-making to a level where everyone can participate in meaningful 'ownership' of land and other resources, including the means of production and participate meaningfully and directly in all significant political decisions. Anarchist organisation starts from something like the Swiss polity as it appears in the smaller Cantons and the fact is that at the height of anarchist movements at the turn of the 20th century, Switzerland was host – not always willingly - to many initiatives involving the various

161

radical tendencies, and specifically to anarchists exiled from other European countries.

Essentially, political theory that developed from the Enlightenment abstracted out decision-making mechanisms from the content of decisions, where these are fundamentally about the distribution of resources. That is to say that representative democracy, simply by creating distance between 'the electorate' and their 'representatives' allows the latter wide scope to hand resources, or the freedom to use resources already in their hands, out to entities — privileged individuals, corporations, bureaucracies etc. — that are far removed, physically and institutionally from the electorate that is, therefore, not in a position to see what is happening let alone to participate in decisions concerning their use.

There is then a synergy between this decision-making process and the growth of the Technostructure: essentially the size and complexity of entities and systems, whilst enhancing the wealth and power of few individuals within the system (owners of capital, corporate directors, technocrats) facilitates the slipping out of the comprehension and control of all but a small elite that itself is incoherent as a class. The failure of Central Planning, as the essence of communist management and distribution of resources, was not simply through the dissatisfaction of the people in not receiving the goods available to consumers in the capitalist world, but rather directly from the failure of the planners to be able to plan on the scale and complexity necessary to produce the same output. The Technostructure took on a life of its own, so that Central Planning became a constraint rather than facilitating its further development.

It is in the first instance difficult for us today to imagine economic activity being on a scale that would allow for a significant degree of decision-making to take place at anything like a local level. However, the Technostructure of today which globalises production and distribution is far more recent than we imagine — even up to the eve of the Second World War, the bulk of locally consumed products (food and building materials, furniture and household goods) in terms of weight if not value (diamonds, electrical goods, etc, being expensive such as to skew the scale) were produced relatively locally even in such 'modern' countries as France and Germany. Britain and the United States were already exceptions to this, going back into the 19th century.

Kropotkin was of the view, growing out of detailed study and analysis, that in the long run local economies would grow at the expense of large scale, distant production and that large-scale production was therefore a temporary phenomenon. As this went into decline, he imagined the door would be opened to the possibility of local populations taking over and managing local resources communally to produce most necessities and indeed satisfy needs well beyond minimal requirements. The problem lay in the skewed ownership of property and the answer was that those people who gained their living from these local resources and means of production should also be responsible for administering them and be the sole beneficiaries, with work carried out according to ability and consumption satisfied according to need without recourse to any system of wages and income and hence no generalised 'surplus' that could be creamed off and spent by an elite as and where it pleased.

We can think of this in terms of local 'cooperative commonwealths' (of which the town of Mondragon in Spain has in recent times gone some way to demonstrate its viability) where workers and consumers are all members, contributing their work and receiving the benefits directly. Communities thus take decisions mutually and confederate to share resources that may be lacking or in over-abundance with neighbouring or more distant communities. Where decisions need to be taken over wider areas, such as the organisation of regional transport systems, these would still require delegation to working groups, the decisions of which would, however, have to be endorsed by whole communities that share an interest in the decisions, i.e. through referendum as is current practice in Switzerland.

At this point one can hear the incredulity of readers, having some idea of the gigantism of productive systems and the global reach of 'the system', rendering such an idea as unrealistic in the extreme. Nevertheless, Kropotkin's ideas of how the world should be organised have been echoed by anarchists throughout the 20th century with many hundreds of small practical projects aimed at demonstrating aspects of how this might work. Meanwhile, literary debate about how today's society as a whole could be transformed abound. Notable manifestations include 'social ecology', associated with Murray Bookchin[195], connecting ecological concerns with Anarchist social organisation, and who also participated in the Town Meetings of Vermont, and 'ParEcon', developing the idea of the comprehensive, local participatory economy, associated with Michael Albert[196].

Above all, we now have to recall that if globalisation is about to come to an end through the systematic diminishing of the energy required to fuel the modern economic system, and the supply of the goods that it has been distributing in increasing measure is radically curtailed, then means will *have* to be found to satisfy needs from local human and physical resources. These are the circumstances in which the anarchist vision becomes immensely, if not uniquely practical. One might envisage – and be subjected to - a return to a local form of capitalism, or even feudalism or a caste system, but at this stage we merely want to point to what was proposed by the turn-of-twentieth-century Anarchists and indicate that this presents a genuine solution to what will become the increasing precariousness of the present global system of resource production and distribution and the system of government that manages it. Centralised authoritarianism of either a Soviet variety or of something akin to absolutist monarchy is even less viable. This assertion, however, needs considerable justification.

Justification and Barriers to Anarchist Arrangements

Upon what grounds should the anarchist proposition for the organisation of society be accepted as 'Right'? In the previous chapter we referred to the fact that Confucian and Hindu societies subsisted over millennia in a sustainable relationship with their environment, which is at least one of the main concerns regarding a 'correct' arrangement for future society. Whether the people, particularly those at the base of the social hierarchy, were in sum less happy than they might have been in a more egalitarian society cannot now and probably never could be tested in any objective manner. We may, however, note how unstable the Confucian arrangements were in the sense of periodically collapsing into widespread violence and famine, thence being rebuilt by new dynasties; and in the Indian case the clear indignity of the lifestyle assigned to the lowest castes

We might, however, go further than this and ask ourselves whether human beings living in societies subsisting in extreme conditions, such as Bedouins in the barren, stifling heart of Arabia or the Inuit subsisting for much of the year in the dark and the cold of the Arctic, are in sum less happy than those living in such luxuriant and easy-going conditions as the South Sea Islands or other tropical 'paradises'.

The conclusion is 'probably not,' in that human beings are amazingly adaptable in their ability to carve out a viable social existence under an almost infinite set of conditions and once reconciled to these can find routes to happiness within the confines of their situation. Hence the fact that class society can become accepted by those who find themselves born into 'lower' classes, in contradistinction to those who find their status diminished within their lifetime. However, societies can certainly be dysfunctional in creating insecurity by being in a permanent state of internal conflict such as, today, New Guinea or Somalia – historically a common feature of nations that were all too often in a state of war, internal or under invasion or fighting against other nations. It is therefore worthwhile to seek a form of society that has the stability and security that will allow it to blossom as a condition that is not merely ecologically sustainable into the distant future, but a place where all can expect to find happiness and self-fulfilment.

It is surely evident to most people who give any deeper thought to the issue that anarchist arrangements are vehemently opposed by most of those who are privileged and possess prerogative in any class-organised society. The history of the opposition to anarchism in the Occident from the mid-nineteenth century to the present is wearisome and manifold, ranging from constant vilification and smear regarding violence and for whatever reason illegitimacy, leading to suppression of all manner of manifestations and to *agents provocateurs* creating violent events that were then attributed to Anarchists. Whilst there have, certainly, been Anarchists who advocated violence and, indeed, practised it, this was but a small minority that established power used as a means to dissuade the mass of the people from embracing anarchism.

In the final chapter of this book we will look into the philosophical and moral grounds concerning the correctness of the anarchist intuition regarding 'ultimate' arrangements for Occidental society (and as we will see, possibly appropriate for other cultures damaged or infected 'beyond repair' by 'globalisation' wrought by Occidental culture). We need, however, already here to discuss this at least in outline. We also need to know why this has not actually come about in the past which includes both arguments against and barriers that in the past have blocked advance into such arrangements.

Egalitarianism

First we discuss the issue of 'equality'. Of course the pursuit of equality has to end at some point, due to the fact that each individual has his or her differences in person and place and different capacities and orientations which no equality of education and enculturation can or should attempt to erase. What is meant by those who are for equality is an openness to hear and be heard and a lack of barriers to access what the community has to offer in terms of resources, broadly defined. There is clearly built into it an acceptance by all members of the community that equality in terms of mutual respect is a fundamental principle of life.

As such, we can see that the rightness of equality is lodged deeply in Occidental society, emanating from the teaching of Christ and experience of Christian communities before the advent of the great Churches - Orthodox, Catholic and then the great proliferation. This is not in itself a justification in a situation where here we are arguing for a rational form of political organisation, free of any purely traditionalist or mystical underpinning. Perhaps the justification can be seen more clearly in moral terms by its obverse, the unjustifiability of some having access to more than others in terms of wealth, privilege, prerogative and other aspects of the wielding of power and access to physical resources. Essentially, this is the moral concept of 'fairness'. It is relevant to the Occident as it is accepted within the culture as a legitimate aim and an Anarchist polity is one that implements this principle consistently.

Certainly there is nothing new in Occidental thinking about the idea that egalitarianism is morally correct and this is not merely in the writing of utopians and political radicals but in countless small initiatives and policies. In recent years the concept has been stopped in its tracks by the notion of 'equality of opportunity', taking off from the notion that we are equal in the eyes of God and that every child born starts its life equal with all others, obscuring the reasons why opportunities in our 'real world' are not equal.

The most compelling argument against inequality, however, concerns the issue of the competition and competitiveness that is bred by inequality, and which destroys reason in the organisation of life. It is a central assertion of liberalism that competition is a fundamental quality of human existence and furthermore that competition is, in principle, essentially good in that it motivates individuals, communities, organisations, cities and nations to Develop. We have argued above at length the fallacy of the liberal assertion that humans are inherently competitive and investigate this further in the final chapter.

Furthermore, if 'Progress' and 'Development' are discredited as laudable aims, as a consequence of the experience of modernisation and the emergent fall, then the issue becomes: what is a viable form of organising for the future that does not involve competition as a motivating principle? How can we arrive at a condition where the constitution of society is one where reason has a chance to prevail and where we can create a genuinely sustainable relationship with the biosphere and in particular the part of it in which we and our descendants may live out our lives in security and happiness?

Copious evidence indicates that the collapse of many cultures in the past has resulted from the inability of societies to foresee the folly of their activity because competition with others has narrowed their horizons to focus on the means to win[197]. On Easter Island the

166

competition was simply over the production of monuments that used up resources to the point of exhaustion[198]. In many empires it was the waging of wars that united the people behind leaders, putting internal competition behind them but ending in destruction and misery. In modern society it has been the pursuit of status through the acquisition of commodities as symbols of success, distracting the attention of the people from the unjustness and dissatisfaction with the privileges and prerogative of those who possess substantial wealth and command power.

It is no secret that the insistence on 'growth in GDP' that dominates the present-day political process is a design to maintain the social peace in a situation of unequal societies. This is, however, leading to collapse, not only of the global economy, but of the political system that holds it in place through the forced reversal of economic growth brought on by the decline in energy resources and in parallel the degradation and destruction of the biosphere, the health of which is the fundamental physical basis of all human existence. This will force a re-evaluation of the issue of competition, where status indicated by increase in commodities will decline for humanity as a whole and so the unjustness of inequality and the dissatisfaction with this and with it the legitimacy of those who rule and the whole machinery through which they rule will come into deep question.

It was noted in Chapter Two that inequality does not necessarily lead to generalised competition, for example in the case of India and China, where over long periods of time the enculturation of the whole population was such as to convince at a deep level those with a lower status that this was the role they should play and that change in role was, in the Indian case inconceivable and in the Chinese case available only through a strictly regulated process of exams that was universally held to be the only legitimate way to improve one's status. Nevertheless, there was for the overweeningly ambitious always the prize of kingship and domination which led to incessant war that has, throughout civilisation, become accepted as a recurrent feature of cultural life. If war can be permanently eliminated through the elimination of the prize of war (kingship or more generally, national domination) then clearly this should be pursued.

The argument from Occidental sensibilities for equality and against fixed roles was, in the Enlightenment context, that hereditary kings may be wise in governing the people but may equally lack the character or inclination to rule well. By extension, why should one expect in the Indian case children born, say, in a village of potters to become good potters when they might have capacities that would make them good musicians, jewellers, doctors or engineers? A society of equals opens the door to everyone pursuing their potential as human beings within the overall confines of the society as a whole, as long as these are not anti-social, and so maximises the possibilities for personal self-realisation.

Finally, inequality restricts the horizons for affection in many societies (and indeed particularly amongst the upper classes) where traditionally marriages are arranged for reasons of maintaining wealth and power within a restricted circle rather than for love. But inequality breeds disrespect and lack of empathy for those not in one's own class. However, admiration on the part of some elements of the lower (or generally lower-middle) classes for their 'superiors' is a widespread perversion that combines aspiration to have what the upper classes have with the desire to emulate their lifestyle that is so prevalent in modern Occidental culture and particularly that of the United States. Indeed, this latter characteristic is a large part of the social-psychological or pathological state of being that is the legacy of Mandeville and Adam Smith, and which is leading us to catastrophe.

Common Pool Resource Management

It was argued above that the attempt in the Soviet Union to eliminate private property had disastrous results. However, what seems clear is that it was not the fact of the lack of private property but rather the collectivisation of it, and with it the relation between the collective and the property that led to its failure. In practice, in spite of today's dominant ideology that asserts that private ownership is the most effective way to ensure that property is well-maintained and in spite of the evidence that peasants throughout the world have craved their own land which they manage more effectively when it is individually owned, there are nevertheless many thousands of instances around the world, both traditional and modern, that indicate situations where communities have preferred to manage resources in common and have devised very effective ways of managing them in this way[199].

The reason for the abolition of private property as a principle of anarchist governance lies in the close connection between private property ownership and inegalitarian social arrangements. In short, the concentration of the ownership of property, in the first instance in land, is the hallmark and indeed the foundation of privilege and prerogative, and of the existence of class distinction in most societies. As with social equality, so also with the management of common pool resources; the population must fundamentally respect the principle and

168

communities must be able to decide how resources are used and, with respect to consumption, distributed. The latter overcomes the problem encountered in communist societies where communities were not party to the decisions on use and distribution and hence considered themselves to have been divested of their land, albeit in much of the Soviet Union, in the first instance, the Communist Government inherited land still under feudal custom or, in some cases, governed communally by peasant communities themselves (*Mir – Obshchina - Skhod*) that had never been in private ownership.

Whilst communal ownership and management of land resources is the root issue, this became over the 19th and 20th centuries increasingly overshadowed in the process of industrialisation by the ownership of a broader range of the means of production. Until the modern era, most manufactures were created by individual artisans, but increase in production meant ever larger factories that were overwhelmingly owned by 'entrepreneurs' and then corporations that created a propertyless 'proletariat' or 'working class'. Since the Owenite invention of cooperatives in the early 19th century, this mode of community self-organisation has been available and practiced in different countries to different degrees, where workers and consumers participate on an equal footing in the decision-making processes regarding what should be produced and how, and then how the produce should be distributed and how, as in the case significantly of housing, it should be managed. The shining example in modern times of a successful 'cooperative commonwealth' is that created in the town of Mondragon in Spain, where banking, factories, housing and higher education are organised on a cooperative basis. The history of this experience teaches essential lessons, indicating also the means, and also the difficulties, of creating and managing such a system[200].

In all cases, the question of scale and complexity arises, and although intensively debated in terms of details, it is prima facie evident that the origins of inequality are closely associated with the way in which the complexity of production processes (initially, according to some, the creation of large-scale irrigation systems[201]) demanded differentiation in skills and functions that extended into differentiation also of power and benefits. Insofar as we will see during the collapse of the Technostructure and radical re-localisation in the coming years, this could, at two extremes, either collapse into a neo-feudalistic state with rigid class structures, or localised economies could be organised on the basis of local and sub-regional cooperative commonwealths. The socio-political struggle in the coming years will circulate

169

essentially around the avoidance of the former and the successful implementation of the latter.

Democracy

The case for democracy hardly needs arguing insofar as it is a principle which everywhere today is lauded. 'The people' should have the opportunity — and indeed the responsibility — to participate in their own governance, which goes well beyond government decision-making and which requires adequate machinery through which they can participate meaningfully, and where they are privy to the issues at stake and in a position to influence decisions regarding these issues in so far as they are affected by them. It was argued above, however, that what today is called democracy is not democracy at all in that the principle and genuine practice is lost in the process of electing representatives who are then free to take decisions on behalf of the people without further reference to their views on issues affecting their welfare.

It should be, but almost never is, clearly understood that representatives do not, and indeed cannot, implement the will of the people once they enter a decision-making forum that is at a distance from the electorate, unless there is adequate machinery for communication and for the people to have the power to sanction the decisions of their representatives. Whilst, as noted above, the issue of scale and accessibility becomes crucial here, it becomes clear that the present machinery of government in most countries falls lamentably short of anything that can be meaningfully referred to as genuine democracy. Upon describing clearly what democracy really means, Rousseau essentially threw his hands into the air and declared:

If there were a nation of Gods, it would govern itself democratically. A Government so perfect is not suited for men (sic)[202].

We need not give up hope, however, and below we discuss the means whereby we can approach the achievement in large measure of genuine democracy.

It is generally contended that democracy is a 'good thing' in that it opens up access to decision-making for the people as a whole. However, it also denotes the distribution of responsibility to the people as a whole. It will be recalled that Plato's scepticism concerning the efficacy of Democracy resided in the way in which it lends to the people a sense that they are free 'to do what they want'. In Plato's view it was this that led to its degeneration into tyranny and eventually

170

widespread abrogation of responsibility led to the need for authority to be asserted to bring political decision-making back into line with the genuine needs of the population. A mature democracy will need to be rooted in a society in which responsibility is commensurate with the freedom that comes with democratic decision-making.

Problems in Implementation

The first problem in attempting to advocate the kind of governance described in the foregoing few paragraphs may seem to concern the question of practicality. The present political conjuncture and the complexity of the global economic and technical systems make it seem that we are too far away from any of what is described so far to be able to even conceive of making a transition of any kind away from the present machinery of governance, let alone designing and managing the steps to get there, even if we had a great urge to do so. It is clearly the case that attempts today to think and act in this direction are pitifully small and/or theoretical: one scours the internet and finds thousands of small-scale initiatives that together add up to very little and in virtually no cases is there any strategic thinking towards constitutional change or the general reorganisation of the political and social settlement. The strategy of Power ('the Powers that be') to deflate and divert critique over the past decades has been extraordinarily successful! Indeed, we might say that the Powers themselves have been subverted by the astronomic freedom and wealth that has overwhelmed even them!

Unlike the turn of the 20th century where social movements thought strategically and had eminently practical suggestions as to how to arrive at more rational arrangements for the governance of society, today's social movements, best expressed in the gatherings of the World Social Forum under the banner of 'another world is possible' and the wave of demonstrations that swept the Middle East (the 'Arab Spring') and thence Europe and the United States in 2011-2012, show pitifully little by way of strategic and theoretically coherent proposals, narrowing down, rather, to hundreds of small ideas, projects and initiatives[203] that, it was hoped, might eventually result in the emergence of a better world.

One of very few exceptions, the formulations of the *International Forum on Globalization* (IFG) attempted to bring together a wide range of 'radical thinkers' to construct an alternative vision to address many of the problems outlined in the first chapter, with a sense of social justice and a broad perspective. Although the authors of their Manifesto — *Alternatives to Economic Globalization – A Better World*

171

is Possible[204] — noted the extremely rapid changes taking place in the world, the presumption was implicit that something like the currently available resources would continue to be available in the future with no thought being given to the possibility of a precipitate fall of the 'modern world system'. This attempted, rather, to set new goals and devise mechanisms to counter what they saw as the radical injustice and environmental failings of neoliberalism, to create a fairer and ostensibly environmentally sustainable world on the basis of current resource flows and with much of the present political, institutional and corporate structures remaining in place. There was no suggestion in this context that alternative forms of government might need to be considered.

There was in this a call for increased democracy – and a fair understanding of the problems of achieving this – and 'subsidiarity', the latter meaning decentralisation of decision-making; and the development of local economies. The question of 'equity' arose but not in any definite terms as regards 'equality' and 'competition' albeit between local enterprises it was seen in a favourable light. Like the Social Forum, however, the IFG manifesto lost perspective out of concern to demonstrate just how many small 'good practices' were already under way which, however, may have added up to very little even if it had been genuinely wise and feasible to 'scale them up'. Ideas were formulated for breaking up corporate empires and to localise production and then a revision of the relative powers of the international organisations, all of which were assumed to continue to operate into a better future, proposed by the IFG.

But with the global economy going into a profound decline, globalisation would be expected to fail of its own accord, probably in stages but relatively rapidly, and in the long run 'localisation' could be expected inevitably to result as movement over distances becomes increasingly difficult. Whether corporate empires of today could survive is extremely doubtful and, as discussed in the first chapter, current complex systems of international and even national administration and with it political structures would be expected to come under strain and metamorphose in some way or other. The principles set out above are designed to address this without yet dictating anything specific. However, the 'impracticality' of what was set out above may not under emergent conditions be at all impractical but, rather, an effective way to reconstruct a viable politics – and as we will see in the last three chapters also a viable system of supplying and distributing resources.

However, we can almost be sure that there will be conflicts and resistances to implementing the anarchist principles set out in relative

172

abstract form above. There are several interrelated headings under which we can discuss these. The first is the issue of the demise of the Commercial Ideology and the way in which today status is promoted through the accumulation of commodities and more generally the problematic of class which expresses itself both by the presumption of the 'upper classes' that they should be privileged and possess prerogative in decision-making and the acquiescence of the 'lower classes' in their powerlessness and exploitation. The cultural confirmation of class is secured through mythologies, traditionalism and the manipulation of the powerful. How to deal with this complex of problems?

All of these situations can be found almost everywhere in different measure and in discussing these in detail it is not possible – and not even very useful – to try to find a universal answer. It was noted earlier that class is deeply built into the sub-conscious of most civilised peoples, so that until the onslaught of Occidental colonialism and thence 'independence', particularly when connected with notions of communist egalitarianism, and now globalisation, there was no thought that social hierarchy might be abolished. The case of Indian castes and Confucian hierarchy were briefly presented as examples but in one configuration or other, class is well-nigh ubiquitous, even in the modern world.

Whilst castes declined in Europe following the end of Middle Ages (but at very different rates in different European countries viz serfdom being abolished in Russia only in the late 19th century) even up to the late 18th century clear class lines continued to exist throughout Europe, in France and some other European countries referred to as 'Estates'. With the massive shift in location and lifestyle of most of the populations of the Occidental countries through industrialisation and urbanisation, the potential for the abolition of class opened up and it is in this context that the radical proposals of the communists, anarchists and other tendencies pushed in the direction of more egalitarian societies.

It was only in Britain, the first country to undergo these changes, that the ruling classes succeeded in forging a culturally well-defined modern 'working class' under the imposed banner of 'ours is not to question why'. The depth of this enculturation became particularly evident when, post Second World War, possibilities for advancement, particularly through advanced education, opened up that the working classes were slow to take advantage of and numbers of sociological studies revealed that 'class consciousness' and class allegiance were overwhelmingly an inhibition rather than rallying cry for emancipation[205].

Elsewhere, obvious distinctions between the new lower classes and their 'superiors' were less marked and were maintained more through the success in using property — those who possessed it in significant measure against those who possessed little or none — and the maintenance and growth in wage labour as capitalist (and in some cases Government) enterprises grew. The extreme was the United States, which feigned classlessness but maintained and extended de facto classes, through the 19th century predominantly by importing labour that thought of itself as better-off than the circumstances from which they came, even though in practice they were subservient to the pre-existing ('WASP') elite.

Given the Marxist assumption that the lower classes would eventually 'cast off their chains' and in the context of social democracy, with its apparent underlying assumption that gradually things would move in the direction of greater equality, the persistence of class appeared anomalous across much of the 20th century. However, there was complex machinery in the Occidental countries that kept things that way, including particularly special education for the elite — being more a ticket to enter the 'upper-' and 'middle classes' than that this made them better or in any meaningful way 'more effective' members of society. But both private enterprises and public authorities to an even greater extent, maintained clear hierarchies and there was, and remains, no doubting who is superior and who inferior within these frameworks, being in most circumstances defined by pay levels and in bureaucracies by letters designating staff levels.

But in general the systems confirm the hierarchy through differences in pay, synergising with the capitalist principle that income and thence wealth be the final arbiter of status. And finally, there were, and still very much are, 'leaders' who, regardless of how well or badly they 'lead', confirm that power and wealth *should* be unequally distributed, using tradition and in the case of constitutional monarchies (however lacking in real powers they might be) and through the Abrahamic religions, mythology to confirm and instil in the lower classes an acquiescence in the legitimacy of hierarchy.

There seems to be an unanalysed impression in the Occident that somehow in recent years, in the atmosphere of post-modernism, class is fading away. However, analysis using census data that actually classify the population by class not only confirms that class continues to be a fact but that there is relatively little movement between classes: most people born in one class stay there throughout their lives[206].

Furthermore, differences in ownership of wealth and property have grown in recent years everywhere, with small, fabulously wealthy elites emerging, the persistence of relative poverty and 'social exclusion' in spite of general 'economic growth' and the stagnation or even decline in many countries (notably the United States) of the broad 'middle classes' that were supposed to be the ultimate destiny of everyone in increasingly egalitarian societies[207]. The complexification and ever finer differentiation of roles in the economy is a further factor obfuscating the actuality of growing class differentiation as stratification.

In short, whilst at an everyday level more obscured than in earlier eras, equality has been declining rather than increasing for the past thirty years throughout most of the Occidental countries. This does not bode well for any proposals for a radically egalitarian society to emerge in the coming years. We can, however, be certain that as the international and local economies decline and the broad middle and economically lower ends of the population become conscious that the current means of expressing growing status are disappearing forever, the people will become aware of their class inferiority. Indications in the United States, where the 2008 'economic crisis' robbed many of their means of income and even their houses, are nevertheless that there was little immediate palpable sense of the injustice that would be expected to foment riots and the rise of coherent outrage at what is happening[208].

As yet, it appears there is a broad assumption-cum-hope that current economic problems are temporary. How long, and through what stages, will it take for the realisation to dawn that this is not temporary and indeed that this is only the start of a radical reduction in living standards? And what manifestations can we expect as this realisation dawns? History would suggest that there would be demonstrations, as already apparent in Southern Europe, that will become violent riots with relatively inchoate demands. What these demands might be and of whom they will be demanded we can only speculate on. But the inegalitarian nature of current society will in all likelihood generate violence as the total wealth diminishes such that those who continue to be able to live the life we have become accustomed to will want to defend this against those for whom it is no longer available and factions will in all probability emerge as governments attempt to counter violence and increasingly coherent demands with violence and subterfuge.

Another spontaneous reaction may, however, be the spread of generalised depression where large numbers of people simply decline into inactivity and suffer starvation, disease and premature death on what we can expect to become a massive scale as the public means and concern to combat these recede. The situation in Russian cities, post collapse of the Soviet Union provides an illustration of this[209] — albeit the alcoholism that has ostensibly killed many, particularly in the context of the economic crises of 1990s and 1998, has had a long prehistory in Russia.

The call for radical equality as an organising principle is designed, as explained earlier, to bring down the walls between people so that they may discuss rational ways to overcome what will be deep problems in the dysfunctionality of the emergent world. This will facilitate cooperation to build new settlements to replace defunct suburbs and centre cities and to rebuild local economies that once again will produce and distribute most of what is locally needed, initially for survival and thereafter for a more comfortable life. Today's struggle for status through consumption that is the defining principle of our age, that essentially isolates classes and individuals, can only hinder the kinds of inventive thinking and cooperative spirit and organisation that will be essential to rebuild a workable and congenial world. The most difficult task will be the rebuilding of affective social and community relations.

But it is by no means only a question of 'seeing the light' and acting accordingly. At the present time, huge and organised resources are being extended by the corporate world and its neo-conservative ideologues into influencing the media, who themselves are largely owned by wealthy individuals and their corporate empires and, through a proliferation of 'think tanks', a barrage of publications and other means of disseminating 'information' concerned with pouring scepticism on radical ideas of any kind, has been effective in curtailing even consideration of ideas counter to their ideology.

Whilst the notion of 'anti-communism' is difficult to sustain in a world where 'communism' is hardly a title used by any national Government, the label continues to be used and, in the United States has a widespread effect of labelling ideas counter to neoliberalism and conservative ideology and simply by doing this closing minds to further consideration or debate on problematic socio-political issues. A very small minority in the United States is thus prepared to talk openly – or even think about – the kinds of ideas presented above or, indeed, to admit the possibility that the United States as a political and economic entity might be about to enter a radical decline and hence that new ideas and new approaches to organising life might be urgently needed[210]. Elsewhere in the Occident such ideas might be approached more openly and creatively but have hitherto been consistently marginalised, nevertheless.

There are those who believe that forces are already in place to suppress not only riots but also movements aimed at restructuring life as the world as we know it falls apart[211]. These would clearly aim at continuing to maintain existing authority structures. As the crisis deepens, however, the present-day means of sophisticated surveillance and repression will encounter escalating incoherence and organised violence emanating from these structures, which will fail for lack of resources and coherence. This is unlikely to stop the repression in its tracks and this will surely find new, perhaps fragmented and local ways of regrouping and focusing aggression on creating hierarchical structures at the local level and recreating class society in new forms.

Movements for reconstruction at the local level will, under these circumstances, need to be clear about what they are aiming to achieve and organise themselves accordingly. However, just as Lenin's dictatorship and the suppression of the anarchists was justified as a defensive strategy against foreign intervention, so movements will have to avoid a new, local, authoritarianism justified as 'defensive', that would surely then establish itself on a permanent basis that could well end in revivals of feudalism - that is, institutionalised rigid hierarchy no longer based on income and money wealth but inserting people into exploitative roles directly to produce wealth for new elites. This situation was, indeed, the origin of European feudalism in the chaos of the Dark Ages, where villages were organised hierarchically as defensive systems against marauding bands that swept across Europe following the fall of Rome, and where 'leaders' supported by the people turned into their exploiters.

We can be almost sure that State sovereignty will come increasingly into question, although in the first place this needs to be defended, not as nationalism but against the incursion of other states. But creative thinking should have its eye on an eventual turning upside down of the notion of sovereignty: that localities should be sovereign and thence to learn at what level confederation should be built, lending powers to counties, provinces and only ultimately at the level of today's states. The determining factor will be the way in which the local economy is able to be rebuilt to satisfy local needs and the extent to which collaboration with neighbouring localities and communities will be effected on all sides to enhance the fulfilment of local needs through, where relevant, collaborative initiatives and trade at the margins.

Urbanisation and thence globalisation (and in Europe the relentless passage towards a united 'European Community') has been accompanied by a receding of consciousness regarding local community as sentiment. Nevertheless, the residue of history should be recovered in terms of memory and in terms of the debates and turning points along the road to modernity. Whilst the English Revolution and the radical movements which it sired may be too far in the past to inspire future alternatives, particularly given the sad history of repression at home and belligerent imperialism of the 19th century, in many nations, at least, the notions of alternatives that were defeated or rejected in the relatively recent past remain in the social subconscious and can be revived and in some cases the actual debates revisited.

There is much, for instance, in the French self-consciousness regarding its history from the end of the 19th century, and the open contradiction that continues in a crassly hierarchical society that displays above the door of every town hall 'Liberté Égalité, Fraternité' — this is not far under the surface, as demonstrated by such repeatedly surfacing movements as Situationism, that can be revived and built upon. Or revival of the anarchist movements in Italy and Spain that also have surfaced from time to time. Or the case of *The Federalist* debates in the United States and how, instead of federation, local autonomy and confederation can be taken up as the route that was rejected at the end of the 18th century. The Russian Anarchist tradition, as the major alternative to communism in the years leading up to the Revolution, should be far fresher in the national imagination. Each nation will have to find its own ideological path.

However, there are many unpleasant and potentially dysfunctional cultural memories that we might expect to be revived that should be actively fought against and decisively rejected. These include the kinds of nationalism that led to fascism and to the carnage following the break-up of Yugoslavia. Racism and belligerent anti-difference emanating from religion are likely to surface, exacerbated by the extent to which, in recent years, populations have moved, particularly from the South to the North in attempts to benefit, even with an inferior status, from what has been seen as the advantages of Development. The immense difficulties that this will almost inevitably raise and the difficulty of re-integrating communities to rebuild a holistic local culture, require that there be longer consideration of this, which is presented in the final chapter.

It is, however, already necessary to add that the anarchist model of governance grows out of the frustrated Christian-based notion of what is right and good, indeed presenting the ultimate solution to the path of Progress, that can be argued, at the same time, as a profound reconstitution of Occidental society in removing the basis of class struggle and all other versions of competition that have been the essential fuel of actual (indeed misdirected and perverse) Progress over at least the last century. But is this appropriate for all cultures or would it be once again an Occidental imposition if advocated for all societies? Actually there have been in very many societies democratic, if not necessarily anarchist, social decision-making mechanisms that were destroyed in the process of modernisation, which might be revived or remembered in the process of rebuilding locally appropriate forms of governance.

Where this is not the case, one might decry the re-emergence of authoritarian and absolutist government in parts of the world, as the power of Occidental modernism recedes (even now, we see this recurring across much of Africa and in a more sophisticated, but nevertheless insistent form, in almost all Muslim States). But what right has any society to determine how another should govern itself? All that can be said is that whilst every society — and in the future we will in all probability be speaking of micro-societies within their own sub-regions — should be secure against invasion from outside with its imposition of economic exploitation and foreign notions and mechanisms of governance. Censure of others should involve no greater force than that of demonstration. Good forms of governance of the future should prove themselves through being demonstrably successful in terms of satisfying the needs of all their members and of maintaining the ecological context in a truly sustainable fashion.

Chapter 4: Ecology – Resources – Production

It is evident that the crisis we face and the fall of modern civilisation that we can expect in the coming decades is a consequence of the lack of an adequate consciousness and understanding we have of our social relationship with the biosphere and more generally the resources of the earth due to the overly-developed self-concern of humanity, and particularly Occidental society, in the context of our progressivist belief that we should strive onwards and upwards, wherever this should lead us. Chapters Two and Three focused attention predominantly on the way in which Occidental, and recently global, culture has developed in terms of social and political evolution and what the options in these spheres appear to be. Although pointed to as an important ingredient of the passage of social evolution, relatively little attention has so far in this book been paid to the physical environment that has nurtured and sustained this social evolutionary passage.

From the outset of this dimension of the analysis we face an ideological problem. From time to time it has been recognised that interest and study of physical things has, in our culture, been carried out separately from interest and study of social and political phenomena. The interface was ostensibly 'economics' which, however, has paid precious little attention to the details of ecological processes and geophysical realities, as these interface and interact with the production of social and political life.

In fact the problem goes all the way back to Christian teaching, which has very little to say about environmental matters, so that these have always hung loose in the moral universe of our culture. Natural science has its roots in certain Greek philosophies where we can already see a sharp divide between the moral and human on the one side and the first attempts to 'understand' nature and the universe on the other. This divide can be seen to be reproduced in the outpouring of the European Enlightenment which, whilst laying the foundations of modern science, Newton, d'Alembert, Buffon, Lavoisier, Helvétius and yet others did so along lines that rarely intersected with the moral and political theory associated with such names as Montesquieu, Voltaire, Rousseau, Adam Ferguson and Adam Smith. From the early years of the Enlightenment, through even well into the 20th century, there was a notion that science, as understanding of the physical world, was a kind of absolute knowledge of how the universe and the earth works with an expectation that even human motivations and actions would eventually be as predictable as following 'natural laws'.

In recent years this messianic vision has mellowed and, with the rise of 'social constructionism'[212] and Feyerabend's 'Anarchist theory of knowledge'[213], there is a broad acceptance that knowledge of natural phenomena and the uses to which this is put interact densely with social forces as expressed in production of the human environment and impacts on nature. However, whilst the insights of Bruno Latour[214] and his social constructionist predecessors might have a small enthusiastic following, the inertia of disciplinary paths and the traditional foci of intellectuals in the social and political fields has been on social and political relations, oppression and social exclusion, human rights, political economy and so on, which leads at the same time to an attitude that physical things and the environment are the concern of environmentalists and natural scientists and not of those concerned with political and moral questions. Indeed, this can be seen as an important ingredient of the ongoing 'denial' of the resource and environmental problems on which this book is focusing so much attention.

In short, socially engaged intellectuals do not see it as their business to try to engage with 'environmental' debates (and hence easily fall prey to those conservatives who would like to dismiss the problems), seeing them as detracting from the urgent need to combat social inequity and violations of human rights. This is very unfortunate insofar as their intense attention to problems they can see today fails altogether to see the far greater human existential, political and moral problems we will be facing in the near future as a consequence of the way in which modern society and politics has misinterpreted the dimensions of our existence where Nature determines what is and what is not feasible. Somehow we need to pull the environmental and socio-political into the same frame of reference if we are to resolve the emerging global problematic. In this chapter we start this process first by clarifying elements of 'how we got to be here' in terms of our social understanding and action to, and in, our environment and in the final chapter we attempt to think more coherently about ethical issues that fuse our understanding and responsibility towards the biosphere with issues of social and political ethics and morality.

From time to time in the paragraphs that follow, we use the term 'nature'. Historically a complex notion, here we use it exchangeable with 'the biosphere', of the sum of global ecosystems, with an implication also for the geological resource base and atmosphere upon and within which the Biosphere evolves.

Human Impacts on the Environment

If humanity is to survive the coming decades and centuries, it will be necessary to adapt to, rather than change, the ecosystems in which human groups live out their social lives, maintaining biodiversity and ensuring that disturbance of the atmosphere and subsoil is radically reduced, insofar as this produces such toxins as atmospheric change and the kinds of residues and pollution that result from mining. Whilst this is prima facie rather obvious and should have been the basic principle upon which programmes for 'Sustainable Development' were built, in practice, those concerned with Sustainable Development almost always seem to hope that small changes in practice could achieve this end, with pitifully little by way of conscientious and honest comprehensive analysis of the consequences – and above all the deeper causes - of what is happening and the implications this has for an adequate level of revision of Development to render our lifestyle and production systems genuinely sustainable.

Ecosystems are in constant flux with metamorphosis of genera and species, in the short term with respect to their geographic location and behaviour, and in the long term through evolution of physical morphology which, in turn, reacts back on the ecosystems and in general the flow of energy and materials within which they subsist. Although some species of plants and animals have survived morphologically almost unchanged for hundreds of millions of years, the changes in the ecosystems of which they are a component is never-ending, responding to changes also in the climate that alter temperatures in particular places over quite wide ranges and this, in conjunction with changes in rainfall patterns, means that vast areas can change over the millennia from rainforest to desert, from tundra to open grassland to dense forest and thence succumb to deep ice sheets as ice ages close in, with species moving and evolving in search of congenial environments, adapting to change or simply dying out.

There has been an immense accumulation of paleoarchaeological information in recent years that, with the aid of a great refinement of tools, has helped to suggest sketches of the path of human evolution. Bipedal animals close to today's human beings emerged some four million years ago in Africa and it is probable that 'Homo erectus', the earliest truly human species that developed basic tools, made use of fire and appears to have lived in bands by hunting and gathering, not dissimilar from today's remnants of hunter and gathering peoples evolved from these perhaps two million years ago. Whilst both predecessors and all the major developments in humanoid species all first appear in Africa, there were various waves of migration out of Africa at least one and a half million years ago, predominantly through the Levant, with evidence of variants of Homo erectus as far apart as Europe in the west and China and Indonesia in the east.

Paleological analysis of the evolution of other animal species over these early periods gives no indication that the advent of Homo erectus and its immediate progeny had any marked impact on the ecosystems which they occupied and it can be speculated that the humanoid niche was relatively insignificant. It is only with the emergence of Homo sapiens something less than two hundred thousand years ago (but an instant in the evolution even of humanoid species) that we see emergence of the capacity of language, and in general the brain capacity and facility that generated what today we would consider to be culture — art, religion and an awareness of the separateness of the human from the rest of nature — as an external framework for organising the life of its members.

Within a few thousand years of Homo sapiens appearing in different parts of the world, spreading out of Africa starting some sixty thousand years ago, there was everywhere a rapid decline in large animal species[215]. Whilst there is dispute as to how much this might have been the result of human hunting, there can be no doubt, as evidenced by many finds of, in some cases massive, graveyards of animal bones dating from the presence of Homo sapiens and with evidence that they were the cause of the devastation, that they were from early on capable of hunting and killing even the largest animals and that as one species after another became extinct, so human bands focused on hunting or trapping the smaller animals. It is estimated that in the two or three thousand years after the arrival of humans in Australia, some 86.4% of the large animal species were exterminated. Across Eurasia the same decimation of animal species can be found and following the human advance into and down the Americas, starting only some fifteen thousand years ago, there was a veritable holocaust of species that meant that following the transition to agriculture, there were few animal species left that might be usefully domesticated. By eight thousand years ago, at the onset of agriculture (which may be in some way connected with this loss of game) some 76 per cent of species that reached over 160 kilos mature weight and that were to be found on the two continents some twelve thousand years earlier, were extinct.

There is a wide supposition in much American literature, extrapolating from this pre-history, adding the marauding and otherwise aggressive episodes of more recent human history and referring the whole argument to a variant of Hobbesian 'human nature', to conclude that Homo sapiens can be nothing but destructive and that the collapse of Civilisation ahead and the eventual destruction of the biosphere through the bloody-minded continuation of greenhouse gas production is par for the course. This does not, however, recognise that in the end, hunting and gathering bands did learn to adapt to most environments, extending from the frozen Arctic to the arid margins of the deserts, and to live sustainably in these over many thousands of years, even into the 20th century. Australia is an excellent case in point, where, following the end of the animal holocaust, for well over ten thousands years a small population developed an easy going lifestyle in harmony with the environment and remaining animal species.

But is this only possible if humans organise themselves into small hunter-gatherer bands and live in their particular ecosystem with a minimum of what we consider to be culture? Joseph Tainter's[216] influential analysis of the collapse of complex societies concludes that there is always a trajectory of growth in human cultures that ends in collapse and that small-scale, simple societies (not well-defined by Tainter) are the only form that can continue in a sustainable manner. Tainter did not see environmental degradation as being the primary reason for collapse — and nor did Jared Diamond in his influential book *Collapse*[217] . Furthermore, whilst civilisations certainly do collapse (the case of Rome is taught in almost every Occidental primary school and the cases of Mesopotamia and of the Maya in Central America are known to every educated citizen) there is nevertheless ample evidence, as demonstrated by the longevity of Egyptian, Indian and Chinese cultures, to indicate that complex civilisations can be sustained over at least a few thousands of years. We might go on to extrapolate this to tens of thousands of years with the aid of the knowledge that modern civilisation has gained about how the biosphere works, if civilisations, in Diamond's words, were to learn to adapt.

However, there is a widespread assumption that there has been a linear, if slow, increase in the pressure of human habitation on the biosphere since the onset of agriculture some eight thousand years ago, and that is another way of confirming that human civilisation as a whole will inevitably end in over-exploitation of the biosphere and the inevitable collapse that will follow from this. The exponential growth in human pressure that we have seen over the past three centuries has not, however, been some kind of continuations of a linear process when looked at in longer perspective. It is, rather, one that is associated, until three hundred years ago, with the growth and decline or collapse of particular civilisations. Whilst we might speak of incipient world population growth over the past two thousand years, that of China went through three periods of decline (3rd to 9th century, 13th to 15th century and 17th and 18th century, with a brief dip also in the mid-19th century) and the population of Western Europe declined by a third in the mid-14th century, reviving again only a century and a half later. The African population is estimated to have remained more or less stable, possibly for thousands of years, until the 19th century and the American population was decimated over the century following the arrival of the Europeans, then rose again slowly until the 18th century.

As already referred to, the massive, exponential growth in human pressure on the biosphere that we see today is closely linked in increasingly complex ways to the exponential extraction and use of fossilised energy resources.

However, the engagement of human populations with Nature in terms of exploitation of ecological resources, with ever more efficient forms of farming and livestock raising, thereby modifying and then displacing whole ecosystems, has been a clear path trodden by humanity over a longer time span that, nevertheless, has resulted in many places in stable relationships between particular societies and their environment over very long periods of time and, if these had been made conscious in the sense of a clear understanding of the limits to particular interventions (for example: stocking of pasture, planting of crops, exploitation of fisheries and forests) could have continued indefinitely. A vast amount of research, wonderfully summarised by Jared Diamond[218], has revealed when and where, species by species, plants and animals were domesticated and thence cultivated and spread by human populations, progressively displacing pre-existing ecosystems[219], and turning nature progressively into a function of human life[220].

In practice, no culture has had any clear or coherent awareness of the impacts it has upon nature in the form of any kind of scientific analysis and set of rules. We might say that it is simply a matter of experience and prudence as a dimension of the innate wisdom embodied in certain cultures that has grown out of this experience – and, it can hardly be denied, also a matter of good fortune — that has facilitated the longevity of some civilisations. Whilst the failure or 'collapse' of particular cultures has been a regular occurrence across the history of civilisation, this has rarely been the consequence of just one cause. Nevertheless, over-exploitation and depletion of local ecological resources — in some sense what economists refer to as 'diminishing returns to scale' — has featured as one, and sometimes an important causal factor[221]. Elsewhere, this has been referred to as 'overshoot'[222], in that the process of depletion is usually evident decades or even centuries before the actual collapse, the eventual collapse being a function of the symptoms being ignored or the society lacking the imagination or political conjuncture necessary to avoid the emerging situation and hence failing to develop a more coherent perspective on the problems and their causes and thence a failure to adapt[223].

It is here that we find ourselves confronted again with the problematic of the ideology of progress in its most virulent form, as it impinges on the instrumental way in which Occidental society has confronted nature. As we will see below in the discussion of science and technology, progress, in terms of the relationship between our society and nature is where the present sustainability crisis comes to as head. Wherever Occidental culture has extended its power and ideology, it has intervened in order to exploit resources to its own end and within this culture the ends of its elites. The role of colonialism and the emergence of the Commercial Ideology (and capitalism), as machinery to yield wealth, has already been referred to. In some cases — notably the early years of the colonisation of what is now Latin America — this was no better than plunder of a kind that could be found right across the history of empires. When deepened to produce streams of wealth over longer periods through more intensive engagement with nature, it came, in principle, in an open-ended way where there was never a notion of an end state where a plateau of 'sustainable yield' might be achieved that could be maintained into the indefinite future.

Whilst today the most proximate break point where this trail comes to an end is in the imminent decline of the availability of fossil energy resources, in practice we can look across a whole series of 'unsustainable situations' that over a relatively short period will, even if energy resources were to continue to be available, result in the decline of yields[224]. Thus whilst many situations can be presented where, following a descent into the exploitation of geological resources until exhausted and the over-exploitation of ecological resources, the general trail leads inexorably back to Bacon's 'extension of power and dominion over nature' that is in reality the rout and plunder of the planet. As warnings have arisen over the past half century with the acceleration of problems — particularly the warnings emanating from the Green Movement — increasingly elaborate technical mechanisms were introduced, ranging from environmental impact assessment and regulations to reduce environmental impacts of industrial production, to recycling of domestic waste and latterly 'carbon trading'.

However, no framework criteria were ever seriously introduced to indicate how effective any of these or other measures might be in reducing environmental impacts in a comprehensive manner, where in practice effective evaluative criteria could have been formulated and thence much less complicated measures introduced to curb impacts. These were, however, simply dismissed or avoided without due consideration. These would, of course, have necessitated a fundamentally different approach to the use of resources and the environment that recognised limits and thus would have brought progress, in terms of accumulation of wealth as presently understood, to a halt and this was simply unthinkable within the Occidental ideological framework[225].

This did not inevitably have to be so in terms of some negative teleology or 'working out of human nature'. There can, indeed, be no doubt about placing the responsibility for this upon the general ambience and sleazy lifestyle generated by the Commercial Ideology and its liberal underpinning. The belief so pithily encapsulated in Adam Smith's famous assertion that we not concern ourselves with the consequences of following our own personal interests because the 'invisible hand' of 'the market' ensures that the interests of society will look after themselves, is constantly reiterated by economistic theory and propaganda (one thinks, above all, of the Economist journal). This has always encouraged a fatal lack of responsibility for the general welfare and the future on the part of Occidental societies. And it should also be evident that this attitude is not an issue of 'human nature,' when almost all other cultures have demonstrated the possibility of organising society in a manner that is self-correcting with regard to the interests of its members.

Later in this chapter we discuss those serious attempts that have been made over the past two centuries to find ways to conceptualise the predicament that has been developing with regard to the systematic depletion of environmental resources and to suggest approaches within the prevailing paradigm that might address the problem of depletion effectively. Here we will see what other approaches could have been taken to construct evaluative frameworks and thence take action to stabilise resource use onto genuinely sustainable tracks. First, however, it is necessary to look in greater detail at the world of thought and action that is driving the world to environmental degradation and collapse — namely the world of modern consumption.

Consumption

Whilst in this chapter we are analysing environmental questions, it is here also necessary to connect these to the social and ideological machinery of what today is the rout of the biosphere. It will be recalled that of the two perspectives that inform modern life as they emerged from the Enlightenment, the Commercial Ideology as propounded at the end of the 17th century most clearly by Mandeville and elevated to a moral outlook by Adam Smith, saw the accumulation of wealth as the ultimate goal of life. Whilst Calvin, in approving of the accumulation of wealth in the eyes of God did, however, call for modesty in consumption and that wealth be used as capital to create more wealth (hence capitalism) after Mandeville and his associates this modesty was called into question and whilst a residue remained in the sense of there being a notion of greed and ostentation beyond which it might be 'bad taste' to venture, step by step conspicuous consumption became increasingly in evidence as an approved characteristic of Occidental culture. Following the failure of the non-revolution of 1968, ostentatious consumption, in the form of the Consumer Society, moved centre stage and it is this that is the true motor of environmental destruction today. Already in 1955, the economist Victor Lebow, in an obscure article in the *Journal of Retailing*[226], expressed the situation perfectly in the following terms:

Our enormously productive economy demands that we make consumption our way of life, that we convert the buying and use of goods into rituals, that we seek our spiritual satisfactions, our ego satisfactions, in consumption. The measure of social status, of social acceptance, of prestige, is now to be found in our consumptive patterns. The very meaning and significance of our lives today expressed in consumptive terms. The greater the pressures upon the individual to conform to safe and accepted social standards, the more does he tend to express his aspirations and his individuality in terms of what he wears, drives, eats- his home, his car, his pattern of food serving, his hobbies.

These commodities and services must be offered to the consumer with a special urgency. We require not only 'forced draft' consumption, but 'expensive' consumption as well. We need things consumed, burned up, worn out, replaced, and discarded at an ever increasing pace. We need to have people eat, drink, dress, ride, live, with ever more complicated and, therefore, constantly more expensive consumption.

The home power tools and the whole "do-it-yourself" movement are excellent examples of 'expensive' consumption.

Before embarking on a 'critique of present day consumption', it is germane to make reference to the way in which this has been debated academically in recent years. Until some twenty years ago, the concept of 'consumption' was a concern that in analytical terms was almost exclusively the purview of economists. Although ostensibly a science and therefore posed as 'value free', the normative foundation of economics is clearly to aid and abet the accumulation of wealth. In fact, whilst ostensibly critical of consumption in the context of capitalism, and despite the apparently critical notion of 'commodity fetishism', Marxism is also concerned with creating a world of affluence, the difference being that this would involve an egalitarian distribution of wealth and hence seemingly have an entirely different meaning from the status-confirming characteristics of consumption in a capitalist world.

The extreme efflorescence of consumption as a social phenomenon emerging globally at the end of the 1960s (albeit in the United States already immediately following the Second World War) became an increasing focus of critical attention of the Green Movement and eventually academic disciplines other than economics. Each of these possesses a different attitude in terms of sympathy or hostility towards the phenomenon and hence different analytical approaches[227]. In this context, there arose a conflict between those participants in the proliferating discourse who insisted on maintaining academic distance ('objectivity') and those genuinely concerned with the increasingly horrific consequences of rampant consumerism in terms of its social and environmental consequences and, indeed, how life, work and the physical world was increasingly structured around it[228]. At this end, the notion of 'sustainable consumption'[229] entered the field and much has been written in an attempt to discover the wellsprings of the phenomenon in order to find tools to diffuse rampant consumerism — or at least its clear negative consequences. The outlook and approach taken in the following paragraphs is one that emerges from the foregoing discussion and should therefore need no further location in the landscape of academic discourse.

'Consumption' denotes in principle the using up of materials and artefacts, destroying them as a stage in the metabolism of life. Humans have to consume to survive. The issue is, however, what and how much. Human societies might be reduced at times to a point where consumption is at a level that it does no more than sustain life at survival levels. However, humans live in communities which evolve ways of life and lifestyles in the context of which consumption takes place, such as the eating of meals, the use of materials to make tools to assist in creating particular cultures that clothe people and build houses and, creating platforms on which to carry out religious rites, organise education and maintain good health. And all of this becomes ritualised and evolves symbolism and aesthetics that give things and processes and artefacts meaning beyond their sheer utility. Indeed, utility is never pure but is always clothed in layers of meaning and value to the consumers, that in total are woven together to constitute an organic culture — even modern culture. We cannot escape from the symbol, ritual and aesthetics through which we make sense of our communal lives, and modes of consumption are an essential dimension subsumed within the whole.

Certainly in hunter-gathering societies, consumption is but a minor dimension of life — unless we talk of the 'consumption of leisure'. Even in more sophisticated societies until very recent times, almost all members of the vast majority of communities consumed at modest levels with consumption as an activity in itself occupying but little mental space and time spent in living. Of course for the most part this was a consequence of the greater time taken up in the work of production and the modest incomes available to the vast majority of populations to indulge in consumption as a discrete activity.

Today, however, in the context of modern society, the concept of consumption has evolved an entirely new meaning, as the vast variety of materials and goods consumed per individual and the process and context in which goods are produced to be consumed reach their final destination. The concept of consumption has further extended to entertainment where time is consumed in the consumption of virtual sights and sounds over a significant part of the day of the average — such that we now refer to people as — 'consumers'.

Consumption as 'consumerism' has become something analogous to religious catharsis with overtones of sexuality and is in general imbued with an emotional undertow associated with the process of status satisfaction, involving enormously elaborated rituals tethered to, and physically sustained by, the complex Technostructure. Key to understanding what is happening is to see this as the goal and apotheosis of the Commercial Ideology and the striving for status: 'to have', or even in the case of children and television or the viewing of sports events or undertaking tourist activities: 'to have participated in'. In most cases, it is not so much consumption that is at issue but rather the question of *acquisition*: The present phase of Modern society is obsessed with acquisition of Stuff as proof of status — much consumption having as little meaning as the disposal of things that have been acquired and to spend time in each of the stages of the consumption event, including, importantly, the movement – most commonly sitting in or driving an automobile - to and from events where money was spent.

At the top of the pyramid of the 'Religion of Consumption', or rather Acquisition, today is the activity of shopping that, recognised in many as an obsessive activity under the title of 'shopaholism', has become an important time and emotion-consuming pastime of the 'consuming classes,' with incomes that facilitate the purchase of a constant stream of materials and goods and participation in vicarious entertainment. Even large sections of urban populations in both North and South with more modest incomes spend time doing no more than wandering the city streets and the corridors of shopping malls, gazing at and absorbing the kaleidoscope of lights and images, logos and commodities, accompanied in supermarkets and shopping malls by a constant stream of music, advertising and other thought-erasing sights and sounds.

Acquisition — be it through the real-estate agent or the car sales outlet, the department store or supermarket, the local store or the weekly market or through internet purchasing at ebay, amazon or a whole world of virtual shopping outlets — is the cathartic moment in what amounts to an orgiastic, quasi-religious experience of shopping today, even when those undertaking the activity pretend that this is but a utilitarian process of satisfying their needs. Clearly, whilst this might have been promoted through the rational decisions of elites in government and commerce, in recent years, perspective has been entirely lost in a mass phenomenon well beyond any structured capacity to control or redirect. The ostensibly functionalist nature of Occidental culture has departed far into the realms of the ritualistic, away from any meaningful notion of consumption as a utilitarian function.

The shopping experience is thus a vitally important expression of our lifestyle and is linked closely to the personal self-expression that is the essential outward manifestation of this. Locke's self-commodification is expressed less in work activity and more in clothing and body language, being seen: moving amongst the crowd, in 'work,' in social situations and gatherings of friends and family. This then extends to the desire to be seen in the public eye, in the vast proliferation of lifestyle magazines, the press and television. Fragments of earlier forms of social and self-expression as lifestyle survive: religious rituals, artistic events and the appreciation of aesthetically created objects with which we are surrounded as human environment. But recent years has seen the ever greater focus on the present hour, the present moment as all-important and all-consuming, with the savouring and contemplation of the aesthetic curtailed by the sheer melange and jostling of the next event, the next commodity acquired, urged on by an accelerating flow of images: the sheer frenetic drive of the modern consumer lifestyle.

It is said that within six months of purchase, ninety nine per cent of that which has been acquired by American consumers has found its way into the waste stream[230]. On average the Occidental citizen eats over ten per cent more food in terms of calorific value than their bodies can absorb, resulting in obesity and eventually serious health problems. However, they consume substantially less than the upper limit so that between a quarter and a half of food purchased finds its way into the waste stream without being eaten. Whilst this could be fed to animals to be recycled as meat, in practice it goes down the 'insinkerator' or into the garbage to be landfilled.

In addition, diets have been progressively increasing the amount of meat consumed, with decreasing amounts of carbohydrate. Americans consume twice the amount of animal protein than is recommendable for a balanced diet and Europeans and even Latin Americans are probably not far behind; even the Chinese diet is rapidly changing in the same direction. Livestock require many times the amount of carbohydrate to produce a given amount of meat and around the world diets have progressively increased meat consumption and decreased carbohydrate which is, rather, being fed to animals to produce meat. Grain fed to American livestock, using vast quantities of agrochemicals and water, could feed as many as 800 million people on a more balanced diet[231].

Where the houses of rich families, from palaces to 'stately homes' were not only in Occidental culture but throughout complex societies almost always the primary expression of superior status, the translation of this into the modern suburban house has become a major component of the Consumer Society, producing endless suburban tracts, increasingly dispersed over vast landscapes beyond the edge of erstwhile cities. Initially in the United States but increasingly also in Europe and starting even on the edges of Latin American and Asia cities, this expression of consumption status is becoming the Achilles Heel of a society about to experience reduction in energy that will rapidly render this lifestyle impossible for an increasing majority to continue[232].

Automobiles have become the second largest expenditure item, after housing, for the average modern consumer. In principle, cars can run quite frugally on as little as a hundred miles per US gallon of petrol, and experimental cars have been run on over one thousand. Cars available on the market, however, generally run between fifteen and forty miles per US gallon. Endless discussion is raised about achieving greater energy efficiency — through 'hybrid cars' or eventually simply with more fuel-efficient engines — and substitutes for petroleum using hydrogen or electric cars are supposed to overcome the problems of rising prices and diminishing fuel availability that we will be facing.

This debate is, however, perfectly absurd in that the latter options actually use considerably more energy per mile driven than conventional smaller cars and the fact remains that few consumers focus much attention on the issue of fuel use as an issue when cars are purchased. Then comes the question of the resources and energy used in producing cars which, again, is well beyond what is necessary to accomplish the ostensible purpose of the car. Finally, few questions are asked about the reasons for continually growing amounts of time spent travelling in cars and the importance attaching to this travel[233]. By now the automobile industry is, in addition, the greatest consumer of a wide range of resources and cars the fastest growing consumer of petroleum worldwide.

The list of absurd levels of wastage that are directly connected to the 'Religion of Consumption' is endless. The purchase of shoes and clothing that are used only once and then discarded — some of which are then shipped to 'poor' countries, putting local tailors out of work — is a further illustration of this wastage; also, the vast proliferation of household goods that may be used once or twice and then accumulate in cupboards or basements or lofts with no further use. And even when used more intensively, the manufacturers see to it that the life of their goods will be limited by 'built-in obsolescence', both through wearing out and non-reliability and through changes in style and specification that is then used to convince consumers to replace items well before these reach the end of their useful life.

It is instructive to obtain perspective on just how grotesquely wasteful this lifestyle is in terms of the use of resources for functions that could be undertaken equally well with far less resources, and how it has spread to elites and new middle classes beyond the Occident, in what only a few generations ago were radically different cultural attitudes. We can observe, furthermore, how vast populations beyond the Occident with very modest incomes, especially in Asia, are able to emulate Occidental lifestyles at as little as a tenth or less of the cost in money terms and in terms of actual throughput of materials and commodities.

What is truly tragic is the way in which these populations are today seduced into emulating not simply Occidental lifestyles as aesthetic, but increasingly also the self-identification with commodities and competition for status that is the ethos and driving force behind the lifestyle, with its obsessive insistence on acquisition and personal accumulation. Mutualism, particularly amongst extended families, remains a significant dimension of life support systems and distribution, but increasingly the dimension of individualistic competition becomes more powerful, particularly when in the process of leaving rural communities and becoming urban citizens.

This brings us back to the fact of consumption and acquisitiveness as core dimensions of Occidental culture, that have grown to grotesque proportions and which, with the demise of modernity, will necessarily, perhaps thankfully, recede again into the background and sadly return for all too many into a desperate struggle for survival which untold numbers will lose. Doubtless, for perhaps most of those for whom it is a quiet retreat rather than a struggle, this will be accompanied by a deep sense of emptiness for the vast majority of modern populations and here we must point to two principles around which consumption will need to be brought back into a reasonable perspective and with a reasonable level of throughput of materials and goods.

Principle One is to understand consumption in terms of the satisfaction of basic needs clearing away the layers of over-consumption and accumulation of the recent past. As communities we might choose to go through a 'final catharsis' following personal and community discussions and decisions as to what 'need' might mean in a post-consumer world, rejecting most of the excess accumulation. This could proceed through the establishment of warehouses where the excess could be deposited. In many cities in the Occident, such depositories (such as the international charity Emmaus that has depository/shops in hundreds of towns and cities across Europe) do in fact exist for second-hand garments and other commodities. A major problem will evolve out of the demise of automobile culture, where increasing numbers of people will no longer be able to afford to drive any significant distances. Depositories will need to be found for the vast numbers of defunct cars that will increasingly be unwanted but already crowd out and infest city streets and car parks. Decisions will need to be taken about where and how these should be reutilised or disposed of.

Substantial employment will emerge to sort, repair and organise the goods. Increasingly much of this, besides cars, will have no further use: already televisions, computers and other electronic and electrical goods are deemed to be 'obsolete' within a few short years, even though still in working order. But as energy supplies decline, they will become strictly unusable. Then as time passes the issue will become more urgent as to how to reuse, how to recycle and remanufacture the materials embodied in these artefacts into goods — there will be vast quantities of steel, plastic and glass embodied in defunct automobiles — to render the materials reusable in the emergent conditions and then how to distribute these to satisfy radically redefined needs. These issues are further aired in Chapter Six, including discussion of how decisions might be taken regarding the administrative aspects of this process.

Principle Two concerns the lifestyle aesthetics within which future consumption will be subsumed. In recent times the aesthetics of everyday life have not only become crowded with goods designed by corporate producers to stimulate and then invade the vicarious whims and fantasies of Consumers, but increasingly, as in the case of cars, subject to individual choice regarding colour, 'trim', accessories, etc. This has produced in the social sphere a cacophony of visual and oral noise, overwhelming the senses and within which there is no longer any space for rest or contemplation. Furthermore, the creative impulse expressed in the past by being in contact with work that actually produced materials and objects and allowed for the expression of workers in terms of aesthetic satisfaction has been smothered, initially through the mechanics of industrialisation, and today by the deluge of Stuff designed and made elsewhere and in such a manner that nobody in the process can have more than an extremely fragmented experience of the joy of creation in their lives.

In the past, in traditional societies up to the present and even in village life in the Occident until into the 20th century, most of the aesthetics of everyday life were a community affair. Diets relied on local produce and changed throughout the year, with the availability of produce by season and cuisines were developed as the translation of available produce into the aesthetics of fine taste. Vernacular architecture might evolve over time but over longer periods, in some cases over millennia, little changed in the commonly accepted way that people expressed their needs in the form of the houses they themselves built and lived in[234]. The clothing and immediate accoutrements of life — furniture, kitchen and tableware, items of pure decoration — were of a common design whilst being open, within the general functional design, to variation and imaginative reworking and could be identified with as the physical extension of an organised life process of the community.

In many parts of the world, in spite of the insistent spread of consumerism, this external expression remained modest, either because of the meagre resources available or because the aesthetic sensibilities remained at a simple level. But, as discussed earlier with the cases of Bali and Bhutan, even at a very modest level of existence in terms of resource availability and use, a highly developed aesthetic life could be achieved and what we know of the European past indicates — particularly in what remains of vernacular villages and farmhouses before the advent of industrialisation — also here a well-developed sense of the aesthetic could be found to be almost universal amongst the common people.

Another insight can be obtained when we view the lifestyle of certain religious communities, notably in the Orient, but including also the Amish and Hutterites who emigrated to the United States in past centuries. These have survived and proliferated as communities that have largely resisted the modernisation process in terms both of industrialisation and especially attitudes to consumption. Of particular interest here is to look more closely at the community decision-making processes that have confirmed the community aesthetic as lifestyle and in terms of the commodities that they choose to produce and use in this context. Most well-known in this context are the horse-drawn carriages of the Amish, where they have resisted the use of the internal combustion engine. However, the attitude of considering very carefully what to allow and what not to allow by way of modifications to the lifestyle, and the community decision-making that controls this, are profound lessons for the future of all Occidental societies.

Ruling classes since the earliest times of civilisation, and in recent centuries the growing urban bourgeois, took the aesthetics of daily life to a more developed level, often distorted as a means to demonstrate their superiority, and then initiated the processes of expressing status through changing styles. None of this is necessary and, as discussed in the final chapter in this book, aesthetics can and should be developed in particular settings to achieve inclusion, cohesion and the good life for all. Consumption will have to be developed almost entirely within the confines of local sub-regional resources and so the revival of local lifestyles following the demise of the global will need to develop dialectically as between resource availability and limits, via production processes to local consumption patterns defined in a common aesthetic.

We cannot end the discussion of consumption and the aesthetic without reference to the transition process as understood in the concept of Transition Towns (and cities). As mentioned above, a key moment in transition will come with the rejection of excess commodities and establishment of warehouses for these. But it is not merely movable goods that may be deposited in warehouses and car graveyards. Even much of the built environment will become increasingly unusable, from high-rise buildings where ventilation, lifts and lighting no longer function, to suburban developments that are too dense to form peasant villages (gardens too small to grow very much and too far from any land where sufficient food can be grown or from any community support facilities) and so will no longer be able to function as residences.

So the transition will involve migrations and the formation of new communities, initially in vast numbers of places in the midst of the now dysfunctional remains of existing built environments or by removing building materials from these to build and consolidate new communities which can easily obtain food from the surrounding countryside and can start to rebuild production systems congruent with an emergent new local aesthetic of life. Scrap materials will become the immediate basis for reconstruction: plastics remoulded, concrete fragmented into hardcore, metals reshaped, glass cut to new sizes, bricks and timber recovered and re-used.

However, this will be transient in that within decades this will degenerate and have to be replaced by genuinely local materials that can be harvested sustainably from Nature and the local stock of mineral resources. Perhaps there will be communities that largely reject the transition, abandoning modern goods and built environments entirely to decay over the years and decades as monumental lessons to the ludicrous absurdity of the modern hubris, immediately searching for an aesthetic of sustainable living from the natural resources of the sub-region.

Environmental Influences on the Construction of Culture

We analysed above how changing climates have, in the past, been an essential dimension of the way in which ecosystems evolved and we might add to this how individual species evolved morphologically to create their own ecological niches. Homo sapiens, however, seemingly broke loose from the tethers of particular ecosystems by developing cultures adapted eventually to almost all the world's ecosystems. So perhaps we should not pay any attention to the notion that environment might be an influence on the character of human beings.

However, this has been a focus of attention since at least the Enlightenment[235], so there is some purpose in enquiring into the debates, and asking what has motivated these and looking at the conclusions that have been drawn by various participants at various times. More to the point, these debates have been deeply contentious, being a foundation for racism over the past two centuries. It is therefore of interest to start from Rousseau, given his critical perspective on his own society. In his *Discourse on the Origin and Foundations of Inequality* discussed earlier[236], he gave some thought to non-Occidental societies, about which little of an empathetic considered kind was known at the time and, in a lengthy appendix (J) entitled *The Diversity of climates, air, foods, way of life and habits in General* laid out a programme for what could have been an unprejudiced programme for anthropology.

Had this programme been developed in the framework of his critical view of inequality, perhaps anthropology would have become a powerful tool for disseminating attitudes of respect for other cultures where the climate was not seen in any way in prejudicial terms, in the hands of those wishing to recreate more equal societies. However, instead, the 19th and early 20th centuries were marked by belligerent Occidental racism, where climate and geography were given as reasons for the putative inferiority of non-European races. It is easy enough to find texts to illustrate and here we present a classic passage from Hegel's philosophy of history:

*The torrid and frigid regions, as such, are not the theatre on which world history is enacted. In this respect, such extremes are incompatible with spiritual freedom. All in all, it is therefore the **temperate zone** which must furnish the theatre of world history... America has always shown itself physically and spiritually impotent.... Even the animals show the same inferiority as the human beings... anyone who wishes to study the most terrible manifestations of human nature will find them in Africa.*[237]

On a less philosophical note, Marx, in reviewing this theme, quoted a London merchant writing 1669 as follows:

Nor can I conceive a greater curse upon a body of people than to be thrown upon a spot of land, where the productions for subsistence and food were, in great measure, spontaneous, and the climate required or admitted little care for raiment and covering.[238]

In Chapter Three we discussed how 19th century British evolutionism justified colonialism and the exploitation of non-European lands and people as a result of 'inevitable evolutionary trends' and arguments concerning the effects of climate and geography were further used to reinforce this attitude and the practices that followed from this.

In the course of the 19th and first half of the 20th century, all manner of means were introduced in Occidental culture to 'prove' the superiority of particular people — white versus black, northern Europeans versus Southern, and even Germans versus the French and Slavs. The 'scientific' disciplines that emerged included phrenology, supposedly 'proving' that some head and face shapes indicate superiority or inferiority of particular races. Then 'intelligence tests' were developed to provide 'objective' means to distinguish between better and worse people. Eugenics was invented by Darwin's cousin, Francis Galton, as the 'science' of 'breeding' superior people as the ultimate corollary to Darwin's dismal interpretation of nature. This remained as the background to the continued ill-treatment of indigenous peoples in Australia and the Americas and the final phases of colonisation of Africa by the European nations.

With the demise of colonialism, the open expression of racism became more muted and the belief was disseminated, particularly in the context of Development in the immediate post-colonial era, that eventually we might expect there to emerge a mutual respect amongst all races. However, even today, with the triumph of a 'coloured' President of the United States, unthinking and unspoken racial prejudice continues as evidenced by the systematically inferior work and wealth of non-Occidentals across the world and in the inane ranking of countries in terms of GDP, which in practice almost universally indicates which peoples are being exploited by which and which are the exploiters, and where there is an absolutely clear hierarchy with very few exceptions to the dominance of Occidental societies. Discussion of the issue of possible environmental influences on culture has, however, been suppressed by a tacit collusion of the oppressed and the oppressors: firstly because it is seen by those suffering prejudice as an insult and secondly because to do so highlights the de facto allocation of inferior status to other races where climate may be implicated and that could become the basis for a structured critique of the global racial hierarchy.

Of course racism is found also in non-Occidental cultures, almost everywhere as part of the problematic of prejudice against difference and the assertion of power, but the Occidental case, elevated to a structural dimension of the international exploitative hierarchy imposed upon the rest of the world, needs to be confronted head on and laid to rest.

Perhaps we should start by turning the messianic prejudice of Occidental culture concerning the issue of 'the theatre of world history' and pride in the progressive nature of capitalism on its head. That is to say that the notion of the superiority of Occidentals, today no longer given words but expressed in their superior economic status, is not merely questionable but is fundamentally flawed insofar as it is they who are bringing the relation between humanity and the rest of the biosphere into ever deepening crisis. In this context the Occidental population is pathological. If the great quest for Progress and Development has brought us only to the edge of the destruction of the biosphere, then it is necessary to consider the temperate climate and in general the European setting from which it emanated in a harshly critical light.

Let us simply state that unlike the tropics, indeed unlike even the southern parts of Europe, the climate of northern Europe is not easy to live in without considerable planning and organisation to survive long winters and to ensure that in the warmer months enough is accumulated to survive through the winter. In fact through much of the Middle Ages, communities were subjected to recurrent famines[239], such that there was clear motivation to find more effective ways to produce a more secure life and to construct more congenial lifestyles. Calvin's 'work ethic' — what Weber in his analysis referred to as 'worldly asceticism' — as religious confirmation of hard work as a moral cause simply gave a commercial orientation to deep-seated anxieties concerning the need to work for survival. This is clearly in contrast to the situation of people living in warmer climates where, turning the above quotation on its head, a good life can be lived with relatively little planning or work, given the fecundity of nature in this climatic setting and relatively light needs for clothing, housing or any more permanent accoutrements of life.

Of course the matter is not simple. Many other peoples experience harsh living conditions that have not turned this into a mission to subjugate other people and the environment. What is being said here, rather, is that environmental conditions have been a further dimension forming the character, ideology and culture of the Northern European. In the case of (northern) China, with similar climatic challenges, a basic philosophy that sought an ultimately satisfactory lifestyle — and on the whole found it — there was no structured attempt at 'improvement' even though, as Joseph Needham's monumental study of science and technology in China amply shows[240], incremental improvements were in fact continually invented. This was within what otherwise was a stable general framework and foundation, and notwithstanding periods where natural resources were depleted, benign in terms of its long-term ecological impact. In the case of northern Europe, with its apocalyptic, 'progressivist' ideology, there was never a point at which it might be said: 'Stop! We have now achieved what for us can be deemed to be 'the good life' in equilibrium with our ecological setting'.

So we can conjecture that climate and ecological conditions have combined with the Progressivist ideology to motivate the (particularly northern) Europeans to 'improve' their living conditions, moving out of what until the end of the Middle Ages was a defensive strategy[241] towards nature to an aggressive stance that went out to plunder nature in the rest of the world's regions and thence, across the past few decades, has continued to coerce and seduce the whole of humanity into participating in the rout and plunder of nature for short-term gains. What we are saying here is that, insofar as the opportunity arises to reconstruct local societies after the fall of modernity, the influence of climate and setting must be seen as proactive partners in the process of reconstruction and not as an enemy to be conquered.

Thus if we want to look for 'superiority' amongst races and cultures then we will find it amongst those peoples that have established a sustainable relationship with their environment, including both cultural and ultimately biological adaptation and thence built 'beautiful' cultural expression upon this. Here Occidental culture certainly doesn't qualify, for all the pride in its cultural legacy in terms of the arts. Of course, the very notion of a hierarchy of peoples and cultures is only meaningful in a world of growing interconnection in which the notion of competition is a vital characteristic. Once the notion of a 'global society' recedes into the background, it becomes ridiculous to talk of superior and inferior where each society is a qualitatively different entity, relevant predominantly to its own particular environment rather than part of any universal, globalised hierarchy of a putative theatre of world history.

Many anthropologists were, indeed, not only sympathetic towards the subjects of their studies but, standing in their situation, were critical of the modernisation process that was destroying all other cultures. The accumulation of anthropological studies over the 20th century revealed, particularly through those anthropologists such as Carl Sauer, Julian Steward, and John W Bennett, and indeed many less known scholars, that specifically focusing on the relationship between ecological setting and the structure and function of particular cultures is instructive in helping us to reflect on how, in the future, following the radical failure of Occidental culture, the reconnection of particular social and environmental systems might be effectuated.

Thus we see around the world how the location of populations, their distribution, their proliferation and migrations and thence harnessing of the possibilities of particular ecosystems in specific locations, was deeply influenced by geography and climate. Hence moving beyond hunting and gathering, into agriculture and then the 'finer' dimensions of civilisation was, in the first instance, overwhelmingly in response to that which nature and geological realities (particularly once industrialisation had taken off) made available. The climatic conditions then moulded the further development of civilisations where survival meant more than the immediate daily harvesting of what nature produced. And finally, the environmental context in which peoples found themselves gently coaxed them to make improvements to lifestyles and moderating local climates through vernacular architecture. This in turn influenced orientation and attitudes of people towards one another – how they might better organise their own societies and relations – and with this attitudes towards others whose own environed attitudes differed from their own.

Of course urbanisation and even suburbanisation — that by now involves over half of humanity living in cities and towns — and with this the process of industrialisation extending across the globe, put at a great distance the relationship between people and environment, creating increasingly man-made environments and mental frames where sensitivity to climate and local ecological and physical resources has systematically diminished. Furthermore, the mixing of peoples that has occurred over recent decades with mass migrations from South to North and people of the North working, living or holidaying in the South seems to have rendered the whole issue of the relationship between people and their immediate environment to be irrelevant.

Meanwhile, 'indigenous people' that had in the past adapted to their environment have moved elsewhere or been crowded out in their own home territory by peoples from quite other environments who are overwhelmingly insensitive to their new environment and/or use technologies (air conditioning, heating, lighting, etc.) to create the kind of environment they originated in and/or wish to live in, largely disregarding the realities of the environment they now inhabit or the sustainability of this artificialisation.

However, both through anthropological studies of how different cultures adapted to their environments and, in turn, were moulded by these, and through the residue of our own past cultures, we can learn much that will doubtless be of use in re-adapting to local environments as the globalised world, and with it the power to distance ourselves from our immediate environment, recedes and the surviving populations have to learn to live in, and generally reconcile themselves once again with, their surroundings. The remains of vernacular buildings that were built with local materials and provided living and working environments for local cultures that evolved over time to be adapted to shelter from rain and wind, heat and cold, are in most cases particularly instructive[242]. Whilst cultures everywhere that created these buildings have been damaged or completely destroyed, the buildings, nevertheless, have survived to surprising degrees as testament to their appropriateness to local conditions. Local searches can surely turn up a wealth of information on how people adapted to their local environments in the past, in most cases having departed from these traditions within this or at most the preceding generation.

Science and Technology

The Occidental Ideology of Progress and quest for Development can be seen historically as the quest to find a systematic route, particularly to unlock the resources of the earth and yield them up to the productive process that would bring progress down from abstraction to concrete reality in terms of lived experience and ways of life[243]. What might be referred to as the mythology of science is that it comprises an 'objective' method to 'explain' the natural world as a basis for accessing resources to turn them into commodities and eventually improve our lives. Although science is popularly seen as yielding pure knowledge, as we will see, scientific knowledge is not of a coherent piece, being made up of a great number of theories and empirical observations which involve many contradictions. In practice it is closer to the truth to see it as being handmaiden to the Commercial Ideology and in general the accumulation of physical capital and supply of consumer goods — and at the same time, the means to assert power by the powerful and thence support the development of the means to win wars and dominate populations.

Interest in a more objective, less ideologically obscured view of how science arose as an important dimension of Occidental culture started in the middle years of the 20th century and expanded into the sociology and philosophy of science, from the 1980s becoming the focus of attention of those concerned with the environmental consequences of science and particularly the technologies that science made possible[244]. Some attention was paid to the notion that modern science might have its origins in Christianity but this essentially drew a blank. Christian texts are quite unconcerned with 'nature', and, in the end merely provide rather weak moral orientation concerning how she should be used (suggesting only a vague concept of 'stewardship', or looking after nature as producing for human needs). This is not, however, the whole story.

The medieval conception of nature, as appearing in the seven days of God's work of the creation, advances out of the Dark Ages and into the Middle Ages in the form of the Great Chain of Being[245]: a hierarchical structure with mankind occupying a place between the angels and the animal kingdom. It was a static, given structure of no particular interest with regard to how nature might be made use of. The practical use of nature was, quite independently, an issue for the common people on the land for whom animistic beliefs continued in Europe even into the 19th century[246], eliminated only through mass urbanisation and the decline in rural vernacular culture generally.

The beginnings of the ideology of science lie in the Renaissance re-discovery of Greek and other ancient speculation about nature. Whilst the main concern of the rediscovery of antiquity was to produce more grand and luxuriant expression of the wealth that was accumulating in Italy, the rediscovery of ancient literature stimulated new trains of thinking, resulting in the founding of new academies outside the established Universities with their deeply Christian-impregnated studies concerned as they were with spiritual/theological matters involving people and society, rather than anything by way of the natural reality that was the physical support of societies. Much speculation on nature found in ancient texts was not far beyond its animistic origins and implied an organicist and contemplative, even reverential attitude (analogous to Taoism) that was only tangentially concerned with the uses to which nature might be put.

In contrast to the medieval concept of nature as the residue of God's creation, the neo-Platonist and Hermetic conceptions that were initially at the centre of Renaissance thought on nature, asserted that Nature *is* God. The theologians were not, however, content to give way to an essentially pagan, animist belief and, in reasserting the separation of nature and God, yielded up what had now come into the foreground of European intellectual endeavour, to a more instrumental attitude.

Francis Bacon, writing at the start of the 17th century, is seen today as the most effective advocate for the early development of science. He proposed an empirical research methodology for unlocking the secrets of nature, proclaiming that whilst conquest of peoples and countries might be a morally questionable undertaking, this was not the case with nature, which was there to be conquered[247]. There was no question as to whether there might be a need to treat nature kindly or awareness that the conquest of Nature might eventually be the destruction of the source of human existence: nature was there to 'relieve man's estate' and in time progressive discovery would yield great wealth and a better life.

Bacon's inductive method proved inadequate as a tool for effective scientific discovery and when Newton came to lay what, until the 20th century, was deemed to be the correct perspective on discovering the truth about nature, he did this coming out of an education in the final flowering of Neo-Platonism, wedded to Baconian empiricism, that essentially laid the foundation of what we might call the dialectic of scientific discovery. Arguably the first systematic scientific research programme can be traced back to the 'Invisible College' (precursor of the British Royal Society) the foundation of which coincided with the mid-17th century English Revolution. The members of the Invisible College were seeking solutions to practical problems facing expanding commercialism: increasing production from mines (investigating scientific problems related to pumping and ventilation), increasing navigational skills (investigations into mathematics and astronomy) and increasing military efficiency (investigations into ballistics).

Thus viewed in retrospect, we see that science became a focused programme to accumulate wealth and power hidden (we might say deeply and hypocritically) behind a facade of the accumulation of knowledge as the source of wisdom. It is quite unabashedly a project to progressively analyse how Nature works in order to take it apart and reconstruct it in the service of 'society' — read power[248]. And furthermore, 'scientific theories' could be used as ideological tools to bludgeon the people into believing that there's should not be to question why. The situation of Darwin described above is a classic case where, being generally portrayed as a scientific sage, he lent an aura of moral authority to what was (and continued to be) in reality a justification for the assertion of power under the title of the 'struggle for existence' and (as interpreted by Herbert Spencer) 'survival of the fittest'. Whilst this has freewheeled even into our own time, this ideology can be seen as nothing short of deeply reprehensible.

Back in 1947, the theologian CS Lewis put this in a well-known aphorism in the following way[249]:

From this point of view, what we call Man's power over Nature turns out to be a power exercised by some men over other men with Nature as its instrument.

Par for the course is the notion that it is 'Man' in general, rather than the particular programme of Occidental culture, and then of the rich and powerful against the poor, that has taken this particular road to conceptualising nature. 'Scientific Progress' becomes in practice the ideological foundation of the accumulation of power and wealth — for some: Knowledge is Power.

Since the more focused idea of science came into currency at the time of the Enlightenment, a notion became current that it is not only Nature that might be subject to study and the accumulation of knowledge but that also 'Man' and 'Society' would eventually be 'understood' and, as philosopher David Hume already put it in the early 18th century:

We may be free, and yet another may be perfectly certain what use we shall make of our freedom.

The disciplines of economics and sociology, psychology and (less so) anthropology were all founded and developed within the ideological framework of this conception.

There was talk, particularly in the early 20th century, about 'social science' being a 'young' or 'inaccurate' science that, with time, would catch up to natural sciences in terms of discovering ultimate truths. However, there was a deep misunderstanding here. As already noted, natural science is basically oriented towards gaining knowledge that will yield wealth and power with relatively marginal, cosmetic concern with wisdom or any possibility of an eventual comprehensive knowledge. In the case of the 'social sciences' this notion simply concealed the direct struggle for power in revealing realities, or formulating ideological precepts, that in fact had direct moral and power implications, as in the case of Darwin's 'theory'.

An important point here is the academic struggle across much of the 20th century around what should or should not be deemed to be science in the context of social theory and, particularly in the Anglo Saxon world much effort went into carefully circumscribing what might or might not be deemed to be science. The term 'science', after all, had great cachet and when Marx came forward with a theory of social evolution that he asserted to be scientific, then all hell broke loose in the field of social theory.

As Stuart Hughes put it:

To come to terms with Marxism, then, was the first and most obvious task confronting the intellectual innovators of the 1890s.[250] '

This overt and covert anti-Marxism ruled the 'social sciences' across the century and into the 1960s, when neo-Marxism at last surfaced as 'legitimate' — though continuing to be seen as 'radical' and hence fringe and, until the eventual demise of 'actually existing socialism', as a challenge to liberal society. What Hughes was pointing to was the urge to discredit Marx's claims which came, on the one hand, in the form of assertions that his theory was not actually science or, in the case of Karl Popper (whose anti-Marxism was an important part of his prestige as a 'philosopher of science'[251]) claiming that whilst Marxism was scientific, the theory was simply false.

Objections might be raised at the notion that science is nothing but handmaiden to the accumulation of wealth and power, with one asserting: 'but science has also produced a better life in so many ways for all of humanity, lightening the burden of work, improving the conditions of health and widening lifestyle and consumption choices and beyond this given us insight that shows in so much more depth the wonders of the creation'. However, such a view is either naive or disingenuous in that inclusion by the ruling elites of the mass of humanity in the 'benefits of science and technology' has been predominantly fuelled by instrumental motivations, at best to make profits but more generally in the framework of a politics of appeasement or seduction of the masses into acquiescence in the political settlement, in recent years through consumerism but at the other end of the spectrum, through police and military oppression and ultimately war.

Unfortunately, furthermore, it is in this respect that we have to return to Bacon's notion of 'the extension of power and dominion of the human race itself over the universe' and see the way in which the 'benefits' have been accomplished at the expense of the health of ecosystems and the sustainability of the exploitation of resources, ultimately resulting in the vanquishing of nature and the exhaustion of nature's bounty, precipitating the collapse of this vaunted culture and loss of most of these putative benefits.

Surely many of these benefits could have been achieved without the dimension of extending power and dominion, to result in destruction and depletion? However, this would have required a different ideological framework (for instance those which informed the improvement of lifestyles in other complex cultures, particularly China) that did not possess such a concertedly aggressive posture towards nature or its focused use to political ends, and yet still managed to develop many useful technologies long before they appeared in the context of Occidental science.

We can see the origins of science in Ancient Greece being quite other than instrumental or aggressive and thus other philosophical strands underlie modern science, that have resurfaced in Occidental thought throughout the Modern era. Insofar as the ideology of science starts life as the rediscovery of Greek philosophy, so we can see that it was not originally analytical or instrumental so much as the result of deep curiosity with a strong sense of mystique at the wonders of nature. Upon its arrival in Renaissance Italy — and as noted above, particularly in the form of Neo-Platonism and Hermeticism — the study of nature was overwhelmingly understood in holistic terms.

Whilst the story then takes us to the instrumental version of science that we know today, there were advocates along the way of alternative ways of interpreting nature that maintained the holistic understanding inherited from the past. Highlights include the debates of the 19th Century German 'Naturphilosophen'[252] starting with Schelling, but hailing back to medieval mystics viz Meister Eckhart and which produced, in the late 19th century, the concept of ecology[253] as a potentially scientific way of looking at the interconnection of species within environmental contexts. Mention should also be made of Alfred Whitehead, whose holistic view of nature insisted that science should not discard the aesthetic and the moral dimensions. Given the effectiveness of positive science in a world organised on a the basis of striving for power and wealth to amplify power and wealth, there was never much of a chance of holistic notions of nature, and any alternative version of science that might be based upon this, making any headway.

In fact, focusing on science without immediately associating it with the technologies that are facilitated by scientific knowledge is problematic. Although, until the 19th century, technologies were developed in Europe relatively independently of science, essentially through the efforts of clever artisans, the aspiration was always one to achieve knowledge that would help to create more effective technologies. And in the end, it is not science but rather technological development based on a scientific understanding that is lethal to the environment.

Chinese culture has also over the centuries developed technologies, albeit in the framework of very different ideological complexion, that did not develop any 'scientific methodology' as an adjunct to a notion of progress and the conquest of nature. When Bacon gave examples of effective technologies in his time, as illustrating the benefits that science could yield, all of these — the compass, gunpowder, paper-making and printing — had been invented and first made use of in

China. Joseph Needham's exploration of the development of science and technology in China over the millennia mentioned above, revealed unequivocally than until at least the middle of the 18th century, European technological prowess remained less well-developed than that arising in China[254]. The drive to invent and develop technology in China was not, however, an adjunct to the millenarian quest that emerged from the ideological conjuncture described in the foregoing paragraphs, thus devoid of the conviction concerning progress that has driven on the Occidental scientific programme.

The recent growth in the sociology of science as 'social constructionism', has demonstrated in detail through countless case studies the way in which scientific enquiry is in practice motivated by the struggle for status amongst scientists[255] and thence the power and profits which it yields to those who finance it. Furthermore, Paul Feyerabend, and more recently a proliferation of other writers, have shown that there is in practice no single methodology of science but that it is simply an orientation, or the application of rationality, towards yielding knowledge that can be used instrumentally. As Feyerabend put it: *anything goes* that can be seen to yield results[256].

Bruno Latour[257], building on earlier analysis of sociologists of science, went on to show in detail not just the social process of 'scientific production' but how the results, through the development of technologies, react back on society that has given us, particularly over recent decades, a radical restructuring not only of research and how it is carried out but of the 'Mode of Production' to which the discoveries, in conjunction with other dimensions of social and economic change, have contributed.

The extreme development of this case is that of Jacques Ellul[258] who conjectured that technological development has a programme of its own, independent of the human will or seduced human compliance, that gives us the Technostructure referred to throughout this book (Ellul used the term 'Technological Society'). We might see this in terms of the 'Faustian bargain' as set out by Christopher Marlowe in the 16th century and thence in the second endeavour of Goethe to present the myth of Faust[259].

A further dimension of Occidental science has been various attempts to solve riddles embedded in the Christian religion. It is a little known fact that Newton, sometimes seen as the father of Modern science, spent half his time attempting to calculate exactly when God created the world[260]. And nor has this dimension of scientific investigation ceased. Where many religions have a pat answer to this, including the Christian myth of God's creation of the world in seven days, the European version of Enlightenment, that wishes to dispel superstition, must seek the true answer to the question of creation. The huge budgets spent on looking into the far corners of outer space and the massive facilities in Geneva (CERN) and elsewhere created to find the fundamental structure of matter, seem to have little promise in terms of yielding wealth and power to anyone[261]. Well, whilst this illustrates the multi-causality and motivation so often to be found in human actions, it does not detract from the centrality of the messianic, aggressive agenda of science, the rooting out and elimination of which must be an important goal of the future reformulation of human endeavour.

Once the mythology that sees science as benign knowledge is replaced with the understanding that it is handmaiden not just of abstract progress but of the Commercial Ideology and fundamentally aimed at the exertion of power over nature as handmaiden to the power of some men over others, then it becomes apparent just how lethal it is with respect to facilitating the passage towards the destruction of the biosphere. It is not just proliferating technology that needs to be questioned but also the ideology of science. Whilst practical knowledge relevant to the emergent situation post-collapse will be desperately necessary, the notion of science as some kind of general method to achieving this knowledge must be abandoned.

In reconstructing viable cultures following the fall of modernity, the lessons of the problematic nature of the ideology of science and its technological progeny will have to be acknowledged and a new morality and ethics established that recognises the need not only for benign social relations but also benign relations with nature. Humanity and human cultures are an inextricable part of the rest of nature and need to recognise the integrity of society and ecology as one entity and process, understanding the role of people and communities in this context and developing an appropriate sense of responsibility that extends to the whole. This becomes the main focus of the final chapter of this book.

Environmental Theory and Philosophy

We might say that over a three hundred year period, science, as ideology, came progressively in the Occident to eclipse both philosophy and religion. The efficacy with which, translated into technology, it changed the world, yielding wealth in general but far more importantly the extension of lifestyles in ways that could never have been imagined in any previous civilisation, yielded any other mode of more profound thought to be of diminishing value. In the past only the gods could fly and only the kings and their entourages could live colourful lives filled with beguiling commodities and entertainment, the frontiers of human health pushed back... What need to reconsider what life is all about or any other way to improve it?

Hence the thoughts of the German Naturphilosophen and a few intellectuals elsewhere dissenting from the scientific mainstream, made no impression, and were lost as historic curios, leaving little trace on society at large. During the 19th century there was, however, still room for speculation and proposals on how society and politics might be run which, of course, yielded the two distinct visions of capitalism and communism that competed through much of the 20th century. And then, from the end of the 1960s, as the environmental problematic began to emerge in increasingly definite form, so theoretical and philosophical speculation revived to enquire into bringing the problems facing humanity into better focus and what, at the level of vision and understanding, might be done to overcome these.

In the United States, across the second half of the 19th century, a line of thought and action that was little more than a continuation of ancient Arcadian notions was articulated, notably by Thoreau, Emerson and Muir, who were unhappy with the way in which Progress and Development were changing the face of the land, as they saw it, for the worse. And as these changes become more pronounced, Gifford Pinchot, the first Chief of the United States Forest Service, was instrumental in initiating a system of environmental management right across the resources of the United States, that has been dubbed the 'first conservation movement[262] and which was concerned to raise the efficiency and hence stem wastage in the economic exploitation of water, land and especially forest resources.

A friendship between Muir and Pinchot in the opening years of the 20th century soon turned into an acrimonious dispute that has characterised to a degree the spectrum of attitudes in the United States with the growth of the environmental movement from the end of the 1960s and with it theorisation and speculation on the problematic of increased negative impacts of development on environments and how to stem these. Already during the 19th century the European bourgeois had been travelling more extensively for recreation — the start of the modern tourist industry —— and part of this involved wonder at particularly the European alpine landscapes but in general a romantic attitude grew that valued aesthetically, wild and other natural landscapes[263]. Muir raised this, with theistic underpinnings, to an insistence on preserving selected wilderness areas against any development, creating what became national parks and other 'protected areas'. In parentheses it should be noted that by the end of the 21st century an international system of land preservation and conservation had extended to an estimated ten to fifteen per cent of the earth's land surface, albeit these are predominantly areas with relatively little economic value.

Theorisation as to what moral or ethical framework might be applied to curb environmental depredation and resource depletion moved in the 1960s into religious exegesis that soon discovered that Christianity had little to say about any particular attitude towards the environment[264] and subsequent investigations noted that with the marginal exception of Taoism there was little in the 'great religions' that might help by way of moral directions in which nature might be understood. Weak attempts were made by Christians to build ideas of the protection of nature into the religion, such as the Pope declaring St Francis of Assisi to be the patron saint of the environment in 1979. And whilst no attempts were made to revive 19th Century 'Naturphilosophie', a few (ex)Marxists did, however, move to adapt radical social theory to address the environmental problematic[265].

The rate of production of work on environmental theory and philosophy, and including much on environmental political theory, accelerated across the 1980s with, by the turn of the century, a truly massive outpouring of literature with numbers of dedicated journals besides the strictly academic, including some more engaged in deeper theoretical debates about change including *Environmental Ethics* (founded 1979), *Capitalism Socialism Nature* (1988) and *Environmental Values* (1992). Less formal journals dedicated to 'deep ecology' included *The Trumpeter* (1983)[266]. However, this has to be seen in the context of the vast recent growth in publishing and in general communications across this period where the environmental and ecological component remained but a small niche with few participants and an extremely small participatory public in all but the most superficial aspects of the discourse.

Within this theoretical discourse, it was generally realised that there remained a spectrum as characterised by the Pinchot – Muir approaches to the environment, gaining a whole range of titles including conservation versus ecology, (where in general the term of ecology rapidly broadened out from its original definition of the study of the relations of biological species within their environments), and then Imperial versus Arcadian; expedient versus sacramental; technocentrism versus ecocentrism and shallow versus deep ecology.

A central issue was to identify the distance that moral (and legal) responsibility or attitudes should extend out from what in the modern world, and going back into religion, had been strictly applied to people and social relations. Animal rights advocates attempted to assert the extension of human rights to all other sentient creatures on the argument that they, too, had feelings and in a few cases possibly even consciousness regarding how they were treated. Others went further to assert that some sort of ethical principles should extend to all components of ecology and finally to the earth as a whole. The background to the discourse was an objection to 'anthropocentrism', meaning that human interests were being pursued against the interests of other species.

The most radical view simply asserted the 'intrinsic value' of other species, ecological systems and of the earth. The Gaia hypothesis of James Lovelock[267], which generated considerable debate, takes the Ancient Greek notion of the earth as a living organism and asserts that it will look after itself and correct any errors that mankind makes by way of altering environments, including the possible elimination of humanity. Whilst widely read and cited, this gained few adherents and was certainly not useful as a guide concerning what might be done to reduce the growing negative environmental impacts of human activity.

More central to the discourse in respect of intrinsic value was a cluster of philosophical constructs around the term 'deep ecology' proposed by the Norwegian philosopher Arne Naess[268]. This generated a wide debate[269] with further developments under other titles including Warwick Fox's *Transpersonal Ecology*[270] and Fraya Mathews' *Ecological Self*[271]. The basic belief of these philosophies is that being human needs to recognise the holistic 'one-ness' of the totality of the earth as the same as ourselves on a level of equality, and develop a view of life from this perspective. The resulting philosophy has also become known as 'ecosophy'.

Although there are here implications of some kind of spiritual dimension to the belief that is being proposed, and that adheres to some of the discussants within the expanding discourse, in practice none of the more prominent theoreticians/philosophers discusses the subject in any kind of mystical terms but rather as both a practical approach to addressing the attack of humanity in our age on the integrity of the biosphere and, indeed, by implication a 'correct' interpretation of the human condition. In the case of Mathews, relating her discussion back to earlier philosophies (particularly Spinoza), she sees the proposed attitude being dependent on the configuration of culture in which people live which, in turn, is in the first instance sculpted to function in particular natural environments, and in the long term interests of the communities that express themselves through this culture.

These debates had almost no resonance in mainstream academic discourse on philosophy or ethics. 'Shallow' environmentalism, concerned with environmental protection in the interest of humanity and of future generations, made more impression on academic disciplines, including 'environmental economics', and to a lesser extent on sociology. Anthropologists certainly took a greater interest in the synergies between particular cultures and their environments, implying models also for modern society. As noted elsewhere in this chapter, government research programmes even supported substantial programmes, albeit mainly in the areas of the 'hard sciences', to investigate the veracity of putative anthropogenic environmental problems and possible technical solutions. However, almost none of this was influenced in any way by the deeper philosophical discourse.

There was, however, some resonance between this discourse and practical action. Participants might play different roles and there was certainly much exchange of views and action amongst environmental campaigning groups from animal liberation through to monkey-wrenching (sabotaging forestry and various damaging development projects) to the everyday activity of the groups and the significant role that they played in pressing for legislation to limit environmental degradation. At the level of international debates and the actions of development agencies, there was significant negotiation and the adoption of developmental and even moral principles regarding the use of the environment[272]. This was all, however, firmly on the side of shallow ecology. The only noticeable exception was where most intentional communities adopted deep ecological attitudes as background to their new lifestyles and the way that they treated the part of the earth and its resources on which they impacted.

Otherwise, the destruction of the environment moved into increasingly higher gear with little or no regard to any environmental theory or other insight: factory farming escalated to a disgusting level of maltreatment of animals on a massive scale; the continued destruction of remaining forests; strip-mining and now the beheading of mountaintops in the voracious exploitation of coal and thence the rubbishing of vast landscapes in Alberta, Canada to obtain even pitifully small amounts of oil from tar sands, made laughable the attempts of environmental theorists and even the groups that heeded their teachings, to make any discernible impact on the reality of modern life.

So we can say that whilst there may be elements of profound thinking going on with the aim of heading off the environmental depredations resulting from Development today, this seems to be making no impact at all on what is happening. We might say that whilst in the past philosophers have often had nothing more than mutually referential debates and discourses, it should be remembered that in the course of the 16th to 19th centuries, Philosophy resulted in significant changes in the course of Occidental culture, including particularly Locke's influence on political life that synergised with the changes in his lifetime in British governance and his influence on the thinkers of the French Enlightenment. The little-known influence of de Mandeville and the better-known influence of Adam Smith in defining the morality of modern liberal consumerism should also be remembered. Then, of course, there was the substantial influence of Karl Marx and his associate Frederick Engels, which provided most of the theoretical basis for the way in which the Soviet Union came to be governed.

Perhaps the problem today is simply one of the sheer din of contemporary life that crowds out any more profound thinking on the part of either political leaders and opinion formers, the media and thence populations at large. Or put more abstractly, what Zygmunt Bauman referred to as the slide from intellectuals as legislators to being interpreters[273]. However, we should also note two key problems here. On the one hand, the grand, overarching philosophical schemes to which some 19th century philosophers, especially Hegel and some of his followers, strove is in no way in fashion today. This means that environmental ethics and philosophy has (and this goes for the whole range of attempts to build environmental concerns into other disciplines) become just another academic niche amongst many. The best achievement amongst all the environmental theoreticians with respect to attempting a more complete ecological philosophy was, arguably, Murray Bookchin in his magnum opus *The Ecology of Freedom: The Emergence and Dissolution of Hierarchy*[274] that explained Bookchin's 'social ecology', analysing not only problems of environmental degradation but also addressing in a structured manner the social problems that need to be effectively addressed if the ecological denouement is to be avoided.

Indeed, the environmental philosophers have failed to take much notice of philosophy in other niches and in particular the vital relationship between the philosophy which informs the present liberal-consumerist world and the way in which the beliefs that this entails, and the almost universal adherence to these surely block any meaningful consideration of environmental philosophy. Unless there is a trenchant critique of the very bases of the philosophy or consciousness that informs current unconsidered, powerfully motivating beliefs, and not just a superficial dismissal of individualism that is the stock in trade of writing on environmental philosophy, then the environmental philosophy and, in particular deep ecology, becomes no more than sentimental wishful thinking and possibly belief in a world where, miraculously, liberal-consumerism and the Commercial Ideology have evaporated.

Furthermore, a key missing element that distinguishes environmental philosophy, however well-argued, is the lack of what Marxists refer to as a 'social subject' in whose interests it is clearly present to take up the philosophy and forge the means to change life in ways that will bring it into harmony with the biosphere. Marxism rose to prominence predominantly as a result of its advocacy of the interests of the working class that, by the end of the 19th century, comprised large parts of Occidental societies and who took his philosophy as the road to their own salvation. However, it is not only the pursuit of the self-interest of the individual or society that brings philosophies to the surface. It may have deeper reasons and involve and even necessitate widespread secular revelation. Understanding and following the principles of deep ecology would, prima facie, seem to be in the interests of all of humanity, but how this might engage populations in an urge to change their lifestyle and, indeed, the very basis of their consciousness of the world they live in is not at all evident and certainly inadequately addressed in the literature of environmental philosophy.

Finally, it would also seem, prima facie, that the 'love of nature' that is at the heart of deep ecology, is an extremely esoteric notion to the masses who have been brought up in recent years in cities with an extremely meagre understanding and almost no direct experience of countryside. Occasional holidays, such as on the beach or skiing, where there happens to be something by way of natural surroundings, especially in a frame of mind that is interested only in vicarious enjoyment of the accoutrements and situations of modernity, is no meaningful opening to any deeper empathy with nature.

The answer to these criticisms is in part for the theoreticians to broaden out their view and thence to realise that, whilst the likelihood of political and business leaders or people to be in the least bit interested in what they have to say is vanishingly small and likely to generate hostility, they need to become clear about what will be happening as modern civilisation falls apart and how their philosophy might be brought into its own under these conditions. In the final chapter, we will be discussing in further detail the context in which 'ecosophy' is likely to become increasingly seen as relevant to emergent circumstances as a route to salvation from a collapsing world.

But the philosophy will need to be transmitted in ways that makes this clearly evident to the populations in transition.

Resources for Development

We can say that by and large, the patterns of use of environments and resources changed little in the context of complex societies from ancient Mesopotamia, Egypt and China up until the 18th century. Densifying populations and the inability to manage accumulating stresses of food production due to soil depletion contributed in a few cases to the decline of Empires and communities that might also have been subject to destruction through invasion[275]. Buildings (using local materials and with architecture producing suitable internal environments) furniture and utensils, clothing and personal and household decoration, made out of much the same materials amongst all 'complex societies' up to the modern era, taxed Nature relatively little. In but a few cases, mining operations were on a small scale, continuing to yield resources over long time spans to supply what amounted to modest demands for mineral resources[276].

Timber resources were, however, overexploited in various parts of the world, starting already in the Mediterranean over two thousand years ago and in some cases, due to the soil erosion which followed, have never fully recovered, despite the decline of Ancient Greece and the collapse of the Western Roman Empire. Shipbuilding in the context of the growth of European commercial and colonial expansion from the 16th century also led to forest depletion in Britain and to a lesser extent, other territories. Then from the late 18th century the toll on an ever-widening spectrum of natural resources began to escalate, impacting ever more heavily on ecosystems and geological resources and this can be seen to have been linked inextricably with the growing exploitation of fossil sources of energy. In the first instance these were used to increase coal production and thence to escalate production of all other goods through mechanisation and industrialisation and eventually through the substitution of many 'natural' materials for coal, oil and natural gas derivatives[277].

Certainly in the early years of the Industrial Revolution, those concerned with the Development process might be forgiven for not having taken the long-term view of the ultimate unsustainability of the exponential use of resources in circumstances where the first indications of exponential use were starting to emerge. However, the economic crisis in Britain following the end of the Napoleonic wars was confronted by two alternative Development visions. Two men, both affluent businessmen well-known in their time, presented their proposals to Parliament. David Ricardo recommended that Britain engage in more intensive trade that would clearly avoid diminishing returns at home by exploiting the resources of other countries. Robert Owen, on the other hand, proposed the creation of a more egalitarian society based on small communities that would have been intrinsically less demanding in terms of resources. It is well enough known that Ricardo's notion of 'the gains from trade' prevailed, and is today the central propaganda pillar for 'economic globalisation', whilst Owen's proposals were simply ignored and remain almost entirely unknown today[278].

As already referred to in Chapter One, the first concerted attempt to conceive of future resource limits of the emerging Development process was that presented by William Stanley Jevons in his book, *The Coal Question* published in 1866. Jevons's book makes extraordinary reading for us today as he thought through the whole problematic of exponential growth in resource use, focusing particularly on energy (which in 19th century Britain was already predominantly from coal) and the way in which this must eventually hit up against limits and in the case of non-renewable resources, exhaustion that must inevitably result in economic decline.

His calculations concerning when Britain would go into decline were not accurate, due both to underestimation of coal resources and, of course, unawareness of the role that an expanding global economy and in particular exploitation of oil and natural gas would come to play. However, the principle and the way in which he worked this into detail remains unassailable. Although not entirely disappearing from view, Jevons's book and his arguments, however, fail to appear even as a footnote in standard economic textbooks today[279]. The arguments, most forcefully put by Barnett and Morse, referred to already in Chapter One, dismissing resource depletion as a significant issue as recently as the early 1960s, have prevailed both within the discipline of Economics and more widely as a problematic deserving wider recognition and debate[280].

Jevons had already identified one of the main problems facing any attempt in a market economy, bent on ever increasing wealth production, to break the exponential growth in demand for resources. The so-called 'Jevons Paradox' which he set out in his book postulates that increased energy efficiency, in bringing down the unit price of energy to produce given goods or services, brings down the price also of the goods and services produced. This is likely to encourage more sales, hence more production, which is likely to lead to an overall increase, rather than reduction in the use of energy. This therefore suggests that encouraging energy efficiency in a market economy can in no way be guaranteed to satisfy a policy aimed at conserving energy use — which was already Jevons's concern.

Of course the core problem lies with the presumption that Progress and Development, and a market economy as the best way to achieve this, cannot, in today's world, be called into question. Rather obviously, if we wish to forestall an eventual 'overshoot' and collapse of our civilisation then thought has to go into attempting to discern the level at which resources can be exploited, so that they can be harvested indefinitely and then measures be taken to restrict resource use to that level. This cannot, however, apply to inherently non-renewable resources that will eventually be exhausted if exploitation continues, no matter at what level they are exploited.

In an obscure article published in 1925, John Ise[281] proposed a principle that non-renewable resources should only be exploited if substitutes can be proven to exist (e.g. fossil fuels exploited in a situation where renewable resources are under development and can be shown to be able to replace fossil fuels before these are depleted). This would clearly have also to take secondary effects of impacts on the environment into account, such as limiting use of fossil fuels to a point short of changing the earth's atmosphere This would not necessarily bring a halt to improvements in lifestyle from innovation but, as in the Chinese case noted above, restrict exploitation to within the 'carrying capacity' of local environments and, more broadly, of the earth.

Of course economic argumentation generally avoids engaging with the messy realities of culture and politics so we have to look elsewhere to understand the problematic of exponential exploitation of resources and why this was, until recent decades, ignored. The contemporary version of the ideology of Progress contains within it a penchant for risk-taking. Where most cultures embody a conservative dimension that cautions against doing things where the risks may be high, progressivism is inherently more prepared to take risks on the assumption that progress will yield solutions in the future to today's problems. It therefore encourages the playing down or disregard of messages of caution[282].

Furthermore, the impressiveness with which technological change led over the 19th and 20th centuries to reductions in resources per unit of production and thence substituted more abundant for less abundant, or eventually renewable for non-renewable resources, and at the same time reduced negative environmental impacts through improved environmental management, encouraged the notion that the ultimate exhaustion of resources and accumulation of environmental problems could be ignored. As made explicit by Barnett and Morse, one could project, or imagine or fantasise such improvements into the indefinite future. And in the 1950s and 1960s there arose a naive assumption that endless energy supplies from nuclear power to unlock all other resources would soon be available with, at the time, little regard for the environmental consequences, should this path be pursued[283].

As long as the more distant future can be 'discounted', formally in economic theory but more importantly as a general cultural outlook, then resource and environmental sustainability worries can be dismissed as an issue that might arise in the distant future but be of no concern today. Finally, certainly until after the Second World War, in the atmosphere of competition, colonialism and then the era of 20th century wars, no thought was given to the notion that other people, be they the lower classes in one's own country or whole populations of colonised countries, might ever aspire to consuming resources at the level being 'enjoyed' by Occidental elites and middle classes. The excitement of the journey, together with the details of the layer upon layer of competition (for resources, for profits, for power, for the ineffable benefits of consumption) quickly banished thought concerning the wisdom of taking into serious consideration the possibility of eventual resource limits to Development.

The first area where concern for possible exhaustion of resources arose in Europe was following the Second World War, and was related to food production. Restricting food supply to enemy populations had been one of the weapons of the warring nations. It was, however, more a psychological reaction based on the immediate past, together with the political pressure of the farming lobby, rather than any structured analysis of future limits that led to the policies that supported food production in Europe. Those who did argue for the conservation of farm land over and against land conversion for urban development etc. were, in this context, attacked by economists with their dogma that 'the market' is the most efficient way of allocating resources[284].

Most Western European countries nevertheless maintained policies of subsidising food production and with the formation of the European Economic Community and thence the European Union, agricultural support under the Common Agricultural Policy (CAP) became the greatest burden upon the budget of the organisation. The perverseness of the whole system of support emerged through escalating over-production whilst pumping food out of the ground in ways that were increasingly unsustainable, both because of damage to the soils and escalating non-renewable energy, and chemical inputs ending, as we have already seen, in a food production system where as much as ninety per cent of the energy going into the food on Occidental tables today comes from non-renewable energy sources.

Eventually the CAP came round to paying farmers to take land out of production, whilst the land continuing in production remained over-intensively farmed. Only in the last few years did the policy process in some European countries begin to acknowledge the unsustainability of this food production system, with civil society initiatives sometimes on a considerable scale running ahead of government, viz Cuba, Russia and Japan starting to support organic farming and to look for further ways to de-escalate energy inputs to the food supply and production system[285].

However, we might say that this is really 'too little, too late' in that the localisation and the changeover to organic production of food can, in the not too distant future, be expected to be progressively forced by the diminution of energy. In the short term, however, there is a danger that intensive development of crops for energy, to maintain current car-based lifestyles, will wring further depredation upon soils before the system collapses into localised, organic farming. Then in the longer term, 'organic by necessity' may also be pursued without adequate concern for soil maintenance out of a combination of ignorance and desperation to produce food to survive.

Farming in countries of the South has also been dragged in stages onto the treadmill of modern production methods. Many countries, already colonial plantation economies, have stripped away their original vegetation and depleted soils, sometimes over wide areas that will take centuries or longer to recover even if their exploitation were to cease forthwith. In other areas, however, where traditional peasant methods of farming have persisted, de-escalation in the creeping application of modern agrochemicals and methods in recent years should be possible, relatively gently, in the coming years. Notwithstanding systematic soil erosion over vast areas of the world today[286], most soils can recover over a relatively short period of time but it remains to be seen at what level of productivity this will stabilise, having also to take consideration of the impacts of climate change. Certainly the progress in constantly increasing tonnage of food per hectare that was achieved from the early 19th through to the late 20th centuries will become a thing of the past.

It was in the 1950s that the first signs arose of a return to the broad concerns of Jevons for the sustainability of the Development path in terms of natural resource availability. In the first instance, official responses were not motivated by concern for absolute limits but rather that the Soviet Union might be able to win in the competition for economic growth and potential war by having access to a larger stock of resources. A first round of publications warning of the impossibility of endless growth , was followed in the course of the 1960s by a new round, focusing particularly on a Malthusian conception of the 'population problematic' and making a greater public impression[287].

This triggered loud altercations over what might be the limit of global population relative to the carrying capacity of the earth, with those believing the limit was approaching urging that policies be implemented to curb population growth. A few governments, notably the Chinese Government but also those of India and Indonesia (together containing half the world's population) did implement concerted attempts to limit population growth. It rapidly became evident, however, that although the world was fast becoming crowded with humanity at the expense of the integrity of ecosystems, a much more pressing issue was the toll on resources made by the more affluent populations, both of the North and the elites in the South.

This could be measured in terms of energy consumption per capita, where today the average sub-Saharan citizen consumes less than a tenth of the energy of the average Western European and one twenty-fifth that of the average citizen of the United States. If the cruder statistic of per capita GDP is used as a measure of differential impacts, then we see that the average sub-Saharan African consumes at a rate of one seventy-fifth of the average US citizen. Whilst the elimination of poverty (however defined) might bring the average sub-Saharan wealth or income to a somewhat larger number, this is not likely to be more than a 50th of that of the average US citizen.

In the case of energy consumption, this calculation has been carried out in terms of the level of per capita energy consumption that correlates with a high 'human development index'. This comes to one fifth of the energy consumption of the average US citizen. That is to say that most countries that have grown to a per capita energy consumption of one and a half tons of oil equivalent per annum already have a high human development index, so that one is led to ask the question of what additional developmental benefits are achieved by Europeans consuming four tons and US citizens consuming eight tons of oil equivalent per capita per annum.

It was Barry Commoner, who was for several decades one of the most effective environmental campaigners in the United States, standing as US Presidential candidate on behalf of the Citizen's Party in 1980, who in the late 1960s criticised the population alarmists, indicating that high population levels might be sustained if only modest consumption levels would be accepted. In other words, it was the rich nations and classes who were primarily responsible for the spoliation of the world's environment and draw-down of natural resources and not 'population' in general[288].

Commoner went on to analyse the way in which, over the period from 1946 to 1968, less sustainable and more energy-intensive materials and processes were systematically substituted for more sustainable processes and material used in production and consumption in the United States[289]. Glaring examples were: reduction in animal and rail power versus increase in fossil fuel powered transport and electricity; reduction in cotton and wool fibre and increase in artificial fibre; modest growth in steel use versus rapid growth in aluminium; reduction in soap and growth in detergents[290]. So, Commoner pointed out, any effective analysis of the problematic of resource depletion should focus on per capita consumption (and thus class) differentials and production processes to gain a balanced perspective on what was happening and why, and maybe help to formulate means to reduce these impacts.

Further research over the past few decades has indicated that there have, nevertheless, been some improvements in terms of the reduction in resource use, and particularly in 'energy intensity' per unit of output and consumption, through continual improvements in production efficiency. We might conjecture that these improvements were slower to come than might have been the case had these been policy-induced rather than leaving matters to the market. However, the overall conclusion of the few attempts made at a macro-analysis of the net impacts of growth versus efficiency gains simply confirmed Jevons's paradox: overall impacts on environments and resource use were growing rather than declining[291]. And by the early years of the new century, the implications were clear with regard to the steady deterioration of global ecosystems as a whole, as revealed by the monumental Millennium Ecosystems Assessment[292].

Analyses did look at the differences between renewable resources, under the heading of 'sustainable yield,' and non-renewable resources. But often enough, whilst no thought was going into any coherent programme to ensure substitutes for failing resources in the foreseeable future (*pace* the economic resource optimists) it became clear that many renewable resources were being systematically depleted, including most notably forests, with their rich biodiversity, and fisheries. Evidently, neither 'market mechanisms' nor ostensible resource conservation policies were working.

Several major research studies were carried out in the 1960s into the potential ultimate availability of mineral resources. The SCEP[293] study undertaken by the Massachusetts Institute of Technology is of interest here because of the clear way in which it indicated that mining for a whole range of minerals is an end-game of relatively short duration at current rates of extraction. By standards of more recent analyses as applied to 'peak oil', the method used was crude. That is to say that exhaustion of each resource was simply portrayed as happening from one year to the next after continuous mining at the current level. In fact, empirical analysis of the exploitation of oil resources indicates clearly that from a single well (or mine) output rises exponentially, levels off at a peak which, without significant improvements in extraction methods can be expected to be half way through extraction of the resource from the particular well or mine, before declining along a downward path that mirrors the rise — in other words, exploitation follows a bell-shaped curve. The decline is characterised by the resource becoming more difficult and expensive to extract as well as becoming rarer: diminishing returns.

The SCEP study might have under-assessed the ultimate amounts of resources in most if not in all cases; Jevons, in the mid-eighteenth century, underestimated UK coal reserves by what eventually transpired as a quarter of what is now known (probably now close to the real ultimate). The point is, however, that whether the peak and thence decline sets in in twenty or fifty or even one hundred years from now, this is but the blink of an eye in historic terms. What seems quite extraordinary, even ludicrous, when taking one step back and contemplating this situation is that no meaningful consideration was given in the face of these analyses concerning what might happen to our vaunted civilisation once the resources *en masse* were on the downward path.

This could only be a matter of two or three generations. And what was supposed to happen after that? If we look backwards, we can get a better perspective on where we stand by thinking simply of our parents and grandparents whom we might have known; now we are looking at our children and maybe grand-children and failing to ask any questions about their welfare once the earth has been squeezed dry of resources. From the mid-1980s, the mantra of Sustainable Development, cited in what has become a vast literature, and as the heading for countless small projects was:

Development that meets the needs of the present without compromising the ability of future generations to meet their own needs[294].

How many people, however, thought seriously about what this might mean for the ongoing growth in the global consumption of non-renewable resources?

A wealth of science fiction writing, particularly in the 1960s and 70s, and thence increasingly movies, conjectured all sorts of future worlds, some thinking seriously about scenarios from here on, presenting contexts in which human dramas could be played out. Most were, however, simple fantasy involving dramatic technical strides having been made and then these being backdrops to adventures of various kinds or alternatively of catastrophe. As the years proceeded, the images presented became ever more refined in terms of the technology of image-making and ever more convincing, as if this could really happen. However, all remained at the level of fertile imagination and entertainment, confirming ever more deeply the illusion of progress in the everyday even when presenting apocalypse on the screen.

Serious thought regarding the depredations of the unsustainable use of resources, on the other hand, was almost non-existent. An apparent widespread concern regarding 'sustainability' fell, with very few exceptions, very far short of anything like a realistic assessment of what needed to be done to reduce consumption and management of environmental resources to levels that could be genuinely sustained over the long term. The 'serious' Green Movement simply gained no meaningful hearing, crowded out by the weak rhetoric of non-serious contributions and with Government committees, Sustainable Development reports, public hearings and an endless array of means to keep the them occupied on the fringes of political and economic life, succeeded in obliterating the obvious truth concerning the inevitable failure of the system in the not-too-distant future.

Somehow there was no space left for mainstream thought on the end state of the patently unrealistic path that was being taken, and the way that the health of the planet's ecosystems and its wealth had to be managed in a responsible way for future generations. Lifestyles evolved with an ever-extending cornucopia of goods available at ever more accessible prices, even for the most modest incomes, but for the global 'consuming classes', fantasy became reality, in what had become a kind of cocoon of a world, of wondrous gadgets and proliferating virtual means of escape from any serious engagement, whether social or environmental.

Already from the end of the 1960s and thence ever more definitely, this could be nothing but an end game. There were hardly even the faintest attempts to produce transition strategies for the event when signs of exhaustion would arise and the downward path – that was

225

never allowed to be seriously contemplated - commenced. 'Sustainable Development' never took exhaustion into consideration but merely made proposals concerning how to live more parsimoniously within current lifestyles and production processes that might extend the resource base a few more decades. And then, de facto, would come the decline and fall which was not allowed to cloud the imagination apart from the frisson presented in simplistic apocalyptic movies.

It is in this context that the efforts of Aurelio Peccei must be seen as a valiant attempt to bring sense and responsibility into the political arena by discussing with politicians, academics and industrialists the fatal trajectory which development was taking. Few young people today are even aware of *The Limits to Growth* initiative and vanishingly few know of the path that Peccei trod from the mid-1960s. Peccei was a senior technocrat at FIAT and later Olivetti, and founded a consultancy concerned with Development planning that advised governments around the world on how they should go about achieving their Development goals. Convinced of the unsustainability of the global development trajectory, he founded, with associates, the Club of Rome, with the objective of convincing 'world leaders' of the folly of what was happening.

He and his associates had access to, and undertook negotiations with, 'senior politicians' both in communist and capitalist countries, but whilst securing a sympathetic hearing, achieved little. In consequence of this, the Club of Rome commissioned academics at the Massachusetts Institute of Technology (MIT) who had already initiated some global modelling, to extend their modelling exercises, with the aim of projecting current global development trends into the future[295]. The model simulated the exponential growth, based on past experience, of global investment, population, resource use and pollution. The initial computer runs indicated that some time before the middle of the 21st century, the global Development path would run into insuperable problems and collapse. Basic policy measures were then suggested and introduced into the model with the intention of seeing what it would take to head off collapse and attain a sustainable world, bringing economic growth and hence *de facto* also what was generally assumed to be 'progress' to a halt.

Peccei did not pretend that this was in any way a definitive exercise and was quite open about the way in which the modelling exercise and the publication of the findings were designed to gain far wider attention than the meagre results of the quiet negotiations with 'leaders' behind closed doors. And this was a correct assessment as the report, published in 1972 as *The Limits to Growth*[296], did raise a very widespread debate in the Occidental media and amongst institutions that took up the challenge to construct their own 'world models' to see whether their own results matched or opposed those of the MIT group, including much nit-picking that successfully obscured the rather obvious message[297]. As noted in Chapter One, by the end of the decade following publication of the report, debate had receded and research initiatives motivated by the report were quietly terminated[298].

These details are spelled out here because the *Limits* process was the nearest the political world came to acknowledging the impossibility of continuing along the present Development path. It is the failure of this that sealed our fate and is leading to the tragic consequences that we will see unfolding in the coming years. The MIT team continued to monitor the global Development process, without their publications making any discernible impact in the political arena, but essentially confirming the original scenario and noting that nothing effective has been done to respond to the strategic policy agenda which the original study had attempted to sketch[299]. No subsequent initiative raising the issue of the need to change the Development path (including the IUCN World Conservation Strategy[300] and the UN Commission on Environment and Development report *Our Common Future[301]*) was as clear as the *Limits* study as to the depth of change that would be necessary to head off the eventual collapse. Today very few of the younger generation have even heard of the *Limits to Growth* study[302].

Environment and Resources in the Context of Lifestyles and Production Processes

The workings of local ecosystems, and through interconnection the whole systems of nature, insinuate themselves into everyone's life at every turn. However, today that encounter is, for the modern citizen, at a great distance in terms of their lived lives. That is to say that work in the urban context, be it high-paying 'service' work in the North or selling in the informal economy in southern cities, has left Nature far behind; for the most part in the case of Occidental citizens this was left behind one or two or more generations ago, when becoming urbanised citizens earning a living and consuming in the matrix of a globalised economy. Modern education systems attempt increasingly, through 'environmental education' to generate a sympathy with 'environmental issues' but this is incorrigibly theoretical and fails almost entirely to reveal the complexity of how the environment is manipulated and converted into what we want by way of a lifestyle. The wonders of nature pass as colourful images across television screens and there remains, as a residue of past lives, a romanticism towards nature that translates into the suburban garden, the urban park, the 'outdoor' activity or eco-tourism. However, this does very little to raise awareness of the serious business of producing our way of life out of nature and the impacts that this yields.

If we consider in detail how resources and the environment were managed in the context of complex societies before the emergence of Modern Europe in the 18th century, then we can see that the vast majority of humanity remained in close contact with nature, predominantly as peasants, and even when under more complex management systems such as feudalism, or in the context of extensive irrigation systems, the impacts of the actions of farmers on the environment and the vagaries of floods, drought and of hard winters had an immediate impact that taught hard lessons about the need to conserve resources and manage them well in order to survive and thence provide the basis of a reasonable life. Insofar as pre-modern societies collapsed as a consequence of resource and environmental problems, this happened in most cases over longer periods of hundreds of years as a consequence of the inability to see the slow, systematic depletion of soils or water resources or of fluctuations in the climate.

A major achievement of modernity that is qualitatively different from all previous cultures in that it progressively severs the direct relationship between an increasing proportion of the population and the environment from which their livelihoods are produced. In general this has been achieved through urbanisation and industrialisation. In the case of the way in which the Soviet leadership collectivised the land, it is clear that those who worked it possessed neither the power nor the incentive to maintain the productive system which they worked; here too was an instrumentalisation of the land as being there purely for production. The net result was that this failed to maintain or conserve the resources of the country or, in the event, even to produce enough food to feed the population[303].

Liberal economic dogma states that as long as resources remain in private hands then these will be managed sustainably for basically the reasons outlined above; property owners can see that it is in their interests to continually make a living from these resources and hence that they should be managed sustainably. Whilst this might hold for the individual peasant owner, unfortunately, in the context of modernisation, new dimensions entered into the relations between owners and resources. These included the fact that corporate owners would be quite happy to exhaust resources as long as they could in the process accumulate the capital to invest in other enterprises. This was exactly the point that Barnett and Morse and at the extreme Kay and Merlees[304] made, being unfoundedly optimistic that this procedure would always result in more resources becoming available, in spite of leaving a trail of destruction and exhaustion behind them. One can see this graphically in areas that have been mined out, where soils have been degraded through plantation monocultures, and irrigation systems have failed through salinisation and waterlogging. As economists, they subscribed to the crass fallacy that money is more real for the sustenance of people and communities than physical resources.

However, more important than the issue of ownership and the maintenance of resources is the simple fact that by the middle of the 20th century, the majority of the population of the 'developed' countries had no idea what the impact of their lifestyle was on the environment and in the first instance little or no interest in the issue. The 'Green Movement' grew out of a widespread intuition, triggered to an important degree by *The Limits to Growth* and the debates that followed from this, that this lifestyle and its production processes are 'unsustainable' in the literal sense, and that it is *systematically* mining out and destroying the global resource base.

Without this intuition and the commitment of a small corps of campaigners, we can be sure that no measures at all would have been taken to analyse the nature of the problems and thence take some kind of action to obviate or at least reduce or rather postpone the depredations. We can see the development of mechanisms implemented with the intention of improving the management of the impacts of the emerging production systems and lifestyle, ranging from 'environmental impact assessments' to pollution control systems based on such notions as 'best available technique' and 'clean production'. Recycling systems have been established, eventually with sophisticated machinery to sort and reinsert 'wastes' into the production system.

However, whilst these represent the brighter side of current relations between our society and nature, they have clearly been inadequate to halt the slide into unsustainability. The simple fact is that these fragmented initiatives could never have added up to a complete system of sustainable environmental management without a fundamental critique of the belief in progress and its practical manifestations. There was some criticism emanating from the Marxist (or, we might say, socialist) critique of capitalism[305]. However, as we have seen, Marxism and the whole orientation of socialism had little to say about society-nature relations and with its general progressivist thrust, was blind to the fundamental contradiction between exponential economic growth and a finite resource base. It was therefore incapable of carrying through a consistent critique of modernity from a resource conservation perspective.

On the one hand, the explosion of the division of labour and the progressive shift out of direct production, first into factory production and then into a predominantly service economy, means in the end that almost no-one living in what the modern world has become, has more than a sketchy idea concerning the physical basis of how their lives are produced[306]. And as a corollary to this there is almost nothing by way of incentive mechanisms to discover how it is being produced and what the negative impacts of this on the resource base might be. Even those very few people professionally involved in environmental management are on the whole specialised in just one or other aspect of this, resulting in growing incoherence between the various components of the system.

Furthermore, increasing reliance has been placed since the early 1980s, in the context of neo-liberal politics, on a pathetically simplistic optimism that 'market mechanisms' could be applied to bring coherence beyond the human understanding – of the invisible hand – to somehow bring the impact of lifestyles gone wild into line with the need to maintain the sustainability of ecosystems and resource base. We might say that the economists were simply cynical or that they were naive in their dogma, beholden to cynical industrial managers and a public that had decisively lost its sense of self-responsibility, addicted to the cornucopia of Stuff that modern industry showered upon them. However this is seen, the net result over recent decades has been a descent into a fatal loss of responsibility of the system as a whole for the future welfare, not just of the resource base but of the populations that are dependent on the ongoing health of this base.

Whilst this describes the progress of Occidental culture, it encompasses at the same time the ever accelerating incorporation of other cultures into the process of losing knowledge amongst the populations at large and thence relinquishing responsibility for the management of the resources upon which they rely. It is extraordinary to behold how apparently serious initiatives continue to be made by 'Development agencies' that ostensibly aim to bring Modern Development to the so-called 'developing nations', severing these from traditional, sustainable lifestyles, with no sense of the longer term, or indeed increasingly short term, unviability and hence the senselessness of these initiatives[307]. The main problem, however, is the way in which the modern commercial world, with its seduction into vicarious consumption, is continually insinuating itself into the interstices of other cultures, undermining any remaining critical capacities.

At the same time, even the serious, if incoherent, attempts at environmental management of the Occidental countries, are largely lacking in the South, so that the depredations of the undoing of the earth's ecology and plunder of its resources become more glaringly evident, with totally inadequate intellectual or technical capacities to reverse or at least halt the process. And we might add that this involves a cynical economic system whereby the rich everywhere and the broad populations of the Occidental countries with a few additions (Japan, Korea) ignore — in more or less full knowledge of what is happening — the obvious exploitation not only of southern resources but also of their people as a subservient workforce.

In the following two chapters, where we reach back into the proposals that have been made over the past decades by those marginal initiatives that *have* attempted to propose real solutions to the destruction of the biosphere and plunder of our resource base, the basis for these solutions is one where responsibility for maintaining the environment and resource base into the future returns to the local community. In practice, as the analysis of the collapse of complex societies in the past makes very clear, we can expect that as our globalised culture falls anyway, so the survivors will be thrown back on their own resources, human and physical, at a relatively local level.

Just how local this will be, will depend on the degree to which local and sub-regional and perhaps also national political and administrative structures hold or metamorphose fast enough to maintain some kind of coherent organisation. The point here is that responsibility will again devolve directly upon the people, no more able to shrug off the responsibility for the maintenance of the environmental resource base that sustains their lives. But where there is the desire to take on this responsibility again, where over the past century most decisions have been inaccessible by the scale and distance involved in production and resource management chains, this will be the measure by which some kind of cultural reconstruction will be successful .

Chapter 5: Life after Modernity – Some General Considerations

We now take a closer look at how we might think about reorganising life after modernity — and more specifically, after 'globalisation'. As we will see, the dissolution of local production systems and local social structures and networks has proceeded at a breakneck pace over the past few decades. Even large cities today produce very little of what is locally consumed and their hinterlands now are more likely to yield most of their resources and produce for export not only to other parts of the country than their neighbouring towns and cities but in some cases for export over great distances.

As the means of transport become increasingly restricted over the coming decades and the world 'closes in' on localities, can we simply expect to pass back along the path that has been taken in the past decades to re-build a rich matrix of local production for local consumption? Can we expect to be able, trouble-free, to rebuild local affective and organisational relationships to satisfy local existential needs without being able to abscond when things get difficult?   To focus on these issues it is necessary to analyse how this process unfolded and this might give us a better idea of the possibilities, and what new directions might be taken where the simple backward passage is blocked or otherwise no longer viable or available.

A Short History of De-Localisation

The first thing we need to consider here is the de-localisation of people. Even today, only three per cent of the world's population lives outside their country of birth — albeit if China and India are omitted from the calculation, the percentage is significantly higher.   Nevertheless, migrations have been taking place since pre-history; with occasional exceptions of mass migrations these were modest in scale and most probably gradual by modern standards until some three thousand years ago.   These people moved into territories that were relatively unpopulated and established rural economies, bringing with them their knowledge of agriculture and their simple production technologies and then, over leisurely time periods, adapting to local conditions and environments and developing technologies or learning these from peoples already present.   Trade goes well back into pre-history but involved tiny proportions by volume of local economies, which might, nevertheless, have made a vital difference in diversity of lifestyles, especially where mineral resources were concerned.

Larger settlements, demanding more bulk resources than their hinterlands could produce, started to appear several thousand years ago — but were very few and far between until just two hundred years ago. Numbers of Chinese cities grew to many hundreds of thousands of people already well over two thousand years ago, with the capital, Chang-An, estimated to have accommodated some two million already 1,400 years ago. However, these overwhelmingly existed in areas which could yield practically all the resources necessary for everyday life and were made possible by highly developed local methods of, particularly agricultural, resource exploitation, including biofuel production and the production of materials for building (these two have always comprised the bulk in terms of weight of what is needed to sustain 'civilised' life) and then materials necessary for the production of household and personal goods, particularly timber. Over the centuries Chinese cities waxed and waned, producing consistently large cities only in the course of the twentieth century.

The Occidental, Egyptian, Mesopotamian, and even ancient Greek cities were very modest in size and we can be sure that the resources and goods necessary to build these and maintain their populations were overwhelmingly locally sourced and produced. The demise of Mesopotamian culture was in part the consequence of the exhaustion of methods to extract local materials were necessary to support larger urban populations, particularly through the salinization of irrigated land. In the case of Ancient Greece, local resources were depleted over time, in Greece itself so that by the time of the Roman Empire, the possibilities for expanding the cities had passed. The culture was maintained over several hundred years by the constant splitting off of populations to build colonies ever further around the Mediterranean coast.

Ancient Rome, and extending throughout its empire, was where for the first time resource demand and supply stretched substantially beyond the capacity of the local resource base, involving significant long-distance trade including import of large amounts of grain from North Africa to feed the city of Rome. It has been argued that the demise of the Western Roman Empire, whilst involving a complex of factors[308], was in the end the consequence of the depletion of distant resource bases and thence the failure of trade networks[309]. Rome also exported people who built small towns and farm estates scattered across the northern reaches of the empire as far as the Scottish borders; these however, 'disappeared' into the local populations upon the decline of

233

the Western Empire with the collapse of the economy that had expanded in the course of the Empire[310].

The western European population was relatively sparse and almost entirely rural until the 11th century, with most of the land fully occupied only by the 14th century, when increasing famines indicated over-population relative to local resource bases in the context of the then agricultural practices. The Great Plagues of the mid to late 14th century decimated population right across Eurasia, accompanied in places by famine and war. The late medieval population was only reached again in Western Europe well over a century later.

European cities remained small with up to ninety per cent of the population residing in rural areas; practising agriculture was the norm until well into the 18th century with London being the first modern European city to surpass one million in population, which it did at the turn of the 19th century, little more than two hundred years ago. Thus in spite of growing trade from expanding empires, this was almost entirely made up of luxuries to enhance the wealth and status of tiny elites, with timber and sugar spearheading the growth of trade in more essential materials and goods in the course of the 17th century. Indeed, the initial sign of environmental stress in Modern times was the depletion of timber resources – started around the Mediterranean over the period of the Roman Empire and then taking off again in the 16th Century - that were the basis of so much of life in Europe, ranging from buildings through to tools and machinery (rakes and ox yokes, wagons and carriages, looms and oil presses etc.) to growing naval and trading fleets. Forests also provided almost all the energy resources fuelling these societies.

Britain was alone throughout the 19th century in substantially reducing the proportion of goods produced locally. Production of different goods became concentrated in different cities — cotton cloth in Lancashire and wool in Yorkshire, shoes in Northampton and stockings in Nottingham, machinery in the Midlands and so on, and by the mid-century Britain was producing and exporting a substantial proportion of the world's traded manufactured goods[311]. At the same time, the opening up of the United States provided grain, and later in the century, with the invention of refrigerated transport railcars and ships, meat was imported from Australasia and the Americas. We should not, however, exaggerate the loss of food self-sufficiency at the national level when, as recently as the 1960s, some 80% of the calorific value of food in the UK was still provided by produce originating within the country and even with a recent decline, today two thirds of calorific value is grown within the country. However, the amount grown within sub-regions where it is consumed is considerably lower with 'food ton-miles' within the country continually growing. It has already been noted that today almost half of these 'food-miles' are, however, accomplished by consumers driving to the supermarket and back[312].

It is clearly the increasing exploitation, initially of coal and thence of oil, that facilitated this de-localisation and the expansion of transportation that was the means to expedite this transformation. However, whilst steam power for shipping, railways and industrial production spread across Europe through the late 19th and early 20th centuries, nowhere else in Europe was there such a marked de-localisation as was experienced in Britain. Even in the 1920s, studies of South Germany (associated particularly with Walter Christaller[313]) indicate substantial sub-regional self-reliance in production through the interconnection of villages with towns and small cities, with the former supplying food and much by way of other raw materials whilst the towns and cities produced the manufactures for the regional population[314]. The potential for trade had been immensely augmented by a dense network of railways, and fossil fuel was everywhere available that might have facilitated specialisation and was, from the 1880s, the basis for the rapid growth of German manufacturing industries mainly, sitting atop the Ruhrgebiet coal mines. However, 'tradition' remained strong and it was not until after the Second World War that substantial numbers of German farmers substituted tractors for horses to plough their fields[315].

The United States might have been expected also to pioneer de-localisation in that immigrant populations, with no roots in any particular part of the territory, poured into the country over the 19th and early 20th centuries and as a consequence, specialisation of cities and the process of industrialisation might have preceded that of the UK. With a few early exceptions, it was only towards the end of the 19th century that specialisation of particular cities became salient in the United States. On the whole there remained a significant dispersal of skills and production right across the country. Whilst farmers in the United States were more likely to produce for export out of their region and abroad than their European counterparts who sold more into local markets, nevertheless, the localities continued into the 20th century to be significantly self-reliant, with the urban population only exceeding the rural population in 1925 — when, by contrast, already by the turn of the 20th century the rural population in the UK was well below ten per cent.

So what we see is that, in historic terms, until very recently indeed — to within the lifetime of today's elderly populations — the idea that most of what we consume might be expected to be produced relatively locally could be assumed. Luxuries and then increasingly also necessities flowed into shops and lifestyles, not just of the rich but increasingly also to the expanding middle classes in cities that were no longer locally sourced or produced. As incomes rose early in the 20th century, so tastes could be flattered and even satisfied by products and produce from ever greater distances. Somehow the Commercial Ideology and the whole process of Development came replete, with the help of increasing advertising, with a notion that something produced elsewhere was better than that produced locally (and cheaper with the scale economies of mass production) and at the same time the range of things that came from distant places expanded, extending from food through to household goods and gadgets to means of transport and places to go to and eventually even to building materials. And this was thought to be a natural process where the idea of wealth and conspicuous consumption, as advocated by Mandeville, Adam Smith and an expanding body of 'economists', had become the ultimate goal of life with nothing by way of critical concern regarding the sustainability of this process.

The fact is that trade by value and volume grew rapidly throughout the 19th century, even whilst representing only a modest amount of the total economic activity of the Occidental countries. This, however, stagnated and even declined during the first half of the 20th century in the context of the Great Depression and two World Wars[316]. What today is referred to as Globalisation started in a relatively modest way immediately after the Second World War and accelerated greatly following the 'neoliberal counter-revolution' of 1979-80. Over the period 1945 to 2005 the global volume of trade increased in money terms by a factor of eight — which, it should be noted, was closely paralleled by an eight-fold increase in the throughput of fossil fuels, so that reliance on these amongst energy sources in the 'industrialised countries' rose to eighty five per cent.

Much ink has been spilled over the absurdities of much of this trade seen as de-localisation. It is not necessary here to provide any kind of complete overview, but examples will suffice to illustrate the phenomenon. Food production has been increasingly concentrated, not just grain and meat but all kinds of other produce. Dutch 'farmers' have succeeded in capturing markets in vegetables, and also flowers, by growing these in vast greenhouses that are lit throughout the night to speed growth, with the produce then shipped to supermarkets right across northern Europe. Potatoes, as a basic source of nutrition, grow easily in urban regions almost anywhere in the north but few are now grown anything like locally; New Yorkers consume potatoes predominantly from Idaho, while Long Island potatoes grown near the city are shipped in great quantity to Florida. By 2005, the inhabitants of Berlin, surrounded by excellent agricultural land, obtained little more than ten per cent of their potatoes from the hinterland of the city, with different varieties available from right across Europe and as far afield as Egypt.

A study of the origins and destinations of yoghurt, which can also be produced anywhere where there is pasture for cows (which, wherever they are located today, are fed mainly on grain shipped over considerable distances) was produced in southern Germany in the 1990s, yielding a map that indicated long-range sourcing of ingredients, including the pots and lids, packaging and labels, and then a wide distribution of the product to supermarkets across the region[317]. Aluminium drinks cans distributed across Europe are economically worthwhile to be recycled. In the British case, recycled cans from all around the country first go to Runcorn to be processed into raw material and then to Germany where they are made back into cans before being distributed to the canning plants and redistributed to retailers across the continent.

Lobsters consumed in New England are cultivated in New England. However, once caught or farmed, they are shipped to Memphis, Tennessee from where they are distributed by air across the USA, including back to New England. The stories are endless, and indeed the bulk of international trade is internal to corporations that are shipping materials, parts and semi-finished produce and final products around and around the world, being processed along the way before reaching the shops where they will be sold. Of course all of this has been fuelled by a growing flow of fossil fuels, and particularly oil. Although the rhetoric of 'unsustainability' was often cast at this phenomenon, even in the few cases where the energy consumption consequences were calculated (such as the British food-miles study referred to above), this was not coupled to any attempt to calculate how long it could continue and what would happen when it could no longer continue as a consequence of the peaking and decline of energy resources.

This de-localisation and particularly the concentration of productive activities has clearly been facilitated not just by cheap energy and massive investment in transport infrastructure and vehicles but in great measure through 'improvements' in technology, that is to say introduction of technologies that can produce greater and greater volumes of particular products in a shorter time and with decreasing workforces and in decreasing numbers of locations. Temporary winners in this end-race have been those who were able to make the investments in these technologies and operated them where they were cheapest to operate in terms mainly of the cost of labour.

And here we reach what we might construe as the main point at issue: de-localisation has been, on the social side, an extreme process of de-skilling — what one school of anthropology refers to as 'the growth of ignorance'[318]. Throughout the Occident, across the 20th century, the proportion of the workforce working in farming decreased to a point where today this involves considerably less than ten per cent. This was followed by a diminution of the workforce involved in manufacturing, to a point where in few countries does this exceed twenty per cent today. 'Services' provide employment for the vast majority of those working in the Occidental countries. In southern countries these services are provided mainly by the 'informal economy,' where the population receives little by way of income and suffers endemic insecurity as a consequence of the rapidity of economic change. Education and health are significant employers but 'financial and business services' have continually increased as sources of employment — in Britain, by 2008 amounting to a quarter of the national workforce.

This translates into very small proportions of populations having any meaningful idea of how things are produced, from what materials and through what methods and hence with what skills. Even manufacturing employment increasingly involves tending and maintaining sophisticated machines that are controlled by electronics, themselves made in highly concentrated factories connected to design offices located in a few centres and locations in Europe and North America, and increasingly in Asia. A further dimension of this 'growth of ignorance' has been the disconnection between urban populations and the natural environment discussed in the foregoing chapter, but that can usefully be underscored in this context. Already starting with the industrial revolution and the decanting of rural populations into urban industries, this can be seen to have been a vital step in nurturing a lack of respect for the natural environment.

In the past, rural populations might at times have abused the land. However, they soon learned the error of their ways through the lowering of production and income. Farming practices had evolved and ways to improve production increased but this took place generally in a leisurely way, with rural populations (everywhere the vast majority) maintaining a necessary respect for the local piece of nature in which they lived. Indeed, traces of Animism or related imputation of spirits into particular places and manifestations in nature persisted in all countries, which only recent urbanisation — and the spirit and practices of modernism — have extinguished[319]. Some would say that this severance of people from the natural setting and herding into concrete jungles (or even suburbs) has involved a catastrophic impoverishment of the spirit as well as precipitating a callousness towards nature that is a consequence not of aggression but of ignorance. The vast majority of humanity simply no longer has more than a fleeting idea, from video clips on television, what the impacts are of our lifestyle upon the environment and the depletion of resources.

We can think of two main dimensions to the forces that have driven urbanisation and with it the construction and reconstruction of the urban workforce. First is the political, that has involved in the first instance the disciplining process of factory work and then, following the rise of socialism and trade unionism and thence the ending of the Developmental era, an extrication of businesses — in the framework of neoliberalism promoted by governments – from the very possibility that 'labour' (in practice trade unions) can hold businesses to ransom through strike activity. In other words, de-localisation and the growth of ignorance has not been a just-so story but has been underlain by processes to disempower and exploit others by those who would gain power and wealth[320]. These are driven, in other words, by the Mandevillian and Adam Smithian principle that wealth creation is the primary goal of life. The impacts in the North appear mainly as the exploitation of people as consumers, but the other side of the equation is the exploitation of cheap workforces in the South. The Commercial Ideology would like to insist that the mechanisms that have created the global economy are benign for everyone. However, whilst in the short term they are in reality impoverishing for vast numbers in the South, in the longer run they are catastrophic for everyone.

The other force driving delocalisation is from the perspective of the workers themselves; once the pride in physical labour and craftsmanship has receded, the pursuit of status translates into a flight from 'labour' into any kind of work that is deemed to be of higher status, meaning in practice out of factories and into offices or stores or street vending. The meaning of 'menial work' and lower wages has shifted into such employment as shop assistants and entertainment workers, secretarial and other 'low-grade' administrative workers, transport operatives and maintenance workers.

As discussed in the previous chapter, this has not obviated class difference, and insofar as income and wealth disparities have grown in recent years, all that has happened is that the whole class system has 'shifted upwards' and become diffused into a complex, multi-layered construct largely constituted of a wide range of service jobs, themselves arranged into hierarchies including the swollen administration of business companies, government bureaucracies, hospitals and so on. This is referred to by anthropological theorists as stratification. Extremely little of a physical nature that is consumed by these workforces is produced in any proximity to where they live and work. But status is achieved by the fact that even the poorest can afford something from the cornucopia of modern production and in this way can claim progress in status.

The Social Relations of Production

The environmental movement never really managed to focus on why the world refused to accept its message about the non-sustainability of current economic processes under way and the fact that this would end either in a fulsome recognition of this and consequent changes in how the world's production and consumption systems work, or, as indicated by *The Limits to Growth,* end in a veil of tears. In earlier chapters we have dealt with the way in which social competition for wealth as status became the central machinery of the way that Occidental (and increasingly global) culture works and with this the understanding of what is the central truth of life, marginalising the social and environmental consequences of this.

Here we want to focus on what might be called the theoretical framework of how societies more generally engage with nature to produce what they need (or in our case mainly what we desire) to sustain life. A useful starting point is Marx's notion of the Mode of Production, being a concept which encompasses both the mechanisms wherein nature is exploited, at the same time pointing to the social formation in terms of who does what and who gains what from the exploitative process.

The concept of Mode of Production (we shall refer to it below simply as MoP) derives from Karl Marx's analysis of social evolution where he was particularly interested in the emergence of capitalism out of feudalism in Europe and thence with helping to define a future stage that we will start by referring to as a Communist Mode of Production. This was assumed by Marx - and the Marxist movement through much of the 20th Century - to be a natural corollary and a 'final stage' in social evolution. With hindsight it is clear that the Communist Mode of Production as it actually unfolded (maybe we should refer to this simply as the Soviet MoP), whilst in certain respects successful in its own terms, at least on the production side, cannot be seen as a 'natural' successor to capitalism. Indeed, with better knowledge today of how non-Occidental societies organise themselves, the very notion of a single line of evolution, whereby Chinese, Indian and indeed all other cultures would be shoehorned into a hierarchy that would end in communist society is clearly a very naïve, or dogmatic, application of the idea of progress — or as it was seen philosophically, 'the triumphal march of history'.

So do we simply reject the very existence of Modes of Production? Maybe not — especially in the light of the force with which the ideology of neoliberalism as the present global MoP, clearly rooted in capitalism, continues to rule the way in which not only Occidental but increasing all societies — at least in terms of their 'formal economies' — are organised. The idea of the Mode of Production is a useful analytical tool to set the scene for the discussion later in this chapter of what we might conceive of as organising principles for a future sustainable world.

Essentially the concept of the MoP, that we can also refer to as the 'social relations of production', links together the way in which societies organise the exploitation of nature and the production of materials and goods, at the same time allocating roles and responsibilities in the exploitation and production process as well as distributing the results across all members of society. Interpreted flexibly we can see how different Modes of Production structure meaning in life in terms of values projected into nature and natural and man-made objects. In the case of the present-day MoP, we have analysed earlier the rise of the concept of the individual and related to this the concept of 'property' and 'ownership' and thence how society is structured, in the ethnographic sense, as a means to allocate responsibilities and rights across families, communities and eventually nations.

The reason for the existence of MoPs is at root clearly the imperative to satisfy human need for sustenance and at the same time to supply meaning with respect to human relations, and provide structures to accomplish this. Culture is, as it were, the strategic structure — given life by basic understanding of what (social) life is all about, that stretches from ideas or notions or concepts ranging from God and spiritual meaning imputed to both abstractions and, in earlier religions, also things-in-nature. It is revealed through the grander artefacts of societies such as monuments and artistic creations, down to details such as food and dress, all imputed with symbolic meaning and value with an important dimension of lending status to people involved in various ways with these ideas and artefacts. The MoP is the structure of activity that *produces* this. Basic to all MoPs in complex societies prior to communism, was the proof of status and the differential lifestyles of different classes and 'lifestyle groups'. In European, under feudalism as well as under Confucian, caste and slave societies, the social allocation process was clearly determined by the MoP. These were and are internally coherent and self-maintaining systems of belief, understanding and action.

What is quintessential about the concept is that definite sets of relations come into being, sometimes evolving slowly through transition periods and sometimes rapidly: the Marxist assumption (and with a very wide 'quiet' following) has been that this could happen overnight through revolutions lasting just a few years — and in the case of the Soviet MoP, this was certainly the case. Marx himself, in line with Enlightenment proclivities, (and this was widely discussed amongst his following) tended to see social evolution as a single, universal path to be trodden by all human societies. Today, few believe this in the light of the extraordinary variety of Modes of Production that have manifested themselves around the globe over the past few millennia and where, today, knowledge of non-Occidental societies is far more extensive than that which Marx could glean from his research in the British Library.

Hence we can speak of a hunting and gathering MOP in which value is imputed to the particularities of nature and environment in which particular small bands lived, where there is very little by way of physical accoutrements of life and where social relations are egalitarian and informal in the sense of roles being largely ill-defined and interchangeable, albeit there being certain marked constant gender roles. There has been something of an assumption (albeit with little concrete evidence) that these matters were unchanging over ninety per cent of the period in which Homo sapiens has graced the earth. Whether true or not, there certainly came a sudden complexification process with the advent of agriculture —the manipulation of nature as 'other' — and with it the condensing out of social hierarchies, the heart of which was the division of labour in the production, and with this the consumption, systems: farmers and pharaohs, building labourers and artisans, kings and warlords with their entourages and armies.

The analysis of Morton Fried of the steps between hunting and gathering and the advent of civilisation discussed in Chapter Three[321] is useful in indicating the internal logic of different modes of human organisation with the Mode of Production, or the exploitation of nature, the processing of materials into commodities and the formulas for their distribution, at their foundation. It is evident that the organisation of large-scale irrigation systems both intensified the relationship with nature, radically altering ecological systems, imposing human organisational principles and at the same time creating definite, hierarchical social relations with the vast majority of these populations subsisting in slave relations. At a relatively early stage the resulting societies already abstracted out 'meaning' in terms of religious beliefs, sanctifying social and political organising principles and organising workforces not only for agriculture and artisanal work but even to construct monuments, such as pyramids, as instruments of complexifying rituals attaching to these abstractions in belief[322]. That this appeared in several places in Eurasia and persisted for thousands of years is testimony to its concreteness as a mode of social organisation and in terms of its sustainability[323].

Marx and the discussions of the MoP which his work inspired tended to see everywhere, as a prelude to the emergence of capitalism, a feudal form of society. European feudalism came in a variety of forms. All of these were hierarchical in a similar way to Indian Caste society where individuals were born into particular classes with particular socio-economic roles and statuses, duties and benefits with regard to what they had to produce — both 'at work' and in the household or royal court or religious institution — and what they could expect to receive from the production system. There was very little hope for the vast majority of populations of escaping the role into which they were born and it was the process whereby the rigidities of this system came to an end, particularly following the Great Plagues of the 14th century, that inspired Marx's notion of an evolutionary trajectory from slave to caste to 'bourgeois capitalist' Modes of Production. This would continue on to a rationally organised society and production system that could only happen through the dismantling of class difference in which different classes possessed different understandings of the world and different interests which underpinned these.

The fact is, however, that social evolution produced very different kinds of society and productive processes in different places that were, in themselves, viable and sustainable over long periods, if short of the particular ideals of the European Enlightenment and the subsequent radical social movements of the 19th century. Mention has been made from time to time in this book of both Hindu and Confucian societies as presenting such alternatives — and perhaps more should have been made also of Islam with its very definite idea on how society and within this the production system should be organised that even today has a major impact on the lives of one and a half billion people. Beyond this, at more local levels, indeed even within the major social organisational systems, there were variations: areas where landlords prevailed and others where peasant holdings were independent or even communally organised. Even under the ostensibly capitalist system of the Occident, we see the latifundia Mode of Production, already discussed, and the slave production system of the southern states of the United States and Latin America.

We nevertheless generally see in each society – being the principle defining feature of that society - an overall set of organisational principles tending to be sanctified by religions, usually rather indirectly (in the case of Islam and Christianity but Buddhism also has nothing direct to say about this with the notable exception of the monasteries) but with definite rules regarding who should do what and who has the right to determine what gets done and who gets what, starting with blood relations and the family and progressing through from the local to the wider society of the nation. Today, Hinduism presents an extreme regarding people born into a particular role with its precise responsibilities and procedures and the benefits attaching to these, as having very little chance to move into another role. However, this can be seen as the last remainder of the deeply divided societies that characterised European and other slave and feudal societies prior to the modern era.

But even in non-caste societies, the vast majority of the population continued until the last several decades within family networks to practise what their forebears had practiced in terms of their role in the production system, with resources flowing between family members in rather precisely defined ways, disrupted only by the forces of Occidental modernisation. Family hierarchies were the dominant mode of self-understanding and organisation everywhere in civilised societies until the advent of modernity as the basic building block of the MoP. Indeed, these continue to matter in societies as diverse as Arab, Overseas Chinese and Latin American; elites that superficially seem to operate on capitalistic principles.

We should be clear that Modes of Production are, on the social side, moral systems. It was the cleric Calvin who opened the door to the notion that making money might be morally just and we should never forget that Adam Smith, whom we might refer to be the prophet of capitalism, was not a professor of economics, but of ethics. The essence of capitalism is that the isolated individual who is prepared to take risks in investing and organising enterprises, is morally just, and is also justified in being superior to those whom he employs to carry out the actual work.

Hierarchy is therefore not explicit, as in caste and feudal society, but implicit as evidenced by the successful accumulation of capital. Economic relationships are then not determined by favours and fixed status positions but by contract in which definite activities are determined within the confines of enterprise. The terms 'crony-ism' and 'nepotism' give the flavour of the way in which extra-enterprise relations, including even family favours, are seen as somehow immoral and, in line with Adam Smith's belittling of the usefulness of government, even the existence, and certainly the moral justification of government, comes into question. By contrast, we note the favourable light in which the words 'enterprise' and 'business' appear in present-day discourse. The de facto impacts on social, environmental and resource terms simply don't figure in this moral system. Hence the incommensurability of economic discourse, about 'economic growth', and social and environmental issues.

Earlier we discussed the evolution of religion and the way in which nature was increasingly ignored as a dimension of human life. When discussing possible political systems in Chapter Three, reference was made to Plato's analysis of different political and economic conjunctures in Hellenic Greece. What was not of concern (and can be found elsewhere in Greek writing in passing) was the way in which Greek development was already losing an effective concern for the interaction between society and nature and hence an ethic that could render the whole sustainable. Christianity paid even less regard to nature[324]. The evolution of European thought and action in terms of organising productive processes was incipiently destructive of nature, not wilfully, but simply because it was there as a resource to be exploited. This may be seen as significant background to the essential ineffectiveness of environmental management and disregard for the limits to resource exploitation today. We might say, however, that post hunter-gatherer Modes of Production tended in general to increasingly underplay the value and to instrumentalise nature as a function of the self-concern of the social hierarchy and the excessive focus on how the distribution of the benefits should be determined.

Turning to the question of commerce, as such an important feature of our world today, we should note that commerce and indeed the aspiration to accumulate wealth was not invented by European culture in the context of the emergence of the Capitalist MoP, but has played an essential role in all the more complex civilisations — though, it needs to be emphasised, *not* in pre-civilised societies[325]. The point, however, is that it has always occupied a particular niche, controlled by the overall framework of social and economic organisation. As already implied in the general division of responsibilities, Hinduism assigned commerce to particular castes and this was also taken on by minority religious groups (Jains and Muslims) and in this context had no chance of greatly expanding its role. Both in Confucian and Islamic societies, small entrepreneurship played an essential role in production and distribution. In the Islamic world this is still the case, where large enterprises are few and never 'out of control' in the way to be found in the Occident. This is underpinned by the socio-religious principle that forbids the use of interest – usury - as a mechanism for accumulating capital.

It is also germane that small enterprises in many pre-capitalist societies were organised into associations and guilds that, far from encouraging free competition in the Adam Smithian conception, cooperated in maintaining standards and, indeed, regulating prices, not in monopolistic fashion but in order to maintain a quality of product and a modest income for all who produced a good product. These 'guilds' were destroyed in Europe, starting in the Renaissance but persisting in many countries into the 19th century and in the German case, carrying through as a remnant into the present-day practice of vocational training. In the Middle East, these can still be found in many cities in western and southern Asia[326] and in Vietnam (the famous 39 streets of Hanoi and their related craft villages are still today a tourist attraction).

The spread of the Commercial Ideology in Europe and particularly the violent destruction of traditional society, the dismissal of workers and the creation in the early 19th century of the factory system, smashed the guilds and created the disenculturated 'working classes' with the degraded living conditions described so well by Marx's colleague Frederick Engels in the Manchester of 1848[327]. The transition of Confucian society to adopting capitalism as an ideology and lifestyle can be witnessed particularly amongst the 'overseas Chinese' (Hong Kong, Singapore and Taiwan) where small family businesses, with the weakening of Confucian values and political structures, at the same time coming under the administration of the British, began to expand the scale of their activity and aspire to the open-ended pursuit of wealth that evolved, after the collapse of Communism and Dung Xiao Ping's famous statement that: *it doesn't matter what colour the cat as long as it catches the mouse* (i.e. accumulate wealth), into the extraordinary explosion of modern production in mainland China that has come to play a key role in the global production system over the last three decades.

At this juncture it is useful to note the many critics today, particularly in the United States, of the obvious depredations, both social and environmental, of the present manifestation of capitalism. These critics overwhelmingly call for a de-escalation of the size of enterprise[328] and some also for the relocalisation of economic activity[329]. Indeed, this has a long tradition in the United States as a minority movement; in the 1930s it was associated with the name of Louis Brandeis, who championed both trade unionism and small business. This movement is edging towards a deeper critique of 'business' and, perhaps the more radical exponents (Albert, DeFillipis, McKibben) will propose more fundamental change in economic structures to address the need for some overarching control at the level of 'community', with implications for ideology (as opposed to the law) and the social matrix that would ensure, if de-escalation were possible, that large enterprises would not re-emerge.

However, none of this identifies the deeper cultural motivation and structures of capitalism. Fundamentally, capitalism is about making money from money, fundamental to wealth accumulation, central to which is the payment of interest on capital, and whilst pre-existing status structures persist weakly (monarchies, patrician bourgeois families, etc.), at the foundation, money accruing to individuals — and thence what it can buy — performs the act of allocating status. The emphasis shifts from the direct identification of status with individuals, as kings and slaves, lords and vassals and even as bosses and workers, to one where flows of money as income and wealth, and the manipulation of money, take on an independent role with religious qualities driving the system, hiding class and all other hierarchical social difference behind a veil, where individual status is what really matters to people as social beings.

Ostensibly money accrues from work and the 'work ethic' gains its meaning from this. The value of different kinds of work determines how much money an individual might obtain from the system, and we all know how perverse this gets where the people who perform the real acts of production and servicing that create the actual world in which we all live today are paid little for their efforts while increasingly esoteric 'professional' and other 'high quality' services (and at the pinnacle, entertainers) are showered with money. We have seen in recent years the increasing degree to which the highest status of work is that which is directly concerned with the manipulation of money — speculation and banking[330]. The 'relationship with nature' in producing everyday life has by now almost entirely vanished from view in terms of 'value', being but a means for an increasingly small proportion of the workforce, given that machines, powered by fossil fuel, are now doing the real work.

Turning now to the 'Communist Mode of Production', we can be sure that Soviet Communism was a genuine attempt to overcome the negative social and related psychological effects of moral individualism and the money machine and the status structures that this has fuelled. Furthermore, it did indeed succeed in introducing a MoP that was radically different from capitalism, destroying the centrality of money which characterised the Commercial Ideology as a 'natural' phenomenon. In its own terms the 'centrally planned economy', ostensibly determining what each person needed for the good life and then organising production in a functionally rationalistic fashion to satisfy these needs, was for much of the 20th century a considerable success in applying such organising principles to the processes of production and distribution.

With its demise, we forget the difficulty with which the ideologues of capitalism were able to justify their system in the face of the rapidity and apparent efficiency with which the Soviets built up their industrial competence and capacity in the 1920s and 1930s over and against the Great Depression. At its end, communism is supposed to have failed as a system because it failed to supply the ineffable benefits of the Consumer Society. This, however, misses the central problem in that although there were at times perceived shortages and thus delays in the satisfaction of consumer desires that were blamed on the planning and production system, the Soviet Central Planning system, nevertheless, developed a modern infrastructure across the vast territory of the Soviet Union and Eastern Europe and manifested a sophistication in its productive capacity to match that of Western Europe and the United States. Above all, by the end, it succeeded in supplying a reasonably comfortable lifestyle for all in a substantially more egalitarian way than has been the case with capitalism — particularly when contrasted with recent conditions where it is increasingly freed of the accoutrements of social democracy and welfare states that prevailed in the immediate decades following the Second World War.

Indeed, in principle the Soviet system was supposed to eliminate social difference and produce a classless society embodied in the ideal of the universal 'Socialist Man' (sic), in which hard labour would be eliminated and a life of comparative ease lived by all. However, no public discussion was allowed as to what that life of ease might consist of and insofar as there remained a gulf between decision-makers (the

Nomenklatura together with technocrats and privileged intellectuals) and those who received the decisions, *de facto* class did exist, even if not expressed in monetary terms. Furthermore, the planning system constantly watched and emulated the twists and turns of developing consumerism in the Capitalist world, with the United States as a role model.

The pursuit of wealth thus continued as a parody of the capitalist process of accumulation, rather than as an end towards the 'good society' that had been the original goal of the radical movements of the 19th century. It may seem pathetic that smuggled Levi jeans and Coca Cola became so easy to sell in the Soviet Union, while copies by state enterprises of goods produced in the capitalist West — from clothing to televisions and cars right down to free holidays organised by trade unions on the Black Sea — were spurned as somehow not so beguiling. So we end up recognising that it was, in the end, the seductive dimension of capitalism, in its guise as the Consumer Society, that triumphed over the Communist MoP, rather than that it was inadequate as a system of production and distribution. And insofar as the privileged class of the Soviet Union did emulate their peers in the capitalist West, there seemed no more reason to pretend that the goals of communism were any different from those of the world beyond its borders. It was this that resulted in the collapse of the Communist Mode of Production: rather than follow capitalism, let's have it directly!

It is well enough known that the rejection of the Communist MoP did not lead immediately to access for the majority of the population to the symbols and objects produced by capitalism. Indeed, it led immediately to economic collapse and the majority of the population has yet to see benefits on a level with those they received under the Communist MoP. It is very sad that the disappointment so widespread in Russia today at the collapse of the Soviet Union fails to motivate concerted constructive criticism of the Soviet Mode of Production that might have saved and built upon what did work. Instead we have witnessed an abject capitulation to a system that does not work for the majority, even on its own terms, by providing access to consumer goods and the status which these can imply. Furthermore, this being the main concern of this book – the whole capitalist system cannot survive too much longer into the future with no notion of what might come after.

What has made capitalism so beguiling, dissolving all effective criticism in its wake. has been the way in which it has promised and eventually supplied the illusion of status for vast populations in the

249

form of an ever growing flow of 'commodities', or Stuff. The 'critique of capitalism' has continually obscured the moral problems of the Ideology of Commerce. The moral critique of capitalism, according to Marxism and its progeny, is that it exploits the working classes in the sense of depriving them of dignity, and at worst renders them physically deprived. But if the working classes are given the opportunity to join the race for status, then they do not see things this way and so this critique loses its force.

Furthermore, over the second half of the 20th century in the capitalist nations, the supplanting by machines of what was once a large working class that understood itself to be exploited, projected them into 'work' that has an ostensible 'middle class' status and hence enlarged the proportion of the population that saw itself as legitimate participants in the race for status even whilst their actual status was that of employees. Arguably a more profound critique of the Commercial Ideology, however, is directly a moral critique that recognises that it is based upon 'sleaze': the striving to possess the symbols of status by whatever means and with no consideration other than that imposed by the law, of the human and environmental consequences, commodifying individuals as competitive entities and distancing feelings of human mutuality. In other words, it turns humans into objects — 'commodities' or Locke's notion of property — as functions of their status and the Stuff that confirms this, over and against the self-identification with community and ultimately mutual love overflowing into love of the place in which we find ourselves: an outward instead of an inward, individualistic, even narcissistic love.

The production system therefore cannot be designed simply as a rational system of the extraction, processing, manufacturing and distribution of materials and goods in isolation from the social relations of production and, above all, consumption on a foundation of the meaning inherent in these social relations as manifest in particular societies. The focus on the Commercial Ideology in earlier chapters indicates how the competition for wealth and status has been the motor of capitalism, and not just as money made from money but, as is ever clearer today, in the struggle to possess and the way in which this defines who we are and how we should relate to our fellow human beings – i.e. the 'social formation'. Any attempt at a considered reformulation of the production system must come to terms with the issue of reconstructing the social psychology and with it the very foundations of social self-understanding as a social project, before even considering how the production system, and beyond this the viability of its use of resources and environment, might be reformed.

It is with this in mind that we may focus a little attention on the 'informal economy' of the Southern countries today. When this was discovered in Africa by the International Labour Organisation in the 1970s, the assumption was that the 'problem' of the proliferation of 'micro-enterprises' that was accompanying the process of urbanisation in the South was simply one of the population growing in advance of modern economic Development and that in time, these workforces would be absorbed into the mainstream of the capitalist (or eventually communist) Mode of Production[331]. One might, however, jump to the conclusion that here is an alternative MoP that has sprung up out of the failure of the two main contending Modes of Production to satisfy the needs, physical and psychological, of the burgeoning urban masses in the South and, given its continuing growth as a percentage of the world's workforce in recent years, that we are confronted with what may, in future, become the predominant MoP.

However, notwithstanding local differences in the structure of the informal economy, in part because of differences in culture, by and large, this is not simply a revival of small-scale production of pre-capitalist societies but, rather, a form of redistribution of the overflowing wealth of capitalism in its fossil-fuelled excess of resources. Little is actually being *produced,* the main activity being street trading, much of it of inexpensive and even recycled produce of the 'formal' economy where a small (in Africa and South Asia very small) capitalist (and state) economy 'leaks' enough material and money (much of it through 'corruption') to maintain massive urban populations in precarious lifestyle conditions.

Pre-existing social relations continue, albeit gradually dissolving, be they caste or other systems of social status and commitment, through the corrosive influence of the Commercial Ideology and more broadly Occidental culture as experienced through urbanisation processes and impacts of global and local media propaganda. Families, tending over much of the South to be extremely large and extended, often straddle the divide with one or more members working in the 'formal' economy, maybe 'moonlighting', and other members active in the informal economy , which itself may involve 'put-out' work undertaken in the home for the formal economy.

As the decline in energy resources sets in, whilst this redistribution mechanism will surely continue, it will do so in conditions of declining urban populations due to the diminishing availability of all goods and materials and, in particular, food. Populations will disperse back to the countryside and rural towns or die in the context of spreading urban hunger, already visible on a small but escalating scale today. The

251

central question will be: through what stages will today's path towards an extreme individualistic (or in the South familial) MoP make the transition to modes of cooperation that will re-establish viable community economies?

What we have been insisting throughout this discussion is that we need to bring together analysis of possible ways of producing what we need from nature in a way that nurtures nature itself, with the social structures that carry out these productive processes. This is not just a technical exercise as might have been understood as the ideal of the Communist MoP. The most difficult dimension involves breathing life into any such invention in the sense of its being emotionally, psychologically and above all socially engaging, that the result has meaning and sense for all the participants, and that it is universally agreed upon (even if only at a relatively local level) — in the longer run without fundamental questions of the kind that demolished the Communist MoP.

In the coming years, with the falling apart of modern production systems, it will be necessary to reconstruct societies in their capacity as systems of production, reproduction and consumption at a relatively local level. As in past eras, there will have to be an empathetic understanding of the environment from which the resources necessary for life are extracted and the social relations of production and reproduction that will have a coherent consciousness of themselves as functioning systems if they are to work. This will call for a universal commitment and a deep, eventually internalised and unquestioned, sense of responsibility.

From the foregoing discussion, insofar as human cultures survive the fall of Occidental Progressivist culture, we would not expect any 'post-capitalist' or revised 'Communist Mode of Production' to emerge in any universal way but, quite possibly, a proliferation of Modes of Production that may cover wider territories in a synergistic manner or may be relatively local as was the case described by Plato in Hellenic Greece. Nevertheless, it is worthwhile, in the spirit of the earlier discussion of communitarianism and Bioregionalism, to consider possible dimensions and components of a post-fall Mode of Production appropriate at least to Occidental circumstances that might be posed as 'neither capitalism nor communism', that could provide a relatively sophisticated life for all, including enjoyable working conditions and relations, and to do so whilst maintaining, even enhancing, the self-reproduction of nature and radically de-escalating reliance on inherently non-renewable resources. There are several key components to this that we discuss separately in the following sections of this chapter.

By way of a general pointer, we can see a relatively clear 'alternative MoP' that has been on offer in many parts of the world historically and in the Occident, in a coherent way, since at least the middle of the 19th century, in the form of 'Cooperativism'[332]. Reference has been made to this on several occasions earlier in this text, indicating that it is a perfectly viable way of organising productive processes from farming through processing to manufacturing and distribution and thence on to the provision of services. The case of Modragon has been mentioned already several times in this text, as the city that advanced the furthest in organising not only production but services and housing on a cooperative basis, but where success ended in degeneration and a merger with the growing Spanish capitalist economy and decay of the cooperative principle of equality. And then recently there has been a proliferation of related and extended sketches and experiments in Cooperativism, such as the notion of the Participatory Economy (Parecon)[333] and l'Economie Solidaire and then the notion of the 'gift economy' that adds community and social economies to traditional Cooperativism, all of which reject individual and corporate 'entrepreneurial' modes of economic organisation, substituting for this community and mutualistic approaches.

These cooperative modes of productive organisation are based on the same principles as participatory political organisation (direct democracy) but, whilst in practice in many countries, the principles of Cooperativism have been distorted, undermined or abandoned whilst continuing to use the word 'cooperative'. If applied consistently, honestly and with integrity, Cooperativism is essentially the practice of anarchism and egalitarianism, extending its ethos from the political arena into all corners of social relations. The rest of this chapter deals with a selection of themes relevant to re-organising life post-fossil energy, and takes as assumed that some kind of 'Cooperative MoP' will provide the organisational principles upon which the activities described and analysed are best undertaken. But in Chapter Seven we will need to look closely into the kinds of social relations compatible with and nurturing of Cooperativism that definitively abolishes the social status machinery that has been inherent in all MoPs produced in the course of civilisation.

Social Movements

Few human cultures expend much, or indeed any, intellectual effort on attempting to analyse and propose what might be appropriate ways to organise political and social life and the place of these arrangements in nature with respect to extracting what it takes to sustain society and more benignly, living respectfully and in admiration of the wonder of nature. The world and the prevailing social and political arrangements are simply accepted as given with, in extreme cases, rebellions that happen with no notion of what the rebels would like to have by way of solutions to their woes. China has been arguably the greatest exception to this, starting with Confucianism as a set of social and political rules and thence the Tao as a romantic, spiritual vision of the human condition in nature. Specific rules, many of which are serendipitous rather than obviously rational, are provided by Feng Shui and the I Ching.

The Abrahamic religions, starting already from Zoroastrianism and thence through Judaism, Christianity and Islam provided moral pillars and some detailed rules[334] which, however, are far short of anything that might be construed as a coherent structure for social and political organisation. The teachings of Christ produced fuel for discourse on what might constitute a 'good society' and the brief 'Greek Experiment'[335] gave us reasoned discussions of issues that have underlain the whole course of political development of European culture over the past millennium, the results of which were discussed in Chapter Three.

In this context, ideas about social and political change in Occidental culture have always been surrounded by a supercharged emotional casing that at times has been millenarian in nature: a mass rushing towards a severely inadequately defined future to take place through revolution or through the establishment of moral communities. Nevertheless, whilst very few people are aware of just how rich the history of such movements is, the fact is that Occidental culture has always possessed this dimension of the search for the ideal society and polity. Regarding the Middle Ages, Norman Cohn's *The Pursuit of the Millennium*[336] is essential reading as is Frank Manuel's research on the more recent centuries, particularly in his compendious *Utopian Thought in the Western World*[337].

Amongst the proposals made and experiments attempted, there have been many sound proposals and social movements that might have given us the kinds of society and political arrangements that would have yielded results that would have satisfied human needs in nature in better ways than has in practice been the case. Here we want to bring the record up to date by analysing recent manifestations that follow from these traditions and then attempt to make sense of them, what we hope for in the end will be a set of social relations and politics to resolve the problematic of civilisation and emerge from the fall that lies immediately ahead, with the right solutions[338].

We start with 1968, being a year that is remembered for the apparent possibility that the nascent global culture was about to fundamentally change direction. Reading the literature of the times, there can be no doubt that there was a strong millenarian atmosphere to the events that generated urban manifestations in many places around the world. Often seen as focusing on Paris, where for a brief moment student revolt and industrial strike brought the Government to the edge of collapse, lesser manifestations erupted in many other cities in Europe, across the Americas and even in Japan. This was not an altogether sudden manifestation but had been building up in demonstrations against the Vietnam War and a variety of fragmented youth movements that seemed to want a different kind of world from the one they were growing up in.

The hoped-for revolution, that was hopelessly ill-defined in terms of what the output was supposed to look like and which prima facie failed abysmally, nevertheless sired two, for us, important strands, producing initiatives and idea that have continued to develop and that can help us here to formulate suggestions and proposals towards the reconstruction of life following the fall of modern civilisation. One of these was the rise of the environmental movement; the initiatives and impacts of which ranged from formal improvement in environmental management, noted as one of the relative success stories of recent decades, to the more radical proposals for fundamental change in understanding human–nature relations and reorganising life accordingly. The other, that overlaps with the radical end of the environmental movement, is the 'communes movement' that in its immediate post-1968 manifestations was in a negative way anarchistic in that it involved 'hippies' asserting 'freedom' as reneging responsibility towards any kind of organised life.

However, from the start, going back to the years leading up to 1968, there were small signs of a general ambience out of which concrete alternatives might emerge, initially amorphous, so it is difficult to find clear edges to what we might consider relevant to useful guidance in the direction in which to take things. We can start by referring to journals that started and then continued to support useful explorations of ideas. In the UK a number of journals of this kind appeared, the first

255

of which (continuing today) was *Resurgence,* founded already in 1964 by a group that included E F Schumacher of *Small if Beautiful* fame and soon found an editor in the person of the Jain ex-monk, Satish Kumar, who continues even today to oversee the content of the journal[339].

The *Ecologist* was founded shortly after *Resurgence,* edited by Edward Goldsmith, who was the brother of a businessman who was at one point the richest man in Britain, accused by the then Prime Minister of representing 'the unacceptable face of capitalism.' It has since then maintained a trenchant critique of the modern world, and in one of its earliest issues presented something of a coherent decentralist utopia under the title of *Blueprint for Survival,* that, as a book, was widely discussed at the time[340]. A more radical journal in the UK, in the political sense, that explored 'alternative lifestyles' albeit with a technological focus closely connected with the then growing organic farming and alternative energy movements, was *Undercurrents* that after some years merged with *Resurgence*; the *Ecologist* is now also merged with *Resurgence.*

In North America this all began with the *Planet Drum* movement, with the *Whole Earth Catalogue* and *Raise the Stakes* as its radical expression of the movement and from 1970, *Mother Earth News* informing the more 'ecological' side of the new movements. It would be wrong to ignore the outpouring of grey literature and quasi-journals, together with all manner of events, 'conferences' and manifestations that arose in this period that seemed, in fragmented ways, to point in radically new directions[341]. In North America, at the forefront was (and remains) *Fifth Column*[342], that like *Undercurrents,* espoused anarchist sentiments that came to conjoin radical ecological concern with 'anti-authoritarian' sentiments. In the UK this slide into joining 'radical ecology' with anarchism was taken on by *Green Line*, starting in 1982 on the Anarchist-inclined fringe of the UK Green Party. Then in 1984 the more radical *Green Anarchist* was launched. These journals linked through to radical action initiatives and groups, including Earth First!, Animal Liberation Front and thence Ecological Liberation Front. Meanwhile, elsewhere in Europe other countries generated their own journals and movement fragments.

Also from the mid-1960s structured experiments in 'alternative living' began to blossom, reviving Utopian movements going back into the 18th and 19th Centuries[343] and of which a few, such as the Anabaptist Amish and Hutterites in North America, survived and spread with a population today estimated at some 300,000. Partly out of a desire to assist these to become more coherent in particular directions, there were also considerable attempts to theorise the different components and directions that these experiments were taking, exploring whether they might be the germ of what eventually would be fundamental change in Occidental outlook and lifestyles[344]. These communities, that have more recently acquired the title of 'Intentional Communities' in that they express 'alternative' ideas about life and the world and then attempt to live by these ideas, gradually proliferated over the years, so that there are today many hundreds scattered across the Occident, with a few also in Latin America and even in Asia[345].

When these manifestations emerged as the 'Communes Movement' in the 1970s, there arose some public interest. This soon, however, died down, giving the appearance that the movement had vanished. Certainly, for many years these communities remained small and with a tendency to come and go, leading Abrams and McCulloch, in their sympathetic analysis of the phenomenon at the time, to remarked harshly that:

...communes face insuperable obstacles in realising their aspirations in capitalist societies and that in the face of these obstacles they tend either to disintegrate or to become as authoritarian and as mystified as the societies from which they are trying to escape.[346]

However, through the 1990s and especially since the turn of the century, not only the numbers but also the size, durability and confidence in what they have been doing has become more evident[347]. Recent surveys have shown that whatever the other dimensions of their activity, an overwhelming first priority is to demonstrate ways of living that obviate the environmental and resource unsustainability of modern society.

Many of these communities are little more than an aspiration of a few, where 'members' are living otherwise conventional family lives, often in urban settings or suburban 'eco-villages', and are aware of their environmental impact but who are inconsistent in practice, having no framework to evaluate what their actual impact is. Some of the initiatives engage in social support for disadvantaged urban inhabitants and/or propagandise for more improvements in the way cities work. However, most of the communities have established themselves in rural areas, ranging in a few cases up to a hundred or more residents striving for self-reliant lifestyles through various approaches to organic farming, whether bio-dynamic or permaculture (of which more in the next chapter) and minimising energy use other than from renewable sources. Some are reviving craft skills that will certainly be necessary as

257

modernity recedes into the past and manufacturing will once again require manual skills utilising relatively simple technologies.

Living arrangements may range from continued stable and more or less private family arrangements to communal eating arrangements, communal distribution of tasks and sharing of income from the produce of the commune, or that members have earned out in the 'conventional' world. Most of these communities are also exploring different 'philosophies of life' in many cases adhering to some inherited religion: some fragment of Christianity or Indian philosophy, and in a few cases 'modern' in the sense of consciously socialist or anarchist frameworks. Private property is eschewed in many cases for some kind of cooperative ownership and common property management arrangements, both on the side of production and consumption, de-escalating the consumer culture and its, status-seeking and passion for Stuff.

Conflict management in the context of improved cooperative, consensus decision-making is an important issue as part of a process of eliminating the modern philosophy of liberalism and individualism. In short, there is accumulating and increasing confidence in working out arrangements that might be seen as precursors of forms of living that could become the basis of the reconstruction of community and ways of life that will be viable and enjoyable following the fall of modernity[348].

But even with a hundred or even two hundred members, these communities remain almost invisible, relative to the wider world in which they are located[349]. However, it might be said that this is a movement that will simply take off when the going gets rough as the global and local economies start an accelerating decline and the way of life which the vast majority of the Occidental population expect, increasingly falls apart. On the other hand, it is likely that even under dire hardship, the vast majority of modern citizens, particularly young people, are not only unaware of these 'alternative' communities and the ideas and lifestyles they espouse but certainly are very far from being able to empathise with, or even understand, what these are trying to do and how this might be an option also for them.

The tent cities that arose in the context of the collapse of the 'sub-prime' mortgage market and the massive evictions and unemployment in the United States that arose in the latter half of 2008 and start of 2009 certainly didn't lead to any dawning amongst the affected population of the possibilities of a positive but very different set of existential arrangements than pursuit of the American Dream, albeit there were reports of cases of spontaneous mutual help arising in the face of hardship. The brief spread of protest movements following in the footsteps of the 'Arab Spring', initially under the title of *Occupy Wall Street,* made no connection to the Intentional Communities movement but tended rather to manifest rhetorical gestures without content and, at worst, wishing to 'rebuild the American Dream' in the context of economic recession. Needless to say, government and corporate media answers to the crisis made no reference to alternative lifestyles by way of a response to the growing challenges, asserting continually the imperative to return to rapid 'economic growth' in the context of the global economy and ignoring the circumstances in which the affected population now found itself.

In practice, whilst Intentional Communities have made some strides in recent years to overcome what is often hostility of the communities amongst whom they have come to locate, and in many cases are seen positively and participate in local community life, it is not as if these can be expected in more than a small number of cases to spread their principles and ways of working to these 'conventional' communities[350]. However, there has also been since the 1970s, a movement thinking along the same general lines as the Communes Movement, that has been exploring alternative organisation of life at the regional scale under the title of 'Bioregionalism'.

Bioregionalism, initially essentially an American movement, started in the early 1970s — so can be seen to be another of the many strands that emerged from the non-revolution of 1968 and the rise of environmentalism in the years that followed. However, it is notable that the Bioregional idea can also be traced back to earlier American romantics who turned against the developmentalist thrust of American society in realising, briefly in each case, the destruction that development was precipitating. Thoreau, Emerson, John Muir, Aldo Leopold: these are all names attaching to a recessive anti-developmental strand in American thinking harking back to the 19th century that, had it become a more powerful force, would have led the society in a very different direction from the world-dominating empire towards which its elite have continually driven it[351].

Again, during the Depression years questions were being asked about the efficacy of the way in which the country was being developed, such as early revelations in the Dust Bowl of destructive agricultural practices and on the other hand thinking arising out of the failure of the capitalistic thrust of Development, and these led also to alternative proposals. Regional planning arose as one way out of the Depression and whilst the Tennessee Valley Authority with its interventionist spirit became a famous component of the way out of Depression, there were voices including Howard W Odum[352] and Lewis

Mumford[353] who had ideas that pointed more forcefully in the direction of internal development for the people where they lived, in situ, and not Development as wealth for an increasingly powerful nation[354].

Growing out of this history, Bioregionalism is thus a concept concerned with empathy with place and of developing a local culture as a socio-political expression of that place. Culture, as being place and environment based, is in this sense not an abstraction but must nevertheless be developed out of the human imagination: there are many ways to build a house out of local materials that synergises with the landscape that, at the same time, solves the environmental and existential needs of the occupants and their wider community, embodying an aesthetic expression of this resolution.

Classically this is returning with this notion to the synergy of traditional societies with their environments and the Bioregional movement was, from the outset, concerned to learn anything that remained of local indigenous 'Indian' cultures that could express things about the local and regional environment. This would teach us how to solve existential problems in particular settings, rather than as was the case with the Occidental society, which invaded and rode roughshod across the land, applying knowledge brought from elsewhere to exploit it. Knowledge brought in from outside would need to be applied with greater wisdom, empathising first with the land and adapting the sensibility acquired more sensitively to the complexities of the local climate, ecology and landscape; exploring possibilities whilst remaining at all times aware of the limits to intervention, the 'carrying capacity' of the region and its particular features and localities.

This is not to say that rationality should not be brought to bear in understanding regions. Bioregionalism has from the beginning a concern to inventory local resources and ecosystems using the tools, mental and physical, inherited from the scientific tradition. However, this needs, according to the literature that has emerged from the movement,[355] to be reoriented to become handmaiden of a process of 'feeling ones way' into the land and its resources and ecosystems, avoiding an approach that has developed in some of the subsequent Bioregional literature that Bioregionalism be interpreted as just a variation on traditional technocratic regional planning[356].

Following the early spread of the basic notion of the bioregion, groups started to form in various parts of the United States to think through the implications for their own region of what management as a bioregion might involve and by the turn of the century there were over sixty such groups[357]. Groups initiated networking activities and national congresses started in the early 1980s with small numbers of participants, to exchange ideas and develop competences with regard to how to understand and intervene in what was happening in the regions.

Following the sixth national congress in 1992, there was evidence of interest beyond the borders of the United States, with a recently formed network in Mexico and from thence the congresses became 'continental', spreading in recent years to other countries in Latin America. Indigenous groups and such radical movements as that of Chiapas in Mexico became involved. Meanwhile, in the past few years, the notion of Bioregionalism, which is sometimes interpreted in extremely contradictory ways as a consequence of the attractiveness of the term as implying 'sustainability' (for instance denoting a region containing a 'cluster' of genetic engineering industries!) has spread also to Europe, Australia and Japan.

In thinking about the fall of modernity and the changes in lifestyle this will necessitate, we can put the notion and experiences in communitarianism and Bioregionalism together to sketch some ideas of how 'collapse' can be turned around into a proactive restructuring of life. First we look at this as one combined movement taking off from small beginnings in the Occident. Bioregionalism and the formation of communitarian living arrangements can certainly be extended to a conversion throughout much of the Occident of existing smaller settlements and towns relatively easily to make the transition to the kind of local way of life in a regional setting that will become a necessity as the modern world falls apart. This can indeed be seen as a natural trajectory, as systematic deepening of the 'Transition Cities' movement discussed further below. For larger settlements, there will, however, need to be stages through which the populations of cities (and suburbs) find their way into such arrangements.

With the collapse of the Soviet Union the 'dacha movement' accelerated spontaneously, with urban populations increasingly growing their own food but without yet any notion of fully dispersing into the countryside. Cities have remained viable as the Russian economy has, haltingly, revived. When, however, urban economies run progressively into deepening unviability, populations will find themselves increasingly not only without food but without work or access to all manner of other materials, goods and implements necessary to continue a reasonable, or survivable lifestyle, at all. Urban and peri-urban agriculture (UPA) will not be enough in itself to solve the problems and proliferating initiatives in local manufacturing will become an increasingly urgent necessity.

We can be sure that, as happened in a small way in Russia following the collapse of the Soviet Union, there will be reductions in population through premature death almost everywhere and through the failure of economic and social welfare systems leading to dislocation, spreading hunger (already a significant problem in many Southern cities)[358] and resurgence of communicable disease and this scourge will be more severe the longer it takes for organised action and the severity, should this arise, of civil conflict.

On the other hand, it is highly likely that much of the population will descend into a deep depression in a way that has been widely observed by sociologists when people become impoverished and come to realise that this is not a temporary state: the motivation to act or even to communicate with others ebbs away. This will clearly be exacerbated with the disappearance of the modern world of virtual kaleidoscopic and ear-numbing entertainment facilitated by electronic wizardry: Hollywood, facebook, twitter, the whole wondrous world of the internet, and that offered by television and frenetic communication by handphone... all this will fall apart in stages, exacerbated by the progressive breakdown of electricity grids and so even light at night will become increasingly sporadic and localised leaving a deep sense of withdrawal and hopelessness amongst younger populations who have been raised in this virtual environment, knowing little or nothing else.

With few connections to the 'alternative movements' described in the foregoing paragraphs, practical steps are described that have been taking place in thousands of communities both ad hoc and, more formally, in the context of collaborative initiatives involving community groups and formal local government and in large numbers of 'development projects' financed by development agencies, to experiment with participatory planning processes that, in the future, can be expected to be the foundation of the rebuilding of communities. In each of the sections below, we describe how such initiatives work – or can work – for particular dimensions of the rebuilding of Community. But first we discuss the general case.

Because of their diversity, it is difficult to focus on what we are looking at here. In general, they are forms of governance that, whilst almost never referred to as such, are initiatives in Anarchist self-management. They can be traced back to the way in which certain small communities managed themselves in the past, where there were no landlords, such as the Russian Obshchina and the Swiss Talschaften. A basic shared principle is the notion of an equality amongst participants in the processes in question — though in practice, locally prevailing class cultures and oligarchies insinuate themselves into the way in which decisions are actually taken.

The idea amongst the early promoters of such processes — we think of Paulo Friere[359] and Anisur Rahman[360] in the South and Saul Alinski in the slums of Chicago[361] — were determined to empower communities and in this way erase differences in the right to participate, even if in practice there were (and always will be) differences in the dynamism, imagination, knowledge and skills of particular participants. Attempts were made to devise ways of implementing such decision making processes over larger populations. Perhaps the most renowned initiative of this kind in recent years has been the 'participatory municipal budgeting process' invented in Porto Alegre in Brazil and which has been reproduced over many hundreds of towns and cities in Brazil and increasingly elsewhere. Whilst initiated with a genuine conscientiousness to hand power to the people, it can be interpreted as an interesting experiment, the manifest shortcomings of which have important lessons for the future initiatives we are speaking of here.

Firstly, the complexities of simply maintaining ongoing urban processes — water and energy supply, waste management, transport systems and the bureaucracy necessary to manage these costs — means that from one year to the next the proportion of municipal resources available to any new planning initiative are small and so participants can quickly descend into a mood of apathy out of feelings that much discussion leads to little power to change things. And in the end, whilst each local community might have something to say about things that affect them, the process of adding each of these into a larger whole that comprises the municipal budget as a whole leads to dilution that doubles the impression of powerlessness felt by the participants. Put simply: the present world and particularly large cities are far too complex for individuals other than technocrats and powerful politicians to make differences for which the people feel they have ownership.

This syndrome undermined very many initiatives ranging from Local Agenda 21 processes where, inspired by the UN Conference on Environment and Development in 1992, throughout the 1990s many thousands of communities initiated sometimes complex participatory planning processes aimed at improved urban environmental management and 'sustainable urban development' that simply died out of feelings of non-achievement. Some of these were due to the lack of commitment of municipalities to finance the initiatives proposed but mainly out of the sheer lack of any sense within municipalities of the need to implement more radical policies and initiatives to head off the genuine unsustainability of contemporary urban metabolism. Where initiatives were entirely independent of the state, these could, and did, persist and make a real difference to a few lives the most coherent being the Intentional Communities discussed above.

The few initiatives that did achieve any significant gains were those amongst disadvantaged urban communities that were able to organise, either spontaneously or with assistance, usually from committed non-government organisations (we might think here of the 'advocacy planners' in US cities in the 1970s), in ways to block evictions and 'urban redevelopment' and thence demand of urban authorities that they improve the provision of urban services.

In the context of 'development assistance' to countries of the South, large numbers of initiatives were undertaken and financed by development agencies and even development banks, from the 1980s, applying participatory planning processes to determine how resources provided by these agencies (grants, but mainly loans, paid off by central Governments) should be spent. The best of these have generally been administered by local NGOs (Non-Government Organisations: voluntary organisations – civil society organisations, etc.) and have succeeded in motivating local communities to continue self-management where resources for Community development are given directly as budgets from central Governments or local authorities disbursed and managed independently with their use unencumbered by official intervention. Of course here the problem is that the communities have little or no resources they can generate internally and so are still contained within structures defined by Governments[362].

Which brings us to the relevance of this discussion to the future of cities and the organisation of a civilisation about to fall into a rapid process of decline. What we can expect is that Governments, both national and local will, with the decline of national economies and hence the decline of incomes, no longer be in a position to support local services. At the same time, the rise in prices of all commodities and rapid disappearance of successive ranges of product will require local initiative to replace what is increasingly lacking. The indirect ways that the impact of energy starvation and hence rising prices will affect business will be complex but in general drive businesses into bankruptcy, possibly in waves, affecting whole industrial sectors.

This will include spectacular failures of famous transnational companies with no less vulnerable companies in place to substitute with more modest production to supply much smaller markets. Unlike such bankruptcies in the past, where governments would bail them out if they were considered to be economically important, the call on government funds from many other problematic areas, such as unemployment benefits, the rising prices of all manner of services paid for by government, etc. may be expected to lead to sudden shortfalls in the supply of different goods and services. In short, both the private economy and at the same time governments can be increasingly expected to fail, leaving local populations to their own devices.

Whilst this sounds exaggeratedly dramatic, mention has sometimes been made in this text of the collapse of the Soviet Union and how cities right across the territory were deprived of supplies and at the same time loss of government mechanisms to fill the gaps and rebuild what had been lost. Whilst within two and three years, a new private economy grew to fill the gaps, in the future, the general collapse of the international and local economies will not be temporary, resulting in the necessity for new forms of local organisation to revive local self-responsibility and production processes to take over from failing global and national structures.

The point here is simply that the many participatory planning processes that have been experimented with in the past few decades will rapidly become the main recourse to rebuilding economic and with it social structures capable of managing production and supply and generally provisioning processes. We can be sure that there will be significant differences in how these impacts unfold in different countries and localities consequent on cultural factors and availability of resources relatively locally. But overwhelmingly important is that preparations be made for the emergent situation and in the next chapter we outline some of the chief considerations with respect to making these preparations so that the transition – difficult in the best of circumstances – can be practically effectuated.

Participatory planning and management processes that in the past supplemented local governments and took on marginal activities in parallel with authority will progressively become the central means to organise local services and coordinate the reconstruction of local economies to produce goods and services that global and national economies will be failing to supply at affordable prices and in time supply at all. Local governments will survive only through institutional fusion with transition groups with the initiative possibly taken from either side (in a few cases, the initial steps have already been taken).

Already starting in the early years of the new century, groups were emerging, explicitly with an understanding of the difficulties ahead and, adopting the name of Transition Towns and thence Transition Cities, rapidly developing networking capacities and the notion of the 'energy descent plan' came into currency[363]. Already by 2013 there were over a thousand initiatives that had expressed some interest in starting down the road, almost half of them in the UK, where the movement started, and thence in the United States, but spreading to Australasia, other European countries and then Latin America and Japan. The 'feel' of the initiatives is that these grow directly out of the alternative movements described above, often with enormous enthusiasm and egalitarian methods of working together. Although there is a surface realisation of what is entailed, in terms of the need to prepare and plan for the 'downward passage', the technical understanding and thence a sense of the enormity of the changes that will be forced on life in the very near future is to be found in very few — though certainly in some — initiatives. The French Colibris movement has a similar feel but focuses overwhelmingly on immediate action without yet a deeper comprehension of the downward passage ahead.

The ideal Transition Town is a small to medium-sized town where face-to-face relations and a wide range of responsibilities can be found in a relatively small space. The town of Totnes in Devon, England, was the first Transition Town and is seen by many as a model. In fact the town, together with neighbouring Dartington Hall and more recently the Schumacher College, had harboured various 'alternative' initiatives back over past decades and in this way, becoming a Transition Town was but a reformulation of past experiences around the problematic of 'energy decline'. Nevertheless, the town gains its present day income predominantly from tourism that will certainly, in the not too distant future, decline and need to be replaced by a radically more sub-regionally self-reliant economy.

In a very few cases, where local authorities of larger towns and small cities have committed some resources to doing research that will everywhere be necessary to carry out any effective planning for transition, serious initiatives are emerging such as to make evident the deeply problematic decisions that will need to be taken even for small cities to survive the transition. But in the modern world relatively small percentages of the population live under these conditions, with most of the populations living in very large cities and the suburbs that spread out from these.

Transition groups in larger cities are often fragmented but communicate loosely, such as New York and London, or try to coordinate through a 'hub' or 'coordination' such as Toronto and Sydney. Some groups undertake ad hoc initiatives around issues felt to be locally relevant whilst the more coherent have working groups, notably on food and energy but also arts and culture, and 'time banks' with 'skills groups' already aware of the need to relearn lost skills that will again in the future be urgently needed. Groups are still but a tiny fragment of local populations even in the best cases, and in larger cities they remain invisible to the vast majority who know nothing of their existence and little to nothing of the future circumstances they will themselves be facing with the collapse of local economies and government services.

Recent urban manifestations from Athens to Madrid - protesting against austerity measures - and on to New York ('Occupy Wall Street'), spreading to other American cities, seem overwhelmingly to assume culprits can be found and held to account for creeping economic malaise, from which modern life will recover and continue as if nothing has happened. Stresses will, however, increase as poverty rises in the face of rapidly rising prices and the loss of livelihoods, incomes and the availability of Stuff. Conflict — further demonstrations and riots going over into violent criminality — can be expected to be almost inevitable, with the two main tasks of transition groups being to induct anomic populations into group activity and becoming increasingly effective in their activities - more productive and providing effective services as formal enterprise and institutions progressively fail.

The greater problems will come in the not too distant future with the larger cities and in the extreme the megacities of the Americas and Asia. In the short term, we discuss in the following chapter initiatives in urban and peri-urban agriculture that have already started to address growing hunger in some cities in the South and which can be more intensively developed, putting off, maybe for a decade or two, the eventual necessity of the majority of the populations of these cities to migrate out to productive land. Other aspects of the transition from global to local economies may very well be pioneered in these cities insofar as access to resources are available with communities or community members with new skills migrating to the regrouped communities out on the land.

Thus Transition initiatives in larger cities will be faced with the problem that in the longer run they will have to vacate the cities to survive. In the short-term, however, there are many activities that they can undertake which in general will help to rebuild a sense of community as transport becomes more difficult and unemployment crises occur with the anomie that results from this state of being, and in the coming years the lack of government resources to support the unemployed. Time and circumstances will tell how urban communities will move out: as ready-formed groups or as individuals or smaller groups perhaps, without hope, but if the networking capacities and efforts of communities develop rapidly enough, then skills learned in the cities may be welcomed in the new rural settlements.

So what will happen to transition groups that have resettled into the countryside? The fact is that in the Occidental world there is little that can today be called 'rural': Urban is everywhere with most people living in cities or suburbs and but few in 'country towns', and even those who do are involved essentially in urban work, given the very small workforce that makes a living from agriculture. And there we are dealing with farmers who have been farming ever larger areas with giant machines, often, particularly in the United States, isolated by the sheer size of holdings, for anything much by way of Community and in the European case, constituting a small minority amongst the urban commuters (or in southern Europe, northern Europeans who occupy the once-farm houses as holiday or retirement homes).

Rebuilding local communities will take time, with local people becoming again involved in farming and with people and sometimes communities migrating into the countryside from cities and suburbs, and in the process the structure of the societies in rapid metamorphosis in terms of occupations and the status attaching to these. The new situation, will happen over several decades though with periods of more and less intensity. It is unlikely to take place without conflicts and in general a diminution of populations in this context and in the framework of the inability of many to adjust psychologically to the new circumstances. Conflict may be minimised both by governments adapting themselves to the situation and assisting it to happen (extremely unlikely) and by transition groups themselves, both already in the countryside and those migrating, working out negotiation procedures for integration.

In much of the South, on the social side, this transition may be less traumatic insofar as much of the urban population is but one generation out of the countryside and still has family connections and allegiances. The major problem here will be the lack of room for urban populations in the rural economy. It will become evident the extent to which cities have simply absorbed excess population and even where there is a reversion to more manual ways of farming (in fact farm mechanisation has not progressed very far in much of Asia or in Africa) the excess population will continue to be evident and it is difficult to see that current populations across much of the South will still be supportable under the emergent condition.

The transition movement is something that is recognisably a child of European utopianism of the past. In the light of the discussion earlier in this section we might expect the movement to continue to spread with a certain ease throughout Europe into Russia and with even more fluidity than we are currently seeing in the Anglo Saxon 'new world'.

It is considerably more difficult to envisage what proactive steps might evolve to anticipate and ameliorate the impacts of the decline in energy resources in non-Occidental societies. The procedures emerging from the transition movement in terms of planning the 'downward passage' from modernity are in principle relevant everywhere. However, this cannot be yet another cultural imposition from the Occident[364]. In some southern societies, traditional decision-making did involve participatory decision-making whereas elsewhere, authoritarian structures back to forms of feudalism and caste have persisted into the modern era and it is not evident that the shock of the demise of modernity will alter these arrangements any more than has modernity itself. Whilst this is certainly not to say that local movements will not emerge, one can say little more than that each society, each culture will find its own way to a sustainable future post the hegemony of Occidental Modernity, with the ebbing away of the insistence over the past four centuries that Occidental ways of organising life are good for anyone.

Re-Localisation

We have archaeological evidence that the collapse of the Roman Empire left local economies, and particularly the British economy, in a worse state in terms of skills and sophistication of products than it had been before the rise of the extended economy of Empire[365]. Quite simply, because local skills had been lost through reliance on imports, once the imports stopped arriving, there was no longer any effective local knowledge to reconstruct local production processes. The dangers of this situation arising throughout the Occident in the coming decades — with failing energy supplies, the failure to be able to operate sophisticated machines demanding energy, the failure of resource flows over great distances and finally as a consequence of the displacement of productive industries and related skills involved to China and elsewhere — is vastly greater than was the case with the fall of Rome.

One should be considering right now how to rebuild local skills and initiatives in production without sophisticated machines and tools and with limited basic resources. But almost nowhere is any consideration being given to this[366]. Perversely, currently many Governments are putting considerable thought into developing skills for the future premised on hi-tech and services that, in practice, will not be in the least bit useful in the future![367] This then becomes an important focus of the following chapter; here, meanwhile, we introduce the theme in general terms.

How re-localisation happens as a consequence of the diminution of energy to support the economy, and where it ends up in a relatively stable state, will be very different in different places as a consequence of the carrying capacity of the local/sub-regional resource base and the means employed to harness this in rebuilding local economies and communities. A concept that has gained considerable interest in the last few years that can help in analysing the 'downward passage' is the notion of the 'ecological footprint'. Invented by William Rees and developed by Mathis Wackernagel at the University of British Columbia, the first test of the idea was for Vancouver, resulting in a calculation of what area of land and water (or 'biocapacity') it takes to satisfy the present lifestyle of the people of the city[368]. The result was to show a far larger need for biocapacity than is actually available in the city and its surrounding territory and that in practice needs are satisfied by importing resources from all around the world — of which fossil fuel is a noteworthy component.

This kind of analysis has now been applied to many cities and indeed whole countries[369] — in the case of European countries, indicating the devastating, unsustainable impacts on countries around the world from which they draw their resources. This has been joined by 'material flow analysis', which is a methodology used to calculate both the import to, and export from, cities of materials including 'wastes', providing perspective on how much of different materials (and goods) is required to sustain the city and what efforts need to go into protecting the environment from the impacts of waste — or, of course, how 'wastes' can be understood as usable materials and goods and hence be recycled. The municipality of Vienna pioneered this method, calculating the gross inputs of resources and output of 'waste' of the metabolising city.

There have so far been but few coherent and concerted attempts realistically to sketch how the downward path of energy might unfold. Graphs have appeared in academic contexts that estimate a general bell-shaped exploitation curve in the first instance for oil — as the world is understood to be currently at the peak — and then to take all fossil fuels into account. These are vociferously disputed — not arguing that the decline will happen at all but just when the peak is likely to occur. However, if the lens is changed from theory to practice, the issue becomes the stages through which the decline is likely to happen in different places and the actions likely to be taken to mitigate or even forestall the event through active substitution of energy sources or of activities that will reduce and eventually obviate the need for inputs of fossil energy, such as the elimination of the vast majority of 'food-miles'.

Two salient points need to be stressed. Firstly the bell-shaped curve does not indicate the way in which progressive exploitation of fossil fuels involves an inexorable diminishing of the ratio between energy input to energy output, generally known as *Energy Return on Energy Invested* (*EROEI*), discussed in Chapter One. What in practice is happening is that increasingly sophisticated and expensive methods are being used to extract the increasingly inaccessible fossil energy resources.

Technological improvements – and even breakthroughs – can and do bring the cost down again but this can only be temporary as the resources are more difficult to extract and eventually, as the energy input approaches the energy output, then clearly extraction diminishes to but a trickle. For individual wells, this is always well above the amount that is actually in the ground but this eventually cannot any longer be extracted without expending more energy than is actually gained and, as conjectured in Chapter One, it is unlikely in the end that much more than ten per cent of the hydrocarbons in the earth will ever be brought to the surface. At a minimum, what we can expect is that the downward passage may be considerably steeper than the upward passage, as more and more of the energy retrieved is spent on the process of extraction and processing before the remainder is in an appropriate state to be used.

There are two possible conditions where production will be halted before the limits of accessibility have been reached. The first is political: if agreement is reached to 'leave the resources in the ground' as a coherent response to the need to halt the production of greenhouse gases. The other is where the economic structures necessary to continue high-tech methods of extraction collapse as a consequence of the failure of the global and thence local financing system and with it a relatively sudden descent into a world of considerably simplified technologies and local production[370]. The latter seems at this juncture more likely than the former — and from the point of view of slowing global warming might be viewed positively. However, the result in both cases will be a point at which accelerated re-localisation can per necessity be expected.

As long as there are global markets in oil, gas and coal, then prices will be global and these fuels will be available wherever consumers can afford to pay for them. We have seen prices fluctuate greatly over the past three years and the impacts have been felt more or less everywhere, and this is an important ingredient of the 'economic crisis' in which the global economy currently finds itself. As global output peaks, – that is to say that output increasingly fails to meet global demand – not only will prices rise more dramatically but it is likely that the global market will become fragmented, meaning that some places will receive the fuel they demand and in others availability will decline – possibly, as noted above, precipitately. Matters may be complicated and time-tables for depletion prolonged, possibly also in a fragmented way, by steps to bring on line 'unconventional sources' of fossil fuel: oil from tar sands, shale oil and gas, and coal liquefaction.

The second point is that the energy we use is not only what can be seen on the surface, such as petrol in vehicles, heating and air-conditioning of buildings, electricity to power lighting, machines and household appliances, but also energy embodied in production processes and the materials used in processing, production and consumption, above all plastics and other fossil hydrocarbon-derived materials but also metals, cement and even food. The vast majority of materials and artefacts that support modern life are now made wholly or partly of fossil hydrocarbon products – and we can add that the vast proliferation of Stuff in our lives today is at the same time a consequence of the availability and exploitation of these.

As shortages in fossil fuels arise, so shortages also of progressively more materials and goods will manifest themselves. This means that as energy supplies decline so will the supply of materials and the goods from which, or with the aid of which, these are made. That is to say almost everything physical that we use and consume. Globalisation has distributed materials that supply and produce all manner of goods around the world so we cannot predict when which materials and goods will become difficult to obtain or cease to arrive.

This is likely to emerge both with gradual difficulties arising and then with sudden discontinuities. Localities, sub-regions and/or countries where emergent problems have been anticipated can certainly be expected to weather shocks better than countries and localities that fail to anticipate the changes. In some cases national and local resources and goods can be rapidly substituted for those that are ceasing to flow. In our neoliberal world, 'the market' would be expected to trigger such substitutions. However, in practice this means particular entrepreneurs being available, having appropriate knowledge and being willing to act or to 'take risks'. Market responses are likely to be exploitative: profiteering from the misfortune of others – a literature of which is already emerging on 'how you can profit from rising oil prices'[371]. Without conscious anticipation or planning, this process will be very uneven and it is probable that many shortages and losses of even vital materials and goods will not be substituted for lack of interested entrepreneurs or of the necessary knowledge and skills where they are needed.

Here we arrive again at the problem of the deskilling that has taken place over the past decades: there will be many quite basic products where, when the flow of international trade in these dries up, there will be no local — even national — knowledge of how to revive supply and production from local resources. Even with partial or sectoral attempts to plan, it will be difficult to anticipate when which resources and goods will fall short. In fact the faster the 'market mentality' is substituted with both strategic national, sub-regional and local planning[372] the more can be done to fend off the depredations of deficiencies and cessation of supplies.

This view implies that little by way of proactive steps will be taken before significant problems start to cascade in a situation where resources are failing to arrive in the local economy. In fact, however, there has been a running debate going back into the history of radical movements that has called for the abandonment of globalisation and the rebuilding of local economies. Of course this harks back to Kropotkin's localism, but in its more recent guise is associated with Schumacher's famous notion of 'small is beautiful'. This is actually articulated considerably more coherently by Schumacher's close associate Leopold Kohr, summarised in his book *The Breakdown of Nations* published in 1957[373]. From the end of the 1980s, increasing numbers of books appeared, advocating re-localisation, many from an explicit or implicit green-Anarchist position[374]. This contrasted with orthodox socialists and even socialist and Marxist 'greens' who distanced themselves from localism in line with the 'world revolutionary/solidaristic' outlook informing their ideologies[375]. The issue, however, is just how effective steps to re-localise economies (and particularly in the 'industrialised' countries) are likely to be before necessity increasingly forces re-localisation. This is, of course, the problematic of the Transition Towns and cities discussed above.

The main focus of action of those initiatives with some activity is increasing local (organic) food production (applying permaculture methods). A very few have also seen the necessity of re-learning manual manufacturing skills. Whilst the 'Transition Handbook' that is the basic text with which the transition initiatives are ostensibly educating themselves calls for the production of 'energy descent action plans', as yet little has been done to produce these[376]. It is clearly of great difficulty prior to the cessation of the flow of goods into localities to advocate that people stop consuming now and even advocating step-by-step changes in consumption patterns ahead of necessity to reduce consumption and abandon actions and consumption that we can well-expect to become difficult to continue in future; the fact is that the deep-seatedness of contemporary consumption-as-ritual reduces to a small minority those who are prepared to listen seriously to what is being said and to take effective steps. Overwhelmingly, active participants are a continuation of 'activists' already attuned to buying organic food, cycling rather than driving, etc.

Transition network communities thus have a long way to go to realise the full extent of the impact of the demise of the global economy and the long and probably steep downward path the townsfolk will have to tread as it unfolds in practice. It is excellent that this action starts at the local level, in accord with the foregoing discussion, but it will surely be necessary for thought also to go not just into how town populations can address the issues but how these will have to collaborate closely with communities in their hinterlands from which, in time, they will (again) be obtaining the bulk of their food and raw materials.

How extensive such hinterlands should and will be can be expected to become a key issue in the unfolding of each re-localisation process: in the densely populated areas of Europe and Asia, it will quickly become evident that the hinterland of one city from which resources might be sought soon overlaps with the hinterland of other towns and at the same time engulfs towns that will be seeking resources in the same area. How to collaborate over the distribution of resources and avoid conflict will become a vital dimension of the reconstruction of local economies in the coming decades.

The dilemma at national level will be that no 'democratic' government will want to inform the public of the problems and certainly not of the fact that these are permanent and will continue to intensify. Many countries or sub-regions (particularly large cities) with ecological footprints substantially greater than their land area and that have been the beneficiaries of the acutely unequal exchange of the global economic system, clearly will not, even in the medium term, be capable of maintaining anything like the resource throughputs they have become used to[377].

With the reduction in fossil fuel, many countries will feel the reduction in food production which, if this happens rapidly and without possibilities of imports due to a fall in global food production, we will be witness within the coming decades to frequent and widespread famines and, as noted, if 'the market' is expected to rectify the situation then, just as in Southern countries today, in the Occident also there will be considerably more suffering amongst the 'ordinary people' than necessary whilst privileged minorities continue to live well. It is this situation that will eventually lead (one can imagine following rioting and other violent manifestations in many countries and localities) to the determination to plan fairer distribution and the reorganisation of agriculture, with primarily local economies to take in hand the steering of the downward passage.

The return of manufacturing to relatively local levels, with some, but relative to today radically reduced, trade over longer distance and hence increasing reliance on local resources, will require great resourcefulness in terms of imagination, re-learning of skills, organisational capacities and re-working of social relations that are difficult to envisage from the current world. The following chapter attempts to supply some more specific ideas aimed at assisting the transition to a different culture in terms of organisation and particularly outlook and social interaction.

Chapter 6: A More Detailed Look at Life after Modernity

The Management of Natural Resources

Until the final stages of modern civilisation over the past few decades, the question of resource management devolved almost entirely upon what could be produced from the land; overwhelmingly agricultural and forest produce and, in addition, mineral extraction. Whilst the wild proliferation in the amounts and kinds of resources used by our society has obscured this fact, rights in the use of land, nevertheless, continue to be of prime importance and in the years to come these will, once again, reveal their centrality to human life. We cannot even start to think of reconstructing communities, post-fossil energy, without addressing the issue – constantly problematic throughout the 'civilising' process - of rights to the use of land and what it yields and finding solutions that are 'sustainably productive' and which must include nurturing ecological systems that serve the needs of all the world's people in an equitable manner.

Historically, and in different parts of the world, all manner of mechanisms have been used for allocating land to different uses, determining how this should be used and how the labour processes are applied in social and technical terms to generate and/or make use of the resources from the land. Thence the concern with how the benefits should be distributed is always intimately connected to the prevailing social system and its moral order. In the Occident today, all countries possess some variant of the capitalist arrangement of individual 'ownership' and variations on this have been imposed on most countries through colonialism or otherwise the pressures to 'modernise'. Land and the individual who owns it are as one entity in the Lockean sense of property.

When Adam Smith referred to 'property' this focused predominantly on land, and in legal and common parlance this is still the case today. Karl Marx's complex discussion of 'Alienation' as a fundamental property of human relations under capitalism derived from the English property law indicating termination of ownership. This concerned how the few owned property over and against the masses who owned none, and how this meant, in mid 19th century Britain, that the emergent working class possessed nothing but their 'labour power' which they were forced to sell, as their very souls, to gain access to anything by way of life-sustaining resources. We should remember that it was Adam Smith in *The Wealth of Nations*, rather than Karl Marx who wrote:

Civil Government, so far as it is instituted for the security of property, is in reality instituted for the defence of the rich against the poor, or of those who have some property against those who have none at all.

The predominant lifestyle that emerged in the capitalist nations throughout the 20th century, and hence dominated the United States, involved the aspiration and increasingly the praxis of everyone becoming property-owners in the sense of possessing a small piece of land on which stands their house[378]. This was a central tenet of Margaret Thatcher's notion of a 'property-owning democracy', asserting that there is no such thing as 'society'. Of course the suburban house-and-garden is but symbolic property, diverting attention from the actuality of the escalating concentration of meaningful property ownership in fewer and fewer hands. By the end of the first decade of the 21st century almost ninety per cent of property in the sense of wealth in the United States was in the hands of just twenty per cent of the population.

By now, the dimensions of 'property' have vastly proliferated, with land reduced to just a small part, albeit land used for mining and forestry rights, large-scale farming, industrial complexes, and buildings in the centres of cities command vast prices per square metre, and are concentrated in very few hands. However, in future decades as the wealth embodied in modern large-scale property ebbs away – meaning the end of large-scale mining and agriculture and the uselessness of large manufacturing and other building complexes deprived of access to resources and power – access to and rights in land as the ultimate source of human existence will, once again, become the centre of the sustenance of populations in direct proximity to the land.

The immediate assumption may be that there will be a return to peasant small-holdings that, in recent centuries, were certainly the aspiration and for vast numbers the reality of how life should be organised. We might conjecture, fancifully, that, except as urban farming as a transitional strategy, suburban plots will be converted from flower gardens to productive plots[379]. In few cases will this, however, be feasible as these lots of suburban houses surrounding cities in the United States and increasingly Europe and even the cities of the South are too small for meaningful production even of enough food for family subsistence.

Furthermore, without cars or the general connections of suburban life, of jobs and hence incomes and thence the supermarkets and in general the enterprises to be found along the 'commercial strip', these seas of suburban development will become totally dysfunctional in terms of the wider connections with sources of manufactured goods and the daily interaction with services and other social intercourse. We have to conclude that this configuration of land use will rapidly become unviable and progressively metamorphose into radical reconfigurations such as to reconstitute relatively local production and social systems within relatively narrow local perimeters[380]. And how rights are allocated in the land under new configurations of land use will become central to the reconstruction of viable ways of life and communities.

Whilst, prior to modernity, land has always been the basis of almost all livelihoods (excepting fishermen and other users of areas of water) it was not, throughout pre-history, an issue or a concern in itself free of the resources on the land that provided for food and other needs of human bands. Animist constructs might make sense out of particular landscapes, but as a dimension of holistic understandings of land, ecology and weather with no notion of 'ownership' of any kind.

Where, throughout this text the argument is for a future where decisions are taken democratically and with outcomes that serve equally well the needs and aspirations of all, there is actually a danger that with a mass return to the land as a basis for income and wealth, there will be a re-emergence of feudal, 'semi-feudal' and even caste arrangements where, as throughout civilisation, small minorities have possessed the power to determine how land should be used, who should work it and how its benefits should accrue to different social groups. The 'great debate' on land in the 20th century concerned the transition from feudal to capitalist understanding and social administration systems.

Whilst the heart of capitalistic understanding is that of individual property ownership, even feudalism in its strict European sense was, in fact, not a single system but a multitude of systems for the social allocation of land and its produce that differed from one place to another and evolved through time. Basically, since the start of the process of civilisation, control of the uses and product of the land has been intimately bound up with social hierarchies, so that the very titles of social classes and subclasses, from emperors and kings to barons to lords to vassals, freemen, copyholders and serfs and their equivalents around the world, already suggest association with powers over the use and allocation of produce of the land.

Hence, the transition from feudal to capitalist systems was at its foundation a question of understanding land being a transition from a complex systems of rights and duties between different classes in particular rural areas, and above this of the gains that distant barons and kings might expect, to the simplified system of property ownership attaching to legal persons, who may be natural persons or legal fictitious entities including commercial corporations but also other institutions. Thus the connection between social position and rights to use or produce from the land, together with duties to give part of the produce up to (land)lords, and to yield up part of the rural population to service in armies was, under feudalism (and indeed whatever we wish to call pre-capitalist socio-political and economic systems) the very basis of both social and economic organisation.

Small areas of land such as woodland and pasture might have been reserved as common land from which the less privileged could retrieve fuel and on which livestock could be fed and which functioned as long as demands were kept within the regenerative carrying capacity of these resources. Furthermore, lacunae of more egalitarian, intensive communal, allocation of rights and duties on the land did exist right across the civilising world (notably with respect to usage of alpine pastures, Balinese Subaks regulating irrigated paddy fields and the Russian Obshchina).

Only in modern society has land become predominantly a commodity[381] and even then economists have found it difficult to treat it in the same way as other commodities, firstly because it is immovable and, related to this, because there are social needs to organise the use of land so that the wider society can function effectively, which necessitates curtailment of private rights under certain conditions, on behalf of the wider society. Furthermore, in the case of nomadic peoples on the great Asian and African plains or the Arabian desert, division of land into plots makes no sense, so that communal means of allocating rights to use of the land have continued from pre-history to the present day[382].

When European colonists arrived in the Americas, Africa and Australasia, already with receding feudal or growing capitalist attitudes and presuppositions, the presumption was that the land was vacant in the sense of being freely available for them to apply their own modes of allocation and they essentially stole the land from indigenous populations and/or changed tenure arrangements to be able to use the local population to provide them with the bounty of the land. In most

279

lands that were colonised, complex systems of land management already existed which were generally ignored. Or they were overridden, in some cases creating dual systems that interacted in complex ways where some local systems were honoured or half honoured, ending today in confusions that continue to create situations where land-grabbing and squatting continue, ending in battles, the outcome of which are extra-legal and depend on the relative, contingent power of the claimants.

Systems imposed by European colonial masters were many and depended on the force applied. In the case of North America and Australia the British simply pushed the indigenous people aside and murdered them if they made any assertion of rights to the product of the land that they, the British, wanted to use. In India, the British, finding an administrative system that included the function of tax collection (zamindar) proceeded to formalise this into a landlord system as a means of consolidating the extraction of 'surplus' and in Java the Dutch introduced what amounted to a form of feudal extraction (*cultuurstelsel* — or, seen from an Indonesian perspective, *Tanam Paksa* — compulsory planting), directing the peasantry as to what they had to deliver, leaving little land for them to provide for their own subsistence.

The Latin American case was described briefly in Chapter Three, where in the first instance economic exploitation and conversion of the population to Christianity through the system of *encomienda* (in practice little more than slavery) did not have an immediate attachment to discrete pieces of territory. This was, however, progressively replaced by the *latifundia* system, the descendants of which are still widespread throughout the ex-Spanish and Portuguese colonies, even in the case of the Philippines, under the titles of *fazenda* and *hacienda*. This extended ownership of more or less large tracts of land to individuals who were free to make whatever use they wished of it, exploiting the resources through various forms of labour relationship, was originally predominantly slave labour but today is given over to modern industrial farming or tenancy of some kind, the rents being determined by tradition or, today, by the market that nevertheless leaves vast populations in abject poverty.

Urbanisation increases the intensity of competition for land as reflected in the considerably higher prices and rents[383]. However, urbanisation pressures on the poor in the South has resulted in increased squatting of land where individuals and families, sometimes helped by 'informal entrepreneurs' simply ignore the question of who 'owns' the land and build their own houses and generally also basic infrastructure. Often this is on marginal publically owned land where the government overlooks the encroachment but increasingly this has also been on less marginal public land and on private land, sometimes with landowners charging some kind of rent, even though the development is not deemed to be legal within the planning and official land registration systems.

The whole area of negotiation over urban land resulting in complex compromises has often rendered the urban land issue in much of the South more or less opaque. However, there remains the question of land ownership independent of those actually using the land and whether and how rent in whatever form is paid. On the other hand, 'amnesties' have been arranged where squatters are granted the land (usually with some payment), spreading the ostensible benefits of ownership of landed property[384].

However, in spite of the fact of today's liberal world being dedicated to the notion of commodification and private ownership of land, the reality is that states, national and local, continue to own land, sometimes in large measure. In the United States, bastion of the ideology of private ownership in all things, the Government actually possesses, mainly at national but also at state and local government level, land which is well over half of the area of the country — equivalent to more than the whole area of Western Europe — leased out as grazing land, used by the military or as national parks, forestry reserves with concessions let to exploit the timber and so on.

Furthermore, for much of the 20th century, communist countries nationalised the land and abolished private property in land, administering this through state-determined organisational mechanisms including both collectives and cooperatives. The fall of the Soviet Union precipitated the reinstitution of private property with different governments using different formulae for this reallocation[385]. In the Chinese case, in rural areas cooperative ownership has survived, albeit under great pressure of liberal ideologues within the country and from the United States, as well as individuals within the country who would greatly benefit (as happened in the ex-Soviet union) to institute a full system of private property rights.

Notwithstanding the notion that governments are beholden to the general public and private business is beholden to shareholders (to make profits), in practice there is, from the point of view of the lessee, no significant difference between leasing State as opposed to private property. Of course in the case of some regimes, the issue is complicated by significant dimensions of graft and corruption in waiving rents or, worse, waiving environmental conditions, notably forest conservation laws. In Russia, where, under the Soviet regime all land belonged to the State, since the collapse of the Soviet Union only 7.6% has been passed over into private ownership, including individuals and institutions, so that the vast majority of the territory still 'belongs' to the State, meaning both national and local government.

Furthermore, in all countries, the state ensures that it is legally able to intervene to purchase or requisition or 'borrow' land in the form of easements and way leaves or via planning regulations in order to ensure the coherence of infrastructure systems such as gas and power lines, roads and railways, schools and hospitals, etc. and in general implement land use planning. By this means, private ownership of land is never absolute and the 'public good' can be achieved through public planning and its implementation. Of course this notion of the 'public good' is not simply a rational and self-evident notion but one that developed in Occidental culture out of the debates of the Enlightenment (in the United States the constitutional debates around the time of independence) and in general subsequent notions of socialist and communist systems of 'public ownership'.

There is thus in the modern mind a duality of private and state property; the latter representing the interests of the public, that would seem to preclude other notions of how land and, indeed other 'commons' including the air, lakes and the seas, might be allocated for purposes of effecting production and distribution of the resources needed to sustain human (individual but also social) life. The issue is thus one of decision-making and thence planning and management of land and water, and the resources that exist and further can be developed under and upon these. The universalism (we can point here to the philosopher Hegel's notion of 'the bad infinite') of the Occidental notions of 'private and public' can be contrasted with the great number of variations on the theme of rights (significantly usufruct) and duties upon the land associated with the notion of 'Common Pool (or 'Common Property') Resource Management Regimes' (CPRMRs).

We have to thank Elinor Ostrom, the recent Nobel economics prize winner, for her diligent work in documenting with her colleagues some five thousand cases where resources have been or are managed by communities, either of particular exploiters and users of resources or more generally by communities that have an interest in ensuring that resources are used optimally and sustainably. This research has been used to discover the circumstances and parameters that lead to the formation and sustainability of such management systems in contrast either to state or privately owned and managed systems[386]. Here we discuss some of the parameters of CPRMRs that will be relevant and even necessary to anything approaching an effective resolution of the land use changes that will be happening with the fall of modern civilisation.

Firstly we can think of CPRMRs as fitting into the general category of cooperative ownership and management. This might suggest the kind of legal format that can be found in all countries defining what a cooperative is, how it should function and how it should relate to the general national rules of corporate organisation. However, it quickly becomes evident that it really depends on the kind of resources in question and the territory (if there is such) over which it is to prevail. From her research Ostrom proposed eight general rules governing successful CPRMRs as follows:

1. The territory in which the regime operates should have clearly defined boundaries (albeit some or all the territory may be available for other purposes — such as forests available for mushrooming or hunting by other groups)
2. There should be congruence between appropriation and provision rules and local conditions
3. Collective choice arrangements should prevail so as to allow for the participation of all or most of the appropriators in the decision making process
4. Effective monitoring by monitors who are part of or accountable to the appropriators
5. Graduated sanctions for appropriators who do not respect community rules
6. Conflict resolution mechanisms which are cheap and easy to access
7. Minimal constitutional recognition of rights to organize
8. In case of larger CPRMRs: organisation in the form of multiple layers of nested enterprises, with small, local CPRs at their bases.

It should be stressed that such arrangements in the past can be understood as a natural response to precarious conditions. Alpine life, and indeed the life of peasants in the areas of Russia with extreme weather conditions that brought the obshchina into existence, encourages cooperation in the face of periodic adversity, the alternative being annihilation. In the future, post-modernity, with the necessity to radically rearrange uses of the land over much of the area of the world, conditions will necessitate intensive community cooperation, with the impacts of climate change adding further grounds for cooperation.

Continuation of private property in the management of land and related natural resources in the coming decades would be guaranteed to exacerbate the hardship and tribulations which we will see unfolding and hence the faster that appropriate forms of community ownership of land and other property are accepted and implemented, the better.

As noted earlier with reference to Mondragon in Spain, it is quite possible to organise all of life on the basis of CPRMRs where neither private nor public – in the conventional sense State - ownership need exist at all, albeit Governments, insofar as they survive the anticipated changes in the perceived need for organised government, should be prepared to facilitate their formation. This does, however, mean a far more dynamic form of community self-management than has been the experience of modernity — decisively rejecting Thatcher's 'property-owning (representative) democracy' and embracing the importance of the notions of society, community and *direct* democracy.

As analysed by Ostrom, such arrangements have widespread manifestations in 'traditional' societies around the world, including throughout the Occident and, indeed, many examples even in modern society. We might say that this is simply a matter of generalising what today have become marginal experiences. This will, however, depend on a decisive rejection of the morality of individualism that has dominated the Occident for the past few hundred years under the ideology of Possessive Individualism analysed in Chapter Three. The moral and cultural aspects of this are further discussed in the final chapter.

Of course, as with any genuinely cooperative regime, this will mean abolition of any substantial personal property and with it an assumption of mutual respect and responsibility amongst communities in their capacity as communal caretakers of the land. This, therefore, means mutual tutoring in fairness, not only in distribution of benefits and outputs of the management of the resources but also of contributions made to producing outputs and in general the responsibility for managing the fecundity of the land. In a future where there will be a return to considerably more manual work than has been the experience of the present generation, assisted as it is by the power of so many machines and the energy required to run these, this will become a central concern for many years to come. From each according to ability, to each according to need: in the medium term, abilities may require considerable (re)development and the satisfaction of needs may often prove arduous to achieve and should not be at the expense of others in a world of scarcity.

Reconstructing Local Economies

Modernity, particularly in its final 'global' phase, has progressively impoverished local economies, even in areas financially rich, as a consequence of exploiting particular niches in the national and/or global economy. This has been a matter of reducing or eliminating sectors that served local needs in exchange for earning money in the larger economy with which to buy what has been lost, plus a cornucopia of Stuff flowing around the global economy. Poverty in this respect is poverty in terms of robustness of the economy and poverty in terms of lost skills. Poor cities and the poor in all cities have suffered these consequences of globalisation absolutely. Where at the start of the foregoing chapter we set out the general parameters of delocalisation, here, following a general discussion of relevant issues, we look in detail at a step-wise approach to rebuilding sub-regional economies that has widespread relevance as a structured response to the coming demise of the global, and to a degree national economies.

Given that unemployment is often seen by municipal administrations as a perennially serious problem (and in the South the growth of the informal economy indicates this fact all too clearly) it is something of an anomaly that local governments across the globe have taken little interest in attempting to steer local economic development[387]. Whilst the development of all manner of vital infrastructure, including water supply, sanitation, gas and electricity supply and many other services vital to comfortable and efficient urban living were pioneered by local governments in 19th century Europe, subsequently many of these services were centralised and/or privatised, taking away local accountability and the experience of building and running these services by the local population.

With the development of urban planning aimed at the management of the use of land, local economic development was not seen as part of this remit. In a few cases, particularly of towns and cities that were at some stage subjected to extreme economic shocks such as one-economy towns where the company or facility upon which it relied was suddenly closed down, concerted initiatives were started with a view to rebuilding viable local economies. Generally, technocratic Development Corporations were established. Today the towns and cities where these have been established in Europe collaborate within a Europe-wide association, EURADA.

Insofar as local governments, through Development Corporations or simply through small local economic development departments or divisions, have attempted to intervene to improve local economic

285

activity and employment, this has been overwhelmingly based on the notion referred to as 'economic base analysis'. This posits that it is local manufacturing industries exporting their products that are the motor of the local economy. Hence local governments have often spent most of their own resources for local economic development and foregone tax income through 'tax holidays' to attract 'inward investment', feeling well-satisfied if one or more large national or transnational corporations have deigned to grace the locality with their presence. It is the competition to attract industries in this way that has fuelled a 'race to the bottom' or a game of 'beggar my neighbour,' creating an atmosphere where industries can pick and choose and then at short notice move on to where the grass is greener, leaving the municipality worse off than before in terms of unemployment and loss of tax income.

This is clearly no foundation upon which to rebuild local economies under almost any circumstances and certainly entirely irrelevant to the local economic conditions that will be prevailing in the coming years. Several roots need to be combined to initiate and grow a process of local economic (re)development appropriate to the fall of modernity ahead. The first looks back over more radical attempts that were made in and by some local authorities in the recent past aimed at rethinking the local economy to satisfy local economic and social needs and which indicate how local economies might be steered through a process of planning and negotiation with diverse interest.

Most prominent here is the output of the short period of the Greater London Council (GLC) — London's then Government — from 1980-85, which produced the *London Industrial Strategy*[388] and a number of related documents as well as initiating a number of participatory planning processes under the title of 'Popular Planning'. Whilst this initiative was lost with the abolition of the GLC in 1986, the notion of rethinking the local economy by sector and determining what sectors and initiatives should be supported by the local government on the basis both of a social calculus and social involvement in decisions, was a pioneering exercise. Whilst environmental considerations were relatively weakly supported and almost no thought given to issues of resource supply, action was nevertheless taken by the GLC in the context of local economic planning to create a framework for local energy planning and the financing of various initiatives arising from this[389].

The second foundation should be based on the subsequent proliferation of 'participatory planning processes' discussed briefly in the foregoing section of this chapter and taken into more detail below.

The third foundation is that of regional economic development and specifically Bioregionalism . That is to say that the redevelopment of local economies (we will refer to this simply as LED), relevant to the kind of re-localisation that will be happening per force in the coming decades, can only expect to achieve significant success if it is carried out on a sub-regional basis. Cities cannot be self-sufficient or even self-reliant in terms of resources. As in the past, resources to support urban life will have again to come predominantly from the hinterland of towns and (insofar as they will survive at all) cities, with these then providing the manufactures to support life in rural areas together, perhaps, with an efflorescence of 'craft villages'. LED in this context therefore necessarily means local sub-regional economic development.

As noted above, the structure of settlements within sub-regions discovered by Walter Christaller in South Germany in the 1920s would seem an eminently reasonable distribution of people across the land in many areas of the world — exceptions being deserts, grazing land and mountains. That is, once this has returned to being the territory from where the bulk of the resource needs of sub-regional populations are again satisfied and with the processing of materials and manufacturing of products consumed in the sub-region and produced in its towns or 'craft villages.' Furthermore, it would also seem to be a sound practice to ensure that all members of the population have the opportunity to live and work for periods both in the town as the quintessentially social – and the countryside, to imbibe knowledge of and to learn to empathise with nature. Whilst half or more of the working hours will be spent in agriculture, virtually all who work will participate in this, whilst also practising other vocations and skills. Over the coming decades, with the continuous reduction in energy to fuel transport systems, the world will return in stages to one where, although trade will doubtless continue, this will supply but modest amounts of materials that may be essential (such as salt) or desirable to broaden somewhat the range of products that can be locally produced and in a very few cases supplying finished products that are better produced elsewhere.

For purposes of organising future coherent and concerted LED processes, at an early stage consideration will need to go into defining regions and negotiating these amongst communities within and without these. Over the coming decades boundaries may be expected to change, in most places radically and rapidly, as a consequence of population movement and depletion, and the availability of resources, remembering the degree to which in the short run the relocation and reconstruction of settlements and the recycling of the detritus of modernity will play a major role, giving way in the longer run to sustainable harvesting and processing of sub-regional natural resources.

Whilst below we summarise the process as a step-by-step procedure, here we provide an overview to outline the logic. Thus new initiatives in LED must start from an agreement amongst local populations that such an initiative is necessary as a conscious, coherent and coordinated process. Such a realisation must follow closely on the realisation of the coming trajectory of decline in energy — entering the 'post carbon era', as it is expressed in some quarters in the United States[390]. One can expect that amongst the Transition Cities working groups and committees, one or more groups will be concerned with redeveloping the sub-regional economy (there may be separate groups for particular places or important themes such as the CPRMR groups suggested above). A process of 'visioning' should be undertaken where community-wide debates should be held, where a desirable future is envisioned but one which is also realistic in the light of what we can expect to be unfolding in the sense of the closing in of the world upon the local. Visioning has been a component of participatory planning exercises for at least a decade, but has all too often suffered from being both vague and unrealistic. From the outset, the difficulties that will need to be faced by the downward passage must be fully faced up to.

A series of relatively informal fora on different topics involving different groups, small and large, within the community will need to be organised, drawing in the whole population of the sub-region and culminating with a fair or conference, lasting one or more days, with many sub-events but achieving the dissemination of the first idea of the need for LED and what this might involve and gathering together a preliminary 'stakeholder group' that will start to set out an agenda defining activities and structures. Eventually this should crystallise into a Local Development Institution – that might adopt any one of many names including 'economic', 'employment', 'social', 'resource', etc. as agreed to be locally appropriate.

Immediately activity can be initiated to obtain a data base on how the economy currently works in sectoral terms (what is being extracted, processed, manufactured, carried out in terms of services and what is not being done but rather being imported and from where). This can be done as a collaborative exercise between local government and local academia but encouraging participation in providing information on the part of existing economic units, groups of occupations and community groups. This must extend also to the 'informal economy' to see what is happening there, what problems are being faced by those active at this economic level and what unrecorded skills are to be found there. In general, an important dimension here is the skills base: what have people done in the past, what are they qualified for, what are they doing now and what might they be interested in doing in a future where abandoned, once relevant skills are needed again? A community will need both to know what its members are prepared to do and to learn and what will become evident as needs for work in the community.

At the same time an inventory will need to be made of the sub-regional resources that will include land in use or otherwise available for growing and the quality of its soil, timber resources, flowing water, lakes and ponds and if there are mineral resources, what are these?[391] As the process of descent becomes evident, there will be changes in the built environment and as the redundancy of the materials of modernity become evident, then these must also be inventoried as potentially available for new uses. But already a new kind of identification with the local landscape should start to develop, as explored by the Bioregional movement, that step by step puts behind us the notion of land as real estate or property, as primarily physical resources as a basis of personal wealth, instead reviving past empathy with particular places and their spiritual, in places even mythological, value, to revise the notion of meaning and value of the landscape and its resources to us as communities in the context of its ecological and aesthetic wealth.

The results of the work of information gathering, which will be ongoing and that in time will reconnect people into the community, will need to find a home. In the first instance computers — university or local government facilities — will accommodate and process data but new methods will need to be explored that will not pass away as the electricity and eventually the machines themselves are laid to rest: the information will not just be 'information' but the knowledge and eventually the wisdom of the community, its livelihood and its ecological and geographical context. But it will be active data in the sense of informing the local transformation process.

Current LED initiatives are pragmatic and opportunistic. This means that discussions are held amongst stakeholder groups to identify local activities or immediate possibilities relating to some local resource and/or skills and how these can be enhanced through quality improvement and marketing. Almost always this is in order to export goods from the region to bring in an income. All too little thought goes into creating work and producing goods and services that will fill local gaps and displace imported goods. LED initiatives thus fail even to consider local needs that are not being served and how these might be addressed through bringing into life local units such as enterprises, cooperatives or any type of organisational form, which employs people to address local needs. This should be the first principle of an LED approach relevant to the transition because we will be seeing a rapid rise in the unavailability, not just of luxuries becoming too expensive for anyone much to afford, but of basic necessities that fail to arrive due to failing transport linkages and falling production as a consequence of steeply rising energy prices and thence sheer unavailability.

It is only a generation ago that most manufactured goods were made directly from materials other than petrochemicals. The vast proliferation of Stuff with no question of its genuine usefulness or durability, but penetrating to the core of what is necessary for our lives, has progressively been invaded by petrochemicals. What does this mean? It means that much of what we pick up in our households is made directly or indirectly from petrochemicals and their derivatives. We may have to ask hard questions as to what we really need to live a reasonably comfortable life in the future with a radical reduction in Stuff.

But the crucial question will then be: out of what are we to produce the Stuff that we genuinely need? Whilst plastics can also be made from wood and other biomass — and we should strive not to abandon, in the context of the demise of the modern chemical industry, the virtuoso knowledge we have of chemistry today — we will nevertheless need to be aware of the consequences of the loss of petrochemical feedstock, not only in their impact on transport and the 'closing in' of economies to the local as a consequence of their absence, but also the impact on our production capacities. Where are the raw materials going to come from? In the case of building materials, discussed further below, we may see our way to relocalisation more easily. But there is so much that we will have to rethink in terms as much of the source of raw materials as of the revival of local production knowledge, capacities and skills.

There needs then to be a more solid conceptual basis around which longer-term plans are made. The present world is one where economic decisions are fragmented and as short-term as possible. This is what informs the 'pragmatism' of present-day LED initiatives, which is simply par for the course. As the global economy and with it national and local economies fall apart over the coming decades, there will appear to be a permanent crisis that will turn this short-termism into a series of panic decisions and actions: how can we obtain fuel for our cars, how can we obtain adequate food, how can we obtain basic household goods and services? All too often there will be no easy answers, perhaps no answers at all, to most of these challenges, many of which will relate back to the sudden restrictions on transport, both personal and, more seriously, bringing the physical means of life into the city, suburb, town or sub-region. It will be no good simply crying for transport, because the goods themselves will, in case after case, no longer be available from anywhere, even if we are privileged to have fuel for a truck or train to go fetch them.

Ad hoc decisions will certainly have to be taken as crisis follows upon crisis. But these should always be related back to a notion of an eventual self-reliant sub-regional economy. This means that most food and raw materials will be generated in the sub-region, most processing of these will be undertaken in the sub-region, most goods will be manufactured in the sub-region and almost all services will be provided in the sub-region. Conceptual thinking about reconstruction of sub-regional economies should be grounded in the notion of the three sectors and progress in systematically refilling each of these.

Primary Sector

Starting from primary produce the first consideration must be to organise the production of food. Already reference has been made to the rapid growth in some countries and cities of urban and peri-urban agriculture (UPA). This should everywhere become an immediate concern as to how to organise sub-regional resources to produce food. The importance of this and the changing methods that can be expected over the coming decades is such that the next section of this chapter is dedicated to more detailed discussion of the matter.

Directly related to food production and underpinning much else of local life are the availability of water and energy. Whilst in temperate regions with adequate rain, water availability should not in principle be a problem, in practice most agricultural and urban water supply systems are dependent on pumping, a prerequisite of which is functioning electricity systems or the availability of fuel, and indeed functioning sanitation systems to ensure that water supplies are not contaminated. In arid regions, the failure of energy supply leading directly to failure of water supplies is likely to become catastrophic to the point of reducing radically the population and economic activity that can be supported in these areas. That is unless ingenuity can be applied to radically reduce the need for energy in water supply systems, with the application, as in the past, of gravity, via aqueducts, to move water to where it is needed.

And where can the energy be expected to come from as fossil hydrocarbon prices and availability rise and electricity systems are subject to increasing failure? Of course new sources of energy will be required, with local energy planning based on the two principles of reduction in need ('energy conservation') and supply from renewable sources. Whilst today there is a widespread hope that sophisticated wind, solar and other renewable energy technologies will become widespread, substituting for the loss of fossil hydrocarbons, in practice we can be quite confident that in the longer run (later this century) there will be an overwhelming return to the use of biofuels. These are still the main source of energy in the poorest countries and were, in spite of access to small amounts of wind and water power (particularly to power ships), the main source of energy everywhere until the harnessing of fossil hydrocarbons. As with food supply, the scope of the water and energy crises that will emerge almost everywhere and the approaches that might be taken to overcome or alleviate them, requires that these be discussed at more length later in this chapter. The emphasis here is upon the degree to which these are basic economic problems that require solving before other aspects of the local economy can be considered in any depth.

Finally, in the primary sector, consideration will have to go progressively into what raw materials are needed to recover the ability to manufacture life locally. Hundreds of thousands of products that come to us via the department store, supermarket and even, where it still exists, the corner store (even the hole-in-the-wall stores in the poorest communities of southern countries) are not only manufactured at the far corners of the world but are made of materials, most of which are mined or otherwise sourced from very specific places, so that any one sub-region possesses but a small fraction of the raw materials needed to manufacture the goods with which we are all surrounded today. Mention has already been made of the extreme degree to which goods today are in part or completely manufactured from petrochemical feedstock. Almost everything else is manufactured from metals and other materials which, in a matter of a few decades from now, will be locally available in only very small quantities.

There will, however, everywhere, be substantial amounts of raw material that can be salvaged from the residue of our over-productive age. Cars, no longer functional as a consequence of dwindling availability of petrol; houses vacated as a consequence of being located in places accessible only by car or high-rise buildings where energy-demanding services are no longer reliable or available; mountains of bric-a-brac from kitchen appliances to ornaments, no longer relevant to people's lives, may be salvaged, in some cases by reuse and remanufacturing, but in the main for the raw materials that may be used to make more essential goods that are no longer arriving from the global economy.

Recycling as an industry existed in the industrial economies from the very beginning and went through various phases in terms of their mode of organisation[392], ending, in recent years, in hi-tech means of sorting materials from waste streams, in part via household separation and in part along conveyor belts at waste processing facilities. In the south, 'waste pickers' usually took on the role of resource recovery at the waste dump site. In few cases were these efforts very effective, with most of the 'waste' that contained substantial amounts of material of potential value finding its resting place in landfill sites, dumps and, in the south, in random dumping on vacant land.

A new, more thorough approach to recycling, including re-use and remanufacturing, will be called for as sources of raw materials necessary for the survival economics of later decades of this century. As now, it is likely to be effective in relatively few places as it is very likely to be difficult for people to focus on, or to believe, what is happening in terms of diminishing availability of materials and goods. This should become a substantive dimension of the local economy in the immediate decades ahead, proactively seeking defunct and unused goods, remanufacturing those that can still be used in order to extend their lives, disassembling those that cannot be used anymore and reprocessing the materials for insertion into the local productive economy. Local research and networking with other local efforts to share discoveries and ideas will be needed to find low-energy ways of processing the materials (such as components of cars) and determining how these can be turned into goods that will fulfil basic needs and be made to last, in stark contrast to today's economy of planned obsolescence. As the global economy ebbs away and materials and goods fail to arrive, this economy will hopefully form a bridge to a future where materials are derived predominantly from the local sub-region and goods are locally manufactured.

The section above concerned with the management of resources focused on the future need to organise production on the land via CPRMRs. The LED process will need to keep watch on the changing requirement for different resources and advise on how changes in land use might be made to ensure that needed resources are produced, balancing the need for food against needs for biofuels, raw material for fibre for clothing, forest products and so on. CPRMRs may be formed for purposes of managing discrete areas ('farm cooperatives') or to exploit particular resources (such as energy production, water supply or mining). The planning process will need to be carried out with a basic concern for the maintenance of ecological systems, via permaculture. The catchment and allocation of water resources will need to be coherent and linked to production and maintenance of ecosystems. Where mining activity becomes significant, this, too, should be carried out with the maintenance of ecological integrity as a general framework condition, ensuring that damaged land is repaired and toxic by-products are disposed of in ways that will have no long-term damaging impacts.

Secondary Sector

Today, in principle, skills to make things have never been so well-developed. In the not too distant past, manufacturing involved very few skills and industries, as expressed by the small numbers of guilds or associations in European cities and their equivalents throughout urban Asia. Beautiful and useful things were made but in practice a very small proportion of what, in any case, were much smaller populations possessed and developed manufacturing skills in the tight confines of particular industries: food processing, building materials generally, metal working generally, fabrics and clothing, shoes, tools and utensils, pottery, glass and glasses, furniture, paper, medicines, jewellery, etc, etc.

And then 'industrialisation' proliferated at first slowly throughout the 19th century and then accelerated both what was being made and the skills necessary to make them. Employment in manufacturing grew in the 'industrialised countries' in the early years of the 20th century and then declined to little more than a fifth of employment — and even there much of this was servicing the needs of the industries whilst increasingly the actual work was done by machines, with the fragmentation of skills and activities that meant that diminishing numbers of people knew anything beyond their narrow field within the total manufacturing process.

The residues of pre-industrial production can still be found, particularly in the back streets of Islamic cities. However, manufacturing has not only produced a cornucopia of Stuff but, necessarily, the skills required to make it. Meanwhile, the global economy has systematically distanced most of the population from the details of manufacturing processes, interceding with lengthening transport routes and the efflorescence of retail outlets. Certain manual skills persist in the form of 'bricolage' or 'do-it-yourself', albeit the things that are being done are increasingly a matter of installing 'black boxes', replacing or adding together ready-made components designed by far-off technicians and manufactured by machines, with little knowledge on the part of the user of what is inside (often including electronic control devices as 'embodied skills') or how and out of what it is made.

The road back to a modest range of local manufactures will be long and hard. This will require, within a few decades, at best radical shifts across skill areas and in practice, for the most part, complete abandonment of current skills and (re)learning of skills appropriate to local manufacture, eventually with only simple machines and without power tools. The prospects are devastating in the sense of the spread over the past decades of what amounts to total incompetence. The immediate response in the coming decades may be incredulity that this could happen and thence complete denial, which makes it near impossible even to start the processes of rethinking production to address the conditions which will prevail in the future. The planning process being discussed here is designed to allow a measured entry into thinking through and negotiating across communities both what is needed and how needs will be satisfied in terms of producing goods.

Planning the re-emergence of local materials and processing and manufacturing, to which construction labour and skills must be added, will become an important component of the future labour force. This will require analysis of emergent shortages; of the materials that will be available within the sub-region to make things to substitute for materials and goods hitherto imported from outside the sub-region; of the skills which will need to be (re)developed to bring local manufacturing into being; and the consumer needs that the sub-regional manufacturing economy will be required to satisfy. This will take up much of the time of local economic planning in the coming years. But without such planning, the loss of manufactured products will result in radical disorientation and impoverishment of populations, particularly in the industrialised countries, and with it a complete collapse of the capacity to organise life at the individual or community level.

Tertiary Sector

Today over half of people in employment are making a living from 'services'. A cynical view sees much of this as no more than redistribution of income in a world where production — real work and the production of use value — is undertaken by an ever dwindling workforce and mechanisms have been found to extract income and wealth with little or no social benefit except for the flattering of status and the preening of the population receiving the wealth thus produced. Insofar as these services are improving the quality of life for populations, including education, health services, and other care and

295

personal services, this may be deemed to be part of the success of modernity, if only temporarily. However, large swathes of 'employment' in services in the North are concerned with managing money, real estate, insurance and other services that would be unnecessary in a world where mutualism prevailed rather than competition for wealth and status.

Significant employment is also to be found in transport of goods, wholesaling and retail to bring the materials and goods of a global economy to where they can be distributed to consumers. It becomes clearer in southern countries how the service economy, as 'informal economy', acts to redistribute income to enable urban populations that no longer have a substantive connection to the productive economy — initially peasants abandoning overcrowded agricultural economies and urban populations that are not able to find 'formal' employment — to purchase the means to survive and even participate in a modest way in the consumer economy (if nothing else, at least televisions can be found even in the most basic hovels of southern slums).

The fact that these populations subsist in what is de facto unemployment and poverty is unfortunate, even tragic, in that they could be producing a better life for themselves, given the necessary support in terms of skills development, capital and organisational frameworks. It should be clear from what has been analysed above concerning the fall of modern civilisation that whilst today it is easy simply to ignore these populations, in time the fact of their being 'superfluous' to any meaningful social and political process will become evident as the means of their existence, the 'economic surplus' that is redistributed to keep them alive in precarious conditions, will cease to flow, with consequences that nobody today is prepared to consider.

Planning for the service sector in sub-regional economies of the future will initially require coherent thought to conserve and reorient the skills necessary to deliver the services in a situation where labour will be increasingly required simply to produce the basic necessities of life: food and basic manufactures. The point here is that as machines become decreasingly available to carry out work as a consequence of lack of fuel, there will be a growing requirement for physical labour — on the farm, in workshops and in the rebuilding of the built environment.

There will be diminishing amounts of surplus labour and loss of access to the means to train those who would deliver basic services of education and health. Local economic planning will have to confront this in terms both of labour strategies and where the resources will come from to continue to provide what are deemed to be essential services, abandoning those services that have little social value — or, insofar as they are necessary, finding more efficient ways of delivering them.

A Summary of Local Economic Planning Procedures

Economic planning was developed, so to speak, overnight, with the establishment of the Soviet Union. The basic techniques of input-output analysis, invented at the end of the 18th century, were used in Soviet planning and may still prove to be useful, in simplified form, to assist local economic planning as 'social accounting matrices'. This technique has been augmented to look at social as well as economic consequences of particular lines of investment. In our globalised world, and perhaps of decreasing importance, a further tool has been 'value chain analysis'[393], which analyses products consumed locally to look back at where these came from and where their components, elements and materials, from which these were made, came from and thence the value added that accrued to the workforces who brought each of these into the stream that eventually produced and delivered the items in question. Yet further techniques, in particular 'material flow analysis' and 'life cycle assessment'[394], have been developed in recent years to help to estimate the resource and environmental consequences of decisions to produce goods in particular ways. At the present time, all of these, and other technocratic planning methods, presuppose computers to operate effectively and in fact assume at the same time that the materials to produce things will come from far afield and so need to be assessed in terms of their longer-term availability and impact on distant environments.

Perhaps this is all part of the over-sophisticated world of today and we can safely revert to simple manual forms of planning as economies 'come home again'. However, difficult choices will need to be made in a situation of diminishing resources, to ensure that the production system can deliver not only today but also into the future. One response may be that the Soviet system is not something to be emulated insofar as it failed. However, the failure was not one directly of ineffectiveness: it did actually deliver to a vast population the means to a reasonably comfortable life. The problems that led to its demise were really two-fold: the growing complexity of the modern economy in terms of things to be produced and the allocation of materials necessary to produce them and secondly the fact that 'the people' were not brought into the decision-making process as to what should be produced and ended up rejecting the products and desiring access to the ineffable wonders of the capitalist consumer economy. Suffice it to say, that focused resource and environmental planning procedures will be necessary tools to minimise the impacts of the decline in energy resources on local production economies and to rebuild local economies that are robust in the face of the real resource future.

It will be easy enough in the future to overcome these two problems encountered by the past planned economies. The first will be necessarily overcome in that the complexity of the productive economy will decline radically as a consequence of the cessation of the flow of materials and hence the radical reduction in what gets produced and so the simplification of the analyses that will need to be undertaken, albeit step-wise and as far as possible in anticipation of the 'closing in' process. The second can be overcome, and in recent years much relevant experimentation has been undertaken, by participatory local economic planning initiatives that involve the people directly in deciding what to produce to satisfy their needs, how this should be done and who will take responsibility for doing it. The basic methodology[395] set out briefly below can be disseminated to all local communities that wish to initiate LED processes and can be adapted to specific local circumstances and needs.

1. The first step may be taken by one or a group of motivated citizens, or an initiative such as a Transition Cities initiative, or by local government. Immediately reconnaissance should take place to see who and which institutions are inclined to come together to take the next steps, whether in fact there are already initiatives which might be augmented to cover the local economic planning process, and whether there may be opposition or blockages to moving ahead. This is currently referred to as a 'stakeholder analysis'.

2. A preliminary action will bring the interested parties together to sketch the initiative ahead and to organise one or more events, open to the public and involving the media, to raise interest and disseminate basic information on what is intended. Where an effective transition initiative is already under way, then this should be undertaken within the overall framework of this initiative. This may be a 'conference' or a fair or other means of drawing the public attention to the initiative and what it aims to do. And the output should be a statement of commitment, or

a 'vision', together with a preliminary group of people who will give a structure to the process.

3. Care is needed in developing ideas concerning early institutionalisation of the initiative. It should be as democratic as possible in the sense of being open to all voices and outgoing in seeking those excluded or who do not benefit from the current arrangements, but at the same time able to be effective in taking decisions that will lead to substantive action. This might therefore involve a 'forum' that lends powers to one or more 'executive' organisations, but which maintains overall power and responsibility to change these arrangements. In the same spirit, government should be involved if it is apparent that they will cooperate as equal partners, but this should not legally be a government-led initiative.

4. The first activity must be to obtain a clear understanding of the local economy and to use this as a basis for policy development and planning. This means generating an account of what materials and goods are flowing into the sub-region and from where they are coming; what resources, physical and human, (skills) the sub-region has to offer; and an estimate of needs currently not satisfied and those which might be expected to emerge as problems into the future. This understanding will come not only as 'data' but as views obtained through public involvement ('action-based research' with 'focus group' discussions).

5. The planning process is, today, well-enough known in terms of ways to identify issues, define projects, prioritise these, analyse their feasibility in technical and financial terms and their impacts on resources and environment, financial and logistical requirements and time-tables for implementation. This is where the technocratic tools mentioned above are applied. Participatory planning essentially means not only broad public discussion throughout the process but, above all, motivating particular individuals and groups in the community to take responsibility for projects. This is no longer a question, as in the past, of governments or of a narrow notion of 'private sector', but should focus on elements of the community taking on activities and functions, with the planning process doing no more than defining, motivating and coordinating.

6. Upon deciding what initiatives are to be pursued, a mutual learning process will need to be engaged in both to determine how to manage projects in a mutualistic/cooperative way (fundamentally at odds with the current notion of 'enterprise') and at the same time to develop the knowledge and skills necessary to rebuild local production capacities. This will need to be part of what may be a fundamental change in education and training at all levels that requires further discussion in the following chapter. The immediate need for knowledge and skills may be technical and vocational, but the means of management will also need to be learned and beyond that the ethos of cooperative working that should start already in primary school, finding its realisation in the cooperative operation of all initiatives given birth by the LED process.

7. Projects will need to be financed. This has meant previously the use of municipal resources or obtaining grants or borrowing money and in the first instance this may be relevant for some initiatives. However, from the outset, the Transition Cities movement — specifically in Totness in Devon, England — introduced a local currency so that capital could be raised and circulated locally. In fact such an idea has a long history not far removed from the Owenite notion of 'labour notes'[396], essentially exchanging hours worked, and LETS and 'time banks' that are a more recent phenomenon based on similar principles. All of this is to note that in the coming decades, the wider international and national money systems can be expected to collapse, so that local capital will become much more directly capital in terms of exchanges of work, food and other basic necessities (a 'barter economy') to facilitate the re-crafting of local economies. And then in the future local economies may be transformed to the 'gift economies' inherent in egalitarian social arrangements, where skills are learned for community gain and personal self-fulfilment, not for the individual to 'earn a living' and are given freely where the community, aka LED or other form, has decided skills are needed. The importance of revising the meaning and content of education to address the emergent conditions requires that this be dealt with in some detail in the following chapter.

8. Implementation and monitoring of progress on each project and the overall programme as set out in the planning process should be an open, public process that allows multiple voices to participate, learn and eventually being drawn into the circle of responsibility in taking action to augment transparency and commitment. Project completion and evaluation should be followed by further rounds of planning and the proliferation of projects.

So what do we mean here by 'projects'? At the narrow end, these will design new production initiatives, defining types of products, determining how these are going to be manufactured, where the raw materials or components are going to come from, what skills will be needed and how these are to be acquired if they are not yet present, also how the initiatives will be managed, how the costs will be met and the benefits distributed.

But 'projects' may involve other aspects of local reconstruction such as initiatives in processing defunct infrastructure and objects to recover useful materials for various local industries. Or even systematic building and infrastructure demolition (such as hacking up of highways to make space for agriculture and ecological restoration) as part of the general restructuring of the use of land and its preparation for intensive agriculture or return to ecological diversity. In exploring possible initiatives and projects, each community will need to define its own limits in terms of capabilities — initially relatively narrow by way of a learning process — and thence move into more ambitious projects out of the learning process and accumulated experience and skills.

And finally, the LED process will need to pay significant attention also to the extension and maintenance of services that hitherto have been seen as a government responsibility. With the retreat of governments as a consequence of lack of resources, new ways will need to be found to motivate and coordinate communities in new approaches to education and health services, but also actions to support initiatives to satisfy local desires and needs in artistic and even spiritual fields of the kind that are discussed in the final chapter.

The Built Environment and the Revival of Community

For most of the time that human beings have peopled the earth, they have been satisfied with accepting the environment they inherited without imposing any significant changes. They lived in caves or in the open or built light structures that left almost nothing by way of evidence that they had existed — their own bones and some small stone artefacts, crafted to support their livelihoods and thence means to adorn themselves and give artistic expression to their lives. There are some writers today who believe humanity will return to this state of existence[397] and there are in addition many who lived amongst the last surviving groups of hunting and gathering people who furthermore believe that this mode of existence provided a happier basis for human life than that which emerged as civilisation[398] — and we can be sure that for much of humanity in many eras this is almost irrefutably the case: conflict, violence and mass-exploitation has been inherent to almost all civilisations.

Nevertheless, the view taken from the outset of this book is that the passage of civilisations has given us, in spite of the multitude of problems described throughout this text, much to be proud of and that can be rescued as ways of human social life that can live in harmony and synergy with the rest of the natural world over very long periods. However, the book also expresses a conviction that today's civilisation has recreated, or rather displaced, the earth's environment over vast areas in ways that cannot be sustained and that in the short term will be abandoned as unusable, however much there might be a desire today to live in the manner in which we have become accustomed in recent decades. Of course we can also look at a little distance at the lifestyles that are yielded by the kinds of cities and suburbs that, by now, the majority of people live in, surrounded by their property, and see these as veritably bizarre, with their chaotic streets, an insistence on transport by car that causes endless congestion and horrific pollution conditions.

As discussed in the introduction, the very term 'civilisation' derives from the Latin word *civitas,* or City, throughout history generally denoting urban life, in spite of the fact that the vast majority of humanity, even in the context of 'high civilisations' lived a rural existence in villages and on isolated farms. Whilst a few large cities emerged in history going back some two and a half thousand years, almost all of these were temporary, fading back into small towns and villages amongst the ruins. Modern urbanisation started just two hundred years ago in Britain, fuelled by increasing exploitation, initially of coal, spreading later in the century to other European countries and North America with European colonists founding modest cities elsewhere in the world, occasionally building on small local beginnings. Only in the course of the 20th century did larger cities emerge in Latin America, Asia and Africa, with the majority of the world's population living in towns and cities by the opening years of the 21st century.

This is to say that today the environment in which the majority of people live is predominantly man-made, where for most people most of the time, the rest of the natural environment has been reduced to suburban gardens and parks, put altogether at a great distance from everyday life. In the first instance, our culture presents us with the built environment as a string of past decisions taken for functional reasons and to fulfil rapidly proliferating and changing aesthetic fashions; buildings are there to ameliorate climatic conditions and to articulate the way in which we organise our everyday lives. The infrastructure that connects buildings together provides basic resources of water and energy and thence removes 'waste' and facilitates movement between buildings, parts of the city and other places in the world, is all seen as responding to needs and to making improvements in life.

However, things could be different — and in the past have been very different in the way cultures have intervened in the natural environment to create human and social environments that responded to what they perceived as their needs. Whilst we might say that nomadic peoples who did not build permanent structures are uncivilised, the Mongols demonstrated a capacity for sophisticated organisation of war that we might associate with civilisation but without significant built environments, even today living in mobile tent structures that make little impact on the natural environment until they are clustered in growing squatter suburbs such as the Ger (tent) communities of Ulaanbaatar.

What in history books are referred to in ancient times as 'cities', for instance in Mesopotamia or ancient Greece, or even the cultures of India prior to the Moguls and subsequently the British, possessed no larger settlements than what by today's standards would be referred to as towns. These nevertheless displayed complex cultures in terms of skills and organisational capacities to build individual religious structures, palaces of the kings and comfortable houses for their citizens. Fine fabrics, musical instruments, paintings and other craft products to reflect the capacity of human beings to create beauty in their lives were even produced in what would be thought of today as no more than villages[399].

In short, built environments in general are contingent, rather than necessary, cultural constructs that arise from multiple decisions of the people who possess or are possessed by particular cultures. We might even say that the building of cities has become the apotheosis of modern civilisation, the goal to achieve which has become the central cause of its fall[400]. Our apparently functional, technologically dominated built environment is thus also a cultural construct, created

303

through time and expanded and complexified in dramatic ways over the past few decades that, when looked as cultural process and artefact, can be taken apart and its components subjected to critique.

Now, on the edge of what will inevitably be a radical change in direction as a result of the decline in energy resources that have fuelled the urbanisation process, with the radical dysfunctionality of recently constructed cities, the time has come to apply a fierce critique. This should not, however, just regret what has happened but above all aim to recreate built environments in ways that will be viable in the long term and which will also satisfy the deeper needs of future communities and cultures to express themselves in terms not only of functional needs but also psychological and aesthetic needs.

The notion of the built environment as 'cultural artefact' is most obvious when we analyse the architecture of buildings and their assemblage as villages, towns and cities. The house of the common people is the start of the process of devising architectural style and, as vernacular, this combines the use of local materials to build the structure with the way in which social relations within the family or group interact through enclosing and articulating space to satisfy privacy and group needs in ways that modify the environment to accomplish this: regulating temperature, protecting against the sun, rain and other inclement weather. Houses relate to one another in specific ways: in groups, along streets that facilitate people to access the public space and eventually the surrounding countryside and thence the facilities created to satisfy communal needs — meeting places, places of individual and community work and ritual that, as these become more elaborate, demand also elaborated structures.

With this comes an 'over-determination' of the style, as art and architecture, that often is a formalisation on a larger scale and with new materials of the simple structure of the house (such as the case of the classic Greek temple that could still be found in 19th century buildings applying 'classical' architecture, or the Oriental temple that in reality is simply a radical formalisation of the peasant house). Eventually new means of expression emerge, relating to the details of religious practices, such as in developed Hindu, Islamic and Gothic architecture.

In parallel, the advent of class society meant that the ruling classes demanded grander expression of their superior power and hence scale and architectural expression to match. With differentiation in power also come wars, and hence city walls and gates. And finally, local society articulates itself in various ways to produce schools, markets, baths and a proliferation of other social functions that further structure the city and give it its full character as an organic whole as was assumed throughout civilisation, as the city, to be the essence of cultural and social self-expression.

From the 18th century, with the initiation of the Modern era, first in Britain and thence spreading in the 19th century to the rest of the Occident, cities became increasingly extensive and complex in the differentiation of parts and the structures that articulated them (in fact, a few cities in the past — notably ancient Rome and other large Roman towns and also some Chinese and subsequently Islamic cities had confronted such an incremental construction process). Problems arose in the supply of resources that required the bringing of water over ever greater distance and transport systems to bring in materials to sustain the cities, creating congestion and pollution and wastes that, insofar as they were recognised as useful resources and 'recycled', needed to be removed. All of this required technological invention to deal with, that arose contingently. The most spectacular achievement was the supplying of the cities with increasing amounts of energy to sustain these, initially directly with coal and then with gas and eventually with electricity. Never with any thought for its longer-term sustainability of the cities, caught in a trajectory totally convinced of its inevitability and, for all the problems that came with it, the rightness of the urbanisation process.

Up to the 18th century, we can recognise how the physical structures of cities throughout Eurasia and Meso-America were invented and re-invented with variations but also limits to such variations: a city was recognisably a city wherever it was found. Locally appropriate vernacular ways of building differed greatly according to climate, local materials and styles in the grander structures; once developed, these often persisted over very long periods, with rational rules for the construction of cities developed in some parts of the world ranging from China over two thousand years ago, through ancient Greece and Rome, to France in the Middle Ages and the Spanish in Latin America, the 16th Century Persian and Mogul efflorescence and yet others.

It is important to reiterate that until the modern era, even where in cities styles evolved beyond the simple farmhouse and modest urban residence, the remains of which can be seen in archaeological sites of, for instance, Machu Picchu or the Roman cities, to the 19th century apartment buildings of continental European cities, the 'vernacular' was achieved with the utilisation of materials found readily to hand and making relatively little impact upon local environments in terms of resource extraction. Indeed, with a few exceptions (again of buildings built to express the power of kings and religions[401]) even into the 20th century, the vast bulk of building materials from which cities were built

— stone, clay, bricks and tiles, timber, plaster and even glass — were locally sourced.

Starting in the early 20th century, a radical break occurred through a combination of the increase in the trade of materials and the advent of the 'modern movement' in architecture. The increasing use of steel and cement and thence aluminium and glass (facilitated by vast increases in the exploitation of coal resources) was at the forefront of this change, followed by the spread of an ever wider range of manufactured materials and components, initially produced and traded within national borders, but increasingly internationally.

Although almost never discussed, 'modern architecture', as ostensibly a rationalisation of building (according to the most renowned of modern architects, Le Corbusier, a house should be understood as 'a machine for living in'[402]) erased the ubiquitous aspect of buildings as expressing the power of the owner or benefactor and in the case of dwellings, erased the cultural familiarity of building style and also substituted the social meaning of the configuration of house interiors for rationally functional arrangements.

Insofar as populations identified with the ideology of modernity, or were otherwise prepared, or forced, to forego their cultural understanding of the built environment as part of the bargain of acquiring increased affluence, so modern architecture prevailed. Neither communist nor fascist governments were prepared to accept this unquestioningly and in both cases insisted that new buildings continue to express power and culture over and above their utilitarian function. This did not, however, obviate the growing use of energy-intensive and non-local materials in construction.

With the waning from the 1970s of the modernist impulse and the failure of 'Developmentalism', the idea of a rationally conceived urbanisation, already weak, disappeared altogether. Increasingly a 'postmodernist' notion arose, together with other fragmented architectural features that re-introduced 'style' (albeit mainly as pastiche upon continuing functionalism, especially of the building configuration) into public and corporate architecture as both expressions of the power and wealth of the corporate or government entities financing the buildings and as sheer entertainment.

In fact modernism by no means erased the urge for cultural expression in dwellings and with the revitalisation and further spread of 'Possessive Individualism' and the 'Commercial Ideology', the formula of the suburb, initially in the United States, came in time to be the primary cultural self-expression of the 'middle classes'. that could be seen as the spread of the values of modern society. Reference was made earlier in this chapter to the way in which for growing populations the possession of a small patch of land with a detached house upon it became a confirmation of arrival as a legitimate member of modern society. If we look at the houses built on these sites, we see endless variations in the designs on the theme of status with the house — and with it today the automobile that connects the house umbilically to the rest of life, itself an important expression of status — having become the primary expression of self-worth of individuals and families in the (post)modern world.

We can say with some confidence that this fact, this epicentre of the lives of untold millions today – the majority of the US and Australasian populations, considerable numbers of Europeans and the burgeoning 'middle classes' of the cities of the South - is the root cause of the lack of ability to raise the issue of the unsustainability and unviability of modern life. It is, indeed, precisely this lifestyle that is the reason for the unviability because together, modern houses and automobiles are the great consumers of a wide range of materials that could never have continued to be supplied for very long and above all, understood as a lifestyle, also the great consumers of energy and particularly petroleum.

Looked at as a built environment, this can then be seen at the centre of the machinery that is destroying the global environment. This starts with the rubbishing of the immediate surrounds of cities, not only ecologically but also in terms of producing food efficiently for the needs of urban populations. It then proceeds to make demands on more distant places; depleting resources and environments well out of sight of the populations consuming them, as revealed in the analyses of 'ecological footprints' discussed in the foregoing chapter.

It is not, however, only suburbia, qua built environment, that pushed continually in unsustainable and unviable directions. High-rise modernity, built from materials transported over great distances and manufactured from non-renewable materials and creating internal environments that would not be able to survive the decline in energy resources, matched suburbia in presenting built environments that will become unusable and uninhabitable in the not-too distant future. Without continuous inputs of energy to drive lifts, ventilation systems and lighting, floors in buildings much above the eighth will be difficult to use and in many cases, with unlit interior spaces and windows that cannot be opened, the interior environments will become highly inconvenient if not entirely unusable[403].

We can, by now, see the immense difficulty we will face in the near future to continue to live functional lives in our existing built environments. On the other hand, we will not be able to recreate our

307

built environments overnight in ways that are viable in the situation of the demise of the 'middle class' world of property[404]. This will require a 'cultural revolution' that jettisons the reasoning, both functional and cultural, encompassing psychological as well as the economic forces driving the creation and maintenance of our present-day built environments. In the following chapter we will discuss in some detail the problematic of jettisoning the Possessive Individualism that gives life to present processes creating and maintaining present-day built environments. Here, we will discuss the aspects that relate to the ecological and functional aspects of rebuilding viable built environments.

There may well be parts of the world where the notion of a built environment fades away almost completely through a return to hunting and gathering or nomadic herding — even in what is now the United States. We assume here, however, that for the most part there will be a decline of the urban to a point where settlements are small enough that the countryside and the resources which it can supply are accessible within walking distance as was the case almost everywhere until two centuries ago. As noted above, planned cities (or maybe we should refer to towns in a world where cities, as we know them today, have become a thing of the past) have emerged very occasionally throughout history, but enough to indicate the possibility of communities being able to agree that this is the best way to solve their mutual existential problems with respect to a created environment and in future this could again become something that community planning groups take on as an ultimate objective.

The modern era had seen, during the Developmental years, the creation of New Towns, particularly in Britain[405] and the Soviet Union, but also with variants in many other countries. These were created as artefacts, technocratically responding to the tastes and ideas of professional planners and architects[406] and with assumptions of future viability that would become increasingly dysfunctional, together with the rest of the recent accretion of built environments due to energy dependence. These cannot, therefore, be expected to be models, in physical terms or in terms of a process of development, for the directions that reconstruction will need to take and so planning-oriented groups will need to be original and imaginative in conceiving of viable forms of settlement for the future.

Over the 20th century, urban and regional planning became elaborated into a wealth of technical procedures learned and practised by professionals from well-staffed government offices, assisted by consultants. Fashions came and went in the configurations of new towns, extensively planned suburbs, urban redevelopments and extensive renewal of urban infrastructure systems; the bulk of planning was fragmented, incremental 'development control' that, particularly from the 1980s, lacked any vision in terms of 'end state'.

In the context of the idea of progress, an underlying assumption was that as particular problems emerged, or new inventions and fashions arose, planning would respond to these in a piecemeal fashion. There was, therefore, no consideration, even when by the 1990s the term 'sustainability' was entering into the planning vocabulary, of where the limits of sustainability might lie and, to use current terminology, how to secure resilience against future potential hazards. We only now are starting to see just how far into the deserts of non-sustainability the urbanisation process has penetrated and hence the dysfunctionality of the putative planning processes.

An essential dimension of the abandonment of the notion of progress will be to adopt, instead, the notion of Utopia. This means to consider how territory (we have throughout this chapter been talking of sub-regions) might be refashioned in terms of human settlements to accommodate a sustainable and congenial way of life for the communities occupying this space but which, at the same time, conserves ecological resources. The discussion of bioregions in the foregoing chapter sketched a format which may be applied as a basis for thinking about long-term sustainable development. But even before any thought can be given meaningfully to configuration and content, it will be necessary to devise an effective planning process.

By now, through the foregoing chapter and this, we should have a coherent idea of how participatory planning processes work. We have presented the general case of the Transition Cities initiative and the formation of community groups that start to think and discuss, 'feel their way', and educate themselves into what local development means. The bringing of land in stages into a process of community decision-making and thence the procedures for LED should prepare us for undertaking a more strategic process of planning of localities and sub-regions.

Planners trained for present day planning may have skills necessary to plan for the future and these will eventually be vital for communities to utilise in the reconstruction of settlements and sub-regions. However, we cannot guarantee that the approaches they take out of an education in the modern world will be appropriate, so technocratic planning will need to recede into the background until the community has become confident enough in understanding what needs to happen to plan for a future without oil, which will mean necessarily abandoning much, if not most, of the existing built environment and creating something more akin to the way life was lived spatially before the advent of modernity. This is not a romantic, but a sheerly practical process of recovering the use of sub-regional resources to serve the needs of people living in these sub-regions.

In the short term, contingent steps will surely be taken to dismantle buildings that have been abandoned and move the materials to where houses and other buildings can be rebuilt in clusters that enable people to cooperate in managing everyday life without travelling long distances. In this way we might expect new communities to appear arbitrarily amongst the detritus of the old, with space cleared to create larger areas to grow food. But as this process proceeds and more people become aware of the permanent nature of the changes taking place, then planning the sub-regional environment to accommodate discrete communities can become a more conscious process. Where do we want to place settlements and where recreate rural landscapes and farms? How should we distribute the various functions within the settlements, ensuring housing that is both convenient and pleasant, but such that all dwellings within the settlements are within easy reach by walking of all social functions and facilities?

In the case of still-existing rural areas, this may not involve decisions that are too difficult. In denser suburban areas, the decisions will be more difficult and in dense urban areas, the decisions will often be impossible and it is here that transition groups will have to look for ways of exiting the cities and finding elsewhere to locate their new life and livelihoods. There is likely to be a steady drift of individuals and groups out of the inner cities, at times more concerted as the availability of resources from outside the cities ebb away.

It is dramatic to realise that whole inner areas of great cities such as Manhattan, Brooklyn and the Bronx, or the inner arrondissements of Paris, London's inner boroughs, the opulent developments of Rio's Copacabana, Ipanema, Leblon, Botofogo and Laranjeiras, the vast spread of down-town Tokyo and the massive new city centres that have sprung up in China over the past three decades will, within the next five decades, have emptied out their populations, leaving ghost cities with tiny residual populations, who will be mining resources for the construction of peri-urban settlements or who will manage to obtain enough water to live and to convert city parks and other lacunae in otherwise concrete jungles into viable farming plots. Meanwhile the vast areas of suburbia will have to regroup into smaller communities, removing most of the existing houses to make way for land usable for agriculture.

In the Americas there is certainly enough land with good agricultural possibilities to support networks of smaller communities. In the United States, areas such as Vermont and New Hampshire once supported such networks that emptied out as farmers left for the cities; these and other areas that are now occupied by massive factory farms with small populations will present possibilities to fill up with new village and small town communities, and in South America also there is much space for such settlement or resettlement. Problems of finding such spaces will, however, be problematic in most of Europe and Asia where the productive countryside almost everywhere is already occupied.

The reconversion and redistribution of the land and the drive to re-plan sub-regions will be too important to leave to individuals or even subgroups under the Transition Towns initiatives. Regular public fora should be held, open to all, to discuss possibilities and community members should be encouraged to make long-term proposals for discussion. Groups responsible for land use planning might be constituted as 'Community Planning Groups', recognising the closeness of reconstruction of the built environment and the reconstitution of community, within the general framework of Transition Town initiatives, but held closely accountable to the more general fora.

Local groups will not be able to decide anything much on their own and it is in the realm of bioregional planning that confederal arrangements will need to be forged, where groups from neighbouring areas meet regularly with proposals to see whether agreement can be reached on long-term strategies that make it possible to decide where houses and community facilities should be clustered, and whether pre-existing villages and towns can be revived as semi-autonomous entities or whether new places have to be found. The unbuilt areas will again become precious: to preserve against built up development, removing roads and other land that has been progressively (even arbitrarily) concreted over, regenerating topsoil for local agriculture and replanting and reviving ecologically rich woodlands — all this in the framework of permaculture, is discussed in more detail later in this chapter.

When we speak of confederal groups, we mean initiatives that today fall under the heading of 'inter-municipal cooperation'. In countries where urban areas overflow their boundaries, inter-municipal initiatives have long since organised more or less ad hoc arrangements for such services as sub-regional transport, 'waste' and water management and, indeed, sub-regional strategic planning. As urbanisation goes into reverse, this mode of organisation will take on greater importance, and will now organise sub-regional resource management: centrally urban

311

and peri-urban agriculture (UPA) and the organisation of wastewater and organic solid waste recovery and supply for UPA and the development of energy supplies to substitute for the loss of fossil hydrocarbons. These are discussed later in this chapter. Here it is necessary to emphasise the way in which settlements will need to conserve these resources and recover vernacular knowledge of living in the particular climate and places in which they will develop.

The formation of effective Community Planning Groups may well take time. Initially individuals should come together informally to explore who, and perhaps what, institutions are bringing the need for transition initiatives into focus. Even where transition group initiatives are in train, as the downward passage accelerates, the enormity of what is starting to happen and the opening up of a clearer perspective on what can be expected to be happening in the coming decades, is likely to precipitate revisions in the structure of these initiatives, with a wide disparity of outlooks on what should be done based on different convictions with respect to the direction, degree and speed of change to be expected. The transition movement already provides a wide menu of possibilities with respect to possible reorganisation of built environments and we can expect a growing proliferation of experiences of towns and cities that will provide demonstration of what might be done, providing lessons from these experiences.

The initial discussions on spatial planning might, indeed, form as one component amongst others of a local network of groups across cities and suburban sub-regions, with different kinds of initiatives being undertaken by different components, perhaps merging and fragmenting over the initial years as issues come into focus and with progress towards formalisation of groups moving forward at different paces. The major problem will be how to organise the use of sub-regional responses, as the supply of resources from afar decreases and hence the intensification of sub-regional resource exploitation can be expected. Measures will be urgently needed to avoid conflict and to arrive at consensus amongst sub-regional groups.

There will be room for all kinds of initiatives and people should be allowed to come to an understanding of the new conditions in their own time and hopefully be active in advancing matters towards the new world order in their own way. The process of group formation and the taking on of activities should be underpinned by a consciousness of the necessity to recover the idea and the praxis of community and consensus that existed in the past but that recent experience of modernisation has progressively destroyed, as people become increasingly mobile in a world that admires competition. It is highly likely that large numbers of people will become totally disoriented by what is happening[407] and transition groups should work actively within their neighbourhood to draw in the disoriented, and motivate everyone in the community to participate in decision-making and the resulting actions.

Insofar as eventually almost everywhere there will be abandonment of buildings — in suburbia, central high-rise districts and modern industrial districts, sometimes the majority of the building stock[408]. At the same time there will be an urgent necessity to rebuild in places and in ways that will be functionally appropriate in terms of location and structure for a real, viable future. Amongst the groups that form within the overall transition initiatives, those concerned with the built environment (or 'urban planning') might initially be relatively marginal but in time take on ever greater importance to the community, relating closely to a group concerned with the management of land. In practice this will be more than one group in the sense of starting from very local, community/neighbourhood core groups (these might even be apartment block resident groups) with (following later) groups that are nested confederations of neighbourhood groups concerned with sub-regional and bioregional issues. In the case of larger cities, there will per force be several levels of confederal groups – building on the present formation of local transition groups in many larger cities - eventually city-specific groups, sub-regional groups taking in peri-urban communities that could become, for a while before the acceleration of the emptying out of cities, the source of most of the city's food and other resources.

These 'nested groups', even at the most local level, should play both a strategic and a very down-to-earth practical role. Strategically the groups should inherit from past planning efforts a data base on land uses, monitoring changes as these take place. The group(s) should conduct ongoing formulations and reformulations of what an ultimate built environment might be like in the longer term as a self-education process in the physical aspects of utopianism. The down-to-earth side of the remit of the group will be to monitor the use of buildings to follow the processes of abandonment, for example negotiating with current owners and users concerning the future of the buildings and the pressures to rebuild, and to match these up with ideas of efficient and effective places and ways to accomplish change. That is, both suggesting demolition and directing where the resources from demolished buildings might go in terms of reuse and recycling.

The dimension of community development that these groups should take on in inner urban areas is the management of specific areas of land, with or without buildings, as cooperative enterprises (CPRMRs) that will formulate ways of reviving abused land and demolishing or changing the use of buildings effecting, where possible, a return to natural conditions or to (urban) agriculture or to new buildings appropriate to the conditions and in line with the ongoing formulation and reformulation of the planning of future settlements. We can envisage, in line with the progressive extension of the principle of common pool resource management, the systematic abandonment of private property in buildings as these, being consolidated into discrete cooperatives of users. In some cities much of the residential building stock is already cooperatively run and this mechanism would simply spread to the rest of the building stock, including non-residential, given the prevalence of absentee landlordism or the necessity of abandoning previous places of residence (suburbia) due to the unviability of the concomitant lifestyle.

The way in which most non-residential buildings are used today can be expected to change as a consequence of the changing structure of local economies. We might think initially of some kind of return to the structure of towns before the event of modernity and industrialisation, with small-scale craft industries woven into the structure of towns, of town squares and markets, and with housing densely built along streets for the convenience of being near facilities. Of course, in the case of even small and certainly larger cities, such a model is irrelevant. We might thus also think of the organisation of towns in a new way consonant with the egalitarian and cooperative, rather than familial and individualistic ways of the past.

Here we also need to refer to the experience of Intentional Communities mentioned in the foregoing chapter. This sees people living a more fluid and communal existence where property and hierarchy are no longer relevant and so 'families' are more contingent and groups share their living space — as many groups of youth have done in recent years — and where education and work take place in less articulated spaces than was the case in past eras and certainly not the rigorous separation of families and functions over extensive space, connected by cars and telephones and the elaborated Technostructure that in the past decades aggressively destroyed the integuments of society and settlements.

In large urban areas, it will almost certainly transpire that life for many inner urban communities becomes impossible to continue as a result of diminishing access to food and other resources, in many cases driven by the lack of water supply, which in many cities is likely to be sudden, with little that Governments can do to maintain supply. Earlier in the chapter we discussed the revival of local economies and, central to this, activity to implement urban agriculture. In dense urban areas, however, there is in almost all modern cities totally inadequate space to grow enough to provide more than a small proportion of the food necessary to feed local populations, even after converting urban parks to agriculture, developing roof gardens and other 'vertical farms' and the planting of road, railway and canal margins and recovering wastewater to irrigate these. Hence, to avoid starvation as the importation of food from afar diminishes, communities will have to migrate, and it will be the Community Planning groups that should assist in the management of this process, first investigating possibilities of migration out into the rural parts of the bioregion and where this is impractical, investigating possibilities of longer distance migration and setting up links with other communities — possibly at a great distance — that will be prepared to assist urban communities to 'transmigrate'.

In thinking about how sub-regions might be structured spatially and economically in the more distant future, we can consider how the social and organisational distortions that arose in the context of modernity might be overcome. We should recall from the foregoing chapter that in the process of specialisation and ascending out of any proximity of the production of their livelihoods into the rarefied realm of service work, the vast majority of urban populations lost touch with anything by way of the details of either the natural environment or the processes of production.

If human communities are to reconnect with their geophysical and ecological context then, in the longer term, even the largest cities will be modest in size, where the healthy citizen can walk into open countryside from anywhere in the settlement within ten minutes. Reasonable living densities could be to a maximum population of perhaps 100,000 souls but with less stress, little more than 50,000. But bioregional populations will no longer be concentrated in large towns but, rather, distributed through a hierarchy of larger and smaller towns and with the large numbers of villages, as in the past, accommodating at least half the population. The arrangement, analysed by Walter Christaller in South Germany as recently as the 1920s (and in the American mid-west as analysed by August Loesch in the 1940s) may once again become the most effective way of linking rural and urban activity into a coherent way of life[409].

As the downward passage accelerates and the flow of modern building materials dries up, virtually all building work will make use of materials salvaged from the detritus of modernity. Whilst modern building materials (concrete, steel, aluminium and highly processed

315

glass) lend themselves poorly to recycling without substantial energy-intensive reworking, or are well-nigh useless (various forms of building board) when compared with older buildings (slates, bricks and solid timber), nevertheless, the existence of an abundance of these materials will allow a transition period to a point, later in the century, when locally sourced natural materials will, once again, be the main source for building construction.

This points in the direction of the land and built environment groups looking back to vernacular models of construction that may indicate how local climatic conditions can be ameliorated with comfortable internal environments in an efficient manner and eventually built entirely from materials obtained from the immediate urban sub-region. The expression of power and status that has accompanied building over recent times should be consciously abandoned whilst seeking, perhaps through a new focus on past vernaculars, a cultural expression that confirms the egalitarian and cooperativist ethos that should underlie the whole process of renewal. One may hope that this will not, however, obviate the construction of more highly developed architecture to fulfil the needs of community and even ritual-associated structures that have always decorated and given structure to towns and cities. Experiments with the arrangement of dwellings in relation to the evolution of social gathering places and facilities, should aim in the longer run to develop formulae for the good life under the emergent conditions.

Thus, maybe Community Planning Groups should discuss and formulate ways in which, ultimately, the new settlements should not be merely functionally appropriate to facilitate convenient community life processes, but that in the end they are also aesthetically enjoyable. The journey to reconstructing modest sized settlements in a rural, farmed landscape will certainly take many decades, or even centuries, but with a constant concern in the reconstruction for some kind of aesthetic unity and artefact that one found in villages and towns and ultimately in a few magnificent cities in the past, should prevail.

Beyond the Occident, some parts of the world still have parts of cities where the vernacular architecture, for all the introduction of modern structures, nevertheless has sufficient remainders of the vernacular appropriate to local climatic conditions and from which the skilled use of local materials can be re-learned. This is particularly notable in Arab medinas and the readjustment of the Caucasian and Central Asian cities to the post-oil world will be but par for the course where cities have grown and declined many times over the past millennia.

China, however, will no doubt suffer dire consequences from the wholesale urbanisation and with it the destruction over just three decades of their traditional city centres, though it is to be hoped that there will be enough of the traditional to teach about local architecture and urban structure to rebuild what, in previous centuries, were urbane and pleasant urban environments.

In Latin America, pre-Colombian urban structures are too scant to teach much, but colonial architecture and planning that can still be found in the cores of cities right across the continent – and that, as discussed briefly earlier, has carried through even to informal settlement planning – may still have useful lessons for a future of modest cities and towns. South Asia, and above all Africa, had little by way of urban traditions pre-colonialism and, given the weak inclination of the majority of their populations even today to embrace modernity (being the 'last hold-outs' of peasant culture), may well revert once again to village life with little by way of larger towns. The decline of cities in these regions, and particularly the Indian megacities, will, however, surely result in radical declines in population.

The 'Nexus': Energy, Water, Food

The relationship between the provision of water and energy connects directly through to the production of food in the modern world. Civilisation began with the construction of irrigation systems that intensified the production of food and with it precipitated the formation of social classes, the competition between which, as Karl Marx pointed out, was the motor of the evolution of civilisations. Much has been made in the earlier parts of this book at the way in which the exploitation of fossil hydrocarbons became the foundation for the radical changes in civilisation that gave us modernity for a very brief historical era. With the decline of fossil hydrocarbons, human societies will revert to obtaining energy from the daily flow of the sun and from the systems of wind and moving water, together with the residues of ecosystems — including human residues.

The availability of fossil hydrocarbons encouraged the development both of water supply and food production systems to become dependent on the increased supply of these sources of energy and reached, today, a point where the decline in energy availability will quickly result in the cessation of water supplies for much of today's irrigation systems to cities and industries, rendering these unviable. Few people realise the extent to which our water supply systems, from the individual house or enterprise pumping up groundwater, to the supply systems of urban

317

areas, even where the resource comes from surface water or reservoirs, to vast areas of irrigated agricultural land, can only function as long as the electric pumps keep turning.

Well into the 20th century, even large cities were supplied predominantly via gravity-fed canals and pipe systems. The Romans built enormous aqueducts, the remains of a few of which, today, are impressive historic monuments occasionally still potentially functional two thousand years after they were built. Modernity installed initially modest (steam-driven) pumps at strategic points to bring water to the cities. Whilst we can remember that gravity-fed aqueducts are still possible and thus can in the future again be the basis of town and small city water supply systems, the road to reviving these will be long and in the interim we can guarantee crises everywhere in urban water supply systems. Indeed, such water crises are already affecting many urban areas in the South, where water is only available for short periods of the day and eventually the week, but in time with the ebbing away of energy, will fail altogether, making life there impossible, leading to forced abandonment of the settlements and eventually whole cities.

Similarly with irrigation systems, traditionally vast irrigation systems ran entirely on gravity feed and many of these areas, particularly Asian rice lands, continue in this way. However, the introduction of ground water-supplied irrigation systems, together with inter-river-basin water transfers using massive pumps, particularly in the United States, led to a dependence on external energy sources that will reduce and certainly by the end of the century entirely cease to be available. Indeed, even without the decline in energy supplies, over-extraction of groundwater and deterioration of irrigated soils, sometimes over vast areas such as the Ogallala aquifer under several states in the United States and the San Joaquin valley in California (providing today a quarter of the US food supply)[410], will under any circumstances decline in availability over the coming decades, even without the reduction of energy supply.

The decline in these systems will clearly lead to reductions in food supply which in turn will, with the reliance of many countries on grain from the United States, mean a reduction in global population. Even as the reduction of water availability impacts on agricultural production, so also will the reduction of agrochemicals that are made from fossil hydrocarbons. More than 95% of agricultural crops worldwide are currently grown with the application of agrochemicals.

Organic production, though spoken of much and apparently on the increase, provides only a very small proportion of agricultural produce. Land in organic production in the United States is but 0.6%; and over 5

% in only three of the EC countries. In the future increasing amounts of agricultural land will necessarily go over to organic production, probably much of it without the benefit of the technologies that can improve productivity and so production per hectare will decline substantially[411]. The global population that can be supported under these conditions is considerably less than the present population and the issue here will be: will communities be able to soften the impacts, slow these down and ameliorate the consequences?

Already at the time of writing, there are small admissions in official development agencies, including the European Commission[412], that a growing crisis is upon us to be able to maintain the supply of the water, energy and food that will be required in the coming years to sustain Development. Under the title of 'nexus', there is a call for improving the integrated planning for the supply of these basic resources. The German Ministry of Economic Cooperation and Development (BMZ) focuses this concern specifically on cities, placing the responsibility on urban authorities. Whilst the focus is upon reducing demand through efficiency measures, the acceleration in the development of renewable energy technologies and increased efficiency also in food production, there is very little by way of concrete acceptance of limits to come and none at all concerning the coming diminution of fossil hydrocarbon resources. The rhetoric is still about increased economic growth.

There is nevertheless purpose on focusing on these issues — however, with a realistic assessment of what we may expect in terms of reducing availability of resources. As long as governments and the institutions responsible for the supply of water and energy remain coherent, then technical steps may be taken to manage these in ways that ensure supply whilst the adjustments are made in lifestyles, the spatial configuration of settlements and the organisation of local economies. Unless there is a realistic acknowledgement of the problems ahead however, national governments will not take relevant decisions and indications are that this acknowledgement will not take place, leading to the decline of the legitimacy of governments and ultimately to the profound transformation of the political world.

The spread of transition initiatives, once these educate themselves adequately on the enormity of the challenges and are able to impress these on local governments to make changes in management approaches, might motivate activities that can help smooth the downward passage. In most countries, however, local governments are not independent agents but, rather dependent on national governments for policy and resources. Furthermore, although local governments pioneered the supply of key resources to cities — gas water and electricity supplied as public transport — throughout the 19th and 20th centuries these were largely disempowered in this respect so that there is no longer experience or interest in managing resource provision.

Where these have been given over to private companies, the ability to influence the ways in which these are managed and so devise ways to ameliorate the results of diminishing resources is very low. The drive to privatise was in many ways dysfunctional and when they are no longer able to deliver for lack of resources, the utilities will revert to the responsibility of the local governments. Another possibility is that transition groups will organise their own utilities, and will be more realistic about the probabilities and perhaps therefore more imaginative about the solutions.

It is notable that most of the genuinely effective measures, discussed further below, have in any case been mainly initiated by civil society organisations with generally weak collaboration from the public sector and almost no response from private utilities that cannot see profits in these without them being guaranteed by governments; private utilities never have any incentive to be inventive, particularly where the principle is to maximise sales, which has always undermined 'ecological' initiatives in cities otherwise ostensibly in pursuit of 'Sustainable Development'.

So as of necessity, local initiatives will grow to become the dominant avenue to maintaining a supply of energy, water and food; the transition initiatives will need to invent new institutional arrangements so that communities manage local and sub-regional resources to obtain the supplies they need, and in the process revive the sustainable management of the sub-regional ecosystems. Many such initiatives already exist, from local water treatment facilities that also generate biogas, to rainwater harvesting systems to provide water for schools and hospitals, to cooperatives that are building and installing energy saving measures including solar water heaters. Urban and peri-urban agriculture initiatives run cooperatively are developing particularly strongly in thousands of cities around the world, North and South[413], with multiple goals including reducing malnutrition and improving the quality of local diets, reducing the use artificial fertilisers through organic production and reuse of wastewater as a means to rebuild a local sense of community through local activity.

All that is discussed in the following paragraphs will not in the long run save the megacities of our age from decline. What these kinds of initiatives can do is, if effectively deployed, ease somewhat the hardship of the decline and return societies to ways of relating to the environment in terms of the need for water, energy and food that are ecologically sustainable into the future without the use of fossilised hydrocarbons.

Energy

A central concern of this book is that in the coming years energy resources will ebb away, insofar as these come from fossil sources. It was argued in Chapter One that attempts to overcome the decline by rapidly proliferating application of renewable energy technologies, can at best make only modest contributions and that nuclear power could, even if developed from today as quickly as possible, make little impact to cushion the decline. Quite simply, the decline in energy resources will be the underlying reason for the retreat from 'globalisation' into local economies. Costs of transport will escalate and energy for transport — almost entirely petroleum products — will become increasingly scarce. Biofuels might be further developed in some countries, but will – perhaps with Brazil as the exception that proves the rule - never supply more than a modest amount of fuel, with escalating competition with production of food.

Electricity and gas grids will survive for some decades, increasingly sporadically and then restricted to particular areas, eventually ceasing altogether to provide supply. This will depend on the sources of electricity but also on the ability of utilities to continue to maintain their systems. Cessation of supply may be sudden for some areas and for others over longer periods of sporadic abandonment and revival, with particularly power stations, including such 'renewable' sources as wind farms, progressively failing as a consequence of lack of fuel or parts or maintenance capacity. Once defunct, these may become sources of materials for other purposes. In the case of nuclear power stations, these will need to be treated as long-term dangers and resources invested in making these as safe as is feasible for the short and medium term, realising that in the long term, populations living in their vicinity will need to know what they are inheriting by way of dangers to be avoided long, long after the memory of what they were built for has receded into the realms of myth.

Planning for sub-regional energy supply should become an important dimension of local economic planning. This is both because energy is a vital component of economy (a fact that will become rather obvious as its availability declines) and because what is available, post oil, will be a basic determinant of most of the rest of the sub-regional economic plan post fossil energy sources.

Essentially energy planning will be, as it has been for those who have been involved in attempting to implement it in a coherent way over the past thirty five years, a matter of seeing how functions that we need can be carried out using less energy (energy efficiency) and how the sub-regional planning initiative can lead to the development of whatever the potential is throughout the sub-region for delivering energy from renewable sources[414]. This will mean eventually – well within this century - almost everywhere a return to the use of biofuels as the main source of energy and hence a management strategy for these that will have to balance land used for agriculture and other functions against land used to grow biofuels, including harvesting of agricultural and forestry residues.

Mechanical ways of harvesting the sun's energy (wind and direct solar, water power and so on) will need to be developed in a way that does not need sophisticated technologies imported from elsewhere. Today's renewable energy technologies, particularly photovoltaics and giant wind turbines, are unlikely to qualify almost anywhere, although these are likely to be part of transition strategies as fossil fuel availability ebbs away and as part of the process of learning what will be viable in the future in terms of local materials and capacities to produce and maintain energy technologies and systems under the emergent conditions.

For many transition initiatives, one of the first working groups to form has been an energy group, mainly to inform itself about energy issues and perhaps initiate pilot projects in home insulation, installation of solar heating and photovoltaic systems. These hark back to the 'energy crises' of the 1970s where local and sub-regional energy planning became temporarily widespread with support from, in Europe and a few 'development projects' elsewhere, the European Commission and local governments establishing energy management departments. These disappeared as the price of energy came down again in the 1980s, with plans and strategies gathering dust on shelves[415]. As in any planning exercise, information will be needed on the present uses and demand for energy and the sources that satisfy these (an 'energy balance').

From here, it will be possible to target actions that will need to be taken to reduce energy need in homes, in workplaces and above all in the transport system by helping a transition out of cars and onto bicycles and foot. Of course in this case, there will be no meaningful solution for so many people who are fundamentally car-dependent, with group transport forming interim solutions pending the movement of people to places closer to where they can gain access to resources, gainful work and community support without having to drive. At the same time, steps will need to be taken to see from where local energy resources can be tapped without unsustainable dependence on sophisticated technologies that will only be available for a decade or two, obviating also the unsustainable use of biofuels in competition with food crops. The rebuilding of local economies, particularly the interim industries that will be turning the detritus of modernity (above all vast numbers of useless vehicles) into goods that will be useful under the emergent conditions, will be dependent on coherently addressing the 'energy descent'.

Much might be learned from looking historically at how local life was lived before the advent of fossil energy sources, adding to this knowledge that might still be useful under the new circumstances, gained over the past century, adapted to whatever might be revealed as realistic. Furthermore, whilst somehow energy, having fuelled modern civilisation, has failed to impress itself as an idea, a concept or a dimension of society, as it ebbs away and the importance that it has had to everything that constitutes our life today becomes increasingly evident, perhaps a new consciousness of what it means to our lives will rise to the surface and become a central theme of the emergent future conception of the meaning of life. Many civilisations in the past, as disparate as Ancient Egyptian, Japanese, Iranian and Aztec, recognised at least the importance of the sun to their lives and placed this in a position of great importance to their concept of the meaning of life. Might this, or some variant that is more complex, post-fossil energy, become central to the way that future cultures conceive of and hence organise life?

Water

Some people consider that the most serious crisis facing global society today is not the energy crisis, but rather a crisis of water supply and sanitation. The crisis is, however, clearly one affecting different areas in different ways and is by no means universal. 'Water stress' (water availability to a region or country, divided by population) and the way in which this has been systematically on the increase over recent decades, is seen as the main indicator of this crisis. In practice, well-managed water resources have, in the past, allayed any very significant indication of water stress in countries where organisational, technical and financial resources have been applied appropriately. London's tap water, although not tasting particularly nice, is not harmful to health in spite of having been recycled six times in its journey down the Thames

River and throughput to the water supply and sewerage systems of the towns along the way. The lack of water in local communities and agriculture is apparently most severe in Africa where, in fact, the unused water resources are at their highest.

However, as outlined above, water supply problems will be increasingly manifesting themselves in the industrialised countries of Europe, North America and Asia in the coming years as the means to manage large volumes of water, using massive pumping, and in the Unites States the use of fossil water for irrigation of extensive areas, will become increasingly inaccessible. Desalination that has allowed large cities to grow up, particularly in the Arabian oil states, will cease to function and these cities will rapidly return into the desert, leaving the massive towers built from the proceeds of oil money as empty monuments to the hubris of global modernity[416]. As noted in passing above: water supply systems everywhere will need to be reviewed urgently as to where these can return to gravity feed, and without access to desalination in arid areas, consideration given when planning future settlements, what the implications are for distribution and morphology. There can be little doubt that this will be the primary cause in the radical reduction in size and in some cases almost complete abandonment of large cities such as in the Gulf States, some Latin American cities (notably Mexico City) and the arid areas of the United States from Texas and New Mexico to Southern California[417].

As with other aspects of the economy, an orientation will need to emerge in areas where there is high rainfall or other means of access to adequate water resources to bring water supply, where this has come in the past from increasing distance where gravity feed cannot work, back into the confines of the sub-region and thence engineered so as to reduce the need for energy in water distribution. In the past, ingenious ways of accessing water were developed, for example, aqueducts over vast distances and in the arid regions subterranean aquifer access tunnels ('qanats'). Whilst these have fallen in recent years into disuse, they should be revived and further developed. Conflicts between and within countries over who gets what water are already ongoing and may only be expected to increase.

Modern urban sanitation systems will also need to be entirely restructured for three reasons: as the morphology of cities changes, with the emptying out of populations from large cities and perhaps concentration, even in smaller cities, in particular neighbourhoods of the remaining populations, the sewer systems will no longer serve where they are needed and be redundant over areas that have been vacated and therefore cease to function. In any case, these systems are in most cities reliant to a degree on electrical energy to operate, that will be increasingly erratic and thence unavailable. The most important reason, however, is that these systems were premised on the aim of removing sanitary waste without regard to the nutrients in the waste that will need to be used as fertiliser in a world where agrochemicals are decreasingly available.

The fact is that until the advent from the mid19[th] century of large cities, human wastes throughout Eurasia had, for millennia, been transported to urban and peri-urban farms for use as fertiliser. A combination of the spread of cholera and other water-borne diseases due to expanding densities of population as cities grew larger, together with the growing expense of transporting human waste from the cities to rural farms, led to the development of water-born sewerage and thence, in spite of ingenious developments to continue to recover human waste, the ebbing away of these initiatives. In Germany these survived into the 1920s and in a few cases (Berlin being the most impressive example) water-born sewage was taken to peri-urban fields and used as fertiliser as recently as the 1970s. In smaller Chinese cities, this practice continues even today and ad hoc recovery of human waste can be found in many Asian cities with inadequate treatment resulting in these being hazardous to human health.

Increasingly in Europe, sewage came to be treated in treatment plants, after which the water is returned to the environment and the sludge incinerated, landfilled or, in most countries significant amounts used on the land — in France, Switzerland, Sweden and UK as much as half. This, however, is contentious for the same reason that sewage farms gradually disappeared: present-day sewage contains chemicals and especially heavy metals that, it is suspected, will build up over time to damage soils and contaminate food grown on the land.

The answer is source separation of domestic waste down to separate collection of urine and faeces in what has recently become known as 'sustainable sanitation' or 'ecosan'[418]. This focuses on retention of human waste, processing and use as fertiliser and soil conditioner in urban and peri-urban agriculture. Initially developed in rural areas, exploring technological components of such systems, particularly in India, methods then started to be developed for appropriate toilets and collection systems, that can be used in urban areas and in the near future these may be 'upscaled' to whole towns or urban neighbourhoods for use in urban and peri-urban agriculture (UPA) to substitute for artificial fertilisers.

Source separation of solid waste also retains the organic component that in quite recent times was collected in European cities from hotels, restaurants and markets to be fed to pigs. This will in future, with little doubt, return as a component of UPA, with chickens, pigs and other livestock, together with in-building fish farming, providing vital sources of protein. Those organic wastes not usable for fodder would then be composted with human and animal waste for use as fertiliser and soil conditioner. Ecosan uses less water, but whatever water is used in urban areas, including storm water and rainwater through the installation of rainwater harvesting from roofs and where appropriate other impermeable surfaces, will need to be increasingly recovered and locally treated both to reduce the requirement for energy in water supply systems and to recover residual nutrients in the wastewater for use in UPA. In many circumstances, treating organic wastes locally opens up the possibility of generating biogas as a stage in the process and such opportunities, already practiced sporadically in some cities, particularly in Asia, should be taken up, with the gas available for electricity generation, community or restaurant cooking and other uses.

With the decline in agrochemicals, the recovery of nutrients from human waste will become increasingly important to maintain agricultural productivity. From the outset, this should be a consideration in the development of UPA, with the step-wise intervention in existing sewerage to recover waste water and, with the morphological evolution of urban areas, building human waste recovery systematically into the construction of the settlements, complete with systems for processing the waste (different possibilities are well-enough known) and delivering the results to the urban farmers and peri-urban fields.

As noted above, a major reason for the cessation in the use of urban sewage as fertiliser in recent decades was the increasing complexity of the wastes contained in the sewage. Chemicals from cleaning agents to pharmaceuticals and heavy metals contaminating the urban wastewater and absorbed by plants, became potentially dangerous as food. The retreat of the chemical industry and hence the return of sewage to a simpler state as organic waste, will open the path again to use of all human wastes in agriculture. Nevertheless, the separation of urine, faeces and 'grey water' to be applied to agriculture in the most appropriate fashion should continue to be developed.

Food

Over the past few decades, food supply everywhere has become increasingly controlled by fewer and fewer enterprises with a national and increasingly global reach. Within countries a few supermarket chains, often purchasing directly from producers at home and overseas, in Organisation for Economic Cooperation and Development (OECD) countries market between two thirds and (Germany) nine-tenths of food, with the alternative small retail outlets and wholesaling companies ebbing away. Even in Southern countries, supermarket chains are supplying increasing amounts of groceries bought by the burgeoning middle classes. Although international trade in grain, as the main staple of most national diets, still represents a relatively small proportion of consumption (18% of wheat, 12.5% of corn and 6.5% of rice — 2007 figures), this is largely controlled by a few giant corporations plus, in the big exporting countries, national grain trading agencies.

However, 'food miles' (the distance that food travels from field to table) have been continually increasing in connection with the growth in food trade and growing disparities between food exporting and self-reliance, and food deficit countries. To some extent this is obscured, and perhaps exacerbated, by the way in which food is increasingly exchanged in the sense of countries both exporting and importing, often the same food products.

Trends are thus towards increase in energy consumption to maintain the global food production and supply system. Rising energy prices are, however, paralleled by rising hunger, particularly in the cities of the South with in 2010 the numbers of the undernourished exceeding one billion[419]. As energy descent takes hold, it is clear that food production will have increasingly to become organic as a consequence of increasing prices and eventually non-availability of agrochemicals and also more local as the energy required to transport food diminishes. The inefficiencies of transporting and feeding grain to animals to produce meat will lead to reductions in meat consumption in places where local pasture is not available, or the land will be required to produce basic food products as grain or potatoes for direct human consumption.

Already a widespread movement, as yet small but which is motivated amongst a significant population by an awareness of the troubles ahead, is towards a return to organising and purchasing locally grown organic food. Mention has already been made, in different contexts, of the importance that urban and peri-urban agriculture (UPA) will increasingly play in the coming years[420]. Already movements are under way in most countries, coming out of different traditions and learning from one another in ways that gives a very different inflection from one country and one city to another but where the basic drive is the same: to overcome emergent or future interruptions in food supply.

In the case of African cities, there is little or nothing by way of intellectual consideration of what is happening and how this might be developed more effectively and efficiently: it is to a significant degree an issue of reduction of malnutrition, with some practitioners benefiting as small enterprises.

But in Eurasia and the Americas, there are multiple reasons given for developing UPA and many different approaches. Already from the 1960s, urban women in Japan were taking the initiative, under the title of *teikei*, to form local groups (Hans) and make agreements with peri-urban farmers to supply them with vegetables and fruit. Here there was a concern for 'safe food', demanding direct supply of 'organic' produce that would bypass what they saw as the potential bad health effects of the corporate food industry. This concern has been widespread in Asian initiatives, also present in Vietnam and China, where, however, local governments are taking the initiative (in the sub-regions of the large cities from the 1960s) to develop UPA with multiple aims: for food security (this was the initial impetus), for food quality and variety, and today also for recreation as 'agro-tourism', promoting continuing awareness and education of the urban population about what is entailed in agriculture and food production.

The Japanese *teikei* initiatives spread to Germany and from there to North America by the late 1980s. 'Farmers Markets' sprang up and are now to be found in many North American cities, where only local farmers (albeit sometimes from considerable distances from the cities) are permitted to sell their products with no access to corporations or produce shipped over greater distances. The North American version of *teikei* under the title of 'Community Supported Agriculture' (CSA), or simply 'the box system', involves informal groups who operate a centre where members can put in their requests for a week's worth of produce which can then be collected once the farmers have delivered. Clearly this also depends on what the farmers are currently growing, providing seasonal variation and, in winter, with less supply.

These vary in terms of their effectiveness for addressing needs and supplying high quality produce and in general are an increment less developed than their Japanese equivalent which, nevertheless, has in recent years encountered increasing problems as the regulations for organic produce have been made more exacting with impacts on farmers that have increased the price of their produce. However, the Japanese experience has been impressive with the national cooperative movement helping to organise local Han groups that undertake self-education exercises and where the cooperatives actually consult with the groups in their development of products (not only in food but also other household products). Some groups are even undertaking social services, especially in the face of ageing populations, indicating how these new local approaches to food provisioning prompt further initiatives in the revival and reinforcement of local community life. As yet, however, there are few signs of reciprocal/exchange activities (barter or gift economies) so that the system is still firmly embedded in the national money system.

In some European countries and cities, town markets have survived from pre-industrial times. Almost all French towns and cities – in fact these are common throughout Europe and Asia - have extensive street markets once or twice a week that sell much of what can be found in supermarkets and although today most of the produce is brought over great distances or imported, generally some stalls continue to sell local produce which remain in considerable demand as a kind of 'local nationalism' and a cultural preference for local produce and food products (cheeses, preserved meats, bread and pastries, some fruit and vegetables).

However, nowhere, not even in Japan, are these initiatives making any great headway against the lengthening average food miles along which food arrives on the tables of the citizens of most of the world's cities. The spread of 'supermarket culture' continues (astounding are the massive French Carrefour hypermarkets in Chinese cities!). The models are nevertheless there, the best of them involved in successful local education and training exercises of citizens and community groups in own-food production that at the same time aims to nurture a new sense of community solidarity through collective substantive activity. And networking is growing so as to spread knowledge and experience from one city to another, promising to become more effective, such as the URGENCI network in France with ambitions to provide an umbrella for CSA around the world.

At present UPA is overwhelmingly about growing vegetables, to a lesser degree fruit, and some livestock including fisheries. Almost everywhere there is a concern to reduce or eliminate agrochemicals so that the produce is organic and hence unlikely to be greatly affected by the dwindling availability of fossil hydrocarbons. In many places this leads to an improvement in the variety of local diets. However, almost nowhere does it make significant inroads to the supply of carbohydrate — the staple of human existence. Much of today's malnutrition is concerned with inadequate carbohydrate consumption. As global food production diminishes with the dwindling of petrochemical-based agrochemicals (and also phosphate), production of grain and tubers, as the main sources of carbohydrate, will be at the forefront of the decline in the supply of food, so that malnutrition and famine are likely to escalate rapidly. UPA will have increasingly to assist in seeking solutions to this problem.

The great grain suppliers of today (the United States and Russia for corn and wheat, Thailand and Vietnam for rice) will retreat back to satisfying the needs first of their own people, leaving countries dependent on imports of staples but unable to find them. Important adjustments can be made in the vast amounts of grain fed to animals to satisfy meat-biased diets in the rich countries. This, instead, can be fed directly to people, with meat consumption contracting with little or no impact on health – for many even an increase in health. However, Japan – only 40% self-sufficient in calorific value of food – and even ostensibly over-productive European countries will nevertheless rapidly find themselves in staple deficits where imports will not be forthcoming. There may well be localist solutions but these will have to be effectively sought by local UPA initiatives.

Farming methods around the globe, whilst over the past decades systematically increasing the productivity of the soil for crops useful to human society, have done so at the expense of ecological diversity and hence, it is widely believed in relevant circles, at the expense of the robustness of the biosphere[421]. Adding to this the draining of marshlands and above all deforestation, in the first instance selective forest depletion and thence clear-cutting for agriculture or simply for biomass as a commercial product, the impacts on the biosphere have been increasingly devastating. The dwindling in fossil energy resources and resulting re-localisation of life will not automatically halt these processes where there could be areas where decline in agricultural production as a result of loss of agrochemicals will encourage attempts at more intensive farming, opening up more ecologically important land for agriculture and further depleting soils.

It must be stressed that even with the development of more effective organic fertilisers, the productivity of grain grown organically is significantly below that of grain grown with the application of agrochemicals. Inadequate work has gone into improving strains for organic production, but for sure, progressively going over to organic production will diminish the quantities of grain being produced with rather obvious consequences for global food supply and its capacity to feed the world's population.

In the industrialised countries and to some degree in the countries of the South, various approaches to organic agriculture (sometimes referred to as 'ecological farming') have been spreading at the margins (so far considerably less than one per cent of production) with what may be the most benign and sustainable method — permaculture. This is a method of farming resulting initially from research in the mid-1970s funded by the Australian Commonwealth Scientific and Industrial Research Organisation (CSIRO) and broadcast by its inventors, Bill Mollison and David Holmgren, which has generated national institutions in some countries and accumulated considerable experience in different parts of the world, adapted to particular ecosystems.[422]. As a particular application of 'organic agriculture', this approach is applicable anywhere in the sense that it is a farming method that encourages cultivation in the context of the biodiversity of local ecosystems and, where diets around the world have tended to focus on relatively narrow ranges of edible plants and animals, encouraged also adaptation of local plants and with it localities to develop diets and cuisines that make use of a wider variety of locally available species.

We should add a note here, pointing to discussion in the following chapter, of the necessity to ensure that farming methods in the future are practiced in the framework of a deep respect and active working with ecological systems that is the intention of permaculture. But, as discussed further in the following chapter, it will go beyond this in the sense that the outlook of all people in the world in the future will need to bring consciousness of the value of ecological systems into focus to become a natural way in which all initiatives in building lifestyles and communities-in-nature are structured[423].

If coordinated UPA initiatives are not already to be found, city sub-regions where local economic planning initiatives are proposed and mounted might well make the first substantive initiative a project to organise UPA throughout the sub-region. Local authorities that have been drawn by their civil society initiators into the forefront of the Transition Cities movement are already turning to 'food planning' that extends from field to table with the aspiration of securing food supply into the years of energy decline. The city of Bristol is probably the first city to commission a comprehensive review of how the urban population is fed, and steps that need to be taken to increase the proportion of food locally grown and the general conversion to organic farming methods[424].

This highlights, *inter alia,* how in the densely populated countries of Western Europe, the peri-urban areas of one city overlap with those of others and how the peri-urban areas of smaller towns are wholly within those of the cities, indicating what in future will become incipient competition over what peri-urban produce should be supplied to which population with the implication that as the global food supply chains deteriorate, food supplied to Western European cities will decline, and as in past eras, be a particularly severe problem in winter. Certainly UPA will in time almost universally become the main pillar of the local economy as reliance increases upon the use of local resources, with the ebbing away of resources imported from elsewhere. If UPA initiatives are already well developed before the initiation of participatory local economic planning, then from the outset this should be seen as pioneering the LED process as a whole and remain central to its further development.

Tying UPA back into the nexus concept, planning initiatives should always look sideways into how these can lower the energy impacts of food production and supply. Just the fact of local production should help in this respect, with produce being distributed directly to local households. Agricultural inputs should also use less energy in that locally produced organic fertiliser and pesticide can and should be produced and directly applied to plots and containers. As discussed earlier, plans should be made, techniques developed and engineering steps taken to recover all human waste and urban wastewater, rainwater and storm water for use in UPA.

In the past, efforts to generate and use urban organic wastes in UPA have been slow, or experiments curtailed for lack of a thoroughly consistent commitment to the concept of reuse and then calculations indicating that such initiatives were 'uneconomic'. What this meant is that cheap energy available to move and treat 'wastes' and to substitute cheap petrochemical-based agrochemicals for human 'waste' could not be justified as long as the market in these products did not take them up. Such economic arguments will surely fail in the future and thence the whole economistic way of assessing what is good for society, that is, ensuring that urban populations have enough to eat, will show itself to be increasingly dysfunctional in the face of failing resource flows[425].

Chapter 7: Changed World, Changed Consciousness, Changed Life

We started this book with a declaration that modern civilisation has come to an impasse and that we can expect as the following decades unfold that it will unwind or 'collapse' in ways that mean that it is not possible to predict in any precise way the steps through which this will occur.   The analysis across the body of the book looked at the dimensions of the impasse, how we arrived here and then what practical steps might be taken to ease the passage into something that might comprise a way of life that is, in the current jargon, sustainable.

However, what becomes increasingly evident is that it will take far more than a series of 'practical steps' to open the passage up to future ways of life that will provide congenial, satisfying, enjoyable lives for humanity in environments that will sustain this into the more distant future insofar as the environmental depredation resulting from modernity allows.   It will be necessary to accomplish a total transformation in the self-understanding of the people who will survive and, we hope, thrive in the world of the future. This chapter therefore comprises an inquiry concerning state of mind and with the deeper understanding of the human condition as a possible guide into a future benign path.

The Advent of Civilisation

In the Introduction to the book, it was noted that enough archaeological evidence has accumulated to be able to say something about how civilisation as such emerged   and of course we can analyse very precisely how modern civilisation evolved from the general case as set out in Chapter Two of the book[426]. What has become evident is that whilst civilisations have been around for less than ten thousand years, human beings like ourselves roamed Africa and Eurasia for tens of thousands of years and in the Americas for many thousands of years prior to the emergence of civilisation and even then until very recently, only a minority of humanity ever made the transition into civilisation.

Whilst Archaeologists have referred to the 'sapiens paradox', which asks why it took civilisation so long to emerge, the important fact is that small bands of humans communicated and probably in some areas cooperated with one another, sometimes making notable impacts upon the world including building monuments and the mass hunting of large mammals to extinction, without yet developing social hierarchies and with this the large-scale capacity for destruction of other civilisations and the natural environment that civilisation made possible and which is evidently one of its defining characteristics.

One might even conjecture that civilisation, as a conjuncture of an interconnected set of conceptions and procedures, mythologies and structures that possessed human groups at times varying by thousands of years, might have emerged far later or, indeed, as was the case in Africa, North and South America and Australasia, might never have happened and that the biosphere and humanity as part of it might have been happier without it[427]. From this perspective, civilisation is a malfunction, an aberration in the evolution of the human presence in nature that is now manifesting its ultimate malignity.

We can see, notwithstanding the depletion of the large mammals, the way in which pre-civilised human bands found homeostatic relationships with the environments which they inhabited that lasted tens of thousands of years. Although there is no written evidence to describe how pre-civil societies functioned, what their beliefs were and how they interacted with one another, enough 'primitive' communities survived into the modern era to be researched to indicate in general terms how these functioned. They may have gone through eras of conflict, particularly as 'big men' and thence hierarchies started to emerge — such as was discovered when New Guinea was explored during the first half of the 20th century[428]. Indeed, the emergence of conflict between bands can be surmised as an important generator of early hierarchy[429]. The general case seems, however, to be one of a simple but evidently fulfilling life hunting and gathering with social relations that were egalitarian[430], transparent and easy-going, even when living in such extremely uncongenial environmental circumstances as the Arctic and the Kalahari Desert[431].

The mental systems that held these homeostatic social systems in place involved what has come to be known as Animism: seemingly involving a reverence for the particular part of nature that communities found themselves in, that presumably as they migrated and as climatic and environmental conditions changed, so also the understanding and relationship with the particular environment changed. Inquiry into how surviving hunting and gathering communities conceived of their existential conditions, social and environmental, indicates how these adapted, always with imagination, to the conditions in which they found themselves and on the whole made an easy living out of the locality[432].

Starting from the mid 19th century, copious research has investigated the belief systems of surviving primitive and transitional societies, up to the time of Christianity, in the first instance as 'religions', aimed at showing the inferiority of these with respect to 'scientific', 'rational' thought with an undertow of attempting to prove the superiority of Christianity[433]. Early in the 20th century outlooks changed. Whilst there was now more empathy for the outlook of primitive peoples, with Christianity no longer seen as a superior way of thinking, nevertheless, these were seen as 'irrational' modes of thought, that made connections that were believed in but empirically, scientifically, false or inadequate.

There may well be ways in which we can be critical of some primitive peoples for their irrationalities, where these could be shown to be dysfunctional — what is referred in the Introduction to this book to the emergence of obsessions. But in the end what is evident is that these enabled primitive cultures to interpret their social condition and their environment and live with these in ways that often indicated levels of creativity that might be admired, woven into what for them was clearly an enjoyable lifestyle. What more could one want? As we progress through this chapter, we might keep constantly in the back of our minds the question: what advantages did civilisation and latterly science truly give us in terms of producing a genuinely good life for all? And how is it that in the twilight of modern civilisation we can ask ourselves the question how, insofar as we are able to re-emerge from the fall of our civilisation, we might be able to produce a good life for future generations?

The coming of civilisation is seen in a multitude of mythologies, from Adam and Eve to the Greek myths of Tantalus and Pandora and in many other societies as a 'fall from grace' and the initiation of some kind of inchoate punishment[434]. Civilisation destroyed the closed internal social relations of primitive communities and the close interconnection between social action and particular corners of nature, initiating a process of complexification and what amounted to the subjugation of the majority of the population – identified now as 'subjects' – by elites that dominated the societies and organised incessant wars, at the same time distancing humanity from the part of living nature from which came their food and which was the foundation and inspiration of their lives, while at the same time broadening out the production of the human-made accompaniments to life.

Over historically a relatively short period, a widening range of materials (above all, metals) were employed to proliferate out of the fine stone tools which had been a feature of human existence for over a million years, to more specialised tools and utensils, to pottery[435] and production of woven fabric, substantial buildings and monumental engineering works — the construction of which remains something of a mystery, as they lacked the energy subsidies that latterly facilitated the modern technological revolution, to produce monuments on a similar and also far greater scale.

Archaeological evidence gives us information on the stage of the domestication of plants and livestock, which is termed the Neolithic Revolution, but how this reflected back on the human mind in terms of the emergence of an incipient relationship of power over nature can only be deduced by contemplating the results. It is clear that the emergence of agriculture opened the way not only to an instrumentalisation and objectification of nature but at the same time the division of labour, where, it appears, a process of differentiation yielded shamans and chiefs that remained the limit of social differentiation over longer periods in some places but in a few others, within a few generations. The Nile Valley, Mesopotamia and thence China and eventually Mesoamerica generated extremes of small elites, seen as possessing divine properties, commanding large populations of food producers and small corps of artisans that swelled with the requisitioning of 'surplus' food production to feed a proliferation of tasks from the production of fine goods and the construction of monuments and infrastructure to the organisation and waging of wars. The invention of writing as a corollary to the instrumentalisation processes facilitated the fixing of social relations and production processes through time.

A certain change in terms of rationality, contrasted with pre-existing societies, was achieved in the capacity and the actuality to manipulate and thus instrumentalise relations with nature. This initiated the understanding of how particular biological species could be domesticated and adapted for human use and consumption[436], and analysis to be able to use the impact of the seasons on nature to yield agricultural produce and how – particularly with the development of irrigation systems and thence broader engineering capacities – to use Nature to change nature in the image of human requirements, for the use and aggrandisement of (some - predominantly) men.

Pausing here briefly, we can see in this process how in the minds of civilising humanity, subject and object became separated out as 'objectivity' through the distancing of nature as a process of manipulation, and when turned back as manipulation of people by people, we get initially class society and eventually, as discussed later in the chapter, the commodification of the individual, that today goes under the title of the 'struggle for identity', and the fetishisation of private property in the context of Possessive Individualism. We see this as the central conundrum of civilised humans and so this becomes the thread that takes us through this chapter.

As noted already, primitive societies are said to have a religious outlook that is 'animistic'. We would, however, do better to see the way in which nature and, as a dimension of this, fellow human beings were understood not as objects but as 'subject', that is to say as undifferentiated self. We will discuss later in the chapter what this means and how it came to be, in the flow of natural evolution. The emergence of objectification as a configuration of human consciousness upon which civilisation has been structured, can be understood as an aberration in the natural sense of 'being human'. The deconstruction of 'objectivity' into a ludic and aesthetic outlook that has deescalated the instrumentality that civilisation gives it, reinterpreting our understanding – or interpretation - of nature and the human condition within this, where, 'I am you before I am myself', becomes a goal, aimed at catching the falling remnants of humanity, post-civilisation and to reconstruct human societies at one with nature.

It is crucial, now that we stand at the edge of the final rout of nature, to focus on the way in which it was this growth in human powers over and against the ecological metabolism of natural systems, that triggered also a certain inward looking aspect to human concerns, where the fear and awe of nature and the elements became secondary to how people should relate to one another. The power over nature was now reflected in the emergence of relations of power between people and with the divine spirits, once fused in a continuous fabric of belief in the life of nature, now separated out as gods and mythical heroes, or quasi-human beings, acting out life in the context of a distanced, partially objectified, natural environment.

Particular places might continue to have divine and spiritual value beyond their simple objective being (and amongst rural working populations even in Northern Europe, this persisted into the 19th century). But nature was now predominantly there to be exploited. And so also palpable, physical humans were separated from the continuity of nature and with empathy waning, became open to exploitation by those who developed the belief in their own superior capacities, and who convinced the rest of their societies of the legitimacy of these powers and seized the chance first to exert power and then to consolidate this around blood relations and establish continuity through inheritance, sanctioned by belief that life this side continued into the future on another unseen side, where resided the gods.

To the modern mind, the 'will to power' seems easier to understand than the acquiescence in accepting inferiority. Perhaps it is easier to understand this as a continuation of the characteristic of Homo sapiens that was the foundation of their success in moving into and forging communities adapted to every kind of environment. Submission to the realities of different environmental conditions is a pre-requisite for successful adaptation[437]. With the distancing and instrumentalisation of the environment, communities turned from nature to other humans as master of their fate and once tricked in this way, layer upon layer of social and ideological structures trapped them into accepting specific tasks and with this identities that would mean they would no longer question their inferior status or when they did, encountering institutionalised and culturally embedded violence (for instance, the maintenance of caste relations in India) to keep them in their place.

The division of labour initially yielded small, articulated, elites over and against the masses whose condition deteriorated into slaves — mere objects of the requirements of the elites. This relationship emerged in different ways in different civilisations — in the Americas re-emerging even in the centuries leading up to, and then well into, the modern era. As a corollary, military hierarchies — which are in a real sense the foundations of rationally organised societies in the context of civilisation, and the root impetus to the development of technology — were constituted to keep slaves, and thence conquered people, in subjection. A common characteristic was the way in which the division of labour calcified into hereditary caste systems where particular human groups lived in particular states of mind and skills from whence the world could be seen only from the vantage point of their function, sanctioned by religious belief and deeply-held social convention. Indian society is the one major survival of this kind of society into the modern era.

Two crucial inventions at the foundation of civilisation, fixing and thence objectifying relations through time, were writing and money. The initial use of writing everywhere was for the purpose of keeping accounts and consolidating the dominance of elites, eventually being the means to give authority to, and propagate religion as, the final authority over society. Formal currency, which emerged in the course of the early development of civilisations, confirmed the objectification and distancing of human relations in the formalisation of exchange. There are indications of trade between human groups going back many thousands of years prior to the emergence of civilisation and even then some form of formal agreement on the value of key commodities may have been achieved under particular social conditions.

But the emergence of metal currency, first appearing in the early phase of civilisation, gives a further twist to objectification both of relations with nature and of what is produced from it and at the same time objectifying unequal social relations. Money is abstract value and whilst even into the modern era, much exchange, often as formal relations between different actors within particular social hierarchies, involved value invested in particular goods with money confirming (local) universal abstract value as deep confirmation of social difference and of commodification as a way of understanding the world.

Thus we see the machinery that encouraged the transformation of thought and understanding, and that blew open both the actuality of human communities and their relationship with particular places, opening up the eventual possibility of ever larger scales of human organisation. The instrumental exploitation of nature, the dynamics of which possessed limiting dimensions, namely the particular moral structures and socio-political conventions that made up particular cultures, and the limits of the ecological and geological resource base to support the structures which were adopted. History reveals that in many cases these emerged at a particular place and time but then failed as systems of socio-political organisation over discrete time periods; the rise and fall of civilisations might almost seem like a Law of Nature[438].

We can refer to lacunae, or 'bubbles' of rationality, where aspects of socio-political life were consciously reasoned as 'laws' that facilitated what were, until the modern era, production processes and institutional structures that were partially systematically rational in nature — the extreme, prior to modernity, being the Confucian system of socio-political organisation. But much that evidently worked for particular civilisations was partially non-rational in the sense of being accepted socio-political structures, including chiefdoms and kingdoms, caste and slave societies, that simply emerged by chance and were held in place by belief systems, with the sacred and profane interwoven. When, in the Introduction to this book we made reference to obsessions, we can see here how even ostensibly rational structures and relations could be carried away by religion or simply accepted convention, and in many cases purely emotional states, that defined the boundaries of rational consideration of the actions and impacts beyond the boundaries of the obsession.

We can say that the religious impulse was in a very general sense no more than making emotional sense out of the circumstances that had emerged, incrementally, out of previous states of being and organisation. We can refer to much of what is presented by religions in terms of signs, symbols and action sequences as being in some way aesthetic: something that has a structure, often (as structural anthropologists often sought) a particular kind of logic that could draw upon human emotions at a very basic level, freed from the need for rationality that might otherwise have destabilised them. And, of course, by doing this, as a fundamental attribute of religion, becoming solace in the face of unjust social relations, or, in Marx's words: 'the opiate of the people'. It is actually difficult to find a single set of characteristics that define all religions, as Emil Durkheim discovered in his quest to find the elementary forms of religion[439]. The fact is that religions have performed different functions in different societies and changes in religious beliefs were, indeed, a vital component in ways in which civilisations evolved[440].

In recent years academic studies in sociology, anthropology, psychology, philosophy and many new branches out of these have proliferated vastly in terms of the production of 'facts' and ideas and opinions, but in the process left behind broader speculative attempts of the 19th and early 20th centuries to grasp what might be the central problematic of human existence and self-consciousness. We might say not just that intellectual life has become buried in details and trivia, not to say empty ratiocinations, but that the liberal mindset which this generated this has achieved something analogous to a religion, conjoined to the machinery of 'scientific investigation' that has over the past century dispersed into all manner of fruitless paths to 'knowledge'.

What we consider to be necessary to achieve an adequate critique to combat the irrationalities and obsessions that have emerged in the present day 'consumerist condition' and with it the systematic destruction of the natural conditions from which civilisation emerged, is a return to some of the broad thinking about the human condition that took place in the 19th century, in the wake of the European Enlightenment.

This does not require any survey of the many branches of these debates but can benefit greatly from a critical return, starting with the speculations of Hegel, the debates that arose out of these amongst the 'young Hegelians' and the eventual attempt to organise society on a new basis under the term 'communism.' We start here with a confrontation of the problematic of hierarchy and the way in which this divides humans into different roles and with this, outlooks that mean that rationality on how to organise society can never be unified.

The Forms of Inegalitarian Relations in the Modern World

Marx and Engels wrote in the first sentence of the Communist Manifesto that: *The history of all hitherto existing society is the history of class struggles.* We must qualify this today by noting that 'social struggle' was not a characteristic of human existence before civilisation, but rather a characteristic of civilisation itself. Furthermore, whilst in the context of Occidental civilisation, with its obsession with progress, we can see how this civilisation had, de facto, evolved in terms of the changing shape of class society in conditions we can refer to as struggle, involving rebellion, revolution and many detailed manifestations right down to trade unionism, while other civilisations did work out means to stabilise social inequalities over long time periods. The most notable are the Hindu caste system and Oriental Confucianism. However, incessant struggle continued even here in the form not of struggle between classes but struggles of elites for power within and between states, involving populations in waging wars on their behalf.

It is useful to take one step back to the philosopher Hegel's highly stylised account of what might be expected of the evolution of civilisation, set out in his work, *The Phenomenology of Spirit.* We might be sceptical concerning the teleological presumption of this work, which saw human civilisation as progressing in three stages, from benighted pre-history to an eventual resolution, that he termed 'Reason[441]', which would be the fulfilment of human potential in the context of the totality of nature. However, the notion of the evolution of what might be called the macro-psychological problematic of what he referred to as the deep malaise in both the human spirit and in the kinds of societies this generated is, as we will be discussing throughout this chapter, a sound working hypothesis of the root problematic of civilisation as it has evolved to the present point in time.

What is meant here is that within civilisation individuals fall on one or other side of a divide, either as possessing power or as being possessed by the power of others and although we might, in the spirit of contemporary styles of investigation, speculate on hybrids, exceptions and other complexities, the main point is that as long as societies are divided internally by existential conflicts or competition, it will be impossible to realise full human potential. Hegel refers to the fact that neither side can ever, at the deepest level, be happy in a world where their existence is over and against other people, producing deep-seated one-sidedness and incipient hostility, mistrust and curtailed fellow-feeling. He termed this the 'unhappy self-consciousness'.

We need not concern ourselves about Hegel's ideas as to how this might be resolved but, rather, move on to the debates that arose amongst the students of Hegel (the Young Hegelians) as to the practical measures needed to achieve a resolution. The centre of Marx and Engel's philosophy, that emerged as the most prominent result of the Young Hegelian discourse, revolved around the problematic of private property. In Chapter Two we discussed how Hobbes and then Locke superseded the older means of recognising hierarchy in terms of religiously sanctified rank, with the notion of realising the self through property: understanding oneself as commodity and extending this to the ownership of private property, that might be land but might also be other means of achieving power and status within society.

Thus, property in its broadest sense became the target of Marx and Engels. 'Alienation' was a word they adapted from the relinquishing or selling of private property in English legal terminology, used already by Hegel to describe the inability of people in civilisation to achieve unfettered self-consciousness as a result of class divisions. This was also the term used by Marx and Engels to describe the malaise that the problematic of property imposed on humanity[442]. Thus a central solution to the problematic of civilisation would be the abolition of private property in all its manifestations (and hence the abolition of Alienation) to free humans from the prison of self-commodification and the desperate struggle for identity and the inability to cooperate effectively to create a world where all could live fulfilled lives free of the fear of the other.

Soviet society was a real attempt to do this. We have seen in Chapter Two why this failed. Basically, this failed because although private property, in the sense of land, buildings and other substantial physical manifestations, was abolished by fiat, the State perpetuated relations of dominance and submission through political and bureaucratic institutions and the production system. Party members, bureaucrats, planners, managers and even artists and intellectuals became the new masters, over and against 'The Working Class' and the propaganda concerning the heroism of workers and peasants was lamentably inadequate to conceal this fact. Furthermore, in its latter years, the elite emulated the strategy of the elites of the United States by attempting to seduce the population into accepting their inferior status through constantly increasing consumption that could be made to seem like improvement in status. What was produced in the Soviet Union under conditions where property did not have the redolently fetishistic, quasi-religious dimension manifest in the United States could never have the appeal of US-made commodities. So if consumerism is what you want, why not accept the system as a whole? And hence the demise.

An important question here is why the majority of the population of the United States continued, and continues, to accept subordinate status and what has become grotesque differentials in terms of the stratification of wealth as the current kernel of hierarchical society. And the answer, confirming the discussion in Chapter Two, is really rather simple. The United States as a nation was built upon the philosophy of liberalism, imported in early colonial times (disputed in the early years by various attempts at socio-political organisation that ranged from neo-feudalism to community self-organisation). This in itself would not have been enough to keep the lower classes in their place, even with the constant propaganda that is put out by elites, real and putative. Liberalism is, de facto, a philosophy and way of organising life that promotes increased stratification that favours elites and increases poverty, as a perception of being, amongst the lower classes.

However, the ethos upon which the majority of the immigrants to the United States in the 19th century, that became the social base of society, was one of improving their status through release from hierarchical relations in their countries of origin and the promise of attaining status through property in their newly adopted society — in the first instance in land (stolen from the indigenous population, which did not count because their pre-civilisation cultures had no concept of property). The vehemence with which 'socialism' and 'communism' have been combated at home and abroad is in part ideology propagated by the elite in defence of their putative privileges and prerogative, but is crucially supported by the lower classes because of their deep commitment to the idea that they have improved their status (now under the title of 'middle class') as manifest today in the frantic accumulation of Stuff. With very few exceptions, such as the inhabitants of some Intentional Communities and perhaps within some marginal religious and social movements, the American population has totally lost any sense of the alienated character of their being, presumably for as long as the supply of Stuff ('economic growth') lasts and hence the illusion that we are all headed for higher status.

Attempts at amelioration of the problematic of Alienation arose already in ancient Greece, recognised by Hegel as partial withdrawal from society to reduce the anxieties of this form of existence. This was Stoicism, which he saw as evolving into scepticism (and we might say also into philosophical cynicism). It is of some interest how under the conditions of caste society in India, Siddhārtha Gautama produced a religion — Buddhism — that has an ambiance that can be felt to have much in common with Stoicism, retreating from the Alienation produced by caste society. Stoicism was also an element entering into Adam Smith's version of Mandevillianism, attempting to reduce the extreme vulgarity and the repugnance of participating in the sleaze that characterises commercial society, but to little effect as the Commercial Ideology unfolded in the late 20th century.

Today, there is a certain appeal of Buddhism to a small minority in the Occident that would seem to reflect this approach to retreating at least some distance from today's condition of Alienation without yet discarding – indeed in some manifestations even increasing – self-commodification of adherents. It should, however, be stressed that these are not real solutions but, rather, retreats from social engagement. Any real solution will have to engage fully with civilisation and contemporary society and find a way out of the Commercial Ideology and the consumerism which it feeds. Many of the contemporary Intentional Communities are attempting just this: to find a *social* way out of the problematic of Alienation.

Here we need to consider the question of freedom as the central idea of liberalism, as a philosophy and as moral orientation. The chief focus of the liberal drive to achieve freedom was, in the first instance, to abolish tyranny and this has been its great achievement in the event of steadily putting rank societies behind us and establishing the form of governance that we refer to as democracy. In Chapter Three we saw that this use of the word does not in fact square with the ultimate practice of democracy, which is face to face discussion and decision making as opposed to *representative* democracy, which is not democracy at all. This is par for the course in political terminology, where words that denote good things are successfully captured to perpetrate bad things hypocritically[443].

What liberalism in the philosophical sense steadfastly ignores but in practice encourages, is a hierarchy which allows those people who are 'better' than others to occupy superior positions in society, rather than hierarchy being defined by inherited rank. Today this means what we might call the idealistic version of liberalism; superiority and inferiority are operationalised through 'meritocracy' but in everyday, – and in practice what is today the dominant – understanding, superiority is defined in terms of wealth. The forms of retreat from society (or the woes of the world) discussed in the foregoing paragraph, could also be looked on as striving to achieve some kind of freedom but the tragic truth is that in the framework of liberal philosophy, freedom is ultimately achieved only through total social disengagement which means a persistent inner loneliness until death. The more one engages in the social struggle for visible status and wealth, the less free one is.

Finally, none of the foregoing looks in any reasonable way at the problematic of the destruction of nature and how this might be analysed in a more philosophical light. Insofar as enlightened Occidental thought was intent on the conquest of nature, there was no realisation and discussion of how we might escape from this problematic. Hegel focused considerable attention on nature, but exclusively as a function of human need and hence he was interested in how science, as part of the dialectic leading to Reason, was in the process of unfolding with a very general overarching notion that nature, as a divine creation, will become fused with the resolution to the problematic of the unhappy self-consciousness in the final achievement of Reason[444]. Marx and Engels also gave little thought to this side of the problematic of Alienation, indicating in abstract terms that the resolution to the socio-political problematic would also enable a clearer understanding of our essential relationship with nature — presumably meaning our relationship with it will be one of wiser management[445]. Nature as sentience – of the importance of life beyond the human - was the concern only of marginal thinkers across the 19th and 20th centuries.

The Evolution of Inegalitarian Relations

We have seen that social hierarchy is not a 'natural' fact but that it emerged with the coming of civilisation and in the course of history has changed in terms of its manifestations, being eclipsed in some areas but re-emerging in new forms. If we wish to contribute toward reducing, minimising and eventually eliminating hierarchy through a wholly new way of understanding what life is all about, then we must first have some clarity of what we mean by social hierarchy. The most obvious definition is that people are identified as particular actors or ultimately objects occupying a particular rank or are contained in a particular stratum within an institutionalised social system. We should be clear that it makes no sense to imagine that *difference* as such can be eliminated and nor is there any problem with institutions as such, insofar as life is organised as a participatory process. The problematic arises where difference is used as mechanism or symbols to distance people inside themselves as the basis of social struggle, however small, for power over others and where institutions, in the sense both of organisations and or organisation as such, are constructed in ways that define the rank or status that people occupy within a society.

We find that within civilised societies individuals identify with particular groups, for example, family, solidaristic associations or organisations or class. The walls of difference are reduced or eliminated and a degree of trust may be extended. It is then the group that is separated and is understood as different and usually hierarchically related to other such groups. Hegel's highly stylised version of the separation of civilised humanity into masters and bondsmen is essentially about class, and was rightly interpreted in this way by Marx and Engels. However, even prior to Hegel, Locke had not merely identified, but promoted, the idea of the individual defining her or himself as separate in a way that isolates them even from the solidarity of class.

And, as we shall see as the following discussion unfolds, it is this – we might say ultimate – version of Alienation, or active self-alienation as Possessive Individualism, that has, since the neoliberal counter-revolution become the dominant mental state of globalised society; in Margaret Thatcher's famous words: *there is no alternative.* Are we finally incarcerated into an individualistic struggle for wealth and power to the end of the world? Later in the chapter we will be fundamentally questioning this.

In a sense the foundational hierarchy that has, since the beginning of civilisation been clearly defined, albeit with different internal structures and titles, is military hierarchy. Although there have been occasionally local and even national militias and guerrilla movements where hierarchy has been greatly reduced over the regular conception of a military force, waging war, which is the function of military hierarchies, is fundamentally about defending or capturing power over peoples, so hierarchy becomes an essential corollary to this. Today almost all States possess armed forces — Costa Rica being a country without, demonstrating that it is possible even in the modern world to dispense with the military.

The existence of the State denotes the existence of hierarchies of power. Over most of the era of civilisation, hierarchies from pharaohs, emperors and kings, through aristocracies to gentry, and often many hierarchically organised ranks beneath, emerged spontaneously in the sense of struggles resulting in heads and their entourages inventing and then fixing titles with rights and functions and lower down the hierarchy also duties and responsibilities. In other words, these were not rational designs for the organisation of human life. Very often the head of state was also the head of the military, even in modern times, such as in many 'underdeveloped' States but also under 20th century fascism in Europe and even in the Soviet Union where the heads of State were *de facto* also heads of the armed forces.

Throughout the era of civilisation, although some religions were about withdrawal from the world of hierarchy (Stoicism and Buddhism were mentioned earlier but Taoism was another such manifestation) religions have generally had functional connection with State hierarchies, determining the moralities pertaining to their operation and then sanctioning and confirming the legitimacy of the hierarchy, thus denying at a deep psychological level that a hierarchy-less society might be a legitimate aspiration. Christianity, in spite of the teachings of Christ, constructed its own parallel hierarchy, and hierarchies emerged also to different degrees in other religions. In earlier times, heads of State were also heads of the religion and as such deified, at the same time sanctifying the social hierarchy (it would seem, anomalously for modern times, in the United Kingdom the monarch is also nominally head of the military and of the State religion, yielding, in the strict definition, a theocracy that only towards the end of the 19th century relaxed the insistence that Government service was only accessible to adherents of the Church of England).

As an adjunct to the State hierarchy, there emerged early on, a distinction between the power hierarchy – the aristocracy – and the administration of the State as bureaucracy. Whilst in some civilisations a sharp distinction emerged between aristocratic and bureaucratic power hierarchies, often enough the distinction was blurred and/or aristocratic power could determine the outcome of otherwise bureaucratic decisions. Everywhere there was evolution, not just of individuals occupying particular roles but of the roles themselves and of the rights, duties and functions of these roles. However, often enough once established, civilisations would roll forward with given structures over hundreds and even thousands of years. Thus we see in Ancient Egypt the configuration of power that, in spite of crises where new rulers attempted to change structures at a basic level, these nevertheless survived until the eventual destruction of the system following the invasion of Alexander and the imposition of Ptolemaic and thence Roman rule.

In China, once the general rules of Confucianism, involving a particular hierarchical distribution of power had been adopted in the Han Dynasty some two thousand years ago, despite the rise and fall of dynasties and even the collapse of the State for a period into warring components, and in spite of the introduction of new approaches to management and in general the complexification (we might even say the refinement) of life through technological change, particularly

347

following invasions from outside (Mongolian and Manchurian) each new dynasty accepted the basic inherited ground rules of military, state and bureaucratic structures and the Confucian moral justifications for these.

Even when these structures were significantly modified for periods, by the time of the collapse of Chinese civilisation in the 20th century, the socio-political structures that collapsed were recognisably those that had been introduced two thousand years earlier. Whilst the key positions would be determined by the Emperor, a significant dimension of the Confucian system was the quasi-meritocratic appointment of the bureaucratic hierarchy that proceeded through examinations that could project individuals of low status right through the system and in its implementation reduced to an extent the traditional authority of the aristocracy.

None of the hierarchies discussed above are necessary for the organisation and happiness of human existence. They are all concerned with the concentration and distribution of power of some people over others. Military hierarchies are not necessary if wars are not waged and if civil disturbances due to discontent amongst social groups have no reason to arise. Even States are an artifice of civilisation that are not necessary for the organisation of human life. Whilst states have existed everywhere in Eurasia, the last being constituted over a thousand years ago, as Europeans advanced their colonial project into the Americas and Africa, relatively little of these worlds manifested states and the people were able to organise life quite adequately without them.

The next kind of hierarchy that needs to be considered is the family. Here we are concerned both with the internal structure of families and then with the role of families within tribes and clans, oligarchies and aristocracies, in providing the detailed internal structure to power concentrated in social and political hierarchies, as the elites that head these. All civilised societies have some notion of social organisation that recognises different ethnographic relations within some notion of family and thence structured relations between families viz marriage, the lineage of children and relations with the resulting other family members — brothers, sisters, aunts, uncles, cousins, nephews and nieces on both sides of the marriage, etc.

With marriage comes initially a minimal division of labour, which is inescapable at the biological level but extending to tendencies to task division, particularly in the first instance between hunting (a male task) and gathering (a female task). Already from here, debates in anthropology have tended to identify difference as necessarily hierarchical and 'male dominance' as a ubiquitous implying 'natural' phenomenon. Whilst this is challenged as being 'a point of view' [446], with the emergence of civilisation, unequal relations between men and women are certainly a fact manifest in almost all civilisations, being reinvented in different situations and manifest both symbolically in dress, lifestyle, etc., allocation of tasks and through general male prerogative. The struggle today continues in the face of a myriad of instances of 'gender discrimination' that must be a central focus in any attempt, programme or movement to reduce and eventually abolish social and political hierarchy.

The forms of social organisation including families, tribes and clans, being the focus of ethnographic studies around the world, could be seen even in pre-civil bands incipiently to develop both informal and formally recognised hierarchical relations in terms of kinship relations, the emergence of religious and concentrated decision-making roles and, in the context of conflicts between bands, tribes and clans, incipient leadership to wage war. With the emergence of civilisation, these roles, that might previously have been temporary, became permanent and thence hereditary, with particular families taking positions of permanent dominance as aristocracies, with the development of unequal access to resources, stratified societies evolving in which oligarchies that might include both aristocratic families and families that have attained wealth, collaborated – and sometimes conflicting – over the exercise of power over the society as a whole.

It is important to realise that whilst modern civilisation, in its manifestation in the homelands of the Enlightenment (Northern Europe and the Anglo Saxon extensions), has, over time, diminished the importance of families as subsets of social hierarchy, emphasising the importance of individuals making their own way in the struggle for wealth and power. Elsewhere in the world, the traditional importance of families as sub-sets of the political and social hierarchy remains extremely important. Amongst the lower classes, the continued active existence of 'extended families', with their internal mutual assistance and reciprocity, is a vital factor in the survival of individual members in the modern world[447]. However, in families that are nearer the head of the political and social hierarchy, the collaboration in the form of nepotism, but also conflict that becomes the source of wars, are key manifestations of the maintenance of hierarchical civilisation as such throughout most of Asia, Africa and Latin America.

Indeed, the fact of hierarchy within families, and extending in some cases to tribes and clans where these have survived into the present time (predominantly in Africa) is hidden below the surface of what is presented today as the way in which modern politics and much of the modern economy actually functions. This needs to be unearthed and fully recognised, because with the fall of modern civilisation, insofar as these family structures survive, they may be expected to become the basis for a resurgence of feudal forms of polity in many countries, rather than the utopian forms of organisation implied in the past two chapters and discussed later in this chapter. Insofar as the rout of nature ends in a world that will still support human life, this resolution would lead to yet another phase in the history of the unhappy self-consciousness, putting off, possibly forever, the Hegelian-Marxist notion of a final happy resolution of the human condition.

Hierarchy in human life doesn't end with state and family. At the outset of this chapter, we discussed how the division of labour underlay and even preceded the development of the state, military and religious hierarchies. Unlike state hierarchies that are not necessary for organised and happy human existence, work does have to be carried out to produce the kind of rich and for many comfortable life that has, in times of peace, been the experience of civilisation. And certainly, hierarchy in the production of life became a corollary to the complexification of the production processes. In caste systems we see clearly the imputed difference in hierarchical position between communities carrying out different functions — dancers, potters, metal workers, rice-farmers, priests. Actually, different civilisations have judged different functions to occupy different strata, so that it becomes clear that the hierarchical ranking of tasks is, in the first instance, arbitrary, fixed by social convention of particular cultures.

Whereas independent peasants in Europe, evolving out of the slaves and surfs of feudalism, have tended to be seen as inferior to urban artisans with 'business people' heading urban non-state elites, in some parts of the Indian caste system, rice producers are well above artisans in rank, with artists at the bottom and Confucianism put merchants in a lower status than artisans. Artists were also generally no more than servants in Europe until the 18th century when they — at least the successful — became cultural heroes: the sky became the limit. Of course farmers also had and still have an ambivalent status in Europe and North America that relates to whether they are 'estate owners' (even without employees) or peasants (and the terminology is also important). The professions definitely have a higher status and indeed different systems of ranking within and between one another even within different European societies. And with the transition to dominance in the 20th century of service industries, rank has become more complex and in some areas of work also formalised, but with rivalry, for instance in the medical and educational systems, between the professional and the administrative ranks.

Everywhere, pure bureaucracies are as rigorously ranked as armies, be they local authorities or international agencies, and as production of goods is increasingly industrialised, so ranking systems emerge also in the commercial world: that amongst the workers as between 'skilled' (and particular skills) and 'unskilled' work (albeit the latter also possessing real, valuable skills but not seen as having any status) and ranks within the administration and management. The point here is that whilst many if not most of these tasks are necessary (unlike the power hierarchies of the state), it is not necessary that these be undertaken within a hierarchy: it is a social decision as to what status attaches to what kind of work — and then wages and salaries are paid accordingly, confirming in economic terms this social decision.

What we can forcefully say is that the decisions as to how things should be produced are taken as decisions concerning power. Industrialisation has been centrally a question of the construction of power hierarchies that employ income and wealth as indicators of status. Within corporate structures we perennially witness the scramble to attain higher status. The fact is that even today, mass production does not in many areas cost less to produce goods when all the costs 'from cradle to grave' are taken into account. Meanwhile, machines (and hence the use of greater amounts of energy) can usually displace labour so as to bring the income that labour would have earned individually into the payment of hierarchically-determined structures, creating new administrative bureaucracies inside the production system and allowing owners and top managers, and thence totally unproductive 'share-holders', to earn ever higher incomes over against those doing the real work.

In Asian countries today one can witness, side by side, production systems producing the same goods for export, including garments, shoes, cigarettes and other commodities, being produced by hand, employing thousands, whilst some are produced by machines in factories employing less than a hundred people for the same volume of production[448]. Essentially, mass production opens up avenues for the consolidation of wealth in fewer hands – and this has become particularly evident in the evolution in recent years of the 'global economy' with work carried out in Asia but most (regularly as much as ninety per cent) of the income accruing to 'the enterprise' in Occidental countries where it is used to fuel extended hierarchy-building and thence a few astronomic concentrations of wealth.

The rise and fall of trade unionism is one of the great social dramas of the 20th century, relating vitally to the issue of hierarchy in modern society. The conviction had grown throughout the late 19th century that class society was unjust. Perhaps at this point we should refer to radical Christian movements back through the middle ages, to the very first years of Christianity that had professed what amounts to total rejection of the mental structures that give us social hierarchy. Known in general as the 'heresy of the Free Spirit', this emerged from time to time in different places, usually as quietist religious sects but sometimes more openly such as with the Ranters of the English Revolution, selections of whose writings, in spite of persecution and attempts made to erase their traces, survived to be published in recent years[449].

Norman Cohn, the historian of these and many other European millenarian movements of the Middle Ages, puts forward the notion that the basic impulse, as 'quasi-mystical anarchism', resides, as with many deeply-held cultural attitudes, in the European 'collective subconscious'[450]. Such could be seen as one dimension that informed sub-consciously even Hegel's notion of the unhappy self-consciousness and the possibility of its supersession, going on to inform the theories of Marx and Engels together with the spread of utopian sensibilities across the second half of the 19th Century, culminating in the growth in the socialist movement and eventually the precipitation of the Russian Revolution[451].

It should, however, be stressed that, as mentioned already in Chapter Three, these were not the only voices that, in the wake of the French Revolution (with its declaration of 'Liberty Equality Fraternity' emblazoned even today across the lintel of every town hall in France) throughout the 19th century groped their way towards a notion and thence proposals of a classless or anarchist society. The legion of utopian, socialist, communist and anarchist theoreticians and activists produced a wide array of possible ways out of hierarchical society. Towards the end of the century it was, however, the trade union movement that grew to dimensions that changed the politics of work and relations in the workplace fundamentally. Modern trade unionism, starting with the meteoric rise and immediate precipitate fall in the 1830s of the English 'Grand National Consolidated Trade Union', inspired by the utopian Robert Owen[452], with its failure followed by attempts of workers of various trades to form associations, eventually exploded in the 1880s as a mass movement[453].

The spread of trade unionism throughout the Occident was complex, initially with the assertion of status differences between trades but eventually uniting into general trade unions that became institutionalised in many countries by the 1920s. The growth of trade unionism was, in a sense, just the surface appearance of a groundswell that, across the second half of the 19th century, had seen a general waning of the presumptions of the inevitability of class in the minds of particularly the 'lower orders'. The notion that things *could* be different had metamorphosed into a notion that things *will* be different if we make them so. We discuss here trade unionism as the most evident change but the extension of the Parliamentary vote step by step to the 'lower orders', eventually also to women, and the changing inflection in formal political life that this brought with it regarding attention being increasingly paid to the interests of the lower classes, and with it also the movement amongst elites to slow and stop this tendency – particularly Bismarck's introduction of social welfare measures mentioned in Chapter Two - must also be made clear.

Branches of the trade union and more radical political movements made more assertive demands for workers to take over control of industry, eliminating the distinction between owners and workers (in the UK the anarcho-syndicalists and elsewhere with their own titles). The most successful action in advancing this was a brief period between 1936 and 1938 when workers in Barcelona took control of, and ran modern industries throughout the city[454]. However, whilst the existence of strong trade unions was essential to raising status and with it economic advance for the working class throughout Western Europe and broadly the Anglo-Saxon countries, regardless of internal hierarchy, no significant attempts were made in the context of trade unions to challenge the social hierarchy at any deeper level. It was only the cooperative movements that made some headway in some countries in securing workers' control so as to further reduce, and even in some cases eliminate, hierarchy, at least in the workplace.

More generally, following the First World War, the results of the 19th century movements were largely settled with two major, ostensibly opposing, 'solutions' to the class question. Russia, under the title of Soviet Union, extended into territories that had been conquered by the tsarist regimes in the course of the 19th century, and further extended, following the Second World War, into Eastern Europe. Ancient aristocracies were annihilated and all power consolidated into reformed politico-bureaucratic structures where hierarchy persisted and even deepened over and against the people outside the hierarchy, subsuming even the independent voice of trade unions. The promise at the outset of the Russian Revolution that eventually the State would 'wither away', whilst erased from discussion early in the life of the Soviet

Union, remained tenaciously as a belief in the minds of many both within and beyond the Soviet Union who were committed to the socialist/communist and antecedent notions of a classless society.

Elsewhere in the Occident, whilst ancient aristocracies had over the past several hundred years gradually been losing power and wealth, almost everywhere they remained at least a presence that could be said to continue to confirm, ideologically, that hierarchy is an essential part of how society should work. But, as in the Soviet Union, throughout the modern world, the power, scope and complexity of bureaucracy increased[455], justified as a means of ensuring that the *de facto* Development processes underway would include some measure of redistribution, as appeasement, if not in any meaningful way egalitarian.

In Chapter Two we discussed how as a political movement, the 'neoliberal counter-revolution' swept aside the developmentalist aspirations of the first half of the 20th century, forthrightly attacking the more egalitarian leanings of the social democratic era. Whilst discussion of the reassertion of class was avoided, or even repressed, *de facto*, policies in the Anglo Saxon countries opened the door to the reassertion of class differentials; over the following decades, other societies followed down the same route and with the collapse of the Soviet Union this trend became universalised and accelerated almost everywhere.

We have to see the layers of hypocrisy that underlay the counter-revolution in terms of *de facto* re-assertion of social hierarchy. On the one hand there were what seemed like forthright attacks on the state and on all forms of bureaucracy. In practice, the bureaucratic state was actually reinforced, but in ways in the British case aimed directly at reasserting class differences and in the case of the United States, aimed at removing inhibitions to the accumulation of wealth by the already rich. And everywhere, over the ensuing decades, we can see how, just as in past centuries aristocracies were weakened in terms of the distribution of power in society, so in the late 20th century, bureaucracy that had triumphed as the prime machinery in the distribution of power, was now superseded by differentials in wealth as the dominant means of expressing status and hierarchical superiority — the promotion of stratification rather than rank.

As so well expressed in his analyses of 'postmodern society', Zygmunt Bauman notes that now populations are seduced into participating in the race for status and hence *de facto* accepting lower rank, rather than this being held together, as in the past, by coercion. The underlying notion is that even the persons at the bottom of the hierarchy have the ambition to achieve higher status, not through appointment[456] but through acquisition of money and commodities, for which the fundamental mental state is self-commodification. Any ambition to abolish hierarchy today, whilst digging down to erase Alienation, has to start from the elimination of self-commodification and the consumption drive which is the machinery that keeps it in place, and then to forestall regression back into a presumption of class, instilled through the years of the triumph of bureaucracy and then further back to the deep belief in hierarchy that sits in the cultural subconscious and in some societies is held in place by its continued existence in the shadows, of hereditary aristocracies and monarchs.

We should also be aware that it is not only the more formal aspects of hierarchy, including the formal and less formal (psychological) structures of capitalism, that 'keep people in their place'. Class self-expression can be found in clothes and manners that, of course, change but are important expressions of residual rank difference. Many languages are endowed with different class accents including English in Britain; in some Asian countries there are different languages between different classes within the same society. Ethnicity and of course skin colour and facial characteristics, although not inherently hierarchical, are perennially applied to distinguish between people deemed within the social subconscious to be superior or inferior. Such class cultures evolved everywhere and express themselves even in retreat from engagement of people from others that they do not recognise as their class, resulting in deeper barriers to any attempt to bring people together to destroy class difference.

Research in the United States shows clearly the extent to which people seek out and spend their time with others whom they feel are in the same class as themselves (what Zygmund Bauman has referred to as 'communities of sameness'). Of course this might be an issue of profession or otherwise work-related. But it has become uncannily refined in terms of the layers of difference sensed by people that keep them confined in groups that incline to interact little with others. Income is arguably the main issue; ethnicity is, however, another and also hobby interest communities – that might both reinforce class boundaries whilst at the same time including people from different occupations and income groups. 'Political orientation' and participation in functions including attendance at religious assemblies or any number of local associations can also be closely class-related and finally participation in entertainment events that in some cases move quite broadly across classes, particularly sports events, but in others are events that confirm class status even when these ostensibly possess no class focus, such as different kinds of music events.

But today there is a substantial fading away of social life as such, that becomes for great numbers in the North, as the ultimate destiny of Possessive Individualism, a devastating loneliness where they are kept barely self-conscious by the Technostructure of technical household services, cars, supermarkets and television; for tens of millions of elderly and significant numbers of long term unemployed in the North, social life has died almost altogether with social and medical services, as a vast machine of people keeping them alive. The younger generation, vast numbers unemployed, meaning only loosely connected to any real social or creative activity, supported by parents and the social service machinery, selects fields and communicates virtually with their friends, part narcissism, part diversion, through the internet, facebook, twitter and electronically created mass entertainment. And in the South, vast numbers urbanising, struggle to find an income to survive but are abjectly attracted to the notion that they, too, are upwardly mobile, with the dissemination of hand-phones and small gratifications produced by the overflow of the global mega-production machine[457].

All of these will have to be questioned in what will surely be painful ways in a future where, with the fall of modern life and the spatial regrouping and necessary self-redefinition that all will be forced to undertake, radical changes in lifestyle will be made, necessitating new attitudes and beliefs in how people *should* relate to one another at a minimum just to participate in the receipt of food and other essentials of survival. It is in this context that debates will need to be raised, bringing hierarchical distinctions out of the subconscious and into the open. In the first instance this will almost inevitably lead to conflict of the kind associated with fascism, of hatred of 'the other' being blamed for growing travail (this we can already see in countries running into the first stages of the emerging fall) and there will need to be a rapid growth in tolerance and willingness to work and live outside today's hierarchies, alongside others whose class culture, ethnicity and other group characteristics are different from one's own.

Over recent decades, the 'relaxation' of traditional class systems has been happening all around the world. To take the extreme case of the Indian caste system, there has been a constant splitting over recent decades with grades between castes and the emergence of what amounts to new castes with less definition in terms of where they belong within the social structure. This is not to say that class or caste has disappeared or even that it is in the process of disappearing, but rather that the cultural influence of the Occident, via the media, is introducing new ways of people defining themselves within the emergent Consumer Society.

All societies have been witnessing this process of decay of traditional social relations, with the consumerist ideology of the Occident making more or less deep inroads everywhere. The most radical changes have taken place in the once-Confucian societies. Perhaps this relates to the high level of rationality with which Confucianism as a system was introduced, coming with a higher level of capacity to apprehend the socio-political system as an artefact than has been the case anywhere else, including the Occident. In any case, the transformation of Chinese society over the years of Maoism was truly astonishing.

The radical turn in Japan, with the Meiji Revolution in the late 19th Century, which, whilst implemented precisely to deflect possibly more radical revolt amongst the Samurai class, ended, with industrialisation and, following the failure of Japan's version of fascism, in a considerably more fluid class system but nevertheless with the creation of new working classes, service classes and bureaucratic and business elites, many of the latter whom can still trace their ancestry back to the post-Meiji aristocracy (*Kazoku*) in spite of the abolition of formal aristocratic rank, post 1946.

The Chinese case has substantial lessons for the radical steps through which it has come over the past century. The attempt across the 20th century on the part of the Communist Party to fundamentally change society was even more radical than that experienced in the Soviet Union, with something closer to a genuine attempt to eradicate classes. Whilst a reformed version of the deeply ingrained bureaucracy was introduced, work was carried out at the local level with an attempt to change fundamentally the outlook of the people that would erase class distinctions[458]. Whilst we might view Hegel's insight into the unhappy self-consciousness as arising from deep-seated critique of hierarchical society (stemming from Christ's teaching and perpetuated through the heresy of the Free Spirit) as having been an impossible thought for Hindus, Confucians and indeed the Islamic peoples, locked into societies where hierarchy had been petrified over thousands of years, China's encounter with Europe understood to a considerable extent, through the communist ideology, what had to be done.

We might talk of the failures of the Maoist experiments in retrospect but this criticism depends greatly on what one believes the outcome should have been — and has thus been vastly exaggerated by the hatred that the new Chinese middle class expresses as a consequence of their adoption today of the Occidental Commercial Ideology and all that goes with it in terms of striving for wealth and status. The fact is, however, that communism well-nigh succeeded in erasing Confucianism and the class system which this had operationalised for two thousand years in China. Although capitulating wholeheartedly into Occidental ideological and politico-social commercial culture today, the unfinished Maoist years have many hidden lessons which, through constructive critique, could yield a route, at least for China, but with some lessons also for us all, down which localised anarchist communities, looking after their own piece of nature, could be built in future years.

More on how we got to be where we are – and its Consequences

We wrote in the early paragraphs of this chapter about the way in which the coming of civilisation involved the instrumentalisation of Nature, which was concerned with the analysis of how species and landscapes could be manipulated to produce food and thence other resources. We then spoke of how this approach to life extended to other aspects of production that created tools and utensils, clothing furniture, houses and more extensive infrastructure. We might ask simply what the purpose of this was. This would need first to answer what the ends are that are being aimed at. We should distinguish at least two kinds of ultimate end: those that concern 'power over' and those that concern 'empathy with'. And it is precisely the shift in balance from the second to the first that is a pivotal characteristic of civilisation in contrast to primitive human existence.

So when we spoke of increased rationality entering into the organisation of life, we are speaking of a clarification of ends and the application of logic and empirical knowledge to devise means to achieve the desired ends[459]. In practice, rationality is not easy to define in that many actions considered to be irrational as a consequence of their being deemed from the perspective of one culture to be dysfunctional, are often but misinterpretations of what the ends of the action might be to those perpetrating them. Hence primitive societies seem to live in irrational worlds that make perfect sense to them in terms of empathetic, rather than instrumental ends. It can thus be argued, as has Feyerabend extremely effectively[460], that any idea of absolute rationality is but a chimera and claims that one's own, or that of one's culture is more rational than another is simply cultural prejudice[461].

However, some sense can be brought to bear on rationality in restricted areas, including the components of the natural sciences and much of daily life. And so here we need to refer to irrationality as arising when the empirical dimension is supplanted by emotion, as in religious revelation or millenarian outbursts, crazes and obsessions. Irrationalities of varying kinds may not be harmful and, indeed, may play a vital role in satisfying human needs. However, in what we might refer to as the genuine interests of society, somehow there needs to a framework wherein societies can contain destructive irrational outbursts or dimensions of the working of the society and ensure that obsessions, that we defined in the Introduction as actions that have negative impacts of particular groups or, indeed, on the whole society once the obsession is played out, do not occur. In hierarchical society where individual interests are in conflict and so decisions at all levels are contested or handed over to individuals or minorities, such a mechanism cannot even be contemplated.

Rationality in the modern sense is connected with the scientific quest in which ends are instrumental and their solution involves making use of empirical knowledge about the physical world to achieve those ends. The owner of a car may in the end empathise, even be head over heels in love, with the machine, but it has taken a vast array of rational processes from the mining of the materials to the finished product with vastly complex management systems to ensure that everything needed gets done to produce and supply the vehicle. Even people subsisting in the simplest primitive societies are 'scientifically' rational in the small everyday things of life, including obtaining food and shelter and extending to knowledge of how to relate functionally to their environment. In primitive life, empathy enters at a very fundamental stage into everything in their lives. In modern culture, rational action in the scientific sense has penetrated every area of life, pushing empathy out, predominantly into the end results.

This was, indeed, a central aim of Occidental culture from the 16th century on, with the notion of rationality being almost the goal of life as the ultimate aim of progress and well enough expressed in Hegel's philosophy as the ultimate achievement of human evolution being a state of Reason. There was, well into the 20th century, a widely-held belief that there will one day be discovered a rational 'theory of everything' from which not only nature will be completely understood but, as a dimension of this, that every human action will be predictable[462]. In a real sense, this was an obsession. And whilst this came with a belief (not rational) that this would be to the benefit of humanity in the sense that nature would yield all her secrets to facilitate the easing of human life, this obsession was actually driven by the will to power. In his propaganda for science as the implementation of rationality as a way of life, Francis Bacon, understood as one of the main prophets of the scientific quest, wrote:

...it would not be amiss to distinguish the three kinds and, as it were, grades of ambition in mankind. The first is of those who desire to extend their own power in their native country, a vulgar and degenerate kind. The second is of those who labour to extend the power and dominion of their country among men. This certainly has more dignity, though no less covetousness. But if a man endeavour to establish and extend the power and dominion of the human race itself over the universe, his ambition (if ambition it can be called) is without doubt both a more wholesome and a more noble thing than the other two [463].

Perhaps he was here being naive — his own self-promotion all the way to Lord Chancellor of England would seem to belie his view of self-promotion as 'vulgar and degenerate', even in his own real opinion. But more seriously problematic for us is the alacrity with which he condoned power and domination over nature and the Universe, seemingly without understanding the essential backward link to power and domination of men by men. To repeat CS Lewis' aphorism on this subject from Chapter Four:

From this point of view, what we call Man's power over Nature turns out to be a power exercised by some men over other men with Nature as its instrument [464].

And above all this lacked any sense of wisdom concerning the need to treat nature kindly, not only so that it survives to nurture future generations but beyond that to understand its essential one-ness with humanity.

The drive for the pursuit of rationality yielded precisely what Bacon and the culture out of which he spoke was aiming at, namely technological advance in pursuit of 'the relief of men's estate' but at the same time fuel for the pursuit of *political* power by individuals and elite classes. The success in the Darwinian sense of Occidental culture, with its insistence on progress, is clearly closely linked with this fusion, with the competition between classes and resulting stratification fuelling the process. The central problematic is the contradiction that increased rationality in relation to revealing how nature might yield up her secrets for the benefit of mankind, only makes the application of rationality in the organisation of society increasingly difficult to achieve.

The development of technology rooted in the scientific-rational mode of thinking, whilst having its more benign moments, is a treadmill towards the fuelling of competition and conflict. Weapons of conflict become more sophisticated but it is the world of consumerism, where the proliferation of Stuff supports the continuation of the belief that 'my life' is improving, in the struggle for status. The power over, and domination of, nature is an essential dimension of this state of being.

A deep irony in this is that increasingly technologies, at the same time as giving status, open the door to retreat from social engagement. Television, the so-called 'social media' of internet, facebook and twitter and above all easy access to modes of transport, actually facilitate the distancing of individuals from social commitment, engagement and responsibility, replaced with a narcissism and communication only with small personal circles, giving an illusion of freedom and (virtual) community. The aspirations of social withdrawal embodied in Stoicism and even Buddhism are supplanted with the world of technological diversion and communication that screens out reality that face-to-face communications finds it difficult to hide. Of course this becomes the final problematic for the supersession of Alienation in the sense that this is buried deeper into the subconscious and hence devoid of critical insight. With the fall of modernity, the shock resulting from the loss of the social media and easy physical escape is likely to be extreme, expressing itself as a form of anomie that can be expected to make social re-engagement highly problematic for the complete present generation.

We already spoke extensively in the previous two chapters of the role that the reconstitution of community groups around the planning of the downward passage could play for youth taking the passage back into social engagement and eventually re-establishing a holistic consciousness of society and nature as one. Later in this chapter we will try to provide a general framework to understand not only how but why to re-engage. First, however, we need to continue to understand where the youthful minds of today will find themselves as the downward path accelerates and if they do not engage in participatory social re-integration of their communities.

In his attempts to make sense of the human psyche in the context of late 19th and early 20th century Occidental society, Sigmund Freud developed a notion of individual self-understanding and how this engaged with the society of his time. Bearing in mind the problematic of the unhappy self-consciousness and specifically the refinement of self-commodification, we see Freud's schema as dividing the individual psyche into three parts which he termed the id, the ego and the super-ego. He saw the id as the inchoate emotions that, in other animals, are satisfied through being linked to instincts — through what is referred to below as 'learning loops' — that initiate actions which connect to the environment, the combination of which operationalise the animals' emotions into actions that will satisfy their needs and desires[465].

According to Freud, in humans, however, the operationalisation goes through the ego that interprets (through what he termed the reality principle) the environment in which the individual is located in a more holistic manner and helps to take decisions and thence actions in more complex ways that will satisfy the needs and desires of the id. The resulting solutions may not be optimal for society or even for the individual in question on the next day or in the next encounter and hence the super-ego is that part of the mental structure that is, as it were, the conscience, and in general the broader rationality as given by parents and teachers that will result in decisions that are 'wiser' in the sense of being more compatible with social and future needs. Freud believed that humans are motivated by very general instincts, including on the one hand a capacity for love and on the other an instinct to kill and that culture intervenes in the form of the super-ego to channel these in ways that preserve the social peace or at least coerce the individual into conforming to the dictates of culture[466].

This requires further discussion in greater depth later in this chapter, where the issue of what the 'I' and its relationship to the social and cultural consciousness is explored with respect to how it may realise its needs and desires. Here the point is that in a inherently competitive and conflict-ridden society, the individual cannot hope to find easy solutions to her or his emotional needs and desires in the social context and so resorts to one or more of a series of strategies to escape the dilemma or retreat into various irrational states. Freud made an initial list of such routes as: denial, displacement, intellectualisation, fantasy, compensation, projection, rationalisation, reaction formation, regression and sublimation. It is not necessary to open these out but simply to note that different situations bring out different defence mechanisms with each individual employing these in different combinations in different situations.

The end result is, in crucial dimensions and in spite of the technological virtuosity that comes from rational thought and action, an irrational world in the sense that solutions to problems large and small, individual and socio-political, are reached at best by compromise but in general through decisions on behalf of the mass of humanity being taken by political processes controlled by elites or planners or via the prerogative of particular interests and beyond that the irrational outcomes of 'the market' and even the rules imposed by a technology-dominated world. More pernicious is the acquiescence of the mass of people who accept, through social convention, living by rules that are none of their making. The fact that, in this situation, obsessions may all too easily arise and be promoted, of which modern consumerism and within this endless numbers of branches and sub-obsessions, are today the most extreme, as being in the ostensible interests of economic elites. These arise with great ease as a mental state where the people have no access to the decisions that bring the obsessions to life and where there is no ethos of critique regarding the arising of obsession.

We can already mention in passing the discussion opened up by the anarchist William Godwin[467] at the turn of the 19th century, arguing how a regime of sincerity could arise in a society without hierarchy, where the defence mechanisms listed by Freud are no longer necessary for the survival of the individual, and could open up the possibility of a society that would take decisions according to commonly-held rationality, through empathetic consensus, in the interest of all its members. Today, every individual is locked into the complexities of a world where no-one can know what will happen tomorrow, as decisions are hidden behind multiple layers of defences and the realisation of the ambitions of distant planners and elites, and so responsibility is systematically abandoned. In the political sphere, ostensible democracies promote the projects and defend the decisions of elites and powerful corporations, making concessions only where groups within society become aware that their interests are being ignored and meanwhile information is withheld and distorted and attention is diverted, resulting in an irrational, even suicidal process at the level of the whole that is destroying the very basis of human existence.

So it is that we come to the end of a particular history of struggle with a series of strategic ideological initiatives on the part of elites, aimed at maintaining what they perceive as their interests and overriding those of majorities. This arises in the context of an assumption of progress and the Enlightenment that might bring this to a world of the 'perfection of man', at least of some men, in a state of Reason that, at the extreme, would be realised in the form of a communist society, meaning a society of equals living in ease and rational exchange, where the pursuit of beauty and the requiting of love become realisable objectives.

To recapitulate the main stages: as the basic process of the evolution of Occidental culture, rationality extended ever further, driven by its efficaciousness for elites to further their power, percolating as a mental state also to the lower orders as a process of secularisation and hence understanding that inferiority and the state of subjection to power was not God-given and could be challenged. And so quasi-rational ideologies were extended to substitute for the loss of religious sanction. Hobbes, Mandeville, Locke and thence Hume (the English philosophy generally) destroyed any hope of solidarity through their notion of individual striving to satisfy the passions and offering instead the false hope that individual struggle could lead to a better life through the acquisition of wealth.

In the dawning consciousness amongst the lower orders that this was no solution for them, the Malthusian and Darwinian attempt arose to assert that superiority and inferiority and the struggle for survival or power was a fact of nature. Thence, in the face of rising social movements amongst the oppressed, the institution of appeasement as a false communism and social democracy that utilised rationality in technological inventiveness for Development processes to demonstrate that the lower orders could also benefit, ended in a return to the Mandevillian-Lockeian ideology of individual routes to higher status, facilitated by a world of technological virtuosity and the increased application of energy as the increase, in all systemic senses, of power.

At the same time, in the course of the late 18th and early 19th century, visions arose that progress would ultimately resolve the social struggle in the world through a true understanding of the human predicament, for example, Condorcet's notion of the Perfectibility of Man, ending in a Utopia where all difference would be erased. Hegel's notion of Reason extending into the philosophy also of Marx and Engels, regarded the return of humanity to their place in the totality of nature and the late 19th century idea of an ultimate socio-political revolution through which this would be achieved.

We should not forget the breadth amongst these visions of the practical arguments amongst legions of utopians, socialists, communists and anarchists[468]: This was not, in the course of the 19th century a minor phenomenon, but a real development of the consciousness of Occidental society, disgorged into rational discourse of the problematic of class-divided society and of Alienation and whilst the Marxist vision that came to fix this discourse in the 20th century insisted that the divide could only be resolved by the Working Class — who had nothing to lose but their chains — the discourse was largely articulated by what were sometimes referred to as 'advanced' intellectuals and politically active elites who understood that they, too, suffered Alienation and hence their real interest lay in the destruction of hierarchy.

So the deep-seated acceptance of hierarchy expressed in so many dimensions was never unchallengeable and in many instances throughout the past two centuries has produced not merely heroic rhetoric but also quite practical and often unsung ways of organising life in various places as lacunae in otherwise traditional structures. The case of Switzerland, as presenting seven hundred years of quasi-anarchist Government, was discussed in Chapter Three. The case of the *Obschina* (or Mir) in 19th century Russia gives us another example. Also, the cooperative movement from the mid-19th century, which has spread to tens of thousands of enterprises around the world today, extending at the extreme to the cooperative commonwealth of Mondragon, where most activity in the town is organised on a cooperative basis. Partial routes, but indicative each in their own way of the practical possibility of egalitarian modes of political and social organisation.

The rich variety of thousands of Common Pool Resource Management initiatives, some of which are inherited from centuries past and others recently adopted, also demonstrate the principle of egalitarianism. Another recent manifestation discussed in detail in the past two chapters is the rapid growth in participatory forms of planning in its various forms. Then again, there is the creation, dissolution and reappearance of utopian (what today are referred to as 'intentional') communities that also go back in time, often under particular religious principles. Today there are many hundreds of these communities, scattered right across the Occident and extending into other cultures as potential seeds of a workable dis-Alienated future. Very few of these attempt to root out at a basic level inherited mentalities of class and hierarchy, though all of them address this in part, usually subconsciously through *de facto* cooperation and the growth in trust that this engenders. The basic conundrum for all amongst these initiatives that have entered consciously into egalitarian relations is how to defend their way of interaction against the aggressive propaganda and the everyday reality of mainstream culture and thence how to broaden out the appeal and propagate their own insights and forms of activity.

An Inquiry into the Source of the Problematic

We now go all the way back to basics to try to understand what it is to be human and to fulfil our needs and desires through social — and eventually political[469] — action. We have discussed the way in which elites have attempted to fix a notion that conflict and competition between people, classes and nations is inevitable, in the distant past through religious sanction and divine right of monarchs and aristocracies. With the emergence of modernity, the religious sanction fell away and ideological means to keep hierarchy in place evolved through the speculation of Hobbes and, in a more sophisticated way, Locke and thence Hume. Subsequently, the Darwinian dogma of 'survival of the fittest' portrayed nature as being made in such a way that individualistic competition and hence hierarchy is a fundamental characteristic of natural evolution and of human society as part of this. The ideological means of keeping inequality in place gave way in the 20th century to the use of the improvement of the conditions of life for the lower orders and eventually was maintained through a constantly increasing supply of Stuff — essentially extinguishing demands for change through a process of seduction.

On the other hand, there have been ideas and movements that are based on a belief that the problematic of class-divided, ergo irrational societies based on the outcome of conflicting interests and hence strategies and contradictory outcomes, is resolvable. Throughout the Middle Ages and into the modern era there were millenarian manifestations and quietist religious movements that either demanded change or closed into themselves as defence against the inhumanity of unequal relations. From the European Enlightenment and secularisation of the idea of revolution, legions of utopians envisioned a teleology where progress of human evolution, as a dimension of natural evolution, would end in a reintegration, following the achievement of Reason and communist society, of a world in which society as an entity, subsuming the interest of all, would supersede hierarchical relations producing a society capable of organising the ideal life through rational choice and hence *de facto* manage relations with Nature in a rational manner. Here, whilst clearly having to abandon the teleological view of the future, given the way in which modern society has, in fact, evolved over the past century, we want to look squarely in the face at what human consciousness is and how it comes to an understanding of the world, with a view to enquiring into whether the achievement of a truly egalitarian and rationally designed society could realistically be a possible state of future humanity.

We start from the biological. It stands to reason that all animals must have something we will call an 'I'. Plants, being stationary, may be assumed to have no such entity, simply producing themselves and waiting for the environment, including the sun and rain, insects and

366

other animals, to act in ways that impact on their life and ultimately facilitate their growth and reproduction. If, however, biota move autonomously, then there has to be a centre that takes the ultimate decision on where to go and why. Even a single celled amoeba must decide, motivated by combinations of external and internal stimuli, for instance to flee from danger or to move towards food, and to coordinate its various parts to make the intended move. More complex organisms have more parts to coordinate in order to act once the 'I' has taken the decision and virtually all of this will be controlled from different parts of the nervous system. In fact much, if not most, of what even human beings do involves processes that don't concern the 'I' at all.

If I get up and walk into the living room, sit down and play the piano, practically all the actions that this involves result from decisions taken in various places within the nervous system that make little or no reference to the 'I', right down — if I have already learnt to play the piece of music I then commence to play — to the decisions as to the sequence of finger movements. But somehow the general decision must be taken to get up and to go play the piano as a kind of summary that sets the process in motion and succeeds in implementing it.

The mystery lies in how and why the ultimate decision was made to go and play the piano at this moment and what the music means as a dimension of my life process. These are the things, strategic in nature, that interest us with respect to 'being human' and the construction of our reality. We can refer to this as our 'stream of consciousness' that formulates what to do at a particular point in time from either internal or external motivations (we have probably, indeed, already mapped out our day beforehand), initiating and supervising the action sequences that follow from this. Somewhere, it seems, there must be an 'I' that takes these decisions.

Earlier in this chapter we mentioned in passing the result of ethological research that shows how instinctual actions on the part of animals stimulate the environment that leads to results which satisfy the animals' needs. For example, terns, walking on beaches will suddenly take instinctually to hopping up and down. This stimulates organisms hidden in the sand to come to the surface that are then eaten by the tern. Woodpeckers, on the other hand, hammer the bark of trees with their beaks, stimulating insects to emerge from under the bark, which the woodpeckers proceed to eat. Ethologists have studied countless numbers of these learning loops, how animals will initiate an action and learn by trial and error to carry these out in places likely to elicit the desired response and then how to respond effectively.

It seems that animals are born with very large numbers of species-specific internal routines which, once operationalised, the animals learn to use to satisfy their needs. The end result for the particular species is their occupation of particular ecological niches, including their relationship with others of their own species that can be said to make up their society. This is, for all species except Homo sapiens, almost unvarying in the ways that it manifests itself. There is no learning how to be sociable in a holistic way, it is just the result of learning through the series of learning loops innate in the animals physiology with the 'I' firmly located in the organism, coordinating and supervising the linking up of the loops through time and responses to others of their species are equally the result of such learning loops.

So animals other than Homo sapiens have almost no concept of time, perhaps memories of the past and certainly of empathy with and fear of particular situations, but no notion of the future; they may have daily and certainly annual routines, classically in migrations, but this is built into the animals, not conceptualised and planned. It seems they have sensitivities to their environment that go (different species in different ways) way beyond those of humans, and that may even anticipate immediate climatic and geological events from environmental signs. But they have no notion of history, of being able to anticipate or, above all, to choose how to organise their lives and to plan the future.

Humans, however, create an almost infinitely variable number of different kinds of society and adapt to almost every environment to be found on earth. They possess and maintain stories from history and are able to plan changes in their lives in coherent ways. Mature humans, once they have learned the basics of looking after themselves at the level of daily activity, are capable of living as hermits or of living their lives with others in small communities. Today, however, almost all live in an insanely complex society that we call 'global', made up of nations and localities, communities, associations and households etc. Boxes within boxes with few firm edges and so, in the modern world, an extreme fluidity with regard to the capacity of humans to adapt and integrate into new social frameworks.

How did it come to pass in evolutionary history that humans do this? Let us conjecture the following: the 'I' in animals almost exclusively coordinates the activities resulting from the various learning loops that spring into action from internal or environmental stimuli as these come into contact with internal needs looking to be satisfied. In the course of human evolution, the location of this coordination process migrated out of the brain and into the outside world, creating what we refer to as human consciousness, this being the totality of what the 'I' discovered and brought back to structure the mind. In recent years there has emerged a whole industry inquiring into 'human consciousness' and how it works with as yet little even by way of an agreed definition of what it is and certainly no agreement on how it functions[470].

There has been a certain struggle to banish the Christian idea, as secularised by Descartes, that the 'I', qua soul, is an actual thing, separate from the body, connecting us to God and we should agree with this banishment. Perhaps it helps to see the 'I' as something akin to our centre of gravity that is somewhere inside the body when it is at rest but can even be temporarily outside the body when this is moving round a corner on a bicycle or skis: it is not a physical nor 'spiritual' thing but it has a concrete existence, nevertheless. Whilst the 'consciousness industry' has generally concluded that there is no 'thing' there to be discovered, the focus has nevertheless been almost wholly on trying to find the mechanisms, biological or psychological, within the individual that might be discovered as producing consciousness as a kind of extended psychology.

It is by now generally agreed that evolution of Homo as a species or genera, presumably through stages but in evolutionary terms rather rapidly (referred to as a cascade[471]), generated the capacity to form concepts and to understand matters in terms of symbols. It seems that apes have this capacity in a very rudimentary way, as demonstrated famously by Wolfgang Köhler, experimenting with chimpanzees and encouraging them to put together simple actions and invent tools to accomplish simple and immediate action sequences which they invented, rather than that these were pre-programmed.

By the time Homo sapiens sapiens was fully evolved, instinctual learning loops had faded into the background, substituted by the capacity to formulate complex idea-structures that start with the simple — defining and recognising physical things in the environment, for example: tables, pens, dogs, mountains, then attaching multiple dimensions of emotional meaning, significance and value (no such concept is totally objective in the sense of being value-free) to these as to their characteristics and how to relate to them and in the process seeing these in relation to time, to other objects understood as being in some way related, and thence to what interaction might take place with these objects. This came indissolubly bound up with the capacity to communicate these ideas and concepts between humans via language, so that the physical facts as received sensually could be shared with others intellectually. More than we realise, language, as a string of symbols, helps us to define the concepts that become what we perceive of and understand as reality[472]. This means that at a very basic level most of what is 'understood' is *social* 'fact' which we inherit in the course of our education. We don't invent our language, we inherit it through our education as the framework of reality for us.

An individualistic interpretation of what this might mean in practice, put forward by Richard Dawkins and widely debated, is the notion of 'memes' that are concepts structured with content that, like animal learning loops, are then operationalised to satisfy human desires and needs: tunes, clothes fashions, the game of football, making pottery and so on and so on[473]. This, however, loses a central point, namely the fact that any fragmentary meme requires a conceptual framework to even be thought — in fact a prerequisite is the need for nested frameworks right up to such abstractions as to why and how to live life in general, how to allocate meaning and invest emotion in the content of concepts all the way from everyday concepts attached to routine activities, through multiple levels of abstraction to notions of God or, in primitive people, notions of life invested in nature as a totality.

It is the totality of these concepts and their referents in the real world that make up human consciousness. The 'real world' surely exists but for us it is that that has been interpreted by our consciousness; in the first instance passively through what we are taught or have otherwise learned, in part confirmed through the senses, and then processed as things and ideas, as symbols, mythologies and scenarios, confirmed and then sometimes held as dogma, and others subject to modification, facilitating the living of our lives.

Very few of the concepts which inhabit our personal stream of consciousness (and indeed subconscious in the sense of dreams and even less choate reactions to external stimuli) are invented by us as individuals, though they will always have a particular colouring that is personally ours. The first years of our lives are spent developing, with help from those closest to us, concepts in the mind which in animals are occupied at birth by 'instincts', or, as it were, pre-programmed concepts. This is far from the 'tabula rasa' (clean slate) that was the notion of British philosophy back in the 18th century but, rather, a dynamic process where the 'I' sends out rudimentary conceptual frameworks at different levels of complexity and concreteness that may be conjectured to be relevant to the particular moment, in search of content that includes ways of manipulating the immediate environment, ways of understanding how to relate to parents and others who enter our life and then growing exploration of the beliefs of people surrounding us, both stated and interpreting unspoken beliefs as evidenced in stray phrases but mainly inchoately theorising upon actions.

The conundrum for the newly-born is that, unlike the animal learning loop, there is nothing, or at best extremely little, by way of pre-existing structures or concepts and so a long process of seeking to build concepts to fit particular situations is learned through the formulation of sending out of 'draft' concepts and receipt of the results of the exercise. The process and the results are fused into what becomes the child's early steps towards joining the consciousness of their culture and forming their own self-consciousness, and with age, the process becomes more self-confident and the results richer as guided both by education and, more importantly, experience of the physical world and, above all, observation of peer actions and words.

It is in this sense that the 'I' is no longer a simple 'centre of existence' of the organism as in animals but is, rather, the sum of socially-given knowledge and understanding that will structure the beliefs and actions of the adult as the individual lives out her or his life. In other words, we identify ourselves through the concept structures that are built up in our heads through the educational process in its widest sense. Mental constructs learned earlier can, of course, change as life moves on, through the efforts of the individual mind as a consequence of the fact of myriads of contradictions and alternatives, internalised over the period of education — indeed, right to the end of life — can be interpreted in complex ways through pre-existing concepts or direct contact with elements of the environment, but in the main from social interaction.

So we can see, to look for human consciousness as a function of the individual mind gives us nothing but the mechanism of externalising the thought process, in what Greek philosophy called the negativity of the human mind. This is the point at issue — we can only refer to human consciousness as overwhelmingly a social or culturally shared phenomenon reflected on and interpreted by the individual as a basis for action[474] to satisfy existential needs and desires. We can even hazard that consciousness is the essence of culture, that our particular way of understanding our being and the world that we call consciousness is then expressed in the outside world as the culture in which each of us lives out our lives.

We must remember that all other animals satisfy their desires and needs through instincts that direct their actions. In the place of instincts, humans must trust the concepts they inherited in their education, in the broadest sense, to supply the means to satisfy needs and desires. In primitive societies, we can speak of a holistic conceptual framework where humans felt in a real way their own presence in the natural environment and in the reciprocity of social interaction within their band; in a real sense *being* themselves. Insofar as members of the band felt at a fundamental level that they were one entity, and one with their environment, so the satisfaction of desires and needs could be transmitted openly and without inhibition with the rest of the band responding in like manner. Subject was all and object non-existent.

In practice, most desires and needs can be satisfied in any one of a myriad different ways and even primitive bands formed different structures of marriage, hunting and gathering and the making of simple tools and equipment where these were deemed to be needed. The decisions as to how to do this worked themselves out, in all probability without formulating what should be done but just doing it, with others following and if not, doing something else, until there was *de facto* agreement as a fixed structure that satisfied their collective and personal needs and desires. No resort to rationality in the instrumental sense becomes necessary and in practice all manner of what modern people consider bizarre (viz the mass of practices documented by James Frazer in *The Golden Bough*[475]) manifested themselves as the imaginative results of primitive social interaction.

What the coming of civilisation did is to build walls, and thence veritable mazes, of barriers between the simple needs and desires of humans and how these might be satisfied within the complex social structures which their expanding societies constructed. In early civilisation, these walls grew to tremendous heights in the sense of people using others in slave relations over and against rulers deemed to be gods, and the convoluted religious structures and rituals all aimed at finding ways through the maze to satisfy their needs and desires. Families, sodalities, proliferating forms of association notably religious communities and in some places and ways class solidarities, emerged as places where the walls could be reduced and at least some trust and empathy built and in these contexts needs and desires more simply, directly and sympathetically satisfied.

Structures for the maintenance of complete societies, as configurations of consciousness understood in different ways by different classes, emerged not through design but contingently, one thing leading to another, ending in objective and thence physical structures as sets of institutions, and the laws that held these in place, which we think of as the components of particular civilisations. As already discussed, some of these lasted for short periods whilst, at the extreme, a few lasted for thousands of years as the accepted framework within which human life would be carried out, with the mass of humanity losing sight of the possibility of more direct and fulfilling ways of addressing their needs and desires. Religions of escape (classically Stoicism and Buddhism) arose not as solutions to the existence of walls and mazes but as means of retreat, to reduce the resulting pain and frustration of the often fruitless search for the satisfaction of desires.

However, as we have discussed throughout this chapter, these structures were essentially compromises in which humans were convinced, through their education, that they would have to live with even if, as we can say was almost universally the case, these were less than satisfactory solutions. As a consequence, these processes never came into more than extremely marginal consideration. Nature as ecosystems was, in the process, increasingly affected by the structures created by civilisation — agriculture, cities and eventually deepening rapaciousness in extraction of minerals and the expanding industries which these fed and thence the impacts of the products that these industries produced that summed to ecological damage in the sense of reducing complexity hence robustness and biodiversity and biomass density.

In earlier times this ecological damage had only relatively local impacts such as the damaged landscapes around mines and, more seriously, deforestation. In the context of modernity, these processes went through an additional twist. There came the recognition that — in Hume's philosophy but following on from Mandeville and Locke and the whole ambience of the times — the purpose of life should focus centrally on the satisfaction of personal 'passions', or desires and at a minimum, basic needs. This call was, however, profoundly hypocritical in that the society which produced the idea was deeply class-divided, and where the lower classes were in no way in a situation where they had any freedom to determine the means to satisfy their desires or even needs without reference to their 'superiors'. But what this philosophy did do was to turn people even more tightly into themselves, commanding them to find their own individual path to sensory and mental satisfaction without hope of finding social solidarity to break down the walls, whence desires might be satisfied through extended trust and empathy. We can say that Freud's discovery of so many means of defence, listed above, against the aggression of others seeking their satisfaction at the expense of one another, was the discovery of the results of the individualist drive of modern society.

We can see how the whole civilising process was fuelled by frustrations resulting from the inhibitions and complexities of humans finding their way to satisfying what, in the end, are simple needs and simple desires of human existence through direct and empathetic social intercourse as play or interaction with the environment to produce the physical necessities of life, food and shelter and then the playfulness and arts that fulfil the creative propensities and deeper satisfactions of the mind of Homo sapiens. Primitive people show us that these can be achieved with little effort in most environments (and if not, why not move to a more congenial environment?) but civilisation created elaborate barriers and frustrations by separating people from one another at a very basic psychological level.

The parts and even the whole are clearly capable of evolving as cultural change. We wrote earlier of the way in which some civilisations had created a foundation for thought that in spite of surface changes, nevertheless returned following crises to the basic structure, so that at the strategic level there was a stability that kept individuals in their places, both socially and physically. Only in the context of the ideology of the progress of modern culture and the impact of the harnessing of fossil energy, has, over the past centuries, much of even the deeper-held foundations of Occidental, and more recently 'global', culture been in almost constant accelerating, and deepening processes of change. However, we wish to emphasise that when the complexity of these changes is analysed in detail, we see that the problematic of Alienation that we have been identifying as the source of the suicidal trajectory of modern civilisation, has refused to become the object of an adequate, sustained focus and hence continues to drive us over the edge and into the fall.

Before focusing further on the nature of the key changes and attempted changes that have characterised the past few centuries, we need first to focus a little on the notion of God as something of the foundation of the consciousness of civilisation that produced modernity. Although not easily identifiable as a single, all-embracing or powerful entity somehow encompassing all of life, in cultures and religions beyond the boundaries of Western Eurasia, this is particularly important in what are referred to as the Abrahamic religions. We refer to cultural life, east to west, from Persia to Britain and extending eastwards also to those parts of Asia where Islam has taken hold and throughout the territories colonised by Europe, above all the Americas. Asking the question: 'What is God?' is not as helpful as asking: 'Why God? What does God do?' Here we can see that 'He' (always tending towards the masculine, however abstractly conceived) is, above all, the notion that gives faith in life, so that it is meaningful and worth living. In the extreme, God *is* Faith, and hence prayer.

But it is the notion of God that is the basic foundation of *social* hierarchy amongst Abrahamic-informed cultures, emerging half way through the evolution of Civilisation, condensing out, we might say, from Mesopotamian religion into Judaism, with the complex features of the Christian Trinity – and evident as determinant of hierarchy in the Middle Ages in the notion of the Great Chain of Being and then honed above all into the Islamic conception of Allah. The centrality of Allah to the whole world of the Islamic people, and thence the insistence on Sharia and other law-determined aspects of hierarchical life, gives us also the present-day Islamic resistance movements against the 'relaxed' notions of hierarchy in (Occidental) modernity, with their origins in Christianity — and, indeed, the fading away of the strength of the notion of God in 'Enlightened' Occidental evolution, seeing through the mists the possibilities of an eventual beatific life of equality[476]. But as we can see, in cultures outside the sphere of the Abrahamic, the ways in which faith finds foundations may be quite other than any conception of a single, mighty (masculine) God. And the notion that nature *is* God seeping in from Ancient Greece through pantheistic heresies[477], peeping out between the insistence on Christian, dualistic orthodoxy and ancient heresies that see God embodied in our community and that we are all a unity that embodies God.

It is clear that there are levels of embeddedness or sedimentation of concepts in the social consciousness, meaning that opinions on some things can easily be changed whilst others, even when open to debate, are tethered to deeper, oftentimes inchoate, beliefs and hence changes may be agreed but not actually implemented. Some deeply sedimented concepts are obvious and necessary in the most functional ways, including the presumptions we make that the physical environment we inhabit is real so that we can negotiate it without having to constantly verify it[478].

But much that is deeply embedded has come as beliefs that have no primary physical referents, to satisfy needs where there is inadequate empirical knowledge to answer the basic questions or the basic rules of social convention, the questioning of which becomes too daunting. This is the life of religion, but also of what was earlier referred to as the 'social subconscious' comprising inchoate notions that can surface in unexpected ways as society evolves, most often to reconfirm existing arrangements over and against the threat or actuality of change and might also be called upon actively to reinforce otherwise rational means of bringing about social change.

Conversely, dissatisfactions at many levels can mount to a point to bring people together to formulate ways to change social and political reality. Classically this is through revolution, which is understood as akin, or even the same as, religious revelation in the sense of discarding over a short period – a few years or even months – deeply-sedimented rules and inhibitions to make space for the formulation and eventual implementation of different ways of relating, and of socio-political structures that will address and break down the problematic of Alienation.

Throughout this text we have noted that modernisation has involved a process of increasing application of rationality, generating ever more complex ways of solving human existential needs and desires. This has not, however, banished irrationalities in the directions taken or in the outcomes, viz the modern obsession with automobiles or the waging of wars using incredibly sophisticated technologies and above all the belief in Progress and Development. However, it is notable that the 'social and political unrest' aimed by groups or classes (particularly in Europe and emanating from Christian apocalyptic beliefs) at changing the socio-economic rules and structures, did, following the Enlightenment, move significantly beyond the realm of religious experience to more concrete ways of reformulating social and political relations. It should be stressed here that this is not some kind of proof of progress. We can point to periods of history where rational debate on ways to organise society flourished and then died, including the years between the life of Confucius and the institution of Confucianism as state morality in China and also the 'Greek experiment'[479] that took place around the same time, the unearthed results of which have been so important to the structuring of European consciousness over the past few centuries.

Thus we see over the past several hundred years all manner of revolts, rebellions and revolutions, as well as reformulations of institutional arrangements from political process to social practices, many of which have not taken place at conjunctures or instances but, in the context of recent progress, have taken place *de facto* as sliding between states apparently on the basis of public discourse but in the main 'irrationally' in the framework of the dissolution of formal society and the insertion into the void of technologies that, together, have been referred to earlier in the book from time to time as the Technostructure.

We will not spend much time going into the details of the theoretical discourse on 'social change' that had a certain vogue during the 1980s and 90s[480]. The issue of revolution does, however, require some attention in the sense that this has been seen as the root concept and potentially the way in which major changes in social self-conception and socio-political structure does or might take place. In Chapter

Three, we discussed the European revolutions that ostensible significantly changed the course of history: the English, French and Russian Revolutions.

What we wish to emphasise from the discussion in Chapter Five, is that insofar as these revolutions might have reduced the inner barriers and eventually the privatisation of the participating populations, in practice this did not happen. The mythology that sees these revolutions, and lesser such socio-political events, as having achieved progress towards some kind of ultimate resolution of the human condition, cannot be upheld. The idea that leaders are no longer sanctioned by God as some kind of improvement in the human condition is of no concrete substance, when in practice new elites assume powers that are *de facto* more contrary to 'ordinary people's' needs in their increased interference in, and dominance of, 'ordinary lives'.

Whilst at the time, the English Revolution raised hopes and debates about real alternative arrangements that could have changed the lives of the 'lower orders', none of this was realised and marginal changes in elite structures persisted all the way down to the present. The French Revolution also opened up the realisation of the possibility of breaking down class barriers and building a society based on 'liberty, equality, fraternity', that continued to be declared as ideology whilst in practice maintaining a discrete aristocracy and introducing the world's first technocracy, managed by a new elite, as supposed machinery for satisfying the needs, if not the desires, of its citizenry.

Whilst the Russian Revolution apparently moved towards the removal of barriers represented by the abolition of private property, this came with an even more severe 'authoritarian developmentalist technocracy' under tyrannical rule little different from that of the kings of the distant past and that had even less regard for simple human needs and desires. It eventually failed due to its capitulation to the Commercial Ideology as surrogate solution to the ostensible aim of revolution to break down barriers created by civilisation and recover the sense and reality of one-ness amongst people[481]. We might say that the Chinese Revolution, or, as called by the Chinese themselves, the 'Liberation', whilst starting down the road and experimenting, in many initiatives with naive enthusiasms that ended in tears[482], did no more than open the door to a more wholehearted acceptance and implementation of the Commercial Ideology than was the case of the failed Russian experiment.

We might go on to say that the whole Occidental, millenarian notion of revolution, whilst still carried in a few modern minds, has totally lost its way as to what it is intended to achieve. The famous manifestations of 1968 that took place over several months, ricocheting around the world, were seen as some kind of emergent revolution. The millenarian spirit was certainly present and can be felt in reading literature produced at this time that had an excitement to it, even when discussing concrete changes that might be implemented.

However, it is not merely that nothing concrete actually changed following the outburst, more problematic is that proposals for change were either formulated at an abstract intellectual level that could not be translated into concrete changes (such as in the literature of the Situationists) or were of a kind where addressing realities lost touch with the spirit of change. Subsequent events considered to be potentially revolutionary, down to the Arab Spring and flickering protests over today's 'economic crisis' and 'austerity measures', display no sense at all of the deeper problematic of the Alienation of people in the context of modern society and what steps would need to be taken to move meaningfully in the direction of reviving the very possibility of reintegration of the isolated modern individual into a condition where empathy becomes the context for addressing needs and desires and beyond this, the opening up of the possibility of understanding empathy with nature as part of the resolution.

Exploring Possibilities for a dis-Alienated Future

As the downward passage from modern civilisation accelerates over the coming decades, we can expect there eventually to be fundamental changes in understanding of what human life is about. Deeply sedimented beliefs that have been confirmed over the past decades and centuries will no longer possess referents in the outside world. Most obviously, with economic decline, the lie will be given to the whole hope and expectation of so much that has been delivered by way of Stuff, ease of communication and movement and simple comforts of home. The apparent confirmation of progress will fade away leaving an emptiness that will, over the decades, force fundamental changes in the outlook and beliefs of the people of the Occident but will also affect the rest of humanity that has had its mind turned by the impacts of modernity, to turn in on themselves and seek new foundations for their self-understanding. As the very basis for survival, there will be no alternative but to seek ways of organising life that are sustainable and which will require imagination to achieve, lifestyles that are congenial in close cooperation with local communities, within the limits of local resources and with modest technologies[483].

In the early stages of the process, the Alienation that has been maintained by so many different means throughout the era of civilisation will surely rise into consciousness as a dominating preoccupation. As our 'globalised' world shatters, so a multitude of solutions will evolve rapidly in different places. Owners of wealth and property will attempt to continue to assert their status and power. However, the basis of wealth in banking and then in industry will progressively collapse and property in land will come to reassert itself as the dominant source of wealth. Bureaucracy could also be converted from the present quasi-meritocratic hierarchies to calcify into new rank hierarchies under dictatorship, eventually even hereditary feudal systems. We can be pessimistic, looking down this path, at the very survival of whole societies in the face of resource depletion and what is left following the modern rape of the earth and the impacts of climate change that will require a flexibility that such hierarchies would never be capable of manifesting.

We can only hope that the resurfacing into consciousness of the Alienation that has been the foundation of civilisation will be confronted systematically and that the wisdom that rarely surfaced over the whole era of civilisation, the wisdom that is aware of the reality of the one-ness of human consciousness with nature that is also the one-ness of humanity, comes to govern our relations and to pervade the solutions which each local community finds to satisfy the existential needs of all its members without exploitation and without the civilisation-created mental walls that divide us from one another and from nature, that incipiently produce conflict and competition. Although from the perspective from which we see things today the road may seem long, in historic terms this will be extremely short, forced to take place in less than a handful of – maybe as few as two - generations.

The immediate reaction to the start of the downward passage that we can see flickering across the world today is demonstrations that are predominantly about complaint — at best objecting to dictatorship (the Arab Spring) or to the unfairness of the discrimination in the redistribution of wealth (Greece, Spain) or to the grotesqueness of massive wealth differentials (Occupy Wall Street)[484]. There is in these, no admission of being on the edge of a downward passage with the predominant, wholly unrealistic demand being for the re-establishment of 'economic growth' and the 'American Dream'.

In short, today we see denial even whilst there is amongst most of the population that allows itself to think on the matter, a foreboding that we are seeing the 'end of economic growth' and hence the end to the increasing supply of Stuff and the vicarious life of Consumerism. And beyond this a deepening denial and screening out of any substantive information that would indicate what the world ahead has in store. Very few people wish to think coherently about this and those in positions of power do not wish to reveal the truth. It is difficult to assess how, as the next decades unfold, the realisation of the very different future ahead will come into focus. Whilst the Transition Movement opens a small window on the real future, this remains a movement involving, today, tiny lacunae of humanity when seen in terms of the total populations that will enter the downward passage in the coming years in, initially, a state of maintained ignorance and pretence that this is a passing state of affairs.

Initially life will seem to become harder and more restricted. In fact over the past decades in terms of income, very many even 'middle class' families in the United States and in some European countries have become poorer in terms of income with the difference being made up by two or more earners per household and because so many beguiling things that money can buy have become cheaper, making it seem as if they are growing more affluent[485]. Pensioners living the last twenty years of their lives, so often in isolation, have seen their incomes ebbing away. But prices will rise, and in general greater numbers feel, as is the case in Greece today, that their livelihoods are becoming increasingly restricted. It is likely, as conjectured in more detail at the end of the first chapter, that there will then be points where conditions, as seen by the mass of people, will suddenly deteriorate markedly, movement becoming restricted and the cost of basic necessities crowding out the hopes of buying all but essentials.

Two immediate reactions, already manifesting themselves, are the spread of anger and frustration that 'the system' and hence 'the politicians' are failing the people, as we can see increasingly expressed in demonstrations amongst poor communities turning into 'food riots'. The other reaction amongst the global middle class that we can define is that a proportion of the population (mainly in the Occidental countries) who are wholly defined by the ideology of modernity in its manifestation as commodification, will close into themselves, even blame themselves for not 'succeeding' and in this attitude resist reaching out to neighbours to start to look for common solutions of the kinds discussed in the foregoing chapter. The state may be expected to entirely lack solutions, repressing 'riots' and abandoning the middle class masses to seek their own solutions.

A different ethos will develop in different cities and urban quarters: we could witness this over the past years where even different neighbourhoods could develop substantial solidarity whilst in others people kept to themselves. Many cities and urban quarters have manifested phases of increased violence, robbery and murder and then peace with 'no go' areas that then over a period 'gentrify' in ways where middle classes introduce their community-free living spaces. Very many people in this condition in cities around the world, who are allowing themselves to imagine deteriorating economic circumstances in the coming years, immediately envisage disorganised violence spreading and deepening, even turning, in conjunction with the propensity to 'riot' into more organised civil war, embodying illusions that someone can solve the problems, melding into attempts simply to gain power and access to dwindling resources in a situation where these simply fail to arrive in the cities. It is the danger of this state of affairs deepening into new class manifestations that those who see future possibilities optimistically will need to find imaginative ways to combat.

We can also be sure that in this context, anomie will spread in the form of a loss of orientation, sense of purpose and self-worth, followed in many places by multiple deprivation resulting in widespread premature death — as in Russian cities briefly in 1990-91, but which might be expected to continue in many cities to be the fate even of substantial proportions of national populations. Many will take individual flight, by whatever means, in search of circumstances in the countryside or cities and towns that seem less impacted.

Elderly populations in Germany and Japan today will recall how this happened in their own cities in the last weeks of the Second World War, and continued for many over the following months and even years; at that time, in the late 1940s, they were overcome with the reconstitution of the state and the reconstruction of economies and cities. This time round, to a different degree in different countries, the state will be in a continually weakening position. As long as national governments hold, there may be attempts to stem the decline for months and even a few years which will not, however, hold for long and the very legitimacy of central governments may be expected to fall apart, possibly like Somalia over the past two decades, falling into sub-regional fiefdoms or, if we look optimistically as discussed in the past two chapters, increasingly organised as smaller self-managed territories seeking confederal relations with neighbouring areas.

Intellectually and practically, the solution is obvious, as set out in the foregoing chapter. Those who do not succumb as drops in the sea of the wasted masses will evolve, for them, entirely new ways of understanding their existential condition. We say entirely new, but in

381

practice there is knowledge and understanding of what will be necessary residing very widely in the social subconscious, that it would be difficult and inappropriate to try to impose but needs to be discovered as revived memory — education in the deepest sense where the very word derives from the notion of 'drawing out'.

The issue will be: at what point, in the sense of secular revelation and resulting action, will individuals experience, or allow themselves to experience, the falling away of the pride and inhibition, the illusions of individual status through which they define themselves as legitimate and self-confident members of modern society? When will they reject the incipient fear of the other, cast off the shell of self-commodification created by the competitive ethos that is the defining characteristic of modern society? It is not in the quiet of the individual home that such revelation can be expected to happen but in the context of the reconstitution of community and the organisation of mutual activities to rebuild life on a truly sustainable basis that can generate deep satisfaction, even joy of discovery, giving the lie to the surrogate satisfactions that have been sustained in recent decades by the Consumer Society. This can be expected to happen for most in the context of social activity where communities cohere around strategies, plans and reconstruction activities.

It is notable that Transition initiatives are already displaying such forms of solidarity, initiated by those who already have a more coherent idea of what makes a dis-Alienated Community. The ethos of solidarity has never been entirely eliminated, with many people gaining at least some insight into this through all manner of associations and societies, religious groups, trade unions and even local branches of political parties. There are two sorts of danger to which most contemporary such communities are subject. On the one hand, active societies exhaust their solidarity in cohering as a group to improve the effectiveness of members in various forms of competition in the larger world. In some cases, such as business associations, which does not involve any real sense of solidarity at all. In many, however, there is a partial sense of solidarity such as radical political groups struggling over rights or, as in cooperatives, working as equals in economic activity.

On the other hand, some such communities, particularly where they are constituted as religious groups, are a matter of escape for part of the day or the week from unhappy social relations and the incipient competitivity of every-day life in modern society. These are not the start of a new outlook that will initiate effective activity to produce a new life. The kind of community that will encourage the education of its members into the new ethos will be like Transition initiatives, bringing people together to cooperate in proactive projects to reconstruct worlds that will be sustainable and congenial for all.

In the light of a broad understanding, discussed earlier in this chapter, that in actuality human consciousness is fundamentally a social phenomenon, the solution must lie in realising that we are one another before we are ourselves, that the 'I' *is* the We, and therefore that all activity should be undertaken with humanity as a whole and more specifically with the community amongst whom we live – at the foundation of our self-consciousness. Solidarity properly interpreted, means us being one with all our existential needs and desires which we solve as answers to social needs and desires. The context of participating in Transition initiatives will not in itself bring about secular revelation but provide an enabling environment, encouraging deep changes in orientation and thinking as a mutual educational process as, step by step, the sincerity of members' words and their translation into actions becomes confirmed as unquestioning trust.

There will surely be community initiatives that break down, where trust is not achieved and where continued mutual effort becomes impossible[486]. Indeed, very many Intentional Communities over the past decades degenerated into conflict and non-workability. Abrams and McCulloch,[487] who produced a rigorous and perceptive analysis of the Intentional Communities in the UK in the mid-1970s, noted the immense difficulty of members of these communities to break out of the context of Possessive Individualism – of self-commodification - in spite of the realisation that this was a problem and the aspiration in many communities was to overcome it[488].

The effort almost always ended in exhaustion and failure of the communities in their attempts to break through to a genuine community of trust and sincerity, with there being no doubt of the fundamental problem being the inability of such communities to escape from the realities and ethos of the society which surrounded them as a constant force and threat[489]. We can expect that the collapse of modern society over the coming decades will, as it progressively fails on its own terms, release this constraint on jettisoning the armour of Possessive Individualism, with the deep competitive mistrust that this generates, and may appear in many communities as secular revelation. But it is less likely to emerge without focused consciousness of the problematic amongst community members and whilst the more coherent Transition initiatives undertake all manner of group activities that combine substantive activity with the building of mutual trust and confidence, in the context of the understanding that 'we' *is* 'me'.

A New Understanding of Nature

This brings us to the question of reconstituting our relations with the totality of our environment, of which the social environment is but one dimension. The truth is that we cannot immediately envisage a return to precivilisation consciousness where humanity identified themselves not as individuals or even as communities but as nature, of which their selves were but a constituent of the whole in place and time. But we *can* aspire towards this as an ultimate goal. In Chapter Four, we discussed the development in recent decades of environmental ethics and philosophy where Deep Ecology and the notion of the Ecological Self re-discovered the one-ness of nature and humanity not as atoms or parts but as human consciousness that creates contingent structures — in the case of civilisation walls and ramparts — to structure life. It was noted that the notion has been one of the individual extending without intermediate structure, to nature as a whole. We should, however, realise the bridge of human community[490] which creates the particular consciousness and thence practical life that is a vital intermediary opens out the passage for all to relate directly to the natural world which they inhabit, not one, as in civilisation, that closes the passage of the individual to nature through the existence of nature as Property.

Earlier in this chapter we discussed the nature of consciousness and concluded that self-consciousness is arrived at through a process of identifying with and understanding the world through the evolving consciousness of our culture or community. The Ecological Self is essentially a recognition of this understanding of 'what it is to be human' and then, clearing aside the walls created by civilisation in the individual self-consciousness, to realise that consciousness is but a dimension of nature, created by nature as the particular quality of being human. Human consciousness writ large is nature's self-consciousness and in this way the individual human self-consciousness is a creation of the self-consciousness of nature through education, enculturation and socialisation.

Freya Mathews, whose concept of the Ecological Self is the base concept around which we should aspire to see ourselves in nature, goes on to write of a 'panpsychist perspective'[491], where the universe and thence the biosphere, coming to focus intensively on the immediate landscape which we come to inhabit, has to become understood as a continuum from the outside in, as the essential us. The sheer fecundity of the universe and of nature, and above all, today, the way that it continues to be reproductive in spite of the aggressive onslaught of modernity, is something of unfathomable beauty that civilisation has progressively blanked out of consciousness in its obsession with Development and Consumption. We forget who, what and where we are in the cacophony of Modern life. A panpsychist perspective is the notion that a sane and healthy human psyche is one that *a priori* understands how consciousness originated as a dimension of nature, and is constantly renewing and evolving, which keeps it alive, and it is also something of great beauty of which our civilisation denies us experience. Acknowledged as our proper perspective on life, it is also something, the details of which we must take responsibility for in the wake of the discovery of the destruction we have demonstrated ourselves as being capable of bringing about.

In various places in this chapter there has appeared what might seem a contradictory view of the role of rationality as a product of consciousness. The contradiction comes from the problematic that, parallel to the aspiration to understand human beings as the same as the consciousness of nature (the Ecological Self) so also comes an aspiration to eliminate the distinction between objectivity and subjectivity. We discussed the way in which the Enlightenment's scientific quest imagined that eventually everything could be resolved into a single objectivity of scientific laws, that everything in the universe and even the thoughts and activities of humans and their societies would be known objectively and hence predictable as the ultimate triumph of human knowledge over nature.

We then went on to give a brief account of the more recent perceptions of the philosophy and sociology of science and of anthropology, that discovered that whilst objectivity can be created momentarily for specific purposes, and has been the basis for the creation of today's Technostructure, that in practice discontinuities abound where fields of objectivity come to an end and new fields open up that are incommensurable and which, in general, signal the way in which objectivity depends in the end on what those practising it aspire to, itself structured through particular cultures. On the small scale this may be in terms of particular scientific experiments and explorations, but which are ultimately created in the context of particular cultures.

We discussed under the heading of science how objectivity and more broadly rationality has been pursued in the context of modern civilisation as handmaiden to the acquisition of power, ostensibly the conquest of nature, but in practice the use of power by some to dominate others with nature as their instrument. Following the aspiration to eliminate hierarchical society, the motivation to pursue science also falls. Whilst this does not mean the sweeping away of all rationality, it does mean that much of the effort that has gone into scientific enquiry will be of no use in the future. The Technostructure that modern civilisation has created and that has come to dominate modern life will also need to be dismantled. In practice, this will occur in any case, as it will simply fall apart due to its reliance on the physical power of fossil energy to function. But what is being said here is that far from regretting this, we should turn away from it and adopt an entirely new attitude towards technology[492] and above all to the issue of what knowledge we actually need to create modest lives in the context of particular communities of people and of nature.

The insistence on objectivity should thus be greatly moderated, understanding the world in the first instance phenomenologically, as intersubjective. Whilst contingently objectivity as usefulness in creating our lives will always be necessary, it should nevertheless always be weighed up with respect to its effect on the environment, with questions asked as to the ethical consequences. Rationality was discussed earlier as embodying thought and action that connects means and ends.

In the first instance we can see that this is the root of all roads to the concentration of power and hence the need always to be aware of the consequences of its use and wary of the ways in which 'one thing leads to another' and hence the possible accumulation of power. Ultimately, for human life, the use of rationality should end in aesthetics, or the creation of life that is deeply satisfying in its resonance with the human need for harmony and beauty. The means of achieving this should be formulated and understood as games, even dances of the transformed human: from Homo sapiens sapiens (intelligent) to Homo faber (productive) and in the process, Homo ludens (playful).

Thus the achievement of the Ecological Self can be expressed most simply as love for nature, including the human community through which this is interpreted. We might start from the romantic love of nature commonly expressed in the appreciation of landscapes that has given us today 'protected areas' and which is not seen at all in terms of use but in terms of satisfaction of human needs precisely through non-intervention and a realisation of the wonder of nature of which we are, after all, an indissoluble part. Some would refer to this as mystical experience. The Ecological Self, however, extends well beyond this, with a structured intervention in nature to fulfil our existential need for food, shelter and the means to create these, while being knowledgeable and empathetic towards the maintenance of rich ecosystems.

Over the past decades, much thought and action has gone into the methodology of Permaculture (and related procedures under other names viz 'ecological farming') which in principle fits well with the implementation of the Ecological Self in active relations with nature. And with regard to shelter, the remains of vernacular architecture around the world give us at least clues of how to rebuild shelter out of the particular environment in which we find ourselves in the future. And finally, it will be necessary to revive hand tools and develop modest technologies – tools, instruments and appliances - to create our new lives, applying a modest rationality but creating even here, things of beauty to carry out activities that are satisfying because they are harmonious with nature, treat her kindly, and are means to satisfying human needs, including the inclination to be creative.

Recapitulation and the Holistic Notion of Community

Scattered across the foregoing text have been references to a return of life in the coming years to communities. It is almost universally acknowledged that, whatever it is, community has been lost in the process of modernisation. Usually this is regretted, even decried. The implication throughout the last two chapters is that the rebuilding of communities will be the only positive way that humanity will be able to find its way, in the coming years, through the fall of modernity. Collapse and chaos may be mitigated through the rebuilding of communities at a local level. And in general this may be seen as a wonderful thing, a homecoming after the adventure of modernity. As Zygmunt Bauman put it in the opening paragraph of his monograph on Community:

Words have meanings: some words, however, also have 'feel'. The word 'Community' is one of them. It feels good: whatever the word 'Community' may mean, it is good 'to have a Community', 'to be in a Community'. If someone wandered off the right track, we would often explain his unwholesome conduct by saying that 'he has fallen into bad company'. *If someone is miserable, suffers a lot and is consistently denied a dignified life, we promptly accuse* society – *the way it is organised, the way it works. Company or society can be bad; but not* Community. *Community, we feel, is always a good thing.*[493]

And yet we have built ourselves societies where community has less and less space or even meaning. Not merely modernity, with its creation of industrial relations and anomic cities, can be seen here as an underlying cause, but going back through civilisation, we can see how this seems consistently to be a destroyer of community relations. Bauman notes Walter Benjamin as going so far as to write that:

Repulsion, not attraction, being history's principle moving force, historical change happens because humans are mortified and annoyed by what they find painful and unpalatable in their condition, because they do not wish these conditions to persist, and because they seek the way to mollify or redress their suffering.[494]

We need to look into this conundrum and undo the problems that have led to the flight from community in the context of the civilising process, if we are to advocate community as the road to saving our future. But before focusing on *human* community, we must look further at how human communities are indissolubly part of the physical environment in which they find themselves and that this also must be understood as being part of Community in the wider sense. Aldo Leopold put it in the following way:

Conservation is getting nowhere because it is incompatible with our Abrahamic concept of land. We abuse land because we regard it as a commodity belonging to us. When we see land as a Community to which we belong, we may begin to use it with love and respect. There is no other way for land to survive the impact of mechanized man, nor for us to reap from it the aesthetic harvest it is capable, under science, of contributing to culture... That land is a Community is a basic concept of ecology, but that land is to be loved and respected is an extension of ethics. That land yields a cultural harvest is a fact long known, but latterly forgotten.[495]

Notwithstanding a particular interpretation of words, we want, in the following paragraphs, to draw out the implications of what is being said here, and then integrate the two concepts of community — ecological and human — that are almost universally seen as subsisting in two separate life compartments, but in practice being one and the same in their implications and need to be understood as such if, as intended in the last section of this book, we are to come to useful conclusions on the 'rebuilding of community'. Here we take first the earth as community and work backwards to human community.

We recapitulate here salient points from earlier in the book that feeds into the discussion to follow. At the outset of his book and further in Chapter Two, we wrote of primitive societies and the unity that they understood between nature, their own small communities and themselves. Whilst we know next to nothing of the path down which particular bands found their way to a sustainable relationship with their ecological setting, we certainly saw even in Modern times the residue of hunting and gathering peoples and the ways of life which they invented to achieve their niche in particular ecological settings.

All appearances are that the extinctions of large species wherever humans penetrated out of Africa was not necessarily a question of hand-to-mouth but could well have been some kind of game[496] — the origins of hunting as sport that is at the same time the discovery of power over nature. When we speak to the issue of Homo Ludens, (human life seen as an interlocking set of games, an eternal dance) we should realise that whilst non-competitive games that might also be dances give aesthetic structure to life, they also open the door to 'power games' that in the future should have the word 'danger' inscribed over the door that leads in this direction. The reduction of large animals throughout Eurasia, Australasia and the Americas was the first major impact on the reduction of biodiversity perpetrated by the presence of Homo sapiens.

Irrigation of extensive land adjacent to major rivers and with it the draining of wetlands are seen as the first step in the construction of civilisation and here already the significant purposeful modification of ecosystems to suit the needs and desires of mankind. The growth of mining, initially small scale but with the development of civilisation more extensive, with mining wastes poisoning surrounding landscapes and the depletion of forests for pit props and the smelting of metals, gradually grew into a significant impact on the ecology of the environs of mine locations. Towns grew into cities, almost always on ecologically rich land, with the surroundings converted to agriculture, again thrusting aside existing ecosystems and evolving new, almost always less diverse, ecosystems with a reduced number of species continuing to survive in the interstices where they could accommodate the new circumstances and a few finding the new circumstances congenial to their spread.

With European expansion across the seas, species from Europe entered local ecosystems around the globe and species were brought home[497]. Sometimes this was intentional with no concern, no understanding for the ecological consequences. This included the introduction of goats to islands that, whilst devastating local ecologies, reproduced such that passing ships would be able to harvest them for meat, and more broadly the crossing of the oceans of species such as corn, potatoes, tomatoes, sugar, coffee and rubber, horses, cattle and chickens, and hundreds of others, from their original ecosystems to places where these could be grown or bred in large quantities to satisfy the consumption desires initially of Europe. But at the same time species smuggled themselves on boats that, once arriving on foreign soils, proceeded to attack or displace local species, in almost all cases reducing biodiversity.

As populations grew, so landscapes were altered, usually in phases, one overtaking the other but always leaving traces with, in most cases, something of the pre-existing ecosystem surviving but eventually with biodiversity devastated. There is much evidence of the way in which Mediterranean cultures, two millennia ago devastated local ecosystems to produce for their needs, which even as less voracious cultures subsequently occupied some of the territories, these never regained anything like the preceding ecological richness. We can assume that as civilisation spread through China, India and subsequently Western Europe, biodiversity gave way to the spread of human civilisations. The evolution of the English landscape over two thousand years was carefully traced by W.G. Hoskins,[498] but only recently has archaeology developed methods to analyse the steps along which the original ecology was reduced. Even today, impacts of modernity are resulting in a steady decline in biodiversity in the British Isles and we can be sure that this is the case almost everywhere, as sketched in the massive Millennium Ecosystems Assessment[499].

Aldo Leopold provides a sketch of intervention in North Central United States in terms of the waves of colonisation starting from trapping, through logging and swidden agriculture to vast intensive agriculture monocultures and, in areas less suited to agriculture, the impacts of hunting and thence tourism. Of course the native population had made their own impacts, which were increased with the introduction by the Europeans of horses and guns, quite independent of the presence of European immigrants. However, the latter came rapidly to make major changes across almost the complete American landscape, at a minimum felling almost the complete original forest. Although significant areas once farmed reverted to secondary forest, the ecology had been irreversibly altered and where lands were opened up and valleys inundated by dams and irrigated fields extended over vast areas, the face of the land had become something unrecognisable with respect to the ecological richness preceding the arrival of Europeans.

Over the late 19th and early 20th century many landscapes of the non-occidental world were transformed by plantations in colonial territories — we think, for instance, of the transformation of the Ceylonese and Malayan landscapes by British enterprise growing tea and rubber — and yet still leaving large areas to the original inhabitants. With the curbing of disease (especially, in tropical countries, malaria) indigenous populations grew rapidly and thus progressively colonised rainforests. In the Thai case, where until the end of the 19th century settlement was confined to the hinterland of Bangkok and then in clearings up the river valleys, the end of feudalism signalled a process of new peasant villages moving progressively into the hinterland, followed as the 20th century progressed by the organisation of the rice processing and export industries[500], with dams and extensive rice monoculture. The wide central plain of Luzon, the main island of the Philippines, the wide deltas of the Mekong and Red Rivers in Vietnam and the whole northern coast of Java became vast, monotonous rice paddies created directly or indirectly by Occidental overlords in the name of Development.

Over massive areas of Latin America, exploitation of ecosystems continued to devastate biodiversity in Brazil, already erasing most of the littoral and hinterland rainforest to make way for coffee plantations that covered the whole state of Rio de Janeiro, resulting after a century in permanent depletion of the soils, that now support only rough grasslands, thinly exploited by cattle. In addition there is the famous continuation of the reduction of the Amazon rainforest for timber, minerals, vast artificial lakes and clearance for cattle farming. The list is endless.

All the while, whilst we see the survival even of small bands of primitive people and the creation of new, what we might refer to as traditional communities — albeit in most cases new also in their autonomy from traditional rules of social rank and responsibilities — the major changes took place in land given over to monocultures, producing for distant markets. Even in traditional villages of subsistence farmers, land became increasingly commodified and the focus increasingly on production for income and profit. The sense of those living on the land, although in many southern countries still with significant peasant communities, became decreasingly one of community with landscape and Nature, particularly as and when peasants became employees, or in communist countries members of a collective. They no longer had any tangible responsibility for, or sense of belonging to, what was happening.

The means of farming were also changing, with mechanisation and the introduction everywhere of agrochemicals. These added significantly to the capacity to reduce biodiversity and then their actual impact. Furthermore, there can be no doubt at all of the role that the exploitation and dissemination of fossilised energy sources is playing in all these process. Industrialisation produced increasingly powerful means of changing agricultural practices and in moving the produce over greater distances. And as we have analysed throughout this book, there really is no substitute for fossil fuels to support these kinds of farming: organic methods could be used and, indeed, biofuels to run the machines, but besides the lack of development of these, simple calculations soon reveal that this progress (fortunately, seen from an ecological standpoint) could not survive the ebbing away of fossilised hydrocarbons.

Changes in landscapes and the means of accomplishing these were constantly accelerating with, over the past fifty years, increasingly devastating impacts upon ecology and, indeed, the very shape of the earth's geography. Whilst mining in the past was often a community activity and one which often involved a hard and sometimes extremely exploitative way of life, with mechanisation these were severed from almost any locally-rooted community, becoming larger and increasingly open cast, laying waste to vast landscapes, wiping out ecosystems and any possibility of local human communities, let alone any idea of community with nature. The capping of a whole mountain range in West Virginia and the rape of the Athabasca river valley in Alberta were referred to earlier as the most shocking of these developments and the possible devastation that will start with the craving to access oil from shale is nothing but a frightful vision of ecological destruction.

But the methods of farming and the extension of monocultures, not only of wide-open spaces of the United States and Canada, Brazil and Argentina but even in the nature of farming in Europe, where fields expanded and massive vehicles race across them ploughing, dispensing agrochemicals and then harvesting the serried stands of rapeseed, corn, sunflowers, grain, vegetables and fruit. In spite of demand in the supermarkets for 'free range eggs' and 'biological milk', animals were predominantly housed in giant warehouses, forced to grow faster and harvested as if they were parts of the machinery, rather than sentient beings. The land that came under these regimes was constantly extending into the last areas of prehistoric landscapes. The love of the land and the gratefulness to nature for yielding produce had almost entirely disappeared.

But a further despoiler of land as nature was the massive extension of urbanisation, the scattering of houses across vast landscapes as suburbia, exurbia and holiday homes and the means to connect these up: roads, power lines, water infrastructure. And even where landscapes were entirely hostile to human developments, these became commodified as targets of hunters and for recreation that included the frenetic activities of skiing and mountain biking, trekking and mountaineering, and then invasion of coastlines for 'relaxation', all with somehow a nostalgia for the love of nature but carried out *de facto* as conquest and ecological devastation.

As the modern world comes to an end and the downward passage starts towards another world that will eventually, the depredations of global warming willing, revive rich ecological processes, the enormity of what has been wrought on nature by modern civilisation may be expected to become increasingly evident to the dwindling human populations. In the first instance, sheer survival and the organisation of life imploding to the local will be a primary preoccupation, with the potential means to plan this with some kind of coherence discussed in the two foregoing chapters. It will be difficult to learn again the love of landscape and the fecundity of nature for almost all of the surviving humanity, both because this is an entirely new kind of thought and feeling to those growing up in urban settings and because the result of developments described above will reveal themselves as devastatingly unlovable in the context of the decay of modern interventions.

If nature revives amongst the ruins of modernity, it will be beholden upon human communities, relearning the production and living of life predominantly at a local level, to learn initially gratefulness to her and thence love of her beauty, returning to the land as the interaction of the community of species, including our own. Over much of the world, and certainly throughout the heartlands of the Occident, the great cities will be abandoned and amongst the ruins of suburbia, new human communities established that will have to quickly learn how to produce their lives from the surrounding landscape. But if this remains instrumental, then the communities will not survive. There will need, purely rationally, to be a sense of the limits of use and abuse of the resources of the landscape. But this cannot last long without the emergence of a deeper sense of responsibility and thence a love of the land and the ecosystems it supports, so that conservation, whilst producing from the landscape, is maintained into the undefined future.

Thus, working the land without the assistance of fossil energy sources and the machines that this has powered will surely in the first instance in most places revert to what it often was in the past: a drudgery of hard work with nature a stern task master made more difficult by the process of clearing away the debris and other legacies of modernity and the revival of natural soils. Love of nature will not emerge automatically but will become possible again by proximity and everyday contact and relations with particular landscapes. It will be necessary in the first instance to gain a living from nature for knowledge of the relations that communities might have with the local flora and fauna: what can be eaten and what is poison, what can be used for medicinal purposes and how these can be managed. Locally exotic and foreign species (as is the case of almost all farmed crops) should be assessed for their compatibility with local species and whether, under a regime of organic farming, these will remain appropriate. But knowledge of nature is also the foundation of a deeper love, such as the witnessing of the changing seasons, the expectation of spring and the way in which nature revives, the return of migrating birds and the appearance of the young; the appearance and unfolding of perennial plants and of the flowers; then the maturing and interplay of multitudes of plants and animals over the summer months....

It will be necessary to organise the revival of local production as an intensively cooperative exercise. But the love of nature, whilst being initiated in community activity, will be something that each individual comes to experience and feel through individual contemplation and solitary communing and discovering of particular local landscapes, investing again with spiritual qualities particular rocks and trees or runs of local streams or hilltops. Whilst the generations experiencing the collapse of modernity will start down the road to the love of nature as something alien and strange, those born into the emerging local communities will have the opportunity to experience from the start of life the facts of nature surrounding them and communities should become aware of the need to encourage all born in them to be intensively exposed to nature. Most children born in the countryside, if given the opportunity and encouragement, will explore and learn spontaneously their surrounding landscape and involvement of all young people also in farming opens the way to a universal sense of the one-ness of Self and nature.

We focus now on the human dimension of community. When we discussed earlier in this chapter the way in which humans send out the 'I' in search of reality, there was an assumption that we would be motivated to do so and that, surely, is one of the wonders of 'being human': the curiosity and motivation and then, when the result returns, the conviction, the commitment and eventually the love that enables humans not just to make sense of the world but to actively empathise with, and thence participate in local society and in the processes of nature and the man-made environment where they find themselves. Hence it is that societies cohere and people cooperate.

But the totality of the result can so easily go wrong and fail to satisfy human needs either contingently or systematically and it is the systematic failure of the vast variety of social arrangements produced by civilisation, which almost always produce social hierarchy and the inner walls, and frustrations of the resulting Alienated condition, that has been a major focus of this chapter. The issue is: can this, in the context of the future we face, be transcended in the creation and institutionalisation of communities without hierarchy?

At the start of this section, we referred to the notion, as posited by Walter Benjamin, that the whole history of mankind (we would add: in the context of civilisation) has been motivated by repulsion, not by attraction, by flight from, rather than aspiration and attraction towards. The watchword of modern civilisation is 'Freedom!' Somehow we all want to be free. But free of what? The main sense of the concept as it arose in the Enlightenment was 'freedom from tyranny', that meant the abolition of the Divine Right of Kings which eventually found its resolution in the creation of today's representative democratic governments. Clearly, however, the story doesn't end there.

Freedom means being free of any kind of domination, however overt, covert and even subconscious and so the 'will to be free' has found itself, today, trapped in the treadmill of competitive society where relative freedom simply means being superior (proven by relative wealth and display of what are considered socially to be symbols of proof) to 'the other'.

Community, and the warmth that the notion evokes, is very far from the concept of freedom as understood today, in fact is ultimately its opposite. But perhaps true freedom is to be found in the casting off of the armour of Possessive Individualism and the rebirth of the individual human being as community. Community is, in prosaic terms, the security against the failure of freedom to produce satisfactory results in terms not just of physical but of emotional needs. At a deeper level it is the merging of the individual into the reality of the community, the personality of which becomes the personality of the individual.

In the real world, individual life has to be organised and executed but this is done by agreement, maybe negotiated but ultimately, in the context of true community, tacit, where the understanding is common and in greater measure mutually understood without rationalisation or words. It can only exist where there is complete sincerity on the part of all and complete trust in the sincerity of others and where the needs of others are felt as one's own needs. Thus the drive for freedom is the flight from the pain and indignity that results from the context of competitive, hierarchical society and the Alienation that this generates. Of course the very existence of civilisation is the result of some people capturing and manipulating the tendency to cohere in communities; we might refer to manipulation of the instinct to love.

So before discussing how in the future we might return to a situation where community can be built without being captured and manipulated, we need to look at how, in the past, this trick has been accomplished, so we are aware of what has to be overcome. 'Traditional' societies in recent centuries, before the discovery of fossil fuels and the acceleration into the 'state of Development', emerged sometimes violently, sometimes by stealth, as tacit agreements of different groups succumbing to particular roles and these becoming fixed and usually subsisting over hundreds if not thousands of years. These were reproduced by assumptions built into families and their associated peers of what people's role in life should be and were always subjected to the domination of elites.

Earlier sketches were presented of the way in which slave, caste and Confucian societies operated in ways that became self-reproducing through a combination of ideology (usually confirmed or tacitly framed by religion) and force. This, it was asserted, was how things should be and to step out of line was to be ostracised or dealt with through legitimised forms of violence. There were always dissidents, including travelling people trading and bringing entertainment and news, and small groups retreated into more or less organised and accepted quietist religious groups, the ultimate retreat being hermits. But for the majority of people work, both for their own subsistence and for the greater glory and comfort of elites, was the everyday reality and society was organised around the prevailing Mode of Production. Community (or maybe we should refer to surrogate community) existed under these circumstances, where some kind of reciprocity existed, even if this was blatantly unequal, and the poor came even to admire, if not to love, their 'superiors'[501], ultimately as 'the love of God'.

We discussed how the very possibility of community seems to have taken its distance from modern society and that it has, indeed, become difficult today even to speak of anything by way of coherent society[502]. So how did this come about and what does it mean to have almost totally diffused the sentiments that in the past built communities — real and surrogate? Focusing on the progress of modernity, we can identify a prehistory in the dissolution of medieval society, and then three distinct phases of social (or anti-community) development in the march towards 'global society'.

The early slide out of rank societies took place as towns in Europe (developing in different parts of the subcontinent at different rates as settlements took on particular economic roles) began to absorb escapees from feudal bonds of the villages. The Great Plagues, spreading from Asia in the mid-14th century, facilitated this escape as the lords were no longer able to hold on to their serfs, increasing numbers of whom were able to find work for a wage. In England this accelerated through 'enclosure' where lords and freeholders divided the land between them, evicting the lower orders to search for a living wherever they could, in order to develop the land more extensively for the production of wool and later crops[503]. 'City air is free' was the watchword of the escapees right across Europe, who could attain higher status and in the process, the production of goods and then the increase in trade initiated what grew into proto-capitalism and what we think of today as the 'middle class', or in Continental Europe the 'bourgeoisie', as the prototype of the Modern, putative ideal citizen.

The first phase of true Modernism, when fossil fuel began to energise the acceleration of economic and with it social change, was the 19th century, as the first century of industrialisation. We can see distinctly how society became divided up in ways that squeezed the very possibility of community out of social relations. On the one hand, the bourgeoisie, already wearing the clothes fashioned by Mandeville and Adam Smith, were adapting themselves to a world of individualistic competition. In England, the birthplace and ideological wellspring of this liberalism, there remained a deep hypocrisy, well-captured in the literature of the late eighteenth century[504], where money was what really mattered to advance status but that marrying into aristocracy, and in general the idea that one came from a family that had long-range status, was what was pretended, to achieve 'deep' status. Under these circumstances, community in the sense of solidarity between classes in particular places faded away and the bourgeoisie became mobile and urban in their search for personal wealth and status, with diminishing room for empathy for the rest. This was made clear by the cleric Thomas Malthus in his 'theory of population' that asserted that if left to reproduce, the poor will always eventually reach the limits of the availability of food to the detriment of the whole society: so no succour should be dispensed to the poor.

On the other hand, community continued in places and in circumstances where the emergent working classes found little or no benefit in the self-commodification of the bourgeoisie. Forced to sell their labour for no more than a subsistence living, solidarity was a natural stance. Of course this came to a head by the end of the 19th century, with the growth of all manner of utopian proposals and organisations that would vindicate the working classes and in some cases would reinstate community to achieve this (Fourier, Kropotkin), in its most radical form as egalitarian utopian communities, and eliminate the pretentions and with it the sordid sleaze and hypocrisies of the bourgeoisie, through revolution.

The containment of trade unionism to make only modest demands and, more tragically, the failure of the Soviet Union to meet the promise of a truly classless society, led nevertheless into a new phase of social relations. The horrors of the First World War broke the growing working class movements of the West but precipitated the creation of the Soviet Union. The elites of the United States and the Soviet Union both declared their societies to be an ideal, each promoting a vision of what modern society should be, with the rest of the world being coerced or seduced into following one or the other of these visions. There were no compromises or alternatives, just modernity in this or that form. Most nations, in pursuing whichever of the ideals they followed (often as not the choice was made under duress) actively suppressed minority cultures, languages and 'traditional' community as being at best, parochial, and at worst, subversive. Allegiance was to the Nation-State and, even where not authoritarian, the ideology was one that manipulated the people into participating in mass-society, reinforced through the growth in size of enterprises and the massification of urbanising populations living in endless suburbs (the United States) or housing estates (USSR), with welfare dispensed through bureaucracies.

On the surface, the ideology of Development justified Government control, operationalised through growing bureaucracies. Beneath the surface, competition not only between systems but through nationalism commanded allegiance and diminished what might otherwise have been overt resistance. In the Soviet Union, the possibilities of resistance were stifled through authoritarian violence. By the 1960s, however, in the United States and to a lesser extent in Europe, dissatisfactions boiled over into urban unrest, indicating rising dissatisfaction and culminating in the non-revolutions of 1968.

Much of this was not actually a problem for elites insofar as it involved conflicts between groups; always inconclusive but facilitating a divide-and-rule approach to social management. The one form of resistance amongst the lower orders (or of an alternative political force) recognised as legitimate through this era was trade unionism which, however, had been channelled into a highly stylised set of rituals that were in no way genuinely threatening to elites and where solidarity rarely came in the form of community[505] but rather as a struggle for a greater share of the accumulating wealth of modern society.

The third phase of Modern development came as the final onslaught of bourgeois ideology to incorporate society as a whole. It is not coincidental that this revolved in the British case, as being the heartland of modern ideology, around Margaret Thatcher's assault on the power of the trade unions, as revenge for the demise of the Conservative Government under the impact of the miner's strike of 1974. From now on, individualist competition would be the basic ideology upon which life everywhere would be organised. Of course legacies of previous phases persisted or died away slowly. For instance Nationalism was very effectively used to bring society in line, notably with the Falklands conflict and then 9/11 and in many parts of the world incipient conflict between nations being used by elites to maintain power in their hands.

Furthermore, increasing globalisation, whilst facilitating the breaking up of community with the extension of urbanisation, nevertheless encouraged ethnic communities to form where significant numbers from one country had accumulated in foreign cities. However, these were not communities in any traditional sense, instead providing little more than mutual entertainment and in some cases policing of traditional values and social relations within the community, with their members increasingly pursuing the consumerist goals of contemporary modernism. Furthermore, whilst 'community' might be inferred in the spread of 'gated communities', in practice these were expressions of the continuing self-isolation of particular layers of the splintering social hierarchy, to decrease the very need to encounter any other kinds of people. Within the walls, few residents would have anything but the most superficial knowledge, feelings or friendship with their neighbours.

And finally, whilst in the area of work, 'easy-come-easy-go' became increasingly the experience of all: forced as 'flexibilisation' on the working classes which, by now, were difficult even to identify as a distinct class, and adopted by those more fortunate who could forego permanent employment and rejected any idea of a 'calling' or career path. The same was increasingly true of friendships that became more temporary and contingent, with family empathies receding and marriage itself becoming increasingly subject to break-up. Physical relocation of families and individuals became ever commoner — in the Occident, being relocated by employers or moving between employment and physically between places (by now between cities, with residence in suburbs of sameness).

Meanwhile, in what were still called 'developing countries', rural-urban migration, both to larger cities and with the expansion of rural towns into cities, was leaving a minority of populations, often enough just the elderly and the very young, in traditional village communities. The urgency of this frenetic movement precluded the formation of any meaningful form of local community. Small groups of friends were forged with continual entry and exit and associations for sport, recreation and hobbies persisted whilst religions provided some kind of group security as surrogate community. But whilst depth could still be achieved in allegiance and love, this was almost always of a fleeting kind, for instance increasingly public mass entertainment events, and with almost no breadth in terms of engagement in making a life together and a coherent creation of a shared environment.

The present condition has for most of humanity floated off into a dream world even in conditions of relative hardship, the facility to move on and the accoutrements of the Consumer Society, complete with continuous forms of entertainment, crowd out any deeper thinking and feeling process about the meaning of life or any sense of direction or purpose. Live now and don't think too hard about what is in store! And yet the beginnings of the end of this phase of modern development presaging the downward passage, is just starting and being felt by some, though as yet immediately reacting to this is assumed to be a temporary state of affairs against which contingent action is taken, mostly individual but increasingly as demonstrations and riots. Minimal thought is yet given to the way in which life will be closing in, movement increasingly restricted and access to the stream of physical comforts and entertainment reduced, step by step.

That life will fundamentally change, that this is more than a new phase of modernity, together with the whole associated mental outlook and processes of self-realisation in the social context, is as yet faced up to by a minute proportion of the global population, even though intellectually there is a widespread sense that we are living an end-game. There can be little doubt that the fall ahead will thrust most of humanity back to life at a very local level and whilst this will certainly be a shocking experience for the present generation, with vast numbers declining and exiting simply from disorientation, in reality it both presents the situation where local community cooperation will be the only solution to the loss of the means to living and at the same time can be understood as an opportunity to rediscover and rebuild community not merely as a basis for individual security but as the mode of understanding what it is to be human.

Clearly, starting to think about how we might form a community with the people in our immediate neighbourhood is, almost everywhere, incredibly daunting. Very few people today have more than the slightest empathetic relations with their neighbours and even where there has been effort, such as in gated communities, to cluster with 'people like us', communication is usually minimal or incipiently hostile in terms of competition or on petty bases of individual enmity.

The idea of working in any meaningful way with immediate neighbours has almost everywhere become virtually incomprehensible. There is no direct formula for recreating community amongst neighbouring strangers and prima facie, where life is becoming more difficult, even within neighbourhoods, some will feel the problems more than others and in a world of universal competition, there will, in the first instance, be very little inclination to provide any mutual assistance. All will fall individually.

However, Transition initiatives have understood the need to rebuild – in most cases build from ground zero – community spirit as an essential prerequisite for undertaking activity that will rebuild the means to survival and, beyond that, enjoyable lives. The past two chapters discussed how the rebuilding of the local organisation of life might be undertaken. And whilst Transition communities are initiating participatory planning processes and activities (it will be recalled that urban and peri-urban farming is a natural starting point) initial groups are self-selected individuals coming from different neighbourhoods and comprising a tiny part of wider town or city. It should be emphasised that there is already a keen awareness amongst some of these groups that it is not only the technical aspects of joint activity with which they should be concerned – such as farming to achieve food security in a world which threatens no longer to supply food – and many, maybe most, of these initiatives spend substantial amounts of time and energy on confirming solidarity and building trust between members[506].

There is, here, already a high awareness of the meaning of, and need for, community and the systematic way in which it has to be built. We might say that this is the ethos on which most Intentional Communities of recent years have been structured and whilst, as noted earlier, there have been great difficulties in realising true community when surrounded by the outside world and its prevailing values and presumptions. We can only presume that with failure in its own terms at the heart of modernity, that the pressures to conform to the values of individualist competitive search for status will fall away and that the need for cooperation for sheer survival will at the same time provide a seedbed for the successful building of mutualistic empathy and community.

Whilst as yet many Transition initiatives are little more than the meeting of small groups, the potential demonstrated by those that are more effective is to draw in more participants. 'Bonding' activities, as they are sometimes referred to, that are games about living and working together can, in the longer run, only be truly effective if the groups undertake real life activities to produce food or manufacture things or provide services of some kind and in general *build* their communities as a way of life[507]. And in this way the ethos of competition between neighbours can be broken down by inviting them to join. Transition groups are predominantly egalitarian, contrasting with associations in the past that have been insistently hierarchical with 'officers' elected to manage activities and where such offices gave status. Clearly some individuals take more initiative and/or dedicate more time to the activities, but the ethos of Transition groups, as with Intentional Communities, is the regular exchange and sharing of roles whilst at the same time promoting skills when these become evident, and encouraging their further development, with the whole group benefiting.

Eventually groups become too large and splinter. This is necessary insofar as group identification becomes increasingly impersonal with size and participation. It is already difficult for some, out of enculturated or character modesty, to feel involved, or take active part. Difficulties can then start to arise from a presumption, on grounds of 'greater efficiency', of the need for leadership, which is then taken on by those who are inclined to be more forceful in their opinions or activity.

It is impressive how many Transition initiatives attempt to reach out across old class and newer ethnic divides to become genuinely inclusive. However, at this stage, this remains symbolic insofar as the bulk of participants are actually from a very narrow stratum of present-day society. As the downward passage accelerates, it will rapidly become evident how little inclination or understanding of what transition means there is amongst the mass of the population, particularly those suffering social exclusion through poverty, ethnic, including language, barriers, and the active self-exclusion on class grounds or of particular religious groups. Even more problematic, however, will be (as, of course already) the self-exclusion of elites who, even as the downward passage increases in evidence with growing poverty and hardship, will attempt, as long as they have the financial and political means, not merely to avoid participation in nascent community-building but to actively destroy it — by stealth or by a resurgence of authoritarianism.

There has, over the past few decades, been a long-running debate on whether integration, or 'multiculturalism', should be pursued. Cities the world over, some to an extreme degree, have absorbed peoples not only from all over the country but from all over the world. Cities in the Americas and Australasia in any case were created through immigration from many countries and whilst sections of these communities became integrated into the 'middle class' mainstream so that only their names indicate their origin, nevertheless more or less large ethnic communities have persisted and in cities that were once peopled more or less exclusively by peoples born in the cities or migrating over relatively small distances, today more or less large, diverse ethnic minorities are to be found in most cities around the world. Whilst forced integration (and hence discrimination against those who for whatever reason have difficulties integrating) must be avoided, the danger of multiculturalism resulting in groups not only performing different roles but with these also possessing different status is everywhere clearly evident as a deeply institutionalised modern expression of class-divided society.

In rebuilding local communities on an egalitarian basis, we can conjecture that different ethnic communities might persist and simply confederate with neighbouring communities. Superficially this seems like a reasonable solution and is certainly held to be sensible by large numbers of those who, for whatever reason — as academics, policy-makers, social service workers and so on — are involved in ongoing discussions on the issue. However, realistically, this cannot work in the longer term and as the globalised world is in a state of collapse, the current situation where ethnic communities can fantasise about going home and actually continue to communicate y with their erstwhile home (visiting from time to time and sending 'remittances' that sustain families back home) will come to an end and there will be a constant danger of some communities, already overtly exploited, falling into caste-like conditions over and against surrounding dominant, indigenous communities.

There are many cases where cities have possessed ethnic or religious neighbourhoods that have remained stable over centuries such as in the medinas of the Middle East, where different religious communities practised their own religions and interacted economically with neighbouring communities inside the city walls over millennia. However, perturbations on various grounds led to perennial conflicts, pogroms and massacres of the kind that one has seen often enough more recently in Africa. However, integration of communities within particular spaces had, until the last two millennia of history, almost everywhere been the eventual norm. Possibly no modern nation can boast populations that have not been forged from more than one (usually many) ethnic roots. Overt ethnic communities continuing through time and sharing countries with mainstream nations are either the consequence of actual separation of territory (such as is the case with primitive tribes in remote areas or migrations from earlier centuries, such as German communities in Romania and Brazil) or through shared ideologies that may be religious or the consequence of tribal and clan affiliations transmitted through families.

We would suggest two matters for future consideration. The first involves agreements to form integrated societies on different territory, perhaps neighbouring, that might develop significantly different 'ethnic' cultures from one territory to another, where these can be self-reliant; that is to say they have sufficient population and resources to be self-sustaining over time without significant dependence on resources from elsewhere. This would never mean autarky and, furthermore, neighbouring communities would ideally confederate or even merge, to provide mutual assistance on issues where this could enhance life and where a renegotiation of the parameters of the culture creates a new unity. Trade will always exist but should be kept within modest bounds (in any case necessitated in the future by the radical decline in means of transport that we can expect in the future) and above all should not cause one community to exploit the people or environment of another. Later we discuss in more detail the basic parameters of such communities, combined with the discussion of the foregoing chapter concerned with the redefinition of territory in the process of the fall of Modern Civilisation.

It should be clear that it is entirely illegitimate to establish such communities on territory already occupied by others. If other communities already exist in areas where single-ethnic communities want to migrate into, then it is beholden upon them to start from a position of being inclined to integration and thus to be entirely open to the second consideration. Today the case of Israel is salient where there is an assumption — we might call it theocratic — that Jews should not only have their own country but that this should occupy a place which their forefathers left thousands of years ago and now systematically insist on usurping the present inhabitants, even though most of those aiding the process have nothing to complain about the place where their forefathers ended, be it in Russia, the United States or Australia, Morocco, South Africa or Argentina, etc. Here it is the insistence on difference that is wholly in the mind that has to fade away if we are to see a future viable world[508].

The second consideration is that within a given territory there be a systematic de-escalation of ideological differences as, in the coming decades, a major objective of all communities. This becomes the difficult point with regard to the 'melting' or 'melding' of ideological differences in a world where so many different ideological standpoints occupy the same urban territory. We have seen, particularly in recent years in the Middle East, that when political disruptions occur, ideological differences can quickly escalate into violent intercommunity struggles between factions, with objectively the most minor differences in terms of outward manifestations of the different ideologies. Indeed many such conflicts involving tribal and clan altercation are amongst people with little or no discernible physical or lifestyle differences and so are a matter of no more than identity transmitted through malformed education and religiously-inspired obsession.

Initiatives and methodologies for conflict resolution have been explored in recent years but have been used only in few conditions. In future the need will grow strongly and methodologies should be learned and applied as an integral process of new community development[509]. In the political sphere, particularly in the Middle East, there are both deeply implicated political forces at national and local level that have created and fuelled ideological conflict for their own purposes in the context of locally specific class lines, consolidating under the surface particular powerful people and oligarchies and used to achieve economic gain for some. As the downward passage from modernity accelerates in the coming years, there will be increasing dangers of such conflict-generating political activity that does no more than define who, within existing political and religious hierarchies, will occupy elite positions. These must be resisted through the use of conflict resolution initiatives and patient work of undoing often deep-seated ideological visions and dogmas.

It cannot be overstressed that the ebbing away of ideological and intercommunity conflict and differences will only work where, from the start, there is a mutual respect between people of different perspectives, at the level of human needs[510]. This, indeed, will be the heart of community-building: the construction of a replacement for old social and religious dogmas by a mutual agreement on what is essential about life and how this should be built to satisfy the psychological and physical needs of all within the constraints of the territory occupied by the community.

We might hazard that success in the long-term will only be achieved through institutionalised mutual respect on equal terms turned to long-run love for the community and all who inhabit it: 'I am you before I am myself', where 'you' is not only all members of the community but also the piece of nature which the community inhabits. Perhaps most of the components that made up religious beliefs of the past will fade away over time in the face of the fundamental change in outlook that the coming circumstances will necessitate: morality and ethics are negotiable on a continuous basis, without dogmatic insistence, along the lines of case law: precedent is accumulated wisdom but can always be changed in the process of social discourse.

Research over recent decades has produced vast accumulated knowledge of origins from the creation and structure of the universe to the history of how we came to be what and where we are. This should be more than enough to satisfy what in the past has been the need for mythological justification and inner self-confidence of communities. The way in which this translated to nationalism in the context of civilisation, driven by the will to power and the frustrations and indignities of hierarchical society, should be definitively expunged through the mutual trust and common purpose and the building of integrated local lifestyles of each community.

The pursuit of personal status or the 'Glory of the Nation' is replaced by the pursuit of the locally productive and aesthetic life, with imagination but modest expectation in terms of physical expression, for instance, the arts of music and dance and the production of objects of beauty on the basis of agreement on what beauty might be through philosophical discourse, involving all who would want to be involved, together with the production of objects by those deemed to possess and prepared to develop the skills and imagination. Aesthetic rules may stabilise, as often happened in civilisations that persisted over millennia, or may evolve as a passage through landscapes, that admire innovation but reject any importance of individuals and innovators: the individual product is understood as being given birth to by the community as the evolving self-consciousness and lived life of the Community.

There will be place or even need for community ritual to confirm the unity of the community in itself and in nature. Festivities, rituals and totems are to be found everywhere around the world, many of ancient origin redefined to suit religious dogmas and confirm the inevitability and legitimacy of hierarchies (such as royal jubilees and weddings). Whilst Asian – viz Chinese and Indian - festivals have a constancy that goes a long way back in history, Occidental festivals have been woven out of many strands, regularly changing their form and appearance. The main festivals of Christianity in the West, i.e. Easter and Christmas, ostensibly to mark moments in the life of Christ, are actually inherited from pagan times. In the case of Easter, in spite of a convoluted history of association with pagan gods and myths and linking through from the Jewish Passover to the death and resurrection of Christ, at its origin was a celebration, adoration and thanks to nature for her rebirth after the winter.

Indeed, Christianity imposed the celebration of Christ's life upon almost all festivities and almost every day of the year is dedicated to particular saints as the basis for celebration — par for the course of a humanistic, hierarchical and individual centred ideology. Neither nature nor community are celebrated in the Christian world, but find their place in secular celebrations such as fairs (also harking back to ancient times) and music and arts festivals of more modern origins. In recent years 'alternative movements' came to organise events, with some in the UK associated with mythical sites such as Stonehenge (banned by the authorities) and Glastonbury. These did indeed become celebrations of nature and community often with music — even catharsis — at the centre of their activities. Whilst these developed into mass events, their fragmentation, with the collapse of the modern world, into local community events may be the rebirth of the celebration of locality as human and natural community.

To find in today's world how community and nature may be celebrated in ways that encourage the expression of beautiful rituals, dancing and the arts, one has to visit those lacunae that persisted and even developed in quiet niches where modern civilisation penetrated only very late. One stands out particularly on the island of Bali in Indonesia, to where the artists and intellectuals of Java retreated from the advance of Islam. What this produced by way of a culture of constant celebration of life that, at the same time, found intensive ways to live with nature that were at once productive for human need and conserving of the ecosystems (leaving extensive areas of rainforest uninhabited) was a marvel even to the late years of the 20th century when massive tourist invasions that included both 'entertainment' and a substantial voyeurism came increasingly to destroy the coherence of community and nature in Bali.

The sophistication of the architecture, with hundreds of 'mansions' and temples, right down to the individual house compound, gamelan music, the perfection of the dancing, the complex weaving of 'double-ikat' fabric to make the most magnificent costumes for the dance... and whilst this was in an ostensibly caste society, 95% of the population were peasants with no use in the present-day world for the aristocracy or warrior caste. In this context there was and still remains intensively participatory decision-making processes with *subaks* where all rice farmers, landed or landless, decide on the management of the rice irrigation systems each planting season and each village with its *banjar* decision forum[511]

Even more protected was the small Himalayan nation of Bhutan that, although a kingdom[512], runs a Tantric Buddhist society[513], with its intensely artistic bent and celebration of sexuality[514] that, as in Bali, is celebrated continually throughout the year with colourful pageants that celebrate both community and nature and bring community concerns regularly to the surface as rituals that are in practice continuing discourse on what is right and good in what, today, is a changing world[515]. This is combined with a wonderful architecture, both at the level of administration (once-fortresses cum monasteries now also 'local authorities') and the fine vernacular farmhouses even of the economically poorest households.

Although taking dangerous decisions in experimenting with modernisation (allowing a few major modern infrastructure and mining projects to obtain income to pay for modern education and health initiatives, the importing of teachers to reform education and carry this out in the English language, and allowing a small influx of tourists to trek the magnificent Himalayan landscapes) the goal is stated as achieving 'gross national happiness' rather than the accumulation of wealth. Peasant life, which is not easy in such a mountainous landscape, persists with minimal urbanisation. It can be conjectured that the demise of modernity will make little impact and that the strong orientation of social self-expression towards community and nature may continue with relatively little readjustment.

Whilst in many other cultures, festivities, rituals and totems did and in many cases still do focus on the worship of nature and celebration of community, we might imagine also in the Occident the return of Easter to the veneration of the annual rebirth of nature, even Christmas, at the deepening of winter. This last, as available energy ebbs away, will, as in the past, become a daunting, even fearful, time of year, but will be celebrated as the closeness of community, and create all the warmth necessary to see its way through to the spring: giving gifts as a sign of solidarity and not, as today, conspicuous consumption and status. Other festivities inherited from the past may be reoriented towards community celebration and individual communities might institute their own festivities specific to the Community as in Bali and Bhutan.

However, there will be need for constant evaluation of the development of festivities and more generally the lifestyle of the community. In many cases in recent years these have overflowed into intercommunity violence that clearly must be avoided. As the orientation and context of festivities, including social expression through styles of dress and habits, constant vigilance will always be necessary so that these do not degenerate into obsessions where subgroups or individuals are excluded and/or subject to pain and violence. This should apply also to issues of justice where individuals and the community deem others to have violated social codes of criminality. Justice should always focus on bringing errant individuals and groups back into the fold of the community.

Utopia

It seems that the majority of people today who allow themselves to think of the future, have in their minds a premonition that modernity is coming to an end; at a minimum imagining a slide into economic depression coupled with deepening environmental problems , and for many people, a foreboding of apocalyptic collapse. However, maybe we should be turning this on its head and seeing that our current world is a kind of giant madhouse and that the future might reintroduce a more sane world. Today everything is on the move, leaving no time to contemplate and, with this, the insecurity of shallow and yet deeply alienated human relations together with an abject dependence on technologies to hold our activities together. We are obsessed by the accumulation of Stuff, which is more of a problem to finance and manage than a real enjoyment, and then, the constant tension of it. Beyond this is the way in which the putative Development of the world in the framework of modernity has dislocated so many, plunging them into poverty and in the global South sordid urban environments, while small elites everywhere live in bizarre forms of luxury that no previous generation would have imagined.

And so whilst we might be apprehensive about the coming collapse, we should also see this as an opportunity. Not of any shallow kind but the opportunity to realise ways of life that overcome deep-seated historic problems that have been with humanity since the dawn of civilisation. With the falling apart of modernity in what will seem as it unfolds to be truly apocalyptic, at the same time doors are opened, for those who will survive the precipitate downward passage, to escape from the chains of unequal societies (Hegel's unhappy self-consciousness) and create forms of community that, in the future, will realise the full human potential of all.

Civilisation, and particularly modernity, have been presented throughout this book as problematic in the sense of destroying in all of us the equanimity, peace and enjoyment of the human potential in nature. Not only violence but also vicarious pleasure, particularly for elites, has put off the day when we would make efforts to create what most of us know deep down are the solutions to the full realisation of human potential. The main reason for the fear of the future lies precisely in the fear of losing the vicarious but ambivalent pleasures that modernity has showered upon most of humanity over the past decades.

But we can allow ourselves to realise that civilisation has also given us the means to understand our predicament, at least in terms of the physical environment and potentially to plan our way to an ideal future. Science and the extension of rationality have been cast in a poor light in the discourse of this book. Here, however, we should give these some credit for having facilitating engagement with nature in ways that have yielded many benefits. The problem has been the abuse of this engagement, both to fight wars and maintain oppression and then to generate the vicarious pleasures of recent decades to which we refer, all with totally inadequate consideration of our interdependent needs and suppressed empathy with nature. The results of science and the use of this in the context of a return to nature and hence a love of her, rather than aggressive and callous abuse, can be legitimately applied in the context of a different, what we might call a benign, future. And rationality, in an appropriate context, can also assist us to solve some of the mysteries that have preoccupied humanity and given us (sometimes engaging and reassuring but often problematic) religious beliefs and practices.

The thinking processes that have been applied in the past to envision forms of society that provide us with what could be the ultimate solution to the riddle of human existence comes under the title of Utopia. In various places throughout this book, Utopia has been discussed. Attempts at a rational design of society starts in Occidental history[516] with the Hellenic Greeks — some of Plato's ideas in particular were briefly discussed, but other fragmentary attempts were also made both in ancient Greece and Rome. Much of this writing was simply fanciful entertainment or ways of presenting political and moral lessons, often as satire, without having to spell them out where these were uncomfortable or politically proscribed.

The beginning, in the prelude to the modern world, of what we might think of as serious descriptions of ideal societies starts with Thomas More's book *Utopia*[517] which, of course, gives us the word that is generally used to describe a putative ideal society. There has been considerable debate concerning how serious More was as to whether a society could really be constructed along the lines outlined in his book which was, after all, a forthright piece of fiction, where in real life, More, as a powerful politician and eventually Lord Chancellor (roughly equivalent to Prime Ministers today) in no way even suggested in his official role that England should be transformed into the Utopia he described.

Nevertheless, although published almost exactly five hundred years ago, in social and political circumstances totally different from the present, it is remarkable how much of *Utopia* we can still empathise with, following the long history of discourse on ideal societies by design that has unfolded over the intervening years. However, there is much by way of detail in More's book that is fanciful and there are certain contradictions in the details and aspects that, today, would be considered definitely un-utopian. Nevertheless, some of the basic principles that have recurred in many if not most Occidental utopian proposals over the centuries are already present. More's Utopia is not yet anarchist, there being a King (albeit his narrator, who describes the country of Utopia and likes to refer to it as a Republic, is extremely critical of Kings) and the usual professional positions and ('just') wars are still being waged. But private property no longer exists, property being managed in appropriate ways as community assets. Also, money is abolished as people are prepared to work hard and take only what they need from the product of the community in the form of what today is referred to as a 'gift economy'.

More's fictitious narrator, who in *Utopia* is describing the society, takes particular exception both to conspicuous consumption, focusing on the absurdity of the value put on gold, precious stones and flamboyant attire, and then opining that money is the cause of much evil in society, including not just poverty but also the majority of crime. Ultimately, More's Utopia is achieved by sincere engagement of people in community life and the pursuit of happiness achieved through modest means.

Whilst we should remember that it was written in an age where religion was a strong presence in life, down to the letter[518], it is notable that More could already write that ...*most Utopians feel they can please God merely by studying the natural world...* and that in Utopia the Supreme Being is identical with nature. The practical side of this is that whilst Utopians learn one or even two sets of practical skills, all spend part of their time in close contact with nature and practising agriculture. As with so many Utopian writers, More writes about the practical arrangements of everyday intercourse and how the living arrangements and governance are woven, which are central to utopianism in the sense that relations between people from what we call families, through to the administration of territories and their resources, have to be reconsidered as an integrated whole.

As the centuries unfolded, utopian practice in the Occident rarely grew out of utopian literature or theory, although there are clear parallels, with utopian writing, describing what radical initiatives

411

attempted to practise. The term 'Utopia', although widely understood as applying to the notion of ideal society, was almost never used by those making serious attempts to change the world: hence the oft-expressed notion that Utopia is and always will be but fiction and the world will go its own way, regardless.

Occasional radical attempts demonstrating different (we might apply to them *post hoc* the term utopian) ways to organise life at the local level occurred, generally in the context of the revolutions discussed earlier in this chapter. Notable cases are the disastrous Commune of Münster of 1534-35[519], which was, perhaps, the last of a long line of religiously-inspired millenarian attempts at instant but unplanned or analysed change. There was also the Digger occupation of St George's Hill, Weybridge, which was accompanied by the writings of Gerard Winstanley's justification of this attempt at communal living, but who were soon evicted[520].

The French Enlightenment and subsequent Revolution laid the ground for what we might conceive of as the modern concepts of Utopia. Many of the 18th century French intellectuals wrote in ways that might be considered proto-utopian in the sense that they were concerned about mending what they considered to be the ailments of their society. With a few exceptions, however, these are incoherent in their proposal for how society should be organised, or rather these looked only at limited dimensions of this. Some kind of Utopia can be gleaned from a reading of different texts of the most radical of the more renowned theorists of the age, Jean-Jacques Rousseau, but his most famous work, *The Social Contract,* is far from utopian. Nevertheless, the idea of common ownership of property was again surfacing in reaction to the deepening of the Mandevillian-Smithian dogmas.

We need not go into any detail on the schemes and proposals of the many utopian ideas, proposals and experiments put into practice in the 19th century — but summarise here a selection of the authors, most of whom have been mentioned somewhere in the foregoing text and are still of interest to anyone caring to make comparisons and see and feel the differences. Frank Manual, who documented the complete history of utopianism 'in the Western World'[521], focused particular attention on 'the Prophets of Paris'[522] over the end of the 18th and into the 19th century, whom we might say, several of them coming from amongst the French elite, brought utopianism into something of the mainstream, in terms of being well-known, even if being marginal in impact until the end of the 19th century.

Turgot and Condorcet, leading up to and into the French Revolution, set out general schemas of an expectation that Occidental society would evolve into a state of the 'perfection of man' but without yet any very clear outline of what the end state might be. Mably and Morelly, lesser known writers prior to the French Revolution, were more explicit with regard to end states. The Compte de Saint Simon is counted amongst the utopians, even though his version of Utopia was one that advocated large-scale industrialism, and was certainly an influence on Marx's thought (Marx's father having been a keen Saint Simonian).

Fourier and Cabet were two utopians who believed in creating real communities in which their version of utopian principles would be realised and several such communities did come into being. August Compte and Pierre-Joseph Proudhon may be counted amongst the French utopian theorists, the first as the inventor of what became the discipline of sociology but with definite ideas of the coming trajectory of society and the latter being seen as a consistent theoretical proponent of anarchist political and social organisation.

In Britain, three names stand out. William Godwin, in his *Enquiry Concerning Political Justice* set out what has been called 'the most complete statement of rational anarchism ever attempted'[523], briefly mentioned in the foregoing text, and which has remained politically contentious ever since[524]. Mary Wollstonecraft, Godwin's partner[525], set out the first comprehensive statement of what she termed *A Vindication of the Rights of Women* in the context of anarchist society. Robert Owen, who made a fortune in industry, spent this on tireless experiments designed to overcome the cultural differences in class society and the vindication of the nascent modern working class, ranging from the initiation of modern trade unionism, the invention of modern cooperativism, and the substitution of labour-based money, to the creation of utopian communities in Britain and the United States and with the movement that he brought to life, promoting the emancipation of women[526]. His own theoretical writings are supplemented with writings of his associates, particularly in the development of a different approach to economics from that which was expounded in the context of liberalism under the tutelage of Adam Smith, and which was an important influence on Karl Marx.

Three Russian aristocrats stand at the summit of the 19th century development of anarchist proposals for the reorganisation of society. Mikhail Bakunin was both a theoretician and philosopher of 'collectivist anarchism' whilst moving around Europe promoting revolution as the spontaneous route to total change in social and political organisation. His confrontation with Marx in the development of the international movement towards an ultimate anarchist society (Marx avowing that eventually the State would 'wither away', whilst

Bakunin and the anarchists believe the State should be immediately abolished) is one of the great political dramas of 19th century political movement.

We might be sure that the fundamental problem with the whole universalist and internationalist approach to radical socio-political change, to dis-Alienation and the reorganisation of human life to realise this, was that it entirely overlooked real people on the ground, so that the eventual creation of what in the Soviet Union became the notion of the 'Socialist Man' (sic) could never be more than a theoretical construct, without flesh and blood, without any real possibility of human warmth and love and the same could obviously be said for any eventual communing with nature, requiring real landscapes and ecological places that had no place in Marxism or its practical manifestations, where Bacon's notion of conquest continued unabated.

It was Leo Tolstoy, and above all Pyotr Kropotkin, who understood the need not merely to abolish hierarchy but to create human community in particular natural settings. Although one might find particular fault with the approaches of these two utopians and wish to interpret and apply their writing and experience in particular ways, they certainly represent the culmination of utopian thought and (in the case of Tolstoyan communities) practice. Kropotkin wrote extensively concerning issues in the organisation of anarchist society that are today (still) accessible and important to read as background to any more substantial theorising and working out of practical moves to construct Utopia[527].

From about the middle of the 19th century, 'alternative communities' sprang up right across the Occident. Perhaps it can be seen as evident that these harked back to religious sect communities going all the way back to the various manifestations of the 'Free Spirit' that emerged from time to time from the Middle Ages, and taking in what became the very successful communities of the Amish and Hutterites in North America. However, whilst some of these communities remained within some kind of religious or spiritual fold (and this is true even of some present-day communities, for instance of the very successful Findhorn Community) most were either ecumenical or forthrightly atheist based on secular principles coming out of the burgeoning socialist, communist and anarchist movements of the times[528].

Following the First World War, the struggle between the two great ideologies of capitalism (liberalism) and Marxist communism ('actually existing socialism') and the authoritarianism of the inter-war years that, although not generally acknowledged, had a deep influence on restricting the 'alternative imagination' around the world, continued

414

after the Second World War within the overall notion that the Developmental State had the answers necessary to build 'good societies'. And it was not until after the events of 1968 that utopian thinking and what became the 'Communes Movement' revived the discourse and activity of the late 19th century[529].

The revival of Utopianism, is of course, totally overshadowed and obscured to the vast majority of today's humanity by the bellicose cacophony of the Consumer Society and the bludgeoning by the media into understanding the world in very narrow ways, forcing a very particular idea of how it should be run, with, for all the propaganda concerning ours being a free society, implications also for how people should behave in terms of social morality. Looking through the tiny window of the revived movement after 1968, we can see a trickle of analytical, academic literature, partly escaping from Marxist orthodoxy and partly anarchist or frankly Utopian — that provides ideas of Utopia as a political ideology and partly as a set of practical principles[530], with a small stream of committed movement literature.

For the two decades of the 1970s and 1980s it seemed there were coherent movements of Intentional Communities that communicated regularly, exchanging experiences and ideas and, at least in the United States, this connected loosely to the bioregional movement, concerned not just with small human communities but how a new vision of human existence could be constructed around empathy with particular corners of nature. From the 1990s, the idea and practice of 'movement' seemed to decline and whilst the approach to communities that were in some way aiming at the utopian continued on much the scale of the earlier decades, the shape and content of these became more varied and in general elements became more partial and fragmented[531].

We come now to the future of utopianism in the context of the fall of Modern Civilisation. We described in sadness the escalating violence and struggles already incipient and that might be expected to escalate as the global economy declines and the seductive capacity of the Consumer Society falls away, leaving almost everyone increasingly exposed to what in previous ages was the relative frugality and necessity for hard manual work in small communities; the degree to which this descends into destitution and premature death can only be speculated on but certainly can be expected. No longer will it be a matter of choosing, as do the members of utopian communities today, to live in close proximity with others and to plan their common life. Now it will become a necessity to re-form communities of some kind, as the means to escape become increasingly unavailable.

415

If taken in the spirit of loss and resistance and continuing attempts to find individualist solutions, the first impression of the re-emergence of community will seem like a prison, with the struggle to stay alive making everyday life nothing but pain. What the intentional Community and the utopian impulse can do, and will do as it becomes increasingly evident that Modernity and the bizarre life that it produced and offered is permanently behind us, is to provide a positive solution to the emerging life-problematic. Now utopianism will not merely be a dream or the experience of a few scattered experiments but, rather, a lifeline to spiritual renewal[532] that will have to reinvent not just how to live together in relative harmony and distribute the tasks and benefits of local production and maintenance fairly, as is the life of present-day Intentional Communities, but to reach an understanding of the human condition in nature in ways that were lost throughout the 20th century but what might eventually be understood as a loss of the 'human essence' that has been the eight thousand-year long nightmare of Civilisation[533].

So what might a positive utopian community look like in the more distant future as the dislocation of the fall of modernity bottoms out? Although there is much that Intentional Communities, not only in the Occident but the few to be found in other parts of the world have in common with regard to everyday life, we have no intention of writing any detailed Utopia of the kind set out by Thomas More and many, others since[534]. And, as made clear early in this book, it is certain that a resurgence of cultures other than Occidental will re-emerge and have to find their own way that will surely be very different from the European notion of Utopia. However, here we present what might be considered certain general principles that result from the discussion running throughout the last few chapters of this book:

1. *Size and Distribution of Communities:*

Often, starting with More's Utopia, an important consideration is the way in which the population is divided up in terms of immediate empathetic community, what we might refer to as village or neighbourhood and thence wider areas of town, city, (bio)region and nation or country.

Empathetic community (or family) is in very many utopian frameworks, and confirmed as 'usual practice' in the majority of Intentional Communities as being made up of more than the nuclear family, but reaching its limit at thirty or forty people ranging across all ages. Members would not necessarily be genetically related in that some will leave and join as a couple or other empathy relations forged through contact of work and recreation with members of other communities. Such communities as long-term empathetic units would then confederate as neighbours, and in more formal relations as villages or neighbourhoods ranging from just a handful to a limit of perhaps forty making a village, but then with a third level of organisation of larger numbers of neighbourhood units that could make up towns.

Some utopian proposals conjecture larger cities. However, we may agree with More that in settlements of much over eighty thousand souls, the issue of anomie begins to arise where overview is lost and administration starts to become a separate set of tasks that Utopia would prefer to avoid. Two important criteria containing the size of cities is that the countryside can be accessed within ten minutes walking distance from any part of the city and that the city, being the largest kind of settlement in regions where most of the population live in towns and villages, produces in terms of processing and manufacturing most of what is consumed in the region. A return to the kind of regional distribution of villages, towns and (small) cities that would be expected under 'central place theory' would seem to be a reasonable distribution of settlements[535].

The point here is that dissolution of community over the past century and thence the growth of megacities and suburbs has been accompanied by ways of organising life, including its special manifestations, that cannot continue to function technically and hence also in terms of human relations. From a sheer practical point of view, there will have to be a return to the distribution of settlements and their relations with the resources necessary to support human life that is at a minimum similar to what was on the ground before the exploitation of fossil fuels. What is being said by utopianism is that there will be a need to go beyond the physical reorganisation, indeed start from the organisation of egalitarian 'extended families', work out how such communities can interact in terms of 'villages', 'neighbourhoods' and 'towns' that have enough person-power to produce a reasonably comfortable and enjoyable way of life for all.

2.   Social Relations:

It is at the level of working out egalitarian social relations that the Intentional Communities can provide advice coming out of intensive experience. The construction of hierarchy and the Alienation that this has produced and reproduced in all cultures in the context of civilisation comes to an end first and fundamentally at this level.

Women are no longer 'chattels', the property of particular males, but equal in every way except the biological, which means also the minimisation of the sexual division of labour. And with it, sexual relations that essentially bind mature humans in love relations and are an essential dimension of joy in life, may also be less structured, and clearly with forced sexual relations (themselves part of the problematic of inegalitarian gender relations) being eliminated so that all can experience 'the joy of sex'.

Patriarchy, 'leadership' of any kind or any hierarchical organisation within communities also falls away, being replaced by true democracy in decisions concerning the organisation of the life of the community and the distribution of responsibilities and respect for all reasoned points of view. The way in which children are educated to participate in such arrangements is of great importance insofar as democracy has had the tendency in individualist society to be interpreted to mean 'I can do as I please'. The issue of 'I am you before I am myself' arises as the foundation of every communal decision and with it comes not only the warmth of cooperation but also the feeling of responsibility carried through to satisfying activity on behalf of the community as social subject.

3. *Living Arrangements:*

The built environments that future societies almost everywhere will inherit are extremely poorly suited to a future of the kinds of communities we might expect. Many millions of high-rise apartments were built to straitjacket and isolate the average nuclear family, with no flexibility for different kinds of families and certainly no idea of larger communities. And finally, as energy ebbs away, they will become impossible to climb beyond modest heights. Similarly, suburban development, whilst ruining vast landscapes all around the world ('gardens' that invited people to dominate their own tiny piece of nature) were also built to accommodate nuclear families.

Many Intentional Communities in the UK acquired old 'country houses' that were, indeed, 'communities' in the past, albeit extremely hierarchical with masters and many servants, but have the space to accommodate today's Intentional Communities. But the classic neighbourhood of towns and small cities of the past, be it around the Mediterranean, in North Africa, in the Hispanic colonial towns of Latin America and, indeed, in traditional Chinese cities, was a courtyard house that allowed for flexible arrangements of larger families. Whilst other arrangements are certainly possible, for instance in Northern

418

Europe, simply larger houses along streets and tenements with apartments of various sizes could be adapted and extended to accommodate larger communities and could become the main form of community accommodation in the future.

But there will also be a need to re-integrate functions that, through modernity, became separated out as a consequence of developments in transport that will be reversed as petroleum resources decline. Thomas More was rather precise about how towns should be arranged (or rather how towns in Utopia were organised). They had to be convenient places to live, with facilities close at hand and the countryside within easy reach. Through the ages, much thought has gone into planning 'ideal cities', from the Hippodamian cities of Hellenic Greece right up to the garden cities and new towns of the 20th century. Communities in the future, as they come together to form larger settlements and overcome the frightful chaos of the detritus left behind by modernity, can learn much from these and certainly should consider coherently how their settlements should be structured[536].

4.   Property:

Little more needs to be said of this in so far as Utopias almost universally advocate the abolition of private property. Of course the Soviet alternative of the state taking over possession is fundamentally contrary to anarchist doctrine and was clearly part of the problem of the failure of the Soviet Union. Earlier we discussed Common Pool Resource Management (CPRMR) as a mechanism for the management of property and this is clearly the practical solution to the problems of property as neither 'private' or 'public' but community managed. In fact the very idea of 'property' as commodity is counter to 'deep utopianism' qua 'deep ecology' where the instrumentality of which property is an essential dimension is replaced by land as natural community in the Leopoldian sense, indissolubly one with social community.

5.   Mode of Production:

Discussed earlier, we emphasise here that capitalism has no place in Utopia; indeed, More's Utopia was in great measure an attack on the evils of emergent capitalism. However, in the case of American proto-utopianism, or 'radical decentralists', the evil is only seen in terms of Big Business and somehow small and family businesses continue to be smiled upon with little understanding of the deep synergy between these and liberal individualism and 'small business'. Elsewhere there is the notion of cooperatives which have a substantial history growing out of Owenite utopianism, with a significant percentage of enterprises in Italy and Spain and lesser numbers in most European countries being run on cooperative lines. Seen under the broader umbrella of CPRMR, management of the complete local economy can come within this mechanism, with all who work in a particular organisation being co-owners in the sense of the saying 'from each according to ability, to each according to need'. Any need to provide tools, instruments, accommodation and other capital for micro-enterprise become the responsibility of the wider community.

Work as such would, in time, cease to be understood as drudgery but instead become recreation. It is a true perversion of human spirit that in modern times, there has been a constant drive to put manual work behind us as being demeaning and of lower status . The constant restructuring of employment has hidden from view the status attached to the position and held that manual work, thanks to the availability of machines powered by fossil fuel, could become both less onerous and, more importantly, diminished resulting in a diminishing size of the 'working class'. Meanwhile, to maintain bodily health, strenuous recreation such as sport, and more ludicrously as 'fitness', accomplished with elaborate machines that produced nothing – became a significant component of middle class lifestyles.

Productive work, when it entails producing beautiful things or farming where one cooperates with nature and is witness to its fecundity, that provides human sustenance can be truly fulfilling, producing at the same time a balance in the maintenance of mind and body. In Utopia (already as mentioned previously, in More's version) everyone participates seasonally and, as agreed between urban and rural communities, in farming. But everyone should also practise at least one calling that, in the future, will predominantly be about making beautiful things. Administration, that became the main occupation in modern society as a consequence of the scale at which everything was done, becomes, like agriculture, something that everyone spends some of their time accomplishing.

The provision of services may become almost entirely an internal matter for the empathetic community, with the knowledge everywhere that where problems arise that overflow the individual community, assistance will be provided by neighbouring communities. Education is further discussed below; healthcare should be organised within empathetic communities, with health education (focusing on the maintenance of healthy living) held in high regard. Legal and religious services dissolve into community relations (where perhaps Quakerism and Jainism have things to teach) and the extensive 'services' that maintain the modern business world have no significant place as Cooperativism learns to provide its own services.

6. *Urbs in Rur:*

Already from the paragraphs above, there is a sense in which all inhabitants have an urban and a rural life — urban in the sense of what today would be called 'town' in a situation where 'city' in the modern sense has vanished as a phenomenon. But life in human communities is vital for the development of the child to maturity for the many activities that can be learned and exchanged and above all the arts and the festivities. Nevertheless, as has already been stressed, love of nature does not develop from the occasional excursion and recreation trip but, rather, from more prolonged contact; living periods of time in nature. Practising agriculture is one dimension of this but also learning about the details of nature (biology and ecology) and spending time beyond study also in contemplation of her incredible beauty as ecological process and its expression in movement and in change through the seasons. Everyone should have the chance to experience this even though, as with everything in life, some community members will derive deeper spiritual experience from this than others.

7. *Governance:*

We discussed government at length in Chapter Three, where the sinews of an egalitarian, that is to say 'without leaders', form of decision-making was an essential dimension of Utopia as it evolved towards the end of the 19th century. This can, however, only work where all essential decisions are taken at a very local level that will allow, logistically, for all to have the opportunity to participate.

The fact is that modern government, in the scale of the way in which it operates, simply cannot logistically accommodate true democracy. The concentrated nature of decisions reinforces and promotes through the globalisation of economic activity was, in the final years, the actual decision-making arena in most of what has really mattered. The automatism of 'the market', as set out by Adam Smith in promoting the individualistic creed was never really automatic but, on the contrary and increasingly over time, run by the elites that controlled and owned corporations. And in a very real sense, as revealed in the vision of Jacques Ellul[537], the Technostructure came to take much of modern decision-making autonomously in the logic of the way the machinery worked. In the process, government became a set of rituals, endorsing decisions taken outside the framework of government with both government and corporate bureaucracies managing the results of elite decisions.

The decline in energy resources that will bring the economy back to the local scale will, at the same time, open up the possibility of true democracy, that is to say participatory, face-to-face democracy, as the way in which decisions are taken, and without technologies taking autonomous decisions out of the necessity of how they work. Elite decision-making can also operate where these are predominantly at the local level, which was the experience of eras before modernity and in other cultural settings once civilisation was on the road. However, utopianism is concerned with ensuring that all voices relevant to each decision that concerns communities, villages, neighbourhoods and (bio)regions can, in principle, be heard and respected on an equal footing. How this is effectuated in practice will need careful design with checks at each stage and level to guard against overt or stealthy concentration of power and thus exclusion of individuals or groups who should be drawn into the decisions — not only because it is fair but more importantly to nurture responsibility. The basic parameters were described already in some detail in the foregoing chapter.

8.   *Education:*

From time to time, in some places, across European history, education has come to be understood not as a process of imparting facts and dogmas, but in the true sense of the Latin term *educare,* a process of 'drawing out'. This means in practice to assist children, and thence adults throughout life to learn how to learn, to instil education as a process of self and mutual education that runs throughout life. Of course there are 'facts' concerning efficient ways of working and concerning the structures in nature that do have to be taught in the traditional sense, but this can be imparted as illustration of how to learn and not as rote learning . As the vast electronic stores of information that have become an essential aid to knowledge over the past few decades fall apart in the future with the diminution of energy resources, it will be vital to rescue those aspects of information that will be of use in reconstructing local worlds.

However, what matters *a priori* is that the curiosity and will to learn is encouraged that will work to rebuild local knowledge and that can result in imagination, inventiveness and the sense of the beautiful things 'out there' and in the satisfaction of producing things made to accompany the lives of the communities. All of the life of human communities becomes a concatenated work of art, including also human relations and the ways in which nature is engaged.

9. *Rites of Passage, Marking Time and the Seasons:*

Most cultures, including those prior to civilisation, have rituals to mark the passage of people through life. As there are so many versions, it makes little sense to set out a particular structure: each community through neighbourhood, village, town and region, and maybe even over greater distances, will inherit ways of celebrating. Changes in the way in which communities and societies revise their self-image and ways of organising life will open opportunities to rethink how the passage of time, and what needs to be celebrated along the way, is structured.

Will baptism be a meaningful activity? Initiation rites and the opening up of life with the coming of adolescence? And marriage? Are the rituals of Christmas and Easter still valid, or might these yet again change their meaning and how they are celebrated? We might speculate on whether similar rituals (Chinese New Year, the Hadj, the multitude of colourful Hindu and Buddhist festivals, the countless African rituals) might also change as a response to other changes that will in all probability ensue from the fall of modernity in which most of the world's population will become implicated. Almost everywhere, the focus that civilisation gave to human life that distanced itself from nature could be reconsidered in the revision of ritual and festivity to celebrate the beauty and the mystery of nature.

All of this relates back everywhere to the religion of the particular place and people. Given the way in which modern cities the world over have come to harbour peoples with very different notions of what is right concerning rites, the starting point for the revision of rites postulated in the foregoing will, in very many places, be an essential aspect of the process of local social (re)integration, the revival of community and the reconstruction of human and ecological life at the local and bioregional level.

10. *Aesthetics:*

Ultimately, being human means that life is an aesthetic experience and process that brings us contentment and happiness. That is to say that every sentence spoken can be seen as well or badly said. The sounds with which we are surrounded and to which we add our own noises and music give us pain or pleasure. The visual images of Nature, of its reorganisation into reordered landscapes, eventually drawn and painted and sculpted representations, are an essential dimension of our equilibrium and our empathy with the world in which we find ourselves. And then every action that we undertake and which we perceive undertaken by others is but a dance and related ritual, well-conceived and executed or, as the case may be, less well-executed, being incompetent in its own terms or ugly with respect to criteria emanating from the social being.

Most people are relatively, or maybe completely, unaware of the role which aesthetics plays in our lives. In the context of civilisation, this has been captured by elites (often entailing struggle between factions), in the end as an essential weapon in holding the people in thrall as the very framework of consumerism. Often enough majorities as lower classes have been impoverished, not because they were physically deprived but through being given models of how life should be lived of which elites have the resources to accomplish, but to which the poor do not have access and so life becomes a functional process without activity or accoutrements that could lend confidence, pride and happiness to their lives. In many places and times, however, particularly in peasant societies, aesthetic ways of life (epitomised by vernacular architecture but also including communal work and the carrying out of local rituals and festivities) became the ultimate expression of life.

Modernity abused the aesthetic impulse savagely as a means to seduce populations into acquiescence in the order of life. The baroque means of self-expression promoted by the global production system and the consumer society withdrew the imaginative impulse from the vast majority of people with 'the creative classes'[538] harnessed to administer a bogus aesthetic life, presented as a means to gain status as the game within which modern life was carried out.

Future Utopias will be of necessity frugal by the standards of modernity. Very many utopian visions, starting with that presented by More, have insisted on this. But frugality need not be aesthetically poor. What matters is for there to be an awareness that life be seen as a series of aesthetic interwoven situations and artefacts. And what will matter is that the means to achieving the aesthetic life is frugal in the sense of energy, materials and, indeed, time necessary in accomplishing means to the designed ends. We could still see at the close of modernity, cultures that have survived the aggressive onslaught of modern life so we could see by travelling how a rich life could be produced by frugal means, within the carrying capacity of the locality. Amongst these are Bhutan and Bali, briefly described above.

The idea of Utopia as a final resolution of the human condition, a kind of arrival at the end of the process of history and of Development, is strictly a child of Occidental culture with its roots in a certain interpretation of Christianity. So the question arises as to whether it might be irrelevant in other cultural settings. We may say, however, with some confidence that many elements of Utopia can be found in the history of other peoples, independent of the name. Classically this involves struggles of peasants to be free of exploitation by landlords and other external powers together with some notion of cooperative management of life. Meanwhile it can further be argued that the idea of Utopia is no more than the terms of reference for a reasonable way of organising human life to satisfy the needs of all in a fair way and treating the local corner of nature inhabited by particular communities in ways that will ensure her continued health. What might be called the 'spiritual' pursuit of Utopia as a coherent approach to the organisation of life is something that will need to develop out of communities themselves in the process of cultural evolution with what will become a wide range of interpretations or versions of Utopia.

One might think of the peasant community of farmers together with artisans who make up a modest but complete way of life in clusters of villages and small towns scattered across agricultural landscapes, as a reasonable starting point for the construction of Utopias in very many places. This, after all, was the way that life was organised for the bulk of humanity over the millennia up to less than a hundred years ago. Problems faced by peasant communities arose almost entirely from the exploitative structures that different civilisations imposed on these settlements, ranging from traditional feudal fiefdoms through exploitative systems introduced by colonial masters, to the walls and structures built up by spreading capitalism involving concentration of property, money-lending and other modern mechanisms that systematically produce wealth for a few and poverty or at best a modest living for the rest. Even within these structures and occasionally almost entirely transcending them were all manner of cooperative arrangements such as community water management and rice transplanting, communal grazing of animals, barn-raising (the CPRMR identified by Elinor Ostrom) sometimes in the context of a gift economies.

Although the sheer variety of situations in different cultural and geographic settings makes it difficult to generalise, we can nevertheless sketch the ways in which modernity has intervened throughout the non-

Occidental world to move systematically away from the possibilities for fair and sustainable local rural communities. What we see everywhere is a retreat from self-reliant settlements with an escalation of production for markets well beyond community borders and buying in necessities with the money acquired from the sale of produce. This has meant, increasingly, reduction to monocultures, sustained and intensified through the application of agrochemicals and mechanisation.

In the process land becomes concentrated as richer farmers can afford inputs and poorer farmers can no longer survive off the product of small plots, becoming landless labourers in a situation of reducing demand for labour — not only in farming but also with the demise of local productive activity where more and more locally consumed products are bought from outside rather than being locally produced[539]. Local vernacular building is displaced by building with imported materials — often enough through local populations being seduced into new, environmentally inappropriate styles of building[540] and losing the skills to produce buildings out of local materials — which, in the case of timber, have already become depleted[541].

So village life even in the poorest areas has become increasingly energy-intensive and locally incoherent, not only in economic terms but also in terms of the richness of community life. The population drift to the cities that is almost complete in Latin America and now in full swing in Asia and Africa is not so much a question of greater chances of formal employment and increased income (when in practice most rural-urban migrants subsist in the precarious informal economy and live in often squalid informal settlements) as the result of the death of vibrant local cultures contrasted with the vicarious, voyeuristic pleasures of the cities.

The fall of modernity will surely have devastating consequences for the southern cities and especially the huge populations that have accumulated in the informal settlements[542]. It will also increasingly affect the new middle classes, whose employment and income will also decline in ways that we are already seeing in the United States [543]. Whilst we might think of villages and small towns in the South as once again becoming the centre of life for the majority of the people, again reliant on local production of food and most of the rest of life, the road to such a life will almost everywhere be a rocky one. In the first instance the population exiting the cities may in many instances overcrowd rural settlements in search of survival. In addition almost everything about producing local life and the revival of communities will have to be relearned or learned in new ways.

But if this path is eventually to produce anything approaching Utopia, then there will be much more to it than re-learning skills and the technical aspects of producing life from local resources and even the rebuilding of community. The main problems will arise in how modern governance and the continued cultural practices that are far from utopian, viz landlordism and other exploitative practices including the mistreatment of women, are avoided or eliminated through the spread of cooperative and sharing ways of life.

In Chapter Two we discussed how the fall of modernity will almost certainly mean also the fall of modern government in the heartlands of Modernity. This may be expected to occur on different timetables and with very different results, with the shape of government (and more generally governance)certainly undergoing radical modification as a consequence of the failure of modern governments to be able to continue to seduce the people into acquiescence in contemporary political and economic life. Whilst some governments can be expected to collapse completely in the relatively short term, devolving de facto to local governance (the case of Somalia was mentioned in Chapter Three as a 'failed state' that might well become a negative model for increasing numbers of States in the coming decades) the arrangements that result will be consequent on the way in which the people intervene in devising solutions that may succumb to warlords or other violent and tyrannical 'leaders', imposing or reinforcing landlordism or other exploitative systems but could also eventually evolve into substantially more benign arrangements if and when active social movements claim the day.

It is in this respect that the lack of traditional indigenous utopian vision may be expected to inhibit benign transitions. In recent years attempts have been made through many 'Development projects' in rural areas right across the global South, to 'empower' communities in 'local economic development' projects and 'participatory planning' instigated by various agents from international Development agencies to local non-government organisations (NGOs), to improve local life in small ways. Perhaps none of this has left anything very meaningful behind but maybe in a few cases there is a residue that local people who have participated in such actions may develop into what will amount to local political movements to defend localities against outside powers and revive local life on an altogether more autonomous basis than in the past.

The model for this that grows directly out of a realisation of what the future holds for us all – the fall of Modernity – is the Transition Movement discussed earlier in this chapter. At the time of writing this is overwhelmingly a movement of the North — initially Anglo Saxon but with rapid development elsewhere across the Occidental world. Furthermore, lights have started to shine also in Latin America and the first few in Asia. The literature of the movement and the mechanisms that are evolving for inducting local populations into active involvement in the movement are strongly oriented towards the reconstruction of community as well as actions that address key issues in re-localisation of economies, reduction in energy and other resource need, and permaculture as a resource-conserving approach to farming, but more importantly an approach to Nature that at a minimum respects ecological systems — just a few steps from an attitude recognising the Ecological Self.

In spreading more intensively into the South, the movement will need to understand in a clearer way the political dimensions of reconstructing local life. Whilst small initiatives in ecological farming and the revival of local production do not upset local interests — and may, indeed, be encouraged by landlords — as the downward passage reveals itself with greater clarity, exploitative powers will certainly become more assertive and local communities will need to evolve political forms to defend the advance of initiatives asserting and practising in accordance with the principles of Transition and push through to fully cooperatively-run local economies and societies. Just as past struggles to attain justice for all had to learn from where oppression was coming (both imposition of personal and institutional power and more problematically, internal acquiescence) so the reformulation of life in the future will require a deep learning process and much fortitude. Even without utopian traditions, some local movements all round the world are, by now, aware of what is at stake in building egalitarian societies and the spread of the Transition Movement should take upon itself to support, even if only by demonstration, the planting and nurturing of utopian movements and initiatives even in the most unlikely cultural environments.

Notes

Introduction

[1] Butterfield (2007); Leakey and Lewin (1996).

[2] Of course for the early millennia of what are referred to as 'cities', populations remained little more than what today would be referred to as villages or small towns with much of the population engaged in agriculture (Childe (1964), Chapter Five).

[3] Whilst the archaeological evidence of human communities indicates clearly that people just like us were already in existence 60,000 years ago, in fact analysis of skeletons and the remains of human settlements as far back as 150,000 years ago reveal nothing of significant difference to humans alive today. Renfrew (2007).

[4] Notwithstanding the hunting to extinction on every continent except Homo's original home, Africa, of most of the large mammals.

[5] Diamond (1998); Renfrew (2007).

[6] Opinion today amongst archaeologists is tending to believe that all major evolutionary steps in the development of species Homo took place in Africa and that at different times, starting at least one and a half million years ago, waves of migrants moved out and across much of Eurasia.

[7] The notion of the emergence of civilisation as a distinct phenomenon came about in the context of the deep conviction of the 'triumphal march of history', starting already with Turgot, Condorcet and Adam Smith in the 18th century and with another wave in the mid-to late 19th century. The Marxist interpretation came to the fore in the course of the 20th century and the present-day definition of civilisation, continuing to be seen as a stage in 'the evolution of mankind', originates in the work of Gordon Childe (1951, 1964, 1965).

[8] See particularly Stanley Diamond (1974).

[9] For a fully-articulated presentation of this argument, see: Cohn (1977).

[10] A very extensive debate on the context of clarifying the evolution of class society as a dimension of Marxism emerged in the 1920s, initiated

by Karl Wittvogel. For a taste of the debates, see: Bailey and Llobera (1981).

[11] Lee and Devore (1967).

[12] Diamond (1998), Chapter Ten.

[13] In line with the inclusive orientation of Oriental religions, contrasting with the exclusive, competitive orientation of Abrahamic religions, Indonesian (Balinese) Hinduism includes the full stretch of beliefs including one almighty God, a pantheon of deities and mythological characters, but locally also much by way of sacred places redolent of an animist past. This is not a fusion under modern influence but a local evolution that has a strong presence today even following a multi-layered invasion of modernity including Dutch colonialism, Indonesian nationalist bureaucratisation and massive tourism.

[14] For a summary of the extensive debate on these issues that took place in the early years of the Green Movement, see Atkinson (1991), Chapter Five.

[15] In his book *What Happened in History*, Childe described the steps from non-class to class societies. For a discussion of the forms of early elite formation, see Fried, (1967).

[16] See the writings of John Zerzan – and particularly: Zerzan (2010); also: Jensen (2006).

[17] Tainter (1988).

[18] Diamond (2005).

[19] See under Wikipedia - 'Extinction Events' - for a long list of events in Nature that can and have characterised fluctuations in ecological conditions on earth.

[20] Of course at the level of immediate life, there were always things that belonged to an individual – even if only the food that was about to be eaten. Sahlins (1974) and Fried (1967) p.63 ff, discuss the forms of private property from 'primitive' to 'civilised' society.

[21] The case of William Stanley Jevons' (2012[1865]) writing in the mid-19th century was concerned about the consequences of an eventual exhaustion of British coal discussed in more detail in Chapter Four below.

Chapter One

[22] Meadows et al (1974).

[23] Even the Local Agenda 21 movement, discussed further in Chapter Four, that eventually achieved initiatives in over 6,000 municipalities across the 1990s had been largely forgotten a decade later – with students in my classes that in principle were more oriented than the average towards 'sustainability issues' having never heard of it.

[24] Bahro (1978,1982,1984,1986).

[25] Carr (2004).

[26] International Forum on Globalization (2004).

[27] IUCN (1980).

[28] WCED (1987).

[29] Quarrie (1992).

[30] Meadows et al (2004).

[31] Jackson (2011).

[32] Ponting (2007).

[33] Galbraith's (1961) essay, *The Great Crash 1929* remains the seminal analysis of what happened and why.

[34] Galbraith was also one of the few academic economists who was prepared to note how well the fascist government in Germany in the 1930s invented mechanisms to manage the economy in order to escape from the Great Depression – which in Germany preceded and was considerably more profound than the Wall Street crash.

[35] Stiglitz (2010).

[36] Barnett and Morse (1963).

[37] WTO (2003).

[38] Hubbert (1962).

[39] Mills (2008); Gorelick (2010).

[40] IEA (2008).

[41] Heinberg (2013).

[42] Lüthi and Schütze (2011).

[43] Allaby (1972); Mallanby (1975).

[44] Ehrlich (1969).

[45] The phenomenon was analysed and discussed in the pages of the British Medical Journal as the result of the privatisation of the Russian economy. Men et al (2003).

[46] Wohl (1983).

[47] Weale (1992).

[48] Lapierre and Moro (2002).

[49] Colborn et al (1996).

[50] Commoner (1966). Throughout his life, Barry Commoner addressed environmental problems in theory in a series of publications and also raised the level of political concern on one issue after another and at least in the case of the atmospheric test ban treaty was successful. His focus on energy (Commoner (1979)) was also path breaking and his candidacy for the US Presidency in 1980, although a total failure, illustrates the difficulties of making any meaningful headway on environmental issues in US politics.

[51] IPCC (2007).

[52] WWF et al (2009).

[53] The most radical – and the same time most realistic – assessment of what would have to be done to maintain the earth's temperature at something below the level at which runaway effects start to manifest themselves, was that of James Hansen (2009). Initially an advisor to the American President, when it became evident just how draconian the measures would need to be to contain global warming, he was cast out of favour. His book discusses his role and lays out a plan for reducing global warming that is considerably more radical than that of the NGOs that attended the Copenhagen conference. He suggests, *inter alia,* that it will be necessary to cease burning coal immediately.

[54] Hoggan (2010).

[55] Hansen (2009).

[56] See Hansen (2009) also for a thorough discussion of probable causes of previous mass extinctions and the depth to which the current human-

caused event might extend, depending on how far fossil hydrocarbons continue to be exploited.

[57] Ponting (2007).

[58] Crosby (1986).

[59] Millennium Ecosystem Assessment (2005).

[60] Diamond (2005)

[61] Beck (1992).

[62] Now somewhat dated but still probably the most detailed analysis of the way in which modern opinions are formed and manipulated - see Herman and Chomsky, (2002). Recently, Joseph Stiglitz (2012 – Chapter Six) deals with key aspects of this phenomenon under the title '1984 is upon us'.

[63] Korowicz (2010).

[64] A classic study in how these politics played themselves out in practice was undertaken by Matthew Crenson (1971) under the title of *The Un-Politics of Air Pollution*. This revealed how in the case of two suburbs of Chicago suffering major air pollution from steel production plants, one with a large plant owned by the American Steel Corporation and the other with a number of smaller steel plants, the issue of air pollution was only raised in the latter case. Once the issue was raised, it became possible to negotiate that the companies install air pollution controls. In the former case, with threats to jobs and in general the sheer political weight of American Steel, the result was that the issue of air pollution was never even raised in spite of the health consequences being equally bad in both cases.

[65] Jacques et al (2008).

[66] Hirsch et al (2005).

[67] Hirsch (2005).

[68] Strahan (2007).

[69] ZfTB (2010).

[70] Bündnis 90/Die Grünen (2010).

[71] Burgbacher, E. Parlamentarische Staatssekretär (2010).

[72] From 2003, a flow of publications on the consequences, at least for the United States, started to appear. See by way of key examples: Heinberg (2003, 2004, 2007); Kustler (2005); Greer (2008, 2009).

[73] Two books that have already dealt with this, at least for the United States, in considerable detail: Kunstler (2005) and Greer (2008).

[74] For one attempt to posit different scenarios of the downward passage, see: Holmgren (2009).

[75] From the early centuries after Christ when Rome had a population estimated at one and a half million, by the first millennium this had declined to just eleven thousand. See: Ward-Perkins (2005).

[76] Ward-Perkins (2010).

[77] Tainter (1988).

[78] Odum and Odum (2008).

[79] Commission on Oil Independence (2006).

[80] Hopkins (2005).

[81] Hopkins (2008); Chamberlain (2009).

[82] Lerch (2007).

[83] Korowicz (2010)

[84] See: Peak Oil Task Force (2009) produced by the City of Bloomington, Illinois for an illustrative list. The report notes Gary Stringer of Northeast Louisiana University as having compiled a list of 500,000 products using oil or oil-based ingredients.

[85] Atkinson and Viloria (2013).

[86] For a full-length exposition of what happened with the collapse of the Soviet Union, comparing this with what might be expected to happen in the United States with the decline in energy, see: Orlov (2008). For the Cuban experience in developing UPA see: Koont (2009).

[87] Atkinson and Viloria (2013).

[88] There are good indications that the second Iraq war was motivated strongly by the attempt by the US state to control the flow of oil from that country. See Strahan, (2007) for a well-researched and useful discussion of the issue. Whilst this appeared to be unsuccessful in this

respect, costing the United States state considerable amounts for little return, whether this experience would deter the Government from further threatened adventures in Iran remains to be seen. In all probability any aggression from the US is likely to result in the Iranian Government 'turning off the spigot', and with Iran being currently the fourth largest supplier of oil, we might exercise our imaginations with regard to the consequences.

[89] One of the early books outlining the fall of our civilisation as a consequence of the decline in oil resources was entitled *The Party's Over* (Heinberg (2003)) This perhaps gives a flavour of the state of mind – a kind of extreme existential hangover – that may be widespread amongst the younger generation in the coming years.

[90] There is solid evidence that such a state of depression descended upon sections of the population in Russia with the collapse of the Soviet Union with, according to the United Nations, some three million 'premature deaths' that can only be accounted for by alcoholism, drugs and deep disorientation. See: Men, et al (2003).

[91] Graham and Marvin (2001).

[92] Debate around the long-term unviability of American suburbia goes back even to the 1980s and since the 2008 financial crash, the growth of suburban poverty and the incipient vacating of houses and support services has gained the title of 'slumburbia'. For a review of the literature and discussion of the phenomenon, see: Schafran (2013). Looking into the future regarding the future acceleration in the decline of suburbia, which may be expected due to energy-starvation, see: Kunstler, (2005). The DVD entitles *The End of Suburbia* concerning the coming demise of suburbia that has been very widely screened in the United States is: Electric Wallpaper Co. (2004). See also: Atkinson (2007).

[93] This is, however, discussed in a proactive way in Chapter Six, suggesting the process has started already in the context of the Transition Movement.

Chapter Two

[94] Carr (1964); Finley (1986). See Atkinson, (1991) Chapter Four for a detailed discussion of this discourse.

[95] For a useful discussion of definitions in this respect, see: Fried (1967) p.5 ff.

[96] Harris (1980).

[97] McLellan (1986).

[98] During the middle years of the 20th century there was a wide discussion of the problematic of ideology ranging from analysis of religion through Marxist notions of 'false consciousness', 'alienation' and 'reification' to psychology with the notion of the 'social subconscious', discussed in Atkinson (1991) Chapter Four.

[99] This is discussed in detail in Chapter Seven.

[100] In recent decades, with the spread of mass media, the slow death of languages turned into a flood with now less than 7,000 discrete languages of which over 500 are spoken by fewer than ten people.

[101] Whilst the transition to the transcendental in the Occident simply eliminated spiritual value in Nature, in the Chinese case Buddhism maintained a residue of value, at least in the animal world through the notion of reincarnation and in China, Taoism and, more instrumentally, the I Ching – and particularly Feng Shui - provided some kind of spirituality and moral order, preventing the reduction of nature to the subject of pure instrumentality. The issue of Occidental attitudes to 'the environment' are discussed in Chapter Four.

[102] Sanderson (1990).

[103] Condorcet, Marquis de (Caritat, Marie-Jean-Antoine-Nicolas) (1976).

[104] Burrow (1966).

[105] The philosopher Hegel in his version of progress, asserted the then German political system to be the end point in cultural evolution.

[106] Marx (1976).

[107] Tainter (1988); Diamond (2005).

[108] The astonishing level of wanton murder and destruction brought about by the amazingly well-organised and strategically and tactically astute military campaigns of Genghis Khan resulted in mountains of loot disappearing into the grass plains of Mongolia and, following weak attempts at more permanent construction of a capital for the empire at, respectively, Karakorum and Xanadu, in the context of the ravages of

the Black Death, those Mongols who didn't merge into the existing cultures of the East, South and West, returned home to fade back into the simple pastoral life we see in Mongolia even today. Weatherford (2005).

[109] Francis Bacon, generally seen as the first propagandist for Occidental science, advocated this by reference to three inventions – the compass, printing, gunpowder - all of which had been invented in previous centuries in China and found their way to Europe via the Silk Route. For a comprehensive history of science and technology in Chinese history, see: Needham (1954-1971).

[110] Albeit the first Christian *States* were respectively the precursors of modern-day Armenia and Georgia.

[111] Almost the whole corpus of modern literature on the evolution of human societies and its various branches of paleoarchaeology, archaeology, anthropology, theories of history and now including a growing literature speculating on the coming collapse of modern civilisation, assumes that progress (and thence collapse) - continuous change - is an inevitable feature of civilisation as such. Whilst this is patently false, it is also pernicious in erasing the possibility of conceiving of how end-states might be organised and hence planning the future in the name of human welfare and environmental sustainability instead of submitting to chaos.

[112] Blumenberg (1983). See also Lasch (1991).

[113] Manuel (1968).

[114] Tuveson (1949); Pollard (1968); Cohn (1970).

[115] Smith (1974).

[116] Marx and Engels (1965 [1848]).

[117] Cohn (1970).

[118] Hill (1975).

[119] A similar technocratic cultural orientation emerged with the modernisation of Japan and more recently South Korea, albeit with very different cultural substructures.

[120] Venturi (1960).

[121] Manuel and Manuel (1979).

[122] Gerth and Wright Mills (1970).

[123] Weber (1976 [1930]).

[124] Anderson (1970). There have been those – notably Joseph Needham who documented the development of science and technology in China - who insist that China was far from stagnant. Whilst the development of technology cannot be denied, this was certainly not accompanied by any general notion of progress but rather incremental improvements on what otherwise remained a static framework.

[125] Greer (2008).

[126] Moore (1967); Gates (1996).

[127] Indeed, the 'overseas Chinese' had been blazing a trail already from the early 20th century and as Sterling Seagrave (1995), noted of this 'nation', comprising four per cent of the Chinese population generating at that time a gross product significantly larger than that of mainland China.

[128] Lubbock (1995).

[129] Horne (1978).

[130] Smith (1976 [1776]).

[131] Hobbes (1968 [1651]).

[132] Locke (1960 [1690]).

[133] MacPherson (1962).

[134] It is interesting to note that in the 'developmental' and 'social democratic' years there prevailed a notion from the other side of the Enlightenment that greater efficiency in the economic system could enable us to spend more time improving our lives through leisure pursuits and, perhaps, through the arts, and average working hours would decline. With the advent of the 'liberal counter-revolution' from 1980 onwards, working hours again began to increase, first in the United States and then spreading to other Occidental countries. No questions were asked as to how meaningful this work might be but in so far as it earned money – and increasingly at the upper end, yielded surreal incomes - this has become the ultimate judge of our individual worth and, indeed, our identity.

[135] A number of further 'axioms' concerning 'markets' and their efficacy in promoting the growth of wealth are built upon the notion of

the competing individual which may have had some truth in the time that Adam Smith devised them but which today are a perfectly ludicrous depiction of how the economic world works. See: Scott Cato (2006), Chapter Two.

[136] Thompson (1963).

[137] Cholera reached England and Wales in 1831 with an epidemic that killed 20,000 people, and a further epidemic in1848-49 killing a further 50,000 people. In mid-19th century England about half of all children died before the age of five (today in sib-Saharan African countries about a quarter of children die before the age of five). Lüthi and Schütze (2011).

[138] Formalised by David Ricardo in the 19th century viz the theory of 'gains from trade' which disingenuously asserts that all parties to trade may gain from this activity, obscuring the actuality where the rich and powerful can, and do systematically, use this 'insight' to exploit the poor and weak through unequal terms of trade.

[139] For the most complete analysis of the role of technology in Europe across the 19th century see: Landes (1969); Berg (1979).

[140] A notable exception being: Debier et al (1991).

[141] Whilst some assert that this is somewhat exaggerated, Joseph Needham's five-volume *Science and Civilisation in China* makes it quite clear that most technologies that appeared in Europe only from the 18th century had been invented and in common use already for many centuries in China.

[142] It was the Mongols, once they had themselves become sinified under Kublai Khan, who took China to its most extensive spatial limits.

[143] See, for starters: Hobsbawm (1962,1968)

[144] Mann (2005).

[145] Braudel (1972).

[146] Sophisticated metallurgy in China and Japan preceded the 'inventions' of the British industrial revolution by hundreds and in some cases even more than a thousand years.

[147] Cohn (1970).

[148] See: Hobart (1993).

[149] Donal and Rattansi (1992).

[150] Garland et al (2007).

[151] Bauman (2002).

[152] Latour (1987, 2005).

[153] Hays (1959).

[154] The nearest thing to a culture that disregarded the drive to modernise was Tibet's neighbour Bhutan. Never colonised and largely ignored, Bhutan went its own way as a Buddhist kingdom that survives even today. However, in 1961 the King decided that the education system should be 'modernised' and from then on imported teachers from English-speaking countries (mainly from India but also from Britain, Australia and Canada) who inevitably started a process of changing minds whilst the principle of 'driglam namzha' – maintaining tradition – became more coercive through legislation. As the decades rolled on, however, surreptitious development unfolded with mines and hydroelectric dams – all for export to India – and slowly restrictions on tourism were relaxed so that by now the country is crawling with voyeuristic tourists who inevitably bring increasing wealth, dissolving tradition at the edges. See Chapter Seven below.

[155] Rostow (1960).

[156] Committee on Resources and Man (1969).

[157] Meadows et al (1974).

[158] Roll (1994).

[159] Harvey (2005).

[160] Vogel (1989); Beder (2000).

[161] From a US perspective, see: Herman and Chomsky (1988).

[162] Bryceson et al (2000).

[163] The use of the word 'Technostructure' here is close to what Jaques Ellul (1964) referred to as the 'Technological Society,' only I wish to stress that the society is *driven* by commerce and *produces* the Technostructure rather than that the Technostructure *is* the society.

Chapter Three

[164] Burrow (1966).

[165] For thorough analyses of the issue of social evolutionism see: Sanderson (1990) and Ingold (1986).

[166] See Fried (1967).

[167] As Stuart Hughes (1959, p.42) put it:

To come to terms with Marxism, then, was the first and most obvious task confronting the intellectual innovators of the 1890s.

[168] Lights in the darkness nevertheless appeared, particularly in the writings of Gordon Childe.

[169] Sahlins and Service (1960).

[170] Fried (1967).

[171] Barclay (1982).

[172] Sahlins (1974).

[173] The most extreme case being the institution of 'potlatch' amongst the Indians of north-western America, where social status was acquired from showing just how much in terms of commodities one was capable of contributing to the community.

[174] Montagu (1978).

[175] Leacock (1981).

[176] Korten (1995).

[177] Galeano (1973).

[178] Occidental intellect is particularly pleased when it can find non-Occidentals to help them to refine their intellectual prejudices - for instance Amatya Sen and Kwame Anthony Appiah.

[179] Blum (2003).

[180] Codding (1965).

[181] Fried (1967).

[182] See in particular: Blum, (2003).

[183] Lenin (1965 [1917]).

[184] Dobb (1946); Hilton (1976).

[185] Ward-Perkins (2005).

[186] Plato (1974).

[187] More (1965 [1516]).

[188] Locke (1960).

[189] Rousseau (1968).

[190] Rousseau (1964).

[191] Wilder Publications (2007).

[192] Marx (1964).

[193] A short bibliography of the Anarchist movement worldwide would need to include: Woodcock (1963), Joll (1980) and Marshall (2010).

[194] Miller (1976).

[195] Bookchin (1982, 1989).

[196] Albert (2003).

[197] Tainter (1988).

[198] Ponting (2007).

[199] Ostrom (1990).

[200] Foote-Whyte and King-Whyte (1988).

[201] This was famously asserted by Wittfogel (1957) in his thesis concerning 'hydraulic society.' that became the subject of extensive academic debate. However, many complex irrigation systems – the 'subak' on the island of Bali provide an excellent example – are managed through democratic decision-making processes involving the whole community of farmers, landed and landless.

[202] Rousseau (1968).

[203] Par for the course being the eighty five 'working groups' that discussed 'what should be done' in the context of the 'Occupy Wall Street' events in New York in the autumn and winter of 2011-12.

[204] Cavanagh and Mander (2004).

[205] Hoggart (1957); McKenzie and Silver (1968).

[206] Giddens and Held (1982); Erikson and Goldthorpe (1992).

[207] According to a detailed analysis presented in 2009 on the web site of the journal Mother Jones, from 1980 to the mid 1990s the average income in the US declined gradually, then recovered slowly so that by 2009 it was, at just over $30,000 a year, barely 10% more than in1980. By contrast, whilst the income of the top one per cent fluctuated wildly over the period, the overall tendency was upward, being, by 2007, 240% greater than in 1980 and standing at over three million dollars per annum. The 2008 financial crisis returned the average US citizen to their situation in the early 1990s, by which time the ideological eyewash of the rich, whilst having become grotesque in its crass lies, still managed to keep the population in an ideological straightjacket that confirmed acquiescence in the notion that present wealth and income differentials are legitimate. See the preface to the paperback edition of: Stiglitz (2012).

[208] The flickering events at the end of 2011 and start of 2012 around the cry of 'Occupy Wall Street!' ostensibly the start of a revolution against the grotesquerie of US wealth and income differentials, involved a minute minority of the US population and quietened down after a few months but rumbled on below the surface and by 2013 had spread to Western Europe as a series of ongoing demonstrations.

[209] Men, et al (2003).

[210] A literature on this is opening up almost exclusively in the United States. Key publications were cited in Chapter One (see endnote 72 for details), significant authors at the time of writing being Richard Heinberg and John Michael Greer with a flow of books by various authors from New Society Press.

[211] Graham (2010).

Chapter Four

[212] This was, arguably, initiated in the work of Robert Merton (1970) in his analysis of the beginnings of the scientific revolution in the 16th and 17th centuries. It was soon followed by what might be called a school of the 'sociology of science' a notable contribution to which was made by Barry Barnes (1974, 1977).

[213] Feyerabend (1978).

[214] Latour (1986).

[215] The view and statistics presented in this paragraph are mainly derived from Sale (2006).

[216] Tainter (1988).

[217] Diamond (2005).

[218] Diamond (1998).

[219] The role of European imperialism in mixing the species of different continents is described in detail by Crosby (1986).

[220] What Bill McKibben (1990) referred to as the end of Nature.

[221] Ponting (2007).

[222] Catton (1982).

[223] See in particular: Greer (2005). This is also Jarred Diamond's (2005) major finding from his extensive research into the collapse of complex societies.

[224] One cannot help but immediately focus on the pathetic abuse of water resources in the United States which is, today, temporarily, the world's greatest exporter of food by a wide margin. Problems of the future of America's water resources include notably the systematic draw-down of the massive Ogallala aquifer stretching under eight states and the progressive threat of waterlogging and salinisation of the San Joaquin Valley in California known as 'the most productive unnatural environment in the world' that currently produces some ten per cent of all the agricultural produce of the United States, both of which are unsustainable in the relatively short term. See: Reisner (1986).

[225] There were in fact numbers of theoreticians who realised this and who worked diligently towards truly effective measures to stem environmental depletion in the context of Modern society. See particularly the work of Herman Daly (1973, 1996) – with his concept of the steady state economy – and the work of Robert Ayers (1994) on resources and industry or 'industrial ecology'.

[226] Lebow (1955).

[227] Fine and Leopold (1993).

[228] At another extreme we see the anti-anti-consumption polemic that accuses, via a series of straw men, a wide range of critics of

consumption as denying the poor and populations of the non-Occident the fruits of modern wealth. See the introduction to: Mille (1995).

[229] Cohen and Murphy (2001); Jackson (2006).

[230] Recently a brilliant and enormously popular cartoon movie under the title of *The Story of Stuff* (Leonard, A: www.storyofstuff.com) was launched on the internet in December 2007 and focused on the importance of consumption to today's politics, the problems that this is raising and ultimately the unsustainability of current consumption patterns.

[231] Over the past decades, David Pimentel has published a steady stream of books and articles that document the evolution of global food consumption habits and the problematic nature of these.

[232] Electric Wallpaper Co. (2004).

[233] Atkinson (2007).

[234] Oliver (1998).

[235] Glacken (1967) demonstrated that in fact interest in the relationship between climate and geography and the culture of those living in different environments goes right back to antiquity.

[236] Rousseau (1964).

[237] Hegel (1975).

[238] Marx (1976) p.649.

[239] Cohn (1970).

[240] Needham (1954-1971).

[241] Thomas (1983).

[242] Paul Oliver (1998) coordinated prodigious work, collecting information on vernacular architecture worldwide and published, with others, a number of books on different aspects of this.

[243] A more detailed account of what is presented in the following paragraphs can be found in Atkinson (1991) Chapter Five.

[244] See in particular: Capra (1982); Easlea (1980); Leiss (1972); Merchant (1980); Roszak (1973).

[245] Lovejoy (1936).

[246] Thomas (1983).

[247] Bacon's (1960[1620]) propaganda for science as set out in his aphorisms and utopian fantasy is, unlike much of the writing of the Enlightenment such as Hobbes, Locke and Hume, still highly readable.

[248] Aronowitz (1988).

[249] Lewis (1947).

[250] Hughes (1959).

[251] Popper's major works, viz *The Poverty of Historicism,* published in 1957 but originally written and circulated in 1936, and thence his *Open Society and its Enemies* published in 1945, were dedicated to destroying Marxism and everything it stood for in terms of any notion of an ideal society, and hence also any form of Utopianism. Popper, who eventually held a professorship at the London School of Economics, had the deep support of the academic establishment in the UK and to some extent in the United States, as a central pillar of the blasting of claims that egalitarianism might be a viable way to organise society.

[252] Coppleston (1965), Chapter 18.

[253] Ecology, conceived by the 19th Century German scientist Ernst Haeckel as an approach to understanding biology seen from the point of view of the interconnection between species in their actual environments, was always a problematic child for science in that it implies holism, rather than disassembly – with fundamentally different philosophical implications (see: Worster (1979)). A colourful figure with a wide set of interests and achievements, Haeckel often produced ideas as facts well before their justification in empirical terms. He was also an unabashed racist in seeing different races in terms of a hierarchy with Caucasian at the peak – par for the course in the 19th century.

[254] Needham (1954-1971).

[255] Latour (1986).

[256] Feyerabend (1978).

[257] Latour (1986) and (2005).

[258] Ellul (1964).

[259] See particularly Marshall Berman's (1994) fine interpretation of Goethe's *Faust* as anticipation of the progress of industry in the modern world.

[260] Manuel (1968).

[261] Such deep research programmes that might not seem to have instrumental value can and do, however, produce knowledge that comes to be applied by commerce and for military purposes. CERN produced the Worldwide Web as a spin-off of their work; the jury is still out as to whether or not this, as 'social media', aids or undermines power relations.

[262] Hays (1959).

[263] For a detailed history of the English case of changing attitudes to Nature – which was extremely influential in the development generally of modern attitudes – see: Thomas (1983).

[264] This discourse starts with Lynn White's famous 1967 essay - *The Historical Roots of our Ecological Crisis*. Important subsequent contributions include: Moncrief (1970); Black (1970); and thence a number of anthologies appeared including: Barbour (1972 and 1973); Partridge (1981) and Passmore (1980).

[265] An early attempt at Marxist exegesis on the issue of environmental conservation or management was Alfred Schmidt's (1971) *The Concept of Nature in Marx*. Key theoreticians were Murray Bookchin (1982, 1989) in the United States, Rudolph Bahro (1978, 1982, 1984, 1986) in Germany – both of whom were directly involved in informing the growth of environmental politics – and Andé Gorz (1980) in France.

[266] It is difficult to make a choice amongst literally hundreds of thoughtful books on these subjects; but at least reference might be made to two compendia that give something of an overview of contributions to environmental ethics and philosophy are: Elliot and Gare (1983); Chappell (1997).

[267] Lovelock (2000).

[268] Naess (1989) first developed his ecological philosophy from earlier stages in his work, expressed in an essay, developed in 1972 and published in various forms and places under the title of *The Shallow and the Deep Ecology Movement.*

[269] An important push to broadening the discourse of *Deep Ecology* can be found in Devall and Sessions (1985) in somewhat rhetorical form, as a critique of the developing environmental debates.

[270] Fox (1990).

[271] Mathews (1991).

[272] The World Conservation Strategy and World Charter on Nature were produced by the International Union for Nature Conservation and Natural Resources (IUCN) in 1980 with a view to influencing the international agencies as they went about the business of development. The International Development Ethics Association was founded in 1987 with a view to developing ethical principles including those concerned with environmental conservation. See: Engel and Engel (1990).

[273] Bauman (1989). In fact Karl Marx complained already in his theses on Feuerbach of 1845 (No.11) that: *Philosophers have hitherto only interpreted the world in various ways; the point is to change it.* It seems we are back to a situation where philosophy is of no significant interest to society.

[274] Bookchin (1982).

[275] Tainter (1988) list of factors contributing to the collapse of complex societies provides a useful structure for considering the range of problems faced by any complex civilisation that can lead to collapse. In the end some broad notion of 'diminishing returns' to investment – including imagination – seems to encapsulate the general case.

[276] But see Ward-Perkins (2010) who presents the archaeological evidence of Roman mining which was capable of wreaking serious local environmental damage that has still not recovered after well-nigh two thousand years.

[277] Peak Oil Task Force (2009). See Endnote 72.

[278] Harrison (1969).

[279] In his magnum opus *The General Theory of Employment, Interest and Money,* John Maynard Keynes (1936, pp.522-524) - the chief architect of post Second World War economic growth - made a disparaging remark in passing to the effect that Jevons' worries about depletion were due to a psychological inadequacy, namely: *a*

psychological trait, unusually strong in him...a certain hoarding instinct.

[280] Indeed, the *Limits to Growth* report met with some amazing invective on the part of some economists, railing against its very legitimacy as if it had infringed some moral principle! See for instance: Kay and Mirrlees (1975).

[281] Ise (1925). This was discussed by Ivor Pearce in the context of a 1974 conference in which some of the more absurd expressions of economists' 'resource optimism' were voiced. See: Pearce and Rose (1975). In reaction to environmentalist concerns at this time, many economists were belligerently declaring that physical resources count for nothing as long as there is enough capital to make the transition to alternative resources when depletion reveals itself. And surely as modernity and with it the resource base fails, economists, locked in their ideological straightjacket, will continue to lament the fact that it was the capital supply that has failed and not the impossibility of endless progress. As Kenneth Boulding put it: *Anyone who believes exponential growth can go on forever in a finite world is either a madman or an economist.*

[282] Where the notion of ours being a 'risk society' arose only recently – especially identified with the work of sociologist Ulrich Beck - we can say that European progressivism has always possessed an over-abundance of risk, adventure and plain gambling which became one of the key traits of 'the discoveries' and subsequent European colonialism and thence of capitalism as an economic system. Beck (1992).

[283] PEP (1955).

[284] Best (1981).

[285] DEFRA (2005).

[286] Middleton and Thomas (1997).

[287] Particularly contentious in this respect was Ehrlich (1969).

[288] Commoner (1972a).

[289] Commoner (1972b).

[290] Peak Oil Task Force (2009). See Endnote 72 above. This proliferation of substitutions of petro-chemicals as a basis for the production of goods continued unabated such that in 2005 Gary Stringer of Northeast Louisiana University counted over 500,000

products in daily use that are made from petro-chemicals or their derivatives.

[291] Wallace (1996).

[292] Millennium Ecosystems Assessment (2007).

[293] SCEP (Study of Critical Environmental Problems) (1970).

[294] Over the years, definitions of 'sustainable development' proliferated into the hundreds, but this definition, presented in the Brundtland Report (WCED (1987).

[295] Recent US literature addressing the coming fall of American civilisation likes to portray the *Limits to Growth* study as the brainchild of the MIT team, completely overlooking its origins in the political activity of the Club of Rome and particularly the heroic efforts of Peccei!

[296] Meadows (1974).

[297] See for example: Clerk et al (1975).

[298] Peccei, however, never ceased with attempts to engage an elite audience through founding a series of institutions and organising initiatives aimed at fundamentally changing the direction of Development. Whilst many of these survived as research institutes and political fora, following Peccei's death in 1984 these made little impact on the political world and none gained any noticeable renown within the growing Green Movement.

[299] Meadows et al (1993, 2004).

[300] IUCN (1980) Although this report is generally considered to be a landmark in the development of the concept of 'Sustainable Development '- and where this term was first brought into widespread currency, it was never formally published.

[301] WCED (1987).

[302] This comes from personal experience when in recent years I asked each new group of students studying planning (i.e. who might be expected to be the most likely to have come across the study) whether they knew of the study and regularly found perhaps one or two amongst twenty who had heard of it but were unlikely to know anything much about its content.

[303] Komarov (1980).

[304] Kay and Mirrlees (1975).

[305] A notable example being James O'Connor's notion of 'the second contradiction of capital' as expounded through debates in the pages of early issues of the journal *Capital Socialism Nature.*

[306] Recently, William Catton (2009) has identified the division of labour – not only in distancing us from Nature but also as a central aspect of exploitative social relations – as a core issue in driving our world to collapse (what he refers to rather euphemistically as a 'bottleneck').

[307] Small numbers of anthropologists had enough distance from modernity to realise the problematic of orienting peoples away from traditional practices and into practices that would, in the medium term, be unusable. A small European group organised conferences under the clearly not 'urban skills' but 'modern skills'.

Chapter Five

[308] Ward-Perkins (2005).

[309] Ponting (2007).

[310] Ward-Perkins (2010).

[311] Hobsbawm (1968).

[312] DEFRA (2005).

[313] Christaller (1966).

[314] Christaller's analysis was subsequently applied, qua 'Central Place Theory', proactively. This included the actual destruction of villages in Poland during the Second World War as not conforming to an 'ideal' rural-urban structure. Whilst this might seem to have been a draconian act to be expected of the German Nazi regime (that also raised most of Warsaw to the ground) but was in fact a policy continued by the subsequent Polish 'communist' regime! The state of Israel also experimented with Christaller's 'theory' to determine where they should locate their new expansion over the land taken from Palestine. To this day, Central Place Theory is an integral part of German regional planning, determining the distribution of Government investments in different classes of settlement. However, globalisation has made nonsense of the distribution of economic activity in space where even

shops sell goods produced at the far ends of the world or at any rate from the far corners of Germany where the cities obtain little by way of materials and goods from the surrounding countryside.

[315] The production of tractors having been delayed by the preoccupation with producing vehicles to wage war!

[316] Torres (2001).

[317] Böge (1995).

[318] Hobart (1993).

[319] Thomas (1983).

[320] For excellent blow-by-blow analysis of the way in which liberalism in trade was promoted, particularly first by the British and then the Americans as a means to exploit the rest of the world, see: Chang (2003, 2007).

[321] Fried (1967).

[322] Gordon Childe, cited above, was the great historian of the emergence of complex divisions of labour and society as 'civilisation.'

[323] For a while, this engendered a huge debate amongst Marxists around the notion of 'hydraulic civilisations' associated with the name of Karl August Wittfogel cited above.

[324] See Footnote 264.

[325] Marshall Sahlins's (1974) work on pre-civilisation economic relations was discussed in Chapter Three.

[326] viz Shiraz and Lahore, visited by myself in 1969

[327] Engels (2009).

[328] Kelly (2001).

[329] Etzioni (1993); Shuman (2000); Albert (2003); DeFillipis (2004); McKibben (2007).

[330] By 2005, 25% of the UK workforce was 'working' in banking and related services including 'real estate' – making money out of property transactions.

[331] One thinks back to (Sir) Arthur Lewis and his theory that the development of the 'underdeveloped countries' required as a

prerequisite the stimulation of the entrepreneurial spirit and the mentality of saving and investment rather than immediate consumption.

[332] With variants under such titles as 'worker's control', ESPOs, etc.

[333] Albert (2003).

[334] Some rules can be read out of 'holy' texts which are not, however, translated into daily life where in other cases, rules have been invented that are said to be associated with the religions that are not, however, found in the texts. This is particularly true of Islam where the role of women, strictly regulated in most Islamic societies down to the details of dress, are not to be found in the Koran or any other original holy text.

[335] Littman (1974).

[336] Cohn (1970).

[337] Manuel and Manuel (1979).

[338] Particularly impressive amongst these was the Students for a Democratic Society (SDS) in the United States that produced the 'Port Huron Statement'. See: Sale (1973).

[339] Satish Kumar has published several books over the years. See particularly: Kumar (2002).

[340] Goldsmith et al (1972).

[341] For anyone wanting to do research on this era, please contact the author to consult a library of many of these quasi-publications.

[342] The journal of this name should not be confused with the Canadian critical – but nevertheless 'establishment' - television programme of the same name.

[343] Hardy (1979); Mercer (1984).

[344] Rigby (1974); Abrams, P. and McCulloch (1976); Moss Kanter (1972). Rosabeth Moss Kanter, following her insightful and sympathetic analysis of communes, subsequently went on to become Professor at Harvard Business School, where she has tirelessly promoted the interests of global capital. A literature also appeared in other European countries. For Germany, see: Hollstein and Peth (1980); Junk and Müllert (1980).

[345] A biannual directory of such communities in the UK has been produced since the late 1980s under the title of *Diggers and Dreamers* that, besides listing and briefly describing the communities, published articles about and relevant to communal living. Since the turn of the century, a European network of communities has been established, publishing the *Directory of Intentional Communities and Ecovillages in Europe* of which three have so far been published. In the United States, the Fellowship for Intentional Community has been promoting community living and cooperative lifestyles since 1986 – growing out of a previous organisation founded in 1948. It issues a journal, organises events and publishes a regularly updated directory with currently entries for well over a hundred Intentional Communities. For a review of circumstances up to 2010, see: Dawson (2010).

[346] Abrams and McCulloch (1976).

[347] Besides the more substantial literature of the movement itself, periodic external attempts to understand and to theorise about them have appeared. For Britain, see: Pepper (1991); Sargisson (2000).

[348] For an excellent overview of the state of the Intentional Communities movement world-wide, based on extensive travels and visits, see: Metcalf (1996).

[349] In 2007, the UK Communes Network listed 93 groups in its directory with 2,781 members. It estimated that there might be up to 23,000 members of related, unrecorded communities and 'ecovillages'. Even this is less than 0.4% of the population of the islands.

[350] Mention was made in passing to the town of Totnes in Devon, as initiating the 'Transition Towns' movement in England: here is a town – and, indeed a sub-region - that has for many decades been oriented as a whole to 'alternative' lifestyle ideas and activities linked to the neighbouring Dartington cluster of initiatives. The Findhorn Community in Scotland has a similar sub-regional impact. Both of these may be seen as linked to 'New Age' thinking.

[351] Leo Marx (1964) analysed American society even back into the years of its discovery, and right through history the story of the development of 'American' culture, stating that there has been a constant tension between the Developmentalist (he doesn't use the concept of capitalism) and what might be termed the bucolic – or even utopian – notion of what America might become as a place, and the society that resides in it.

[352] Mention should also be made of Odum's son Howard, mentioned in Chapter One, who spent his career studying how energy moves through and animates ecological and human systems. He was alone already from the 1970s in his sharp awareness of the end-game which our civilisation was playing with energy and was the first in recent years to spell out – if idiosyncratically - the way in which our civilisation is about to peak and proceed downhill because of shrinkage in the availability of energy. Odum (1971); Odum and Odum (2001).

[353] Luccarelli (1995).

[354] Friedmann and Weaver (1979).

[355] Sale (1985).

[356] Brunckhorst (2002).

[357] For a recent detailed history of the Bioregional movement, see: Carr (2004).

[358] In 2010 the World Food Programme estimated that the population suffering undernourishment had cross the one billion mark. The figure was, however, revised downwards by the UN Food and Agriculture Organisation (FAO) in a recalculation that showed that globally undernourishment has been on the decline almost continuously since 1990.

[359] Friere (1993).

[360] Rahman (1993).

[361] Alinski (1971).

[362] For almost twenty years the journal *Environment & Urbanization* has championed the lot of the urban poor in the South, bringing their problems and initiatives to overcome these to the attention of those who may be concerned with the issues involved.

[363] To learn what Transition Towns and cities are about, copious information is available at the present time on the internet but in published form is best found in: Hopkins (2009); Chamberlin (2009).

[364] Having been involved with others in developing participatory planning methods in Britain in the early 1980s, from the early 1990s I was funded by development organisations to work up similar methodologies in various Southern countries – in the main in Asia. Indigenous development workers – such as Paulo Friere (1993) and

Anisur Rahman (1993) developed methodologies for participatory planning – and more broadly empowerment of 'the poor' - that were designed to fit the cultures of Southern countries and in each country and particular cities, methods were tried often with local 'civil society organisations' funded by international agencies to spread the efforts and in principle even with national Government backing. Larger programmes including UNDP's LIFE programme, UN-HABITAT's Sustainable Cities Programme and the City Development Strategies of the Cities Alliance, housed in the World Bank and funded by a number of bilateral agencies (European 'donations'). However, there was little by way of deeper cultural bases for these initiatives and little residue once the 'assistance' had come to an end. In any case, the assumptions of the agencies and most of the development workers structuring these projects was one that was 'developmentalist' rather than in any way informed by 'utopianism' or other 'cultural change' model.

[365] Ward-Perkins (2010).

[366] Recently working for the International Labour Organisation on 'skills for green jobs', I had the opportunity to look at national programmes for skills development around the world. Significant resources are going into this which, however, stress 'competitivity' at the hi-tech end and even in quite basic skills such as in construction, means to install sophisticated technologies and apply new materials, rather than any realisation of the need to 'regress' to the use of local materials and manual skills that will be required (again) in the not too distant future!

[367] Working regularly for the ILO, as I do, I become keenly aware of this anomaly, but find it difficult to bring the real future into focus for the staff and hence to start a process of radically revising the direction which 'skills development' should take!

[368] The idea was developed by William Rees at the University of British Columbia For a description of what this is about, see: Wackernagel and Rees (1996).

[369] The Worldwide Fund for Nature (WWF) calculated the per-capita ecological footprint for seventy two countries broken down into seven use categories. Hails (2006).

[370] This situation is conjectured and the consequences discussed in the report produced by the German Defence Department research division referred to in Chapter One: ZfTB (2010).

[371] Leeb (2006).

[372] 'Market solutions' are likely increasingly to lead to dislocation, deprivation and starvation.

[373] Kohr (1957), an Austrian professor of economics, described himself as a philosophical anarchist, sharing a prime place with Schumacher in writing for the early issues of the journal Resurgence, described in the following chapter.

[374] Good examples include: Dauncey (1988); Lang and Hines (1993); Trainer, T. (1995); Hines, C. (2000); DeFilipps, J. (2004); Scott Cato (2006); McKibben, B. (2007). There is also an emerging literature of personal ways to adapt lifestyles that includes: Astyk (2008); Baker, C. (2009).

[375] Good examples include: Wall, D. (2005); Kovel (2007).

[376] Hopkins (2009).

[377] Wackernagel and Rees (1996) p.97.

Chapter Six

[378] In emulation of the rich and powerful where, as the saying went: 'An Englishman's house is his castle'.

[379] In Russia this has become a significant reality in the shape of 'dachas' that are second homes of urban citizens, often at some distance from the cities, where today they are a significant source of food – described further below.

[380] Electric Wallpaper Co. (2004).

[381] Albeit incipient move towards the creation of trading in land plots began to emerge in the 'proto-modern' era of China 1,500 years ago. This resulted, through consolidation of land holdings, in what amounted to feudalism under landlords owning massive holdings.

[382] Par for the course in forcing conformance to what we Occidentals (Americans) think is correct in the face of any kind of rational argument is a current USAID-funded programme to privatise the Mongolian steps. One commentary had the following to say:

Before the freewheeling 1960s, before Mao led China to revolution in 1949 and before the Soviets took control of this country in 1921,

Mongolia was already one giant commune. "Land here never belonged to anyone; it belonged to everyone," said Davasuren, 50, a self-described retired nomad.

Many local politicians and economists now say that Mongolia's traditional land regime is the core cause of its backwardness and want to replace it with a Westernized property management system under which land would be parcelled out and privatized.

"Our plan is, every citizen gets some land free once, in one area", said Myagmarsuren Dechinlkhundev, consultant to the Government's standing committee on environment and rural development in Ulan Bator.

There are nevertheless legitimate objections to land-privatization in Mongolia (or anywhere else). To wit, there are (to simplify grossly) three: First, it goes against traditional Mongolian notions of land use. Second, it would create instability in the livelihoods of well over half of Mongolia's population that derives its subsistence from nomadic herding. Third, it would go a long way toward destroying an ancient, thriving, and irreplaceable culture.

However, the argument of the Modernisers is simply: "... the Mongolians are just going to have to adapt to the way things work in the modern world, just as all advanced civilizations have."

[383] For an extensive discussion of issues involved in land ownership in squatted areas in the urban South, see: Durand-Lasserve and Royston (2002).

[384] This was strongly promoted by the Peruvian Liberal economic ideologue Hernando de Soto and enthusiastically taken up by the World Bank so that many national Governments have initiated 'titling' programmes for urban squatter settlements.

[385] In Russia, certain individuals were in a position to grab vast resources, leading to the creation of a class known as the oligarchs. By contrast, in the case of the German Democratic Republic, archives existed on who the owners of land had been prior to communist times and with the reuniting of Germany, the authorities proceeded to hand the land back to the pre-war owners.

[386] Ostrom (1990).

[387] A clear indication of this lack of interest, it seems to me, is the lack of any committee or working group on LED or employment amongst the twelve thematic groups established by the members of the UCLG –

the international support organisation for local governments – to promote the interests of the citizens of member cities.

[388] Economic Development Department (1985).

[389] In the framework of the then newly-created Economic Development Department, I was employed by the Popular Planning Unit to liaise both with relevant sections of the council bureaucracy and to organise public meetings to educate citizens and promote energy conservation policies and initiatives – primarily to recover waste heat from London's power stations to substitute for the use of natural gas in heating the city's building stock.

[390] Albeit this is a rather strange notion, given that biofuels, which can be expected to become the main source of energy once again, are also carbon fuels...

[391] Urban and regional planning departments should already have this data albeit, as outlined below, a new approach needs to be taken – and the bioregional literature already indicates approaches that might be taken, e.g. McGinnis (1999); Thayer (2003).

[392] I remember in my student days in London how the trucks came round to hotels and restaurants at night, collecting food waste to take to pig farms on the edge of the city. And how 'totters' combed the streets with horse-carts, crying, 'any old iron!' to collect metals for recycling. These died by the 1980s and the new approach, engaging local authorities to separate household waste, came into being in stages.

[393] Kaplinsky and Morris (2001); Schmitz (2005).

[394] Although little known outside the circle of professionals who have developed and who use the method, Life Cycle Assessment has nevertheless been developed by large numbers of institutions in many countries, with computer data bases that can analyse the resource inputs, 'wastes' and environmental impacts of almost any industrial product. It has been applied particularly in the design of buildings – though, being nowhere compulsory, it is ignored by the majority of architects.

[395] There are by now many manuals and other sources indicating such procedures. A relevant example might include: ILO (2012).

[396] The focused inventiveness – and the use of his fortune made from the cotton industry in Manchester – of the Utopian Robert Owen goes sadly unacknowledged in that he pioneered, during the first half of the

19th century, much that provided experience relevant to our real future, starting with trade unionism, and thence including labour notes (even constructing labour banks), cooperativism and the promotion of equal rights for women and the development of economic theory that fed into Karl Marx's thoughts on the subject. See: Harrison (1969).

[397] These writers might be referred to as being 'anti-civilisation', starting with Stanley Diamond's (1974) *In Search of the Primitive* recently further developed by the 'neo-primitivist' John Zerzan (2005) and other 'green anarchists' but extending also to erstwhile radicals such as Kirkpatrick Sale (2006) and in the extreme Derrick Jensen (2006).

[398] A seminal conference was held at the University of Chicago in April 1966 under the title of *Man the Hunter,* bringing together a large number of anthropologists who had been researching hunting and gathering peoples. Published under the same tile and edited by Lee and Davore (1967) the book gave considerable insight into a wide range of aspects of the life of hunting and gathering peoples.

[399] The remnants of such craft villages can still be found in India and, better known, in the countryside surrounding Hanoi in Vietnam.

[400] Arguably the clearest critique of modern cities, contrasted with an idea of urban living at a moderate scale that can be expected to satisfy a rich set of human needs and aspirations, is that of Murray Bookchin (1987).

[401] The timber to build the Forbidden City in Beijing and the temples of Angkor, being hauled over considerable distance and the massive columns of the Parthenon in Rome – that still stands after 2000 years – having been transported from Egypt, the other end of the Mediterranean sea.

[402] Entirely forgotten today is the enthusiasm that reigned in the early decades of the 20th century for the machine imagery and the possibilities of machines woven into social life. One of the most impressive texts on this was Sigfried Gideon's (1948) *Mechanisation takes Command.* Of course, subsequently mechanisation sank beneath the consciousness of (post)modern society, undoing the very tissues of society and replacing this with an ever more coherent Technostructure that, like a supra-organism increasingly facilitated and thence determined how people should and did run our lives...

[403] In parts of the ex-Soviet Union (notably Georgia), energy supplies were cut for considerable periods and upon my enquiring as to whether the large number of high-rise apartment buildings continued to be occupied, I was answered in the affirmative. However, the upper floors of twelve storey towers would certainly have been impossible for elderly and disabled people to negotiate and the lack of light and heating, particularly in the stairwells in winter, must have been daunting for the inhabitants – who presumably only continued to live in the apartments because there was nowhere else to go and because there was an expectation that sometime soon the power would come back on. But what will happen when it becomes evident that in future the power will fail permanently?

[404] This problematic was first identified in the United States in the early years of the century and discussed in a number of books, the authors and associates coming together to make the 90 minute video, *The End of Suburbia* referred to above, that actually circulated and was viewed widely in the United States without yet generating a social movement to address the problem.

[405] Starting from utopian roots, first the Garden Cities and then later in the century the New Towns, whilst losing the details of utopia, were intended to represent towns of a reasonable size and a degree of self-reliance which, however, faded away with the deepening of the global economy and ever further commuting distances. The Russian New Cities were an integral part of the Developmentalist impulse of communism as ideology.

[406] British planners, having seen the hill towns of Italy and found these attractive, decided to plan new towns in their image without too much thought about environmental appropriateness (Cumbernauld); thereafter planning for an automobile-dominated future (classically Milton Keynes).

[407] There is much evidence upon the collapse of the Soviet Union that large numbers (particularly men) became disoriented by the loss of employment and the forced reorientation of society, and who died of alcoholism or of no particular cause. Research published in the British Medical Journal, The Lancet, estimated over three million such premature deaths that were attributed to the peremptory 'privatisation' of the economy. See: Stuckler and McKee (2009). What is being discussed here is an analogous rapid change in the whole structure and functioning of the society on a considerably larger scale even than the

collapse of the Soviet Union, that will now have its most dire effects in the high capitalist societies. See: Orlov (2008).

[408]   Whilst this may sound unbelievable and even shocking to many readers, those who know US cities will be aware of whole districts that became derelict as a consequence of deindustrialisation and the abandonment of inner suburbs already in the 1970s-90s.

[409]   Whilst originally no more than research, the results of Christaller's findings were thence used as a basis for regional planning. During the Nazi era, the theory was even used in Poland to eliminate villages that didn't fit the model. Application subsequently in Israel was not so effective as the country is not an undifferentiated plain where the expected hierarchy is clearly irrelevant to the desert. Research carried out in Thailand, however, discovered a Chistallian hierarchy of settlements. Even today, the German planning system designates different settlements according to their position in a Christallian hierarchy – which, however, means very little in a globalised world where rural areas no longer provision adjacent urban areas and with rural and small town populations now commuting to work in cities right across regions.

[410]   Schoups et al (2005).

[411]   A recent analysis of yields per hectare of crops grown organically indicated on average about 20% lower yields than 'conventional' agriculture applying agrochemicals (de Ponti et al (2012). However, it is evident that much larger differences in yields are due to the efficiency of production plus the availability of water with, according to World Bank statistics analysing cereal production by country, 'industrial' countries producing crops at between six and nine tons per hectare and 'poor' countries (evidently an aspect of their poverty) producing less than two tons – and in some cases even less than one ton per hectare. 'Efficient' production in the industrialised countries is achieved with vast inputs of energy and as this ebbs away and as methods of farming change with the diminishing of energy and re-localisation, yields are likely to reduce considerably with obvious consequences in terms of being able to feed the world's population.

[412]   European Union (2012).

[413]   Atkinson and Viloria (2013).

[414] In the early 1980s, the European Commission financed many initiatives that resulted in the development of methodologies for local energy planning. Once the oil price collapsed in the mid-1980s, interest at the local level declined and initiatives ceased. At the time, I was financed by the South East Economic Strategy Association, a collection of local authorities in Southeast England, to develop a simple local energy planning methodology that was applied to seven towns in the region.

[415] I still have a very large library – representing just a small offering – of the documentation that poured out of these initiatives.

[416] Recently on a visit to Sana'a, I was invited to lunch at the house of my driver (in fact an engineer trained in Abu Dhabi) where I encountered his uncle who had just returned from working in Dubai. His opening remarks were to casually note the temporary nature of the Gulf cities, remarking that these will not survive the end of oil: this is certainly no secret to the local population enjoying but briefly the luxuries offered by modern life. The massive investments currently being made by the enlightened leaders of Abu Dhabi in the hi-tech Mazda Community that uses radically less energy to run than conventional local developments is but impressive window-dressing that will equally return to the desert post-modernity.

[417] Marc Reisner's (1986) *Cadillac Desert* provides a wonderful history of the colonisation of the arid areas of the United States through aggressive diversion of water resources from the north.

[418] A number of development organisations have formed the *Sustainable Sanitation Alliance – SuSanA* that has, for a number of years, been developing theory and practice of urban sanitation systems that are more in harmony with ecological systems, returning nutrients to the soil. See: Lüthi and Schütze (2011).

[419] Methodologies used to achieve such gross estimates require what amounts to arbitrary decisions regarding definitions. Whilst the UN Food and Agriculture Organisation had in its annual report up to 2010 been warning of growing undernourishment, in 2012 a new methodology was devised that showed undernourishment to be a more modest problem and even, overall, to be falling. Presumably there were certain political pressures brought to bear on this refocusing.

[420] Atkinson and Viloria (2013).

[421]   The *Millennium Ecosystems Assessment* provides a detailed overview of the depredations upon the Biosphere of human activity over the past decades.

[422]   There is by now a substantial literature on the method – see, for starters: Mollison (1988).

[423] Permaculture is superficially a technical approach to farming that circulates nutrients and creates robust farming against the insecurities of monocultures that encouraged infestations and produced famines in the eras before the advent of agrochemicals. But at a deeper level, discussed in the next chapter it involves an entirely different thinking process to that of modern farming. To get an impression of this, see: Holzer (2004).

[424]   Carey (2011).

[425] For an amusing article on the need to revive the use of human waste in urban farming and the cultural impediments to this in the Australian context, see: Richardson (2012).

Chapter Seven

[426] For an excellent analysis of civilisation over against pre-civilisation, see: Heinberg (1995a).

[427]   This was, of course, Rousseau's contention in his two famous essays on Civilisation!

[428] Archaeological evidence shows that Homo sapiens has been present in New Guinea (presumably migrating when the sea levels were low) for some 40,000 thousand years without any signs of developing civilisation. Sub-Saharan Africa is, of course, fascinating in having been the origin, it is now thought, of *all* 'refinements' of genus Homo, going back millions of years, and yet having never developed more than the first steps towards civilisation.

[429] A hotly debated theme in anthropology. See the exchange between Elman Service (1962) and Morton Fried (1967).

[430] Much of this chapter deals with the complex hierarchical socio-political and economic structures that civilisation has built. Whilst anthropologists generally accept that pre-civil humanity lived in egalitarian bands, one must realise that 'egalitarian' is not actually a simple concept, as 'difference' existed even in the simplest societies.

So it becomes necessary to think through what 'egalitarian' means in terms of any future society where 'difference' will continue but the many dimensions of hierarchy are laid to rest. See Fried (1967, Chapter 2) for a very useful discussion of what 'egalitarian' means in the context of social organisation.

[431] As noted in the General Introduction: Lee and Devore (1967).

[432] Surely many 'primitive' peoples/cultures didn't adapt easily or at all, ending in extinction. The anthropologist Colin Turnbull made many studies in Africa that indicated clearly the spectrum of well-adapted, poorly adapted and on-the-way-to-extinction tribes. Of course, a central theme of Jared Diamond's book *Collapse,* (2005 - op.cit.) embedded even in the title, is how many cultures simply do not adapt and in the process are extinguished. Although Diamond is concerned with 'civilised' cultures and by implication warns of the incipient non-adaptation of modern civilisation, we may presume that over the millennia, thousands of 'primitive' cultures failed to adapt.

[433] The most elaborate and famous of studies of this kind were those conducted by Sir James George Frazer, published in his twelve-volume compendium entitled *The Golden Bough.* See the condensed version: Frazer (1922).

[434] This is well captured by Richard Heinberg (1995b).

[435] Individual materials and products sometimes were invented or learned from neighbours well before the broad range of civilised products came together. An extreme anomaly is the invention of pottery in Japan some 10,000 years before the emergence of civilisation in that country.

[436] See particularly Jared Diamond's *Guns, Germs and Steel* (1998) for a systematic analysis of the archaeological evidence on the time scale and processes of domestication.

[437] As Bacon put it pithily in the third aphorism of his *New Organon: 'Nature to be commanded must be obeyed.'*

[438] See Ponting (2007); Tainter (1988); Diamond's (2005).

[439] Durkheim (2008 [1912]).

[440] Recall the work of Max Weber, discussed in Chapter Three, where he analysed the close interconnection between the outlook and

organisation of different civilisations including the ostensibly secular outlook of Occidental culture.

[441] There is no 'accurate' English translation of the German word 'Geist' – and indeed much of Hegel's terminology, so here we adopt what are the words commonly used in translating his ideas – and subsequent related debates in German – into English.

[442] The term 'Alienation' has a long and eventful history in philosophy starting with St Paul's reference in his Epistle to the Ephesians to the lack of faith in God (see: Schacht, R. (1970). See also Atkinson (1991) Chapter Three for a critical discussion of the concept. Following heated debate in the 1960s, the word – and indeed the whole idea - went entirely gone out of fashion.

[443] The most absurd case today is the way that in colloquial usage in the United States, 'liberal' denotes a certain increase in Government intervention to achieve 'social' ends whilst in more focused and 'theoretical' discussion, 'liberal' means exactly the opposite: of lessening of government intervention.

[444] Coppleston (1965).

[445] Marx and Engels (1975).

[446] Leacock, E. (1981); Dobbins (1978).

[447] Today, the economies of many poorer States obtain essential support – sometimes as much as twenty per cent of GNP – from 'remittances' of family members working in rich countries and sending part of their earnings back to family members in the country they left behind.

[448] An Indonesian cigarette manufacturer (witnessed by myself) employs 58,000 women to make cigarettes by hand, whose income is vital to the economy of the local town. It also operates thirty two machines, each of which produces 2.8 million cigarettes a day. In fact all the women could be replaced by employing another forty machines. The machines are tended by a small number of foreign (so well-paid) engineers and the rest of the income from selling the cigarettes goes to the owners and management. The continued employment of the women is a function of 'tradition' and politics where the company grew in the town from small beginnings and is, in addition to being a factory, a local social institution.

[449] Morton (1970); Smith (1983).

[450] Cohn (1970).

[451] The growth of 'radical' movements in late 19th and early 20th century Russia is a particularly forceful case of the growth of such movements throughout Europe. See: Venturi (1960).

[452] Harrison (1969) pp.208-216.

[453] Matters are slightly more complicated than this in that certain trades had been organised as 'guilds' going right back into the middle ages, looking after the interests of skilled workers in different branches. Trade unionism, however, concerned itself with a much broader movement of the interests of all workers in the context of industrialising civilisation. For the British case – which was, of course, where industrialism and with it 'general trade unionism', arose: see Pelling (1971)

[454] Seidman (1982).

[455] The German sociologist Max Weber, referred to earlier with respect to his seminal analysis of capitalism, saw bureaucracy negatively, as the fate of the modern world.

[456] Albeit it is common to find, in countries where government pay is below subsistence, that the status of a government job is still attractive even though money must be found somewhere in the 'informal economy' to achieve subsistence and, hopefully, also basic symbols of status that are expressed through possession of hand-phones, motorcycles, electronic gadgets and stylish attire.

[457] For an excellent insight into these worlds, see: Bauman (2004, 2011).

[458] William Hinton's (1966). He revisited the area in 1971, reviewing his original impressions in a further book entitled *Shenfan*.

[459] A major debate on how to understand rationality erupted in the 1970s. See: Wilson (1970); Hollis and Lukes (1982).

For a more recent discussion of ways of understanding the meaning of rationality, see Searle (2001).

[460] Feyerabend (1987).

[461] This is generally self-evident amongst anthropologists, where Lévi-Strauss (1972 p.3) put it in the following way:

Every Civilisation tends to overestimate the objective orientation of its thought and this tendency is never absent. When we make the mistake of thinking that the Savage is governed solely by organic or economic needs, we forget that he levels the same reproach at us, and that to him his own desires for knowledge seem more balanced than ours...

[462]   The early 19th century French mathematician and astronomer Laplace wrote:

We may regard the present state of the universe as the effect of its past and the cause of its future. An intelligence which at a given moment knew all the forces that animate nature, and the respective positions of the beings that compose it, and further possessing the scope to analyse the data, could condense into a single formula the movement of the greatest bodies of the universe and that of the least atom: for such an intelligence nothing could be uncertain, and past and future alike would be before our eyes. Quoted in Powers (1982 p.138).

[463]   Bacon (1960 [1620] – op.cit.) Aphorism CXXIX. Seventeen years later, Descartes' *Discourse on Method* was published in which he used the phrase – arguably better known than that of Bacon and certainly more belligerent - that men should become "Masters and possessors of Nature"!

[464]   Lewis (1947).

[465]   Whilst there has been much critical debate on the methodology whereby ethologists have approached the issue of instinct in animals, the notion of pre-programmed action sequences – that Conrad Lorenz referred to as *Leerläufe* – are in some cases obvious whilst, clearly, many animal actions may be less clear in their motivations and so less easy to categorise as governed by specific instinctual 'instructions'. NB: in German 'leer' means 'empty', hence Leerläufe might be translated loosely as 'empty runs'. The use here of 'learning loops' is analogous to ' Leerläufe' – and might fancifully derive from the German 'Lehrläufe' - but indicates that these initiate a learning process rather than that they are empty shells.

[466]   Whilst elaborating on the relationship between the individual psyche and the workings of civilisation and, indeed the function of religion interested Freud greatly, resulting in two books on these issues (*Civilisation and its Discontents* and *The Future of an Illusion*), he had no interest in the notion that the coming of civilisation might in fact have *created* the psychological problems on which he focused his

attentions. He was, indeed, entirely cynical regarding the possibility of ever resolving these problems in the form of a differently structured society, opining that the *...masses are lazy and unintelligent, they have no love for instinctual renunciation, and they are not convinced by the argument of its inevitability...*i.e. beyond redemption in his terms. His attention was chiefly focused on coaxing the bourgeoisie to accept their fate in terms of a rule-based class society.

[467] Godwin (11976[1798]).

[468] Even Britain, the heartland of liberal philosophy, had its Owenite utopian initiative and then became a haven for radical refugees from across the water, including amongst others Marx and Kropotkin.

[469] Or maybe in the future, where sincerity is the guiding principle of social life, 'politics' no longer has a place. We should remember that where the term 'civilisation' originates in the Latin work for city, so the term 'politics' derives from the Greek word for city – polis - the advent of cities being where intrigue and duplicity start...

[470] See Searle (1997) *The Mystery of Consciousness* for a series of chapters on what different current thinkers on the subject think it is about, criticising these from his own point of view. Stuart Sutherland even managed to assert, in the 1989 version of the Macmillan Dictionary of Psychology, that: 'Nothing worth reading has been written on it (i.e. on the concept of consciousness.)

[471] Campbell (1966); Crook (1980 p.96).

[472] Mannheim put this in a beautiful way when he wrote:

The word and the meaning that attaches to it is truly a collective reality. The slightest nuance in the total system of thought reverberates in the individual word and the shades of meaning that it carries. The word binds us to the whole of past history and, at the same time, mirrors the totality of the present. Mannheim (1936 p.74).

[473] This is much the same notion as Roland Barthes' (1973) idea of mythologies as the basis for the study of semiology.

[474] Many an 'action' in this sense is carried out entirely in the head, ranging from planning to day-dreaming.

[475] Insofar as he could understand what he was documenting, what he saw absolutely petrified Frazer (1922) who saw the irrationality of primitive thinking as 'a standing menace to civilisation.'

[476] Notions of subsidiarity, participatory planning and the like.

[477] Hermeticism, Neoplatonism, the thought of Jakob Böhme. Whilst pantheism existed in Ancient Rome – surviving in the amazing building of the Pantheon, representing the unity of the collection of polytheistic gods, rather than more broadly 'the creation' – in more recent times it is associated with Spinoza whose 'monism' continues to be debated into modern times.

[478] We can see how embedded general assumptions are concerning the reality of the environment when we encounter people traumatised by having lived through major earthquakes.

[479] This is the title of one of two wonderful books on what Ancient Greece was all about: Littman (1974) and Dodds (1951).

[480] For a small selection of contributions, see: Touraine (1981); Boudon (1986); Maheu (1995); Jenkins and Klandermans (1995); Johnson and Klanderemans (1995).

[481] It must surely be considered an arcane joke, making nonsense of Occidental political heroics, that the Swiss, in their revolution of 1291, achieved more in their implementation of face to face democracy and hence a consensus politics than any of the revolutions discussed here and that could have been a model for other revolutions (as Rousseau, himself a Swiss, suggested).

[482] For a sense of the early attempts of the Chinese revolutionaries to transform their society in ways that would create genuinely egalitarian local communities and what happened to these, see the books of William Hinton: *Fanshen* and *Shenfan* referred to above.

[483] In 1974 René Dumont published one of the earliest books on the current crisis of civilisation which, in the English translation, had the arresting title of *Utopia – or Else!*

[484] For an entertaining romp through these manifestations, see: Mason (2013).

[485] In 1998 (p.83), Richard Rorty wrote: *America is now proletarianising its bourgeoisie...* Already in the early 1990s, Wallace Paterson (1992) referred to twenty five years of decline of the middle classes in his book *Silent Depression*.

[486] An early video made by the Transition Network (*In Transition*) gives the example of how first attempts to form a transition initiative in

Lancaster broke down in acrimony. A later attempt was then successful.

[487] Abrams, and McCulloch (1976).

[488] David Pepper (1991), carrying out a survey amongst Intentional Communities in the UK at the end of the 1980s, came to similar conclusions, quoting from one of his informants as the final word of his book:

To move to the left is difficult – you have to push everyone else. To move to the right is easy – all you have to do is opt out of the collective struggle. And in the end you think: "fuck it, it's easier to opt out."

[489] More recently Zygmunt Bauman (2001) ridiculed the very idea that anything vaguely like community could be achieved in the context of modern society – albeit it the aspiration is laudable.

[490] Aldo Leopold (1949), in his *Sand County Almanac* expressed what he called the 'land ethic' as the community of all living things within a particular ecological setting. This has been extremely influential and is indeed extremely valuable in developing attitudes to particular natural surroundings, but does not include the need for *human communities* to develop these attitudes and understand their surroundings as a component of the natural community.

[491] Mathews (2005).

[492] A substantial literature on the critique of technology arose between the 1960s and 1990s. Jaques Ellul's (1964) opening thesis has already been referred to. Murray Bookchin (1965) then opened a debate about new directions that technology should – would – take in an anarchist society. Notable further texts include: Boyle and (1976); Winner (1977); Collingridge (1980); Norman (1981); Albury and Schwartz (1982); Hill (1988). This discourse is summarised in: Atkinson (2004).

[493] Bauman (2001) p.1.

[494] ibid, p.19.

[495] Leopold (1949) p.viii.

[496] Sale (2006) pp.35 and 90.

[497] Crosby (1986).

[498] Hoskins (1991).

[499] Large numbers of country profiles of environmental destruction have appeared in recent years. Attempts are made to gain accurate figures for each country on endangered species and the attrition in biodiversity, documented in the annual *World Resource,* produced by the World Resources Institute (New York). The *Millennium Ecosystems Assessment* (2005) involved a large number of researchers attempting to map the trajectory of ecological change across the entire globe.

[500] Phongpaichit and Baker (1995).

[501] The German sociologist Thönnies defined clearly the relationship between society and community – in German Gesellschaft and Gemeinschaft - that became the basis for sociological discussion of the nature of these entities and their role in structuring human intercourse and activity.

[502] Bauman (2002).

[503] It was in response to the inhumanity of the early enclosures that Thomas More wrote his sketch of an ideal society/community under the title Utopia – and that gave the title to subsequent attempts to invent societies and communities that genuinely answer the needs and desires of humanity.

[504] Epitomised by the cult novels of Jane Austen.

[505] Strike action often generated community feeling and organisation that, however, did not persist beyond the settlement. Most famous were the strikes around coal mining as some kind of community did persist as a consequence of the hardship and danger of mining. Emil Zola's novel *Germinal,* describing a coal strike at the end of the century, contrasts the warmth of community in hardship amongst the miners with the coldness of individualistic competitive struggle, even within the bourgeois families of the mine owners.

[506] Atkinson and Viloria (2013).

[507] Many ostensible local planning initiatives are also – sometimes mainly – about community-building rather than anything resembling technical planning exercises. Already in 1999, the NEF (1999) New Economics Foundation documented twenty one methodologies of this kind.

[508] The case of Israel is truly bizarre, held in place by Jews in the USA as a kind of puppet state that continuously – but unsuccessfully –

attempts to eject Palestinians (of more than one religion, but just not Jews), including the imprisonment in their enclave of the population of Gaza, then inviting 'Jews' from around the world to 'come home.' This results in a severely class divided society due to the dominance of the ex-Occidental (Ashkenazim) Jews over the Sephardic Jews from North Africa and even from Ethiopia. It would seem that the resolution of the convoluted problems of this people would be to recognise the irrelevance of the Old Religions to their lives, abandon the control asserted over their country by American Jewry and commence active attempts to create an integrated local culture that would – maybe in a three or four generations – learn mutual respect and love and a common identification with their piece of nature, learning from both the Palestinian traditions and the experience of the Kibbutzim.

[509]   See for starters: Kellett (2007); Bercovitch and Jackson (2009); Hicks (2011).   Amongst the international development agencies, conflict resolution methods have generally been linked to new initiatives in participatory local development planning of the kind discussed in the foregoing chapter. Rahman (1993); Stiefel and Wolfe (1994).   For background, illustrated by specific situations, see the groups of essays edited respectively by Fals Borda (1985) and Reason (1988).

[510]   Bauman (2001) Chapter Nine analyses this matter in detail.

[511]   Whilst truly an ancient civilisation with some building complexes well over a thousand years old and the survival of a significant animist sensibility towards nature, in fact the island was always ruled as a number of constantly squabbling petty kingdoms where the efflorescence of the arts came through competition to produce the best. Arriving in Indonesia already in the 17th century, Dutch colonialism only took an increasing interest in Bali over the latter half of the 19th century, eventually eliminating the kingdoms and their social relations and emasculating the ruling classes, giving us the intense, Hindu-centred and autonomous community-organised peasant society we see today – albeit today rapidly succumbing to modern life.   Nor were social tensions and conflict thereby eliminated where Bali suffered the worst from the communal massacres that took place with the fall of Sukarno and the elimination of the Indonesian Communist and Socialist parties.

[512]   Albeit the King abdicated at the start of the new millennium to establish a more 'modern' form of Government.

[513] Perhaps we should not be over-enthusiastic in Tantra per se in that its intensity – and in the more strictly Hindu case intimate involvements of the multiple Hindu gods – easily slides into obsession such as the practice of Black Magic and Witchcraft that, in turn, leads to witch-hunts that have a long a horrific history also in Europe and North America.

[514] Shocking to those used to the image of the seated Buddha upon a lotus leaf to see now a naked woman seated on his lap, her legs around his waist, head bent up to kiss his lips... and the houses in many villages with painted decoration including huge erect, ejaculating penises. Where civilisations almost universally pervert the sexual through its connection with the transmission of women as property and as means to consolidate unions of power and wealth, in Utopia, sexuality becomes the ultimate sacrament of the one-ness of humanity and nature through sexual pleasure and the orgasm that, in civilisation, has been abstracted in the union of the individual with an empty notion of God.

[515] Witnessed in one pageant, clowns copulating with wooden penises in an act designed to insist on the use of condoms and a banner across the village street saying: 'LET'S FIGHT AGAINST AIDS NOT PEOPLE WITH AIDS'

[516] We should not forget that Confucius lived at the same time as the great Greek philosophers and that his version of the rational design of society, further debated and embellished by subsequent 'sages', was actually implemented and survived for 2,000 years!

[517] More (1965 [1516]).

[518] In practice, More was a strict Catholic in a world where the Reformation was in full swing and, as Lord Chancellor (something like today's Prime Ministers) was instrumental in the burning of a number of 'heretics'. In the end he was also executed for refusing on religious/moral grounds to recognise the King's taking of a second wife.

[519] Cohn (1957) Chapter 13.

[520] For a detailed account of the many radical movements and activities of the English Revolution, see: Hill (1975). For the writings of Gerrard Winstanley, see: Hill (1973).

[521] Manuel and Manuel (1979).

[522] Manuel (1962).

[523] Cited in introduction to Godwin (1976 [1798]).

[524] See Philp (1986).

[525] ...who died giving birth to Mary Shelley, whose youthful novel *Frankenstein* not only remains popular today but in a certain kind of way is a mythical critique of the emergence of industrialism.

[526] The definitive history of Owen and the Owenite Movement is set out in: Harrison, (1969).

[527] The best-known of these writings today are: Kropotkin (1979[1902]; 1985[1912]; 1985[1913]).

[528] For a history of many such communities in 19th Century England, see: Hardy (1979).

[529] Within the Soviet Bloc, anything approaching utopian thought remained proscribed until 1990. The imprisonment of Rudolph Bahro in the German Democratic Republic for the publication in 1977 in West Germany of his utopian *Alternative* well-illustrates the point. With the collapse of the Soviet Union there are few signs of any utopianism in the Russian Federation or other CIS countries.[529] We should not forget that Confucius lived at the same time as the great Greek philosophers and that his version of the rational design of society, further debated and embellished by subsequent 'sages', was actually implemented and survived for 2,000 years!

[530] Of particular note are: Goodwin and Taylor (1982); Kumar (1987); Levitas, R. (1990). Specifically on Anarchism, see: Woodstock, GW. (1963); Marshall (2010 [1992]).

[531] For the case of Intentional Communities in the UK, see: Coats, C. (2007) pp.5-15. In fact the biennial 'guide' published by Diggers and Dreamers has, since1990-91, documented many aspects of the content and ideas circulating amongst Intentional Communities and their supporters in the UK. For a history of the bioregions movement, see: Carr (2004).

[532] We recall, earlier cited, the wonderful title of Rene Dumont's 1975 book *Utopia – Or Else!*

[533] Zerzan (2005).

[534] By way of an exception to this statement, an interesting attempt by a theoretician who has gained a widespread following among radical

(particularly reformed Marxist) intellectual circles. See: Harvey (2000) pp.263-281.

[535] More's Utopia, on the other hand, contained fifty four cities all of the same size: also a possibility.

[536] I would express a prejudice for learning from the Hellenic Greeks – particularly post-Hippodamus - referred to earlier in passing. A pilgrimage I made to some of these at the end of the 1960s revealed to me not only their being planned for convenience but also in some cases the settings that brought the beauty – often dramatically – of the surrounding landscape into the everyday view of the citizens.

[537] Ellul (1964).

[538] Florida (2004).

[539] A dramatic case of the systematic death of local industry is the shower of second-hand clothing into Africa which has killed off local tailors by the thousands – with South Africa actually banning the imports in order to save the local industry.

[540] A very sad aspect of rural modernisation has been the progressive displacement of traditional building that almost everywhere evolved to provide, inter alia, a comfortable environment within particular climatic conditions. Preference is given to materials that look modern and are more expensive than local materials, providing what are prima facie worse internal environmental conditions and are more precarious in terms of robustness against earthquakes and other natural hazards. See: Atkinson, A. (2007) *Grassroots Action to Address Emerging Sustainability Threats to Cities in the South.* 8th N-AERUS Conference: Grassroots-led Urban Development – Achievements; Potentials: Limitations. Development Planning Unit, University College London.

[541] The EIDOS group of anthropologists that set themselves the task of looking critically at the impacts of development on traditional societies, discussed briefly in Chapter Four, referred to this characteristic as 'the growth of ignorance'.

[542] Atkinson (1993).

[543] Discussed by Stiglitz (2012). Predicted already in the 2003 video film *The End of Suburbia* (Electric Wallpaper Co. (2004)) with already creeping decline of US suburbs, a cynical debate is emerging around the notion of 'slumburbia'. See Schafran, (2013)

References

Abrams, P. and McCulloch, A. (1976) *Communes, Sociology and Society.* Cambridge University Press, Cambridge.

Albert, M. (2003) *Parecon: Life after Capitalism.* Verso, London.

Albury, D. and Schwartz, J. (1982) *Partial Progress: The Politics of Science and Technology.* Pluto Press, London.

Alinski, SD. (1971) *Rules for Radicals: A Pragmatic Primer for Realistic Radicals.* Random House, New York.

Allaby, M. (1972) *Who will Eat? The World Food Problem: Can we solve it?* Tom Stacey, London.

Anderson, P. (1970) *Lineages of the Absolutist State.* Verso, London.

Aronowitz, S. (1988) *Science as Power: Discourse and Ideology in Modern Society.* Macmillan Press, London.

Astyk, S. (2008) *Depletion and Abundance: Life on the New Home Front.* New Society Publishers, Gabriola Island, British Columbia.

Atkinson, A. (1991) *Principles of Political Ecology.* Belhaven, London.

Atkinson, A. (1993) *Are Third World Megacities Sustainable? Jabotabek as an Example.* Journal of International Development, Vol.4, No.2, pp.605-622.

Atkinson, A (2004) *Appropriate Technologies in a Globalizing World?* Paper presented to the conference: *Scientific Cooperation Balancing Social Demands with Technological Challenges North-South Sustainable Development – What is at Stake?* École Polytechnique Fédérale de Lausanne, 12th – 15th February.

Atkinson, A. (2007a) *Grassroots Action to Address Emerging Sustainability Threats to Cities in the South.* 8th N-AERUS Conference: *Grassroots-led Urban Development – Achievements; Potentials: Limitations.* Development Planning Unit, University College London.

Atkinson, A. (2007b) *Cities after Oil – 2: Background to the Collapse of 'Modern' Civilisation.* City, Vol.11, No.3, pp.291-310.

Atkinson, A. and Viloria, J. (2013) *Readjusting to Reality 2 – Transition?* City, Vol.17,No.5, pp.622-638.

Ayres, RU. And Simonis, UE. (Eds)(1994) *Industrial Metabolism: Restructuring for Sustainable Development.* United Nations University Press, Tokyo.

Bacon, F. (1960 [1620]) *The New Organon and Related Writings.* Anderson, Fulton H. (Ed.) Bobbs-Merrill, Indianapolis.

Bahro, R. (1978) *The Alternative in Eastern Europe.* Verso, London.

Bahro, R. (1982) *Socialism and Survival.* Heretic, London.

Bahro, R. (1984) *From Red to Green: Interviews with New Left Review.* Verso, London.

Bahro, R. (1986) *Building the Green Movement.* Gay Men's Press, London.

Bailey, AM. and Llobera, JR. (Eds)(1981) *The Asiatic Mode of Production – Science and Politics.* Routledge and Kegan Paul, London.

Baker, C. (2009) *Sacred Demise: Walking the Spiritual Path of Industrial Civilization's Collapse.* iUniverse Inc., New York.

Barbour, I. (Ed.) (1972) *Earth Might Be Fair: Reflections on Ethics, Religion and Ecology.* Prentice-Hall, Englewood Cliffs, New Jersey.

Barbour, I. (Ed) (1973) *Western Man and Environmental Ethics.* Addison-Wesley, Reading, Massachusetts.

Barclay, H. (1982) *People without Government: An Anthropology of Anarchism.* Kahn and Averill with Cienfuegos Press, London.

Barnes, B. (1974) *Scientific Knowledge and Social Theory.* Routledge and Kegan Paul, London.

Barnes, B. (1977) *Interests and the Growth of Knowledge.* Routledge and Kegan Paul, London.

Barnett, HJ. and Morse, C. (1963) *Scarcity and Growth: The Economics of Natural Resource Availability.* Johns Hopkins Press, Baltimore.

Barthe, R. (1973) *Mythologies.* Paladin Grafton Books, London.

Bauman, Z. (1989) *Legislators and Interpreters: On Modernity, Post-Modernity and Intellectuals.* Polity, Cambridge.

Bauman, Z. (2001) *Community – Seeking Safety in an Insecure World.* Polity, Cambridge.

Bauman, Z. (2002) *Society under Siege.* Polity Press, Cambridge.

Bauman, Z. (2004) *Wasted Lives: Modernity and its Outcasts.* Polity, Cambridge.

Bauman, Z. (2011) *Collateral Damage: Social Inequalities in a Global Age.* Polity, Cambridge.

Beck, U. (1992) *Risk Society: Towards a New Modernity.* Sage Publications, New York.

Beder, S. (2000) *Selling the Work Ethic: From Puritan Pulpit to Corporate PR.* Zed Books, London.

Bercovitch, J. and Jackson, R. (2009) *Conflict Resolution in the Twenty-first Century: Principles, Methods, and Approaches.* University of Michigan Press, Ann Arbor.

Berg, M. (Ed)(1979) *Technology and Toil in Nineteenth Century Britain.* CSE Books, London.

Berman, M. (1984) *All that is Solid Melts into Air.* Verso, London.

Best, RH. (1981) *Land Use and Living Space* Methuen, London.

Black, J. (1970) *The Dominion of Man: The Search for Ecological Responsibility.* Edinburgh University Press, Edinburgh.

Blum, W. (2003) *Killing Hope: US Military and CIA Interventions since World War II.* Zed Books, London.

Blumenberg, H. (1983) *The Legitimacy of the Modern Age.* MIT Press, Cambridge, Massachusetts.

Böge, S. (1995) *The well-travelled yogurt pot: lessons for new freight transport policies and regional Production.* World Transport Policy & Practice, Vol.1, No.1, pp. 7-11.

Bookchin, M. (1965) *Towards a Liberatory Technology,* in Bookchin, M. (1974) *Post-Scarcity Anarchism.* Wildwood House, London, pp.85-139.

Bookchin, M. (1982) *The Ecology of Freedom: The Emergence and Dissolution of Hierarchy.* Cheshire Books, Palo Alto, California.

Bookchin, M. (1987)*The Rise of Urbanization and the Decline of Citizenship.* Sierra Club Books, San Fransisco.

Bookchin, M. (1989) *Remaking Society.* Black Rose Books, Montreal.

Boudon, R. (1986) *Theories of Social Change.* Polity Press, Cambridge.

Boyle, G. and Harper, P. (Eds)(1976) *Radical Technology.* Wildwood House, London.

Braudel, F. (1972) *The Mediterranean and the Mediterranean World in the Age of Philip II.* Harper and Row, New York.

Braun, E. (1995) *Futile Progress: Technology's Empty Promise.* Earthscan, London.

Brunckhorst, DJ. (2002) *Bioregional Planning: Resource management beyond the new millennium.* Routledge, London.

Bryceson, D., Key, C. And Mooij, J. (2000) *Disappearing Peasantries? Rural Labour in Africa, Asia and Latin America.* Intermediate Technology Publications, London.

Bündnis 90/Die Grünen (2010) *Kleine Anfrage: Vorbereitung Deutschlands auf Peak Oil und seine Folgen.* Deutsche Bundestag, Berlin.

Burgbacher, E. Parlamentarische Staatssekretär (2010) *Vorbereitung Deutschlands auf Peak Oil und seine Folgen (Beantwortung).* Präsident des deutschen Bundestages – Bundesministerium für Wirtschaft und Technologie, Berlin.

Burrow, JW. (1966) *Evolution and Society: A Study in Victorian Social Theory.* Cambridge University Press, Cambridge.

480

Butterfield, NJ. (2007). *'Macroevolution and Macroecology through Deep Time'* Palaeontology Vol.50, No.1, pp41–55.

Campbell, BG. (1966) *Human Evolution: An Introduction to Man's Adaptations.* Aldine Publishing Company, Chicago.

Capra, F. (1982) *The Turning Point: Science, Society and the Rising Culture.* Flemingo, London.

Carey, J (2011) *Who feeds Bristol? Towards a Resilient Food Plan.* Bristol City Council and National Health Service, Bristol.

Carr, EH. (1964) *What is History?* Penguin Books, Harmondsworth.

Carr, M. (2004) *Bioregionalism and Civil Society: Democratic Challenges to Corporate Globalism.* UBC Press, Vancouver.

Cavanagh, J. and Mander, J. (Eds)(2004) *Alternatives to Economic Globalization: A Better World is Possible.* Berrett-Koehler Publishers, San Francisco.

Catton, WR. (1982) *Overshoot: The Ecological Basis of Revolutionary Change.* University of Illinois Press, Urbana.

Catton, WR. (2009) *Bottleneck: Humanity's Impending Impasse.* Xlibris Corporation.

Chamberlain, S. (2009) *The transition timeline for a local, resilient future.* Chelsea Green Publishing, White River Junction, Vermont.

Chang, H-J (2003) *Kicking away the Ladder: Development Strategy in Historical Perspective.* Anthem Press, London.

Chang, H-J (2007) *Bad Samaritans: The Guilty Secret of Rich Nations & the Threat to Global Prosperity.* Random House, London.

Chappell, TDJ. (Ed)(1997) *The Philosophy of the Environment.* Edinburgh University Press, Edinburgh.

Childe, G. (1951) *Social Evolution.* Watts, London.

Childe, G. (1964) *What Happened in History.* Penguin, Harmondsworth.

Childe, G. (1965) *Man Makes himself.* Watts, London.

Christaller, W. (1966) *Central Places in Southern Germany.* Trans. Baskin, CW, Prentice Hall, New York.

Clerk, J. and Cole, S. with Curnon, R. and Hopkins, M. (1975) *Global Simulation Models: A Comparative Study.* John Wiley, Colchester.

Coats, C. (2007) *Within these Communities.* In: *Diggers and Dreamers – The Guide to Communal Living.* Diggers and Dreamers Publications, London.

Codding, GA Jr. (1965) *The Federal Government of Switzerland.* Houghton Mifflin Company, Boston.

Cohen, MJ. and Murphy, J. (Eds)(2001) *Exploring Sustainable Consumption: Environmental Policy and the Social Sciences.* Pergamon, Amsterdam.

Cohn, MN. (1977) *The Food Crisis in Prehistory: Overpopulation and the Origin of Agriculture.* Yale University Press, Newhaven.

Cohn, N. (1970) *The Pursuit of the Millennium.* Paladin, London.

Colborn, T., Dumanoski, D. and Myers, JP. (1996) *Our Stolen Future: Are we Threatening our Fertility, Intelligence and Survival? – A Scientific Detective Story.* Abacus, London.

Collingridge, D. (1980) *The Social Control of Technology.* The Open University Press, Milton Keynes.

Commission on Oil Independence (2006) *Making Sweden an Oil-Free Society.* Prime Minister's Office, Stockholm.

Committee on Resources and Man (1969) *Resources and Man: A Study and Recommendations.* W.H. Freeman and Company, San Francisco.

Commoner, B. (1966) *Science and Survival.* Victor Gollancz, London.

Commoner, B. (1972a) *The Closing Circle.* Bantam, New York.

Commoner, B. (1972b) *The Environmental Cost of Economic Growth.* In: Schurr, SL. (Ed.) *Energy, Economic Growth, and the Environment.* Resources for the Future, Johns Hopkins Press, Baltimore. pp.30-65.

Commoner, B. (1979) *The Poverty of Power: Energy and the Economic Crisis.* Bantam Books, New York.

Condorcet, Marquis de (Caritat, Marie-Jean-Antoine-Nicolas). (1976) *Selected Writings.* Baker, KM. (Ed.). Bobbs-Merrill, Indianapolis.

Coppleston, FS J. (1965) *A History of Philosophy, Volume VII, Modern Philosophy, Part 1, Fichte to Hegel.* Image Books, Garden City, New York.

Crenson, M. (1971) *The Un-Politics of Air Pollution.* Johns Hopkins Press, Baltimore.

Crook, JH. (1980) *The Evolution of Human Consciousness.* Clarendon Press, Oxford.

Crosby, AW. (1986) *Ecological Imperialism: The Biological Expansion of Europe, 900 – 1900.* Cambridge University Press, Cambridge.

Daly, HE. (1973) *Towards a Steady-State Economy.* W.H. Freeman, San Francisco.

Daly, HE. (1996) *Beyond Growth: The Economics of Sustainable Development.* Beacon Press, Boston.

Dauncey, G. (1988) *Beyond the Crash: The Emerging Rainbow Economy.* Greenprint, London.

Dawson, J. (2010) *Ecovillages: New Frontiers for Sustainability.* Green Books, Totnes.

Debier, J.-C., Deléage, J.-P. and Hémery, D. (1991) *In the Servitude of Power: Energy and Civilization through the Ages.* Zed Books, London.

DeFillipis, J. (2004) *Unmaking Goliath: Community Control in the Face of Global Capital.* Routledge, New York.

DEFRA (2005) *The Validity of Food Miles as an Indicator of Sustainable Development.* Department of Environment, Food and Rural Affairs, London.

de Ponti, T., Rijk, B. and van Ittersum, MK. (2012) *The crop yield gap between organic and conventional agriculture.* Agricultural Systems. Vol.108, April, pp.1-9.

Devall, B. and Sessions, G. (1985) *Deep Ecology: Living as if Nature Mattered.* Gibbs and Smith, Salt Lake City.

Diamond, J. (1998) *Guns, Germs and Steel: A Short History of Everybody for the last 13,000 Years.* Verso, London.

Diamond, J. (2005) *Collapse: How Societies Choose to Fail or Succeed.* Viking, New York.

Diamond, S. (1974) *In Search of the Primitive: A Critique of Civilisation.* Transaction Publishers, New Brunswick.

Dobb, M. (1946) *Studies in the Development of Capitalism.* George Routledge, London.

Dobbins, P. (1978) *From Kin to Class: Speculations on the Origins of development of the Family, Class Society and Female Subordination.* Signmaker Press, Berkley.

Dodds, ER. (1951) *The Greeks and the Irrational.* University of California Press, Berkeley.

Dumont, R. (1974) *Utopia – or Else!* Andre Deutsch, London.

Donald, J. and Rattansi, A. (1992) *'Race', Culture and Difference.* Sage Publications, London.

Durand-Lasserve, A. and Royston, L. (2002) *Holding Their Ground: Secure Tenure for the Urban Poor in Developing Countries,* Earthscan, London.

Durkheim, E. (2008 [1912]) *The Elementary Forms of Religious Life.* Oxford University Press, Oxford.

Easlea, B. (1980) *Liberation and the Aims of Science.* Scottish Academic Press, Edinburgh.

Economic Development Department (1985) *The London Industrial Strategy.* Greater London Council, London.

Ehrlich, PR. (1969) *The Population Bomb: Population Control or the Race to Oblivion?* Sierra Club-Ballantine Books, San Francisco.

Electric Wallpaper Co. (2004) *The End of Suburbia: Oil Depletion and the Collapse of the American Dream.* The Electric Wallpaper Co.

Elliot, R. and Gare, A. (Eds)(1983) *Environmental Philosophy.* Open University Press, Milton Keynes.

Ellul, J. (1964) *The Technological Society.* Vintage, New York.

Engel, JR and Engel, JG. (1990) *Ethics of Environment and development: Global; Challenge and International Response.* Belhaven, London.

Engels, F. (2009) *The Condition of the Working-Class in England in 1844.* George Allan and Unwin, London.

Erikson, R. and Goldthorpe, JH. (1992) *The Constant Flux: A Study of Class Mobility in Industrial Societies.* Clarendon Press, Oxford.

Etzioni, A. (1993) *The Spirit of Community: Rights, Responsibilities, and the Communitarian Agenda.* Crown, New York.

European Union (2012) *The 2011/2012 European Report on Development, Confronting Scarcity: Managing Water, Energy and Land for Inclusive and Sustainable Growth,* Overseas Development Institute (ODI), European Centre for Development Policy Management (ECDPM), Deutsches Institut für Entwicklungspolitik (GDI/DIE). Brussels.

Fals Borda, O. (1985) *The Challenge of Social Change.* Sage, London.

Feyerabend, P. (1978) *Against Method: Outline of an Anarchistic Theory of Knowledge.* Verso, London.

Feyerabend, P. (1987) *Farewell to Reason.* Verso, London.

Fine, B. and Leopold, E. (1993) *The World of Consumption.* Routledge, London.

Finley, M.I. (1986) *The Use and Abuse of History.* The Hogarth Press, London.

Florida, R. (2004) *The Rise of the Creative Class: And How It's Transforming Work, Leisure, Community and Everyday Life.* Basic Books, New York.

Foote-Whyte, W. and King-Whyte, K. (1988) *Making Mondragon: The Growth and Dynamics of the Worker Cooperative Complex,* ILR Press, Ithaca, New York.

Fox, W. (1990) *Towards Transpersonal Ecology: Developing new Foundations for Environmentalism.* Shambala, Boston.

Frazer, JG. (1922) *The Golden Bough: A Study in Magic and Religion.* Abridged Version. Macmillan, London.

Fried, MH. (1967) *The Evolution of Political Society: An Essay in Political Anthropology.* Random House, New York.

Friedmann, J. and Weaver, C. (1979) *Territory and Function: The Evolution of Regional Planning.* Edward Arnold, London.

Friere, P. (1993) *Pedagogy of the Oppressed.* Penguin Books, Harmondsworth.

Galbraith, JK. (1961) *The Great Crash 1929.* Penguin Books, Harmondsworth.

Galeano, E. (1973) *Open Veins in Latin America: Five Centuries of the Pillage of a Continent.* Monthly Review Press, New York.

Garland, AM., Massoumi, M. and Ruble, BA. (Eds)(2007) *Global Urban Poverty: Setting the Agenda.* Woodrow Wilson International Centre for Scholars, Washington DC.

Gates, H. (1996) *China's Motor: A Thousand Years of Petty Capitalism.* Cornell University Press, Ithaca.

Gerth, HH. and Wright Mills, C. (1970) *From Max Weber: Essays in Sociology.* Routledge, London.

Giddens, A. and Held, D. (Eds)(1982) *Classes, Power and Conflict: Classical and Contemporary Debates.* Macmillan Publishers, London.

Gideon, S. (1948) Mechanization Takes Command: A Contribution to Anonymous History. **WW Norton, New York.**

Glacken, CJ. (1967) *Traces on a Rhodian Shore.* University of California Press, Berkeley.

Godwin, W. (11976[1798]) *Enquiry Concerning Political Justice.* Penguin Books, Harmondsworth.

Goldsmith, E., Allen, R., Allaby, M., Davoll, J. and Lawrence, S. (1972) *A Blueprint for Survival.* The Ecologist, Vol.2, No.1, January, pp.1-43.

Goodwin, B. and Taylor, K. (1982) *The Politics of Utopia: A study in theory and practice.* Hutchinson, London.

Gorelick, SM. (2010) *Oil Panic and the Global Crisis.* Wiley-Blackwell, Chichester, West Sussex.

Gorz, A. (1980) *Ecology as Politics.* South End Press, Boston.

Graham, S. (2010) *Cities under Siege: The New Military Urbanism.* Verso, London.

Graham, S. and Marvin, S. (2001) *Splintering Urbanism: Networked Infrastructures, Technological Mobilities and the Urban Condition.* Routledge, London.

Greer, JM. (2005) *How Civilizations Fall: A Theory of Catabolic Collapse.* http://www.dylan.org.uk/greer_on_collapse.pdf

Greer, JM. (2008) *The Long Descent: A User's Guide to the End of the Industrial Age.* New Society Publishers.

Greer, JM. (2009) *The Ecotech Future: Envisioning a Post-Peak World.* New Society Publishers.

Hails, C. (Ed)(2006) *Living Planet Report 2006.* Worldwide Fund for Nature (WWF), Gland.

Hansen, J. (2009) *Storms of my Grandchildren*. Bloomsbury, New York,

Harris, M. (1980) *Cultural Materialism: The Struggle for a Science of Culture*. Vintage Books, New York.

Harrison, JFC. (1969) *Robert Owen and the Owenites in Britain and America: The quest for the new moral world*. Routledge and Kegan Paul, London.

Hardy, D. (1979) *Alternative Communities in Nineteenth Century England*. Longman, London;

Harvey, D. (2000) *Spaces of Hope*. University of California Press, Berkeley.

Harvey, D. (2005) *A Brief History of Neoliberalism*. Oxford University Press, Oxford.

Hays, SP. (1959) *Conservation and the Gospel of Efficiency*. Harvard University Press, Cambridge, Massachusetts.

Hegel, GWF. (1975) *Lectures on the Philosophy of World History. Introduction: Reason in History*. Duncan Forbes (Ed.). Cambridge University Press, Cambridge.

Heinberg, R. (1995a) *The Primitivist Critique of Civilization*. Paper presented at the 24th annual meeting of the International Society for the Comparative Study of Civilizations at Wright State University, Dayton, Ohio, June 15 at: http://www.primitivism.com/primitivist-critique.htm

Heinberg, R. (1995b) *Memories and Visions of Paradise: Exploring the Universal Myth of a Lost Golden Age*. Revised Edition. The Theosophical Publishing House, Wheaton, Illinois.

Heinberg, R. (2003) *The Party's Over: Oil, War and the Fate of Industrial Societies*. New Society Publishers, Gabriola Island, British Columbia, Canada.

Heinberg, R. (2004) *Power Down: Options and Action for a Post-Carbon World*. New Society Publishers.

Heinberg, R. (2007) *Peak Everything: Waking up to the Century of Decline in Earth's Resources*. Clairview Books, Forest Row.

Heinberg, R. (2013) *Snake Oil: How Fracking's False Promise of Plenty Imperils our Future*. Post Carbon Institute, Santa Rosa, California.

Herman, ES. and Chomsky, N. (2002) *Manufacturing Consent: The Political Economy of Mass Media*. Second Edition. Pantheon Books, New York.

Hicks, D. (2011) *Dignity: The Essential Role it Plays in Resolving Conflict*. Yale University Press.

Hill, C. (1975) *The World Turned Upside Down: Radical Ideas during the English Revolution.* Penguin Books, Harmondsworth.

Hill, S. (1988) *The Tragedy of Technology: Human Liberation Versus Domination in the Late Twentieth Century.* Pluto Press, London.

Hilton, R. (Ed.) (1976) *The Transition from Feudalism to Capitalism.* New Left Books, London.

Hines, C. (2000) *Localisation: A Global Manifesto.* Earthscan, London.

Hinton, W. (1966) *Fanshen – A Documentary of Revolution in a Chinese Village.* Monthly Review Press, New York.

Hirsch, RL. Bezdek, R. and Wendling, R. (2005) *Peaking of World Oil Production: Impacts, Mitigation and Risk Management.* Department of Energy, Washington DC.

Hirsch, RL. (2005) *The Inevitable Peaking of World Oil Production.* Bulletin of The Atlantic Council of the United States, Vol.XVI, No.3.

Hobart, M. (1993) *Introduction: The Growth of Ignorance.* In Hobart, M. (Ed) *An Anthropological Critique of Development.* Routledge, London. pp.1-30.

Hobbes, T. (1968 [1651]) *Leviathan.* Penguin Books, Harmondsworth.

Hobsbawm, EJ. (1962) *The Age of Revolution.* Weidenfeld and Nicolson, London.

Hobsbawm, EJ. (1968) *Industry and Empire.* Penguin Books, Harmondsworth.

Hoggan, J. (2010) *Climate Cover-up: The Crusade to deny Global Warming.* Greystone Books, Vancouver.

Hoggart, R. (1957) *The Uses of Literacy.* Chatto and Windus, London.

Hollstein, W. and Peth, B. (1980) *Alternativ-Projekte: Beispiele gegen die Resignation.* Rowohlt, Reinbek bei Hamburg.

Holmgren, D. (2009) *Future Scenarios: How Communities can adapt to Peak Oil and Climate Change.* Chelsea Green Publishing, White River Junction, Vermont.

Holzer, S. (2004) *Sepp Holzer's Permaciulture: A Practical Guide for Farmers, Smallholders & Gerdeners.* Permanent Publications, East Meon, Hampshire.

Hopkins, R. (Ed)(2005) *Kinsale 2021:An Energy descent Action Plan.* Kinsale Further Education College, Kinsale, Ireland.

Hopkins, R. (2008) *The transition handbook: from oil dependency to local resilience.* Chelsea Green Publishing, White River Junction, Vermont.

Horne, TA. (1978) *The Social Thought of Bernard Mandeville: Virtue and Commerce in Early Eighteenth-Century England.* Columbia University Press, New York.

Hoskins, WG. (1991) *The Making of the English Landscape*. New Edition. Penguin Books, Harmondsworth.

Hughes, S (1959) *Consciousness and Society*. Macgibbon and Kee, London.

Hubbert, MK. (1962) *Energy Resources. A Report to the Committee on Natural Resources of the National Academy of Sciences-National Research Council. Publication 1000-D*. National Academy of Sciences-National Research Council, Washington DC.

IEA (2008) *World Energy Outlook 2008*. International Energy Agency, Paris.

ILO (2012) *Formulating Projects and Studies Concerning Labour Issues in Greening the Sectors of the Built Environment Guidance Manual*. Sectoral Activities Department, International Labour Office, Geneva.

Ingold, T. (1986) *Evolution and Social Life*. Cambridge University Press, Cambridge.

International Forum on Globalization (2004) *Alternatives to Economic Globalization – A Better World is Possible*. Second Edition. Berret-Koehler, San Francisco.

IPCC (2007) *Climate Change 2007: Synthesis Report*. Intergovernmental Panel on Climate Change, Geneva.

Ise, J. (1925) *The Theory of Value as Applied to Natural Resources*. The American Economic Review. Vol.15, No.2, pp.284-291.

IUCN (1980) *World Conservation Strategy*. International Union for the Conservation of Nature and Natural Resources, Gland.

Jackson, T. (Ed)(2006) *The Earthscan Reader in Sustainable Consumption*. Earthscan, London.

Jackson, T. (2011) *Prosperity without Growth: Economics for a Finite Planet*. Routledge, London.

Jacques, PJ., Dunlap, RE. and Freeman, M. (2008) *The organisation of denial: Conservative think tanks and environmental scepticism*. Environmental Politics, Vol.17, No.3, pp349-385.

Jenkins, JC. and Klandermans, B. (Eds)(1995) *The Politics of Social Protest: Comparative Perspectives on States and Social Movements*. University of Minnesota Press, Minneapolis.

Jensen, D. (2006) *Endgame: The Problem of Civilisation*. (Two Volumes) Seven Stories Press, New York.

Jevons, WS. (2012[1865]) *The Coal Question: An Enquiry Concerning the Progress of the Nation, and the Probable Exhaustion of Our Coal-Mines*. Ulan Press,

Johnson, H. and Klanderemans, B. (Eds)(1995) *Social Movements and Culture*. University of Minnesota Press. Minneapolis.

Joll, J. (1980) *The Anarchist* (2nd Edition), Harvard University Press, Cambridge, Massachusetts.

Junk, R. und Müllert, NR. (1980) *Alternatives Leben.* Signal Verlag, Baden-Baden.

Kaplinsky, R.and Morris, M. (2001) *A Handbook for Value Chain Research.* IDRC, Ottowa.

Kay, JA. and Mirrlees, JA. (1975) *The Desirability of Natural Resource Depletion.* in: Pearce, DW. and Rose, J. *The Economics of Natural Resource Depletion.* The Macmillan Press, London.

Kellett, Peter M. (2007) *Conflict Dialogue.* Sage Publications, London.

Kelly, M. (2001) *The Divine Right of Capital: Dethroning the Corporate Aristocracy.* Berrett-Koehler Publishers, San Francisco.

Keynes, JM. (1936) *The General Theory of Employment, Interest and Money,* (1936) Harcourt Brace, New York.

Kohr, L. (1957) *The Breakdown of Nations.* Routledge and Kegan Paul, London.

Komarov, Boris. (1980) *The Destruction of Nature in the Soviet Union.* Pluto Press, London.

Koont, S. (2009) *The Urban Agriculture of Havana.* Monthly Review, Vol.60, No.8, pp.44-63.

Korowicz, D. (2010) *Tipping Point: Near-Term Systemic Implications of a Peak in Global Oil Production. An Outline Review.* The Foundation for the Economics of Sustainability & The Risk/Resilience Network, Dublin.

Korten, DC. (1995) *When Corporations Rule the World.* Earthscan, London.

Kumar, S. (2002) *You Are, Therefore I Am: A Declaration of Dependence.* Green Books, Totnes.

Kovel, J. (2007) *The Enemy of Nature: The End of Capitalism or the End of Nature?* 2nd Edition. Zed Books, London.

Kropotkin, P. (1979[1902]) *Mutual Aid − A Factor of Evolution.* Extending Horizons Books, Boston.

Kropotkin, P. (1985[1912]) *Fields, Factories and Workshops Tomorrow.* Freedom Press, London.

Kropotkin, P. (1985[1913]) *The Conquest of Bread.* Elephant Editions, London.

Kumar, K. (1987) *Utopia and Anti-Utopia in Modern Times.* Basil Blackwell, Oxford.

Kunstler, JH. (2005) *The Long Emergency. Surviving the Converging Catastrophes of the Twenty-First Century.* Atlantic Monthly Press, New York.

Landes, D.S. (1969) *The Unbound Prometheus: Technological Change and Industrial Development in Western Europe from 1750 to the Present.* Cambridge University Press, Cambridge.

Lang, T. and Hines, C. (1993) *The New Protectionism: Protecting the Future against Free Trade.* Earthscan, London.

Lapierre, D. and Moro, J. (2002) *Five past Midnight in Bhopal: The Epic Story of the World's deadliest Industrial Disaster.* Grand Central Publishing, New York.

Lasch, C. (1991) *The True and only Heaven: Progress and its Critics.* WW Norton Co. New York.

Latour, B. (1987) *Science in Action: How to follow Scientists and Engineers through Society.* Harvard University Press, Cambridge, Massachusetts.

Latour, B. (2005) *Reassembling the Social: An Introduction to Actor-Network-Theory.* Oxford University Press, Oxford.

Leacock, E.B. (1981) *Myths of Male Domination: Collected Articles on Women Cross-Culturally.* Monthly Review Press, New York.

Leakey, R. and Lewin, R. (1996) *The Sixth Extinction: Patterns of Life and the Future of Humankind.* Anchor, New York.

Lebow, V. (1955) *Price Competition in 1955.* Journal of Retailing. Spring.

Lee, RB. and Devore, I. (Eds)(1967) *Man the Hunter: The First Survey of a Single Crucial Stage of Human Development – Man's once Universal Hunting Way of Life.* Aldine Transaction, New Brunswick.

Leeb, S. (2006) *The Coming Economic Collapse: How you can thrive when Oil costs $200 a Barrel.* Warner Business Books, New York.

Leiss, W. (1972) *The Domination of Nature.* George Brazillier, New York.

Lenin, V.I. (1965 [1917]) *The State and Revolution.* Foreign Languages Press, Peking.

Leopold, A. (1949) *A Sand County Almanac and Sketches Here and There,* Oxford University Press, Oxford.

Lerch, D. (2007) *Post carbon cities: planning for energy and climate uncertainty.* Post Carbon Institute, Sebastopol, California.

Lévi-Strauss, C. (1972) *The Savage Mind.* Weidenfeld and Nicolson, London.

Levitas, R. (1990) *The Concept of Utopia.* Philip Allen, Hemel Hempstead, Hertfordshire.

Lewis, CS. (1947) *The Abolition of Man.* Geoffrey Bles, London.

Locke, J. (1960 [1690]) *Two Treatises of Government.* Cambridge University Press, Cambridge.

Lovejoy, AO. (1936) *The Great Chain of Being.* Harvard University Press, Cambridge, Massachusetts.

Lovelock, J. (2000). *Gaia: A New Look at Life on Earth.* Oxford: Oxford University Press.

Littman, RJ. (1974) *The Greek Experiment: Imperialism and Social Conflict 800-400 BC.* Thames and Hudson, London.

Lubbock, J. (1995) *The Tyranny of Taste: The Politics of Architecture and Design in Britain 1550-1960.* Yale University Press, New Haven.

Luccarelli, M. (1995) *Lewis Mumford and the Economical Region: The Politics of Planning.* Guilford Press, New York.

Lüthi, C. and Schütze, T. (Eds) (2011) *Sustainable Sanitation in Cities: A Framework for Action.* Papiroz Publishing House, Rijswijk, The Netherlands.

MacPherson, CB. (1962) *The Political Theory of Possessive Individualism: Hobbes to Locke.* Oxford University Press, Oxford.

Maheu, L. (Ed)(1995) *Social Movements and Social Classes: The Future of Collective Action.* Sage Publications, London.

McGinnis, MV. (Ed) (1999) *Bioregionalism.* Routledge, London.

Mckibben, B. (1990) *The End of Nature.* Penguin Books, London.

Mckibben, B. (2007) *Deep Economy: The Wealth of Communities and the Durable Future.* Oneworld Publications, Oxford.

McKenzie, RT. and Silver, A. (1968) *Angels in Marble: Working Class Conservatives in Urban England.* Heinemann, London.

McLellan, D. (1986) *Ideology.* Open University Press, Milton Keynes.

Mallanby, K. (1975) *Can Britain Feed Itself?* Merlin Press, London.

Mann, CC. (2005) *1491: New Revelations of the Americas before Columbus.* Vintage Books, New York.

Mannheim, K. (1936) *Ideology and Utopia.* Routledge and Kegan Paul, London.

Manuel, FE. (1962) *The Prophets of Paris.* Harvard University Press, Cambridge, Massachusetts.

Manuel, FE. (1968) *A Portrait of Isaac Newton.* Belknap Press, Cambridge, Massachusetts.

Manuel, FE. and Manuel, FP. (1979) *Utopian Thought in the Western World.* Basil Blackwell, Oxford.

Marshall, P. (2010) *Demanding the Impossible: A History of Anarchism.* PM Press, Oakland, California.

Marx, K. (1976) *Capital Volume 1.* Penguin Books, Harmondsworth.

Marx, K. and Engels, F. (1965 [1848]) *Manifesto of the Communist Party.* Peoples Publishing House, Peking.

Marx, K and Engels, F. (1975) *Economic and Philosophical Manuscripts*. Penguin Books, Harmondsworth.

Marx, L. (1964) *The Machine in the Garden: Technology and the Pastoral Ideal in America*. Oxford University Press, New York.

Mathews, F. (1991) *The Ecological Self*. Routledge, London.

Mathews, F. (2005) *Reinhabiting Reality: Towards a Recovery of Culture*. State University of New York Press, Albany.

Meadows, DH, Meadows, DL, Randers, J. and Behrens III, WW. (1974) *The Limits to Growth*. Pan, London.

Meadows, DH., Meadows, DL. and Randers, J. (1993) *Beyond the Limits: Confronting Global Collapse, Envisioning a Sustainable Future*. Chelsea Green Publishing Company, White River Junction, Vermont;

Meadows, DH., Randers, J. and Meadows, DL. (2004) *Limits to Growth: The 30-Year Update*. Chelsea Green Publishing Company, White River Junction, Vermont.

Men, T., Brennan, P., Boffetta, P. and Zaridze, D. (2003) *Russian mortality trends for 1991-2001: analysis by cause and region*. British Medical Journal, Vol. 327:964.

Mercer, J. (1984) *Communes: A Social History and Guide*. Prism Press, Dorchester.

Merchant, C. (1980) *The Death of Nature: Women, Ecology and the Scientific Revolution*. Wildwood House, London.

Merton, R. (1970) *Science, Technology and Society in Seventeenth-Century England*. Howard Fertig, New York.

Metcalf, B. (1996) *Shared Visions, Shared Lives: Communal Living Around the Globe*. Findhorn Press, Forres, Scotland.

Middleton, N. and Thomas, D. (1997) *World Atlas of Desertification*. Second Edition, Arnold, London.

Mille, D. (Ed)(1995) *Acknowledging Consumption*. Routledge, London.

Millennium Ecosystem Assessment (2005) *Ecosystems and Human Well-being: Biodiversity Synthesis*. World Resources Institute, Washington, DC.

Miller, M.A. (1976) *Kropotkin*. The University of Chicago Press, Chicago.

Mills, RM. (2008) *The Myth of the Oil Crisis: Overcoming the Challenges of Depletion, Geopolitics, and Global Warming*. Praeger Publishers, Westport, Connecticut.

Mollison, B. (1988) *Permaculture: A Designers' Manual*. Tagari Publications.

Montagu, A. (1978) *Learning Non-Aggression: The Experience of Non-Literate Societies*. Oxford University Press, Oxford.

Moncrief, LW. (1970) *The Cultural Basis of Our Environmental Crisis.* Science, **170**, 30 October, pp.508-512.

Moore, BJr. (1967) *Social Origins of Dictatorship and Democracy.* Penguin Books, Harmondsworth.

More, T. (1965 [1516]) *Utopia.* Penguin Books, Harmondsworth.

Morton, AL. (1970) *The World of the Ranters: Religious Radicalism in the English Revolution.* Laurence and Wishart, London.

Moss Kanter, R. (1972) *Commitment and Community: Communes and Utopias in Sociological Perspective.* Harvard University Press, Cambridge, Massachusetts.

Naess, A. (1989*) Ecology, Community and Lifestyle.* Cambridge University Press, Cambridge.

Needham, J. (1954-1971) *Science and Civilization in China.* Five volumes. Cambridge University Press, Cambridge.

NEF (1999) *Participation Works! 21 Techniques of Community participation for the 21st century.* New Economics Foundation, London.

Norman, C. (1981) *The God that Limps: Science and Technology in the Eighties.* WW Norton, New York.

Odum, HT. (1971) *Environment, Power and Society.* John Wiley, New York.

Odum, HT. and Odum EC. (2008) *A Prosperous Way down: Principles and Policies.* University of Colorado Press, Boulder.

Oliver, P. (Ed)(1998) *The Encyclopedia of Vernacular Architecture of the World.* (Three Volumes) Cambridge University Press, Cambridge.

Orlov, D. (2008) *Reinventing Collapse: The Soviet Example and American Prospects.* New Society Publishers, Gabriola Island, British Colombia.

Ostrom, E. (1990) *Governing the Commons: The Evolution of Institutions for Collective Action.* Cambridge University Press, Cambridge.

Partridge, E. (Ed.) (1981) *Responsibilities to Future Generations: Environmental Ethics.* Prometheus Books, Buffalo, New York.

Passmore, J. (1980) *Man's Responsibility for Nature.* Second Edition, Duckworth, London.

Paterson , W. (1992) *Silent Depression.* Norton, New York.

Peak Oil Task Force (2009) *Redefining Prosperity: Energy Descent and Community Resilience Report of the Bloomington Peak Oil Task Force.* City of Bloomington, Illinois.

Pelling, H. (1971) *A History of British Trade Unionism.* Second Edition, Penguin Books, Harmondsworth.

PEP. (1955) *World Population and Resources.* Political and Economic Planning, London.

Pepper, D. (1991) *Communes and the Green Vision.* Green Print, London.

Philp, M. (1986) *Godwin's Political Justice.* Duckworth, London.

Phongpaichit, P. and Baker, C. (1995) *Thailand Economy and Politics.* Oxford University Press, Kuala Lumpur.

Plato (1974) *The Republic.* Desmond Lee (translation), Second Edition. Penguin Books, Harmondsworth.

Pollard, S. (1968) *The Idea of Progress: History and Society.* C A Watts, London.

Ponting, C. (2007) *A New Green History of the World.* Penguin Books, London.

Powers, J. (1982) *Philosophy and the New Physics.* Methuen, London.

Quarrie, J. (Ed) (1992) *Earth Summit 1992 (Including Agenda 21).* The Regency Press, London.

Reason, P. (1988) *Human Inquiry in Action: Developments in New Paradigm Research.* Sage, London.

Reisner, M. (1986) *Cadillac Desert: The American West and Its Disappearing Water.* Penguin Books, London.

Renfrew, C. (2007) *Prehistory: The Making of the Human Mind.* Weidenfeld and Nicolson, London.

Richardson, A. (2012) *A New World Ordure? Thoughts on the use of humanure in developed cities.* City, Vol.16, No.6, pp.700-712.

Rigby, A. (1974) *Alternative Realities: A Study of Communes and their Members.* Routledge and Kegan Paul, London.

Roll. E. (1994) *From Heaven to Earth: Images and Experiences of Development in China.* Routledge, London.

Rorty, R. (1998) *Achieving our Country; Leftist Thought in Twentieth-Century America.* Harvard University Press, Cambridge, Massachusetts.

Rostow, WW. (1960) *The Stages of Economic Growth: A Non-Communist Manifesto.* Cambridge University Press, Cambridge.

Roszak, T. (1973) *Where the Wasteland Ends: Politics and Transcendence in Post-Industrial Society.* Anchor Books, New York.

Rousseau, J-J. (1964) *The First and Second Discourses.* Roger D. Masters (Ed), St Martin's Press, New York.

Rousseau, J-J (1968) *The Social Contract.* Maurice Cranston (Trans). Penguin Books, Harmondsworth.

Sahlins, M. (1974) *Stone Age Economics.* Tavistock Publications, London.

494

Sahlins, Marshall. D. and Service, Elman. R. (Eds.) (1960) *Evolution and Culture.* University of Michigan Press, Ann Arbour.

Sale, K. (1973) *SDS.* Random House, New York.

Sale, K. (1985) *Dwellers in the Land: The Bioregional Vision.* Sierra Club Books, San Francisco.

Sale, K. (2006) *After Eden: The Evolution of Human Domination.* Duke University Press, Durham, North Carolina.

Sanderson, SK. (1990) *Social Evolutionism: A Critical History.* Basil Blackwell, Oxford.

Sargisson, L. (2000) *Utopian Bodies and Politics of Transgression.* Routledge, London.

SCEP (Study of Critical Environmental Problems). (1970) *Man's Impact on the Global Environment.* MIT Press, Cambridge, Massachusetts.

Schacht, R. (1970) *Alienation.* Doubleday, New York.

Schafran, A. (2013) *Discourse and dystopia, American style: The rise of 'slumburbia' in a time of crisis.* City, Vol.17, No.2, pp.30-48.

Schmidt, A. (1971) *The Concept of Nature in Marx.* New Left Books, London.

Schmitz, H. (2005) *Value Chain Analysis for Policy Makers and Practitioners.* International Labour Office, Geneva.

Schoups, G., Hopmans, JW., Young, CA., Vrugt, JA., Wallender, WW., Tanji, KK, and Panday, S. (2005) *Sustainability of irrigated agriculture in the San Joaquin Valley, California.* Proceedings of the National Academy of Sciences, Washington DC.

Scott Cato, M. (2006) *Market, Schmarket: Building the Post-Capitalist Economy.* New Clarion Press, Cheltenham.

Seagrave, S. (1995) *Lords of the Rim: The Invisible Empire of the Overseas Chinese.* Bantam Press, London.

Searle, JR. (1997) *The Mystery of Consciousness.* The New York Review of Books, New York.

Searle, JR. (2001) *Rationality in Action.* Massachusetts Institute of Technology Press, Cambridge, Massachusetts.

Seidman, M. (1982) *Work and Revolution: Workers' Control in Barcelona in the Spanish Civil War, 1936-38.* Journal of Contemporary History, Vol.17, No.3, pp. 409-433

Service, E. (1962) *Primitive Social Organisation: An Evolutionary Perspective.* Random House, New York.

Shuman, MH. (2000) *Going Local: Creating Self-Reliant Communities in a Global Age.* Routledge, New York.

Smith, A. (1976 [1776]) *An Inquiry into the Nature and Origin of the Wealth of Nations.* Two volumes. R.H. Campbell, A.S. Skinner and W.B. Todd (Eds.). Clarendon Press, Oxford.

Smith, DH. (1974) *Confucius.* Paladin, London.

Smith, N. (Ed)(1983) *A Collection of Ranter Writings from the 17th Century.* Junction Books, London.

Stiefel, M. and Wolfe, M. (1994) *A Voice for the Excluded: Popular Participation in Development, Utopia or Necessity?* Zed Books, London.

Stiglitz, JE. (2010) *Freefall: America, Free Markets, and the Sinking of the World Economy.* WW Norton & Company Inc., New York.

Stiglitz, JE. (2012) *The Price of Inequality.* Penguin Books, London.

Strahan, D. (2007) *The Last Oil Shock: A Survival Guide to the Imminent Extinction of Petroleum Man.* London: John Murray.

Stuckler, D., King, L. and McKee, M. (2009) *Mass privatisation and the post-communist mortality crisis: a cross-national analysis,* The Lancet , Vol.373, No.9661, pp. 399–407.

Tainter, J. (1988) *The Collapse of Complex Societies.* Cambridge University Press, Cambridge.

Thayer, RL. (2003) *LifePlace: Bioregional Thought and Practice.* University of California Press, Berkley.

Thomas, K. (1983) *Man and the Natural World: Changing Attitudes in England 1500-1800.* Allen Lane, London.

Thompson, EP. (1963) *The Making of the English Working Class.* Penguin Books, Harmondsworth.

Torres, R. (2001) *Towards a Socially Sustainable World Economy: An Analysis of the Social Pillars of Globalization.* International Labour Office, Geneva.

Touraine, A. (1981) *The Voice and the Eye: An Analysis of Social Movements.* Cambridge University Press, Cambridge.

Trainer, T. (1995) *The Conserver Society.* Zed Books, London.

Tuveson, EL. (1949) *Millennium and Utopia: A Study in the Background of the Idea of Progress.* University of California Press, Berkeley.

Venturi, F. (1960) *Roots of Revolution: A History of the Populist and Socialist Movements in 19th Century Russia.* Weidenfeld and Nicolson, London.

Vogel, D. (1989) *Fluctuating Fortunes: The Political Power of Business in America.* Basic Books, New York.

Wackernagel, M. and Rees, W. (1996) *Our Ecological Footprint: Reducing Human Impact on the Earth.* New Society Publishers, Gabriola Island, British Columbia.

Wall, D. (2005) *Babylon and Beyond: The economics of the Anti-Capitalist, Anti-Globalist and Radical Green Movements*. Pluto, London.

Wallace, D. (1996) *Sustainable Industrialization*. Earthscan, London.

Ward-Perkins, B. (2005) *The Fall of Rome and the End of Civilisation*. Oxford University Press, Oxford.

Ward-Perkins, B. (2010) *We'll cope. Mankind always has: The fall of Rome and the Cost of the Crisis.* in: Levene, M., Johnson, R. and Roberts, P. *History at the End of the World? History, Climate and the possibility of Closure.* Humanities-Ebooks Penrith, pp.46-52.

WCED. (1987) *Our Common Future*. Oxford University Press, Oxford.

Weber, M. (1976 [1930]) *The Protestant Ethic and the Spirit of Capitalism*. George Allen and Unwin, London.

Weale, A. (1992) *The New Politics of Pollution*. Manchester University Press, Manchester.

Weatherford, J. (2005) *Genghis Khan and the Making of the Modern World*. Crown Publishers and Three Rivers Press, New York.

White, L. (1967) *The Historical Roots of our Ecological Crisis.* Science, **155**(3767), pp.1203-1207.

Wilder Publications (2007) *Foundations of Freedom*. (Including *The Federalist* papers). Wilder Publications, Radford, Virginia.

Wilson, BR. (Ed.) (1970) *Rationality*. Basil Blacknell, Oxford.

Winner, L. (1977) *Autonomous Technology: Technics-out-of-Control as a Theme in Political Thought*. MIT Press, Cambridge, Massachusetts.

Wittfogel, K. (1957) *Oriental Despotism*. Yale University Press, Newhaven.

Wohl, AS. (1983) *Endangered Lives: Public Health in Victorian Britain*. Methuen, London.

Woodcock, G. (1963) *Anarchism: A History of Libertarian Ideas and Movements*. Penguin Books, Harmondsworth.

Worster, D. (1979) *Nature's Economy: The Roots of Ecology*. Anchor Press, Garden City, New York.

WTO. (2003) *World Trade Report 2003*. World Trade Organization, Geneva.

WWF. et al (2009) *A Proposal for a Copenhagen Agreement by Members of the NGO Community*.
http://assets.panda.org/downloads/treaty_vol1_web_compl_1.pdf

Zerzan, J. (ed)(2010) *Against Civilisation: Readings and Reflections*. Feral House, Port Townsend, Washington.

ZfTB. (2010) *Peak Oil: Sicherheitspolitische Implikationen knappe Ressourcen.* Zentrum für Tranformation der Bundeswehr, Strausberg.

Index

123, 124, 127, 130, 134, 135,
143, 166, 182, 183, 191, 199,
206, 207, 215, 218, 221, 231,
232, 240, 243, 245, 253, 268,
280, 303, 304, 309, 315, 323,
326, 328, 335, 346, 356, 375,
376, 389, 405, 417, 422, 436,
437, 438, 439, 457, 470

Chomsky, Naom, 433, 440, 485

Christaller, Walter, 234, 286,
314, 451, 461, 480

Christianity, 19, 20, 102, 124,
142, 202, 210, 243, 244, 253,
257, 279, 334, 346, 350, 373,
405, 423

clan, 347, 348

Cohn, Norman, 253, 351, 437,
439, 445, 453, 466, 474, 481

Commercial Ideology, 25, 26,
96, 107, 108, 121, 136, 141,
151, 154, 171, 185, 186, 187,
189, 209, 214, 235, 238, 245,
247, 249, 250, 305, 343, 356,
376

Commodity Fetishism, 25

Commoner, Barry, 221, 222,
432, 449, 481

Commune of Münster, 410

Communism, 29, 99, 126, 127,
131, 139, 144, 152, 153, 154,
159, 160, 172, 175, 177, 210,
241, 245, 247, 248, 251, 339,
342, 356, 363, 413, 461

Communist, 26, 103, 122, 124,
127, 128, 129, 130, 131, 144,
145, 152, 153, 154, 161, 167,
172, 239, 247, 248, 250, 251,
280, 351, 352, 356, 362, 365,
390, 413, 473

Communist Manifesto, 339

Communist Party, 152, 154

Compte, August, 411

Condorcet Marquis de, 98, 119,
363, 411, 429, 436, 481

Confucianism, 19, 20, 100,
103, 106, 107, 108, 143, 144,
163, 172, 241, 242, 245, 253,
338, 340, 346, 347, 349, 355,
356, 375, 395

consciousness, 12, 13, 15, 18,
28, 34, 37, 41, 97, 99, 100,
101, 106, 115, 130, 155, 172,
176, 177, 179, 211, 214, 215,
251, 311, 321, 330, 336, 360,
361, 363, 365, 367, 368, 369,
370, 371, 373, 374, 375, 377,
378, 381, 382, 383, 384, 405,
436, 460

Constitutional Monarchy, 147

Constitutions, 146

consumer society, 29, 31, 37,
40, 75, 109, 124, 154, 187,
191, 247, 248, 355, 381, 398,
413, 414, 423

Consumerism, 96, 378

Consumption, 383

cooperativism, 459

Cooperativism, 32, 120, 121,
252, 412, 419

Costa Rica, 345

CPRMR (Common Pool
Resource Management
Regime), 32, 281, 282, 283,
287, 292, 312, 418

Crenson, Matthew, 433, 481

CSA (Community Supported
Agriculture), 83, 327, 328

Cuba, 83, 99, 220

Darwin, Charles, 99, 138, 139,
141, 198, 204, 205, 363

Dawkins, Richard, 368

deep ecology, 211, 212, 214,
215, 418, 447

336, 345, 348, 349, 352, 356,
373, 379, 388, 389, 391, 395,
397, 412, 417, 439, 466, 473
European Enlightenment, 20,
21, 29, 34, 98, 135, 144, 179,
242, 339
facebook, 35, 85, 261, 355, 360
Fals Borda, Orlando, 473, 483
family, 24, 73, 74, 97, 103,
116, 136, 144, 149, 156, 190,
191, 193, 240, 243, 244, 245,
246, 256, 267, 276, 279, 302,
305, 313, 344, 347, 348, 349,
394, 396, 398, 402, 410, 415,
416, 417, 418, 466, 472
FAO (UN Food and
Agriculture Organisation),
59, 61, 455
fascism, 177, 345, 355, 356
Faustian bargain, 208
FEASTA, 74
Ferguson, Adam, 179
Feudalism, 99, 103, 105, 109,
146, 155, 156, 157, 162, 167,
168, 176, 239, 241, 242, 243,
244, 277, 278, 279, 348, 377,
395, 424, 486
Feyerabend, Paul, 180, 208,
357, 443, 446, 467, 483
Findhorn, 413, 454, 491
First World War, 121, 125,
126, 352, 396, 413
Fordism, 126
Fourier, Joseph, 120, 139, 396,
411
Fox, Warwick, 212, 447, 483
fracking, 54, 66
France, 16, 45, 51, 65, 96, 119,
128, 161, 172, 304, 324, 328,
351, 447
Frankfurt School, 20
Frazer, James, 371, 465, 469

Freedom, 105, 110, 122, 214,
343, 393, 394, 442, 479, 496
Freud, Sigmund, 360, 361, 362,
372, 468
Fried, Morton, 149, 241, 430,
435, 441, 452, 464, 483
Friedmann, John, 454, 483
Friere, Paulo, 261, 455, 483
Fukushima, 66
Galbraith, John Kenneth, 431,
483
Galeano, Eduardo, 441, 483
Galton, Francis, 198
GDP (Gross Domestic
Product), 123, 127, 166, 198,
221
Geneva, 108, 148, 158, 208
Genghis Khan, 24, 436
Germany, 39, 41, 45, 48, 52,
66, 115, 128, 148, 161, 234,
236, 286, 314, 323, 325, 327,
380, 431, 447, 451, 453, 458,
475
Ghandi, Mahatma, 124
Giddens, Anthony, 442, 484
gift economy, 140, 252, 410,
424
GLC (Greater London
Council), 285
global economy, 53, 80, 83, 89,
166, 171, 217, 238, 258, 270,
272, 284, 289, 291, 292, 293,
295, 350, 414, 461
global warming, 28, 36, 44, 55,
67, 69, 70, 71, 75, 76, 135,
270, 391, 432
Global Warming, 61, 67, 432,
486
globalisation, 82, 96, 113, 115,
132, 137, 149, 162, 164, 171,
172, 176, 217, 231, 235, 271,
272, 284, 319, 397, 420, 451

507

participatory municipal budgeting, 262

participatory planning, 364, 426

peak oil, 49, 50, 53, 69, 77, 78, 79, 222

peasant society, 130, 134, 142, 167, 227, 282, 295, 341, 349, 390, 406, 423

Peccei, Aurelio, 224, 225, 450

permaculture, 42, 60, 256, 272, 292, 329, 426

Persia, 373

phenomenology, 384

Philp, Mark, 474, 492

Pinchot, Gifford, 210, 211

Plato, 30, 156, 157, 158, 169, 244, 251, 409, 441, 493

Polytheism, 18, 97

Ponting, Clive, 431, 433, 442, 444, 451, 465, 493

Possessive Individualism, 29, 109, 113, 116, 119, 120, 122, 283, 305, 306, 335, 345, 354, 382, 394, 438, 490

Primitive, 459, 464

Primitive Society, 15, 20, 21, 114, 138, 139, 141, 333, 334, 336, 357, 358, 369, 370, 371, 372, 387, 390, 402, 429, 482

private property, 113, 149, 157, 167, 280, 282, 312, 335, 341, 376, 409, 418

Progress, 11, 13, 21, 22, 26, 29, 97, 98, 99, 100, 101, 102, 103, 104, 105, 106, 107, 110, 114, 116, 119, 120, 121, 124, 125, 132, 135, 138, 143, 144, 165, 177, 185, 186, 199, 202, 204, 207, 209, 210, 217, 218, 224, 225, 228, 240, 340, 358, 359, 362, 363, 365, 373, 375, 377, 436, 437, 438, 449, 489, 495

Proudhon, Pierre-Joseph, 120, 411

Rahman, Anisur, 261, 455, 472

rationality, 20, 33, 72, 76, 93, 96, 119, 121, 155, 156, 164, 170, 175, 190, 208, 249, 253, 259, 281, 304, 334, 335, 338, 339, 345, 355, 357, 358, 359, 361, 362, 363, 365, 371, 374, 375, 384, 385, 408, 409, 412, 457, 467, 474, 475

Reason (Hegel), 340, 344, 358, 362, 363, 365, 445, 485

Rees, William, 268, 456, 457, 495

Reisner, Marc, 463

Renaissance, 102, 203, 206, 245

renewable energy technologies, 38, 41, 50, 51, 52, 53, 57, 58, 117, 134, 217, 218, 219, 222, 223, 251, 256, 290, 306, 317, 319, 320

Renfrew, Colin, 429, 493

Revelation, 357, 374

Revolution, 16, 59, 95, 99, 104, 109, 115, 121, 126, 129, 131, 147, 152, 158, 159, 160, 176, 177, 204, 253, 254, 258, 340, 351, 352, 356, 363, 374, 375, 376, 396, 397, 411, 412, 437, 470, 474, 475, 485

Ricardo, David, 216, 439

Rigby, Andrew, 453, 493

risk society, 72, 449

Rome, 21, 79, 80, 102, 117, 156, 176, 183, 225, 232, 268, 303, 304, 346, 409, 434, 460

Rostow, WW, 493

twitter, 35, 85, 261, 355, 360
Tyler, 138
UNCED - United Nations
Conference on Environment
and Development, 40
unconventional oil and gas
resources, 53, 55, 66, 81, 270
undernourishment, 36, 59, 63,
83, 250, 260, 266, 326, 455,
463
UNEP - United Nations
Environment Programme, 40
UNFPA (UN Population Fund),
62
unhappy self-consciousness,
340, 344, 349, 351, 356, 360,
408
United Nations, 40, 59, 63, 68,
128, 141, 147, 151, 435
United States, 16, 38, 39, 45,
48, 49, 50, 52, 54, 56, 61, 65,
66, 68, 76, 80, 82, 86, 88, 89,
111, 115, 121, 122, 123, 126,
127, 129, 130, 131, 134, 143,
144, 148, 150, 152, 158, 159,
160, 161, 167, 170, 173, 174,
175, 177, 188, 191, 195, 198,
210, 221, 233, 234, 243,246,
247, 248, 257, 259, 264, 266,
276, 280, 281, 287, 305, 306,
309, 317, 323, 328, 341, 342,
353, 354, 379, 389, 391, 396,
397, 403, 412, 414, 434, 435,
438, 443, 444, 447, 453, 460,
463, 465
UPA (Urban and Peri-Urban
Agriculture), 83, 89, 260,
290, 310, 324, 326, 328, 330,
434
Urbanisation, 14, 26, 47, 64,
87, 115, 125, 133, 154, 172,
176, 201, 203, 227, 238, 250,

279, 301, 302, 304, 305, 307,
310, 315, 391, 397, 407
Utopia, 20, 29, 34, 74, 119,
120, 156, 157, 158, 165, 253,
255, 267, 348, 351, 363, 364,
365, 396, 409, 410, 411, 412,
413, 414, 415, 416, 418, 420,
423, 425, 426, 427, 437, 446,
459, 461, 468, 474, 475, 490
Vancouver, 268
Vietnam, 143, 245, 254, 326,
328, 389, 460
Voltaire, 179
Wackernagel, Mathis, 268,
456, 457, 495
war, 17, 22, 23, 24, 25, 45, 48,
72, 84, 86, 103, 113, 114,
126, 133, 145, 149, 157, 165,
166, 202, 206, 216, 219, 220,
233, 301, 303, 334, 335, 340,
345, 347, 348, 374, 379, 408,
409, 413, 434, 451
Ward-Perkins, Bryan, 434, 441,
448, 451, 456, 495
WASP (White Anglo-Saxon
Protestant), 173
Weale, Albert, 432, 496
wealth, 23, 25, 26, 32, 72, 75,
98, 104, 106, 107, 108, 109,
110, 111, 112, 113, 114, 115,
116, 119, 122, 134, 154, 161,
164, 166, 167, 170, 173, 174,
176, 185, 186, 187, 188, 198,
203, 204, 205, 207, 208, 209,
217, 221, 223, 224, 233, 235,
238, 239, 244, 245, 246, 248,
249, 250, 258, 276, 277, 288,
294, 305, 307, 342, 343, 345,
348, 350, 352, 353, 356, 363,
377, 378, 394, 396, 397, 407,
424, 438, 440, 444, 473

511